2395

48364

17382

EQUIVA

an

A RES

EQUIVALENCE RELATIONS and BEHAVIOR: A RESEARCH STORY

MURRAY SIDMAN

Authors Cooperative, Inc., Publishers
P. O. Box 990053
Boston, MA 02199-0053

For information, address:
Authors Cooperative, Inc.
Publishers
P. O. Box 990053
Boston, MA 02199-0053

ISBN 0-9623311-6-3
Library of Congress Catalogue Card Number 93-073793

Printed in the United States of America

*To all of the coworkers, colleagues, and subjects
who made this story happen*

Preface

In addition to bringing together a number of the papers my co-workers and I have published on equivalence relations, I have added new material to each chapter as Introduction and Commentary. Readers will find that the pages with double columns contain the reproduced papers, with the newer material in single-column format. For the most part, the added Introduction and Commentary did not repeat points considered in the papers unless new developments made additional discussion desirable. The very process of adding the new material forced me to rethink some of the earlier work; this rethinking led me to write Chapter 10, which contains no previously published work. (Other chapters, of course, also refer to the developments that Chapter 10 introduces.)

Space did not permit inclusion of all of our work on equivalence. In most of the omitted papers, the dominant themes were methodological. For example, although the papers that analyzed the two-comparison protocol (Carrigan & Sidman, 1992; Johnson & Sidman, 1993) do contain some startling corroborations of our analysis of equivalence relations in behavior, these papers derive their main importance from methodological considerations. Nor does the book contain a comprehensive review even of the modern work on equivalence relations. It is largely a personal story of a research program as my collaborators and I actually lived it. I have cited others' work when it has influenced my own thinking. Methodological flaws in some published experiments prevented me from adopting conclusions that their authors drew—unless those conclusions were later verified under more exacting conditions—and I have simply left that work uncited.

Some of the previously published text has been altered in minor ways: wherever detected, typographical errors and references to original publications have been corrected; some stylistic inconsistencies have been adjusted; where possible, "in press" citations have been changed to actual publication dates, even though the cited references may have appeared after the papers in which they were cited; most of the original figures and tables were remade; reference lists have been deleted from each article and gathered into a single list at the end of the volume. Also, rather than put a trademark symbol in every occurrence of trademarked names, I point out here that the names are being used only in an editorial fashion, and to the benefit of the trademark owner, with no intention of infringement of the trademark.

Many people contributed to this book—so many that I cannot begin to list them. The paper citations that begin on the next page do include the coauthors and original acknowledgments. In addition, all my friends know that my wife, Rita, not only made life possible during the preparation of the book but also contributed to its content and tone. My children and grandchildren have been extraordinarily patient with my preoccupation; I look forward now to some quality time with them all. And Garth Fletcher has continued to teach me what I had to know in order to work effectively on the computer, and to help me when I did not have the resources to do some of the things that had to be done in preparing the text.

The research discussed in this volume was supported by and carried out in the Joseph P. Kennedy, Jr., Memorial Laboratories, Neurology Service, Massachusetts General Hospital; the Behavior Laboratories of the E. K. Shriver Center for Research in Mental Retardation; the Psychology Department of Northeastern University; and the Research Laboratories of the New England Center for Autism. It was supported at various times by the following grants: NS 03535 from the National Institute of Neurological Diseases and Stroke; HD05124, HD04147, and HD20688 from the National Institute of Child Health and Human Development; MH30063 from the National Institute of Mental Health; NE-G-00-3-0011 from the National Institute of Education; and RR07143 from Northeastern University, Biomedical Research Support.

I am grateful for permission from publishers and authors to reprint the following papers in the indicated chapters:

Chapter 1: Sidman, M. (1971). Reading and auditory-visual equivalences. *Journal of Speech and Hearing Research*, 14, 5-13. Osborne Cresson, Jr., Martha Willson, and James Sidman provided technical assistance in this research.

Chapter 2: Sidman, M., & Cresson, O. (1973). Reading and crossmodal transfer of stimulus equivalences in severe retardation. *American Journal of Mental Deficiency*, 77, 515-523. F. Garth Fletcher and Martha Willson provided technical assistance, Nan Haar and Helen Beier performed the IQ evaluations, and George Toomey helped in obtaining the data in Figure 2-1.

Chapter 3: Sidman, M. (1977). Teaching some basic prerequisites for reading. In P. Mittler (Ed.), *Research to practice in mental retardation: Vol. 2. Education and training* (pp. 353-360). Baltimore, MD: University Park Press. This paper was presented at the Fourth International Congress of the International Association for the Scientific Study of Mental Deficiency, Washington, D.C., in August, 1976.

Chapter 4: Sidman, M., Cresson, O., Jr., & Willson-Morris, M. (1974). Acquisition of matching to sample via mediated transfer. *Journal of the Experimental Analysis of Behavior,* 22, 261-273. (Copyright 1974 by the Society for the Experimental Analysis of Behavior.) F. Garth Fletcher provided technical assistance, and Nan Haar performed the IQ evaluations.

Chapter 5: Sidman, M., Rauzin, R., Lazar, R., Cunningham, S., Tailby, W., & Carrigan, P. (1982). A search for symmetry in the conditional discriminations of rhesus monkeys, baboons, and children. *Journal of the Experimental Analysis of Behavior,* 37, 23-44. (Copyright 1982 by the Society for the Experimental Analysis of Behavior.) Special thanks are owed to Steve Brown, Gary Dubois, Wendy Mackay, and Karen Oeschger for technical assistance; to F. Garth Fletcher for apparatus design, construction, and maintenance; and to Betsy Constantine for suggesting a conceptual link between stimulus equivalence and the mathematically defined equivalence relation. Joseph V. Brady and his associates and staff provided facilities and a congenial atmosphere for the conduct of Experiment 5 during the first author's sabbatical year at the Behavioral Biology Laboratories, Department of Psychiatry and Behavioral Sciences, Johns Hopkins University Medical School; particular thanks are owed to Alan Harris and Robert Hienz for their generosity with equipment, space, and time; Frank Grollman for apparatus construction; and Chris Bowers and Deborah Sheckler for their competent day-to-day conduct of the experiment and maintenance of the baboons' feeding and health regimen.

Chapter 6 (first paper): Sidman, M. (1981). Remarks. *Behaviorism*, **9**, 127-129. Willard Day honored me greatly by asking me to contribute a "column" to *Behaviorism*, the fine journal that he founded and edited for many years. "Remarks" was his title for the column. I was able to contribute remarks on an intermittent schedule; those reproduced here appeared in the Spring of 1981.

Chapter 6 (second paper). Sidman, M., & Tailby, W. (1982). Conditional discrimination *vs.* matching to sample: An expansion of the testing paradigm. *Journal of the Experimental Analysis of Behavior*, **37**, 5-22. (Copyright 1982 by the Society for the Experimental Analysis of Behavior.) Special thanks are owed to F. Garth Fletcher for apparatus design, construction, and maintenance.

Chapter 7: Sidman, M., Kirk, B., & Willson-Morris, M. (1985). Six-member stimulus classes generated by conditional-discrimination procedures. *Journal of the Experimental Analysis of Behavior*, **43**, 21-42. (Copyright 1982 by the Society for the Experimental Analysis of Behavior.) Special thanks are owed to F. Garth Fletcher for apparatus design and construction, to Charles Sidman for computer programming, and to Ben Wallace for apparatus maintenance and programming support.

Chapter 8: Sidman, M., Willson-Morris, M., & Kirk, B. (1986). Matching-to-sample procedures and the development of equivalence relations: The role of naming. *Analysis and Intervention in Developmental Disabilities,* **6**, 1-19. Special thanks are owed to F. Garth Fletcher for apparatus design, construction, and maintenance, and to Charles Sidman for computer programming.

Chapter 9 (first paper): Sidman, M. (1986). Functional analysis of emergent verbal classes. In T. Thompson & M. D. Zeiler (Eds.), *Analysis and integration of behavioral units* (pp. 213-245). Hillsdale, NJ: Lawrence Erlbaum Associates.

Chapter 9 (second paper): Sidman, M. (1990). Equivalence relations: Where do they come from? In D. E. Blackman & H. Lejeune (Eds.), *Behaviour analysis in theory and practice: Contributions and controversies* (pp. 93-114). Hillsdale, NJ: Lawrence Erlbaum Associates. (Only pages 104-113 are reprinted here.)

Chapter 11: Sidman, M., Wynne, C. K., Maguire, R. W., & Barnes, T. (1989). Functional classes and equivalence relations. *Journal of the Experimental Analysis of Behavior,* **52**, 261-274. (Copyright 1989 by the Society for the Experimental Analysis of Behavior.)

Chapter 12: Bush, K. M., Sidman, M., & de Rose, T. (1989). Contextual control of emergent equivalence relations. *Journal of the Experimental Analysis of Behavior,* **51**, 29-45. (Copyright 1989 by the Society for the Experimental Analysis of Behavior.) Special thanks are owed to F. Garth Fletcher for assistance with apparatus and with computer programming.

Contents

Contents

Contents

Introduction

All of the investigations described in this book arose out of more complex backgrounds than the original published reports acknowledged. No publication in a scientific journal ever describes the whole set of circumstances that led up to an experiment. In extreme instances, the reasons authors give for initiating a study may be unrelated to anything that really happened. The authors may even have invented a rationale after the fact. Perhaps they had to see their study's outcome before they could appreciate its significance—the outcome may have been unexpected—or they may have known that their original reasons for doing the work—sometimes, mere curiosity—would not convince potential journal reviewers that it was important. I and my research collaborators have on occasion published a post hoc rationale instead of the original one, but the papers that are included here were not extreme in that respect. The omitted background in the original reports of these studies of equivalence relations would have contributed little or nothing to the evaluation of their reliability, validity, or importance.

Still, I think it is worthwhile to record some of that unwritten history. To acquaint readers with the social context in which a particular piece of research originated adds a bit of spice to the account. Also, historians, sociologists, and philosophers of science are always concerned with the larger question of where ideas come from. Perhaps most important, students worry about how to decide which of the many experiments that need doing should be done now. They are always looking for models that they might find congenial or that might allay their fears of doing something foolish.

And so, I have tried to present this series of studies as a story, gathering together papers that were originally published at different times and in various journals or books, and adding previously unpublished material that gives a more complete picture of why the experiments were done. Later developments, of course, often

altered the significance and value of earlier work or our way of looking at the earlier work. I might have just presented my current thinking about equivalence, and left out all the false paths and blind
alleys that were encountered. There is something to be gained, however, from following the course of a program's development. I have
therefore tried to clarify the continuity of the experimental program, pointing out changes in the way we talked about our procedures and data and explaining how we were led to make those
changes. In the course of writing the story, I found still more changes
taking place in my own thinking, and those culminated in what
turned out to be Chapter 10, which contains nothing but new material, presenting no old experiments but proposing many that still
have to be done..

What Is Interesting About Equivalence Relations in Behavior?

A more relevant introductory question for this section might be,
"Why should you, a potential reader, be interested in equivalence
relations?" Because you will come from many different backgrounds
and will have many different interests, I cannot answer that question directly. The best I can do to indicate why you might find
equivalence relations worth reading about is to tell why I find equivalence relations worth experimenting and writing about.

Words and other symbols versus things and events. A major source of
my own interest has been what seems to me a central role of equivalence relations in making language such a powerful factor in our
everyday social intercourse with each other. I think we can agree
that words have meanings, even while we recognize that the term
meaning may itself have many meanings (for a more extended discussion of the problem of meaning, see Epilogue, pp. 561-573).
One kind of word meaning is symbolic reference: many words are
symbols; they *refer* to other things or events. As Skinner pointed out
in arguing against what he called reference theories of meaning (1957,

pp. 7-10, 86-89, 114-129), statements about meanings, symbols, and referents do not explain verbal behavior. Such statements *are* verbal behavior, and as such, they themselves require explanation. Nevertheless, they summarize real observations. We can—and do—specify the referent of a word or other symbol by giving the referent other names, by pointing to it or acting in other ways with respect to it, by specifying its opposite in a name or another action, by speaking or otherwise acting differently in its absence, and so on. But to me, one of the most fascinating observations is that we often react to words and other symbols as if they *are* the things or events they refer to. Even though we do not treat word and referent as equal in all respects, we attribute some of the same properties to both. This treatment of linguistic forms as equivalent to their referents permits us to listen and read with comprehension, to work out problems in their absence, to instruct others by means of speech or text, to plan ahead, to store information for use in the future, and to think abstractly—all of these by means of words that are spoken, written, or thought in the absence of the things and events they refer to.

On the other hand, the substitution of words and other symbols for their referents may also bring about some extraordinary, even bizarre, conduct. Let me just touch on some examples of that type, ranging from magical thinking to the highest realms of human creativity. I bring these up not because they are usual but because they illustrate the power of symbolic reference.

During recent years, two instances in which people reacted to nonlanguage symbols as if they were the things they represented were so spectacular that the news media featured them prominently for a long time One of these was the flag-burning controversy in the United States. In response to the destruction of a few American flags, mobs gathered to defend the country against attack and to mount counterattacks. Members of our governing bodies interrupted the processing of much needed legislation and other governmental functions so that they could make themselves popular and gain votes by declaiming in outrage against the fiery destruction of our institutions. The burning of flags was not just a threat; it was actual war.

Those who burned the flags knew this would be the reaction; that is why they chose flag burning as their way of protesting. Although flag burning is in itself a nonviolent act—it touches no person; it destroys nobody's property—they knew it would receive the kind of public notice that is ordinarily provoked by actual violence against people or property and against our system of government.

A second media-celebrated event occurred during the hectic days when the Communist government of Russia was falling. I watched TV in fascination as a crowd of enraged Russian citizens hurled both invective and stones at a famous statue of Lenin and then wrestled it to the ground, jumped on it, kicked it, and pounded it with hammers. The statue, of course, was not alive—was not Lenin himself—but people were still trying to kill it.

Happenings analogous to these are not confined to nonlinguistic representations. The treatment of language symbols as if they are the things they represent is so strongly and deeply ingrained that we often react to words with feelings of pain, and we use words to inflict pain. A familiar adage, meant especially but not exclusively for children, is intended specifically to counteract this feature of words: "Sticks and stones may break my bones, but names can never hurt me." In fact, words *are* considered to be hurtful. Witness what has now become commonplace in our daily news: first, killings after the receipt of actual or imagined verbal insults; and second, such killings then being justified even in the courtroom as self-defense.

An insightful picture of words being taken as their referents comes from the description of a character in a novel by David Grossman (1989):

> [He] lives totally in a world of words, which means, I imagine, that every word he utters or hears has for him a sensual quality which I cannot perceive. Is it possible, then, that the word "supper" is enough to satisfy his hunger? That the word "sore" cuts his flesh? That the word "living" enlivens him?…Could it be that [he] became a fugitive from human language in order to protect himself from all the words that cut his flesh? (p. 283).

Introduction

B. F. Skinner (1957) pointed out that many distinctive characteristics of verbal behavior come from the fact that words have no power in themselves to change the environment: "Rarely do we shout down the walls of a Jericho or successfully command the sun to stop or the waves to be still. Names do not break bones" (p. 2). Any physical effects that our utterances accomplish must be mediated by the actions of listeners or readers. Still—what about the newspaper article (Mehegan, 1994) in which I read with amazement that:

> A famous and controversial legal scholar clashes with a book critic, throwing a spotlight on a philosophical question: Is talking about committing a violent crime, even pretending to commit it, the same as actually doing it?
>
> ...In his fiercely negative review of MacKinnon's new book...Romano begins with a complex hypothesis that he has raped MacKinnon in his imagination, then written about it as if he had done it. In an argument that mirrors her book's central thesis, an outraged MacKinnon charges that Romano's hypothesis in itself constitutes rape.
>
> ...[MacKinnon has argued for] a model law that would outlaw graphic words and images that tend to subjugate women. In her new book, MacKinnon advances the argument with...such statements as, "To say it is to do it...."

Writers and book reviewers live in a world of words, so it is perhaps not surprising that many of them endow the source of their influence and livelihood with great importance and power. But it is certainly true that what we say can mirror our feelings, may be predictive of nonverbal actions we would take if we had the opportunity, or may incite or encourage others to take action, so words may realistically be reacted to with resentment and even fear. The prevention of such resentment and fear in everyday intercourse is one of the functions of society's rules of common courtesy, and a book review or any other verbal interaction may indeed go beyond those rules, as may a listener's or reader's verbal reactions. Nevertheless, we forget that no matter how outrageous or threatening they may be, no matter what they reveal about a speaker's or writer's attitudes or intentions, words can themselves produce no direct damage or hurt; for words to exert physical force requires nonverbal action by listeners or readers. Even though words may indicate intentions or desires, to say it is *not* to do it. What is perhaps to be legislated against is not the mere utterance or writing of words but the performance of hurtful actions that words often warn us of, or the verbal provocation of others to perform hurtful actions.

I believe that equivalence relations underlie all these examples: the flag has become equivalent to our nation itself and its institutions; under some conditions, statues become equivalent to their models; a dent in the rear fender of one's car is equivalent to a slap in one's face; to complain about such a dent is equivalent to initiating a bodily assault; verbal hostility is taken as the equivalent of physical aggression; sharp words are the equivalent of sharp instruments; hypothesizing an action is equivalent to performing the action.

Examples of nonverbal symbols becoming equivalent to events and things in reality abound: advertising agencies have long recognized and promoted the equivalence of automobile size and penis size; changing a company's logo is expected to change the company itself, transforming it from an economic failure to a success; "clothes make the man," and the emperor unclothed is a mere mortal; pins are inserted into a doll in order to bring pain to a far-away person; property trespass is the equivalent of a threat to the property owner's life, thereby justifying the trespasser's destruction.

Examples of verbal symbols becoming equivalent to events and things in reality also abound: as we have learned from many of our political leaders, saying that poverty does not exist is equivalent to doing away with poverty as a problem, or saying that everybody has access to health care is equivalent to everybody actually receiving health care; in general, saying that poor is rich, war is peace, and offense is defense are equivalent to the elimination of poverty, war, and aggression, so nothing further need be done about these matters; for many theorists and model makers in science, the theories and models themselves, rather than the observations they are

6

supposed to explain, become the primary subject matter (see, for example, Chiesa, 1994, pp. 52, 70, 158); in both science (Hineline, 1980) and religion (Schoenfeld, 1994, pp. 32-35, 96), verbs are often transformed into nouns or things, which are then dealt with as though they actually existed apart from their lexical status. *Acts of remembering* become a thing we call *memory*. Having been represented by a noun, memory can then be talked about as if it had qualitative and quantitative characteristics of its own, independently of the acts sit refers to. Similarly, *the origin of life*, *life after death*, *the birth of the universe*, and so on are events that no living person has experienced; they must therefore be purely verbal constructions— words that are defined only by other words. But then, having invented those words, we go on to build scientific and religious systems around them. Words become equivalent not only to observed but to hypothesized reality.

The treatment of words as equivalent to their referents is not necessarily disadvantageous or deceptive. Great accomplishments arise from our ability to manipulate words in the absence of their referents and even to manipulate words that have no referents except other words. Because of the equivalence of words to things and to other words an Einstein can come up with a verbal construction like $E=mc^2$ that results not just in more words but in the creation of an atomic explosion or the sending of a rocket into outer space; we can translate architectural drawings into real buildings and bridges; we can categorize things and events by verbal labels so that we do not have to remember every experience uniquely; we can store data, specifications, descriptions, instructions, and many kinds of knowledge in books, disks, and tapes so that these can be passed on for use by future generations; we can communicate poorly understood but common and even universal experiences, feelings, and emotions by means of poetic and other forms of artistic expression.

In addition to instances of word-referent equivalence that can be culled from everyday experience, we have seen some striking examples in some of our laboratory studies of aphasic patients (Leicester, Sidman, Stoddard, & Mohr, 1971). Although these observations were published in the same year as our first equivalence paper (Chapter 1), they actually antedated that work by more than ten years, but even after we had started our direct experimental attack on equivalence phenomena, the significance of the earlier data took a while to sink in. Those data should have made us take a closer look.

Our subjects were people who had recently suffered stroke-induced brain damage and, in consequence, were having problems speaking, writing, and understanding spoken and written language. To help analyze their problems, we gave them simple matching-to-sample, naming, and writing tests. Here is a condensed account of the test methods (from Leicester et al., 1971):

> The patients were tested in a quiet, softly lit room. They sat before a panel of nine translucent windows, each 2-in square, arranged in a 3 x 3 matrix. Each trial began by presenting the sample stimulus. Visual samples (for example, printed words) were projected from the rear onto the center window of the matrix. Auditory samples were dictated from tapes over a speaker, and tactile samples were presented for palpation inside a screening box. In tests of matching to sample, the patient touched the center window to bring choice stimuli (for example, pictures) onto the outer windows of the matrix. One choice, the correct one, corresponded to the sample; the others did not. The patient selected and touched one of the choice windows. Correct selections caused a chimes to ring and a nickel (5 cents) to be delivered. After incorrect choices, there were no chimes or nickels. In some tests the sample remained after the choices appeared (simultaneous matching); in others, the sample disappeared when the subject touched the center key, and the choices appeared 0-40 sec later (delayed matching). The sample stimulus was presented in the same way for writing and oral naming tests. For writing tests, the patient had a new sheet of paper for each trial. Correct responses caused the ringing of the chimes and payment of a nickel.
>
> The patient was given many trials with each type of task, the trials differing in the specific stimuli presented and in the arrangement of the stimuli on the windows. This was essential to avoid pitfalls of window-pressing preferences, learning of trial sequences, imperfectly designed sets of trials, and so on. The methods are described in greater detail in Sidman, Stoddard, Mohr, and Leicester (1971).

Figure IN-1. Tests with numerals and dots. Illustrative trials, simultaneous matching: A. visual numeral sample, dot choices; B. visual dot sample, numeral choices. Different patterns of dots were used on other trials.

In one type of test, the subjects matched printed numerals and quantities of dots. When the sample was a numeral, the choices were various quantities of dots, and vice versa, as illustrated in Figure IN-1. Other tests offered the subjects the dots as choices but the samples were auditory (dictated) instead of visual. What we were asking the patients to do was to relate certain symbols (visual numerals and auditory number names) to some of their referents (quantities). The matching tests were of particular interest because they permitted us to examine how aphasic patients related symbols and referents to each other without having to speak.

Our test methods allowed us to observe not only that subjects made mistakes with these simple materials, which they would have matched perfectly before their illness, but that their errors were not random. For example, Figure IN-2 shows one subject's generalization gradient in which the choice on any trial is specified by its numerical deviation from the sample. For example, when the sample was the written numeral, 7, or the written or dictated number name, "seven," a subject's choice of 8 dots had a deviation of +1; nine dots, a deviation of +2; 6 dots, -1; 1 dot, -6; and so on; correct choices had a deviation of zero. This subject's actual errors are listed below the gradient. The main finding here was that the subject's incorrect choices were related to the samples by proximity in the number sequence. Other subjects also showed a preponderance of errors with small deviations from the sample.

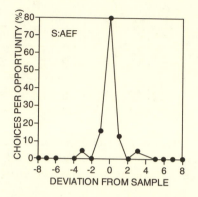

Sample	7	8	6	7	4	8
Error	6-dots	5-dots	7-dots	6-dots	5-dots	7-dots

Sample	"three"	"seven"	"seven"	"four"	"eight"
Error	4-dots	8-dots	6-dots	7-dots	7-dots

Figure IN-2. Subject AEF. Generalization gradient with numerals and dots, showing the relation of the subject's choices to the sample in the number sequence.

These tests required subjects to match stimuli that were only arbitrarily related—numerals, printed or dictated number names, and quantities of dots bore no physical resemblance to each other. Lissauer (1890), in his studies of what he called "mind-blindness," characterized such symbolic reference as an "inner relation" that depended on language. One might, instead, take a more parsimonious view of our test results: perhaps the subject's errors were due not to any problem with symbolic reference but simply to imprecise counting of the dots. A second kind of test, however, suggested a more interesting possibility. In these tests, subjects matched numerals to number names; no actual quantities (dots) were involved. When the sample was a numeral, the choices were printed words, and vice versa, as illustrated in Figure IN-3. Other tests offered the subjects the same choices but the samples were auditory (dictated) number names.

A		
2	6	1
4	one	3
8	7	5

B		
seven	four	six
five	1	two
three	eight	one

Figure IN-3. Tests with numerals and number names. Illustrative trials, simultaneous matching: A. visual number-name sample, numeral choices; B. visual numeral sample, number-name choices

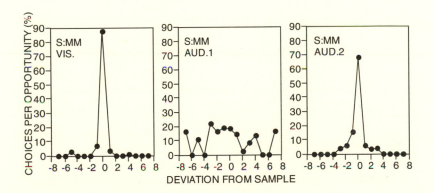

Figure IN-4. Subject M.McL. Generalization gradients showing the relation of a subject's choices to the sample within the number sequence: A. visual samples and choices; B and C. auditory samples and visual choices.

Again, patients had problems doing these tasks accurately. And again, their errors were not random. One subject, for example, when tested a week after her stroke, showed only slightly less than normal accuracy (88% correct) in the simultaneous matching of numerals to printed digit names, but there was still a definite relation of proximity in the number sequence between each error and what would have been the correct choice (Figure IN-4, left). The actual errors, in order of occurrence, were:

Sample	4	5	6	9	3	2	3	6	2	five	7
Error	three	four	seven	four	two	six	two	eight	three	6	six

In other tests, this patient was quite unable to match dictated number names to printed numerals or number names (18% correct), and the early generalization gradient showed no relation within the number sequence between errors and correct choices (Figure IN-4, center). When the tests with auditory samples were repeated three weeks later, however, her accuracy was much greater (67% correct) and her errors were now related to the correct choices by proximity in the number sequence (Figure IN-4, right). The actual errors were:

Sample	"five"	"seven"	"five"	"four"	"seven"	"five"
Error	three	six	seven	five	six	3

Sample	"six"	"four"	"seven"	"five"	"two"	"three"
Error	3	3	6	8	3	2

These test results were interesting not simply because they provided a quantitative description of patients' stroke-induced difficulties but because they showed patients to be making the same kinds of errors when matching symbols to each other as when matching those symbols to their referents. The patients were reacting to numerals and number names as if those symbols were actual quantities.

We saw similar results when we tested some aphasic patients who had problems matching color names to colors. The most prevalent errors were confusions among red, orange, and yellow and between green and blue. Perhaps these errors were due to physical resemblances among the colors. But then, we saw the patients making the same kinds of errors when matching dictated color-name samples to printed color-name choices. Although the latter tests involved only the color names, the patients' errors were like those they made in tests that involved the actual colors. These patients were reacting to auditory and visual color names as if those language symbols were the colors themselves.

We summarized our findings as follows (from Leicester et al., 1971, with some modifications):

> Relevant stimulus characteristics are those that relate the sample to the correct choice; by their use the task can be done correctly....[A] distinction among relevant characteristics is between physical characteristics and language characteristics. Physical characteristics describe the shape, [quantity], color, [brightness], size, etc. of visual stimuli; the loudness, pitch, etc. of auditory stimuli; the shape, etc. of tactile stimuli;...Language characteristics describe nonphysical aspects of language symbols. They are arbitrary, learned by convention, and transfer between auditory and visual modalities. We were surprised to find that language characteristics could be studied by the same methods as physical characteristics, by generalization gradients, for example, and that responses related to language characteristics were governed by similar laws to those that govern responses to physical characteristics....[Language] characteristics governed aphasic errors in a manner similar to the way physical characteristics govern non-aphasic errors....Language symbols apparently come to be governed by the physical properties of the things they represent. (pp. 152, 153).

We were almost there. Our patients had demonstrated strikingly that they were giving language symbols the properties of their referents, and we had the methods at hand to produce laboratory analogues of that phenomenon. If we had been more venturesome, we would have begun our work on equivalence relations at that point, but we were not yet ready. The notion that we might be able to describe equivalence relations in a way that could account for our observations about symbols and their referents was still too great a conceptual leap. We had to wait until other considerations led us up that research path (Chapter 1).

Equivalence and creativity. Even if I were to stop at this point in my list, I think I would have justified my interest in equivalence relations. But there is still more substance to my reasons both for writing this book and for the more than twenty-five years of research that preceded it. The early chapters, for example, may be regarded as the beginnings of a functional analysis of elementary reading comprehension, auditory comprehension, and oral reading. Our basic experimental paradigm provides a method for defining "comprehension": when the relation between words (written or spoken) and things can be shown to be an equivalence relation, then we can say that the words are understood. We have, here, an empirically verifiable method for distinguishing between meaningful and meaningless behavior-environment relations. The comprehension of written and spoken language, of course, involves much more than we have dealt with in our experiments, but we have laid down the foundations for the analysis of more complex cases.

And, as will be seen as early as Chapter 1, one outcome of the early work on reading comprehension and equivalence relations is a method for generating new cognitive performances without having to teach each one separately. The very definition of equivalence relations—which we did not arrive at until the work that is described in Chapters 5 and 6—requires the emergence of new performances from a baseline of explicitly arranged contingencies. Chapter 7 highlights the incredible efficiency of the experimental paradigm as a method of teaching. Even by itself, this practical outcome of the research is exciting, although its utility has gone largely unappreciated by the education establishment. The potential contribution of the equivalence research to instructional technology is for me one of the most compelling reasons for continuing the research, but the educational relevance of the procedures and data has been noted in the original papers and in the additional discussion in the Epilogue; it need not be stressed again here.

In addition to its significance for the methodology of teaching, the emergence of new behavior that has not been explicitly taught is also the defining feature of *creativity*. Because creativity always involves the production of something new, it is feared by those who find change threatening, and respected by those who recognize change as a prerequisite for progress. But whether one wants to rein in or promote the creative process, knowledge about how it works is necessary. Largely because we do not even recognize an ongoing creative process until it yields a new product, the process itself remains little understood; by the time we become aware of it, it is over. Many therefore consider creativity an unapproachable mystery, beyond our power of understanding.

Clearly, creativity involves more than just equivalence relations. Just as clearly, insofar as equivalence relations can underlie the emergence of untaught behavior, equivalence relations can also underlie creative acts. The more we understand equivalence, the more we understand creativity. To the extent that we can say, "Teach a person that A is related to B, and B to C, and then, without further teaching, you will find the person relating C to A, A to C, B to A, and C to A," we are predicting acts of creativity from a set of specified circumstances. This is exactly what has happened over and over in the research on equivalence. In the very process of testing for equivalence relations, we see creativity being displayed even by people who have been classified as nonlearners. The more we find out about equivalence relations, the better we will understand and thereby become able to generate desirable creative performances.

The problem of induction. Creativity has long occupied the attention of philosophers and logicians, but they call it *induction*. The classical definition of inductive inference is "the derivation of general principles from particular facts or instances." Why is this creativity? Inductive generalization entails the bringing together of a group of particulars into a set. At some point in any particular instance of inductive reasoning—in our classification of particulars into a set that is differentiated from other sets—an act of faith must occur; except when the particulars resemble each other physically, we have no reason for classifying them together except the generalization itself. We then go on to test the utility of the generalization, often by *deductive* inference, which is defined classically as "the derivation of particular facts or instances from general principles." It remains ever possible that the original inductive leap may turn out to have been unjustified. That is why an inductive inference—a generalization that is induced from particulars that seem unrelated on any other grounds—can never be proven indisputably. Inductive inference is therefore a pure act of creativity in the sense that the reasoning from particulars to generalization involves no purely logical or physical necessity.

This illogical feature of what has been called logical induction led me many years ago to state, "Induction is a behavioral process, not a logical one" (Sidman, 1960/1988, p. 59). Now, I think we can take an additional step. The behavioral work on equivalence relations permits us to describe and to demonstrate and investigate under controlled conditions at least one of the processes underlying the behavior that is called inductive inference.

As we pointed out in the work that is described in Chapters 5 and 6, when features of the environment become related through behavioral contingencies, their relation is an equivalence relation if it possesses the properties of reflexivity, symmetry, and transitivity. There are several ways to find out empirically whether a given relation possesses these properties. One of them goes like this: we start with Stimulus A being related in a particular way to Stimulus B, and B being related in the same way to C; then, if that relation is an equivalence relation, A will also be found to be related in the same way to C, C to A and to B, B to A., A to itself, B to itself, and C to itself. In some of our empirical work, we used conditional-discrimination procedures to establish a relation that included stimulus pairs that we may call AB and BC; then, we provided evidence that the relation our procedures had established was an equivalence relation by showing that it also included the stimulus pairs AC, CA, CB, BA, AA, BB, and CC. Once explicit reinforcement contingencies had established the original AB and BC relations, all the other relations were emergent—not having been involved in any reinforcement contingency. Their emergence was predictable by deductive inference, but the deductions were made possible only by a previous act of induction, a generalization from particulars—the particulars being the AB and BC stimulus pairs, and the generalization being the inclusion of these pairs in an equivalence relation. The generalization therefore provided the only basis for expecting the untaught relations to emerge. Given the inductive generalization, the deductive inferences were built in; the new relations *had* to be there.

What does all this say about inductive inference as a behavioral process? We have here an example of an inductive inference—that the AB and BC pairs are included in an equivalence relation—an inference that is required by no logical or physical necessity and is supported only by the subsequent observation of new related pairs, the emergence of which we have deduced from the definition of equivalence. *Emergence of the new pairs tells us that our subject has made the same inferences, both inductive and deductive, that we have made.* Although we express our inferences in words, our subjects need not verbalize their inferences; all of the environmental relations we teach a subject explicitly and those which emerge without having been explicitly taught show themselves in the subject's nonverbal selection of stimuli from a number of alternatives. I believe, then, it is fair to say that our empirical behavioral studies of the equivalence relation are at the same time empirical behavioral studies of inductive inference.

The statement, "If A is related to B, and B to C, then C is related in the same way to A," is based on inductive inference. The problem for mathematical set theory is to answer the question, "What general conditions will justify this induction?" Although I have taken a behavior analytic definition of equivalence from mathematical set theory, behavior analysis has a different question to answer: "What specific acts will justify this induction?" The behavioral problem is not to define the noun, *induction*, but to account for the verb, *to induce*. To the extent that our studies of equivalence relations help to solve that problem, we confirm the supposition that induction is a behavioral process. In bringing the study of equivalence relations into the behavior laboratory, we are at the same time submitting the problem of logical induction to an experimental analysis.

1

The First Experiment

Background

The laboratory in which this first study took place was a unit of the Neurology Service of the Massachusetts General Hospital. One of our research directions was the behavioral study of language. With the encouragement of Raymond D. Adams, who, as Chief of the Neurology Service, was responsible for our being there, we approached the study of language by examining patients in whom normal language processes had, to some extent, broken down. Most of these patients were aphasic, showing language disorders as a result of brain damage from disease, accident, or cerebrovascular stroke.

Since many of the patients could not speak or write intelligibly, we had to devise ways to investigate their language comprehension without requiring them to speak or write. To this end, we adapted the matching-to-sample procedure, which was originally developed to study the behavior of nonhumans (for example, Yerkes, 1928). Using this procedure, we were able to evaluate how well the patients could relate text, objects, and pictures to words that they heard, saw, or touched (for example, Sidman et al., 1971). Because we were doing this research, we had available the test materials that were needed for our first study of equivalence relations. Since that study was, for us, a diversion, it might never have been done if our ongoing research had not made the necessary apparatus, stimulus materials, and procedures readily available.

Where did the idea for the experiment come from? Behavior analysts had done little in the field of aphasia, so the literature from which we worked was largely neurological in nature. Also, the immediate reinforcers for our own behavior were coming at that time not from behavior analysts but from the medical community, largely clinical and experimental neurologists and pediatricians. Like anyone else, we were responsive to our environment and we looked there for much of our inspiration.

At the same time, we felt a certain alienation, because the medical community's language about behavior was based on ordinary rather than scientific knowledge (Lee, 1988). We, on the other hand, were convinced that our systematic orientation would be more likely to produce the kind of behavioral-neurological synthesis that we were all interested in achieving. It was important, therefore, not only to work cooperatively but to take every opportunity to demonstrate that our approach would prove more productive than the "person in the street" conception of behavior.

One such opportunity presented itself in the writings of the late Norman Geschwind, a neurologist whose work we followed with great interest. Geschwind was a master of inductive theorizing about relations between brain structures and behavior, and much of what he had to say seemed relevant to the kinds of behavioral data we were seeing in our lab. We had the uncomfortable feeling, however, that he was sometimes trying to relate real neuroanatomical structures to unsubstantiated behavioral processes. An occasion to check the reality of a behavioral process whose existence Geschwind took for granted came from his discussions of reading comprehension.

Like many others, Geschwind subscribed to the common wisdom that auditory comprehension is a prerequisite for reading comprehension—people usually learn to understand words they hear before they understand words they see. Unlike most others, however, he often stated this wisdom in ways that suggested the possibility of experimental test.

For example, with reference to a simple test in which one shows a patient an object and several written words and asks which of the words is the name of the object, he wrote: "It is obvious that the ability to select the correct word depends on there being some connection between the site of perception [in the brain] and the speech area.... [the patient] in some way compares the images or memories aroused by [the] word with the sensations he is receiving from the object" (Geschwind, 1965b, p. 589). Again, "...it is the left angular gyrus that converts the visual pattern of a word into the auditory pattern; without such conversion, a seen word cannot be comprehended" (Geschwind, 1972, p. 82). Still later, "...The comprehension of a written word seems to require that the auditory form of the word be evoked...." (Geschwind, 1979, p. 187).

From statements like these came the idea for our first equivalence experiment. For Geschwind, a person's ability to match a written word with an object indicated whether the person comprehended that written word. This definition of reading comprehension did not, of course, originate with Geschwind; teaching word-object or word-picture matching is the standard method for giving school-children simple reading vocabularies and for testing simple reading comprehension. For the same reason, we routinely evaluated picture-word matching in our tests of aphasic patients. What was new in Geschwind's formulations was the notion that reading comprehension requires *only* that a picture and its written name be "connected to" or "arouse" the same spoken name. We should, therefore, be able to produce reading comprehension indirectly by teaching children to relate both a picture and its written name to the same dictated word. Reading comprehension—matching the written picture name to its picture—should emerge without our having to teach it directly.

Because we were routinely testing our aphasic patients on all of these kinds of matching-to-sample tasks, we had all the necessary procedures available. All we had to do was to bring in a subject who did not already know how to read and understand printed words.

As far as we were concerned, the experiment was to deal with a specific question about the origin of reading comprehension. We had not yet formulated the concept of equivalence in any rigorous way and we had no thoughts as yet that the experiment might have more general implications. Furthermore, we did not really believe that the experiment was going to work, that our subject would learn by this indirect route to understand text. Geschwind's formulation had too many assumptions about mediating processes, assumptions that were common enough to have entered our everyday vocabulary but which a scientific analysis did not require. We were, therefore, out to prove that naive theorizing about behavior was not the path to travel.

Still, if the experiment were successful, it would give us a new and quite powerful way to teach reading comprehension. If that were to happen, we would be delighted; we could deal with the theoretical implications later. And so, when the final test came, we waited with bated breath. Whichever way the experiment went would be exciting.

Reading and Auditory-Visual Equivalences

A retarded boy, unable to read printed words orally or with comprehension, could match spoken words to pictures and could name pictures. After being taught to match spoken to printed words, he was then capable of reading comprehension (matching the printed words to pictures) and oral reading (naming the printed words aloud).

Reading may be regarded broadly as a type of stimulus-response relation in which the controlling stimuli are visual words—written or printed text. Within this general type of stimulus-response relation, several subcategories may be identified. One is oral reading. A simple example: If we show a child the word, *boy* and he says "boy," he indicates that he can read the word orally. Oral reading may or may not involve comprehension; for example, one can read words in a foreign language aloud without understanding them. Oral reading may, in fact, be more appropriately called "oral naming of words." As such, it may be no different than the oral naming of objects or the pictures of objects. A common observation, however, is that children generally learn to name objects or pictures aloud before they learn to name the corresponding printed words.

To demonstrate reading comprehension, we require a different kind of stimulus-response relation. A simple example: If we show a child the printed word, *boy*, and he is then able to select a picture of a boy out of several other pictures, we say that he understands the word. One simple kind of reading comprehension, then, may be demonstrated by the child's accurate matching of printed words to pictures. Defined this way, reading comprehension is a purely visual task. Note that one may be capable of this kind of reading comprehension without being able to read the words orally.

A third stimulus-response relation, rarely discussed explicitly, might be termed, *auditory-receptive reading*. For example, we say the word *boy* to a child and he is then to select the word *boy* out of several other printed words. This differs from oral reading in that the word is spoken to and not by the child. Nevertheless, discussions of the role of auditory-visual equivalences in reading often confuse oral reading and auditory-receptive reading under some such common heading as word recognition.

Like oral reading, auditory-receptive reading may or may not involve comprehension, either of the auditory (spoken) or the visual (printed) word. As noted before, simple visual comprehension can be tested by a visual word-picture matching task. Similarly, simple auditory comprehension can be tested by matching auditory words to visual pictures: we say the word *boy* to a child and he is then to select the picture of a boy out of several other pictures.

Several lines of converging evidence and theory have led many writers to postulate that reading comprehension, a visual task, evolves from the previous learning of auditory-visual equivalences (Birch, 1962; Geschwind, 1972; Wepman, 1962). First, there are certain common observations of normal developmental sequences: (1) Children normally understand words they hear before they learn to read with comprehension; auditory comprehension of words usually precedes visual comprehension. (2) Children usually name objects or pictures of objects before they learn to name the printed or written words that correspond to those objects; object naming precedes word naming (oral reading). Most children break through the "sound barrier" in the first or second grade and learn to understand not just words they hear but words they see. They also learn not just to name pictures but to read words orally. A large group of retarded children and dyslexic children, however, has not made the transfer from auditory comprehension and picture naming to visual reading comprehension and oral reading. It is likely that this transfer marks a critical point in the development of behavior and the central nervous system.

A second indication that auditory-visual equivalences and

reading are closely linked comes from correlational studies by Birch and his co-workers (Birch & Belmont, 1964, 1965; Kahn & Birch, 1968). Using a test of auditory-visual integration (matching sound patterns to visual patterns), they found positive correlations between scores on this test and scores on standard reading achievement tests.

A third set of considerations comes from the neuroanatomical theories of Geschwind (1965a,b), who takes as his starting point the observations, like those noted above and others, that cross-modal equivalences and language are closely linked. He has proposed that cross-modal equivalences, particularly auditory-visual, actually make language possible. Furthermore, he has suggested that the evolution of the angular gyrus region, strategically located at the junction of auditory, visual, and somesthetic association cortexes, makes that region the prime candidate as the central-nervous-system site for the mediation of crossmodal equivalences. As a consequence, the angular gyrus is held to be critical for language in general and for reading in particular. Geschwind has proposed that developmental dyslexia may be correlated with the slow maturation of the angular gyrus bilaterally or perhaps even with its failure to develop.

In spite of these empirical and theoretical considerations and in spite of the educational practices (e.g., the "look-say" method of teaching reading) that are based on them, the question of whether auditory-visual learning is indeed a necessary or even a sufficient prerequisite for the development of oral reading or reading comprehension seems not to have been studied experimentally. The experiment to be described now will demonstrate that certain learned auditory-visual equivalences are indeed sufficient prerequisites for the emergence of reading comprehension, even without explicitly teaching reading comprehension. Although the data raise a number of unanswered questions, the major finding is sufficiently provocative, and relevant to both theory and teaching practice, to warrant this report in advance of more extended studies.

METHOD

Subject

The subject of the experiment was an institutionalized 17-year-old boy, microcephalic and severely retarded. During the past two years, he had extensive experience with the apparatus and matching-to-sample procedures described below. The following findings are a relevant background for the present experiment: He was able to match pictures, colors, and printed numbers to picture names, color names, and number names that were spoken aloud to him. But he was unable to do the matching correctly when the names were presented to him visually rather than spoken. Also, he could name the pictures aloud but not the corresponding printed words. Therefore, he showed good auditory comprehension and picture naming but little if any reading comprehension or oral reading. He could not write.

Apparatus and Procedures

The subject sat before a panel of nine translucent windows, each 5.48 cm square, arranged in a 3 x 3 matrix. Visual stimuli were projected from the rear onto the windows (Rosenberger, Mohr, Stoddard, & Sidman, 1968). Each trial began by presentation of a sample stimulus. Visual word or picture samples appeared on the center window of the matrix; auditory word samples, repeated at 2-s intervals, were dictated from tapes over a speaker (Figure 1-1, left column).

In matching tests, the subject pressed the center window to bring choice stimuli, always visual, onto the outer windows of the matrix. Schematic examples of the displays are in the second column of Figure 1-1. On each trial, one choice, the correct one, corresponded to the sample; the other seven choices did not. The subject selected and pressed one of the choice windows. His correct choices were rewarded by chimes ringing and delivery of a candy and a penny. No rewards followed incorrect choices. The stimuli disappeared after each choice, and 1.5 s later a new sample began the next trial.

In oral naming tests, the subject had simply to name the sample picture or word aloud.

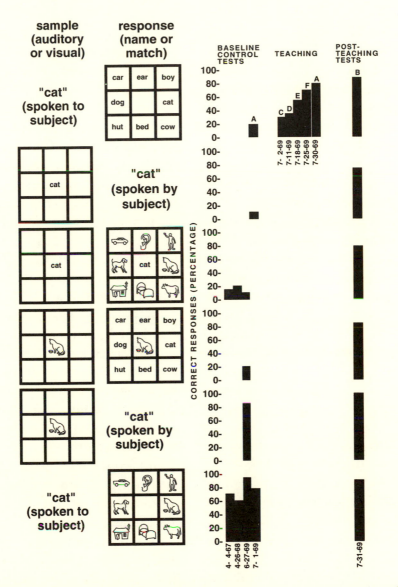

Figure 1-1. In the two left columns are examples of the sample stimuli and responses that comprised each type of test. Choice stimuli and correct window positions in the matching tests varied from trial to trial. The three columns of bars represent scores in each depicted test during the three phases of the experiment. Absence of a bar means no test on the indicated date. Letters identify the six auditory-visual word matching sets (uppermost row).

Reward procedures were the same as in the matching tests.

Each test had 20 trials. The sample and choice stimuli, taken from a list of 20 pictures or the printed (lower case) or spoken names of the pictures were: *axe, bed, bee, box, boy, bug, car, cat, cow, dog, ear, hat, hen, hut, hoe, man, pie, pig, saw, zoo.*

Preliminary tests evaluated the subject's proficiency at simple comprehension and naming tasks; then, he was taught to match spoken to printed words; final tests evaluated the effects of this teaching on his reading comprehension and word naming.

RESULTS

Each row of bar graphs shows the subject's test scores on the task depicted at the left.

Baseline Control Tests

The results of preliminary tests are in the left column of bar graphs in Figure 1-1. Bars at the lower left show the subject's scores in tests that required him to match spoken word samples to picture choices. In four tests, administered from April 1967 to July 1969, he scored from 60 to 95% correct, demonstrating a

fair proficiency at this type of auditory comprehension. He also scored 85% in naming the pictures (second row from bottom).

In reading—all tests that involved printed words—the subject scored poorly. Continuing up the left column, these tests were: Matching picture samples to printed word choices; matching printed word samples to picture choices (three tests over two years); naming printed words; and matching spoken word samples to printed word choices.

The possibility that the subject could not distinguish the printed words from each other was ruled out by his score of 95% in matching printed word samples to printed word choices (not shown in Figure 1-1). The words in this test were the same 20 that comprised the other tests. Also, the two types of control tests at the bottom of Figure 1-1 (matching spoken words to pictures, and picture naming) show that the subject could already distinguish the pictures from each other and the auditory words from each other and that he could say the words aloud. His difficulties were neither with the discrimination of the stimuli used here nor with the oral responses but were specifically with the stimulus-response relations that operationally define simple reading comprehension, oral reading, and auditory-receptive reading.

Teaching Auditory-Receptive Reading

Teaching the subject to match auditory to visual words was the critical experimental operation. Figure 1-2 will illustrate the logic of the experiment and will serve as a basis for later discussion. The three boxes at the left and center of Figure 1-2 represent the three types of stimuli and the arrows represent stimulus equivalences as defined by the matching performance. The arrows connecting the center boxes to the right hand box represent the two naming performances, picture naming and oral reading.

The subject came to the experiment knowing the equivalence of spoken words to pictures (Equivalence I). Would teaching him auditory-visual Equivalence II, spoken words to visual words, suffice to establish reading comprehension, the purely visual equivalence of printed words to pictures (Equivalences III and IV)? He also came to the experi-

ment able to name the pictures (V); given this ability, would teaching him auditory-visual word matching suffice for oral reading (VI) to emerge?

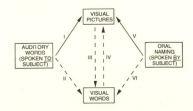

Fig. 1-2. Schematic summary of the experiment. Of the stimulus equivalences, I-IV, the subject came to the experiment knowing I. Of the naming tasks, V and VI, he could do V. After being taught equivalence II, he could then do III, IV, and VI.

In the teaching procedure, sample stimuli were words spoken to the subject; choices were printed words (Figure 1-1, top row). Teaching differed from testing in several ways. (1) A correction procedure was used; when the subject chose a wrong printed word, the display remained unchanged until he pressed the correct window. (2) Errors had different consequences; if the subject made one or more errors on a given trial, the chimes rang when he finally pressed the correct window but he did not receive candy or a penny. (3) Each phase of the teaching procedure started with only two kinds of trials (sample-choice combinations), the two being repeated until the subject's first choices on both were correct. Then a third trial was added; when his first choices on all three were correct, a fourth was added. This progressive enlargement of the set continued as the subject attained each criterion of mastery until his first choices were correct on the full set of twenty trials; (4) Six versions or sets of auditory-visual word matching materials were used. Each set presented the same 20 sample words in different trial sequences and displayed a different combination of seven wrong words along with each correct word.

Set A was used for the preliminary control test. Then the subject was taught Set B until he scored 100% and was tested on Set C. His low score on Set C (Figure 1-1, center section, first bar), suggested that his learning of Set B had been specific to the particular sequence of correct window positions and to the particular wrong words displayed along with each correct word. The subject then learned Set C,

reviewed Set B to the same 100% criterion, and was tested on Set D. The process of learning, reviewing, and testing on a new set continued through Set F, and the center section of Figure 1-1 shows the gradual improvement on each new test. (The teaching process itself is not shown; only the test scores on each new set.) Finally, the subject was retested on Set A, which he had not seen since the preliminary test. The change from 20 to 80% correct on Set A, one month after the preliminary test, demonstrated his new proficiency at the task.

Post-Teaching Tests

After the teaching, all comprehension and oral naming tests were administered once more. Scores are in the right column of Figure 1-1. The subject maintained his good performances on the first auditory-visual word matching set he had learned (upper right), in matching spoken words to pictures, and in picture naming (lower right).

Of major interest are the subject's reading comprehension and oral reading tests (visual word-picture and picture-word matching; word naming). These improved greatly. Having learned to match spoken word samples to printed word choices, he was then able, without additional teaching, to match picture samples to the printed word choices, to match printed word samples to picture choices, and to name printed words.

Given the subject's initial ability to match spoken words to pictures and to name the pictures, teaching him the second auditory-visual equivalence, spoken to printed words, sufficed for the emergency of purely visual reading comprehension and oral reading.

DISCUSSION

The findings will be discussed with reference to Figure 1-2. A simple connectionistic interpretation of the emergence of reading comprehension might be that the visual words and pictures became equivalent to each other (III, IV) because each, independently, had become equivalent to the same auditory words (I, II). This would be entirely consistent with the theoretical suppositions of Geschwind (1965b), particularly with respect to the integrating functions of the angular gyrus region. It is not clear from this experiment, however, whether equivalences I and II need be cross-modal. Suppose, for example, that visual nonsense syllables were substituted for the auditory words and that arbitrary equivalences between these visual symbols and the words and pictures were taught to the subject. Would the words and pictures then emerge as equivalent to each other, even with a common intramodal, rather than a cross-modal linkage? That deaf children learn to read suggests an affirmative answer. There is no need, however, to assume only a single mechanism for reading comprehension.

The emergence of visual-word naming or oral reading (VI), complicates the simple connectionist view, since the equivalence of visual words to pictures may have been mediated by naming (V, VI) rather than by auditory words. This, too, is testable. It should be emphasized, however, that even if the emergence of word naming permitted reading comprehension to develop, it did not do so through the auditory channel. The subject did not name the words or pictures aloud during the reading comprehension tests;

Chapter 1

the only auditory stimuli were the words spoken to him in previous tests and teaching sessions. Furthermore, whatever proves to be the role, if any, of the subject's ability to read orally in mediating the transfer from the cross-modal to the purely visual equivalences, the experiment has demonstrated that matching auditory words to pictures and to printed words are sufficient prerequisites for the emergence of both types of stimulus-response relation, reading comprehension and oral reading.

The identification of these sufficient prerequisites for reading comprehension suggests a most important practical consequence. Both auditory-visual equivalences (I, II) can be taught completely without the intervention of a teacher. Reading comprehension is usually taught by way of oral naming and this does require that a teacher participate actively. Automated programs to teach reading comprehension via purely receptive auditory-visual training (Equivalences I and II) would permit a far larger number of children to be reached than is now possible. Furthermore, the technique provides a rapid method for

determining whether a child who has not yet made the transfer from the auditory to the visual comprehension of words is actually incapable of passing through this apparently critical developmental stage.

Independently of comprehension, one may ask whether oral reading (VI) will always emerge, in a child capable of speech, after the child has learned auditory-visual word matching. Guess (1969) has shown that receptive language training need not facilitate the learning of productive speech. The auditory stimuli Guess used were singular and plural object names and he taught the children to match these spoken names to singular and plural objects, analogous to our Equivalence I. The children were unable, then, to use the correct singular and plural forms in naming the objects, analogous to our oral naming Task V. In addition to the differences in stimulus materials and responses (simple nouns versus singular and plural nouns), a likely reason for the discrepancy between Guess' experiment and the present experiment is that our subject was taught Equivalence II and tested on Task VI (word naming) after he had demonstrated his ability to do Task V (picture naming). If receptive training is to facilitate oral speech, it may be necessary for the child already to have the words in his own speech repertoire.

✳ ✳ ✳ ✳ ✳ ✳ ✳ ✳ ✳ ✳

Commentary

Early Stages of the Experimental Program

The joy of discovery. Our subject in this experiment was a severely retarded boy with whom we had been working for several years in the context of an intensive teaching project at the Walter E. Fernald State School (Mackay & Sidman, 1968; Sidman, 1970). We had taught him step by step—agonizingly slowly—to dress himself, to feed himself, to make his bed, to help with chores, to draw simple figures with pencil and crayon, to name pictures, objects, and features of objects like colors, sizes, and quantities, and to speak some of his needs instead of using violence to draw our attention. We had not yet been able to teach him to read with comprehension. In the experiment, it took us more than 15 hours of instruction over a four week period to teach him to match 20 spoken to printed three-letter words. And then, at the end of that month, we watched him suddenly matching the 20 printed words to pictures and vice versa without having been directly taught to do so.

During the final test session, the excitement in the laboratory was palpable. We were all outside the experimental cubicle, jumping up and down with glee as we watched correct choice after correct choice registering on the recorder. My son, who was helping in the lab that summer, said to me, "Dad, I never saw you lose your cool like that before." Looking inside the cubicle through a one-way window, we could see Os Cresson, good lab technician that he was, sitting quietly behind the subject, hands folded in his lap, not moving—hardly breathing, saying nothing, only his eyes, wide open and unblinking, betraying his tension. But when the boy had completed the tests, Os could contain himself no longer. He grabbed the retarded boy in a bear hug and cried out, "Goddammit, Kent, you can read!"

Os was right, of course. By matching each printed word with its appropriate picture, the boy showed us that he had learned to read and to understand what he was reading, We had not expected this to happen but there was no disappointment. To be sure, we had failed to make our point that the behavioral theorizing of Geschwind and others was too naive to be useful but the very proof of our failure was the emergence of what looked like a startlingly efficient teaching technique. Our subject, having learned to relate 20 dictated words to their corresponding pictures and printed words—40 relations in all, then proved able, *without any additional teaching,* to do nearly 40 new tasks, relating text to pictures and pictures to text. Overriding any theoretical disappointment was the prospect of using the technique not only with normally bright children but with people who needed special help to overcome their impaired learning abilities.

The unimportance of theory. Later developments were to show that Geschwind's theorized progression from auditory to textual comprehension, although not incorrect, was oversimplified. To be fair to Geschwind's memory, I note here that he did not postulate the auditory path to reading comprehension as necessary but only as the way most people develop. He did recognize, after all, that deaf people can learn to read. But because the design of our first experiment has led some to assume that one *must* learn auditory-visual relations before reading comprehension can emerge, I emphasize once more that auditory-visual relations like I and II in Figure 1-2, although *sufficient* to bring about simple reading comprehension, are not *necessary*.

For example, visual-visual stimulus relations (like III and IV in Figure 1-2) that are used to demonstrate simple reading comprehension can be taught indirectly without involving the auditory modality at all; visual or tactile stimuli can be used instead of dictated words (for example, Bush, 1993; Lazar, Davis-Lang, & Sanchez, 1984; Sidman, Kirk, & Willson-Morris, 1985; Spradlin, Cotter, & Baxley, 1973). It is also possible to produce the emergence of new relations when gustatory stimuli are involved (Hayes, Tilley, & Hayes, 1988) and even when all of the stimuli are auditory (Dube, Green, & Serna, 1993) or tactile (O'Leary, 1994). The sensory modalities are not critical. What is critical is that teaching a subject two sets of conditional discriminations can cause new conditional discriminations to emerge. The generality lies in the process, not in the stimulus modalities and, as we shall see, goes beyond just the comprehension of meaningful text.

It is also worth noting at this point that the emergence of reading comprehension does not require subjects to enter the experiment already capable of matching dictated words to pictures. As later studies were to show (for example, Chapter 2), subjects become capable of relating printed words to pictures even if they have to be taught to match the pictures to dictated words during the experiment. More generally, performances III and IV will emerge even if subjects have to be taught *both* sets of prerequisites (for example, Chapters 6 and 7).

Some early naiveté. In this first paper (and some of the next ones, too), major oversimplifications were reflected in my own uncritical use of certain terms and phrases. Chief among these was *stimulus equivalence*. Just once, out of the many occasions on which I talked about this first experiment to academic audiences, someone asked me what I meant by equivalence. I did not even understand the question. Furthermore, I was unaware that I did not understand it. The term *equivalence* had, for me at that time, no technical significance. On later reflection, I realized that without having given it any special thought, I was using the term as a synonym for the phrase *substitutable for*, automatically assuming that any stimuli a subject matched were substitutable for—equivalent to—each other. It had not yet occurred to me that the experiment actually tested that supposition (Chapter 5).

This assumption—that the matching-to-sample procedure generates equivalence relations—was so ingrained that I did not even know I was making it, and I stumbled through an answer that my questioner in the audience must surely have considered incoherent. Several years were to elapse before I came to understand the question and to realize that a rigorous definition of equivalence was basic to the almost dormant field of research that this experiment was to help rejuvenate. Not until our 1982 papers (Chapters 5 and 6) did that rigorous definition appear in print. And so, in reporting this first experiment, I labeled the sets of conditional relations as if each denoted a separate equivalence relation (Equivalences I, II, III, and IV). Later, I came to understand what the experiment really showed: that each group of three related stimuli comprised a single equivalence class, with all related pairs within a class—both in the baseline and in the emergent conditional discriminations—being members of just one equivalence relation. But more about this in Chapters 5, 6, and 10.

Also reflecting my uncritical acceptance of a vocabulary that did not really describe what we were seeing was the application of the terms *stimulus-response relations* and *connectionistic interpretation* to performances that the matching-to-sample procedure generated, especially those performances said to demonstrate simple reading comprehension. It subsequently became clear that a fundamental outcome of the matching-to-sample procedure was its establishment of relations among features of the environment; *stimulus-response relations* therefore gave way in later publications to the more descriptively accurate *stimulus-stimulus relations*, and the relatively sterile notion of *connection* gave way to the more productively defined *equivalence relation*.

Getting published. Before becoming involved in the work on equivalence—starting with the first report from my doctoral dissertation (Sidman, 1953)—I had published several papers in the journal *Science*. One function of this prestigious journal was to publish preliminary reports that would quickly alert a broad range of researchers to important, useful, or exciting findings. Experimenters were expected to follow up those preliminary findings with more extensive studies. In that spirit, I originally submitted our first paper on equivalence relations to *Science*, but this time I was rebuffed. The reviewer wrote:

> The report should not be published. The primary reason for rejection is inadequate control for 'learning-to-learn' or learning set.... In order to distinguish specific from general bases of transfer, at least one control is necessary: presentation of an equivalent

set of words under conditions similar to those of teaching but without experience with the specific [auditory-visual] relationships. Without such control, extent of transfer, of 'reading' due to specific stimulus-response relationships, cannot be estimated…. With increasing familiarity with the situation and the general kinds of material but no specific training on sound-match relationships, [the subject's] performances on these and other relationships might have improved.

The reviewer apparently wanted a demonstration that non-specific factors would not have caused the subject to learn the reading comprehension and oral naming tasks more rapidly anyway, even if the tests had presented words and pictures that were unrelated to the dictated words used in the critical teaching. Such a demonstration would indeed have been necessary if the tests, like those commonly used in paired-associate studies of equivalence relations, had shown the subject learning the tested relations gradually but in fewer trials than would have been expected without the critical teaching. Our tests, however, gave the subject only a single opportunity to match each printed word or picture sample, and one opportunity to name each stimulus. What we observed was not just faster learning but rather, the *immediate* emergence of almost every tested relation.

This was an instance, common enough in Psychology, of the unthinking application of evaluative criteria to kinds of research that make those criteria irrelevant. Fortunately, the editors of the Journal of Speech and Hearing Research, to whom I submitted the manuscript next, were not burdened by a history of paired-associate research and were able to see the data for what they were—a demonstration, still to be fleshed out in detail but clearly relevant to and perhaps even important in the process of learning to read.

We were, however, lucky. Our first subject proved immediately capable of doing the tests after learning the auditory-visual relations but this was not true of all subsequent subjects. Some required several tests. If our first subject had not shown the immediate emergence of the tested relations, we would probably have reported that the learning of auditory-visual relations did not suffice to produce reading comprehension, and we would have shifted our attention to other research problems. But because our early data were so strong, our later observations of delayed emergence caused us not to abandon the area but to rethink our conceptual orientation and to modify our experimental techniques—for example, testing without reinforcement.

But that is a story to be told later. For now, we did recognize that replication was necessary and we moved next in that direction.

2

A Systematic Replication

Background

Although the first experiment had only one subject, the findings were so strong that we had no doubt about the likelihood of successful replication. Also, if the indirect teaching technique that we used could bring about reading comprehension in a subject who had shown such severe learning difficulties, then it should certainly work with people who had no such difficulties. Because of the controls we had built into our procedures, because of the robust findings, and because we knew the boy who was our subject so well, we were convinced that the results of the first experiment were valid.

We realized, however, that many who did not know us, our experimental methods, or our subject, would need more convincing, so we worked some additional controls into the next study. The principal change was to teach only a subset of the auditory-visual relations before testing for the emergence of all 20 of the possible new visual-visual relations; then, to teach a few more of the auditory-visual relations before testing the complete visual-visual set again; and finally, as in the first experiment, to teach all 20 auditory-visual relations before testing a third time. The expectation was, of course, that the only new relations to emerge in each test would be those which required the particular auditory-visual relations that had been explicitly taught.

The traditional kind of control would have had us comparing groups of subjects, all given the same final tests but different training experiences. Instead, we looked at individual subjects and compared groups of stimulus words; all words were involved in the tested relations but during the early teaching phases, only some were related to auditory samples. This design permitted us to avoid the intersubject variability that might otherwise have obscured our data (Sidman, 1960/1988).

In addition to making a science of individual behavior possible, individual-subject experimentation produces another kind of spinoff: immediate reinforcement for the experimenter. In this instance, for example, we were able to observe both positive and negative instances of emergent relations within a single test, and to attribute both kinds of outcome to the particular learning experiences we had given the subject. We did not have to wait for control group data before we could know the results. Such immediacy makes for a kind of joy of experimentation that those accustomed to group comparisons experience only rarely.

Because we were convinced that we had happened on a teaching technique that could be useful in working with handicapped people, we wanted to present our findings to a wider audience. That is why we sent the second paper to the *American Journal of Mental Deficiency.* That audience would want to know whether subjects who were more severely retarded than our first one would also be capable of reading comprehension after having learned auditory-visual stimulus relations.

This is a difficult kind of question. When we first met our original subject, and for a long time after, his behavioral repertoire was in very bad shape. There was no doubt that he was to be classed as severely retarded. But the alert reader will note that we referred to him in the second paper as only moderately retarded. Compared to normal youths his age, he was still severely handicapped but compared to those of his friends who were subjects in the second experiment, he had improved so much more that it no longer seemed appropriate to place them all in the same category.

None of these boys had enough behavior to permit their evaluation by standardized intelligence tests. The subject in our first experiment had, since then, probably become capable of profiting from instruction in a normal classroom if he was given special attention and instruction and if the class contained children much younger than he. The subjects in our second experiment were not ready even for that. Their vocabularies were much more severely limited, as indicated by their poor performances on our simple tests of picture naming and of matching dictated words to pictures. We even wondered whether an inability to transfer automatically from auditory to textual comprehension might be a defining feature of their retardation. The experiment ruled this possibility out; they were clearly capable of learning much more than anyone had previously succeeded in teaching them.

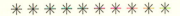

Reading and Crossmodal Transfer of Stimulus Equivalences in Severe Retardation

Two severely retarded Down's syndrome boys were first taught to match printed words to each other (visual discrimination) and to match dictated words to their corresponding pictures (auditory comprehension) but were still incapable of matching the printed words to their pictures (reading comprehension) or of reading the printed words orally. They were next taught to match the dictated to the printed words and were then able to read the words orally and with comprehension. The learned equivalences of dictated words to pictures and to printed words transferred to the purely visual equivalence of printed words to pictures. The success of the mediated-transfer paradigm suggests that inability to achieve crossmodal transfer of stimulus equivalences is not necessarily the cause of reading deficiency in severe retardation and provides a technique for introducing severely retarded children to simple reading skills.

In the normal course of child development, auditory comprehension of words generally precedes visual comprehension or reading. That is to say, children ordinarily learn to understand words spoken to them before they understand written or printed words. In some unpublished experiments on matching to sample we verified this developmental sequence by testing intellectually average preschool children's auditory and visual comprehension of simple words. The children had to match pictures, colors, and numbers to their spoken (dictated) or printed names. If they could match dictated names to the visual pictures, colors, and numbers, they demonstrated simple auditory comprehension; if they could match printed names to the pictures, colors, and numbers, they demonstrated simple reading comprehension. The left side of Figure 2-1 shows that

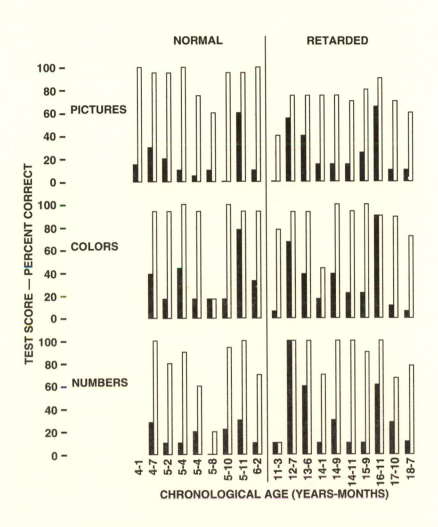

Figure 2-1. Scores of individual normal and retarded subjects in visual-visual (solid bars) and auditory-visual (clear bars) matching-to-sample tests. Each test consisted of 20 (pictures) or 18 (colors and numbers) trials. Each of 20 picture names was presented once; each of six color names was presented three times; and each of nine number names was presented twice. In response to dictated or printed sample names, the subjects had to select the correct choice out of eight (pictures and numbers) or six (colors) available choices on each trial.

preschool children's auditory comprehension (clear bars) was almost invariably superior to their reading comprehension (solid bars) for all three types of words.

Successful performance in the tests required the children to have learned equivalences between auditory and visual stimuli (auditory comprehension) and between different types of visual stimuli (reading comprehension). The data support the widely accepted proposition that learned equivalences between auditory and visual stimuli are at least helpful and perhaps critical in the development of reading comprehension (Birch, 1962; Birch & Belmont, 1964, 1965; Geschwind, 1965a,b, 1972, 1979; Kahn & Birch, 1968; Wepman, 1962). The assumption implicit in this view is that the auditory-visual equivalences involved in simple auditory comprehension transfer in some way to the purely visual equivalences (e.g., printed words and pictures) involved in simple reading comprehension

The same tests were given to a group of severely retarded boys, all institutionalized and all untestable by standard IQ tests. Their scores, depicted on the right side of Figure 2-1, show the same superiority of auditory over reading comprehension. The major difference between the two sides of Figure 2-1 is not in the scores but in the ages of the subjects. No intellectually average child we have tested in the age range of these retarded boys has ever made more than a single error in any of these simple tests. This suggests the possibility that the transfer from auditory comprehension to reading comprehension marks a critical developmental step. Most children achieve it by the end of the first or second grade but some retarded children appear incapable of achieving it.

An alternative possibility is that some retarded children who have not achieved the transfer from auditory to visual comprehension have the capability of doing so but have simply not been taught effectively. The possibility received some support from an experiment in which a retarded boy, after learning certain auditory-visual equivalences, transferred this learning to the purely visual equivalences that define simple reading comprehension (Sidman, 1971b). The boy, who could not read but could match auditory (dictated) words to pictures, was taught to match the same auditory words to their printed counterparts. Then, without any additional training, he was able to match the printed words to the pictures (reading comprehension).

This finding provided experimental evidence, heretofore lacking, for the proposition that learned auditory-visual stimulus equivalences play a constructive role in the development of reading comprehension. Although the experiment did not prove the necessity of such a relation (the fact that deaf children learn to read suggests that the relation is not a necessary one), it did demonstrate that appropriate auditory visual learning is sufficient for the emergence of simple reading comprehension. The present study was an attempt to replicate this finding with additional control procedures and with two children more severely retarded than the original subject.

METHOD

Subjects

The subjects were two institutionalized Down's syndrome boys, one (B.A.) 19 and the other (J.W.) 18 years old at the start of the experiment. Both boys were participants in an ongoing behavior modification project (Mackay & Sidman, 1968; Sidman, 1970) but received no instruction in reading during the period covered by the experiment. Their experimental sessions, however, were scheduled so as not to interfere with their activities within the project and the pennies they earned were spent in accord with the contingencies prevailing in the project. Subject B.A. was tested on the Stanford-Binet L-M immediately after the experiment and achieved a mental age of 4-2, Basal at year III and scatter through year V. No numerical IQ could be calculated since his score was below the Binet's minimum. Subject J.W., also tested after he completed the experiment, achieved a mental age of 4-0, Basal at year III and scatter through year V and could not be assigned a numerical IQ. These performances were considerably below those of the first subject in this series (Sidman, 1971b), who achieved a Wechsler Adult Intelligence Scale Full Scale score of 49 one year after completing his experiment.

Apparatus and Test Procedures

The subject sat before a panel of nine translucent windows onto which visual stimuli could be projected from the rear. In the early sessions of the experiment, the windows, each 5.07 cm square, were arranged in a 3 x 3 square matrix (Sidman et al., 1971). A new apparatus, introduced later in the experiment, had nine round windows, each 7.32 cm in diameter, arranged in a circle of eight with the ninth in the center (Figure 2-2). The diameter of the circle, from outer edge to outer edge, was 32.72 cm; the center-to-center distance was 9.53 cm between adjacent windows on the perimeter and 12.7 cm between the center window and each of the others. The change from the square to the circular matrix had no effect on the data (see below).

Each trial began by presentation of a sample stimulus. Visual word or picture samples appeared

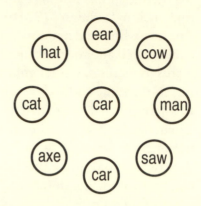

Figure 2-2. Schematic diagram of the circular display matrix, illustrating one trial from the identity word-word matching test. In other kinds of tests, the sample window (center) or the choice windows (periphery) contained pictures or were blank.

on the center window of the matrix; auditory word samples were dictated and repeated through a speaker at 2- to 5-s intervals by a continuous loop tape system (Fletcher, Stoddard, & Sidman, 1971).

In matching-to-sample tests, the subject pressed the center window to bring choice stimuli, always visual, onto the outer windows of the matrix. On each trial, one choice, the correct one, corresponded to the sample; the other seven choices did not. The subject selected and pressed one of the choice windows. His correct choices were rewarded by chimes ringing and delivery of a penny. No rewards followed incorrect choices. The stimuli disappeared after each choice and 1.5 to 2 s later a new sample presentation began the next trial. Sample stimuli, choice stimuli, and correct window positions varied from trial to trial.

In oral naming tests, the subject had simply to name the sample picture or word aloud. Reward procedures were the same as in the matching tests.

Each test had 20 trials. The sample and choice stimuli, taken from a list of 20 pictures or the printed (lower case) or dictated names of the pictures, were: *axe, bed, bee, box, boy, bug, car, cat, cow, dog, ear, hat, hen, hut, hoe, man, pie, pig, saw, zoo.*

A series of seven different tests, administered to the subjects at several strategic points, provided the experimental data. The left columns of Figures 2-3 and 2-4 list the types of sample stimuli and the responses required of the subjects in each of the seven tests. Reading from bottom to top, the tests were: *(a)* identity matching (selecting the printed word choices that matched the printed-word samples); *(b)* audi-tory comprehension (selecting the picture choices that corresponded to the dictated-word samples); (c) picture naming (naming the picture samples aloud); *(d)* auditory receptive reading (selecting the printed-word choices that corresponded to the dictated-word samples); *(e)* reading comprehension (matching the appropriate printed-word choices to the picture samples); (f) reading comprehension (matching the appropriate picture choices to the printed-word samples); and *(g)* oral reading (naming the printed-word samples aloud).

Visual and auditory samples never occurred together in the same test. When samples were dictated, the center window of the matrix was always blank; when visual words or pictures were presented as samples on the center window, no auditory stimuli were presented.

Teaching Procedures

Teaching sessions took place between administrations of the test series; the teaching and testing sequences will be described in conjunction with the results. The teaching always involved matching to sample but details

49

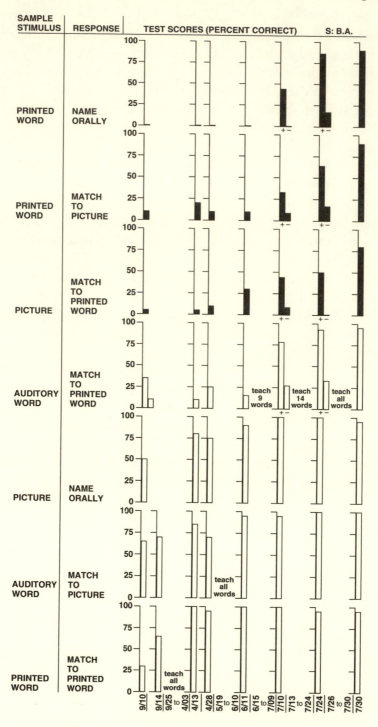

of the methods were changed several times to meet difficulties encountered in teaching the subjects the various materials. For example, sometimes the procedure was correction, sometimes noncorrection; sometimes reinforcement was delivered for any correct response, sometimes only if the first response in a trial was correct; usually the subjects had to learn two new sample words at a time and then the newly learned words were rehearsed together with words they had learned earlier, but sometimes previously learned words had to be retaught individually; the number of teaching sessions per week varied from one to three. Because of such irregularities, data describing the course of learning the various materials by the subjects will not be presented. Instead, test scores after the completion of each teaching procedure will attest to the effectiveness of the teaching.

RESULTS

Subject B.A.

Pretests. This subject's test scores before any explicit teaching had taken place appear in the left columns of bar graphs, dated 9/10 and 9/14 in Figure 2-3. In the four tests at the top—oral reading, the two reading comprehension tasks, and auditory receptive reading—the subject scored poorly. Subsequent scores on these four reading tests provided the critical data.

In picture naming and auditory comprehension the scores were better but considerably short of perfection. In the identity matching task (printed word to printed word; bottom of Figure 2-3), the subject scored poorly on 9/10 but improved on retest (9/14), perhaps because of reinforcement during the tests themselves. The poor scores on the word-word matching tests raised the possibility that his

Figure 2-3 (facing page). Subject B.A. The two left columns identify the sample stimuli and responses that comprised each type of test. The row of bars to the right of each test represents the subject's scores in successive administrations of the test. The dates of each test and of the interpolated teaching are given below each column of bars. In the final three test series, each of the four reading tests has two scores: The bars marked + represent the subject's performance with sample words he had been taught to match in the auditory-visual word word matching task; the bars marked − represent his performance with words he had not yet been taught.

inability to distinguish all the printed words from each other, even on the basis of their form alone, underlay his reading deficits.

Teaching word-word identity matching. During the period 9/25 to 4/03, the subject was taught to select each of the 20 printed words from different sets of eight alternatives in response to printed-word samples, as in Figure 2-2. As might have been expected, most of his problems occurred with words that looked alike, for example, car-ear, car-cat, hat-hut, pie-pig.

When Subject B.A. had learned the identity matching task with all 20 words, he again went through the test series; the results are in the column dated 4/13 (Figure 2-3). His newly learned skill was confirmed by a score of 100% on the identity matching test. Some improvement after the six-month teaching period also appeared in auditory comprehension and picture naming but there was little change in any of the four reading tests.

The column of test scores dated 4/28 represents the change from the square to the circular matrix of windows. No consistent differences in performance appeared consequent to the apparatus change, although a slight decline in auditory comprehension suggested that the previous improvement had merely represented uncontrolled variability in this marginal performance.

Teaching auditory comprehension. Matching dictated words to pictures provides a measure of auditory comprehension and is one of the stimulus equivalences presumed to underlie reading comprehension. The next task to be taught to the subject, therefore, was to match each of the 20 dictated sample words to six variations of its appropriate picture. This was accomplished in slightly less than one month (5/19 to 6/10).

After he had learned the auditory comprehension task, the subject received the test series again (6/11). He achieved a score of 95% on his newly learned skill and maintained a perfect score on the previously learned identity matching task. Learning to match the dictated words to pictures also appeared to improve his picture naming. The changes in auditory comprehension and picture naming, however, were not accompanied by appreciable improvement in any of the four reading scores. Subsequent data showed that the slight changes in the two reading comprehension scores represented only uncontrolled variability; both of these scores were actually close to the chance level for tests with eight possible choices per trial.

It is possible at this point to make certain assertions about the subject's reading deficits and to clarify the logic of the remainder of the experiment. First, the subject's excellent performance in matching printed-word samples to printed-word choices demonstrated that mere inability to distinguish the printed words from each other did not cause his poor scores in the reading tests. Second, his good auditory comprehension and picture naming demonstrated that he could distinguish the pictures from each other and the dictated words from each other and that he could say the words aloud. The subject's reading problem, therefore, stemmed neither from poor discrimination of the stimuli nor from inability to say the words aloud. His problems were specifically with the stimulus response relations that comprised the tests of simple reading comprehension, oral reading, and auditory receptive reading.

Third, the development of auditory comprehension did not by itself generate reading comprehension. The role of auditory receptive reading— matching dictated words to printed words—remained to be evaluated.

Teaching auditory receptive reading. The experiment went on to investigate whether the mediated transfer paradigm that was used in the earlier experiment (Sidman, 1971b) would generate reading comprehension even in subjects as severely retarded as these. An additional control also evaluated the specificity of the transfer.

The mediated-transfer paradigm may be summarized as follows: Teach the stimulus equivalences A-B and A-C; then, test whether the learned equivalence of A to both B and C has caused the equivalence B-C to emerge on the very first trial. In this experiment, A represents the 20 dictated words, B the 20 pictures, and C the 20 printed words. The equivalence A-B, therefore, represents auditory comprehension—matching dictated-word samples (A) to picture choices (B);

the equivalence A-C represents auditory receptive reading—matching dictated-word samples (A) to printed-word choices (C); the equivalence B-C represents one form of reading comprehension—matching picture samples (B) to printed-word choices (C); the equivalence C-B, also tested, represents the matching of printed-word samples (C) to picture choices (B), the reverse of the first reading comprehension task.

The subject was first taught to match only nine of the dictated-word samples to their printed-word equivalents (6/15 to 7/09); the other 11 printed words appeared in the displays among the wrong choices. After this teaching, the subject once more received the complete series of seven tests and his scores appear in the column dated 7/10 (Figure 2-3). Double bars in each of the four reading tests distinguish the scores for the nine dictated sample words the subject had been taught to match to printed words (+) and the scores for the 11 words he had not yet been taught (-).

The direct effect of the teaching was a large increase in the subject's accuracy in matching the nine dictated sample words to their printed equivalents, an increase not reflected in his score for the 11 untaught words. The major factor contributing to the less than perfect score for the nine critical words was probably the subject's confusion because of the mixture of taught and untaught words in the test.

The three upper sets of bars in the same test series (7/10) show that the subject improved also in reading comprehension and oral reading, tasks in which he had received no direct instruction. The latter scores increased slightly for the nine critical words only and the major evidence for transfer was this selectivity of the improvement.

The subject was then taught to match five more dictated words to their printed equivalents. During this teaching (7/13 to 7/24), he also reviewed the original nine words, so that he had been taught 14 of the 20 words when he again took the test series (7/24). This time he scored almost perfectly in the auditory receptive reading task on the 14 words he had been taught, with little if any improvement in the six untaught words. The evidence for transfer to reading comprehension and oral reading (the three upper sets of bars) was even stronger than before, both in the scores for the 14 taught words and in the difference between the taught and untaught words.

Finally, the remaining six words were added in teaching the auditory-visual, word-word matching task (7/26 to 7/30), and the final test series (7/30) continued the trend of the earlier tests. The subject maintained his good performance on all the prerequisite skills he had been taught, as well as on picture naming, and clearly demonstrated his newly and indirectly acquired ability to read aloud and to comprehend the printed words. Having learned to match dictated-word samples to printed-word choices during the final three teaching periods, Subject B.A. was then able, without additional teaching, to match picture samples to printed word choices, to match printed-word samples to picture choices, and to name the printed words aloud.

Subject J. W.

This subject replicated the major results obtained with Subject B.A. but his rate of progress was slower. After his pretests (Figure 2-4, 9/09 and 9/15), Subject J.W. was taught identity word-word matching and auditory comprehension (bottom two rows of Figure 2-4) and did not transfer this learning to any of the reading tasks (7/07 and earlier). He differed from Subject B.A. in showing little if any improvement in picture naming after learning to match dictated words to pictures (7/07). He also took about a month longer to learn auditory comprehension (Figure 2-4, 5/19 to 7/03, as compared to Figure 2-3, 5/19 to 6/10).

Subject J.W. lagged still further behind Subject B.A. in learning to match dictated to printed words. It took three months (7/09 to 10/06) to teach him the first nine words of this task, as opposed to one month for Subject B.A. On his next test series (10/07), he showed no transfer to reading comprehension or oral reading. He then required nearly seven months to learn 14 words of the auditory receptive reading task (10/21 to 5/12); during this time, he actually had to be retaught to match several of the

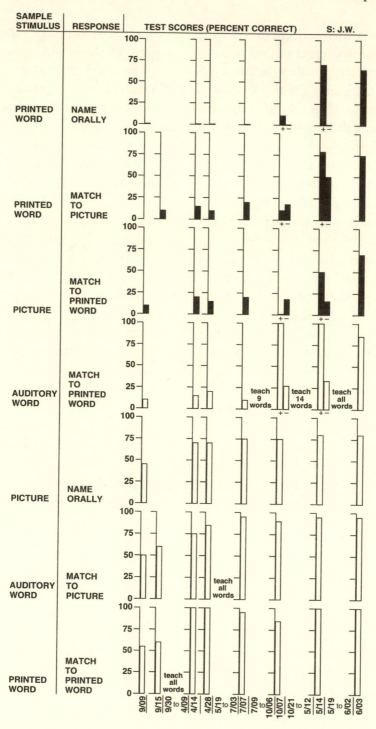

sample words in the identity matching and auditory comprehension tasks. After learning the 14 words, however, he displayed considerable transfer to reading comprehension and oral reading. Finally, after learning to match all 20 dictated to printed words (5/19 to 6/02), his scores on the other reading tests (6/03) were considerably higher than the pretests, although not as high as those of Subject B.A. It is clear, however, that a considerable ability to read orally and with comprehension had emerged from his learning of the auditory receptive reading task.

DISCUSSION

The moderately retarded subject in the earlier experiment (Sidman, 1971b) initially could not read but could discriminate printed words and match dictated words to pictures. After he was taught to match dictated to printed words, he was able, without additional teaching, to read the words with comprehension. The two severely retarded Down's syndrome boys in the present experiment had first to be taught identity matching and auditory comprehension; then, teaching them to match dictated to printed words also caused reading comprehension to emerge. The conclusion seems inescapable that profound reading deficit, even in boys as severely retarded as these two, need not signify an inability to achieve the normal transfer from learned auditory-visual stimulus equivalences to the purely visual equivalences that define simple reading comprehension.

Still to be tested is the size and complexity of the reading vocabulary such severely retarded subjects can attain. The difficulties encountered in teaching 20 simple words suggests that the transfer process may have been

Figure 2-4 (facing page). Subject J.W. The two left columns identify the sample stimuli and responses that comprised each type of test. The row of bars to the right of each test represents the subject's scores in successive administrations of the test. The dates of each test and of the interpolated teaching are given below each column of bars. In the final three test series, each of the four reading tests has two scores: The bars marked + represent the subject's performance with sample words he had been taught to match in the auditory-visual word-word matching task; the bars marked − represent his performance with words he had not yet been taught.

approaching its limits. On the other hand, studies now in progress suggest that the teaching procedures, rather than the subjects' deficiencies, may have set the limiting conditions, even at this level of retardation.

The transfer process itself presents some unsolved problems. A major one is the nature of the mediation. Was the equivalence between printed words and pictures mediated by their common equivalence to the dictated words spoken *to* the subjects? Or did the words spoken *by* the subjects (oral reading and picture naming) mediate the equivalence between printed words and pictures? The first possibility would imply pure stimulus mediation via receptive channels; the second would require active or implicit response mediation via the oral names.

This problem has been a persistent one in the experimental and theoretical literature (Jenkins, 1963; Jensen, 1971; Peters, 1935) and the present experiment does not solve it. It does, however, add two new considerations. First, the transfer demonstrated here was crossmodal, from auditory-visual to visual-visual stimulus equivalences. Second, all of the teaching was accomplished via matching to sample—the direct teaching of stimulus equivalences without requiring names—in contrast to the explicit teaching of oral or written names in the paired-associate tasks usually used in studies of mediated association. If, in the present experiment, the emergent visual word-picture equivalences were mediated by oral names, such mediation would have to be viewed as a second-order process: the subjects learned oral reading indirectly as a by-product of auditory receptive reading. The conditions under which receptive language training facilitates the learning of productive speech are only poorly understood (Guess, 1969). Although both of our subjects learned to name words orally as a consequence of learning to match dictated to printed words, only one of them improved in picture naming as a consequence of learning to match dictated words to pictures. Until further work clarifies the problem, an empirical description of our results would appear prudent: The learning of auditory comprehension and auditory receptive reading are sufficient to generate both reading comprehension and oral reading; the relation between the latter two performances remains to be evaluated.

This empirical view highlights a cogent practical consideration. The two auditory-visual matching tasks that are sufficient for the emergence of reading comprehension can be taught by teaching machines, as they were here; they do not require active participation by a teacher except to construct the teaching sequences in advance and to enhance the effectiveness of the reinforcers. Similarly, the more basic prerequisites, identity word-word and picture-picture matching, can also be taught by machine. This means that a practical method and an effective teaching sequence are available for introducing many severely retarded children to reading, children whose training has hitherto been precluded by the scarcity of teachers and by the seeming profundity of their own deficits.

∗ ∗ ∗ ∗ ∗ ∗ ∗ ∗ ∗ ∗

Commentary

Our technique for teaching simple reading comprehension was clearly applicable to retarded youths who had been ranked close to the bottom of the ladder. We even had to teach these boys to distinguish printed three-letter words from each other. But then, after we taught them to relate words they heard both to pictures and to printed words, they were able right away to relate the printed words to the pictures—they could read the words with understanding. It was clear that their previous inability to read with comprehension had not been caused by an inability to accomplish the transfer from auditory-visual stimulus relations to purely visual relations.

By testing all of the possible word-picture and picture-word relations after we had taught the auditory-visual prerequisites for only a few, we were able to show that the subjects' emergent performances were not brought about by some nonspecific aspect of the procedures (Chapter 1, pp. 37-38). I have been asked, however, whether the subjects' poor test performances on control trials might have come about because they simply continued to select only those pictures and words they had become familiar with on the teaching trials. On checking our data, we found no evidence that this had happened. We also wondered whether the control-trial scores might have been inflated because the subjects avoided choices that they had learned were correct only with specific samples (the *exclusion* phenomenon: Dixon, 1977; McIlvane & Stoddard, 1981), but again, our data did not support this possibility.

So it really looked as though we had a tiger by the tail: new performances emerging that we had not specifically taught, of a type that was important in everyday life, and that our background had not prepared us to consider. We were off on a long-term adventure.

An Apparatus Note

Some readers might wonder why we changed the matrix of windows during this experiment. The original matrix, designed and built by Ron Ray, contained nine "floating" windows (not attached to the frame). When pushed, these windows activated small mechanical switches. This ingenious system, which worked well for several years, eventually became unstable; like most mechanical devices, it came to require constant repair and adjustment. Another of its disadvantages was the small space between windows. Many of our subjects were unable to move their hands and fingers accurately and steadily and sometimes inadvertently touched a wrong window or two adjacent windows at the same time. Therefore, instead of replacing the original matrix with an exact copy, we made the new windows larger and put more space between them. The windows were also sensitive to touch, so that they required no switches or any other mechanical action. By making the windows circular and arranging them in a circle instead of a square, we thought we might be deemphasizing position cues like corners and edges that often seemed to distract subjects from observing more relevant aspects of the stimuli.

On the whole, the new system worked well but its larger dimensions created new problems. We noticed that some retarded subjects and some normal children six years of age or younger often made errors because they failed to scan the whole matrix. We wished many times that we had stayed with a smaller matrix and in later experiments we sometimes did not use all eight comparison windows. We often wondered whether some of the seeming learning deficits shown by retarded people might have reflected inadequate scanning behavior that was brought about either by incomplete educational experiences or by central nervous system damage (for example, Kirshner and Sidman, 1972). We finally did replace the large matrix with a smaller computer-generated display but there is still much need for investigation of the scanning problem.

Some Terminological Notes

Although we appreciated the relevance of our data to an understanding of reading and to the practical task of teaching reading, our conception of the basic process that was involved—the formation of equivalence relations—was still primitive. Researchers and others who are acquainted with subsequent developments in this line of research will note, once more, the uncritical use of *equivalence* and *stimulus-response relations,* the latter to be abandoned later in favor of *stimulus-stimulus relations* and the former to be defined more rigorously (Chapters 5 & 6). Statements like "auditory-visual equivalences transfer to purely visual equivalences" have probably been the root of much needless confusion and controversy in the literature. We shall show later that it would have been more accurate to say something like, "Emergence of the purely visual conditional relations proves that the auditory and visual stimuli were related by equivalence."

The terms, *receptive language* and *productive speech,* the former referring to auditory-visual matching (nonvocal) and the latter to oral naming (vocal), were adopted from the literature on language and reading. We did not make the mistake of assuming that both reflected a single underlying process or entity; to make such an assumption would have been to ignore our earlier findings that stroke-induced brain damage could affect matching and naming differentially, and within the naming category, could affect oral and written naming differentially (for example, Mohr, Sidman, Stoddard, Leicester, & Rosenberger, 1973; Sidman, 1971a; Sidman et al., 1971). Realizing, however, that the terminology led inevitably to theoretical postulation of an underlying entity, we eventually dropped the concepts of productive and receptive language, particularly after Lee's cogent reminder that we were dealing with the speaker's behavior in the one case and the listener's behavior in the other (Lee, 1981a,b; Skinner, 1957). (But see pp. 114-116.)

The terms, *mediation* and *mediated transfer,* adopted from the literature on stimulus equivalence as studied mainly by paired-associate techniques (for example, Jenkins, 1963; Peters, 1935), have also contributed to misunderstanding and controversy. Not until later did we discuss some of the limitations of these terms (Sidman, Cresson, & Willson-Morris, 1974). We subsequently abandoned the concept of mediation, in the belief that it obscured rather than added to our understanding of equivalence relations. Others, however, continue to talk about and look for mediating processes as causal factors in the development of equivalence relations (for example, Dugdale & Lowe, 1990; Hayes, 1986, 1991; Lowe, 1986). This remains a matter of continuing concern and I shall have more to say about it later (Chapters 4, 8, and Epilogue).

3

A Teaching Sequence

Background

Teaching Some Basic Prerequisites for Reading is included here out of sequence. Like the first two papers, this one was concerned with the teaching of reading and because of this orientation it belongs with the other two.

One might have thought that our second paper, confirming the original findings, would have inspired widespread applications, but that was not to be. Nearly twenty-five years later, we and others have extended the phenomenon's generality far beyond anything our first experiments had foreseen. Several publications have been oriented specifically toward teachers (for example., Hollis, Carrier, & Spradlin, 1976; Spradlin, Karlan, & Wetherby, 1976; Stromer, Mackay, & Stoddard, 1992). In addition, the general availability of computers now permits the technology to be extended almost without limit—an exercise well within the capability of reasonably skilled computer programmers (Dube & McIlvane, 1989). Still, no school that I know of is systematically applying this simple technology to help retarded or normal children learn even an elementary reading vocabulary. To be sure, taking deliberate advantage of the equivalence phenomenon would advance the total instructional process only a small step. And yet, what help it could provide teachers who are overburdened with unchangeable curricula, with schedules and tasks that benefit administrators rather than pupils, and with classes so large that they can reach no individual pupil.

Teachers and applied behavior analysts (who are also teachers but have found that they cannot say so without setting off turf wars) often claim that scientific jargon makes it impossible for them to understand research papers and they fault researchers for not getting out of their laboratories and applying their discoveries themselves. Several writers have provided excellent summaries of the general problem and have given practical suggestions for overcoming the resistance of teachers and administrators to effective educational technology (for example, Axelrod, 1992; Fawcett, 1991; Fantuzzo & Atkins, 1992; Lindsley, 1992). Perhaps change is on the way. But how different from other fields! Practicing physicians are quick—sometimes, perhaps, too quick—to apply new discoveries from basic research in genetics, biochemistry, pharmacology, immunology, and so on. Engineers and architects are always on the alert for new construction materials, design principles, and fabrication techniques.

Many individual teachers, too, are always looking for effective instructional techniques but the educational establishment—schools and administrators of education—resists change. Schools of education do not teach prospective teachers to understand the science that is basic to their profession. As a result, by paying no attention or by attending only superficially, teachers and educational administrators guarantee the failure of every promising new teaching tool that emerges from basic or applied behavioral research.

We were not part of the educational establishment. We had no official credentials for teaching except in colleges or universities; attempts to introduce our discoveries into the educational curriculum were considered intrusive. Working teachers had not been taught to understand, evaluate, appreciate, or apply laboratory findings. Any move by us to share our discoveries with them was regarded, at worst, as an invasion of turf, and at best, as well-intentioned but irrelevant. They politely informed us that their pupils' programs were already too busy. It quickly became apparent that whether we wanted to show them how to do it or to do it ourselves, we were unwelcome. Puzzled and disillusioned, we soon turned our attention almost exclusively away from applications. Instead, we concentrated our efforts on studying some of the more basic and systematic ramifications of the fascinating phenomenon we had happened upon.

As the saying goes, however, hope springs eternal. Perhaps a few teachers—even better, a few teachers of teachers—will happen upon this book and find something worth attending to. If they do, they will certainly wonder how to give pupils, particularly retarded pupils, the kinds of basic skills they will need in order to do the kinds of tasks we have described: match to sample, discriminate shapes and sounds, pay attention, remain motivated, and so on. It would take much more than just a few words to teach all this but the *Basic Prerequisites* paper indicates at least that methods are available. Any reasonably skilled and motivated teacher can find out about them, modify them where necessary, and apply them.

Teachers should not be put off because the methods are discussed in the context of laboratory refinements, particularly the automation of stimulus presentation, reinforcement, and data recording. Automation makes the procedures easier to carry out and easier to describe and has the advantage of freeing the teacher to teach what is *not* amenable to automation, but it is not critical. Matching-to-sample and discrimination procedures, performance recording, and reinforcement were all being done "on the tabletop" long before experimenters brought them into the laboratory. Translating the automated procedures to manual table-top procedures is not difficult. All prospective teachers should receive practice in adapting teaching methods from research to practice.

✳ ✳ ✳ ✳ ✳ ✳ ✳ ✳ ✳

Teaching Some Basic Prerequisites for Reading

This paper describes a linguistic paradigm for evaluating a child's ability to learn a simple form of reading comprehension. Methods are presented for teaching prerequisite skills for this performance even to children who are so severely retarded that they are usually considered incapable of learning to read.

At sophisticated levels of analysis we tend to overlook some of the behavioral processes that are necessary for the development of reading and we often take for granted the large number of basic skills a successful reader must bring to the task. When we study reading in retarded people, however, we are forced to ask questions that do not arise with normal readers who have already developed the basic skills through exposure to natural contingencies. Our interest here, therefore, is not in the level of complexity at which you and I operate when we read, but rather in skills and processes which by themselves may not be considered reading but which are prerequisite if the retarded student is to take advantage of an existing capacity.

Here is a laboratory version of a simple reading comprehension task. The right side of Figure 3-1 shows a display panel of nine windows onto which stimuli can be projected from the rear. A three letter word is first projected on the center window (left side of Figure 3-1); this is the sample. The student responds to the sample by touching it, and pictures then appear on the outer windows; the pictures are the comparison stimuli. The student's task then is to touch the comparison picture which corresponds to the sample word. If the student selects the correct picture, a reinforcer is delivered into a tray beside the windows and a new trial begins with another sample word. If the student has selected the wrong picture, there is no reinforcer.

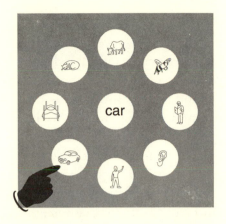

Fig. 3-1. The nine-window matching-to-sample apparatus. Visual sample stimuli will appear in the center window; dictated samples are presented via a loudspeaker. Comparison stimuli will appear in the eight outer windows. Reinforcers will be delivered into a tray at the right. Left side: student touching the sample word. Right side: student touching the comparison picture which corresponds to the sample.

When a student can match each of a set of pictures to its appropriate printed name, we have reason to suspect that he is reading the names with comprehension. But can we be sure? Pigeons and monkeys have been taught matching tasks that are just as arbitrary as picture-to-word matching, but we are somehow skeptical about classifying their performance as reading. How can we tell whether matching to sample is a linguistic performance or whether it represents an arbitrary stimulus-response chain that has no linguistic relevance?

The feature of matching to sample that is critical to its status as a linguistic process is the development of stimulus classes. In a well learned matching-to-sample performance, each comparison stimulus and the sample to which it is matched become a pair of equivalent stimuli. They become substitutable for each other, as is implied by the term "matching."

This distinction between the human and the lower-animal matching-to-sample performance, although real, does not show up in the performance itself. To determine whether or not stimulus classes have become established requires something more. We can set up an independent test of stimulus equivalence in the following way, as is diagrammed in Figure 3-2. We begin by teaching the student to match each of a set of pictures not to its printed name but rather to its dictated name (A–B in Figure 3-2). For example, the student hears the word "boy" and is then to pick out the picture of a boy from several choices; when the word "car" is dictated, the student must pick out the picture of a car, and so forth.

Next, we teach the student to match each of a set of printed words to the same dictated names to which he has learned to match the pictures (A–C in Figure 3-2). Now, for example, the sample word "boy" is dictated and the student must select the printed word *boy* out of several available choices.

Suppose the matching-to-sample tasks have indeed caused each comparison to become equivalent to its corresponding sample. Equivalent stimuli are by definition substitutable for each other. It should be possible then to substitute the printed word

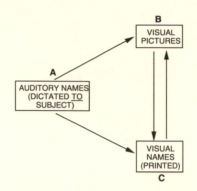

Fig. 3-2. The matching-to-sample tasks. Arrows point from sample to comparison stimuli.

boy (C) for the dictated word "boy" (A) and the student should now be able to match pictures to appropriate printed words (B–C in Figure 3-2) *even though he has never learned explicitly to do this.* Similarly, we should be able substitute the picture of a boy (B) for the dictated sample word "boy" (A) and the student should be able to match the printed word to its picture sample (C–B in Figure 3-2).

We found that some retarded students, who had only the indirect training described above, were indeed able to match picture comparisons to printed-word samples and printed-word comparisons to picture samples (Sidman, 1971b; Sidman & Cresson, 1973; Sidman et al.,

1974). The emergence of these two performances confirmed the formation of stimulus classes in the original matching tasks and provided us with a legitimate basis for regarding the two emergent tasks as reading comprehension. The teaching sequence provides a test for the formation of stimulus classes, a process that is fundamental to linguistic competence because it makes it possible for words to mediate the emergence of new behavior that has never been directly taught.

Furthermore, the test is itself a vehicle for teaching. We have taught this elementary form of reading comprehension to retarded youths whose formal IQs were 30 or less and who had been given up as hopeless prospects for any type of preacademic training. The students emerged with a reading comprehension vocabulary of 20 words, a substantial starting point for a teacher who would otherwise be at a loss as to how even to begin to teach such students to read. It should also be noted that the use of dictated words spoken *to* the students, rather than the usual method of requiring students to name the pictures and words themselves, permits the teaching to be accomplished via teaching machines. In view of the general shortage of teachers who are skilled in working with severely retarded students, teaching-machine techniques make it possible to introduce a larger number of such students to reading than would otherwise be feasible.

However, such children cannot simply be exposed to the test with the expectation that their scores will reveal their actual capabilities. Students functioning at this retarded level usually do not possess the behavioral prerequisites that are necessary to render the test valid. Although many of these prerequisites are nonverbal, they are necessary for a meaningful evaluation of the student's linguistic competence. Where does one start with a severely retarded student who has none of the required skills?

A major problem is to motivate the student to work at the learning tasks. Students who have no history of successful learning cannot be expected to be motivated by learning for its own sake. Normal children discover early that learning is useful; it increases their options. Everything they learn helps open up new worlds of exploration, environmental manipulation, and social interaction. Severely retarded students, especially those residing in institutions, have not yet made this discovery and their learning must at first be motivated from sources extrinsic to the learning tasks themselves. It is necessary to make it worthwhile for such students to sit, attend, and learn effectively for reasonable periods of time. To this end, one may take advantage of reinforcers discovered through careful observation and test—food, candy—or one may go to the effort, time consuming at first but more efficient in the long run, of establishing a generalized reinforcer such as tokens or points. The establishment of generalized reinforcers is not usually regarded as a necessary teaching skill, because normal children come to the classroom with such reinforcers already available. The teacher of severely retarded students, however, must know how to establish and use generalized reinforcers if advanced teaching is to succeed.

Given an effective reinforcer, it is still not possible simply to expose the student to the matching-to-sample tasks. The student must learn the procedures; they require specific behavior—for example, touching the relevant stimuli, waiting for stimuli to appear, scanning the display and searching for relevant stimuli, and discriminating the stimuli from each other. First, therefore, we teach the student some skills that do not involve matching to sample but that are prerequisites for the matching-to-sample performance. We start by teaching something easy and then build upon that, step by step. We teach the student simply to touch whichever window of the stimulus display is lighted—reinforcing each correct response along the way. Then, by shifting the bright stimulus from position to position on different learning trials, we teach the student to scan the display in order to locate the relevant stimulus.

Next, we teach the student not simply to touch a bright window, but rather to touch only the bright window that also has a form on it. We superimpose a circle on the bright window and dimly illuminate the other windows without superimposing a form on them. By gradually increasing the brightness level of the incorrect windows from trial to trial, it is possible to teach the student, often errorlessly, to select only the bright window that has the circle on it and never to choose any of the blank bright windows. We now have a more advanced discrimination—form versus no form.

Next, we want to teach the student to select only a particular form and to reject other forms; we gradually fade a flat ellipse onto the incorrect windows. At the end of this teaching phase, which the gradual fading often causes to be errorless, the student selects the window that has a circle on it and never chooses any window that contains an ellipse. We now have s simple form discrimination—circle versus ellipse (Sidman & Stoddard, 1966; 1967).

We can then change the circle and the ellipse into other forms and by making these changes extremely gradual, we can teach the student to discriminate other forms from each other. For example, the circle may be collapsed into a vertical line and the ellipse to a horizontal line and the student will end up, often without any errors, always selecting the vertical and rejecting the horizontal line. Many such transformations can be made and in this way students can be taught to tell the letters of the alphabet from each other, stimuli that are critical for the learning tasks we are eventually to set for them. This may be a long process, even with a teaching machine, but it is necessary if severely retarded students are to be given a fair chance to demonstrate their true capacities.

Only now can we begin to teach matching to sample. By programming the steps carefully and reinforcing each correct response, we can instruct the student even if we are unable to communicate verbally. We must first teach the student that two responses are now required for reinforcement; touch the sample (to tell us the student has observed it) and then touch a comparison stimulus. To teach this double response, we first present a sample alone, so that it looks bright. When the student touches the sample, a single comparison window is illuminated with the same stimulus that is on the sample window. When the comparison appears, however, the seemingly bright sample is seen to be relatively dim. Therefore, instead of continuing to touch the sample, the student shifts to the brighter comparison window. We then gradually increase the sample brightness until it is exactly the same as the comparison and at the end of this stage we have established the two-response chain—touch the sample and then the comparison.

Adapting a technique that was first reported by Moore and Goldiamond (1964), we next teach the student to refrain from touching any comparison window unless it contains the same stimulus as the sample. Along with the matching stimulus, we also present a nonmatching stimulus on one of the other comparison windows. But the nonmatching stimulus at first is not nearly as bright as the matching stimulus, so the student continues to select the bright matching comparison. From trial to trial we gradually increase the brightness of the incorrect stimulus, By the time the incorrect and correct comparisons are equally bright, the student will have learned to choose only the one that matches the sample. Then, we gradually introduce

additional nonmatching stimuli on the other windows.

The student is now doing identity matching and we are ready to teach arbitrary matching tasks. The first to be taught is matching dictated picture names to pictures (A–B in Figure 3-2) and we use a variation of the delayed-cue technique (Touchette, 1971). Again, we build upon what has already been learned, making use of identity matching to instruct the student how to respond to the unfamiliar dictated picture names. At first, the dictated samples are accompanied by picture samples; even though the student does not yet know how to respond to the dictated names, he can use the picture samples as instructions. Later, the presentation of the picture samples is delayed for progressively longer periods. So long as the student has not yet learned which comparison picture goes with a dictated name, he can still respond correctly by waiting for the sample picture. But once the student has learned which comparison picture is appropriate to a dictated name, he can select the correct picture without waiting for the visual instruction. By eventually anticipating the delayed instruction, the student indicates that he has learned to match a picture to its dictated name and we can go on to teach new dictated names and pictures in the same manner.

The same method is then used to teach the student to match printed to dictated words (A–C in Figure 3-2). The instruction stimuli now are the identical printed words, and as long as the student is unable to match printed to dictated words he can wait for the instruction and make a correct choice on the basis of the identity match. When he has learned the correspondence between printed and dictated words he will no longer need the instruction and will inform us of his new skill by anticipating its appearance.

The delayed-cue technique permits students to apply previously acquired knowledge to the solution of new problems. Lengthy and discouraging trial-and-error learning is circumvented by teaching students instead to use instructions that they already understand.

Having learned the two crossmodal matching tasks (A–B and A–C), the student is now ready for the critical test: Can he now match the pictures to their printed names (B–C and C–B)? If the student proves capable of these reading comprehension tasks, he is a likely candidate for additional language teaching. If the test shows the student incapable of reading comprehension, there is reason to doubt his basic linguistic capability. In any event, such a failure cannot be attributed to inadequate preparation.

This description of a test for an elementary but fundamental form of linguistic competence and of methods for preparing severely retarded students for the test exposes the tragedy inherent in the usual assumption that such students are not amenable to language teaching. Changing their behavior is no easy task, but it can be accomplished if we as teachers will learn first to change our own behavior.

* * * * * * * * *

Commentary

It is to be hoped that testing and teaching programs like those described here would now be done on a computer. The presentation of stimuli and the recording of data would be more precise, and the machine, undisturbed by temper tantrums and other manipulative behavior that characterizes many pupils with "behavior problems," would perform its task without responding to irrelevancies. Also, sophisticated techniques for presenting graphics on the computer screen and for computer/video integration now make it possible to teach reading comprehension not just of nouns but of verbs, adverbs, prepositions, phrases, and sentences. But one does not always have the appropriate computer program available and sometimes it is even desirable first to try out materials and methods that are constructed and presented manually. Stimuli can be drawn and shown on cards instead of on a computer screen; rather than fading stimuli by increasing or decreasing their brightness, one can change lines and forms gradually from bold to thin, from solid to broken, from long to short, from large to small. Given an understanding of the basic principles of behavior analysis, one's ingenuity need not be limited (for example, Sulzer-Azaroff & Mayer, 1977).

Prerequisites

The sequence of steps that was described here for teaching the prerequisites for matching to sample will suffice for many children but will not work for all. Some will have to be taught additional skills, and any automated program will have to include options for pupils who need more preparation. Matching to sample is a blend of several elements: simultaneous discrimination of comparison stimuli (two or more comparisons are present at the same time), shifting comparison discriminations from trial to trial (different comparisons are correct on different trials), successive discrimination of sample stimuli (only one of the samples is present at any given time), and samples serving as instructional cues (the correct comparison on each trial is cued by the sample). To discuss all of these processes would take us beyond the scope of this book (see, for example, Dube, McDonald, McIlvane, & Mackay, 1991; McIlvane, Dube, Kledaras, Iennaco, & Stoddard, 1990; Saunders & Spradlin, 1989, 1990; Sidman, Rauzin, Lazar, Cunningham, Tailby, & Carrigan, 1982). Also, a true appreciation of the prerequisites for the emergence of equivalence relations will require a thorough grounding in the principles of stimulus control (see, for example, Cumming & Berryman, 1965; Goldiamond, 1962; Holland, Solomon, Doran, & Frezza, 1976; Ray & Sidman, 1970; Sidman, 1969; 1980; Skinner, 1953, 1968; Stoddard, 1982; Stoddard & Sidman, 1967; Terrace, 1966).

Once equipped with basic principles, teachers will not have to confine themselves to rote instructional sequences, but will be able to modify procedures to overcome unexpected problems and to meet the needs of individual learners. For example, in the teaching sequence that was described in the *Basic Prerequisites* paper, pupils are taught identity matching (a sample and its correct comparison are the same) before arbitrary matching (a sample and its correct comparison are different). Sometimes, however, being exposed to identity before arbitrary matching makes it difficult for pupils to learn arbitrary matching. Faced for the first time with a display in which every comparison stimulus differs from the sample, some pupils nevertheless continue to look for similarities. They choose comparisons that share elements with the sample—perhaps a line with a particular slant, an arc, a broken perimeter, a dot (Gibson, Gibson, Pick, & Osser, 1962). When they find that choosing on the basis of similarities in form does not work, they often look instead for consistencies in the sequences of correct windows; they try going around clockwise or alternating between left and right positions or, in the case of normally intelligent adults, sometimes looking for repeating position sequences that extend over many trials.

The problem here is not necessarily that the pupil is unable to learn arbitrary matching, but that the teacher has to instruct the pupil more clearly about the nature of the task. Teachers can tell even nonverbal pupils what is expected of them by moving from identity to arbitrary matching gradually. One way of doing this is to start with identical samples and comparisons and, from trial to trial, alter the samples slightly until the pupil ends up matching each comparison to an unlike sample (Zygmont, Lazar, Dube, & McIlvane, 1992). With some pupils, all the samples can be "shaped" at the same time, but with others, the teacher will have to shape just one sample at a time.

The delayed-cue procedure, too, often requires modification. This procedure is worth working on because it gives pupils a way to find answers to problems without having to go through a prolonged learning process. When they do not know the answer, all they have to do is wait for the cue. Then, when they have seen and learned the answer, they can anticipate the delayed cue, thereby obtaining their reinforcers more quickly and at the same time demonstrating that they know how to do the task. It may be difficult, however, to teach some retarded pupils to take advantage of the delayed cue. Sometimes a pupil will continue to wait for the cue without ever anticipating it, even though the delays extend beyond 20 seconds. One can often help such pupils learn how to use the delayed cue by starting with something they already know how to do. For example, if a pupil can already match dictated color names to colors, introduce the delayed-cue procedure in the context of that task, rather than trying to teach both auditory-visual word-picture matching (A–B in Figure 3-2) and the delayed-cue procedure at the same time.

Questions will also arise about the wisdom of teaching reading comprehension by what appears to be a whole-word method. A pupil who can match individual sounds to their textual counterparts and can combine the elements appropriately will be able to read new words orally upon first encountering them. A whole-word method of teaching reading leaves to chance a pupil's recognition of the correspondences between sounds and textual elements (Sidman, 1993, pp. 54-56).

The method I have described does, nevertheless, have several advantages, not the least of which is that a pupil can rapidly acquire a preliminary but substantial reading comprehension vocabulary, even while leaving the teacher free to work with other pupils. That vocabulary can then be used as the basis for teaching correspondences between the components of sounds and the components of words that have already become meaningful to the pupil. It will not be necessary to teach the pupil meaningless phoneme-grapheme pairs.

Once pupils have learned correspondences between sounds and textual units, the equivalence phenomenon will make it possible for them to progress efficiently beyond mere sound recognition to reading comprehension. For example, in Figure 3-2, the teaching that is represented by A–C would become unnecessary once a pupil had learned the correspondences between sound components in A and visual components in C. If combinations of those sounds had "meaning," —if the pupil could match them to pictures (A–B)— then reading comprehension, as indicated by the relations between pictures and text (B–C and C–B) would emerge just from sight-reading. With that background, printed or written words will take care of themselves. By first teaching correspondences between sounds and units of text, whatever those units may be (Gibson, 1965), a teacher could increase the practicality of the equivalence paradigm in the teaching of reading.

Instead of dropping a program because it does not work with all pupils or because all of its ramifications are yet to be demonstrated, knowledgeable teachers will modify the program until it does what they want it to do. This is real teaching. The modification of instructional tools is to be viewed neither as educational reform nor as curriculum design; it is the nitty-gritty of the educational process. And yet, one never sees instructional techniques among the lists of practices that are complained about by a public that is disillusioned with our educational system. And one never sees the development and improvement of instructional techniques among the sweeping reforms advocated by educational administrators and politicians. The need for effective teaching goes unrecognized. No redesign of the curriculum, however, no increase in standards, no allocation of funds for school buildings, and no shifts from public responsibility to free-market competition can have any beneficial effect on educational quality without the simultaneous application of an effective teaching technology.

The Research: Hints of Change

Besides outlining a method for teaching reading comprehension, the *Basic Prerequisites* paper gives some hints of the changes that were taking place in our conception of equivalence and of the significance of our basic experiment. Although not yet fully developed, the language indicates that refinements were on the way. Here, for the first time, is a presentation, albeit sketchy, of the view that the emergent B–C and C–B performances (Figure 3-2) test the nature of the A–B and A–C baseline relations: The new B–C and C–B conditional discriminations tell us that the original A–B and A–C discriminations are something more than they seem to be.

Later, instead of oversimplifying this "something more" as just *substitutability*, we will emphasize a distinction between conditional relations and equivalence relations. Substitutability will be seen to be derivable from the very definition of equivalence relations. Also, the concept of stimulus classes will be refined in order to take account of differences between equivalence relations and other kinds of relations between stimuli.

Also introduced here is the conception that equivalence relations between sample and comparison stimuli mark a matching-to-sample performance as linguistic in nature. Testing for emergent B–C and C–B relations can be viewed as more than just a way to demonstrate reading comprehension. It can be viewed as a test for A–B and A–C equivalence and more generally, as a test for the linguistic relevance of any conditional-discrimination performance. This is the sense in which the teaching and testing procedures constitute a "linguistic paradigm."

4

Embarking on an Experimental Analysis of Equivalence: A Second Kind of Transfer Triangle

Background

The Mediation Paradigm

The *Mediated Transfer* paper (reproduced below), actually the third in the series, marked a transition from our initial emphasis on reading. We were beginning to appreciate both the greater generality of the phenomenon we were dealing with and the need to elucidate that phenomenon in its own right, apart from its practical implications. Here, we introduced the question of whether the emergent stimulus relations have to be mediated by responses.

A few years ago, when I went back to Keller and Schoenfeld (1950) to see if they had said anything about mediated generalization, I found the following (p. 163): "Among the first to recognize the importance of a systematic attack upon the problem of 'mediated generalization' were Cofer and Foley, in 1942 and later. *The problem has not yet been investigated, however, to the degree that its importance would seem to justify*" [emphasis added]. Soon afterward, however, the problem did become the subject of intensive investigation, largely in the context of the paired-associate technique (see below). By the time we began our studies, a considerable literature existed on what was variously called *mediated transfer*, *mediated association*, *semantic generalization*, or *mediated generalization*.

In an early review, Cofer and Foley (1942) characterized mediated generalization as depending not on physical similarities among stimuli but on arbitrary stimulus equivalences that have been established by "previously conditioned (usually language) behavior" (p. 519). They suggested the following as a simplified Pavlovian conditioning schema of mediated or semantic generalization:

> At some pre-experimental time, the subject has become conditioned, either by direct reinforcement or by higher order conditioning, to make R_x to CS_1, CS_2, CS_3 ... CS_n. The subject is next experimentally conditioned by reinforcing CS_1 with UCS_y, setting up a conditioned response, R_y. Generalization is now found to CS_2 ... CS_n... (p. 520).
>
> ...It should be emphasized that the schema...is an operational account of what descriptively occurs in mediated generalization. Hypotheses regarding further, non-observable mechanisms could be introduced.... (pp. 520, 522).

It is often difficult to recognize that what seems an operational description may actually depend on unstated theoretical assumptions; we sometimes describe processes that we have inferred rather than observed. Cofer and Foley (1942), for example, based their description on a respondent (Pavlovian) conditioning paradigm. Today, we are more likely to attribute the behavioral practices to which we give the name *language* to operant rather than to respondent conditioning processes (Skinner, 1938; 1957; 1974, Chapter 6; 1989, p. 37). If we were to construct a schema similar to that of Cofer and Foley, we would derive mediated generalization from the three-term operant contingency (Skinner, 1938).

The operant-respondent distinction, however, is probably not critical for the discussion here. Cofer and Foley's main point was that when several stimuli have somehow come to control a single response, then if one of those stimuli comes to control a second response, the other stimuli will also be found to control the second response. This proposition can be stated more conservatively: when several stimuli control the same response, those stimuli may form a functional class (Chapter 11). To find out whether the stimuli are indeed functionally equivalent, one can establish a relation between one of them and a new response and then determine whether the other stimuli have also acquired control over the new response. If they have, then the functional class will have been confirmed. The schema Cofer and Foley proposed is actually a test for functional equivalence.

Cofer and Foley's second unstated assumption was that generalization among physically dissimilar stimuli *has to be* mediated by a response. That is to say, stimuli—in their schema, $CS_1...CS_n$—become members of the same class because each controls the same response, R_x. To account for this, they hypothesize the following non-observable mechanism: when CS_1 is conditioned to a new response R_y, it also produces the original response R_x; thus, the stimulus consequences of R_x come also to elicit R_y; and so, when the stimuli $CS_2...CS_n$ are tested, they will first produce R_x, which in turn will produce R_y. This set of assumptions—that responses and response-produced stimuli are responsible for mediated generalization— was a major focus of the experimental design and the discussion in our *Mediated Transfer* paper.

The Paired-Associate Tradition

Underwood (1949) described the paired-associate technique as follows:

> The paired associate technique, used primarily with verbal material, is a method wherein S [the subject] is presented with a series of pairs of words, the first member of the pair being the stimulus and the second member the response. S is to associate each response with its stimulus, so that when he sees only the stimulus he can make the response. Thus, in the instance, *DESK—ARMY*, he would learn to say *ARMY* when *DESK* is presented.
>
> Paired associates are customarily presented on a *memory drum*, a device which can expose one pair of words at a time, and each successive pair for the same time interval. Typically, the stimulus word of a pair is presented for 4 seconds. During the first 2 seconds of this period the stimulus appears alone, but during the last 2

seconds the response is shown with the stimulus. Then, the stimulus word of the next pair is shown, and so on down through the list. S is to learn to call out the appropriate response to each stimulus word before the response word appears. He has 2 seconds (when the stimulus is presented alone) in which to anticipate the response. These time intervals are arbitrary, of course, but are the ones which have become fairly standard.

The number of pairs in a paired-associate list has varied, but from 8 to 15 have commonly been employed. Before the first presentation of any list S cannot know what the correct responses are. So, he merely studies the pairs on the first trial and tries to associate each response with its stimulus. On the second trial he may remember some of the responses and will call out the responses during the 2-second anticipation period. E [the experimenter] records correct responses as well as incorrect ones. S goes through the list time after time until he has reached the criterion of performance which E has established. The words are presented *in a different order* on each trial so that S cannot learn which stimulus is coming into the aperture of the drum before it actually appears, and so that he will not learn the response words serially by ignoring the stimuli. (pp. 286-287).

A paired-associate experiment analogous to our first experiment (Sidman, 1971b) might go as follows. Subjects would first learn AB. That is to say, given each word in List A (one at a time, on the memory drum), they would learn to say an arbitrarily corresponding word in List B before the List-B word appeared on the drum. The subjects would then learn AC. That is to say, on being given each word in list A, they would learn to say—in anticipation—a corresponding word in list C. Having learned the AB and AC pairs, the subjects would then be asked to learn BC pairs, orally anticipating a List-C word in response to the visual presentation of each List-B word. Each BC pair to be learned would consist of the two words that had been related to the same List-A word. The crucial measurement would be the number of trials the subjects took to learn BC, in comparison to control groups that had not had the AB and/or AC experience. Mediated transfer would be demonstrated if the experimental group learned BC faster than the control group.

A Second Kind of Transfer Triangle

Jenkins (1963), Jenkins and Palermo (1964), Kjeldergaard (1968), and Postman (1971) have presented thorough empirical and theoretical reviews and critiques of this kind of research, its antecedents, and its rationale. The paired-associate work on mediated generalization eventually fell victim to limitations that are inherent in the experimental practices and theoretical orientation of methodological behaviorism and that still characterize much of experimental psychology (Day, 1992, pp. 61-70). Jenkins (1963) has described some particular circumstances that led to an eventual decline of interest in mediation paradigms, and I shall have more to say about this (pp. 179-181). Here, I want simply to point out that most investigators and theorists, following the lead of Cofer and Foley (1942), took it for granted that any instance of acquired stimulus equivalence had to be mediated by a response that each of the equivalent stimuli controlled in common. Although paired-associate learning tasks require the subject to relate *stimuli* in one list to *stimuli* in another list, the subject has to name aloud at least one member of each pair. Investigators and theorists maintained the obligatory S-R conditioning framework by actually calling the named stimulus a *response term*. In AB learning, for example, A was designated as the *stimulus term* and B as the *response term*, but then, in a BA test, B became the stimulus term and A the response term. Depending on the explanatory requirements, the members of any list could be called either stimuli or responses.

For example, in the BC transfer test described above, the BC relations were held to be mediated as follows (Jenkins & Palermo, 1964, p. 147):

> If a stimulus elicits two responses, the responses will acquire a tendency to elicit each other. That is:
>
> | Given that: | A elicits B; |
> | and that: | A elicits C; |
> | Then: | B will tend to elicit C and |
> | | C will tend to elicit B. |
>
> This may be called the "response equivalence" paradigm....

An example…would be the learning of *zug-dol* followed by the learning of *zug-gex* facilitating the learning of *dol-gex*….

We talk of this as a mediational paradigm because it…may be derived from simple S-R associations given the use of the implicit response:

A—B learning;	A—C learning;
A—(B)—C learning;	A—(C)—B learning;
B—C results.	C—B results.

…The key to this paradigm is…in the second stage. It is assumed that A as a stimulus elicits (B) as a covert response. The stimulus consequences of (B) then have an opportunity to become attached to the response C. Similarly, in the other order of the first two stages, the stimulus consequences of (C) become attached to the response B. Thus, if both orders are experienced, B and C come to elicit each other.

The above formulation, outlined by Jenkins and Palermo (1964), does not even require that the members of each B and C pair control the same response. It is actually a chaining model, in which the learning of the BC pairs is hypothesized actually to take place during the second-stage AC experiences, and the learning of the CB pairs during the AB experiences. During the second stages: (a) because of the subject's previous AB learning, the stimulus A is assumed to elicit the mediating response/stimulus B, and B thereby becomes "attached" to C; and (b) because of the subject's previous AC learning, the stimulus A is assumed to elicit the mediating response/stimulus C, and C thereby becomes "attached" to B. These complex assumptions, all postulating response mediation, led those working in the paired-associate tradition to overlook the possibility of direct stimulus-stimulus relations.

✳ ✳ ✳ ✳ ✳ ✳ ✳ ✳ ✳

Acquisition of Matching to Sample via Mediated Transfer

Two severely retarded Down's-syndrome boys learned a matching-to-sample performance through mediated transfer. The transfer paradigm involved three sets of stimuli, one auditory set (A) and two visual sets (B and C). The subjects were taught directly to do AB and BC matching but experienced no direct association between A and C. They acquired the ability to do AC matching without having been taught that performance directly. They also learned indirectly to name some of the visual stimuli but naming was apparently not the mediator in the emergent AC matching. The use of words and letters as stimuli highlighted the possible relevance of mediated associations in the indirect acquisition of elementary reading comprehension and oral reading. The acquisition of matching via mediated transfer also raised some new considerations concerning the role of coding responses in arbitrary matching to sample.

In his germinal paper on mediated association, or mediated transfer, Peters (1935) cited early associationist philosophers and psychologists in his description of this phenomenon: "...the successive appearance of apparently unrelated ideas in consciousness can be accounted for only on the basis of a third idea which is definitely related to both of them...the term 'mediate association' refers to an indirect associative connection between two items of experience, ideas, or mental acts, as opposed to a direct type of associative connection. And this indirect associative connection is one supposedly mediated by a third item that has been directly associated with both of them. When we find two ideas A and B appearing in succession with no possibility of their previous, direct association, we will usually find that both A and B have formerly been associated with an item C. Thus, the connection A—B is the result of two other connections, A—C and B—C" (pp. 20-21).

Subsequent experimentation, usually using paired-associate techniques in the verbal learning tradition, has amply confirmed the existence of mediated transfer, although the descriptive language has tended away from ideas and mental acts to stimuli and responses (Jenkins, 1963).

We have recently demonstrated mediated transfer by using matching-to-sample procedures with retarded subjects (Sidman, 1971b; Sidman and Cresson, 1973). In these earlier experiments, the subjects first learned to match sets of 20 pictures and 20 printed picture names to corresponding dictated names. They then proved able for the first time to match printed words to the corresponding pictures, with word-picture matching never having been taught directly.

The relation of the matching-to-sample experiments to the familiar mediated-transfer or mediated-association paradigm can be seen in Figure 4-1. A, B, and C are three sets of stimuli. Arrows point from sample to comparison stimuli. Subjects first learned to match A to B and

A to C; they were then able to match B to C and C to B.

In this example, matching printed words to pictures and pictures to printed words may be regarded as simple reading comprehension; matching dictated words to pictures as simple auditory comprehension; and the matching of dictated to printed words may be called auditory receptive reading. The earlier studies thus had some relevance both to the principles and practicalities of teaching elementary reading.

The present experiment, however, was concerned with the nature of the mediated-transfer process itself. One interpretation of the original finding is that the subjects' emergent ability to

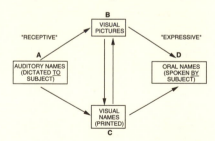

Figure 4-1. Stimuli, responses, and mediated-transfer paradigms for Subject J.C. In the *receptive* triangle, arrows point from sample to comparison stimuli. On the *expressive* side, arrows point from visual stimuli to oral naming responses.

match printed words to pictures was mediated by their previous training to match both of these sets of stimuli to the same auditory stimuli. For example, in the course of learning the crossmodal matching, they had learned to match the dictated word "car" both to the picture of a car and the printed word *car*; they were then able to match the picture to the printed word through the mediation of the dictated word.

A second interpretation is also possible. Before they learned the auditory-visual matching tasks, the subjects had some proficiency in naming the pictures but could not name the printed words. After they had learned the crossmodal matching tasks, they proved able for the first time to name the printed words—to read them aloud. The emergence of oral reading raised the possibility of a different mediation path for the indirectly learned word-picture matching. This path is illustrated by the triangle on the right of Figure 4-1. For example, subjects had learned to say "car" in response to pictures of cars (BD) and to the printed word car (CD); they were then able to match picture with printed word (BC and CB) through the mediation of the spoken word.

Was the subjects' emergent reading comprehension (matching printed words to pictures) mediated by the dictated words spoken *to* them? Or did names spoken *by* the subjects, either aloud or implicitly, mediate their word-picture matching? The first possibility would imply stimulus mediation via receptive channels. The second would require response mediation and would be consistent with stimulus-response models of mediated transfer (Jenkins, 1963; Schoenfeld and Cumming, 1963). To emphasize the distinction, the mediation triangle on the left side of Figure 4-1 has been labeled *receptive*, and the triangle on the right *expressive*.

A major purpose of the present experiment was to determine whether mediated transfer, demonstrated within the context of matching to sample, requires a response as the mediator or whether stimulus mediation is sufficient to carry the explanatory burden. Are the prerequisites for the emergence of BC and CB to be specified as AB and AC or as BD and CD (Figure 4-l)?

If naming mediated word-picture matching in the earlier experiments, it becomes necessary to explain how word naming itself emerged. A possibility was suggested (Sidman & Cresson, 1973) when one subject's picture naming improved as a consequence of learning auditory comprehension (matching dictated words to pictures). Could he also have learned oral reading (naming printed words) simply as a consequence of learning auditory receptive reading (matching dictated to printed words)? If so, printed-word naming and picture naming might then have mediated reading comprehension (word-picture matching).

Although the conditions under which receptive training facilitates expressive speech are still unknown (Guess, 1969; Guess and Baer, 1973), it seems reasonable to suppose that the subjects learned to read the words aloud because of their receptive training in matching printed words to dictated names. In the present experiment, we eliminated this avenue for the learning of oral reading, in the hope that we could assess the likelihood of receptively mediated transfer.

By proceeding around the receptive triangle (Figure 4-1) in another direction, we prevented the subject from experiencing any direct association between printed words and their auditory counterparts. He was taught auditory comprehension (AB) and reading comprehension (BC) directly and was then tested for the emergence of auditory receptive reading (AC) and oral reading (CD). If the absence of direct AC training prevented the subject from learning to name the printed words but AC itself still emerged from the AB and BC training, the possibility of receptive mediation would have to be seriously considered.

Attainment of this objective involved the assumption that the outcomes of the mediation paradigm used in the previous studies (AB, AC, test for BC) and in the present experiment (AB, BC, test for AC) would be similar—that mastery of the first two stages would result in mastery of the third. On the basis of paired-associate experiments (Jenkins, 1963), this assumption appeared reasonable but its test in the contexts of matching to sample and crossmodal associations was a second objective.

A third objective was to use another set of stimuli, upper- and lower-case letters, to test the generality of mediated learning of matching to sample. Two experiments are described; each used different stimuli and differed in certain procedural features.

METHOD

Subjects

The subjects were two institutionalized Down's-syndrome boys, one (J.C.) 14 yr and 9 months and the other (P.A.) 18 yr old at the start of the first complete test session. Both were participants in a behavior modification project (Mackay and Sidman, 1968; Sidman, 1970) but received no reading instruction during the period covered by the experiment. Their experimental sessions were scheduled so as not to interfere with their project activities and the pennies and tokens they earned were spent in accord with contingencies prevailing in the project. Approximately two months after

the experiment was completed, Subject J.C. achieved a mental age of 3-4 on the Peabody Picture Vocabulary Test, 4-11 on the Stanford-Binet L-M Intelligence Test and 6-9 on the Leiter Performance Scale. Subject P.A. did not undergo such formal testing but all who were acquainted with him during the 8 yr of the project judged him considerably less advanced than Subject J.C. in all areas of functioning.

General Experimental Design

The subjects were to be taught two legs of the receptive mediation triangle, the crossmodal matching task AB and the visual matching task BC. They were then to be tested for the emergence of the third leg, the crossmodal matching task AC. Also to be tested was the effect of the teaching on the two oral naming tasks, CD and BD. First, the subjects' pre-experimental capabilities were assessed by pretesting them on all these tasks. They were also pretested on, and if necessary, were taught identity matching (Subject J.C.: printed picture names to printed picture names; Subject P.A.: printed upper-case to upper-case and lower-case to lower-case letters) in order to ensure that they could discriminate the visual stimuli. The left columns of Figures 4-3 and 4-4 list the types of stimuli and the responses required of the subjects in each kind of test. This test battery, administered before, during, and after the teaching (see below), provided the experimental data.

After the pretests, teaching was accomplished gradually, first one leg of the receptive transfer triangle (AB) and then the other (BC). Tests interspersed at various stages of the teaching evaluated the requisite baseline behavior and evaluated nonspecific transfer effects arising from the teaching procedures themselves, apart from the associative transfer with which the experiment was concerned. Variations in this general procedure are described below.

Apparatus and General Test Procedures

The subject sat before a panel of nine translucent windows onto which stimuli were projected from the rear. The windows, each 7.32 cm in diameter, were arranged in a circle of eight

with the ninth in the center (Figure 4-2). The display diameter, from outer edge to outer edge, was 32.72 cm; the center-to-center distance was 9.53 cm between adjacent windows on the perimeter and 12.7 cm between the center window and each of the others.

Each trial began with a sample stimulus. Visual samples (black letters, words, or line drawings on a white background) appeared on the center window. With auditory samples, words or letter names were dictated and repeated through a speaker at 2.0- to 2.5-s intervals by a continuous-loop tape system (Fletcher et al., 1971); the center window was illuminated but blank. Each sample, visual or

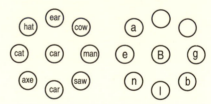

Figure 4-2. Schematic diagrams of the display matrix, illustrating one trial from the identity word-word matching test and one trial from the test of matching upper-case to lower-case letters. In other kinds of tests, the sample window (center) or the comparison windows (periphery) contained pictures or were blank

auditory, remained present throughout the trial, and trial durations had no time limit.

In matching-to-sample tests, the subject pressed the center window to bring comparison stimuli, always visual, onto the outer windows. This "observing response" was always required, even when the sample was dictated. On each trial, one comparison stimulus, the correct one, corresponded to the sample. Subject J.C. had seven incorrect comparison stimuli (words or pictures) on every trial. Subject P.A. had five incorrect comparison stimuli (upper- or lower-case letters) and two blank windows on every trial (Figure 4-2). Sample stimuli and window positions of correct and incorrect comparison stimuli varied from trial to trial.

After the comparison stimuli appeared, the subject pressed a comparison window. Correct choices caused chimes to ring and a penny (Subject J.C.) or a token (Subject P.A.) to be delivered. Neither chimes nor penny or token followed an incorrect choice. All stimuli disappeared after each choice, and 1.5 to 2.0 s later a new sample began the next trial (noncorrection procedure).

Any window press during the intertrial interval postponed the next sample for 2 s. Solid-state logic scheduled the procedures and recorded the responses automatically. Test sessions lasted about one hr.

In oral naming tests, the subject had simply to name the sample picture, word, or letter aloud. He was asked, "Tell me what you see." He pressed no windows and no comparison stimuli appeared. Oral responses of both subjects were clear and there was no ambiguity in determining whether they were correct. After each response, the experimenter pressed a handswitch to activate the reinforcement (if correct), intertrial-interval, and slide-change apparatus.

Visual and auditory samples never occurred together. With dictated samples, the center window was always blank; with visual word, letter, or picture samples, no stimuli were dictated.

Subject J.C.'s tests each had 20 trials. The stimuli, taken from a list of 20 pictures or the printed (lower case) or dictated names of the pictures, were: axe, bed, bee, box, boy, bug, car, cat, cow, dog, ear, hat, hen, hut, hoe, man, pie, pig, saw, zoo.

Subject P.A.'s tests each had 24 trials. The stimuli were six letters, A, B, E, G, L, and N, presented in upper-case or lower-case form or as dictated letter names.

General Teaching Procedures

Teaching, which took place between each administration of the test battery, always involved matching to sample, sometimes with a correction and sometimes with a noncorrection procedure (see below). In the correction procedure, an error produced the usual intertrial interval, after which the same sample and comparison display were presented again. In both the correction and noncorrection procedures, chimes and a penny or token followed any response to the correct comparison window.

Each test listed in Figures 4-3 and 4-4 had six versions, differing in their sequence of sample presentations and in the arrangements of stimuli on the panel. Also, each test set used a different variation of each picture. For example, the car in one set was a VW and in another was an MG; the cat in one set was standing and in another was lying down; and so forth. One version of each

test was used only in the test battery. A systematic rotation through the other five sets during teaching prevented the subjects from learning display configurations, irrelevant display features, and sequences of samples or window positions, all of which would have permitted them to achieve high scores without observing the samples. Varied numbers of sets were presented during teaching sessions, which lasted 20 to 65 min and occurred one to five times a week.

Order of Conditions and Detailed Teaching Procedures for Subject J.C.

Table 4-1 summarizes the subject's testing and teaching sequence. Dates correspond to those at the bottom of Figure 4-3.

Pretesting. Three and two years before the experiment began, Subject J.C. received the tests of auditory and reading comprehension. During these years he also had considerable matching-to-sample and oral-naming experience with other kinds of visual, auditory, and tactile stimuli, including colors and color names, numbers and

Table 4-1
Testing and Teaching Sequence for Subject J.C.

Procedures	Dates
A. Pretesting	
1. Test: Matching printed words to pictures (C-B) and pictures to dictated words (B-A)	7/07/67
2. Test: Same	9/27/68
3. Test: Complete battery	8/26/70
4. Test: Complete battery	9/10/70
B. Preteaching	
1. Teach: Identity matching of printed words to printed words	9/30/70 to 11/12/70
2. Test: Complete battery	11/15/70
C. First leg of transfer triangle (B-A)	
1. Teach: Matching pictures to dictated words	11/17/70 to 12/04/70
2. Test: Complete battery	12/08/70
D. Second leg of transfer triangle (C-B)	
1. Teach: Matching 9 printed words to pictures	12/09/70 to 12/30/70
2. Test: Complete battery	12/30/70
3. Teach: Matching 14 printed words to pictures	1/05/71 to 1/24/71
4. Test: Complete battery	1/24/71
5. Teach: Matching 20 printed words to pictures	2/03/71 to 2/15/71
6. Test: Complete battery	2/15/71
7. Reteach: Matching 20 printed words to pictures	2/18/71 to 2/24/71
8. Test: Complete battery	2/26/71

number names, nonsense trigrams, and geometric forms. In preparation for the present experiment, he received the complete test battery twice. The early scores have been included in order to show that mere exposure to the tests did not appreciably improve his reading and auditory comprehension or his oral reading.

Preteaching. Some of Subject J.C.'s low pretest scores (see Results) might have been caused simply by an inability to distinguish the printed words from each other. He was therefore taught word-word identity matching, selecting each of the 20 printed words from different sets of eight alternatives in response to printed-word samples. A typical display is in the left side of Figure 4-2. The teaching involved sets of noncorrection trials with all 20 samples, and correction trials with subsets of those samples he found troublesome. After 1240 trials, he achieved a criterion of 95% correct in 120 trials of word-word identity matching and was given the test battery again.

First leg of transfer triangle. He next learned auditory comprehension, matching each variation of the 20 pictures to its dictated name. Again, a mixture of correction and noncorrection procedures was used, the correction procedure being applied to special sets of sample stimuli with which the subject had difficulty. He required 540 trials to reach a criterion of 95% correct in 120 trials, and then received the test battery again.

Second leg of transfer triangle. The critical teaching involved the matching of picture samples to printed-word comparisons. Five variations of each picture were presented in mixed sequences. The correction procedure was used throughout. Subject J.C. was first taught to match only nine of the printed words to their equivalent pictures. He was initially given sets of 10 trials with only two sample pictures, axe and zoo. When he achieved a score of 100% in a set of 10 trials, he was then given a second pair of pictures, hen and saw, to learn. After achieving 100% with the second pair, he was given variations of all four pictures as samples until he reached a criterion of 19 correct trials in a set of 20. This system of teaching the subject to match new words and then adding those to the previously learned set continued, with the following sequence of pairs: axe and zoo, hen and saw, man and bug, bug and dog (only one new word at this point), hoe and cow. He required 545 trials to meet the criterion for matching the first nine printed words to their corresponding pictures, after which he received the test battery again.

Subject J.C. then learned to match five more printed words to their equivalent pictures. These were taught in the following pairs: hut and hat, bed and bee, bed and boy. Each pair was presented until he achieved perfect performance in a set of 10 trials. He was then given a complete set of 20 sample pictures, including the six he had not yet been taught. If he did not score perfectly on all 14 samples he had been taught, he was given remedial trials with those he had matched incorrectly. When he achieved perfection on the remedial set, he was retested with the complete set of 20 samples. This process of testing with the complete set and then giving remedial teaching on those he had been taught but found difficult continued until, when given the complete set, he correctly matched all the words he had been taught. The subject met this criterion for the 14 samples in 640 trials and received the test battery.

The next teaching phase, carried out in the same manner as the preceding phase, added the last six pictures in the following sequence of pairs: boy and box, cat and car, car and ear, pig and pie. The subject required 380 trials to reach the learning criterion which, by this time, included all 20 samples. He then received the battery of tests again.

The final teaching stage involved special remedial sets of samples the subject sometimes still matched incorrectly. This teaching used all six sets of word-picture matching trials, including the test set, and the subject achieved 100% on all six sets after 380 trials. The final test battery followed this reteaching.

Order of Conditions and Detailed Teaching Procedures for Subject P.A.

For this subject, all six letters were comparison stimuli on every trial. He was taught to match six dictated letter names to printed upper-case letters and the six printed upper-case letters to corresponding lower-case letters (Table 4-2).

Pretesting. Like Subject J.C., Subject P.A. had considerable matching-to-sample and oral-naming experience with a variety of stimuli other than those used here. He was pretested twice on the complete battery

Table 4-2
Testing and Teaching Sequence for Subject P.A.

Procedures	Dates
A. Pretesting	
1. Test: Complete battery	10/30/72
2. Test: Same	1/23/73
B. Two legs of transfer triangle	
1. Teach: Alternate auditory-visual matching (A-B) and visual-visual matching (B-C) for each letter consecutively	1/26/73 to 5/11/73
2. Test: Complete battery	5/11/73
3. Teach: Review previously taught matching, and teach the other visual-visual matching task (C-B)	5/14/73 to 5/30/73
4. Test: Complete battery	5/30/73

and did not have to be taught identity matching.

Two legs of transfer triangle. First, the subject learned to match two upper-case comparison stimuli, B and L, to their dictated names. When he reached 100% in a set of 24 trials, he then learned to match the two upper-case letters to their lower-case equivalents. A typical display is in the right side of Figure 4-2. When he reached 100% in the visual-visual task, he returned to auditory-visual matching. This alternation continued until he went through 96 consecutive trials, two sets of each task, perfectly within a single session.

A third sample, "A", was then added. When all three upper-case letters were matched perfectly to their dictated equivalents, the subject was given the visual-visual task of matching the three upper-case samples to their appropriate lower-case comparisons. When he reached criterion on each task the other was reintroduced, the alternation continuing until he achieved perfect scores in four consecutive 24-trial sets, two sets of each type, within a single session.

The same procedure then continued, one new letter being added in each teaching step. The final samples to be introduced were "G," "N," and "E." After achieving a perfect performance with all six letters in both matching tasks, the subject had to meet additional criteria before receiving the test battery. First, he had to perform perfectly again on four alternating 24-trial sets, two of each type, within one session. Then, on the day of the test battery, he had to perform perfectly on one 24-trial set of each type. He required 5768 trials to meet these criteria.

In the final teaching phase, Subject P.A. received additional experience with the two tasks he had been taught. He also learned to match lowercase sample letters to upper-case comparisons. With all six letters and letter names as samples, the teaching proceeded as before, with the addition of the third matching task. The subject again had to proceed errorlessly through a 24-trial set before going on to the next task. He also had to perform errorlessly on six consecutive 24-trial sets, two of each type, within a single session. Then, in the same session as the final test battery, he had to perform three 24-trial sets perfectly, one of each type. This teaching phase required 1824 trials.

RESULTS

Subject J.C.

Pretests. The sequence of teaching procedures and test results can be followed by scanning the dated columns in Figure 4-3. The subject's test scores before explicit teaching are in the four left columns of bars. In 1967 and 1968 (the first two columns), he matched dictated and printed words to pictures poorly, although he did somewhat better in auditory than in reading comprehension. His poorest performances on the complete test battery (8/26/70 and 9/01/70) were in the four tests at the top, all involving printed words. He did better, although short of perfection, in picture naming and auditory comprehension, which did not involve printed words. In identity matching of printed word to printed word, he scored no higher than 70%.

Tests after teaching identity matching (preteaching). After being taught visual word-word matching (9/03/70 to 11/12/70), the subject displayed his new skill by scoring 100% on the identity matching test (11/15/70). The other scores changed little; his poor reading did not reflect an

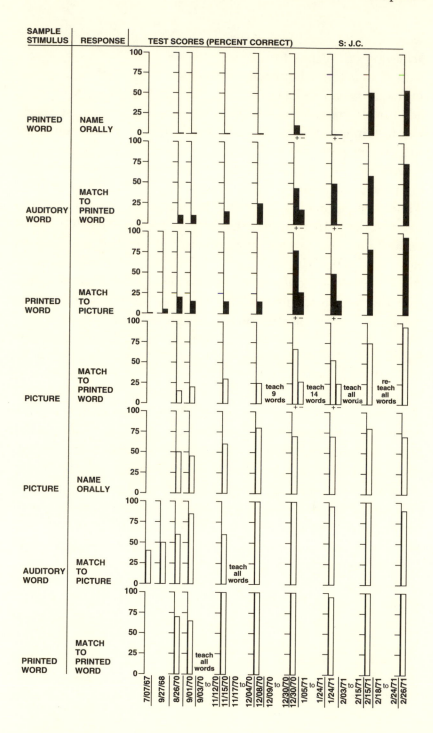

inability to discriminate the printed words.

Tests after teaching auditory comprehension (first leg of transfer triangle). After he had learned auditory comprehension, Subject J.C. scored 100% on his newly taught skill (12/08/70). Learning to match dictated words to pictures also seemed to improve his picture naming slightly, although he did not consistently do as well in later tests. The change in auditory comprehension was not accompanied by appreciable increases in any of the reading scores. Learning one leg of the mediation triangle (AB) did not cause the other legs to emerge. In the three matching tests of reading, his scores were close to the chance level for eight comparison stimuli per trial and oral reading remained at zero. These poor scores apparently did not stem from an inability to distinguish the pictures from each other or the dictated or printed words from each other. Although some difficulty in oral reading may have stemmed from an inability to say the words aloud, the subject's picture naming indicated that this problem could have been only minor and could not have accounted for his complete lack of oral reading.

Tests after teaching reading comprehension (second leg of transfer triangle). Would the establishment of this performance, matching pictures to printed words, cause the emergence of the third leg of the triangle, matching dictated words to printed words?

Double bars in the four reading tests (12/30/70) distinguish the scores for the nine words he was first taught to match to pictures (+) and the scores for the 11 words he had not yet been taught (–). The direct effect of the teaching was a large increase in the subject's accuracy in

Figure 4-3 (facing page). Subject J.C. The two left columns identify the sample stimuli and responses that comprised each type of test. The row of bars to the right of each test represents the subject's scores in successive administrations of the test. The dates of each test and of the interpolated teaching are given below the columns of bars. In some test series, each of the four reading tests has two scores: The bars marked + represent the subject's performance with words he had been taught to match in the word-picture matching task; the bars marked – represent his performance with words he had not yet been taught.

matching the nine printed words to their equivalent pictures, an increase not reflected in his score for the 11 untaught words. The reason for his less-than-perfect score on the nine critical words is unclear. Accuracy also improved considerably in matching printed-word samples to picture-comparison stimuli, although he had not received explicit training on this task.

In matching dictated to printed words, the subject improved modestly on the nine critical words. This improvement did not extend to the 11 untaught words and the selectivity of the change provides evidence that the improvement was a transfer effect from the previous teaching.

In oral reading, the subject named one of the printed words aloud for the first time but his score did not show an improvement comparable to that of the matching tasks.

Although the subject's scores after he had been taught 14 of the 20 words (1/24/71) were similar to those of the preceding tests, the percentages represent a larger number of correct responses. Furthermore, all of his correct choices in response to

dictated samples were printed words learned in picture-word matching. In spite of his improvement in matching dictated to printed words, he still showed no ability to read the printed words aloud.

Having learned to match picture samples to all 20 printed words, the subject correctly matched 12 (60%) of the dictated samples to printed words (2/15/71).

Also, for the first time, his oral reading improved distinctly. The way this came about is of interest. In the first seven trials of this test, he responded to the printed words by uttering nonsense syllables or letter names unrelated to letters within the words. On Trial 8, with *bee* as the sample word, he said, "bee-fire." On Trial 9, with *box* as the sample word, he suddenly sat up straight, clapped his hands, laughed, said, "I get it," and responded correctly. A similar "aha" reaction occurred on Trial 10. After failing the first seven trials, he went on to name nine of the next 13 words correctly. The first seven trials were then repeated and he read three of those words aloud correctly. The correct responses upon retest were included in the score shown in Figure 4-3.

Although transfer to auditory receptive reading and to oral reading did occur, this transfer was far from perfect. Furthermore, the subject fell short of 100% even on the picture-word matching task he had been taught. Therefore, he was retaught picture-word matching and received the test series once more (2/26/71).

This time, Subject J.C.'s picture-word matching was almost perfect, as was word-picture matching, which had not been directly taught. Along with this improvement was an increased accuracy in matching dictated to printed words. Oral reading, however, remained at its previous level.

Subject P.A.

Pretests. The subject did visual-visual identity matching of upper- and lower-case letters perfectly in pretests and continued errorlessly in every administration of the test battery. These consistently perfect performances were therefore omitted from Figure 4-4.

The two initial administrations of the test battery, nearly three months apart (Figure 4-4, 10/30/72 and 1/23/73), yielded consistent results. His best scores, less than 50%, were on the two tasks he was to be taught directly. The other matching tasks were within the range of chance performance for a display of six comparison stimuli. He showed a slight ability to name upper-case letters aloud but was completely unable to name the lower-case letters.

Tests after teaching two legs of the transfer triangle. Although the subject maintained an almost perfect performance on the auditory-visual task he had been taught, visual-visual matching deteriorated from the relatively rigorous learning criterion he had attained (5/11/73). On the reverse visual-visual task, lower-case samples and upper-case comparisons, in which he had not received direct training, his performance was still less satisfactory. Nevertheless, he did better on these tasks after the teaching than before, and the improvement was reflected in considerable transfer to the critical auditory-visual task—matching dictated names to the lower-case letters.

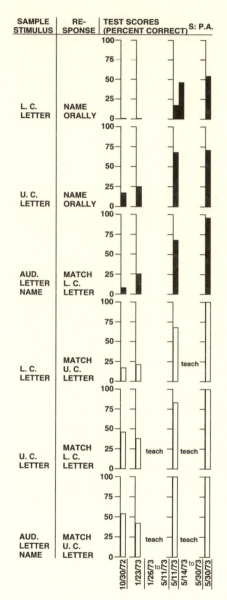

Oral naming of upper-case letters also improved considerably over the pretest performances.

Oral naming of lower-case letters was tested twice. For the first time, Subject P.A. named a few lower-case letters correctly but his score was still quite low, as indicated by the first of the two bars in the uppermost row (5/11/73). This test was administered before the upper-case naming test, and because he did so much better in the latter we suspected that he might have learned something about naming that could help him with lower-case letters. For this reason, the lower-case test was readministered. His score did improve, as indicated by the second of the two bars in the uppermost row but was still quite low.

Teaching the subject two matching tasks brought about a much improved performance in the third matching task, as well as in oral naming of both sets of letters. The incompleteness of

Figure 4-4. The left two columns identify the sample stimuli and responses that comprised each type of test. The row of bars to the right of each test represents the subject's scores in successive administrations of the test. The dates of each test, and of the interpolated teaching, are given below the columns of bars.

the transfer might have reflected his less-than-perfect matching of lower- to uppercase and upper- to lower-case letters. He was therefore retaught the two tasks he had previously learned. He was also taught explicitly to match upper-case comparison letters to lower-case samples.

The final column in Figure 4-4 (5/30/73) shows Subject P.A. maintaining perfect performances on all three matching tasks he had been taught. In matching dictated samples to lower-case comparisons, he also scored almost perfectly. His oral-naming scores, however, were practically the same as in the preceding tests.

DISCUSSION

Matching to Sample

In previous experiments (Sidman, 1971b; Sidman & Cresson, 1973), the ability to match printed words with pictures emerged after subjects had learned to match each set of visual stimuli to a set of auditory stimuli, dictated words. This learning sequence was consistent with the commonly observed developmental sequence in which auditory comprehension precedes reading comprehension. It was also consistent with the suggestion that the ability to perform crossmodal tasks is helpful in learning reading comprehension (Birch, 1962; Birch & Belmont, 1964, 1965; Geschwind, 1965a; Kahn & Birch, 1968; Wepman, 1962).

The present and the earlier experiments together, however, have shown that the receptive mediation triangle (Figure 4-1) can be bidirectional. Facilitation can apparently work both ways; the normal developmental sequence is apparently not a necessary sequence.

The present data suggested also that oral naming need not mediate the emergence of auditory-visual matching. After Subject J.C. had learned to match pictures to nine and then 14 printed words, he showed a substantial ability to match dictated to printed words and almost no ability to read words aloud. Oral reading could not at this stage have mediated the emergent matching of dictated to printed words.

After Subject J.C. had learned to match pictures to all 20 printed words, he named a substantial number of words for the first time. His "aha" reaction during the oral reading test suggested that although he had failed to read the words aloud up to that point, he had actually been capable of doing so and exercised his new capability only in the course of this test. Nevertheless, even though he may have been capable of naming the printed words, he clearly had not been doing so.

Practically all of Subject P.A.'s ability to name upper- and lower-case letters can be attributed to the teaching procedures. After learning the two matching-to-sample performances, his performance improved considerably in matching dictated names to lower-case letters. Correlated with this improvement in crossmodal matching was a corresponding improvement in upper-case letter naming, but on first testing, only a slight development of lower-case naming. The emergence of crossmodal lower-case matching in the absence of lower-case naming indicates that the emergent matching was not mediated by naming but was fostered rather by the receptive training in the other two matching-to-sample tasks.

The improvement in lower-case letter naming upon retest was analogous to Subject J.C.'s "aha" experience. Subject P.A. was apparently capable of naming more lower-case letters than he actually did upon initial testing but he had not been using those letter names to mediate the crossmodal matching of lower-case to dictated letters.

On the second posttest, Subject P.A.'s matching of dictated names to lower-case letters had become almost perfect but the two naming performances remained at their previous levels. This again indicated that the mediation was independent of oral naming.

The Emergence of Printed-Word and Lower-Case Letter Naming

It was possible for Subject P.A. to learn upper-case names in the course of learning to match dictated to upper-case letters (AB). None of the subjects' training, however, involved the association of dictated letter names with printed lower-case letters or of dictated with printed words. The interesting possibility here is that receptively mediated matching (AC) might, in turn, have fostered oral naming of the words and lower-case letters (CD); oral naming, rather than mediating the emergent auditory-visual capability (AC), might itself have been a product of that capability.

This possibility received some support from the data: (1) Oral naming did emerge *after* crossmodal matching. (2) In his test on 2/15/71, Subject J.C. matched 12 dictated words with their appropriate printed words; he also named nine of these 12 correctly. Of the eight words matched incorrectly, five were also named incorrectly. On 2/26/71, 10 of the 15 words that he matched correctly were also named correctly. Four of the five words matched incorrectly were also named incorrectly. These data are consistent with the possibility that the receptively mediated matching of printed to dictated words actually generated oral reading.

On the other hand, oral naming might be explained by the expressive mediation paradigm. For instance, teaching Subject P.A. directly to match upper-case letters to their dictated names (AB) partially established BD in the expressive mediation triangle. Then, teaching him

directly to match lower- to upper-case letters established a second side of this triangle, CB. At this point, the third side of the expressive triangle, CD, would have emerged, making the subject capable for the first time of naming some of the lower-case letters.

This second possibility was suggested by two of Subject J.C.'s naming errors. He gave the incorrect response, "hammer," both to the picture of an axe and to the printed word axe; in response to the picture of a pig and to the word pig, he said, "cow." In these instances, he gave the same incorrect name to the picture and to the corresponding printed word. Similarly, Subject P.A. consistently said, "Seh," in response to both upper- and lower-case G during his final test. It is difficult to attribute such naming errors to any process other than that illustrated by the expressive mediation triangle.

Mediation by Stimuli or by Responses?

The present study has suggested that new matching-to-sample performances, not directly taught, were generated by an apparently receptive mediation process. The suggestion that an untrained association can be mediated by a stimulus is not consistent with stimulus-response theories, which require differential responses to intervene between stimulus terms in the mediated-transfer paradigm (Jenkins, 1963; Schoenfeld & Cumming, 1963). Even stimulus-stimulus association theories postulate intervening representational processes (Estes, 1969) whose functions are difficult to distinguish from those attributable to response processes.

In arbitrary matching to sample, however, no differential responses to the individual stimuli are required. The necessary overt response is pointing or touching, which is the same for all sample and comparison stimuli. Matching to sample has been accommodated into a stimulus-response framework by hypothesizing that each sample generates a differential coding response; the stimulus consequences of these coding responses then control appropriate comparison responses (Schoenfeld & Cumming, 1963). Without such coding, matching to sample would have

to be viewed as a direct stimulus-stimulus association.

Although it is plausible for each sample to generate its own coding response, the transfer tests in our earlier experiments (Sidman, 1971b; Sidman & Cresson, 1973) did not involve the original sample stimuli. The stimuli in the transfer tests, B and C, had training histories only as comparison stimuli. To explain the mediated transfer of matching to sample, a coding hypothesis would therefore have to assume that each sample and its correct comparison generated the same coding response. For example, the dictated sample word "boy," the comparison picture of a boy, and the comparison printed word boy would all have to be coded the same way. The common coding response could then mediate the matching of the comparison stimuli to each other.

In the present experiments, the mediation of AC matching via identical sample and comparison coding would require an additional step. In AB matching, each B comparison stimulus would have had to generate the same coding response as its corresponding A sample. In BC matching, these same B coding responses would have had to persist and, in addition, transfer to the C comparison stimuli. Coding responses common to the A samples and the C comparisons could then mediate AC matching.

Names can clearly serve as coding responses and can meet the requirement of identical sample and comparison coding. To maintain the coding hypothesis in the present experiments, however, one must assume some class of coding responses other than names. Then, each comparison stimulus would have to generate the same unknown coding response as its appropriate sample, even though the matching relation was arbitrary.

Schoenfeld and Cumming (1963) presented a strong argument for nonverbal mediating processes, although such processes become difficult to identify in matching-to-sample tasks that involve large numbers of stimuli. The additional assumption of identical sample-comparison coding, required if mediated transfer of matching is to be interpreted as other than stimulus-stimulus learning, does not seem to have been considered and is under investigation in this laboratory.

Until these issues have been clarified, it would seem desirable to restrict the term *mediation* to its procedural sense. If an association between stimuli B and C is established by their common association with stimulus A and we cannot identify actual events or processes that intervene between B and C, the utility of postulating such events or processes will remain debatable. In the procedural sense, the term *mediation* refers to the observation that the BC association, for example, was brought about by some form of prior learning that involved elements other than B and C. The critical aspects of that prior learning are matters of primary concern.

* * * * * * * * * *

Commentary

Even though the *Mediated Transfer* paper took exception to the kinds of response-mediation theories that had arisen out of paired-associate research on equivalence, our language in this paper was greatly influenced by the earlier work. After the *Mediated Transfer* paper, however, several years elapsed before our lab's next published report on equivalence relations (with the exception of Ron Lazar's dissertation [Lazar, 1977]). During this publication hiatus, ongoing experimental studies and wonderfully productive weekly lab meetings were gradually refining our conception of the equivalence relation and our way of talking about it.

The developments that took place during that period were eventually reflected in two 1982 publications (Sidman et al., 1982; Sidman & Tailby, 1982). The conceptual refinements were significant and explain why we never again talked about our experiments in the same way as in the *Mediated Transfer* paper. Other investigators, however, unaware of the changes that were taking place, adopted the more or less traditional language and conceptual framework of that paper. It is important, therefore, to indicate why interested readers should not stop at this point in our story.

The Language of Association

For one thing, in describing matching-to-sample procedures and the behavior those procedures generate, we never again talked about *associations*. Association theory has a long and respectable history (for example, Rescorla, 1980). Probably because of this history, even investigators without a rigorous commitment to association theory often talk—as we did—about *associations* between sample and comparison stimuli.

The concept of association, however, turned out to have nothing of explanatory value to add to our description of equivalence relations. The defining temporal and sequential properties of associations are so vague that they add only a deceptive aura of explanatory usefulness to a discussion of equivalence relations. They are simply not relevant to the mathematically derived definition of equivalence relations that we finally arrived at (Chapters 5 and 6). The criteria we were to propose for defining equivalence relations between stimuli required the demonstration of the relational properties of reflexivity, symmetry, and transitivity. Those properties have never played a role in the definition of associative connections between stimuli or between stimuli and responses.

In classical conditioning, for example, which formed the basis for S-R interpretations of mediated association, there is no reason to expect symmetry in the presumed stimulus-response associations. Indeed, when it was realized that some of the mediated-generalization data required associations to be symmetric (for example, Ekstrand, 1966), it was found necessary to account for the symmetry by postulating "backward conditioning," a phenomenon that was at best only weakly supported empirically. Jenkins (1963) assumed that "backward associations exist following paired-associate learning" even though the conditioning processes underlying paired-associate learning did not necessarily yield backward associations.

Paradigms of Mediated Transfer

Hindsight permits us to recognize several other shortcomings in the *Mediated Transfer* paper. For example, in our eagerness to test the necessity for response mediation, we ignored the significance of the change we had made in the experimental paradigm—what we called "proceeding around the receptive triangle in another direction" (p. 90). We did not yet realize that the BC and CB tests in the original paradigm (teach AB and AC) did not possess the same significance as the AC tests in the revised paradigm (teach AB and BC). The former tested for both symmetry and transitivity, and the latter for transitivity alone. We still did not comprehend the difference between transitivity and equivalence. By the time we arrived at the 1982 papers (Chapters 5 and 6), we had seen that transitivity is just one of the defining properties of an equivalence relation, and that a demonstration of both symmetry—another defining property—and transitivity is a more conclusive indicator of equivalence.

Similarly, we now realize that the CB test in the *Mediated Transfer* paper was actually a symmetry test. If the tested CB conditional discrimination emerged, this would indicate that the original BC conditional relation possessed one of the required properties of an equivalence relation. By explicitly teaching Subject P.A. the CB conditional discrimination, we negated the validity of the CB test as an indicator of symmetry. We now see, therefore, that this subject's data become equivocal with respect to the emergence of the AC conditional discriminations.

We also referred to the identity-matching procedure simply as a way to test the subjects' ability to discriminate the stimuli we were using. This conception was not incorrect but we now know that testing for identity matching is also the way to evaluate reflexivity, another of the defining properties of equivalence. Using the experimental stimuli, as we did here, to teach Subject J.C. to do identity matching destroys its validity as a test for reflexivity.

Therefore, although the *Mediated Transfer* experiment met its objective—to test for the necessity of response mediation—its conclusions are relevant only to the transitive property of equivalence relations. The experiment suggested that the transitive property of a relation does not require response mediation, but whether that is also true of the more general equivalence relation remains to be seen.

It is only fair to point out, also, that the distinctions among various experimental paradigms for evaluating mediated transfer had been well worked out in the earlier work on mediated associations. For example, Jenkins (1963, pp. 216-219) described four types of paradigms, based on the linear associations and the response-mediation that were presumed to underlie the observations: simple chains (A→B→C), reverse chains (A←B←C), stimulus equivalence (A→B←C), and response equivalence (A←B→C). As we shall see, however, the mathematically derived description of equivalence relations that we were to propose in the 1982 papers made it possible to distinguish among the paradigms descriptively, without having to invoke any explanatory theory.

A Second Kind of Transfer Triangle

Tests of Naming

The problem of response mediation continued to occupy our attention and became a major focus of experimentation in other laboratories (for example, Dugdale & Lowe, 1990). We shall discuss the problem more thoroughly in Chapters 7 and 9. Relevant at this point, however, is a note concerning the validity of tests for naming as indicators of response mediation.

In our laboratory, unlike several others (for example, Lowe, 1986), subjects rarely name stimuli aloud while they are being taught matching-to-sample tasks or while they are being tested for emergent performances. Why this is so is not at all clear, although I have often wondered whether it has something to do with the brevity of the intertrial interval that we customarily use (.67 s). Perhaps the rapidity with which each new trial begins leaves subjects with little time to react to the stimuli in any way except to do what the procedure demands. Although subjects do not have to react quickly, the controlling stimuli come up fast, and in that sense, the procedure demands action. Subjects who act quickly have only limited opportunity to reflect upon and to talk to themselves about what they are doing. I think this conjecture is worth checking out.

In any event, the absence of overt speech in our experiments, whatever the reason, does not rule out the possibility of subvocal naming. Frequently, therefore, after the completion of all tests, we ask subjects to name the stimuli. We show them one stimulus at a time and ask, "What is it?" One assumption underlying this test is that a subject who does not name a stimulus consistently when asked to do so will also not have been naming that stimulus consistently while performing the matching-to-sample tasks.

Dugdale and Lowe (1990), Lowe (1986), and Stoddard and McIlvane (1986) have pointed out that this assumption may not be valid. The instruction may not indicate clearly what the subject is to say, or subjects who have never been told by the experimenter what to call the stimuli may be unwilling to reveal what their guesses had been. After all, those guesses may have been wrong and experience has taught many subjects that our culture often deals unkindly with those who answer wrongly.

In the *Mediated Transfer* experiment, it seems unlikely that these possibilities account for the inaccurate and inconsistent naming in the tests. The subjects did, after all, name at least 50% of the stimuli correctly in every test, a performance that could hardly have come about if they had failed to understand what was wanted of them or were unwilling to reveal their guesses. These data, therefore, cannot easily be dismissed when discussing whether response mediation is necessary to account for emergent matching-to-sample performances. (See pp. 305-307 for additional discussion of this matter.)

Good-bye *Mediation*

For all the above reasons, this was the last paper in which we used the term *mediation*. Other reasons are indicated in the final paragraphs of the *Mediated Transfer* paper. I simply want to emphasize here that our decision to drop the term was quite deliberate. Procedurally, mediation can be defined clearly: when two stimuli become related to each other because each has been related to a third event, that third event can be called a *mediator*. Unfortunately, the term is rarely used so cleanly. Eventually, and perhaps inevitably, mediating processes are hypothesized to account for the observations. As the resulting theories that require those processes encounter empirical or logical difficulties, the mediating processes sink further and further from view. In our experience, that kind of theorizing has not proven useful.

The Receptive-Expressive Dichotomy

The *Mediated Transfer* paper was also the last occasion on which we used the *receptive-expressive* terminology. Something is to be said in favor of that terminology, however, as it is applied, for example, in Figure 4-1. It distinguishes between two quite different procedures for establishing the kinds of stimulus-stimulus relations that we look upon as a form of simple reading comprehension.

The *expressive* triangle illustrates a procedure in which B- and C-stimuli might become related if they control the same response (which, in the general case, need not be a name). For example, students may be taught to produce the same sounds—to say the same name—when they see either the picture of a car or the written word, car. In the *receptive* triangle, those same stimuli might become related if each is related to a third stimulus; students are asked to match both the picture and the written word to sounds that they hear spoken to them—the procedure does not require them to say anything.

The terms *receptive* and *expressive* capture the procedural distinction nicely, clearly delineating two different ways to teach simple reading comprehension. The expressive triangle depicts the method that educational systems have used exclusively since time immemorial; the receptive triangle depicts a method which, as we have indicated several times, can take advantage of modern technology to free teachers for more creative tasks than listening to students recite new letters or words as the students laboriously add these to their repertoires by "looking-and-saying."

The receptive-expressive terminology, however, is commonly held to signify more than the precise procedural distinction we make here (for example, Bloom, 1974). Lee (1978, 1981a) has pointed out that we can maintain the procedural distinction without having to assume two different cognitive processes; we can talk instead about the behavior of a person as speaker (*expressive*) and as listener (*receptive*). Unlike the expressive-receptive dichotomy, the speaker-listener characterization of the two sides of Figure 4-1, compatible with Skinner's (1957) formulation of verbal behavior, raises new questions about the role of the listener in verbal episodes.

The possibility also exists that the process—distinct from the procedure—that the *expressive* triangle in Figure 4-1 depicts does not really take place. Every response, after all, produces some kind of effect which, itself, may control subsequent behavior. When we say words, for example, we also produce sounds. If those sounds, rather than the acts that produced them, are responsible for emergent BC relations, then both triangles in Figure 4-1 may actually represent the same receptive process. Even if a subject gives B- and C- stimuli the same names, the emergent BC relation may still come about because both B and C are related to the same auditory stimulus. That stimulus may be presented by the experimenter or may be a product of the subject's own act. Indeed, it is not far-fetched to propose that in order to be a speaker, one must first become a listener.

Some Notes on Generality

We had been finding our early experiments exciting, partly because we saw practical applications to the teaching of reading comprehension and partly because we saw theoretical significance in a paradigm that created new behavior without our having to teach it directly. Lazar (1977), in his Ph.D. dissertation, made a reasonable case for the possibility that equivalence could help explain how syntax developed. (For later developments along this line, see Green, Sigurdardottir, and Saunders, 1991; Lazar and Kotlarchyk, 1986; Sigurdardottir, Green, and Saunders, 1990; Wulfert and Hayes, 1988). Our excitement, however, did not guarantee that the paradigm was significant. We had to consider the possibility that the phenomenon we were observing was just a laboratory curiosity, interesting to be sure, but perhaps not important.

For example, what kinds of generality did the phenomenon possess? Was it limited just to a few subjects or to a particular type of subject? As we shall see, subject generality has since been established by continued replication, in our laboratory and elsewhere. Equivalence relations have been demonstrated by various types of subjects, ranging from severely retarded people like those we reported in our early experiments, to the less severely retarded (for example, Spradlin et al., 1973; Wetherby, Karlan, & Spradlin, 1983), to normal children of various ages (Devany, Hayes, & Nelson, 1986; Lazar et al., 1984; Lazar & Kotlarchyk, 1986; Sidman et al., 1985; Sidman

& Tailby, 1982), and to adults of varying educational and cultural backgrounds (Bush, Sidman, & de Rose, 1989; Lazar, 1977; Wulfert & Hayes, 1988). More specific questions about the relevance of other kinds of developmental or acquired disabilities (for example, Green & Sigurdardottir, 1990; Joseph & Thompson, 1990), of age or aging (Gershenson & Joseph, 1990), and of species membership (Chapter 5) are beginning to receive satisfactory answers.

Another kind of generality concerns the kinds of stimuli that will support the emergence of new matching-to-sample performances that have not been directly taught. Our first experiments used words and pictures; was the phenomenon we had demonstrated limited to those kinds of stimuli? The *Mediated Transfer* paper extended this type of generality by using upper-and lower-case letters. Later studies in our lab and elsewhere showed that the procedures could also teach children to relate colors to color names and numbers to number names (Mackay & Sidman, 1984), coins and coin values to coin combinations—for example, a quarter to five nickels or to two dimes and five pennies (McDonagh, McIlvane, & Stoddard, 1984), hours of the day to medicinal doses (Green, 1991), words in one language to words in another (Joyce & Joyce, 1990; Sigurdardottir, 1992), and a great variety of forms, shapes, or nonsense syllables to each other in ways arbitrarily specified by the experimenter. Stimulus generality seems firmly established. Chapters 6 and 7 will substantiate yet another important kind of generality, one that firmly established the importance of the phenomenon we were looking at.

5

Conditional Discrimination and Matching to Sample: Are They the Same? Nonhuman and Human Subjects

Background

Some Publication History

The year 1982 saw the publication of the *Search for Symmetry* paper (this chapter) and the *Class Expansion* paper (Chapter 6). One objective of these papers was to show that behavior-analytic principles and techniques of experimentation could be brought to bear on matters that many considered to require a cognitivist orientation. I have often been asked, therefore, why we published in JEAB (the Journal of the Experimental Analysis of Behavior), a journal that cognitive psychologists shunned

The decision to seek a behavior-analytic rather than a cognitivist readership was deliberate, arrived at after much consideration. First of all, it became clear to us that behavior analysts, unlike cognitive psychologists, would find our approach to data collection, description, and interpretation congenial; they would not have to revise their general systematic approach in any fundamental way. We did bring up matters that were new to Behavior Analysis. Among these were: (a) our demonstration that more might be going on than meets the eye in the conditional-discrimination procedure; (b) our application of the concept of stimulus-stimulus relations; and (c) our explicit use of the concept of classes to account for the first-time occurrence of behavioral units more complex than responses or acts. But all of these new considerations were outgrowths of or additions to existing behavior-analytic formulations. They did not call for new beginnings. Behavior analysts were therefore more likely than cognitive psychologists to accept our findings and build on them. *Build* is the crucial word here.

Second, although I would have liked to introduce cognitive psychologists to our methodological and conceptual approach—after all, Behavior Analysis did grow out of Psychology—I realized that it was too late. As I have noted elsewhere (Sidman, 1989, pp. 4-5), Behavior Analysis has evolved as a science separate from Psychology. I saw no more point in trying to contribute to Cognitive Psychology than to any other science in which I claim no particular competence.

Despite these strong convictions, I was tempted to try to achieve the impossible. What tipped the balance was the recognition that publishing in a cognitive journal would, at best, generate a lot of organocentric theory; publishing in JEAB would, at best, generate a lot of experiments. With the advantage of hindsight, we can see that the latter expectation, at least, was correct.

Why publish at all? These 1982 papers seemed finally to convince behavior analysts that the phenomenon we and a few others had been working on for more than ten years was worth active attention. Although portions of the research had been presented at conventions, seminars and colloquia, and other occasions, those presentations apparently aroused only enough interest to produce more invitations to give the same talks. The only other visible effects were a few unpublished M.A. and undergraduate honors theses. It took publication of the two 1982 papers in a journal with a well-deserved reputation for thorough and critical peer review to generate a ripple of activity in the research community.

All this was as it should have been. I have always told students and colleagues, "If you have not published your research, then as far as the rest of the world is concerned, the research has not been done." Two considerations underlie this advice. First, it is fine to spend one's life satisfying one's own curiosity, searching for the answers to questions that seem important or perhaps merely interesting or challenging, but if one does not share the results of that search with students and other colleagues, then from the point of view of science, one has not contributed. Science—even basic science—is a social enterprise. It depends on social interaction for its very survival. At its best, an individual's scientific activity influences what basic and applied scientists in related areas do and say, what scientists in different areas do and say, and what nonscientists do and say. Failing to share the results of one's inquiries, however, even though one may have used scientific methods of the highest quality, means that one has achieved no effects on the behavior of others; one has not done any science. (The same, of course, may be said of other social enterprises like Philosophy and the Arts—both, broadly defined.)

Second, without textual and often pictorial representation, scientists may find it impossible to compare the work of others with their own. The results of experiments, the methods used to obtain those results, and a context that helps other scientists integrate those methods and results into their own repertoires of conduct must all be converted to text. Without recorded methodological details one can neither evaluate another's experimental arrangements nor tell whether one has replicated them; without quantitative details one can neither evaluate another's results nor tell whether one's own results differ in any important ways; without context, it is sometimes difficult to recognize the connections between someone else's work and one's own. Unless a rationale is brief, the methods uncomplicated, and the results concise and easily evaluated, members of the scientific community will await publication before they allow someone else's findings to change their own conduct.

Submission of research to a respected journal for publication does entail a risk. As often as not, reviewers find reasons to recommend that a paper not be published, and sometimes express those recommendations tactlessly. After laborious experimentation and perhaps even more laborious writing, it is not easy to expose one's work to possible rejection. It is certainly not pleasant to undergo a cold or hostile rejection.

The best reviewers, however, not only evaluate manuscripts but also criticize them constructively. As might be expected, constructive reviews take longer and cause publication delays, leading some investigators to search for ways to circumvent the review process. Although our laboratory has had its share of nonconstructive reviews from impatient or ill-informed reviewers, our publications have, on balance, benefitted from the review process. The 1982 papers were no exception.

Although those papers were published together, they were not submitted to the journal at the same time. The *Search for Symmetry* paper was the first. The reviewers recommended publication, at the same time offering excellent suggestions for clarifying the presentation. Tony Nevin, who was then the editor of JEAB, recommended that the manuscript be reduced by 50 percent. That turned out to be a fine suggestion, considerably enhancing the readability of the paper and removing a mass of data that were interesting but not directly relevant to the main points. By the time we completed the revisions, however, the journal had accepted the second paper also, and Nevin suggested that we delay publication of the first so that the two could appear together. Again, a wise and constructive editorial recommendation, probably responsible to a large extent for bringing other investigators into contact with our work on equivalence.

Delayed acknowledgments. My only regret about publishing the two papers together is that our formulation of equivalence relations is now often attributed only to the two authors of the second paper (which dealt only with human subjects) rather than to all of the authors of the first paper (which dealt largely but not wholly with nonhuman subjects). Our practice was to give authorship of a paper only to those who had both contributed creatively and were involved in the day-to-day conduct of the reported experiments but in this instance, that practice may have been ill-advised. All of the authors, those named in the accompanying footnote, and several others (notably, Susan Ott, Terry Burch, and Gregory Stikeleather) contributed in lab meetings and on other informal occasions to the emergence of our formulation of equivalence relations.

A particularly important contribution was made by Betsy Constantine, who, in an early dissertation proposal, noted that equivalence, a concept that we had been bandying about uncritically, had a mathematical definition. Modern high-school math courses now include equivalence relations among their foundation concepts but this was not so in my day. So I searched for a math book that would tell me about equivalence and I found two elementary texts that did the job quite well (Polis & Beard, 1973; Scandura, 1971). I used them to bone up on high-school math, brought my new knowledge into our lab meetings, and the relations between the mathematical and behavioral definitions of equivalence relations were then honed into what we presented in the 1982 papers. Later, when it became apparent that I had to learn some elementary concepts in the mathematical theory of sets, I found it helpful to read (many times) relevant pages in a summary of mathematics for the lay person(Gellert, Küstner, Hellwich, & Kästner, 1977).

Beyond Reading Comprehension

In our early experiments, the emergent relations between spoken and printed words and between printed words and pictures led almost inevitably to reading comprehension as an appropriate framework within which to present our findings. In experiments that led up to the 1982 papers, however, the arbitrary nature of the emergent relations made it evident that more was involved than reading comprehension. Clearly, we were dealing with more general processes. Our data had brought us to the point where we were ready to talk not just about relations that help to define reading comprehension but about equivalence relations that might help provide a behavioral basis for everyday correspondences between words and things, between what we say and what we do, and between rules and contingencies.

In the process of widening our horizons, we became aware that what we came to call "true" matching to sample represented a semantic process but that conditional discrimination did not. And so, in addition to introducing our formulation of equivalence relations in the *Search for Symmetry* paper, we used that formulation to define a behavioral distinction between conditional discrimination and matching to sample. Until then, our publications had referred only to matching to sample. Both terms, however, can signify either a procedure or its outcome in conduct. Conditional-discrimination and matching-to-sample procedures are identical but the resulting actions—conditional discriminations and true matching—are demonstrably different.

As we pointed out in the paper, one outcome of any conditional-discrimination procedure that does its intended job is a conditional, or *if...then* relation between sample and comparison stimuli, but another possible outcome is an equivalence relation to which each sample-comparison pair belongs. Our experimental paradigm provides a way to find out whether or not the procedure has generated equivalence relations. (In Chapter 10, we shall see that the paradigm provides a way to find out whether *any* procedure has generated equivalence relations.) If a conditional-discrimination procedure has indeed produced equivalence, tests for the properties of equivalence relations will prove positive. That is to say, the tests will show new conditional discriminations emerging, discriminations derived from those that were explicitly taught to the subjects and predictable on the basis of the assumption that the explicitly taught *if...then* relations were also equivalence relations. Positive tests for equivalence permit us to say that the original conditional-discrimination procedure had generated true matching-to-sample performances.

When we have reason to infer that a conditional-discrimination procedure has generated equivalence relations, conceptual clarity would probably be served best if we used the term *matching to sample* to specify the resulting conduct and refrained from using the term to specify the procedure itself. The terminology in our subsequent publications was not quite so pure, but whenever we did use *matching to sample* to specify the procedure, we indicated that we were doing so. I highly recommend this practice.

My concern here is not just terminology. Given the demonstrations in the *Search for Symmetry* paper and elsewhere that conditional discrimination and matching to sample are conceptually and empirically separable, a failure to recognize and consider the distinction may do a disservice to readers who are unaware of it. The assumption that a conditional-discrimination or matching-to-sample procedure has led to a matching-to-sample performance may lead to erroneous interpretations of data and to invalid extrapolations. Interpreting conditional discrimination as matching to sample is especially likely to lead to questionable extrapolation in research that compares the conduct of human and nonhuman subjects, since the use of standard conditional-discrimination procedures with nonhuman subjects has not usually produced matching-to-sample performances.

Even as brilliant an investigator as B. F. Skinner was unaware of this pitfall. Epstein, Lanza, and Skinner (1980) showed that linguistic-like performances engaged in by chimpanzees (Savage-Rumbaugh, Rumbaugh, & Boysen, 1978) could just as easily be taught to pigeons by means of standard behavior-analytic procedures and could be interpreted without introducing any new principles. Skinner and his colleagues exposed their pigeons to conditional-discrimination procedures but assumed that the resulting actions denoted matching to sample. This assumption led them to infer that a symmetry test would be positive—that the birds' performances would not be disrupted if former sample stimuli were presented as comparisons and former comparison stimuli as samples: "…We believe that this can be done but is not essential to the demonstration of interanimal communication" (p. 545).

We know now that this assumption was probably incorrect. Pigeons have not shown their conditional discriminations to be symmetric. To interpret what those pigeons were doing as *reading comprehension* or to attribute any semantic significance to their performance would be unjustified. The pigeons were certainly demonstrating complex conditional discriminations but they were probably not doing true matching to sample.

Epstein, Lanza, and Skinner, of course, claimed no special linguistic significance for their pigeons' conduct. For Skinner, language and verbal behavior were two different subject matters (Skinner, 1957, pp. 461 ff.; 1974, pp. 88 ff.). Still, in accord with Skinner's definition of verbal behavior (Skinner, 1957), they did consider the behavior of both the pigeons and chimpanzees to be verbal. If the pigeons were behaving verbally, however, the aspects of the environment that controlled their verbal behavior were related by conditionality and not by equivalence. To the extent that equivalence defines a relation to which we apply the everyday term *symbolic* (see Introduction), the pigeons' behavior, if it was verbal, was nevertheless not symbolic.

Their mistaken assumption that the pigeons were doing matching to sample does not negate the force of Epstein, Lanza, and Skinner's main argument, since the work with chimpanzees was subject to the same qualification. There, too, conditional discrimination was the basic teaching procedure but whether the procedure generated equivalence relations was not verified. Later, Dugdale and Lowe (1990) reported a failure to demonstrate symmetry in conditional discriminations by the same chimpanzees that had been reported to learn linguistic constructions, but it is to be regretted that they were not able to pursue their studies further. The importance of the pigeon demonstration rests on the assumption that the chimpanzees' conditional-discrimination performances were linguistic in nature. As matters stand now, however, the possibility exists that neither chimpanzees nor pigeons have shown true matching to sample in the laboratory. That demonstration will be necessary before any conditional-discrimination performance can be endowed with linguistic, verbal, conceptual, or any other "higher-level" characteristics. Indeed, why those concerned with the possibility of linguistic performances by nonhumans have not engaged in intensive efforts to demonstrate true matching is puzzling; it would greatly enhance the validity of the work on language with nonhuman subjects and would endow that work with considerable credibility in the research community (Schusterman, 1988, 1990; Schusterman and Gisiner, 1989; Schusterman, Gisiner, Grimm, and Hanggi, 1993; Schusterman and Kastak, 1993).

✳ ✳ ✳ ✳ ✳ ✳ ✳ ✳ ✳ ✳

A Search for Symmetry in the Conditional Discriminations of Rhesus Monkeys, Baboons, and Children

Procedures for generating arbitrary matching-to-sample performances may generate only conditional discriminations. Rational grounds for this distinction are proposed, based on the properties that any equivalence relation must possess. Empirical tests are described for determining whether subjects trained on conditional discriminations are also doing true matching to sample. A series of studies then leads to the conclusion that proof of true matching to sample by monkeys, pigeons, or baboons is yet to be provided. Whether the absence of such proof reflects experiential factors or species-defined limitations is not presently clear.

A commonly used experimental arrangement presents a subject with two discriminative stimuli simultaneously, perhaps a vertical and a horizontal line, while a third stimulus, perhaps a green or red hue, determines the positive or negative function of each line. Procedurally, the relation of the hues to the lines is that of conditionality or *if...then...* (for example, *if green, then vertical; if red, then horizontal*). The line discriminations are conditional; hues are the conditional stimuli.

Assumptions that extend the relations between stimuli beyond the procedurally defined conditionality reveal themselves when we call the behavior generated by the procedure *matching to sample*. An important special case is identity matching. The vertical discriminative stimulus (comparison) may be positive when the conditional stimulus (sample) is also vertical, with the discrimination reversing when the sample changes to horizontal. Experimenters often assume that for their subjects, too, these stimuli bear a relation to each other not only of conditionality but of sameness or identity. This need not be so. Carter and Eckerman (1975) have presented data which suggest that *identity matching* can be a misnomer. For pigeons, a red sample and comparison may be as different from each other as a red sample and a vertical comparison. For experimenters working with pigeons, then, matching to sample may be a case of mistaken identity.

The distinction between conditional discrimination and matching holds also when all the stimuli are different—to subjects and experimenter. By adding the qualifiers, *nonidentity, arbitrary,* or *symbolic* to the term, *matching to sample*, investigators reveal their assumption that the procedure generates another stimulus relation besides conditionality. Although the assumed relation cannot be identity, it can be equivalence. Matching to sample, therefore, sometimes refers not simply to the identity relation between a conditional and a correlated positive stimulus but to the more general equivalence relation. (Identity

itself can be shown to be an equivalence relation.)

An example may suggest why many of us have overlooked the possibility that the conditional-discrimination procedure may generate nothing more than conditional relations, assuming instead that the procedure also generates equivalence relations. Suppose the conditional stimuli, hues, control discriminations not just among simple tilted lines but among lines of greater complexity—the printed words *red, green* and their like. By calling a subject's performance *matching* we imply that each color and its correlated word comprise a class of equivalent stimuli, permitting us to say, "The words are *symbols* for the colors," or "The colors are the meanings of the words," and to include such tasks in tests of simple reading comprehension. Equivalence is a tempting assumption, transforming a conditional discrimination into a semantic process and supporting the notion that arbitrary matching to sample is a linguistic performance. If the assumption were valid, it would permit us to adopt conditional discrimination as a procedural model for studying aspects of language even in nonhuman animals.

The Equivalence Relation

We cannot tell by looking at a subject's conditional-discrimination performance whether or not it involves true matching to sample. Although conditionality is directly inferable from current behavior, additional tests are necessary to validate an inference of equivalence.

Suppose conditional stimulus *a* controls a discrimination in which *b* is positive. The procedurally defined relation R between stimuli *a* and *b* is the conditional relation *a*R*b*. If *a*R*b* also satisfies the properties of an equivalence relation, the stimuli will be members of a class of equivalent elements and we can call the subject's performance *matching to sample*. Table 5-1 summarizes the mathematical definition of the equivalence relation. A relation R must possess all three listed properties, reflexivity, symmetry, and transitivity, in order to fulfill the definition of an equivalence relation.

The reflexive property requires the relation R to hold between

Table 5-1
The Equivalence Relation

Equivalence Relations must be
1. Reflexive: *a*R*a*
2. Symmetric: If *a*R*b*, then *b*R*a*
3. Transitive: If *a*R*b* and *b*R*c*, then *a*R*c*

---

each stimulus and itself. If R were the relation *larger than*, reflexivity could not be satisfied; a stimulus cannot be larger than itself. If R is the conditional relation, reflexivity requires *if a then a, if b then b*, and so on, to hold true. Successful identity matching is a necessary consequence of reflexivity, which therefore conveys the notion of sameness.

The identity-matching procedure, however, does not definitively test reflexivity unless we have correctly identified the stimuli that control the subject's behavior. If, for example, control by the lines depended on their location on the left or the right key (given the usual arrangement in which the conditional stimulus is on the center key and the others are on the outer keys), the subject might not match vertical to vertical and horizontal to horizontal but rather, vertical/center to vertical/left and vertical/right, and horizontal/center to horizontal/left and horizontal/right. The experimenter's presumption of identical stimuli would then be incorrect and a performance that looked like identity matching would not be; to conclude that one was testing the relation R for reflexivity would be invalid. A definitive indicator of true identity matching and therefore of reflexivity is generalized identity matching. Successful generalized matching confirms reflexivity for each relation that is tested.

Symmetry requires the relation R to hold bidirectionally between two different stimuli. If sample a bears a conditional relation to comparison b (aRb), the relation must also hold when b is the sample and a is the comparison (bRa); symmetry requires sample and comparison to be interchangeable. A subject who has learned to select *vertical* when the sample is *green* should, given the opportunity, select *green* when the sample is *vertical*.

The final requirement, the transitive property, must hold for the relation among three stimuli. Before one can test R for transitivity, the subject must acquire a second conditional discrimination

in addition to aRb; the former comparison b, now a sample, must control a discrimination in which a third stimulus c is positive (bRc). If the relation R is transitive, a subject who has learned, for example, to select *vertical* (v) when given a *green* (g) sample (gRv) and to select a *triangle* (t) when the sample is *vertical* (vRt), should, when given the opportunity, also select the *triangle* when the sample is *green* (gRt).

A subject's failure in any one of these tests—generalized identity matching (reflexivity), sample-comparison interchangeability (symmetry), or appropriate sample-comparison recombination (transitivity)—would force a conclusion that the conditional-discrimination procedures did not generate matching-to-sample performances; R would not be an equivalence relation. If the tests verified all three properties, the conditional relation R would have met the requirements for an equivalence relation, thereby justifying the *matching-to-sample* terminology. One could then regard each sample and its matching comparison stimulus as equivalent members of a class and the procedure as a model for studying the development, relevance, and other aspects of such classes.

With human subjects, generalized matching tests for reflexivity, along with a test that permits symmetry and transitivity to be evaluated simultaneously, have demonstrated equivalence relations in conditional discriminations (see Sidman and Tailby, 1982, for the rationale underlying this combined test). Retarded youths became able to match pictures to their printed names after being taught to select each picture and its printed name (separately) conditionally upon the corresponding dictated name (Sidman, 1971b; Sidman & Cresson, 1973). The emergence of new relations between printed words and pictures attested to the formation of three-member stimulus classes, each containing an equivalent dictated word, picture, and printed word. Numerous experiments in this laboratory (e.g., Lazar & Kotlarchyk, 1986; Sidman & Tailby, 1982; unpublished data) have systematically replicated this finding with normal children also.

We have, however, been unable to demonstrate to our satisfaction that monkeys' conditional discriminations can properly be called matching to sample. The major purpose of this paper is to describe some experiments that failed to reveal equivalence relations in the conditional-discrimination performance of Rhesus monkeys—a failure that was confirmed with baboons. The experiments to be described represented our first approach to this problem; we asked whether the animals' performances satisfied the symmetric property of an equivalence relation. In the course of these experiments, we also obtained some data on transitivity. Although Hogan and Zentall (1977), Holmes (1979), and Rodewald (1974) have reported failures to find symmetric relations between the stimuli in pigeons' conditional discriminations, several variables that might have contributed to the absence of symmetry still require investigation. The present experiments, in addition to testing for symmetry with other species of subjects, will provide some of the information needed for a more definitive judgment.

GENERAL METHODS

The general subject, apparatus, and procedure specifications will apply to all experiments unless specific exceptions are noted.

Subjects

In all but two experiments the subjects were adult Rhesus monkeys, *Macaca mulatta.* Before becoming experimental subjects, and later, when nearing the end of "vacations" from experimental regimens, animals were fed, at fixed times, enough to maintain weights as close as possible to free-feeding levels. With any remaining food being removed one hour later, animals learned to take their full ration. An animal that did not obtain its full ration in an experimental session received the remainder one-half hour after returning to its home cage. Up to Experiment 4, the monkeys underwent five experimental sessions, each no more than two hr long, in successive two-week periods; one week, sessions took place on Monday, Wednesday, and Friday and the monkey received its daily ration in the home cage on Sunday; the next week, sessions took place on

Tuesday and Thursday, with a home-cage feeding on Saturday. During Experiment 4 the animals had a 1.5-hr session every weekday. Both schedules maintained sufficient deprivation to ensure several hundred trials per session and at the same time kept the animals' weights close to free-feeding levels. In the event of excessive pausing or high error rates late in training sessions, the daily ration was reduced slightly until the performance became more stable.

Apparatus

The animals' experimental environment, a sound-attenuating, fan-ventilated chamber, was in the same room as the programming and recording equipment. The portion of the chamber that held the monkey was 63 cm high, 61 cm wide, and 59 cm deep. One stainless-steel inner wall, opposite the access door, contained a five-key touch-sensitive stimulus-response matrix, a trial-initiation key that operated a limit switch, two pellet dispenser trays, and a houselight. Figure 5-1 diagrams the keys and feeder tray. The trial-initiation key, 3.2 cm in diameter, was mounted on the vertical midline, its center 16 cm

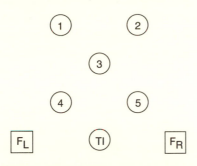

Figure 5-1. Diagram (not to scale) of keys and feeder trays in the monkey chamber. The trial-initiation key (TI) was located below the matrix of stimulus-response keys (1-5). Sample stimuli always appeared on Key 3 and comparison stimuli on Keys 1, 2, 4, and 5 (two per trial). If the correct stimulus was on Key 1 or 4, the pellet was delivered to the left tray (F_L); if the correct stimulus was on Key 2 or 5, the pellet was delivered to the right tray (F_R).

above the grating floor. The five stimulus-response keys were each 3.0 cm in diameter. Four were located at the corners of a 9-cm square (measured from the centers of the keys), with the fifth in the square's center. The matrix, on a circular black Plexiglas surround, was mounted with the center of the middle key at the vertical midline, 35.5 cm above the floor. Pellet trays on each side of the matrix, 22 cm above the

floor and 19 cm to the left and right of the vertical midline, received Noyes 1-g banana pellets. A 60-W Sylvania Lumiline houselight, protected by an aluminum grill, was mounted above the key matrix, its top 55 cm above the floor.

An IEE projector (Grason-Stadler #A509-2A, Stimulus Pattern 156) behind each key of the matrix provided the stimuli, red or green patches filling the key or a vertical or horizontal white line, 0.3 x 1.8 cm, on a black background. The trial-initiation key could be illuminated from the rear by two clear 7.5-W bulbs. A punched-tape reader programmed sequences of stimuli and trial types; solid-state equipment programmed the procedures. Events of interest were recorded on electromechanical and electronic counters, with temporal relations and other details being preserved by an Esterline 20-pen event recorder.

Procedures

Five minutes after an animal entered the experimental chamber the houselight signalled the start of a session and remained on until the session ended. The animal stayed in the darkened chamber for an additional five minutes before being taken back to its home cage.

Preliminary training. Animals first received magazine training, with pellets delivered unpredictably to either the left or the right tray. An autoshaping procedure (Brown & Jenkins, 1968; Sidman & Fletcher, 1968) then taught them to press the keys. All stimuli to be used later appeared on each key in a mixed sequence, one stimulus and one key per trial. If the stimulus appeared on the center key, the pellet was delivered alternately to the left or the right tray; on other trials the pellet dropped into the tray on the same side as the lit key. Once the animal reliably pressed the lit key and only the lit key within 8 s, autoshaping contingencies ceased.

Each trial in the next stage began with a stimulus on the center key. By pressing the center key the animal produced a stimulus on one of the four outer keys of the matrix but no pellet. The center key stayed on. Pressing the outer key then produced a pellet and a 5-s intertrial

interval. Only one comparison key had a stimulus on it, the stimulus which was to be correct for the sample during conditional-discrimination training. In this and all subsequent training and testing procedures, pressing a dark key during a trial had no consequence except to activate a recorder pen.

The next stage required the animal to press the illuminated trial-initiation key to produce a sample; when the sample came on, the trial-initiation key became dark. Pressing the center key then produced a comparison, and pressing that key produced a pellet and the intertrial interval. The animals then learned to press the trial-initiation key five times to produce a sample and thereby initiate a trial. The trial-initiation key permitted animals to pace their own trials.

The final step introduced one incorrect stimulus along with the correct comparison after the animal pressed the sample key. This marked the start of conditional-discrimination training. The sample remained on Key 3 (Figure 5-1). Comparisons, only two per trial, appeared on outer Keys 1, 2, 4, and 5; on any conditional-discrimination trial, two outer keys had stimuli projected on them and the other two were dark.

Each combination of stimuli and keys occurred equally often. With only two kinds of trials, as in the green/red identity-matching procedure, no more than three of the same type could occur consecutively. With more than two kinds of trials, all sample-comparison combinations had to occur before any could repeat. Also, all four comparison keys had to be scheduled as correct before any could be correct again. With those exceptions, all trial types and correct keys were equally probable on successive trials. Tape loops programmed sequences of 192 to 640 trials, depending on the number of trial types. Each session began with the trial that would have come up next at the end of an animal's previous session. Session durations and trials per session varied from animal to animal and in different stages of the experiments. Fewer trials had to be scheduled in sessions when a food pellet followed each correct trial than when leaner reinforcement schedules prevailed (see below).

When an animal pressed the correct comparison key a pellet dropped into the tray on the same side of the matrix as the correct key, all keys became dark, and the intertrial interval began. Except for the pellet, the same consequences followed an incorrect response. The procedure was noncorrection; errors did not cause trials to be repeated. Intertrial intervals lasted at least 5 s but could not terminate sooner than 5 s after the animal pressed any dark key.

Conditional-discrimination training. Monkeys R46 and R47 first had line-line training (line sample and line comparisons). The animal received a pellet if it pressed the vertical comparison when the sample was also vertical and the horizontal comparison when the sample was horizontal. Because Monkeys R46 and R47 had great difficulty learning the line-line task, they were taught to respond differentially to each sample line. Five responses (FR) were required to vertical samples, and a pair of responses spaced 2 s apart (DRL) was required to horizontal samples before the comparison stimuli would be presented. The animals' accuracy quickly rose above 90%, confirming the facilitative effect of sample schedules reported by Cohen, Looney, Brady and Aucella (1976), who used pigeons. Both monkeys then learned hue-hue (hue sample and hue comparisons) without differential sample schedules, pressing the green comparison when the sample was also green, and red when the sample was red.

Before starting the present experiments, Monkey R44 had learned successive reversals of green/red and vertical/horizontal simultaneous discriminations. Perhaps because of its history, Monkey R44 learned the line-line task without differential sample schedules.

All animals finally had sessions with line-line and hue-hue trials mixed. Before starting the experiments to be reported here, they underwent tests with simultaneous- and delayed-matching procedures in which sample schedules, where used, were removed and reinstated.

Symmetry testing. In symmetry tests, new trial types were inserted as probes into a baseline of previously learned conditional discriminations, with all types of trials occurring equally often.

Some experiments provided reinforcement on all correct trials, baseline and probe. Others provided reinforcement only on correct baseline trials, never on probes. In preparation for these extinction tests, before probes were actually inserted, the reinforcement probability on correct baseline trials was gradually reduced from 1.00 to 0.2. This reduction usually took place in steps of 0.1 and at least 90% of the trials had to be correct before a change. Occasional decreasing accuracy trends were halted by increasing the reinforcement probability and then using a stricter criterion while bringing the probability down again. At the final level, 0.2, at least 90% of each baseline trial type had to be correct in each successive 25-trial block during two consecutive sessions. Then, since no probes would be reinforced, the reinforcement probability on baseline trials during the test was increased sufficiently to maintain the overall probability at 0.2. The output of a probability gate (BRS/LVE PP-201) was modified to permit no more than nine consecutive correct baseline trials to go unreinforced.

EXPERIMENT 1

In asking whether monkeys' conditional discriminations satisfied the symmetric property of an equivalence relation, we at first simply added a few control features to the basic procedures used in the pigeon experiments (Hogan & Zentall, 1977; Holmes, 1979; Rodewald, 1974). Table 5-2 summarizes the conditional discriminations. The stimuli in each numbered line— a sample and two comparisons— define a trial type. Each pair of trial types, numbered 1 to 4, is a conditional discrimination with two components, A and B.

The line-hue trial types, 3A and 3B, were of particular concern. Having learned this conditional discrimination, was an animal also doing arbitrary matching to sample? Was the relation between each line sample and its correct hue comparison just *if-then* or was it also equivalence? Had *vertical* and *green* become members of one stimulus class and *horizontal* and *red* members of another class?

Table 5-2

Conditional discriminations and sample schedules (where used) in Experiments 1, 3, and 5. Where neither FR nor DRL is indicated, a single sample response sufficed to produce the comparisons. (Monkey R44 never had sample schedules, and in Experiment 3, only Subjects J.G. and A.B. had sample schedules.) Trial types 1A, 1B (line-line), 2A, and 2B (hue-hue) were to provide discriminative prerequisites for the symmetry test. The starred Trial Types 3A and 3B (line-hue) constituted the critical conditional discrimination that was to be tested for symmetry. Trial types 4A and 4B (hue-line) constituted the symmetry test. Symmetry-test sessions included all eight trial types.

	SAMPLE		COMPARISONS	
	STIMULUS	SCHEDULE	CORRECT	INCORRECT
1A	Vertical	FR	Vertical	Horizontal
1B	Horizontal	DRL	Horizontal	Vertical
2A	Green	—	Green	Red
2B	Red	—	Red	Green
* 3A	Vertical	FR	Green	Red
* 3B	Horizontal	DRL	Red	Green
4A	Green	—	Vertical	Horizontal
4B	Red	—	Horizontal	Vertical

Trial types 4A and 4B constituted the symmetry test. Hues, formerly comparisons, now became samples; lines, formerly samples, became comparisons. If the sample-comparison relations were symmetric, the animal would now select vertical when given a green sample, and horizontal when given a red sample.

Symmetry might fail to emerge in trial types 4A and 4B simply because a subject lacked experience with lines as comparisons, or hues as samples. Line-line (trial types 1A and 1B) and hue-hue training (2A and 2B) gave subjects experience with lines and hues in a context of conditional discrimination. Then, maintaining conditional discriminations 1, 2, and 3 during the symmetry test provided an ongoing baseline of prerequisite discriminations from which symmetry might emerge, and permitted the experimenters to monitor those discriminations.

Although test procedures differed for each monkey (see below), the general training and testing sequence went as follows: animals first had line-line and hue-hue training, trial types 1A, 1B, 2A, and 2B. This gave them experience with lines and hues

as samples and comparisons. They then had line-hue training; 3A and 3B were interspersed among the four previously learned trial types. With vertical samples, animals learned to select green and with horizontal samples, to select red. Finally, with all six trial types mixed together as a baseline, the last two, 4A and 4B, were inserted as symmetry probes. If the line-hue relations in conditional discrimination 3 were symmetric, the animals would now select vertical when the sample was green, and horizontal when the sample was red, although they had never been explicitly trained to do so.

METHOD

Subjects

Monkeys R44, R46, and R47 were subjects. Monkey R44 had a previous symmetry test in Experiment 2 before taking part in Experiment 1.

Training and Testing Procedures

Sample schedules. Table 5-2 also shows sample schedules, which, as noted earlier, were introduced because of difficulty in training Monkeys R46 and R47 on the line-line conditional discrimination (1A and 1B). This difficulty persisted for conditional discrimination 3, in which lines again were samples, so schedules were used also in teaching them the line-hue task.

Cohen, Brady, and Lowry (1981) and Urcuioli and Honig (1980) have suggested that schedule-generated behavior may actually take over the sample function from stimuli projected on the keys, in a manner reminiscent of coding responses (Lawrence, 1963; Schoenfeld & Cumming, 1963). Before Monkey R47's first symmetry test, therefore, attempts were made to remove the schedule requirements—by turning on the comparisons as soon as the animal pressed the sample key just once. Monkey R47 was unable to maintain both the line-line and the line-hue performances without schedules, but with schedules for line-line only, the line-hue performance eventually met criterion. After the schedules had been used during original acquisition, therefore, they were maintained as shown in Table 5-2 for Monkey R46 only; Monkey R47 kept the schedules in trial types 1A and 1B but not in 3A or 3B. Monkey R44 never had differential sample schedules.

In the course of attempts to remove the sample schedules, Monkey R47's comparison keys were permanently reduced from four to two. Samples still appeared on Key 3 but comparisons only on Keys 4 and 5 (Figure 5-1); Keys 1 and 2 remained dark and without function.

Symmetry Tests. After Monkeys R44 and R46 had learned the line-hue conditional discrimination, the reinforcement probability for all six trial types was reduced. Trial types 4A and 4B were then inserted into the sparsely reinforced baseline as unreinforced probes for symmetry. Monkey R47 had two symmetry tests, both of which provided reinforcement on all correct trials, baseline and probe. On probe trials, responses indicative of symmetry were arbitrarily designated as correct.

RESULTS AND DISCUSSION

Figure 5-2 contains the probe-session results for Monkeys R44 and R46. Individual scores for each trial type make it possible to detect patterns of stimulus control that the customary accuracy measure might obscure (Sidman, 1980). Because each nonoverlapping pair of bars represents a conditional discrimination, averaging the pair would yield the usual accuracy score. The first three pairs of bars for each subject show baseline performances within the test session and the final two bars the symmetry probes.

All baselines were above 90% correct. Line-line performances

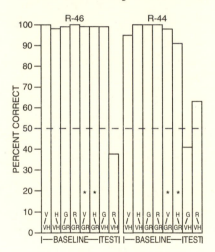

(the first two bars for each animal) were nearly perfect, as were hue-hue(the second pair of bars). Bars with asterisks show the maintenance of high line-hue scores—vertical samples matched to green comparisons and horizontal samples to red comparisons. The final two bars for each animal represent the hue-line probes for symmetry. (Probe-trial responses indicative of symmetry were arbitrarily designated as correct. Subsequent figures will follow this practice.) One animal slightly preferred the vertical comparison and the other the horizontal; average scores on symmetry trials were 55 and 52% for Monkeys R46 and R44, respectively. The animals did not reverse the sample-comparison roles of lines and hues; they gave no evidence of symmetry.

Monkey R47's first hue-line probes averaged only 56% correct but line-hue trial type 3A in

Figure 5-2. Performances by Monkeys R46 and R44 during the symmetry-probe session of Experiment 1. Bars depict the percentage of correct responses for each trial type. Stimuli for each trial type are identified at the bottom of the bars and a line connects each sample to its correct comparison. The bars, from left to right, correspond to trial types that are listed, from top to bottom, in Table 5-2. Asterisks denote the line-hue trial types tested for symmetry and the two right-hand bars for each animal depict the hue-line symmetry probes. Probes were unreinforced. Each bar represents approximately 95 trials for Monkey R46 and 65 trials for Monkey R44. Only Monkey R46 had line-sample schedules.

the baseline also dropped to 76%. After another criterion session of baseline trials alone, summarized in the left side of Figure 5-3, the animal received a second test. The right side of Figure 5-3 shows an average of only 49% correct on the probes. Correct probe trials did not become more frequent as the sessions progressed. Again, there was baseline disruption, most severe this time in the hue-hue trials. Even in its second session with reinforcement on correct probe trials, this animal performed no better on symmetry probes than did the others in their extinction tests.

Probing in extinction, however, did not affect the other animals' baselines, even though they received only infrequent reinforcement. The left side of Figure 5-3 shows that all trial types were above 90% during the session before the probes; this typical stability indicates that the baseline deterioration during the next session came about because of the reinforcement on correct probe trials and was not a paradoxical effect of reinforcement on the baseline trials. It seems reasonable to assume that reinforcement on probe trials would

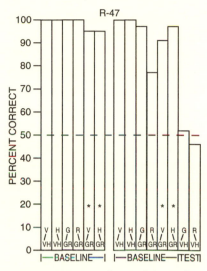

Figure 5-3. Monkey R47's performances during Experiment 1's symmetry test (right side) and the preceding baseline session (left side). Trial types are as depicted Figure 5-2. All correct trials, including probes, were reinforced. Each bar represents 35-40 trials. Only line-line trials had differential sample schedules.

not have disrupted the baseline if the conditional relations being tested were symmetric. The significance of the probe performance itself is somewhat diminished by the poorly maintained baseline but insofar as the baseline deterioration can be attributed to the probe-trial reinforcement, the test does bolster the evidence against symmetry. Hogan and Zentall (1977) used a similar rationale for the design of some of their symmetry tests.

In line-hue trial types 3A and 3B the animals had apparently learned only a conditional relation between each sample and its correct comparison and gave no evidence for the formation of equivalence relations. They were unable to match the stimuli when the original samples became comparisons and the original comparisons became samples, and provided no justification for calling their performance *matching to sample*.

EXPERIMENT 2

Is it sufficient to say that the conditional relation is, "If the sample is vertical, then green is the correct comparison," or must one also specify the incorrect comparison? Would it be more correct to say that the conditional relation is, "If the sample is vertical and the comparisons are green *and red*, then green is the correct comparison"?

Farthing and Opuda (1974) presented pigeon data indicating that the incorrect comparison is irrelevant to the relation between sample and correct comparison.

Nevertheless, the problem requires specific resolution in the present context. If a complete definition of the conditional relation had to include incorrect stimuli, then a valid symmetry test would require sample and correct comparison to be interchangeable only when the original incorrect comparison was also present. Experiment 1, however, not only interchanged samples and correct comparisons but also changed the incorrect comparisons from hues to lines (Table 5-2). In Experiment 2, therefore, the symmetry test substituted samples and correct comparisons for each other while incorrect comparisons remained unchanged.

Table 5-3 summarizes the conditional discriminations. Trial types 1 and 2 were the same as in Experiment 1. Asterisks mark the relations to be tested for symmetry: in 3A, the sample was vertical and the correct comparison green, as in Experiment 1, but the incorrect comparison was now horizontal instead of red; in 4B the sample was horizontal and the correct comparison red but the incorrect comparison was now vertical instead of green. The symmetry test, 5A and 5B,

Table 5-3

Conditional discriminations in Experiment 2. Trial types 1A, 1B, 2A, and 2B are the same as in Experiment 1. The starred trial types 3A and 4B maintain the same line samples and correct hue comparisons as the starred trial types in Table 5-2 but now the incorrect comparisons are lines instead of hues. Trial types 3B and 4A were included in order to maintain conditionality in the line-hue relations. Trial types 5A and 5B, the symmetry test, now maintain the same incorrect comparisons as trial types 3A and 4B. Symmetry test sessions included all ten trial types.

	SAMPLE	COMPARISONS CORRECT	INCORRECT
1A	Vertical	Vertical	Horizontal
1B	Horizontal	Horizontal	Vertical
2A	Green	Green	Red
2B	Red	Red	Green
* 3A	Vertical	Green	Horizontal
3B	Horizontal	Horizontal	Green
4A	Vertical	Vertical	Red
* 4B	Horizontal	Red	Vertical
5A	Green	Vertical	Horizontal
5B	Red	Horizontal	Vertical

again had former correct comparisons, green and red, as samples, and former samples, vertical and horizontal, as correct comparisons. The incorrect comparisons, horizontal and vertical, remained unchanged from trial types 3A and 4B.

What was the function of trial types 3B and 4A? Without 3B, animals might have learned to respond correctly on 3A even while ignoring the sample simply by selecting green whenever a green and a line comparison were present together. Inclusion of 3B required control by the sample if the animals were consistently to choose correctly between green and horizontal. Similarly, trial type 4A made control by the sample necessary for correct choices between red and vertical.

METHOD

Subjects

Monkey R44 had its first symmetry test in this experiment. The probes, carried out in

143

extinction, will not be described here. Its second test, also in extinction, was reported in Experiment 1. Then came two delayed-matching tests (zero delay), the first in extinction and the next with reinforcement on all correct trials. These, also, will not be reported here. The baseline for Experiment 2 was then reinstated in preparation for the test to be reported next.

Procedures

The sequence of training and test procedures was similar to Experiment 1. After line-line and hue-hue training, trial types 3A, 3B, 4A, and 4B, with mixed line and hue comparisons, were interspersed among 1A, 1B, 2A, and 2B. Symmetry probes (5A and 5B) were introduced into this baseline of eight different trial types, with reinforcement on all correct trials.

RESULTS AND DISCUSSION

The right side of Figure 5-4 presents percentages of correct trials of each type during the probe session. Again, asterisks denote baseline trial types that were tested for symmetry. The animal performed no better on the symmetry probes than it did during Experiment 1. (These results were also consistent with the probes in the unreported delayed-matching tests.)

Reinforcement on correct probe trials, however, disrupted the baseline. Each line-line trial type dropped to 89%, trial type 3B (H-HG) dropped to 59%, and 4A (V-VR) to 83%. Although 3A and 4B remained high, the decreases in 3B and 4A indicated considerable change in conditional discriminations 3 and 4 during the test. Probing in extinction had never affected this animal's baseline. Because of the disruption, the left side of Figure 5-4 shows the preceding baseline session. As with Monkey R47 in Experiment 1, the baseline disruption appeared to be a consequence of reinforcing the symmetry probes and provided additional evidence against symmetry. Baseline performances most severely affected by the reinforcement on correct probe trials involved identical sample and correct comparison lines but failures to replicate this relation obscured its significance.

Even with incorrect comparisons held constant, a sample and

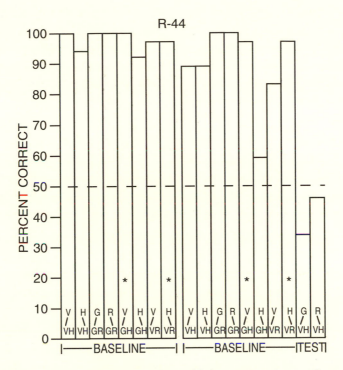

Figure 5-4. Performances by Monkey R44 during Experiment 2's symmetry test (right side) and the preceding baseline session (left side). Bars depict the percentage of correct responses for each trial type (corresponding to Table 5-3). Stimuli for each trial type are identified at the bottom of the bars, and a line connects each sample to its correct comparison. Asterisks denote the line-hue trial types (with lines as incorrect comparisons) tested for symmetry, and the two bars at the extreme right depict the hue-line symmetry probes. All correct trials, including probes, were reinforced. Each bar represents approximately 35 trials.

its correct comparison were not substitutable for each other. The revised test was no more successful than the test in Experiment 1 in demonstrating symmetry. The conditional discriminations did not generate classes of equivalent stimuli and the term *matching to sample* did not appear applicable.

EXPERIMENT 3

A major justification for stressing the importance of symmetry has been the demonstration that the conditional-discrimination procedure does establish equivalence relations when the subjects are retarded teenagers (Sidman, 1971b; Sidman & Cresson, 1973; Sidman et al., 1974; Spradlin et al., 1973), normal children (Lazar & Kotlarchyk, 1986; Sidman & Tailby, 1982), and normal adults (Lazar, 1977). The human subjects, however, did not learn the same conditional discriminations as the monkeys, nor were the methods of testing for equivalence relations the same. Is it possible that the techniques used with monkeys would have failed to produce symmetry even with humans? Experiment 3 attempted to answer this question by repeating Experiment 1 reasonably closely with children.

METHOD

Subjects

Six normal children, five boys and one girl, participated. Their ages(years-months) at the time of their symmetry tests were: 4-8 (C.H.), 4-8 (J.G.), 4-11 (P.L.), 5-2 (A.B.), 5-2 (J.L.), and 5-9 (K.O.). Each child, recruited by newspaper advertisements, came several days a week with a parent who was paid after each session. The number of sessions, each 15 to 30 minutes long, varied because the children required different amounts of baseline training.

Apparatus and General Procedures

The child sat before a stimulus-response matrix of nine translucent keys onto which stimuli were projected from the rear. The keys, each 7.3 cm in diameter, were arranged in a circle of eight, with the ninth in the center (Figure 5-5). The display diameter was 32.7 cm; the center-to-center distance was 9.5 cm between adjacent keys on the perimeter and 12.7 cm between the center key and each

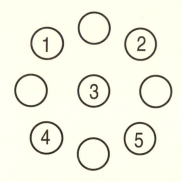

Figure 5-5. Diagram (not to scale) of the key matrix in Experiment 3. Samples always appeared on Key 3 and comparisons on Keys 1, 2, 4, and 5 (two per trial). The other keys were never used.

of the others. Sample stimuli always appeared in the center and comparison stimuli for a given trial appeared only on two of the four outer keys that formed the corners of a square (numbered 1, 2, 4, and 5 in Figure 5-5). A Kodak Carousel projector presented the stimuli, red or green patches filling the key, or a vertical or horizontal black line, 0.2 x 7.3 cm, on a white background. Solenoid-operated shutters were mounted between projector and keys. There was no trial-initiation key.

When the subject pressed a key, a limit switch signalled the programming and recording equipment. A response was not defined until the key had been released for .2 s; this permitted simultaneous pressure on more than one key to be defined as incorrect. Unless a reduced reinforcement probability or an extinction probe precluded reinforcement, correct trials were followed by the sound of chimes, the delivery of a penny into a receptacle below and to the left of the key matrix, and a 1.5-s intertrial interval. The children kept all pennies they received. Only the intertrial interval followed incorrect responses.

Training and Testing Procedures

Training. Three children (C.H., P.L., and K.O.) had already taken part in an experiment on delayed hue-hue matching and needed no preliminary training for the present study. With the three experimentally naive subjects (J.L., A.B., and J.G.), the delivery of three pennies sufficed to accomplish magazine training. The experimenter then provided nonvocal instruction by pressing the keys appropriately for several trials in which a sample and only a correct comparison stimulus (see below) appeared. Each trial began with a stimulus on the center key. Pressing the center key produced a stimulus on one of the four outer keys, while the center-key stimulus remained on. Pressing the outer key then produced chimes, penny, and a 1.5-s intertrial interval.

The experimenter then ceased all demonstration and the children themselves pressed the keys, with instructions provided only by the reinforcement contingencies. Finally, both an incorrect and a correct comparison came on when the subject pressed the sample key. This marked the start of conditional-discrimination training, which followed the pattern of Experiment 1, as summarized in Table 5-2. Three children (P.L., A.B., and J.G.) learned hue-hue first and the others learned line-line first. All four trial types (1A, 1B, 2A, and 2B) were then mixed together. The children then learned the line-hue task that was to be tested for symmetry.

Subject J.G. experienced great difficulty with the line-line conditional discrimination and Subject A.B. learned line-line but then seemed unable to master line-hue. The sample schedules used with the monkeys (FR 5 and DRL 2–s) were introduced to help the two children and these had their intended facilitative effect.

All six trial types were then mixed, providing a baseline for the symmetry test. Subject A.B.'s sample schedules were removed and he was able to maintain his performance. Reinforcement probability for correct baseline trials was then gradually reduced to .2.

Symmetry Testing. Hue-line trials (4A and 4B, Table 5-2), were interspersed among the six types of baseline trials as unreinforced symmetry probes.

Each test contained 72 trials, nine of each type.

At this point, only Subject J.G. still had sample schedules. After his test, reinforcement probability for baseline trials returned to 1.00 and sample schedules were eliminated. When he continued his criterion level of baseline performance, the reinforcement probability was once again reduced and he had two additional tests.

Subject K.O. also had an additional probe. After her first test, she had baseline training with a delayed-matching (zero-delay) procedure. Reinforcement probability was then reduced once more and the symmetry probe was repeated at zero delay.

RESULTS AND DISCUSSION

Figure 5-6 summarizes four of the six children's probe sessions. As before, asterisks mark the trial types being tested for symmetry and the final two bars for each subject show the symmetry probes. Only Subject J.L. made as many as two errors on any trial type, baseline or probe. Unlike the three monkeys, these four children reversed the sample and comparison roles of lines and

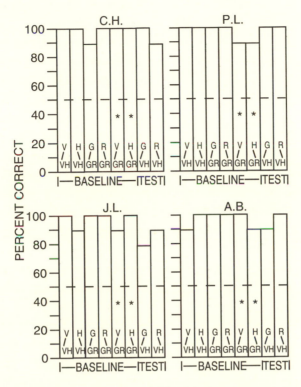

Figure 5-6. Performances by four children during symmetry tests in Experiment 3. Trial types are as depicted in Figure 5-2. Symmetry probes were unreinforced. Subjects had no differential sample schedules during test sessions.

hues. Symmetry in the conditional relation between line samples and hue comparisons thereby satisfied one of the requirements for an equivalence relation.

A possibly major difference between the monkeys' and the children's symmetry tests was the smaller number of trials (only nine of each type, for a total of 72) given to the children. Examination of the first 72 trials in the monkeys' probe sessions, however, did not reveal any need to change our conclusion that they had failed to demonstrate symmetry.

The data for two children failed to prove symmetry. Figure 5-7A summarizes Subject K.O.'s first symmetry test. Although her

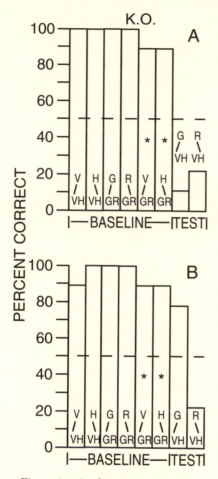

Figure 5-7. Performances by Subject
K.O. during symmetry tests in Experiment 3. Trial types are as depicted in
Figure 5-2. Symmetry probes were
unreinforced.

"chance" level, might have
suggested that the training actually
generated strong "antisymmetry."
The score, however, was deceptive; on one-third of the probe
trials Subject K.O. did not select
the antisymmetric comparison
but rather, pressed both comparisons simultaneously.

Figure 5-7B summarizes Subject K.O.'s second symmetry test,
with the zero-delay matching
procedure. During probe trials,
which this time averaged 50%
correct, she strongly preferred
the vertical comparison. Although Hogan and Zentall
(1977) and Gray (1966), who
tested pigeons with zero delay,
adduced statistical evidence for
symmetry, their conclusion was
not confirmed by Subject K.O.
(or by the data, not presented,
of Monkey R44). The zero-delay
procedure did not suffice to
transform the conditional relation into an equivalence relation.

In Subject J.G.'s first probe
session (Figure 5-8A), he averaged only 56% on probe trials.
In his second test (Figure 5-8B),
after the sample schedules had
been removed, his probe-trial
performance did not improve,
but because of his decreased accuracy (78%) on line-hue

baseline remained quite stable,
she clearly did not reverse the
sample and comparison roles of
lines and hues. Her average score
of only 17% on probe trials, considerably lower than the 50%

baseline trials, he was retrained and tested once more. The third test (Figure 5-8C) shows a more adequate baseline but no improvement in the probes. With or without sample schedules, Subject J.G. gave no evidence of symmetry.

Unlike the three monkeys, four children showed symmetry in the relation between lines and hues. To the extent that Experiment 3 replicated the essential features of Experiment 1, one might conclude that the absence of symmetry in the monkeys' performances was not attributable to some procedural artifact. Two children, however, failed to show symmetry under conditions like those of Experiment 1. The possibility remained, therefore, that some aspect of the procedure was still responsible for the absence of symmetry in the performances of Subjects K.O. and J.G., and the monkeys. A reappraisal of the training and test procedures and their rationale led to changes in the baseline conditional discriminations, and the two children who had been exceptions joined the other four in yielding positive results in subsequent symmetry tests. Although the absence of

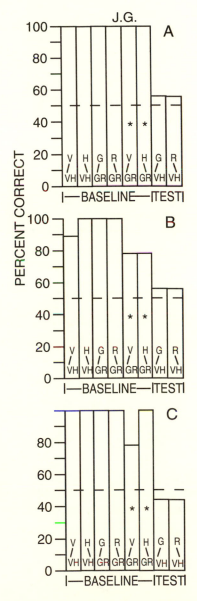

Figure 5-8. Performances by Subject J.G. during symmetry tests in Experiment 3. Trial types are as depicted in Figure 5-2. Line-sample schedules were required only in Panel A.

controls for repeated testing clouded the relevance of these changes (Spradlin et al., 1973), the mere possibility that the new baselines might have been responsible for symmetry mandated similar training and test procedures for the monkeys.

EXPERIMENT 4

Among the prerequisites for the symmetry test were a successive discrimination between green and red samples, and simultaneous discriminations between vertical and horizontal comparisons. Experiment 3 brought about a reevaluation of the assumption that hue-hue and line-line training provided subjects with this prerequisite repertoire.

Consider first the successive green-red discrimination (4A and 4B, Figure 5-2). Probe trials presented either a green or a red sample and the subject never viewed them together—the hallmark of a successive discrimination. Like the probes, trial types 2A and 2B also presented a separate green or red sample. Unlike the probes, once the comparisons had come on, green

and red stimuli were present simultaneously. Although one was a sample and the other a comparison, a subject could view them together. At probe-trial choice points, either a green or a red stimulus was present but not both; at hue-hue choice points, the subject could compare green with red directly. For this reason, the hue-hue task may not have required the subject to learn the particular successive discrimination that the probes demanded.

To help ensure that the monkeys learned a truly successive green-red discrimination in preparation for the symmetry probes, Experiment 4 changed trial types 2A and 2B from hue-hue to hue-form. Samples remained green and red but the comparisons were now X and + (Table 5-4). Because of the change in the comparisons, green and red were no longer present together. Subjects now had to discriminate temporally separate instances of green and red stimuli, the same kind of discrimination that the probe trials required.

Probe trials also required simultaneous discriminations between vertical and horizontal

Table 5-4

Conditional discriminations in Experiment 4. Trial types 1A and 1B, with X and + as samples, were to establish the simultaneous comparison-line discriminations and trial types 2A and 2B, with X and + as comparisons, were to establish the successive sample-hue discriminations required for the symmetry test. The starred trial types 3A and 3B (line-hue) constituted the critical conditional discrimination that was to be tested for symmetry. Trial types 4A and 4B constituted the symmetry test. Test sessions included all eight trial types.

	SAMPLE	COMPARISONS	
		CORRECT	INCORRECT
1A	X	Vertical	Horizontal
1B	+	Horizontal	Vertical
2A	Green	X	+
2B	Red	+	X
* 3A	Vertical	Green	Red
* 3B	Horizontal	Red	Green
5A	Green	Vertical	Horizontal
5B	Red	Horizontal	Vertical

comparisons. Although trial types 1A and 1b (Table 5-2) were supposed to teach these prerequisites, the discriminations in the line-line trials did not have to be the same as those in the probe trials. The probes required discriminations between lines that were located only on comparison keys, but a subject could learn the line-line performance by discriminating between the line on the sample key and the line on a comparison key. This discrimination would not be available on probe trials and the subject might fail to show

symmetry simply because it had never learned the necessary discriminative repertoire.

To give the monkeys discrimination training more like that required for line comparisons in the probes, Experiment 4 changed trial types 1A and 1B from line-line to form-line. The comparisons remained vertical and horizontal lines but the samples were X and + (Table 5-4). Subjects now had to learn the same simultaneous line discriminations that were required during the probe trials; they had to discriminate between lines that were located only on comparison keys.

Subjects

Monkeys R44 and R46 were subjects. Although they underwent different training procedures, they yielded similar probe results and only Monkey R46's experiment will be described.

Procedures

The animal started with the hue-form conditional discrimination(Table 5-4, 2A and 2B) and learned it rapidly, but then had enormous difficulty with form-line (1A and 1B). Several procedural changes were instituted, both singly and in combination: trial types 1A and 1B were scheduled both with and without other baseline trial types; the sample was permitted to remain present for as long as 2 s after the animal had selected a comparison; and nine responses to the X and + samples were required before the comparison stimuli could appear. None of these had any clear beneficial effect and all were terminated. A *yes-no* procedure, which Constantine (1981) had

already analyzed extensively, was then used to teach Monkey R46 the successive discrimination between X and + samples.

In the *yes-no* procedure, trials began as usual with a sample presented on Key 3, but when the animal pressed the sample only one comparison stimulus appeared on Key 4 or Key 5. Sometimes the comparison was positive in relation to the current sample (Figure 5-9, A and C) and sometimes negative (Figure 5-9, B and D). The *yes* response, correct for positive and incorrect for negative trials, was to press the comparison stimulus within 3 s of its presentation; the *no* response, correct for negative and incorrect for positive trials, was to refrain from pressing the comparison for 3 s after its presentation. Either a correct *yes* (press within the 3-s limited-hold period) or a correct *no* (3 s without pressing) produced a food pellet; an incorrect press or wait ended the trial without a pellet.

The *yes-no* procedure was introduced in three steps, starting with trial types A and B (Figure 5-9), then adding the C-types, and finally the D-types. These steps also included temporary variations in the durations of

POSITIVE
TRIALS
(RESPOND)

NEGATIVE
TRIALS
(WAIT)

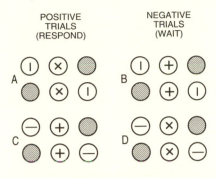

Figure 5-9. Representations of stimulus displays in the *yes-no* procedure after a subject had responded to the sample and brought on a comparison stimulus. Samples (X or +) are depicted in the center and comparisons (vertical or horizontal lines) on either side. Shading indicates a blank key.

the limited-hold and the waiting periods and in the proportion of trials of each type given during a session. A correction procedure was also used for a few sessions. When the performance met the usual criteria, form-line training with the *yes-no* procedure was complete; the animal successfully learned the intended sample discrimination.

Normal form-line trials (Table 5-4, 1A and 1B) were then interspersed among the *yes-no* trials. Although the animal had not learned trial types 1A and 1B in 130 previous sessions, it now exceeded the learning criteria almost immediately and main-

tained excellent form-line performances even after *yes-no* trials were no longer presented. This positive transfer from the *yes-no* to the two-choice conditional discrimination confirmed Constantine's earlier finding with harbor seals (Constantine, 1981).

The other trial types were then added and the animal met the performance criteria relatively rapidly on the full form-line, hue-form, and line-hue baseline (Table 5-4). Monkey R46 then had great difficulty maintaining its performance at reduced reinforcement probabilities, meeting the criteria only after the maximum number of consecutive unreinforced correct trials was limited to nine for each trial type individually. Symmetry-probe trials were then introduced, first in extinction and then with reinforcement on all correct trials.

RESULTS AND DISCUSSION

On probe trials in both sessions (Figure 5-10) the animal almost always selected the vertical (incorrect) comparison when the sample was red. A vertical (correct) preference in the presence of the green sample was less

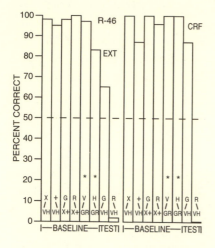

Figure 5-10. Monkey R46's performances during its two symmetry tests in Experiment 4. Trial types are as depicted in Figure 5-2. In the session shown at the left, symmetry probes were unreinforced (EXT); in the session shown at the right, all correct trials were reinforced (CRF). Each of the left-hand set of bars represents 65 trials; each right-hand bar, 23 trials.

pronounced during the extinction test but increased markedly when a pellet was delivered on all correct trials. Baseline error patterns differed during the two tests, with trial type 3B showing some disruption in the extinction test and trial type 1B slightly below criterion in the test with reinforcement. In neither test did the baseline errors seem severe enough to affect probe trials. Even the new baseline discriminations, therefore, which more explicitly required the kinds of stimulus control that the probe trials called for if symmetry were to emerge, did not bring out symmetry in the line-hue conditional discrimination.

The animals' low scores on hue-line probes also revealed the absence of transitivity (Table 5-1) in the baseline conditional discriminations. If the stimulus relations in conditional discriminations 1 and 2 were transitive, then, even without line-hue training, hue-form and form-line should have permitted the emergence of hue-line relations in the probe trials.

EXPERIMENT 5

Whether the different outcomes in the experiments with monkeys and children arose from species-related or experiential factors or both is not at all clear at present (see General Discussion). Because tests with other species might help resolve the question, Experiment 5 repeated Experiments 1 and 3 reasonably closely with baboons as subjects.

METHOD

Subjects

Two baboons (*Papio anubis*) were subjects. At the time of their symmetry tests, Subject Bab-Sim was adolescent and Subject Bab-Win was adult. Bab-Sim was experimentally naive; Bab-Win had been confined in a restraint chair during a study that involved hue discriminations but had never been exposed to the chamber or the stimuli used in the present experiment or to conditional-discrimination procedures. Experimental sessions took place every weekday and on occasional weekends.

Apparatus

During experimental sessions a cage, like that used in the monkey studies but with dimensions appropriate to the larger animals, held the baboon within a sound-attenuated, fan-ventilated chamber. A portion of one chamber wall, accessible to the animal through an opening in the cage, contained a horizontal row of three stimulus-response keys, each operating a limit switch when pressed. The keys were 3.2 cm in diameter, with a center-to-center distance of 4.4 cm between adjacent keys. Samples always appeared on the center key and comparisons on the outer keys. Line and hue stimuli were the same as those in the monkey experiments. A pellet tray, located immediately below the center key, received Noyes 1-g banana pellets. Except for illumination provided by the projected stimuli, the chamber was always dark. There was no trial-initiation key.

Training

The baboons had preliminary training like the monkeys but had no trial-initiation key. Conditional discriminations were the same as those in Table 5-2 but the baboons never had sample schedules.

Subject Bab-Sim learned line-line first. Hue-hue trials were then mixed with line-line. Adding line-hue trials then disrupted the line-line performance, so the animal was trained on line-hue alone before mixing all six trial types again. Reinforcement probability was then gradually reduced, as with the monkeys, and Subject Bab-Sim's first test had no reinforcement on probe trials. A second test on the next day gave reinforcement on all correct trials. Since some baseline disruption occurred during the first two tests, the animal had three more baseline sessions with 100-percent reinforcement, followed by a third probe like the second (reinforcement on all correct trials). Reinforcement on all eight trial types then continued for 20 more sessions.

Subject Bab-Win started with both line-line and hue-hue trials, then had line-hue alone, and finally had all six trial types mixed together. During this final baseline phase, the intertrial interval was increased to 10 s and remained at that duration. Subject Bab-Win had a single test, with reinforcement on all correct trials.

RESULTS AND DISCUSSION

Probe trials during Subject Bab-Sim's first test in extinction (left section of Figure 5-11) averaged 46% correct, with the animal manifesting a slight preference for the horizontal comparison on both hue-line (probe) and line-line (baseline) trials. In the second test, with reinforcement on all correct trials (center section of Figure 5-11), probes averaged 44% and the horizontal preference grew larger in both sets of trial types. Criterion baseline performances were then reestablished, in the hope of ruling out loss of the discrimination between vertical and horizontal comparisons as the source of the animal's difficulty with the probes. During the third test, with all correct trials again reinforced, probes still averaged only 48% (right section of Figure 5-11). Although the animal's comparison preference had now shifted strongly to vertical, the score of 88% on trial type 1B did not indicate sufficient baseline disruption to implicate a generalized loss of the line-line discrimination as the source of the animal's difficulty with the probes. It seems reasonable to conclude that baseline disruption was not responsible for the probe-trial performances but rather, that unspecified control generated in probe trials was responsible for the baseline disruptions. For example, a comparison-line preference that developed during probe trials might have caused the animal occasionally to ignore the sample and, instead, to select the preferred

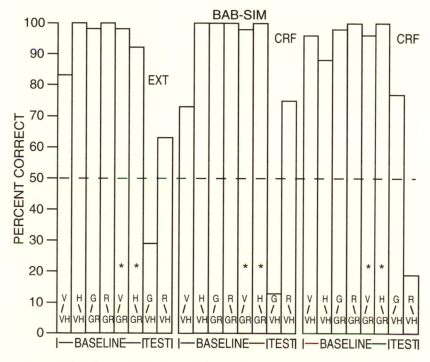

Figure 5-11. Baboon Bab-Sim's performances during its three symmetry tests in Experiment 5. Trial types are as depicted in Figure 5-2. In the session shown at the left, symmetry probes were unreinforced (EXT); in the sessions shown in the center and at the right, all correct baseline and probe trials were reinforced (CRF). Each bar represents 48 trials.

comparison even during baseline trials 1A and 1B.

Subject Bab-Sim's failure to reverse the sample-comparison roles of lines and hues was confirmed during subsequent training sessions, even with reinforcement on all correct trials (Figure 5-12). Throughout these sessions the animal maintained scores of 90% or better on hue-hue and line-hue trials (topmost and third panels, respectively). The

line-line baseline and the hue-line probes (second and bottom panels, respectively) continued to fluctuate until Session 13, with the probe scores always lower and more variable than the baselines. Generally, the comparison-line preference during line-line trials reflected the probe-trial preference but in reduced magnitude.

Subject Bab-Win's symmetry test, with reinforcement, showed

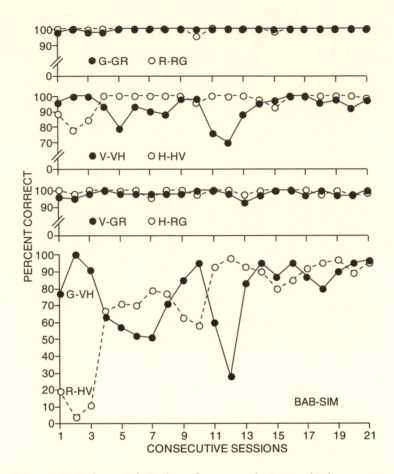

Figure 5-12. Baboon Bab-Sim's performances during its third symmetry test (Session 1) and the subsequent 20 training sessions. All correct baseline and probe trials were reinforced. Hue-hue (G-GR and R-RG), line-line (V-VH and H-HV), and line-hue (V-GR and H-RG) trials appear, respectively, in the topmost, second, and third panels; probe trials (G-VH and R-HV) are in the bottom panel. Each session had 300-360 trials.

the animal maintaining an excellent baseline while averaging only 49% correction probes (Figure 5-13). The baboons, therefore, confirmed the monkeys' data both without and with reinforcement. They gave no evidence that their conditional-discrimination training had established symmetric relations between samples and correct comparisons.

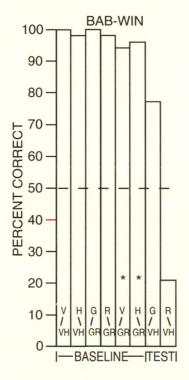

Figure 5-13. Subject Bab-Win's performance during its symmetry tests in Experiment 5. Trial types are as depicted in Figure 5-2. All correct baseline and probe trials were reinforced. Each bar represents 48 trials.

GENERAL DISCUSSION

Procedures that have become more or less standard (e.g., Cumming & Berryman, 1965) generated symmetry in the conditional discriminations of 5-year-old children but not of monkeys or baboons. The failures confirmed and extended findings with pigeons (Hogan & Zentall, 1977;

Holmes, 1979; Rodewald, 1974). Experiment 4 also proved transitivity to be absent in monkeys' conditional discriminations. Because symmetry and transitivity are necessary properties of equivalence relations (Table 5-1), the absence of either was sufficient to disprove the inference that each sample and its arbitrarily corresponding comparison stimulus had formed a class of equivalent stimuli. The monkeys', baboons', and pigeons' conditional discriminations could not legitimately be called matching to sample. By extension, any previous interpretations of conditional discriminations (*if…then* relations) as matching to sample (equivalence relations) must be viewed skeptically, particularly perhaps, if the subjects were not humans.

It is of course impossible to prove by failures alone that conditional-discrimination procedures are incapable of establishing symmetric relations for any organism. Such a conclusion would demand an understanding, which we currently lack, of the prerequisites for symmetry and an explanation of the organism's inability to meet one or more of the requirements. On the other hand, the data have

161

made it clear that symmetry cannot be taken for granted. This demonstration by means of empirically specifiable behavioral techniques is perhaps the most significant contribution of the present experiments.

If failures to demonstrate symmetry are to be attributed to experiential rather than to genetically related variables, proof that the subjects lacked one or more of the necessary experiences must be provided. Whether or not subsequent investigation succeeds in identifying critical gaps in the subjects' behavioral histories, shifting the burden of proof and thereby provoking the search may prove constructive.

Perhaps the most relevant experience to provide would be additional symmetry tests, with initial test failures being followed by explicit reinforcement of the desired performance, as was done with Subject Bab-Sim (Figure 5-12). One might argue that pigeons, monkeys, and baboons, unlike humans, do not ordinarily experience enough exemplars for them to appreciate the concept of symmetry. Demonstrations of symmetry with normal 5-year-olds who had not yet started school

(Experiment 3), and of equivalence relations with severely retarded, institutionalized, environmentally restricted subjects, who had little language and no constructive academic experience (Sidman, 1971b, unpublished data; Sidman & Cresson, 1973), somewhat blunt the force of this suggestion but do not disprove it. If the animals were taught consecutive pairs of conditional discriminations, with the second of each pair always the symmetric version of the first, would the subjects eventually perform a symmetry test accurately the first time they encountered it? Would they learn the general principle, *sample and correct comparison are interchangeable?*

Whether or not the provision of enough exemplars would bring about the emergence of symmetry is still an open question. Yet symmetry's very complexity should temper one's optimism. The principle of symmetry, or generalized sample-comparison interchangeability, requires also the existence of the stimulus classes, sample and comparison. Unless these functional classes have been established, so that individual sample stimuli are also members of the sample class and individual comparison stimuli are also members of the comparison class, no exemplar of symmetry will extend beyond the particular stimuli being tested; the general principle will never emerge. Therefore, subjects who do demonstrate generalized sample-comparison interchangeability (symmetry) should, when tested appropriately (e.g., Mackay, 1979), also demonstrate equivalence relations among functional samples and among functional comparisons.

Whether the functional classes, sample and comparison, are prerequisites for sample-comparison symmetry remains to be tested empirically. The procedure used here, however, may have obscured the functional classes by confining the potential members of each class to particular locations on the key matrix—samples always in the center and comparisons on the outer keys. Location, perfectly correlated with function, might have become a defining characteristic of the classes. In that event, even if the sample and comparison functions of the experimenter-specified stimuli were exchangeable, the locations correlated with those functions could not be shifted; a symme-try test that attempted to change both the stimulus functions and their locations would not have provided a valid evaluation of functional reversibility. A resolution of this problem may come from a training procedure in which sample and comparison stimuli can appear in any location.

Incorrect specification by the experimenter of the controlling stimuli in the conditional discriminations may be the most fundamental factor underlying the absence of symmetry. The number of testable differences between the experimenter's specifications and the actual controlling stimuli is limited only by one's ingenuity. One cannot rule out the possibility that continued attempts to sharpen a monkey's training history will succeed in achieving congruence between the experimenter's and the subject's definitions of the controlling stimuli, thereby permitting a valid and successful test for symmetry. Equally difficult to rule out, however, is the possibility that species-related factors will prevent the development of such congruence. It may, for example, not be possible for some species to abstract certain stimulus features from the environment, or to form certain functional classes, or even to separate stimulus features from stimulus functions. Such species differences need not be absolute but may depend on the ethological validity of the stimuli and functions being examined. The present experiments might have yielded positive evidence of symmetry if they had used monkey odors and monkey sounds as stimuli instead of lines and color patches, or if the functional classes had been *edible* and *safe* or *inedible* and *dangerous* rather than *sample* and *comparison*. In that event, the species differences would lie in the arbitrariness or in the variety of the equivalence relations that could develop.

When the conditional-discrimination procedure does generate true matching to sample, the formation of stimulus classes defines a semantic correspondence between each sample and its matching comparison stimulus. The procedure therefore has features that recommend it as a model for the study of complex behavior, and the discovery that children, chimpanzees, monkeys,

and pigeons could be taught conditional discriminations fostered the hope that such relatively simple organisms could be used to develop experimental and theoretical models even for language (e.g., Davenport & Rogers, 1970; French, 1965; Nissen, Blum, & Blum, 1948; Riesen & Nissen, 1942; Weinstein, 1941, 1945). If nonhuman species fail to develop true matching performances or prove limited in comparison to humans, then studies with nonhuman subjects take on a somewhat different significance. Rather than accept the nonhuman performance as a model, homologous to the human, a thorough analysis of failures of the procedure to generate true matching offers the opportunity to specify the missing components and thereby to identify elements that are unique to the normal human performance. Then, attempts to build into the subjects' repertoires those components that would make nonhuman and human matching-to-sample behavior homologous might yield practical methods applicable to humans with developmental deficiencies.

* * * * * * * * * *

Commentary

Negative Results: When To Publish Them?

The *Search for Symmetry* paper described research that had gone on for almost ten years before being submitted for publication. Much of our effort during that time had been devoted not to a search for symmetry but to a search for techniques that would effectively teach monkeys the conditional discriminations that would be needed as baselines and prerequisites for symmetry tests. That effort, however, does not fully explain the long publication delay. The major factor contributing to the delay was the nature of the results we were seeing. For us, the data were unexpected and exciting; for most others, they were just negative results.

A general skepticism toward negative results is easily justified. Negative instances of any sort are not usually interesting unless positive instances had been anticipated. As Skinner (1957) noted, "…there must be some reason for saying *It IS raining* whenever we say *It is NOT raining*" (p. 322). Was there any good reason for expecting conditional discriminations to show symmetry? Although the literature contains many instances in which conditional discrimination and matching to sample are uncritically equated, no theory that I knew of had required conditional discriminations to show symmetry or any other property of equivalence relations. Our demonstrations of an empirically verifiable distinction between conditional discrimination and matching to sample therefore provided a context in which the negative results we were obtaining in experiment after experiment might also become meaningful to others. Publication had to await the development of such a context.

The Species Or the Procedure?

Another well-recognized difficulty in interpreting negative results arises from the number and complexity of the variables, past and present, that influence conduct. Because conduct is always multiply determined, a seemingly obvious variable may really have little or nothing to do with failures to observe the expected. This is the major problem that currently limits the generality of conclusions we may draw from the *Search for Symmetry* paper about species membership as a variable that limits equivalence relations.

The *Search for Symmetry* paper, along with previous and subsequent reports by others (D'Amato, Salmon, Loukas, & Tomie, 1985; Dugdale & Lowe, 1990; Hogan & Zentall, 1977; Holmes, 1979; Lipkens, Kop, & Matthijs, 1988; Rodewald, 1974), did establish that standard laboratory procedures for teaching conditional discriminations do not also teach nonhuman subjects true matching to sample. This is a solid finding, important methodologically and with inescapable implications for those who would extrapolate from currently available conditional-discrimination data to linguistic and other higher-order processes.

The finding, however, does not permit any generalization about the ability or inability of nonhuman subjects to do true matching to sample—to demonstrate equivalence relations. The possibility remains—and in my opinion, it is a strong possibility (see below for corroborating evidence)—that features of the standard conditional-discrimination procedure, rather than the species of the subjects, have been responsible for the failures to demonstrate equivalence relations with nonhumans. The *Search for Symmetry* paper described a number of unsuccessful attempts to identify some relatively obvious procedural variables that might have been responsible for the negative findings but many more possibilities remain to be looked into (see, for example, Dube, McIlvane, Callahan, and Stoddard, 1993).

Identifying the controlling stimuli. Experiments 2 and 4, for example, manipulated the baseline trial types in different ways; a combination of Experiments 2 and 4, however, has not yet been tried. We also suggested that the actual controlling stimuli in the standard conditional-discrimination procedure may include both the experimenter-specified sample or comparison stimuli and the locations (keys) in which those stimuli appear. This suggestion was confirmed by Constantine (1981), who showed that characteristic scanning patterns by harbor seals gave special status to particular stimulus locations; by Iversen, Sidman, and Carrigan (1986), and Iversen (submitted), who showed with monkeys and rats, respectively, that changing the sample and comparison locations severely disrupted ongoing conditional discriminations; and by Sidman (1992b), who showed with monkeys that location could adventitiously become a controlling aspect of the comparison stimuli.

Relevant to these data is the observation that the conditional-discrimination procedure has not yet unequivocally shown pigeons and monkeys to do generalized identity matching (Cohen, 1969; Cumming & Berryman, 1965; Davenport & Rogers, 1970; Eckerman, 1970; Farthing & Opuda, 1974; Ginsburg, 1957; Mackay & Brown, 1971; Urcuioli & Nevin, 1975; Weinstein, 1941, 1945). That is to say, these subjects have not shown reflexivity in their conditional discriminations. Perhaps that is why they have not shown equivalence relations.

Reflexivity is one of the defining features of equivalence relations but at the time of the *Search for Symmetry* paper, we had not yet come to appreciate completely its fundamental importance. We still viewed the generalized identity-matching test for reflexivity largely as a control for the necessary stimulus discriminations; we regarded it as a way to make sure that subjects could distinguish among the stimuli we planned to use in baseline conditional discriminations and equivalence tests. Not until much later did it occur to us that if reflexivity tests were to be maximally informative, they had to be done after the subjects had learned the critical baseline conditional discriminations, and not before (Carrigan & Sidman, 1992; Saunders & Green, 1992). Reflexivity tests must be given after the baseline has been established because the arbitrary relation, R, that defines reflexivity—*a*R*a*, *b*R*b*, and so on—must have been generated in the baseline conditional discriminations (Johnson & Sidman, 1993). But because reflexivity requires the arbitrary baseline relation to hold between a stimulus and itself, physical sameness—which, as Hayes (1991, p. 32) pointed out, is a nonarbitrary relation—is inextricably bound up with reflexivity.

Because it entails physical identity, then, reflexivity is not only a definitional requirement but is also a behavioral prerequisite for equivalence. If, for a subject in the conditional-discrimination context, the relation of physical sameness does not hold between a sample and comparison that we, as experimenters, consider identical, then it should not come as a surprise when the subject fails to show equivalence in that context.

It is entirely possible that failures of nonhumans to show generalized identity matching—reflexivity—have been caused by a basically irrelevant feature of the standard conditional-discrimination procedure. The usual practice has been to present sample stimuli on only one key in the display and to present comparisons on the other keys. Some subjects may therefore come to identify stimuli not only by their physical characteristics and by their functions—as the experimenters do—but also by their locations—which the experimenters have learned to ignore. For such subjects, a stimulus on the center key will be a different stimulus when it appears on an outer key.

If the fixed locations become defining features of sample and comparison stimuli, then the usual symmetry test, which necessarily changes the location of stimuli along with their sample or comparison function, cannot possibly yield positive results. For example, if the sample stimulus is not just *vertical* but rather, *vertical in the center key*, then a test that presented vertical on an outer key would have removed a critical feature of the sample; it would no longer be correct to say that the sample is being tested as a comparison. Under those circumstances, it would not be valid to call the test a symmetry test; for the subject, the relevant stimuli in the test would not be the same as in the original conditional discrimination. (This problem does not exist in the transitivity test, in which sample and comparison stimuli maintain the same locations as in the baseline. Perhaps this is why D'Amato et al. [1985], with monkeys as subjects, were able to document transitivity even in the absence of symmetry.)

A valid symmetry test, therefore, must ensure that the controlling stimuli for the subject are the same as those specified by the experimenter. Future attempts to search for symmetry (and reflexivity) in the conditional discriminations of nonhuman subjects should avoid the usual practice of correlating stimulus function with stimulus location. Teaching and testing procedures should present sample and comparison stimuli equally often in many locations.

Having given this advice, I must now qualify it by pointing out that varying the sample and comparison locations may still not prevent location from becoming a defining feature of the stimuli. We were led to this conclusion by the failure of our key matrix to achieve its intended aim of reducing the likelihood that subjects would develop comparison-key preferences. At the time the equipment was designed, we had not yet come fully to appreciate the principle that some of our own data had revealed: position preferences, far from *causing* subjects' failures to learn (Harlow, 1959), are usually *produced* by their failures to learn (for example, Sidman & Stoddard, 1967; Stoddard & Sidman, 1967).

We had designed a five-key display (Figure 5-1) because it would permit us to vary the positions of comparison stimuli from trial to trial. The sample was always presented on the center key and comparisons on two of the four outer keys. Our notion was that with every pair of comparison stimuli appearing equally often on each of six possible key combinations, key position would become irrelevant as a controlling aspect of the stimuli.

This assumption proved incorrect. Pairs of key positions became units unto themselves (Sidman, 1992b). When each pair's course of learning was plotted separately, the pairs demonstrated different patterns of progress; and when conditional discriminations were disrupted, pairs of keys differed in their pattern of disruption. Instead of simply learning one set of conditional relations between two sample and two comparison stimuli, subjects seemed to have learned six sets of conditional relations, one for each pair of comparison-key locations.

So, even varying the location of comparison stimuli among six different pairs of keys did not eliminate key position as a controlling aspect of the stimuli. The variations just increased the number of compounds of key positions and experimental stimuli that subjects learned. Similarly, interchanging the sample and comparison locations may not suffice to eliminate location as a controlling aspect of the stimuli. A different kind of training history may be necessary if nonhuman subjects are to learn to dissociate stimulus features and functions from stimulus locations. They may have to be taught explicitly to do so.

Training history. McIntire, Cleary, and Thompson (1987) reported an experiment that they interpreted as showing that monkeys with an appropriate training history can form equivalence relations. This study has caused considerable controversy (Hayes, 1989; McIntire, Cleary, & Thompson, 1989; Saunders, 1989). McIntire et al. (1987) taught monkeys conditional discriminations in which the animals had to respond in the same way to each stimulus within a potential set, and to do so both when the stimulus functioned as a sample and as a comparison. Conditional discriminations then emerged in which the stimuli that the experimenters specified as samples and comparisons had never previously been related to each other by the subjects. That this could happen was an important demonstration, independently of its controversial relevance to equivalence phenomena. But in response to the criticism that the seemingly emergent conditional relations were actually stimulus-response-stimulus chains that the subjects had been explicitly taught, McIntire et al. (1989) argued that they had simply placed under explicit control the process that underlies all demonstrations of equivalence.

Does teaching the same response to different stimuli necessarily establish an equivalence relation or might the common response serve simply as a link in stimulus-response chains (Hayes, 1989; Saunders, 1989)? In fact, the observation that different stimuli control the same response does not suffice to define a stimulus class. Stimuli that control the same response may remain independent of each other in every other way. If the *class* concept is to be useful in describing behavior and its environmental determinants, the members of a class must share more than one feature in common; operations that are applied to one member of a presumed class must be shown also to affect the other members (Goldiamond, 1962, p.

303; also Chapter 11, pp. 447-448). It will be important to attempt such a demonstration in the context of the McIntire et al. (1987) procedures.

Also, the question we posed in Chapter 4 is still relevant: in learning a conditional discrimination, why should any subject, human or nonhuman, respond in the same way to sample and comparison stimuli that are physically different? Such a common response is particularly unlikely when the stimuli have never explicitly been related to each other—for example, the A- and C-stimuli when a subject has learned AB and BC conditional discriminations (as in the *Mediated Transfer* paper, Chapter 4).

It is possible, however, that common responses do not develop until the baseline conditional discriminations are tested for the properties of equivalence relations. One would then have to ask why this should happen. If we were to find that a common response to conditionally related stimuli does develop during tests for reflexivity, symmetry, and transitivity, we would only have moved the question about the origin of equivalence one step back; we would still have to explain where the common response that accounts for equivalence comes from.

For all of these reasons, it is not clear that the McIntire et al. (1987) experiment dealt with the same phenomenon as the equivalence studies with human subjects. An interesting possibility, however, is that this study did generate true matching to sample by monkeys but that it did so for a simpler reason than has yet been considered. The animals were required to respond in the same way to a given stimulus regardless of whether that stimulus was currently functioning as a sample or as a comparison and, therefore, regardless of its current physical location. Did the consistent "labeling" of each stimulus, independently of its placement, suffice to eliminate location as a controlling stimulus feature? This possibility might be tested as follows: require the animal—like the subjects in the McIntire et al. study—always to respond to a particular stimulus the same way both when it serves as a sample and as a comparison, but also require the animal—unlike the McIntire et al. subjects—to respond differently to every stimulus, regardless of its potential class membership. Then, even without a common response to all members of a potential class, equivalence might still be demonstrable.

Zentall, Hogan, and their coworkers, using pigeons as subjects, have presented a considerable amount of evidence that may signify equivalence relations (see Zentall and Urcuioli, 1993, for a review of this work). In this series of experiments, the subjects not only received different training histories but were also tested differently.

The evidence they present for symmetry, however, is, at best, still weak. Also, the experiments on reflexivity and transitivity have used "savings" and "interference" techniques. For example, birds that have learned to match, say, red samples to red comparisons, and green samples to green comparisons, have more difficulty in learning subsequently to match blue to yellow and yellow to blue than do birds who had originally been taught to match red to green and green to red. But why are savings and interference measures (and group comparisons) required to yield data consistent with equivalence? That is to say, why do the techniques used in most of the human research fail to work with pigeons? This problem requires more attention than it has received.

For example, when inferences about equivalence relations are drawn from demonstrations that a task is learned more (or less) rapidly because of the previous learning of another task, one must wonder about the influence of irrelevant aspects of the tasks (irrelevant, that is to say, not to the subject's performance but to the question the experimenter is asking). Might a new performance be learned more rapidly because experience with the first task taught the subject how to deal with irrelevant aspects of the tasks? Or might the new performance be learned more slowly because irrelevant aspects of the original task had changed? Suppose that the similarity of sample and correct comparison had little or nothing to do with a bird's original "identity-matching" performance, but that it had learned to select the larger stimulus—sample plus comparison—in the display (or the smaller, in the case of "oddity matching"). Then, because size or area would remain unchanged when the experimenter substituted new stimuli for the old, the seeming positive or negative "transfer" to "new" discriminations would actually represent little more than a repetition of the same performance the subject had learned originally. The real problem here would be the difference between the subject's and the experimenter's specification of the controlling stimulus aspect. Such problems can, of course, be dealt with, and when they are, unequivocal demonstrations of equivalence may yet be forthcoming from pigeon subjects.

An important study with chimpanzees was reported by Savage-Rumbaugh, Rumbaugh, Smith, and Lawson (1980) and was summarized by Cerutti and Rumbaugh (1993, pp. 815-818). The subjects' final performances could probably have come about only through the development of equivalence relations. Some of the animals' behavior in these experiments was called "labelling," but all of the procedures seem actually to have involved conditional discriminations. The animals had first learned to match a number of foods and tools to individual "lexigrams"—arbitrary forms. Then, in brief, in the most convincing of the experimental procedures, the animals first were taught to match individual lexigrams of three foods and three tools to a general "food" or "tool" lexigram. In subsequent tests, subjects correctly matched individual lexigrams of other foods and tools to the appropriate general lexigram even though they had never been taught directly to do so. The outcome of the Savage-Rumbaugh et al. (1980) study should encourage systematic replications—in particular, continued attempts to produce explicit demonstrations of reflexivity, symmetry, and transitivity with individual chimpanzees.

Direct evidence for each of the properties of equivalence relations with nonhumans as subjects has finally and quite convincingly been reported by Schusterman and Kastak (1993), who worked with a sea lion. Although it is possible that a species variable was involved here, I find it difficult to believe that being a sea lion makes one more capable of equivalence relations than does being a monkey, a baboon, or even a pigeon or a rat. Procedurally, this experiment incorporated many features that were not present in our *Search for Symmetry* studies or in other related work, and the feature(s) responsible for the positive Schusterman and Kastak (1993) results can at present only be speculated on. This work, however, must be followed up if nonhuman subjects, with their advantages of experimentally controllable histories and environments, are to be used more frequently in equivalence research.

In its first tests for symmetry of some of the baseline AB conditional discriminations, Schusterman and Kastak's sea lion did not perform consistently on the tested BA conditional discriminations; like the monkeys and baboons in our *Search for Symmetry* studies, the sea lion failed its first symmetry tests. Then, however, after explicitly teaching the animal the BA performances, the experimenters saw positive results in subsequent tests of other baseline pairs for symmetry, transitivity, and equivalence. That is to say, after being trained on AB, BA, and some BC conditional discriminations, the subject did well on its first CB (symmetry), AC (transitivity), and CA (equivalence) tests; although some of those test performances were reinforced, explicit training after the animal's earlier experience with AB and BA pairs did not seem necessary for the later emergence of symmetry, transitivity, and equivalence.

Nevertheless, Schusterman and Kastak (1993, p. 836) cited the experience with exemplars as the critical factor in their subject's success with subsequent tests. As noted in the *Search for Symmetry* paper (p.154), however, there is some reason to question the likelihood that specific experiences with symmetric relations will be generalized. This point will be considered again (pp. 364-365; 566-567) in connection with the role of exemplars in general and in relational frame theory's account of equivalence relations (Hayes, 1986, 1991).

And again, one must reckon with the possible relevance of stimulus location as a controlling aspect of the experimental stimuli for the subject, even though location is irrelevant as far as the experimenter is concerned. Because the usual symmetry tests exchange sample and comparison locations, such tests cannot yield positive results if fixed locations have become defining features of the original sample and comparison stimuli. Is it possible, then, that the major effect of a history of reinforced experiences with examples of symmetry (or reflexivity) is to reduce or eliminate the salience of stimulus location? Could the varying stimulus locations rather than the varying stimulus functions be the critical aspect of a subject's history with exemplars of symmetric relations? To test this possibility, one might give a subject more experiences like those described in Experiment 4 in the *Search for Symmetry* paper (Table 5-4: trial types 1A, 1B, 2A, and 2B). This would provide the subject with a history of conditional discriminations in which stimuli sometimes served as samples and at other times as comparisons, but would not provide any exposure to symmetric relations. Might such a more limited history—one that did not involve examples of symmetry—nevertheless lead eventually to successful demonstrations of symmetry?

Other procedural factors, too, may have been critical in the Schusterman and Kastak (1993) study. One that seems worth special mention is reflexivity: the sea lion, unlike other nonhuman subjects that had been tested for equivalence, demonstrated reflexivity; it showed itself able to do generalized identity matching. As noted before, reflexivity is not only an integral part of the definition of equivalence but is also a behavioral prerequisite; without reflexivity, a subject would be incapable of the derived conditional discriminations necessary to verify equivalence. A key to the sea lion's successful demonstration of equivalence may therefore come from a closer examination of the conditions that brought about generalized identity matching (Kastak & Schusterman, 1992; 1993).

6

A Giant Step: Expanding Classes of Equivalent Stimuli from Three to Four Members

Background

In my years at the Walter Reed Army Institute of Research, where I had opportunities to observe in action investigators of the highest caliber in many fields, and sometimes even to work with them, I had learned to keep a number of projects going simultaneously. Running several experiments concurrently ensured that something would always be paying off. Fortunately, therefore, the long and unsuccessful (although informative) series of attempts to demonstrate symmetry with nonhuman subjects (Chapter 5) constituted only one wing of our research program. We had other irons in the fire. Consistently successful demonstrations of all of the properties of equivalence relations with human subjects kept us going in spite of our failures in the nonhuman lab.

In the course of this work, we found ourselves discussing the role of equivalence relations in reading comprehension, auditory comprehension, oral reading, symbolic representation, and even creativity and meaning. All of this was at simple levels but still, was far-out talk for hard-nosed radical behaviorists. What excited us was our newly found ability to deal empirically with such matters by changing the environment in specifiable ways and observing the subjects' actions directly.

Was it possible, however, that by providing verifiable definitions for these "cognitive processes" we were robbing them of their significance? I have never believed that simplification has to trivialize. At its best, analysis strips away nonessentials and reveals fundamentals; the results can be elegant and sometimes breathtaking. Analysis can show where we have to start if we want to construct more complex and perhaps more interesting kinds of conduct. Still, a nagging doubt remained. Was our success in applying a behavioral definition of equivalence relations a consequence, perhaps, of the *unimportance* of the phenomenon we were observing?

Class Size: A Matter of Generality

The only way to settle that kind of doubt was to push on. Time would tell whether we were going to turn up anything useful and informative. On the plus side, we and others found that our ability to test for and reproduce equivalence relations was valid for many kinds of subjects and was not limited to particular kinds of stimuli. Also, our original experiments with retarded youths had shown the emergence of 20 classes of equivalent stimuli; the phenomenon did not seem limited to some impractically small number of classes.

But how about class size? So far, we had seen only three-member classes. Each class, for example, might consist of a dictated word, a printed word, and a picture; or a dictated letter name along with upper- and lower-case printed versions of the letter; or a dictated and printed color name along with the color itself; and so forth. Is there a limit to the number of equivalent stimuli that a class can contain? If such a limit does exist, it surely must be greater than three. But if our way of defining, producing, and measuring equivalence relations could not deal with classes that contained more than three members, the utility of our approach would be severely restricted. We certainly would not be able to elucidate the significant role that equivalence relations must play in language and other complex human conduct. Therefore, in the research that led to the *Class Expansion* paper (below), we turned our attention to the possibility of four-member classes.

Within the context of the mediation theory that prevailed in the earlier paired-associate approach to equivalence relations, Jenkins and Palermo had come to a similar conclusion about the importance of equivalence classes of more than three members (1964, p. 149):

> Now, given the processes of chaining, response equivalence, and stimulus equivalence, how are they to be applied? What constitutes a unit or element in one of the paradigms? Certainly, we do not want to hold that the paradigms apply only to nonsense syllables or to discrete lever presses. Nor do we wish to limit ourselves to items taken two at a time. At the risk of making the processes inapplicable, we must say that they apply to any functional stimulus classes and any functional response classes at any level of complexity made up of any number of items and that all processes may operate on all levels at the same time. In essence we are saying that subjects have integrated both stimulus and response units at many levels and that these processes may apply to all of these units.

More specifically, Jenkins described the 16 paired-associate paradigms that would have to be shown to produce four-member ("four-stage") classes if the mediation theory of stimulus and response equivalence was to be validated (Jenkins, 1963, pp. 217-220):

> Encouraged by their findings [three-stage mediation paradigms], we went on to a test of the reasonable four-stage paradigms which seemed to be of importance in the general questions of acquired stimulus and response equivalences....
>
> The four-stage paradigms are of particular interest because of the close resemblance which some of them bear to natural language models....
>
> A classic example of such an equivalence paradigm is the following:

[PA1]   Learn A→B
                         Learn C→B
                    Now learn A→D
                       Test C→D

> It is here assumed that A and C become functionally equivalent stimuli during the first two stages. When a new response to A is

learned in the third stage, it should more likely occur to C in the test stage. It is presumed that the transfer is mediated by the implicit occurrence of B during both of the last two stages.

The case in which the functionally equivalent items shift position in the sequence is similarly the minimal case of language transformation.

[PA2] [Learn] A→B
  [Learn] C→B
  [Now learn] D→A
  [Test] D→C

Here, what were originally functionally equivalent stimuli must become functionally equivalent responses, an occurrence which is almost exclusively a linguistic event....the four-stage equivalence paradigms...appear to furnish the most elementary approach to the development of functional classes in language and a beginning attack on the problems of linguistic transformations.

Having made his case for the importance of the four-stage paradigms, Jenkins went on to a dramatic denouement:

...16 subjects were studied in each of the 16 paradigms. When the data were subjected to analysis, no mediation effects whatsoever were found. Furthermore, *no individual paradigm showed mediation effects significantly different from chance.*

At this point an agonizing reappraisal took place. While we had expected that many of the paradigms would show little if any facilitation, we were unprepared for the total collapse of the enterprise....the experiment had failed completely. Obviously, explanations were required....

Jenkins is to be admired for his open, honest, and thorough exposition of the failure and its significance. Later, he wrote (Jenkins, 1965, pp. 85 and 94):

As more studies appear, we will be able to specify more clearly the circumstances under which stimulus and response equivalence are achieved and the conditions that afford an occasion for their manifestation. We know that a mere specification of the paradigms themselves and their coordination with ostensible stimuli and responses is not in itself any guarantee that the critical behavior showing the equivalence will ensue. In an extensive series of experiments in our laboratories we have found more ways *not* to get the equivalence effects than we have found ways to achieve them (Jenkins, 1963)....

It may appear odd to the reader that one should choose such a fragile and incompletely understood device to make the center of such a powerful set of behaviors as those involved in language. Nevertheless, I believe that the principles involved in these simple paradigms will prove to be adequate to the task in the long run. As we come to understand the controlling variables and as we begin to bring these paradigms under multiple stimulus control (...as must be true in the case of natural language), demonstrations of their effectiveness will become commonplace, and their extensive application will be revealed....

My faith is that [the simple system represented in the four-stage equivalence model] represents a minimal cornerstone in linguistic process and that it will be productive for us to determine those conditions which maximize its effectiveness.

In spite of the faith that Jenkins expressed, the paired-associate research on equivalence had ended. Little more was published. Why did the four-stage paired-associate experiments fail? I believe there were two major causes, one stemming from too early and too strong a commitment to a theoretical formulation based on response mediation (Chapters 8, 10) and the other from methodological considerations.

Some Methodological Background.

As I noted in Chapter 1, one reason for our entrance into this research area was the ready availability in our laboratory of methods that struck us as appropriate for obtaining answers to our first questions about reading comprehension. Conditional-discrimination procedures seemed made to order for revealing possible relations among spoken words, written words, and pictures—relations that appeared to us to define simple reading comprehension.

It turned out also, although we did not realize it at the time, that conditional-discrimination procedures eliminated a problem that was inherent in paired-associate paradigms. For example, in Paradigm PA1 (above), the facilitation of C→D learning in Stage 4 required the A→B and C→B pairs that the subject had learned in Stages 1 and 2 to be maintained during Stages 3 and 4. In learning A→D in Stage 3, however, a subject who is shown an A-stimulus would at first give the previously learned B-response. This response would go unreinforced; the previously learned A→B pairs would necessarily undergo a certain amount of extinction during Stage 3. Similarly, in testing C→D in Stage 4, the C→B pairs would undergo extinction. Thus, the relation of both A and C to B—the basis for AC equivalence—would be severely weakened, thereby making the expected facilitation of C→D learning less likely.

A similar problem arises in Paradigm PA2 (above). In Stage 4, a subject is likely to respond at first with previously learned A-responses to the D-stimuli; the resulting extinction of D→A will weaken the basis for transfer to D→C.

Conditional-discrimination procedures preclude this problem of nonreinforced baseline performances because they restrict the choices that are available to subjects during training and testing, by that means preventing the extinction of prerequisites for the final performances. For example, in a DC conditional-discrimination test, a subject would be given only C-stimuli as comparisons from which to make a selection and would not have the A-stimuli available. DA relations, therefore, which are prerequisites for the final DC test, would remain intact, enhancing the likelihood of demonstrating four-member classes of equivalent stimuli. A study by James and Hakes (1965) indicated that even with paired-associate lists being taught in the first three stages, the use of a matching task during the test can bring about four-member classes.

Because a subject's choices are limited to stimuli that are actually presented on any given trial, the conditional-discrimination procedure also makes it possible to *maintain* the prerequisite relations as a baseline even while testing potentially emergent relations. Maintaining a baseline of previously established conditional discriminations makes it possible to observe whether the prerequisites remain intact during the tests. With the paired-associate procedure, baseline maintenance can be facilitated by reteaching the lists that subjects learned in the earlier stages (Grover, Horton, & Cunningham, 1967; James & Hakes, 1965), but this does not permit the observation of baseline deterioration during the test stage. If the prerequisites were to degenerate during a test and this degeneration could not be observed, a failure to demonstrate emergent relations might easily be misinterpreted.

In paired-associate and serial-learning studies of equivalence relations, comparisons between groups of experimental and control subjects provided the critical data. The final tests, if successful, would show an experimental group learning a new list of paired associates more rapidly than a control group. In contrast, our research did not involve the comparison of experimental and control groups. We possessed an abiding conviction that a science of individual behavior differs fundamentally from a science of group averages (Johnston & Pennypacker, 1980; Sidman, 1960/1988, 1990a). Our aphasia research had shown us that conditional-discrimination procedures yielded orderly individual data (for example, Leicester et al., 1971; Mohr et al., 1973; Sidman et al., 1971). A great advantage of individual data is, of course, the elimination of intersubject variability. If it had been possible to use individual subjects as their own controls in the paired-associate experiments, enough subjects might have been found to show enhanced learning in Stage 4 to justify the conclusion that the method *could* produce four-member classes, even though it did not always do so. The disappointing results that Jenkins (1963) reported might have been a false negative, arising not because four-member classes were absent but because group comparisons prevented the observation of individual successes.

Besides these general characteristics of our approach—the use of conditional discriminations and individual subjects—we found that we had to develop other more specific kinds of methodological practices. As we came to appreciate the potential behavioral importance of equivalence relations, we embarked on what came to be a full-fledged research program. While the program was evolving, we occasionally felt that we had fallen into a methodological vacuum. The use of conditional-discrimination procedures to study equivalence relations with individual subjects had little background that we could refer to; we had to work out a new methodology ourselves. Our initial successes in the human lab, therefore, led to gradual refinements in our research techniques. The 1982 papers not only presented new data; they laid out our new research methodology in painstaking detail.

For one thing, the use of words and pictures as stimuli was making experiments much more difficult than they had to be. The validity of our conclusions depended on the assumption that everything our subjects knew about relations among the stimuli that we were using came from our experimental procedures, but even the youngest subjects might already have had experience with the particular sounds and text we were presenting to them. If we were to continue using stimuli that might be familiar to our subjects, we would therefore have had to maintain the practice of pretesting all of the conditional discriminations that were supposed to emerge from our teaching procedures.

By then, however, the phenomenon of emergent relations based on the formation of equivalence relations was well established. Although we never lost sight of possible extensions outside the laboratory, our research interest was shifting toward the attainment of a greater understanding of the process itself. For that reason, we no longer felt the need to use stimuli that had obvious face validity for the analysis of reading comprehension. We decided to use arbitrary stimuli that clearly had no prior "meaning" for the subjects. With arbitrary forms like unfamiliar shapes or Greek letters, or even with familiar stimuli that our procedures caused to be related in unfamiliar ways, pretesting would be unnecessary. By eliminating pretests, we would be able not only to save considerable time but also to spare our subjects the unpleasant and often disruptive experience of being asked to do things that they could not possibly know how to do.

Procedures for testing emergent relations brought up a second methodological problem. In our original experiments (Chapters 1 and 2), we reinforced what we considered to be correct choices during the tests. Fortunately, most of the 20 new relations emerged the very first time they were tested, so reinforcement during the tests could not have been responsible. In later work, however, we used fewer stimuli and had to repeat test trials many times before we could be sure that a subject was choosing reliably. Reinforcement on test trials would have clouded the issue. Also, we found that new performances sometimes did not emerge right away. The need to give repeated tests forced us to reconsider our procedures. I discussed our dilemma in the following essay (Sidman, 1981).

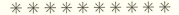

Remarks

I am always somewhat disconcerted when colleagues, telling me about their research, describe the experimental design before acquainting me with the problem the experiment is addressing. They seem not to recognize that an experimental design is empty until it is applied to a problem. Introductions to recent research reports, particularly in applied behavior analysis, seem also to emphasize experimental design at the expense of the study's substantive aims. It is sometimes difficult to brush away the uncomfortable impression that investigators are devising problems to fit the designs. Therefore, before resuming the thread of my earlier Remarks columns on "stimulus control and cognition," I should like to air a methodological problem to which some of my recent research has sensitized me. The problem, actually an old one, is particularly interesting because the adequacy of its solution cannot be evaluated until after the experiment has been done.

In the general research area called "transfer of training," the basic questions deal with the influence one kind of learning experience may exert upon some other performance: Will learning to write with the right hand transfer to the left hand? Or, if a pigeon has learned to peck a key that is illuminated by red light, will it also peck when the key is yellow? Or, in the example to be pursued here, will a subject who has learned a conditional discrimination be capable also of the symmetric counterpart of that discrimination? Answers to such questions will depend critically upon conditions under which the transfer tests take place.

Let us suppose our subject in the conditional-discrimination experiment is faced on various occasions or "trials" with three stimuli, arranged in a horizontal row. In the center is a line, vertical on some occasions and horizontal on others. The two outer stimuli are hues, one red and one green, their left or right positions varying randomly from trial to trial. By providing reinforcement appropriately, we teach the subject two discriminations, one with green positive and red negative, the other with red positive and green negative. These discriminations are conditional upon the line: The subject learns to touch the green stimulus if the center line is vertical and to touch red if the line is horizontal. Thus, we build the arbitrary conditional relations, *if vertical, then green; if horizontal, then red.*

Now, we want to know whether the conditional relations have the property of symmetry. Having learned, *if vertical, then green; if horizontal, then red,* will the subject, *without further training,* be capable also of the conditional discrimination, *if green, then vertical; if red, then horizontal?* To find out, we change the center stimuli from lines to hues, green on some occasions and red on others, and we replace the two outer hues with the lines, one vertical and one horizontal. Will the subject now touch vertical when the center hue is green and horizontal when the hue is red? In the laboratory, five- to six-year-old children who had been

taught explicitly to select hues conditionally upon lines were immediately capable of selecting the lines conditionally upon the hues. Pigeons, monkeys, and baboons, however, have so far shown no transfer to the symmetric versions of the conditional discriminations they had explicitly been taught. Teaching these subjects to select green conditionally upon vertical and red conditionally upon horizontal has not sufficed to enable them to select vertical conditionally upon green and horizontal conditionally upon red.

Since this experiment requires a relatively large number of test trials before we can be sure whether or not the subject's original training has transferred to the symmetric conditional discrimination, we have to specify the reinforcement contingencies that will prevail when we test. This is the methodological problem—to reinforce or not to reinforce during symmetry test trials. Even if transfer has not occurred, the subject's behavior will often seem to be consistent with transfer. By "chance," on 50% of the trials the subjects will select vertical when the center hue is green and horizontal when the center hue is red. We have the option of reinforcing or not reinforcing on such trials. The nature of the problem is highlighted by the discrepant experimental findings. If we reinforce, seemingly successful transfer might be attributable to reinforcement during the test rather than to the subject's training history. If we do not reinforce, a seeming failure of transfer might be attributable to extinction during the test rather than to an inadequate training history.

It is not possible, therefore, to choose the reinforcement contingency to be applied during the symmetry test on the basis of any rules of experimental design. We can only make a best guess and hope that the experimental results confirm the wisdom of our choice. If we test in extinction and the subjects do, like the children, show transfer, then we shall have made a fortunate choice; when subjects' previous training transfers to a new performance, even during extinction, the absence of reinforcement cannot be held responsible for the new behavior. If, however, we test with reinforcement on correct trials, the subject must, like the monkeys, fail to show transfer if our judgment is to be supported; when subjects' previous training fails to transfer to a new performance, even with reinforcement, the reinforcement for the new behavior cannot be held responsible for its absence.

A four-celled matrix can therefore summarize all combinations of test conditions and results: each of the alternative test conditions, reinforcement or extinction, might or might not yield evidence of transfer. Two of the combinations will be definitive. Evidence of transfer even during extinction or the failure of transfer even with reinforcement will provide unequivocal positive or negative answers, respectively, to the original experimental question. The other two combinations will, at the least, require additional clarification. A failure of transfer during extinction or evidence of transfer during the reinforcement condition will raise questions about the relative influence of the subjects' training history and the test conditions themselves in producing the experimental results.

Many of us, experimenters and philosophers both, would like to believe that a set of rules for the conduct of experiments exists independently of any particular experiment, that there is a "higher law," so to speak, on the basis of which one can know beforehand whether a particular experimental procedure is capable of yielding valid conclusions. The example cited above, however, demonstrates that the validity of an experimental procedure sometimes depends on the data the procedure yields. An experimenter does not just scan a list of "sound" methodologies and select a procedure that will guarantee unequivocal data. A logician of science cannot hope to provide such a list on the basis solely of logical criteria. Although rules can, of course, be formulated, any logic of experimentation will always be confounded by instances in which procedural decisions must take into account the substantive content of particular experimental questions. In reporting experiments, therefore, one will enhance readers' or listeners' appreciation of the methodology by clarifying the experimental problem before introducing the procedures.

Background (continued)

Since we had become accustomed to positive tests for equivalence in our research with human subjects, we chose the option of testing in extinction as our standard procedure, as in the following *Class Expansion* paper. (With continued successes, however, I grew careless and eventually fell into the trap of attributing negative results to other sources than the extinction procedure itself. I shall tell that part of the story in Chapter 11.)

* * * * * * * * *

Conditional Discrimination vs. Matching to Sample: An Expansion of the Testing Paradigm

A subject's performance under a conditional-discrimination procedure defines conditional relations between stimuli: *If A1, then B1; if
A2, then B2.* The procedure may also generate matching to sample. If
so, the stimuli will be related not only by conditionality but by equivalence: A1 and B1 will become equivalent members of one stimulus
class, A2 and B2 of another. One paradigm for testing whether a conditional-discrimination procedure has generated equivalence relations
uses three sets of stimuli, A, B, and C, three stimuli per set. Subjects
learn to select Set-B and Set-C comparisons conditionally upon Set-A
samples. Having been explicitly taught six sample-comparison relations, A1B1, A1C1, A2B2, A2C2, A3B3, and A3C3, subjects prove
immediately capable of matching the B- and C-stimuli; six new relations emerge (B1C1, B2C2, B3C3, C1B1, C2B2, C3B3). The 12
stimulus relations, six taught and six emergent, define the existence of
three three-member stimulus classes, A1B1C1, A2B2C2, and
A3B3C3. This paradigm was expanded by introducing three more
stimuli (Set D), and teaching eight children not only the AB and AC
relations but DC relations also—selecting Set-C comparisons conditionally upon Set-D samples. Six of the children proved immediately
capable of matching the B- and D-stimuli to each other. By selecting
appropriate Set-B comparisons conditionally upon Set-D samples, and
Set-D comparisons conditionally upon Set-B samples, they demonstrated the existence of three four-member stimulus classes,
A1B1C1D1, A2B2C2D2, and A3B3C3D3. These larger classes were
confirmed by the subjects' success with the prerequisite lower-level
conditional relations; they were also able to select Set-D comparisons
conditionally upon samples from Sets A and C, and to do the BC and
CB matching that defined the original three-member classes. Adding
the three DC relations therefore generated 12 more, three each in
BD, DB, AD, and CD. Enlarging each class by one member brought
about a disproportionate increase in the number of emergent relations. Ancillary oral naming tests suggested that the subjects' application of the same name to each stimulus was neither necessary nor
sufficient to establish classes of equivalent stimuli.

Given two discriminative stimuli, B1 and B2, a subject selects B1 if a conditional stimulus, A1, is present and selects B2 if the conditional stimulus is A2. This conditional discrimination provides a procedural definition of conditional relations between stimuli. In their simplest form, the conditional relations are: *If A1, then B1*; *if A2, then B2.* Although additional considerations may lead to a more precise description of an *if...then* relation, its existence is directly observable by reference to the subject's ongoing interactions with the procedure. Testing for the existence of a conditional relation requires no modification of the establishing procedure.

A well-established conditional discrimination is often assumed to demonstrate not just conditional relations between stimuli but equivalence relations also. In addition to their *if...then* relation, Stimuli A1 and B1 are also supposed to be equivalent; similarly, A2 and B2 are supposed to be related both by conditionality and equivalence. Investigators who have assumed, explicitly or implicitly, that the conditional-discrimination procedure generates equivalence relations often call the subject's performance *matching to sample*. Stimuli B1 and B2 become comparisons, to be compared to Samples A1 and A2 and matched appropriately. When all sample and comparison stimuli are physically different, equivalence is suggested by calling the performance *nonidentity, arbitrary*, or *symbolic* matching.

Unlike conditionality, equivalence is not definable solely by reference to the subject's ongoing interactions with the establishing procedure. To determine whether a performance involves something more than conditional relations between sample and comparison stimuli requires additional tests. Suppose, for example, a relation, **R**, between Stimuli *a* and *b* fulfills the procedural requirements for conditionality, or *if a, then b*. Is the relation between *a* and *b*, *a***R***b*, also an equivalence relation? The subject's current performance gives no clue. Appropriate tests can, however, be derived from the three properties that modern elementary mathematics texts specify as the definition of the equivalence relation: reflexivity, symmetry, and transitivity.

To determine that the conditional relation, **R**, is reflexive, one must show that each stimulus bears the relation to itself; aRa (*if a, then a*) and bRb (*if b, then b*) must hold true. Reflexivity can therefore be tested by an identity-matching procedure that requires the subject to match Stimulus a to itself and b to itself.

It will not suffice to *teach* the conditional relations, aRa and bRb. One does not know whether a subject to whom the relations had to be taught is matching each stimulus to itself (if matching is involved at all) or is perhaps controlled by one feature of the sample and another feature of the correct comparison. For example, instead of matching *red* to *red* and *green* to *green*, a subject might be matching *red* to *bright* and *green* to *dark*. Only if the subject matches each new stimulus to itself without differential reinforcement or other current instructions can one be certain that identity is the basis for the performance. Given a subject who is familiar with the stimuli and procedures, the proof of reflexivity is generalized identity matching.

To demonstrate that the relation, R, is symmetric, one must show that both aRb and bRa hold true. A subject who matches Sample a to Comparison b is then required, without further training, to match Sample b to Comparison a, reversing *if a, then b* to *if b, then a*. Given a subject who is familiar with each of the stimuli separately, both as sample and comparison, the proof of aRb symmetry is functional sample-comparison reversibility (Sidman et al., 1982).

To determine whether R is transitive requires a third stimulus, c. Once *if a, then b* and *if b, then c* have been established, transitivity requires *if a, then c* to emerge without differential reinforcement or other current instructions. Given a subject who has learned two conditional relations, aRb and bRc, with the comparison in the first serving as the sample in the second, the proof of transitivity is the emergence of a third conditional relation, aRc, in which the subject matches the sample from the first relation to the comparison from the second.

Calling a conditional relation *matching to sample*, then, requires proof that the relation possesses all three properties of an equivalence relation, as listed in the upper section of Table 6-1. Successful generalized matching will prove the relation reflexive, a property that must hold for each stimulus. Sample-comparison reversibility (Lazar, 1977) will prove symmetry, a property that must hold for each pair of related stimuli. Emergence of a third relation, in which the subject matches the sample from one of two prerequisite relations to the comparison from the other, will prove transitivity, a property that must hold for at least three interrelated stimuli.

Table 6-1
The Equivalence Relation

_____

Equivalence Relations must be
 1. Reflexive: $a\mathbf{R}a$
 2. Symmetric: If $a\mathbf{R}b$, then $b\mathbf{R}a$
 3. Transitive: If $a\mathbf{R}b$ and $b\mathbf{R}c$, then $a\mathbf{R}c$

_____

Combined tests for symmetry and transitivity are
 A. Teach $a\mathbf{R}b$ and $a\mathbf{R}c$.
    Test $b\mathbf{R}c$ and $c\mathbf{R}b$.
 B. Teach $b\mathbf{R}a$ and $c\mathbf{R}a$.
    Test $b\mathbf{R}c$ and $c\mathbf{R}b$.

_____

Symmetry and transitivity can be evaluated simultaneously. To prepare for one kind of combined test (A, in the lower section of Table 6-1), first teach the subject two relations, $a\mathbf{R}b$ and $a\mathbf{R}c$, that share the same sample. Then test for the emergence of the conditional relations, $b\mathbf{R}c$ and $c\mathbf{R}b$. If $\mathbf{R}$ is symmetric, so that both $a\mathbf{R}b$ and $b\mathbf{R}a$ hold true, then $b\mathbf{R}a$ and $a\mathbf{R}c$ will yield $b\mathbf{R}c$ via transitivity. Similarly, if both $a\mathbf{R}c$ and $c\mathbf{R}a$ hold true by symmetry, the combination of $c\mathbf{R}a$ and $a\mathbf{R}b$ will yield $c\mathbf{R}b$ via transitivity. Emergence of the new conditional relations, $b\mathbf{R}c$ and $c\mathbf{R}b$, requires the explicitly established relations, $a\mathbf{R}b$ and $a\mathbf{R}c$, to be both symmetric and transitive.

In early experiments that used these tests to determine whether conditional-discrimination procedures had generated matching-to-sample performances (Sidman, 1971b; Sidman & Cresson, 1973), retarded youths first proved capable of generalized identity matching, thereby meeting the reflexivity criterion. They then learned (or demonstrated that they were already able) to select pictures (comparison stimuli) conditionally upon any of 20 dictated picture names (sample stimuli); AB in Figure 6-1 represents 20 conditional relations (A1B1, A2B2...A20B20). A

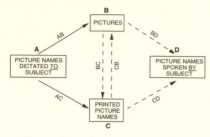

Figure 6-1. A basic equivalence paradigm. Boxes A, B, and C represent stimuli and Box D represents oral naming responses. Arrows AB, AC, BC, and CB point from sample to comparison stimuli and represent sets of conditional relations. Arrows BD and CD point from stimuli to naming responses. Solid arrows represent conditional relations that are explicitly taught to the subjects. Broken arrows represent conditional or oral naming relations that emerge after others have been explicitly taught.

determination of whether the AB relations involved equivalence, in addition to conditionality, required another set of conditional discriminations. The subjects learned to select printed names conditionally upon the same 20 dictated names; AC in Figure 6-1 represents the 20 new relations (A1C1, A2C2...A20C20). At the completion of their AB and AC training, the subjects could select any of 20 pictures or printed picture names conditionally upon a dictated name.

It was then possible to find out whether AB and AC were

equivalence relations by giving a combined test for symmetry and transitivity (A, in Table 6-1). Proof of equivalence required the subjects to select an appropriate printed word conditionally upon a picture sample (BC) and to select an appropriate picture conditionally upon a printed word (CB). The retarded subjects did relate the pictures and printed names correctly, even though they had not been explicitly trained to do so and had demonstrated in pretests that they were unable to do so before learning both the AB and AC conditional discriminations. The conditional relations therefore met the criteria of reflexivity, symmetry, and transitivity and the performances could be called *matching to sample*.

The subjects' emergent ability to do two new sets of matching tasks, BC and CB, confirmed the creation of 20 three-member classes of equivalent stimuli: A1B1C1, A2B2C2...A20B20C20. One of the classes, for example, contained the dictated word "boy," pictures of boys, and the printed word *boy*; another contained the dictated word "car," pictures of cars, and the printed word *car*. A necessary consequence of the establishment of classes of equivalent stimuli will be the subject's ability to match members of a class to each other even without ever having done so before. The testing process itself can therefore cause new matching-to-sample performances to emerge without explicitly teaching them. Stimulus-class formation permits an impressive economy and efficiency in teaching and learning. The direct teaching of 40 conditional relations (20 AB and 20 AC) caused 40 more to emerge (20 BC and 20 CB). Actually, the spinoff was considerably greater; subjects also became capable of naming the pictures (BD) and the printed words (CD) aloud. Although matching to sample does not require subjects to name the stimuli and they usually did not, oral naming emerged when tested. The original teaching of 40 conditional relations created 40 new conditional relations and 40 naming relations—80 new performances.

A major purpose of the present experiment was to add one more stimulus to each class and thereby test the power of equivalence relations to generate a larger network of interchangeable stimuli.

Figure 6-2 shows the stimuli and illustrates the experiment's rationale. Previous studies using English language symbols had required extensive pretests to ensure that the subjects could not already do the critical matching and naming. In order to eliminate both the time required for pretests and the problems created by giving children tasks they are unable to perform, and to avoid the methodological dilemma of whether or not to reinforce correct responses during pretests, this experiment used Greek letters and letter names, stimuli that could be presumed unfamiliar to the subjects and therefore not requiring pretests at all. Reducing the number of stimuli from 20 to three in each set achieved additional simplification.

The upper "triangle" ABC in Figure 6-2 represents a smaller replication of the experiments summarized in the left triangle of Figure 6-1. Subjects learned to select letters in Sets B and C conditionally upon dictated names (A). If the conditional relations, AB and AC, were also equivalence relations, Test A (Table 6-1) would reveal the subjects' ability to match Set-B and

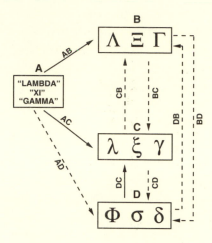

Figure 6-2. The equivalence paradigm in the present experiment. The
stimuli are a set of dictated Greek letter names (Set A) and three sets of
printed Greek letters (Sets B, C, and
D), three letters in each set. Arrows
point from sample stimuli (only one
presented at a time) to comparison
stimuli. The solid arrows AB, AC, and
AD represent conditional relations that
are explicitly taught to the subjects. The
broken arrows CB, BC, AD, CD, BD,
and DB represent conditional relations
that are tested after others have been
explicitly taught.

Set-C letters to each other (BC
and CB). Three three-member
stimulus classes should emerge,
each containing a dictated letter
name, a Set-B letter, and a Set-
C letter.

Subjects were also taught to
select comparison letters in Set
C conditionally upon samples

from Set D. Would the new DC
relations expand the ABC
classes? If they did, each three-
member class would gain a
fourth member from Set D: upper-case phi would join the
lambda class; lower-case sigma,
the *xi* class; and lower-case delta,
the *gamma* class. Subjects would
be able to match each stimulus
to any other in its class. Having
explicitly been taught only the
AB, AC, and DC relations, they
would then prove capable of
matching samples from Set B to
comparisons in Set D (BD) or
samples from Set D to comparisons in Set B (DB). The first goal
of the present experiment was to
carry out these tests for the emergence of the four-member stimulus classes, ABCD.

Spradlin et al. (1973) successfully demonstrated the emergence of relations analogous to
DB in Figure 6-2 but did not test
for BD. Because the DB relations
did not require DC symmetry
but the BD relations did (a point
to be elaborated later), both DB
and BD were required for proof
that the procedures had generated four-member classes. The
present experiment also extended the Spradlin, Cotter, and
Baxley findings by testing the

subjects' ability to name the stimuli and to perform other conditional discriminations besides DB and BD. For example, teaching AC and DC would establish the lower triangle ACD in Figure 6-2, once more making it possible to test for equivalence by evaluating symmetry and transitivity simultaneously. Equivalence tests in the lower and upper triangles, however, differed in at least two respects. First, the explicitly taught relations in the upper triangle, AB and AC, shared the same samples; analogous relations in the lower triangle, AC and DC, shared the same comparisons, like test B in Table 6-1. The logic of both combined tests, however, was similar. If the DC relations were symmetric, so that conditionality also held for CD, then AC and CD could yield AD by transitivity; subjects would prove capable of matching auditory samples from Set A to comparison letters in Set D. Therefore, in addition to testing for four-member ABCD classes, the present experiment also tested for the emergence of two sets of three-member classes, ABC and ACD. Tests for BC and CB relations evaluated the ABC classes;

tests for AD relations evaluated the ACD classes.

A second difference between the upper and lower triangles in Figure 6-2 stemmed from the inability to present several auditory comparison stimuli simultaneously without altering their individual intelligibility. This technical feature of the conditional-discrimination procedure used here precluded a validation of AB- and AC-symmetry that was independent of the combined symmetry/transitivity tests. Testing BA or CA would have required the presentation of consecutive rather than simultaneous auditory comparison stimuli. Such a major procedural modification, although feasible, would at that time have disrupted the continuity of the experimental program. In the lower triangle, the DC relations involved only visual stimuli and could be tested for symmetry independently of the combined test. The present experiment, therefore, not only tested for equivalence relations by means of combined symmetry/transitivity tests but also provided the independent evaluation of symmetry that the lower triangle in Figure 6-2 permitted.

The development of equivalence in all three sets of explicitly taught conditional discriminations—AB, AC, and DC—should create six sets of new matching-to-sample performances, summarized by broken arrows in Figure 6-2. The experiment tested all of these possibilities. Subjects were also tested for oral naming. Accurate naming of the letters in Sets B and C was perhaps to be expected, since the subjects were explicitly taught conditional relations between these letters and their auditory counterparts. Set-D naming was less surely predictable, since the subjects were never taught any direct relation between Set-D letters and the dictated names in Set A.

METHOD

Subjects

Eight normal children, all male except Subject A.D., participated in the experiment. Their ages (years-months) at the time they completed training and underwent their first tests for equivalence relations were: 5-0 (A.D.), 5-9 (J.L. and J.O.), 6-3 (D.B.), 6-5 (E.M.), 6-11 (D.W.), 7-4 (E.W.), and 7-5 (I.C.). Subjects A.D., J.L., D.B., and E.M. attended kindergarten and Subjects J.O., D.W., E.W., and I.C. were in first grade. No other educational or test data were available. All children had at least one parent who completed high school and all except Subjects A.D. and J.O. had at least one parent who had gone beyond high school. Each child, recruited by local newspaper advertisements, came to the laboratory several days a week with a parent who was paid after each session. The total number of sessions, each 15 to 30 minutes long, varied because the children differed in the amounts of training they required to learn and maintain the baseline conditional discriminations.

Apparatus and General Procedures

The child sat before a stimulus-response matrix of nine translucent hinged keys (windows) onto which stimuli were projected from the rear. Stimuli for a given trial had all been photographed on a single slide, and solenoid-operated shutters were mounted between projector and windows. The windows, each 7.3 cm in diameter, were arranged in

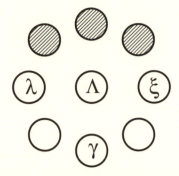

Figure 6-3. Schematic representation of the stimulus-response matrix, illustrating a sample from Set B (center window) and the three comparisons from Set C (outer windows). Positions of stimuli and blank windows varied from trial to trial but stimuli never appeared in the three uppermost windows.

a circle of eight, with the ninth in the center (Figure 6-3). The display diameter was 32.7 cm; the center-to-center distance was 9.5 cm between adjacent windows on the perimeter and 12.7 cm between the center window and each of the others. Sample stimuli always appeared in the center and comparison stimuli in the outer windows but the present experiments did not use the three uppermost windows (shaded in Figure 6-3). Whenever the child pressed a window a limit switch signalled the solid-state programming equipment, impulse counters, and a 20-pen operations recorder.

Each trial began with a sample stimulus. Visual samples, black line drawings of Greek letters on a white background, appeared on the center window. Auditory samples, Greek letter names, were dictated by a master tape and were repeated at 2-s intervals by a continuous tape loop (Fletcher et al., 1971); the center window was illuminated but blank. Each sample, visual or auditory, remained throughout the trial (simultaneous matching) and trial durations had no limit. Visual and auditory samples never occurred in the same trial.

In matching-to-sample trials, after the sample was presented the subject had to press the center window to bring comparison stimuli onto the outer windows. Even dictated samples required this "observing response" but pressing the blank center window could not produce the comparisons until at least one complete sample word had sounded. No trial presented more than three comparison stimuli; at least two of the five functional comparison windows were blank on each trial, as indicated in Figure 6-3. Positions of correct, incorrect, and blank comparison windows varied from trial to trial. In sequences that included only two different sample stimuli, no more than three trials with the same sample could occur consecutively. With more than two samples, all possible trial types—sample-comparison combinations—had to occur before any could repeat. Also, all five functional comparison windows had to be scheduled as correct before any window could be correct again. With those exceptions, all trial types and all correct windows were equally probable on successive trials.

After comparison stimuli appeared, the subject had to press a comparison window. Unless a reduced reinforcement probability or an extinction probe (see below) precluded reinforcement, correct choices were followed by the sound of chimes, the disappearance of all stimuli, the delivery of a penny into an open receptacle below and at the left of the window matrix, and a 1.5-s intertrial interval. Neither chimes nor penny followed an incorrect choice. The children kept all pennies they received.

Any window press during the intertrial interval postponed the next sample for 1.5 s. Once the sample had come on, the subject could not produce comparison stimuli by pressing sample and comparison windows simultaneously; after any such simultaneous response the subject had to release both windows before a sample press could be effective. Once the comparisons had come on, sample presses no longer had any programmed consequences but if the subject pressed correct, incorrect, or blank comparison windows simultaneously the trial was treated as incorrect. The programming apparatus arbitrarily specified simultaneity by waiting to define any response until the subject had released the window for .2 s; pressure on another window during the preceding press or within .2 s of a release defined a simultaneous response.

In oral naming tests, the subject had simply to respond to the instruction, "Tell me what you see," or "What is it?". The child pressed no windows and only samples were presented, with no comparisons. After each oral response the experimenter, seated behind the child, pressed a handswitch to initiate the intertrial interval and the slide change. No chimes or pennies were presented, even for correct names (see below). Test sessions were recorded on magnetic tape and the experimenter also recorded the child's naming responses during the tests. A secretary's transcription of each tape, in the absence of the visual stimuli to which the subject had been responding, never differed from the experimenter's record by more than one naming response in any 90-trial test.

Teaching and Testing Phases

The general plan of the experiment (details are provided below) was, A: first, acquaint the children with the procedures and confirm their ability to do visual-visual and auditory-visual conditional discriminations by pretesting them with stimuli that were presumably familiar, hues and hue names. Then, test identity matching with all of the Greek letters to be used in the experiment. These letter-letter (sample-comparison) tasks served as generalized matching-to-sample tests for reflexivity. B: next, teach the children the three sets of relations denoted in Figure 6-2 by the solid arrows, AB, AC, and DC. This established the baselines to be tested for symmetry and transitivity. C: finally,

without additional teaching, evaluate the children's performance on the six sets of relations denoted in Figure 6-2 by the broken arrows, DB, BD, AD, BC, CB, and CD. Emergence of these new relations or their failure to emerge would prove whether or not the explicitly taught conditional relations were also equivalence relations and whether the performances could be called *matching to sample*. Also, test the children's oral responses to the B-, C-, and D-stimuli.

Table 6-2 outlines the planned sequence. All subjects went through Phases A (Pretests) and B (Teaching) in the indicated order. At the end of Phase B the children were performing the three sets of baseline conditional discriminations, AB, AC, and CD at high levels of accuracy, although only a small proportion of their correct trials terminated with reinforcement (see below). Then, in Phase C (Final Tests), unreinforced probe trials, inserted among these infrequently reinforced baseline trials, constituted the tests for symmetry and transitivity, thereby evaluating the formation of equivalence relations in the baseline.

Table 6-2

Sequence of teaching and testing phases. The identifiers, AB, AC, DC, etc., refer to the sample-comparison relations diagrammed in Figure 6-2.

A. Pretests—Matching to Sample
  1. Hue samples and hue comparsons (Identity)
  2. Hue-name samples (dictated) and hue comparisons
  3. Greek-letter samples and comparisons (Identity)
B. Teaching—Matching to Sample
  1. AB: Set-A samples (dictated) and Set-B comparisons
  2. AC: Set-A samples (dictated) and Set-C comparisons
  3. AB and AC: Trials from Teaching Phases 1 and 2, mixed
  4. DC: Set-D samples (visual) and Set-C comparisons
  5. AB, AC, and DC: Trials from Teaching Phases 3 and 4, mixed
  6. Gradual lowering of reinforcement probability
C. Final Tests—Matching to Sample; Oral Naming
  1. DB: 4-stage equivalence probes, in baseline of AB, AC, and DC
  2. BD: 4-stage equivalence probes, in baseline of AB, AC, and DC
  3. AD: 3-stage equivalence probes, in baseline of AC and DC
  4. BC: 3-stage equivalence probes, in baseline of AB and AC
  5. CB: 3-stage equivalence probes, in baseline of AB and AC
  6. CD: Symmetry probes of DC relations, in baseline of DC
  7. B-, C-, and D-naming

Pretests

After the delivery of two or three pennies had sufficed to accomplish magazine training, the experimenter provided nonverbal instruction by pressing windows appropriately for several hue-hue trials (hue sample and hue comparisons, with the sample hue the same as the correct comparison hue). Each subject then imitated the experimenter, meeting a criterion of 90 % correct in a set of 25 hue-hue trials (Phase A1), followed by a similar criterion performance in matching dictated hue-name samples to the hue comparisons (Phase A2). These first tests with hues established the children's ability to cope with the experimental procedures. In the final pretest procedure (Phase A3) the stimuli were the Greek letters illustrated in Figure 6-2. On individual trials the sample and correct comparison were the same and the two incorrect comparisons were always the other members of the same set (B, C, or D); comparisons from different sets never appeared together. This identity matching evaluated generalized matching to sample and thereby served as a test for reflexivity.

Teaching and Maintenance Procedures

Teaching the three sets of baseline conditional discriminations went according to the sequence summarized in Table 6-2, Phases B1 through B6. Each teaching phase itself, however, was composed of a carefully programmed series of steps.

Teaching Steps. Figures 6-4 and 6-5 depict the sample and comparison stimuli that comprised the trial types in each step. Starting with the AB relations, the children first had to match only two dictated samples, A1 and A2, to the comparison letters B1 and B2. The same two comparison letters, one correct and the other incorrect, appeared on every trial, as illustrated in the uppermost frame of Figure 6-4 (Task AB12). The children rotated through six balanced sets of 20 trials until they achieved at least 19 correct trials in a set. Then, in the second step, they went through sets of 20 trials with another pair of samples and correct comparisons, matching A1 and A3 to B1 and B3 (Figure 6-4, Task AB13) until they met the same criterion. Both steps included Sample A1 and Comparison B1. In the third

TASK	SAMPLE	CORRECT	INCORRECT
AB12	"LAMBDA"	Λ	Ξ
	"XI"	Ξ	Λ
AB13	"LAMBDA"	Λ	Γ
	"GAMMA"	Γ	Λ
AB23	"XI"	Ξ	Γ
	"GAMMA"	Γ	Ξ
AB123	"LAMBDA"	Λ	Ξ,Γ
	"XI"	Ξ	Λ,Γ
	"GAMMA"	Γ	Λ,Ξ
AC12	"LAMBDA"	λ	ξ
	"XI"	ξ	λ
AC13	"LAMBDA"	λ	γ
	"GAMMA"	γ	λ
AC23	"XI"	ξ	γ
	"GAMMA"	γ	ξ
AC123	"LAMBDA"	λ	ξ,γ
	"XI"	ξ	λ,γ
	"GAMMA"	γ	λ,ξ
AB1	"LAMBDA"	Λ	Ξ,Γ
AC1	"LAMBDA"	λ	ξ,γ
AB2	"XI"	Ξ	Λ,Γ
AC2	"XI"	ξ	λ,γ
AB3	"GAMMA"	Γ	Λ,Ξ
AC3	"GAMMA"	γ	λ,ξ

Figure 6-4. Each line depicts a trial type—sample stimulus, with correct and incorrect comparison(s). Each of the three main sections (bounded by solid lines) shows the trial types used in Teaching Phases B1, B2, and B3 (Table 6-2)—AB relations first, then AC, and then both together. Frames within sections show the trial types used in each consecutive step. The numbers 1, 2, and 3 refer to the auditory stimuli shown from top to bottom in Figure 6-2 and to the visual stimuli shown from left to right.

step, the children learned to match the final pair of samples, A2 and A3, and Comparisons B2 and B3 (Task AB23). Each of these combinations—sample and correct comparison—had already been presented along with a different partner in Step 1 or 2.

Trials in these first three steps presented only two comparison stimuli (balanced with respect to window positions), one related conditionally to the current sample and the other to the second sample in the current pair. The fourth AB teaching step (Task AB123) mixed all three samples in sets of 30 trials and presented all three comparisons, one correct and two incorrect, on every trial. When the children met a criterion of at least 29 correct trials in a set, they went on to learn the AC relations (Phase B2 in Table 6-2).

The central frames of Figure 6-4 show teaching Phase B2 broken down into steps like those of Phase B1. The children first learned pairs of AC trial types with only two comparisons per trial (Tasks AC12, AC13, and AC23). Then, sets of trials were given with all three samples, three comparisons per trial (Task AC123). Phase B3 then mixed the six AB and AC trial types, as depicted in the bottom frame of Figure 6-4, into balanced sets of 30 trials. By meeting a criterion of 29 correct trials in a set of 30, the children demonstrated that they could select either Set-B or Set-C letters conditionally upon dictated letter names from Set A.

Phase B4 (Table 6-2) consisted of a similar sequence in which the children learned the DC relations. The upper three frames of Figure 6-5 show the three pairs of DC trial types the children learned first and the fourth frame shows the three-comparison DC trial types. Finally, Phase B5 mixed the nine AB, AC, and DC trial types (bottom section of Figure 6-5) in balanced sets of 45 trials. To complete Phase B5 the children had to meet a criterion of 44 correct trials in a set of 45. Later, sets of these nine trial types would constitute a baseline into which probe trials would be inserted to evaluate the formation of equivalence relations.

Reinforcement Probability. Before inserting unreinforced probes, the reinforcement probability on correct baseline trials was gradually reduced (Phase B6)

TASK	SAMPLE	CORRECT	INCORRECT
DC$_{12}$	Φ	λ	ξ
	σ	ξ	λ
DC$_{13}$	Φ	λ	γ
	δ	γ	λ
DC$_{23}$	σ	ξ	γ
	δ	γ	ξ
DC$_{123}$	Φ	λ	ξ,γ
	σ	ξ	λ,γ
	δ	γ	λ,ξ
AB$_1$	"LAMBDA"	Λ	Ξ,Γ
AC$_1$	"LAMBDA"	λ	ξ,γ
DC$_1$	Φ	λ	ξ,γ
AB$_2$	"XI"	Ξ	Λ,Γ
AC$_2$	"XI"	ξ	λ,γ
DC$_2$	σ	ξ	λ,γ
AB$_3$	"GAMMA"	Γ	Λ,Ξ
AC$_3$	"GAMMA"	γ	λ,ξ
DC$_3$	δ	γ	λ,ξ

Figure 6-5. Each line depicts a trial type—sample stimulus, with correct and incorrect comparison(s). The frames show the trial types used in each consecutive step of Teaching Phases B4 and B5 (Table 6-2). DC trial types were taught first (upper four frames) and were then combined with the previously taught AB and AC trial types (lowest frame). The numbers 1, 2, and 3 refer to the auditory stimuli shown from top to bottom in Figure 6-2 and to the visual stimuli shown from left to right.

from 1.00 to .20. The sequence of probability steps was 1.00, .75, .50, .40, .30, and .20; subjects had to meet the 90% baseline accuracy criterion at each step before the probability

could be lowered. It was occasionally necessary to halt a decreasing accuracy trend by increasing the reinforcement probability and then reducing it again. Since no probe trials would be reinforced, the reinforcement probability on baseline trials during subsequent tests was increased sufficiently to maintain the overall probability at .20. Probabilities were controlled by a probability gate (BRS/LVE PP-201), its output modified to permit no more than nine consecutive baseline trials to go unreinforced.

Before any set of trials in which the reinforcement probability was to be less than 1.00, the subject was told, "You won't always get a penny from now on but you will have a chance to get more later." Then, at the end of the session, the child was given enough hue-hue matching trials, with all correct choices reinforced, to make up for the earlier correct baseline trials that had gone unreinforced.

Maintenance and review. Each new teaching session began with a review of the most advanced performance the subject had achieved, and the subject had to meet the learning criterion again before going on to the next step. For example, Tasks AB12, AB13, and AB23 (Figure 6-4) were reviewed at the beginning of each teaching session until the child had learned AB123; then, AB123 was reviewed at the beginning of all sessions in which the subject was learning the next four tasks; since the final task (bottom frame of Figure 6-4) included all AB and AC trial types, this was all that needed review during the next teaching phase; and so forth. Finally, after the reduction in reinforcement probability, each session in which a test was scheduled began with a review of the trial types that would serve as the sparsely reinforced baseline for the insertion of probes (each of these baselines is described below). To proceed with the test, subjects had to meet the usual accuracy criterion on this review; if they did not, reviews continued for the rest of the session. A child who failed frequently to meet a review criterion returned to an earlier teaching step and advanced through the sequence again.

Tests

Phases C1 through C7 in Table 6-2 summarize the tests with

reference to the relations outlined in Figure 6-2.

Four-stage equivalence. Phase C1 inserted DB trials (samples from Set D, comparisons from Set B) as unreinforced probes into a sparsely reinforced baseline of AB, AC, and DC trials. Phase C2 inserted BD probes into the same baseline. Because emergence of the DB and BD performances required conditional relations within four sets of stimuli (A, B, C, and D), Phases C1 and C2 in Table 6-2 are called "four-stage equivalence probes." This *n-stage* terminology is consistent with a similar usage in conjunction with analogous paradigms that have been studied largely by means of paired-associate techniques (e.g., Jenkins, 1963).

Figure 6-6 shows the trial types (sample-comparison combinations) in the four-stage tests, with each of the three kinds of DB probes below its prerequisite AB, AC, and DC trial types. For example, emergence of the DB1 (probe) relation (Sample D1, Comparison B1) required the subjects to have learned the AB1, AC1, and DC1 relations that are shown just above DB1. In Phase C2, the three BD probes

TASK	SAMPLE	CORRECT	INCORRECT
AB$_1$	"LAMBDA"	Λ	Ξ,Γ
AC$_1$	"LAMBDA"	λ	ξ,γ
DC$_1$	Φ	λ	ξ,γ
DB$_{1(probe)}$	Φ	(Λ)	(Ξ,Γ)
AB$_2$	"XI"	Ξ	Λ,Γ
AC$_2$	"XI"	ξ	λ,γ
DC$_2$	σ	ξ	λ,γ
DB$_{2(probe)}$	σ	(Ξ)	(Λ,Γ)
AB$_3$	"GAMMA"	Γ	Λ,Ξ
AC$_3$	"GAMMA"	γ	λ,ξ
DC$_3$	δ	γ	λ,ξ
DB$_{3(probe)}$	δ	(Γ)	(Λ,Ξ)
BD$_{1(probe)}$	Λ	(Φ)	(σ,δ)
BD$_{2(probe)}$	Ξ	(σ)	(Φ,δ)
BD$_{3(probe)}$	Γ	(δ)	(Φ,σ)

Figure 6-6. Each line depicts a trial type—sample stimulus, with correct and incorrect comparisons. The upper section shows the AB, AC, and DC baseline trial types and the four-stage DB probes used in Final Test Phase C1 (Table 6-2). Each DB probe is just below its three prerequisite baseline trial types. The three lines in the lower section show the four-stage BD probes that were inserted in place of DB trials during Final Test Phase C2 (Table 6-2). The numbers 1, 2, and 3 refer to the auditory stimuli shown from top to bottom in Figure 6-2 and to the visual stimuli shown from left to right. Because probe trials were never reinforced, correct and incorrect probe comparison stimuli are enclosed within parentheses.

TASK	SAMPLE	CORRECT	INCORRECT
AC$_1$	"LAMBDA"	λ	ξ,γ
DC$_1$	Φ	λ	ξ,γ
AD$_{1(probe)}$	"LAMBDA"	(Φ)	(σ,δ)
AC$_2$	"XI"	ξ	λ,γ
DC$_2$	σ	ξ	λ,γ
AD$_{2(probe)}$	"XI"	(σ)	(Φ,δ)
AC$_3$	"GAMMA"	γ	λ,ξ
DC$_3$	δ	γ	λ,ξ
AD$_{3(probe)}$	"GAMMA"	(δ)	(Φ,σ)

Figure 6-7. Each line depicts a trial type—sample stimulus, with correct and incorrect comparisons—used in Final Test Phase C3 (Table 6-2). Each three-stage AD probe is just below its two prerequisite AC and DC baseline trial types. The numbers 1, 2, and 3 refer to the auditory stimuli shown from top to bottom in Figure 6-2 and to the visual stimuli shown from left to right. Because probe trials were never reinforced, correct and incorrect probe comparison stimuli are enclosed within parentheses.

depicted at the bottom of Figure 6-6 replaced the DB trials. Each DB or BD test had 120 trials, 10 of each trial type (90 baseline and 30 probe trials).

Three-stage equivalence. Phases C3, C4, and C5 in Table 6-2 summarize the three-stage probes—those requiring subjects to have learned conditional relations within three sets of stimuli. AD probes (Phase C3) involved stimulus Sets A, C, and D (Figure 6-2). Because emergence of the AD relations required subjects to have learned only AC and DC, AD probes were inserted into a baseline of only AC and DC trials. Figure 6-7 shows the trial types in the three-stage AD tests, with each AD probe below its prerequisite AC and DC trial types. AD tests had 90 trials, 10 of each trial type (60 baseline and 30 probe trials).

The three-stage BC and CB probes (Phases C4 and C5) required subjects to have learned conditional relations within stimulus Sets A, B, and C (Figure 6-2). Because the emergence of BC and CB demanded only AB and AC as prerequisites, Phases C4 and C5 were combined into a single test, with probes inserted into a baseline of AB and AC trials. Figure 6-8 shows the trial types, with each pair of BC and CB probes located below the prerequisite AB and AC trial types. These combined BC-CB tests had 120 trials, 10 of each type (60 baseline and 60 probe trials—30 BC and 30 CB probes).

Symmetry. In Phase C6 (Table 6-2), CD probes tested the DC relations for symmetry. Figure 6-9 shows the trial types in this symmetry test, with CD probes inserted into a baseline that contained only DC trials. CD tests had 60 trials, 10 of each type (30 baseline and 30 probe trials).

TASK	SAMPLE	CORRECT	INCORRECT
AB$_1$	"LAMBDA"	Λ	Ξ,Γ
AC$_1$	"LAMBDA"	λ	ξ,γ
BC$_{1(probe)}$	Λ	(λ)	(ξ,γ)
CB$_{1(probe)}$	λ	(Λ)	(Ξ,Γ)
AB$_2$	"XI"	Ξ	Λ,Γ
AC$_2$	"XI"	ξ	λ,γ
BC$_{2(probe)}$	Ξ	(ξ)	(λ,γ)
CB$_{2(probe)}$	ξ	(Ξ)	(Λ,Γ)
AB$_3$	"GAMMA"	Γ	Λ,Ξ
AC$_3$	"GAMMA"	γ	λ,ξ
BC$_{3(probe)}$	Γ	(γ)	(λ,ξ)
CB$_{3(probe)}$	γ	(Γ)	(Λ,Ξ)

Figure 6-8. Each line depicts a trial type—sample stimulus, with correct and incorrect comparisons—used in Final Test Phases C4 and C5 (Table 6-2), which were combined into a single test. Each pair of BC and CB probes is just below the two prerequisite AB and AC baseline trial types. The numbers 1, 2, and 3 refer to the auditory stimuli shown from top to bottom in Figure 6-2 and to the visual stimuli shown from left to right. Because probe trials were never reinforced, correct and incorrect probe comparison stimuli are enclosed within parentheses.

Oral naming. The final tests, Phase C7 of Table 6-2, were oral naming, in which the subjects named the B-, C-, and D-stimuli aloud. Naming tests had 90 trials, with 10 presentations of each visual stimulus.

Test sequence. Table 6-3 shows the sequence of tests for each subject. Six went through

TASK	SAMPLE	CORRECT	INCORRECT
DC1	Φ	λ	ξ,γ
CD1(probe)	λ	(Φ)	(σ,δ)
DC2	σ	ξ	λ,γ
CD2(probe)	ξ	(σ)	(Φ,δ)
DC3	δ	γ	λ,ξ
CD3(probe)	γ	(δ)	(Φ,σ)

Figure 6-9. Each line depicts a trial type—sample stimulus, with correct and incorrect comparisons—used in Final Test Phase C6 (Table 6-2). Each symmetry probe is below its prerequisite DC baseline trial type. The numbers 1, 2, and 3 refer to the visual stimuli shown from left to right in Figure 6-2. Because probe trials were never reinforced, correct and incorrect probe comparison stimuli are enclosed within parentheses.

Phase C with minor variations in the order given in Table 6-2. Two subjects, J.O. and J.L., required major departures from this sequence; their tests and data will be noted separately.

RESULTS

Each row of bars in Figure 6-10 represents the matching-to-sample test and baseline scores for one of six subjects. Column headings (BD…DC) refer to the relations diagrammed in Figure 6-2. Although there had been no differential reinforcement on probe trials, responses indicative of equivalence relations were arbitrarily designated as correct in summarizing probe-trial results. The three bars at the extreme right side of each row combine the scores for each indicated kind of baseline trial across all tests

Table 6-3

Sequence of tests given to each subject

	Four-stage		Three-stage		Symmetry	
				BC-		Nam-
Subject	DB	BD	AD	CB	CD	ing
E.W.	1	2	3	4	-	5
A.D.	1	2	3	4	5	-
D.B.	2	1	3	4	5	6
E.M.	1	2	4	5	-	3
I.C.	1	2	5	4	6	3
D.W.	1	2	3	4	5	6
J.O.	1	2	(see text)			
J.L.	1		2	3	(see text)	

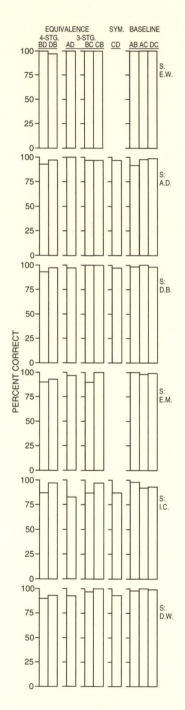

that included it (Figures 6-6 to 6-9). The first six bars (only five for Subjects E.W. and E.M.) each represent a probe-trial score for one four-stage, three-stage, or symmetry test.

Baseline performances were uniformly excellent. A finer analysis of each baseline relation into its three individual trial types (for example, those listed in the lower section of Figure 6-5) showed that these children rarely made as many as two errors, and never more, in 10 baseline trials of any type. Inserting unfamiliar probe trials among the explicitly taught trial types did not disrupt the baselines.

The children also behaved remarkably consistently in probe trials. In four-stage probes for the relations BD and DB, only Subject I.C. selected an "incorrect" letter in as many as four out of 30 probe trials. All subjects

---

Figure 6-10. Each row of bars gives one child's scores on the equivalence probes (four-stage BD and DB; three-stage AD, BC, and CB), symmetry probes (CD), and baseline trials (AB, AC, and DC) summarized in Table 6-2, Final Test Phase. Probe scores represent individual tests and baseline scores are combined for all tests. Two children did not have symmetry tests.

distributed their errors relatively evenly among the trial types. In three-stage AD tests, five of the children ranged from zero to two errors in the 30 probe trials, but Subject I.C. did give an indication here of incompletely established equivalence relations. Although he made only five errors in the 30 AD probes, four came in the 10-trial set with "gamma" as the dictated sample and three of those were selections of the letter that was appropriate for "lambda" (Figure 6-7). In the three-stage probes for the BC and CB relations and in the CD symmetry probes, Subject I.C. was again the only one of these six children to make as many as four errors in any set of 30 trials but these did not concentrate in any particular trial type.

When asked to identify the letters, the subjects named them almost perfectly, none making more than two errors in the 90-trial test. Within each set of letters shown in Figure 6-2 (B, C, and D), the children consistently called the one at the left, "lambda," the center one, "xi," and the letter at the right, "gamma." (The correlation between class membership and position of the letters in Figure 6-2 is simply an expository device; during naming tests the letter was always in the center window and during matching-to-sample tests the positions of comparison letters varied from trial to trial.) This consistency was perfect in trials with the D-stimuli, even though the children's selection of D-stimuli conditionally upon dictated names (AD) had never been reinforced.

Subject E.W., however, differed from all the others in his manner of responding to D-stimuli. Table 6-4 reproduces the first half (45 trials) of his oral-naming test, including the instructions. (Unlike the actual transcript, Table 6-4 does identify the stimulus on each trial.) Although Subject E.W. gave all the expected names, his responses indicated that the D-stimuli differed from the B- and C-stimuli; it is possible to scan Table 6-4, even without observing which trials had D-stimuli and to pick out the D-trials. On trial 2, the first presentation of a letter from Set D, the child expressed doubt, not even venturing a guess until prompted. Although later responses were not as lengthy, he

Table 6-4

Subject E.W.'s responses on his first 45 oral-naming trials, including the pre-test interaction between Subject and Experimenter. Trials are listed consecutively and the stimulus is identified with reference to its portrayal in Figure 2 as the left (1), center (2), or right (3) member of Set B, C, or D.

Subject	Experimenter
What's it going to be like?	O.K. Now this time,…, there aren't going to be any pennies.
Yes.	No pennies this time.
Yes.	I'd like you to keep your hands in your lap like they are.
Mmmm.	And I don't want you to push anything, O.K.?
O.K.	Now when something comes on, you tell me what it is that you see.
O.K.	O.K.?
O.K.	Now remember, don't push anything; you just tell me what it is that you see.
O.K.	

Trial	Stimulus	Subject's Responses
1	1C	……………LAMBDA. (Experimenter: You don'—You don't have to yell into the microphone like that. It'll—It'll hear you alright, O.K.?) O.K.
2	3D	…………Hmmmmmmmmm. Oh, somethin', but—I don't know. It's kinda—Well I—don't really have any idea—One little idea, but I don't know what it is. (Experimenter: What's that?) Well,—I have an—a slight idea that it might be GAMMA.
3	2D	Hmmmmmmmmmmmm. I think that might be XI.
4	3C	That's GAMMA.
5	2B	That's XI.
6	3B	That's GAMMA.
7	1D	Hmmmmmmmmmmmm. — I think that might be LAMBDA. Or somethin' like it.
8	1B	That's LAMBDA.
9	2C	THAT'S XI.
10	1C	That's LAMBDA.
11	2B	That's XI.
12	3C	That's—GAMMA.
13	3B	That's GAMMA.

Trial	Stimulus	Subject's Responses
14	2D	I—I have a slight feeling that might be XI.
15	2C	I think that's XI.
16	3D	It might be GAMMA, but I'm not too sure.
17	1D	I—I thin'—It might be LAMBDA, but I'm not sure.
18	1B	That's LAMBDA.
19	1D	I like the LAMBDA, but I'm not too sure.
20	1C	That's LAMBDA.
21	2D	That might be XI.
22	2B	That's XI.
23	1B	That's LAMBDA
24	3B	That's GAMMA.
25	2C	That's XI.
26	3C	That's GAMMA.
27	3D	Mmmmmm. I have a sl- slight feeling that just might be GAMMA.
28	2C	XI.
29	1D	It might be LAMBDA, but I'm not sure.
30	2B	XI.
31	1C	LAMBDA.
32	3C	GAMMA.
33	1B	LAMBDA.
34	3B	GAMMA.
35	2D	XI.........I think.
36	3D	Mmmmmmm, I think that might be GAMMA, but I'm not too sure.
37	1B	LAMBDA.
38	2D	XI.........I think.
39	1D	Like LAMBDA, but I'm not too sure.
40	3D	That might be GAMMA.
41	3C	That *is* GAMMA.
42	2C	That's XI.
43	1C	LAMBDA.
44	3B	GAMMA.
45	2B	XI.

expressed some doubt about the name of each subsequent D-stimulus. In contrast, with the exception only of trial 15, he named B- and C-stimuli without qualification. In trials 40 and 41, the child even emphasized the contrast himself. During the second half of the test, 45 more trials, Subject E.W. continued consistently to indicate uncertainty in naming the D-stimuli.

If the four-member classes, revealed by the four-stage BD and DB tests, arose through equivalence relations, the data must also possess certain internal consistencies. Reference to Figure 6-2 will help clarify the prerequisites for four-member classes. Given the explicitly taught relations, AB, AC, and DC, the following transitivity paradigm (TR1) constituted the simplest route for the emergence of the DB relations, in which the children matched Set-D samples to Set-B comparisons:

(TR1) *If DC and CB, then DB*

Any child able to do DB must also have been capable of DC and CB. The explicitly taught DC relations were easily verified in the baseline but CB, never explicitly taught, had to be tested. All six children who were able to do DB performed well in their CB tests.

The CB relations, in which the children matched Set-C samples to Set-B comparisons, could have emerged through the transitivity paradigm:

(TR2) *If CA and AB, then CB.*

Any child able to do CB must also have been capable of CA and AB. Again, the baselines verified the AB relations. The CA relations could have emerged through symmetry paradigm SY1:

(SY1) *If AC, then CA.*

The current procedures precluded direct tests of symmetry in the auditory-visual relations, AB, AC, and AD because the children would have been required to match visual samples to auditory comparisons; presenting several auditory comparisons simultaneously was not feasible. The CA relations, indicative of AC symmetry, were therefore not tested.

The other four-stage test, BD, called for different prerequisites. Matching the Set-B samples to Set-D comparisons could have emerged by transitivity through:

(TR3) *If BC and CD, then BD.*

Any child able to do BD must also have been capable of BC and CD, although neither had been explicitly taught. All six children who were able to do BD performed well also in their BC and CD tests. The

BC relations could themselves have emerged by transitivity:

(TR4)   *If BA and AC, then BC.*

Here, the baselines verified the AC relations. BA would have been indicative of AB symmetry:

(SY2)   *If AB, then BA.*

Again, however, auditory-visual symmetry could not be tested directly.

Emergence of the second BD prerequisite, the CD relations (see TR3), proved the visual-visual DC relations to be symmetric:

(SY3)   *If DC, then CD.*

CD relations, indicative of DC symmetry, were prerequisite not only for the four-stage BD relations (by TR3) but for the three-stage AD relations also. The simplest route for the emergence of the AD relations was:

(TR5)   *If AC and CD, then AD.*

Baseline performances verified the AC relations, and children who proved capable of both AD

and BD did well also in the CD test (two did not have the CD test; see Figure 6-10).

All children, therefore, whose DB and BD performances signified the establishment of four-member stimulus classes also provided the necessary internal consistencies in their other data. The prerequisite lower-level relations were intact.

Subjects J.L. and J.O. failed to replicate the other six children's results, their BD and DB performances revealing the absence of the transitive properties (TR3 and TR5) required by four-stage equivalence relations. Might an absence of lower-level symmetry or transitivity have been responsible for the failure of these higher-level relations to emerge? Additional tests given to the two children who did not exhibit four-member stimulus classes are summarized sequentially in Table 6-5.

Subject J.L., whose failure to confirm four-stage equivalence occurred before the desirability of systematic followup had become evident, did not receive all of the tests needed for a complete evaluation of the relations between higher- and lower-level

Table 6-5

Subjects J.L. (upper section) and J.O. (lower section). Scores (percentage correct) during successive tests. Column headings refer to relations in Figure 6-2. 'Nam' denotes oral naming tests with the Set-B, C, and D stimuli. Starting with Subject J.O.'s Test 8, baseline and probe trials were unreinforced.

| | Equivalence | | | | | Sym | Nam | Baseline | | |
| | Four-stage | | Three-stage | | | | | | | |
Test No.	BD	DB	AD	BC	CB	CD	B,C,D	AB	AC	DC
J.L.-1	—	47	—	—	—	—	—	100	100	97
J.L.-2	—	—	40	—	—	—	—	—	100	97
J.L.-3	—	—	—	97	93	—	—	100	100	—
J.L.-4	—	17	—	—	—	—	—	97	100	100
J.O.-1	—	83	—	—	—	—	—	100	97	100
J.O.-2	50	—	—	—	—	—	—	100	87	97
J.O.-3	—	57	—	—	—	—	—	100	100	90
J.O.-4	—	60	—	—	—	—	—	100	97	100
J.O.-5	—	—	60	—	—	—	—	—	100	100
J.O.-6	—	43	—	—	—	—	—	100	100	97
J.O.-7	—	—	50	—	—	—	—	—	97	100
J.O.-8 **	—	50	—	—	—	—	—	97	93	100
J.O.-9	—	—	—	57	30	—	—	97	90	—
J.O.-10	—	—	—	—	—	37	—	—	—	67
J.O.-11	—	—	—	—	—	—	90	—	—	—
J.O.-12	—	10	—	—	—	—	—	83	97	93
J.O.-13	—	—	—	—	—	—	97	—	—	—

performances. The upper section of Table 6-5 shows that he scored only 47% in his first four-stage DB test and 40% when tested for the three-stage AD relations (Tests 1 and 2). Then, he achieved 97 and 93% in the other three-stage probes, BC and CB (Test 3). Repetition of the four-stage DB probes (Test 4) yielded a score of only 17%.

Subject J.L. failed to demonstrate four-member classes or three-member ACD classes (denoted by the lower triangle in Figure 6-2) but did substantiate the formation of three-member ABC classes (the upper triangle in Figure 6-2). Strong DC relations in the baseline (righthand column of Table 6-5) and solid CB performances (Test 3)

216

showed the prerequisites for four-stage DB equivalence (see TR1) to be intact. Subject J.L.'s followup tests, therefore, did not supply any obvious explanation for the failure of DB to emerge. Unfortunately, the other four-stage relations, BD, were not evaluated, nor were the CD relations, absence of which would have clarified the failure of AD (see TR5) to emerge.

The other subject, J.O., had a more adequate series of followup tests (lower section of Table 6-5). His first four-stage test yielded 83% correct; he gave no more than two incorrect responses in 10 opportunities with any Set-D sample. When BD was probed, however, he scored only 50% (Test 2). Then, in two more DB tests, his score dropped to 57 and 60% from its initially high level. Whether the BD test had somehow degraded the DB performance or whether DB would have deteriorated anyway cannot be determined. Nevertheless, Subject J.O.'s first four tests provided no convincing evidence of four-member stimulus classes. A series of tests then undertook to determine whether these failures to document four-stage equivalence were

accompanied by the absence of one or more of the prerequisite lower-level relations.

AD probes came next (Test 5) and the low score of 60% indicated that the three-member ACD classes (lower triangle in Figure 6-2) had not formed. Because the auditory-visual AD probes might have helped to reinstate the DB relations, DB was tested once again; the outcome this time was only 43% (Test 6). Repetition of the AD probe (Test 7) then yielded another low score (50%).

Since reinforcement occasionally followed baseline trials but never probe trials, the deterioration of Subject J.O.'s performances after his first test might have come about because he had discriminated these contingencies. Subsequent tests therefore omitted reinforcement after all trials, probe and baseline. The child was told, "No pennies this time—we'll do colors with pennies later." To accustom him to the extinction procedure, he was given sets of unreinforced baseline trials, with no probes, until he maintained the requisite accuracy. Then, with baseline accuracies remaining high during his first extinction test

(Test 8), the DB probes again gave a score of only 50%.

BC and CB, the next probes (Test 9), yielded 57 and 30% correct, indicating that three-member ABC classes (upper triangle in Figure 6-2) also had not formed. The child's low CB score could have accounted for the failure of the four-stage DB relations to emerge (see TR1). His low BC score revealed the absence of prerequisites for BD, the other four-stage relations (see TR3). Then, a score of only 37% in Test 10's CD probes revealed that the DC relations were not symmetric. (CD probe trials actually disrupted the child's DC baseline—Table 6-5's righthand column shows no other test in which the DC baseline fell below 90%.) The absence of DC symmetry (see SY3) could by itself have accounted for the failures both of the four-stage BD and the three-stage AD relations to emerge (transitivity paradigms TR3 and TR5, respectively).

Subject J.O.'s poor performances on the four-stage DB and BD tests and on the three-stage AD test had therefore proven consistent with the absence of one or more prerequisites. Indeed, none of the testable

prerequisites had emerged. When tested for naming, however, he scored 90% (Test 11). Since naming the letters might have helped establish the equivalence relations, he was given the DB test once again; this time, he achieved only 10% (Test 12). A repetition of naming (Test 13) then yielded another high score (97%).

DISCUSSION

Having learned three sets of conditional discriminations, AB, AC, and DC (solid arrows in Figure 6-2), six of the eight children proved capable of six new sets of conditional discriminations they had not been explicitly taught: DB, BD, AD, BC, CB, and CD (broken arrows in Figure 6-2). Their BD and DB performances documented the emergence of three four-member stimulus classes, and all six children demonstrated the necessary lower-level transitive and symmetric properties in the relations among class members. Without such consistency in the prerequisites, the stimulus-class formulation would need major modification if it was to remain useful. When asked what the letters were, the children called them "lambda," "xi," and "gamma," in accord with class memberships the procedures had established. Each *if...then* relation was also an equivalence relation; the conditional-discrimination procedures had generated matching-to-sample performances.

The efficiency of the four-stage equivalence paradigm in generating new performances endows it with considerable practicality; the very process of equivalence testing yields a remarkable teaching spinoff. After the children were explicitly taught nine different sample-comparison relations (three represented by each solid arrow in Figure 6-2), 18 new stimulus relations (three represented by each broken arrow in Figure 6-2) and nine new oral naming relations emerged. The ratio of emergent to directly taught performances was 27/9.

Teaching efficiency increased as the stimulus classes grew in size. For example, the three-stage paradigm denoted by ABC in Figure 6-2 depicts six directly established stimulus relations, three represented by AB and three by AC. Six more stimulus relations (three in BC and three in CB) and six oral naming

relations (B- and C-naming) emerged from this teaching; emergent performances exceeded those directly taught by a factor of two. Then, building the four-stage paradigm by teaching the children to match three samples from Set D to comparisons in Set C added 12 more stimulus relations (three each in AD, CD, DB, and BD) and three additional oral naming relations (D-naming) to their repertoires; three directly taught performances now generated 15 emergent performances, a factor of five. This 2.5-fold increase in teaching efficiency with the addition of a single member to each stimulus class hints at the potentially explosive nature of the process.

The performances involved here are in principle far from trivial. Matching auditory to visual stimuli (AB, AC, and AD) can represent simple auditory comprehension—understanding spoken words in reference to text; matching visual stimuli to each other (BD, DB, BC, CB, CD, and DC) can constitute simple reading comprehension—understanding text in reference to other objects; naming textual stimuli aloud can be simple oral reading. Most tests designed to evaluate aspects of reading include similar tasks. Nevertheless, formal resemblances between conditional discrimination and reading do not prove one relevant to the other. The establishment of stimulus classes does prove this relevance. Pointing to a picture in response to a printed word denotes reading comprehension only if the word and picture are related by equivalence and not merely by conditionality. Stimulus classes formed by a network of equivalence relations establish a basis for referential meaning. The equivalence paradigm provides exactly the test that is needed to determine whether or not a particular conditional discrimination involves semantic relations.

Linguistic analysis has challenged functional behavioral analysis to account for new behavior that has no apparent reinforcement history (e.g., Chomsky, 1965; Fodor, Bever, & Garrett, 1974). The equivalence paradigm takes a short step in this direction by specifying procedures for generating new and seemingly unreinforced matching to sample and oral naming.

In revealing a class whose members are related by equivalence, the paradigm also exposes a source of reinforcement for the new behavior. By definition, the existence of a class of equivalent stimuli permits any variable that affects one member of the class to affect all members. Even when stimuli bear no physical resemblance to each other, their inclusion within a class provides a route for extending the influence of reinforcement and other variables. Direct reinforcement of the AB, AC, and DC relations (Figure 6-2) extends also to all of the other possible relations within each four-member class. It is therefore not correct to assume that the new matching and naming performances emerged without a reinforcement history.

The children's ability to name the letters in Sets B and C confirmed earlier experiments that used other kinds of stimuli (Sidman, 1971b; Sidman & Cresson, 1973; Sidman et al., 1974). Their consistent naming of the Set-D letters was of special interest since they had never been taught explicitly to select those letters conditionally upon dictated-name samples. Two subjects (E.M. and I.C., Table 6-3) even did the naming test before their ability to match Set-D stimuli to dictated names was tested. The production of Set-D names that were consistent with classes revealed in the matching-to-sample tests raised the possibility that naming might have been needed to mediate the emergent conditional relations. An earlier study, in which a few new conditional relations emerged before subjects were able to name the stimuli, suggested that stimulus equivalence was independent of naming (Sidman et al., 1974). Here, Subject E.W. gave all the stimuli names that were consistent with their class membership but his hesitations and expressions of doubt (Table 6-4) indicated strongly that although he was capable of naming the Set-D letters, he had never done so until the naming test. The new conditional discriminations involving the D-stimuli emerged before he had ever applied names to those letters.

Subject E.W. was the only one of the eight who yielded such a finding but his demonstration that the stimulus classes could form in the absence of naming cannot be dismissed. Although naming, when it occurs, may indeed facilitate equivalence relations, Subject E.W.'s responses argue strongly against the necessity of such a role. Given that naming is not necessary for class formation, the likelihood and nature of a facilitative role remain matters for experimental study.

Table 6-4's naming transcription indicated that stimulus classes could emerge via equivalence relations even before a subject had applied a consistent name to each member of a class; naming was not necessary. Subject J.O.'s naming tests (Table 6-5) showed that consistent naming was not sufficient to establish stimulus classes via equivalence relations. He applied "lambda," "xi," and "gamma" to the letters of Sets B, C, and D in accord with the very four-member classes that the equivalence tests had failed to substantiate. He named the Set-D letters consistently in spite of his inability to match those letters to their dictated names. A response that is common to several stimuli may define a class (Goldiamond, 1962) but does not by itself establish equivalence relations among the class members. Upon reflection, the dichotomy shown here between classes defined by naming and classes defined by equivalence is not surprising; the relation, *is the name of,* does not possess the defining properties of an equivalence relation (Table 6-1).

It might have been tempting to view naming as an indirect test of symmetry in the auditory-visual relations, AB, AC, and AD. Instead of presenting dictated-name comparisons, oral naming tests permitted the children to produce the names themselves in response to the printed letters. It seems reasonable to presume that children who could name printed letters aloud would also be able to select those names when they heard them spoken by someone else. Subject J.O., however, proved this reasonable presumption to be incorrect. His accurate production of the Set-D letter names, after showing himself unable to match those letters to their dictated names, demonstrated that emergent naming did not constitute a valid test of auditory-visual symmetry. Again, a possible relation between naming and equivalence proved illusory.

Formal resemblances exist between the accounts of stimulus equivalence arising from conditional-discrimination and paired-associate procedures. The paired-associate literature refers to symmetry as *backward association* (e.g., Ekstrand, 1966), to transitivity as *chaining,* and to equivalence paradigms A and B (Table 6-1) as r*esponse equivalence* and *stimulus equivalence,* respectively (e.g., Jenkins, 1963). A thorough comparison of the formulation derived from the paired-associate tradition and the one proposed here must await a more appropriate vehicle but at least one fundamental distinction that the terminological similarities might mask is relevant here. Paired-associate methods, which often require a subject to respond differentially to each stimulus by producing its "name," have led to widespread acceptance of response mediation as the mechanism responsible for the establishment of equivalence relations (e.g., Jenkins, 1963, 1965; Jenkins & Palermo, 1964). Although it is clear that differential responses can mediate the emergence of new stimulus relations, the successful use of conditional discriminations to generate equivalences raises considerable doubt about the necessity for postulating the existence of mediating responses. Conditional discrimination requires no differential responses to individual stimuli; the only necessary overt response is pointing or touching, which is the same for all sample and comparison stimuli. It is sometimes said that the subject responds differentially to each sample by choosing a particular comparison but this "choosing" response can be defined only with reference to a stimulus (Sidman, 1978). Conditional discrimination therefore involves relations between stimuli. It is not possible to obviate this conclusion, as some have attempted, by reserving the term, *stimulus*, for sample stimuli and applying the term, *response*, to comparison stimuli. Thus, in addition to evidence cited above that shows naming to be neither necessary nor sufficient for generating stimulus equivalences, the very logic of the conditional-discrimination procedure suggests also that no other kind of mediating response need be postulated.

* * * * * * * * *

Commentary

We had taken our giant step. Moving from three- to four-member classes significantly expanded the potential practical and theoretical utility of our way of analyzing equivalence relations. In the next ten years, the number of publications, symposia, and convention presentations on equivalence relations also expanded significantly. It was almost as though others—both students and established researchers—had been waiting for just such a demonstration of significance before looking more closely at the phenomenon we and a few others had been trying so carefully to define. Behavior analysts had been under intense attack—not always justified—for failing to extend their science to ever more complex kinds of human conduct. Equivalence relations began to look like a new and constructive reply to that criticism.

The Combined Test for Equivalence

In discussing Tests A and B in Table 6-1, we pointed out that these required not just transitivity in the baseline relation but symmetry also. The emergence of BC, for example, requires the baseline AB conditional discrimination to be symmetric and the emergence of CB requires AC symmetry. This can perhaps be seen more conveniently in Figure 6-1. Because these tests evaluated transitivity and symmetry simultaneously, we called them *combined* tests for *equivalence* (and later, *abbreviated* tests). The intention here was to differentiate tests for individual properties of an equivalence relation from tests that required two or even all three of those properties. (A full appreciation of the place of reflexivity was not to come until later, in Johnson and Sidman, 1993.) Eventually, we dropped the term *combined*; when a test required all of the properties of an equivalence relation, we just called it an *equivalence test*.

Justification for substituting a combined equivalence test in place of individual tests for specific properties rested on the assumption that the combined test does indeed reflect the presence or absence of the individual properties. To validate this assumption, it was necessary to show that when an equivalence test proved positive, individual tests for reflexivity, symmetry, and transitivity were also positive. It was also necessary to show that when an equivalence test proved negative, one or more of the individual tests was also negative. The data in the *Class Expansion* paper were consistent with these requirements and in later chapters we shall see additional confirmations. Not only are negative equivalence tests accompanied by negative tests of individual properties but when continued testing brings in the individual properties, the equivalence tests also become positive. At the time, we experienced these observations as breathtaking confirmations of the validity of our analysis, but we and others have now replicated them so frequently, both in published and unpublished studies, that they have become commonplace.

Class Size and Nodality

Several paradigms for increasing class size are available and many remain to be investigated. All are interesting but some more so than others. The simplest paradigm is CD1, below (assume that all stimuli are visual, with the left-hand member of each pair being the sample and the right-hand member the comparison). If an originally taught baseline of AB and AC conditional discriminations creates three-member ABC classes, adding AD conditional discriminations to the baseline might establish four-member ABCD classes; A-, B-, C-, and D-stimuli could become equivalent members of the same class. Subjects would then prove capable of all of the tested conditional discriminations, each derived from the original baseline.

[CD1]	Teach AB	
	Teach AC	
	Teach AD	
Test BA	Test CA	Test DA
Test BC	Test CB	Test DB
Test BD	Test CD	Test DC

Emergence of the BA, CA, and DA conditional discriminations would demonstrate that the baseline relation was symmetric. The other emergent conditional discriminations would demonstrate that the baseline relation was both symmetric and transitive, with transitivity coming about because each stimulus in a related pair was also related to the same A-stimulus. The A-stimuli therefore constitute training *nodes* (Fields & Verhave, 1987; Fields, Verhave, & Fath, 1984); they are the only stimuli that are conditionally related to more than one other stimulus in the baseline. Thus, even though the paradigm can generate four-member classes, the baseline contains only one node per class.

This paradigm is called "simple" only in comparison to other possibilities. The baseline in the *Class Expansion* paper contained two nodes. If all of the stimuli had been visual, the paradigm would be described by CD2, below. Here, both the A- and C- stimuli are related to two others (A to B and C; C to A and D). The baseline therefore contains two nodes, A and C, and consists of two sets of single-node relations: AB/AC and AC/DC.

[CD2]	Teach AB	
	Teach AC	
	Teach DC	

Test BA	Test CA	Test DA
Test BC	Test CB	Test DB
Test BD	Test CD	Test AD

Emergent conditional discriminations that would explicitly document symmetry in the baseline relation are BA and CA, as before, and now, CD also. Again, derived BC and CB conditional discriminations would imply both symmetry and transitivity in the one-node AB/AC segment of the baseline, and now, the AD and DA conditional discriminations would imply symmetry and transitivity in the one-node AC/DC segment. DB and BD are the most interesting tests, since the derivation of these conditional discriminations requires the A- *and* the C-nodes. If DB and BD are to emerge, the relation in *both* one-node baseline segments must be symmetric and transitive.

The DB and BD conditional discriminations, however, are not just symmetric versions of each other. If BD is to emerge, both AB and DC symmetry (BA and CD) are required. The derivation of DB, however, presupposes neither AB nor DC symmetry but only AC symmetry (CA). Because DB has fewer prerequisites, it can be considered a simpler two-node test than BD. Although we did not observe differences between DB and BD tests in the *Class Expansion* paper, we should not be surprised if differences do come to light in experiments that are designed to reveal them. (See pp. 541-542 for further discussion of this aspect of nodality.)

If I were to hazard a prediction about possible limits to the number of equivalent stimuli that a class could contain, I would guess that the existence of such a limit would become more likely as the number of nodes in the baseline conditional discriminations increased. In the next chapter (pp. 267-271), I shall describe an attempt to capitalize on this possibility, but definitive experiments on class-size limitations have yet to be carried out.

Naming and Auditory-Visual Matching: Symmetrical Relations?

In the *Class Expansion* paper, we discussed the notion that the visual-letter naming task might be the symmetric version of matching the visual letter to its dictated name. The naming task involved relations between letters and names spoken by the subject; the matching task involved relations between letters and names spoken to the subject. In spite of the reasonable expectation that naming stimuli aloud and matching those stimuli to names spoken by others would be two sides of the same coin, Subject J.O. named letters accurately even though he failed to match the letters to their dictated names.

In everyday observation, too, a distinction is commonly made between *recognition* and *production*. For example, when meeting someone, we are often unable to produce the person's name, but if given the name, we are able to pick that person out of a crowd of others. This is an instance of name-face matching in the absence of face-naming. In the laboratory, we have observed additional instances of accurate auditory-visual matching and auditory-visual equivalence in the absence of consistent naming (Chapters 2 and 8).

We cannot, therefore, automatically take accurate naming to imply accurate auditory-visual matching. Nor can we automatically take accurate auditory-visual matching to imply accurate naming. In testing for equivalence, neither of these will serve as a substitute for the other.

7

More on Expanding Classes: A Coup

Background

Because the conditional-discrimination procedure we were using required correct and incorrect comparisons to be present at the same time, we could not make a direct test for symmetry in any conditional discrimination that involved auditory samples. Having taught someone AB and AC conditional relations in which the A-samples were auditory, we could not then test directly for the emergence of BA and CA conditional discriminations; only with great difficulty would subjects be able to discriminate among several auditory A-stimuli that were sounded simultaneously as comparisons. We could, therefore, only infer symmetry from the emergence of the BC and CB conditional discriminations. It would be good to be able to test each property of equivalence directly, without having to rely on inference. (See Dube, Green, and Serna, 1993, for a conditional-discrimination technique that permits the presentation of auditory stimuli as comparisons.)

Although all of our previously published studies had involved auditory stimuli, we had little doubt that a purely visual paradigm would give us the complete analysis we needed. This conviction was strengthened by our experimental analysis of the visual triangle in the *Class Expansion* paper (Figure 6-2). Indeed, several investigators had already extended the analysis to purely visual classes of equivalent stimuli (Lazar, 1977; Lazar et al., 1984; Spradlin et al., 1973; Stromer & Osborne, 1982; Wetherby et al., 1983). Still, equivalence relations based on auditory-visual and visual-visual conditional discriminations might differ. We therefore did an experiment not only to determine whether our analysis was applicable to visual-visual conditional discriminations but to compare the outcomes of equivalence tests in auditory-visual and purely visual baselines. That experiment produced the *Role of Naming* paper, which is to be presented in Chapter 8 but is mentioned here because it set the occasion for the following *Six-Member Classes* paper. The later paper is presented out of sequence because it continues the main theme of the *Class Expansion* paper (Chapter 6).

In the *Role of Naming* study, we taught individual subjects two independent sets of conditional discriminations: AB and AC, in which the A-samples were auditory; DE and DF, in which all stimuli were visual. When the *Role of Naming* study had been completed, therefore, we had several subjects with whom we had worked long and hard to develop and test the baseline depicted in Figure 7-1. Experimenters rarely have an opportunity to study complex human behavior whose origin has been so well controlled. What could we do to take advantage of the repertoires we had painstakingly constructed in the laboratory?

An elegant possibility presented itself. If our analysis was valid, a relatively small amount of additional teaching should bring about a veritable explosion in the size of a subject's repertoire of conditional discriminations. After teaching only one more set of conditional discriminations (EC in Figure 7-2), we should be able to observe the emergent performances that are diagrammed in Figure 7-3.

Before this experiment was published, I described it and its background many times in convention and seminar talks. I used to say, presumably in jest, that if the structure depicted in Figure 7-3 actually emerged, I would have to believe I had reached the pinnacle of my career and should retire. Fortunately (for me), even though the experimental results did confirm the utility of our analysis of equivalence relations, enough complications arose to make more studies necessary; I did not have to retire yet.

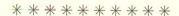

Six-Member Stimulus Classes Generated by Conditional-Discrimination Procedures

In conditional-discrimination procedures with three sets of stimuli, A, B, and C, three stimuli per set (A1A2A3, B1B2B3, and C1C2C3), subjects (children and adults) learned to select Set-B and Set-C comparisons conditionally upon Set-A samples (A1B1, A1C1, A2B2, A2C2, A3B3, A3C3). If the conditional-discrimination procedures also generated equivalence relations, three three-member stimulus classes would be demonstrable, A1B1C1, A2B2C2, and A3B3C3. In addition to these three sets, the present experiments used three other sets of stimuli—D, E, and F. The subjects learned to select Set-E and Set-F comparisons conditionally upon Set-D samples (D1E1, D1F1, D2E2, D2F2, D3E3, D3F3). This established a second group of three three-member stimulus classes, D1E1F1, D2E2F2, and D3E3F3. In all, two groups of three three-member classes were established by teaching subjects 12 conditional discriminations. The two groups of three-member classes were then combined (successfully for five of eight subjects) into a single group of three six-member classes by teaching the subjects three more conditional relations (E1C1, E2C2, and E3C3). With three other children, enlarging the classes one member at a time also produced six-member classes. As a consequence of class formation, 60 untrained conditional relations emerged from 15 that had been explicitly taught. Six of the subjects also proved capable of naming the stimuli consistently in accord with their class membership, but two subjects demonstrated class formation even in the absence of consistent naming.

Procedures for teaching subjects conditional discriminations may also generate equivalence relations; sample stimuli may become equivalent to their corresponding comparison stimuli. If they do, the three defining properties of equivalence relations—reflexivity, symmetry, and transitivity—will be demonstrable. In brief, one can test directly for those properties as follows (see Sidman et al., 1982, for a more detailed derivation). Reflexivity requires generalized identity matching. Symmetry

231

requires the subject to be capable of reversing the sample and comparison function of stimuli in the conditional discriminations; after having been taught AB (selecting Comparison B conditionally upon Sample A), the subject will be capable of a new conditional discrimination, BA (selecting Comparison A conditionally upon Sample B). If transitivity applies, a new conditional discrimination, AC, will emerge after the subject has been taught two other conditional discriminations, AB and BC, in which Stimulus B served as a comparison in one and as a sample in the other.

Figure 7-1 outlines a method for determining whether conditional relations, taught to subjects who can do generalized identity matching, also possess the other properties that define equivalence. In the upper "triangle," subjects are first taught to select Greek-letter comparison stimuli in Sets B and C conditionally upon dictated letter-name samples from Set A; they learn to choose upper- and lower-case delta when "delta" is the sample, upper- and lower-case sigma when "sigma" is the sample, upper- and lower-case xi

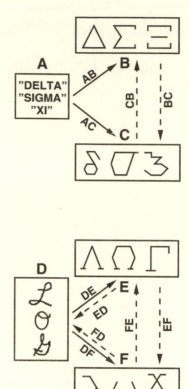

Figure. 7-1. Each box represents a set of three stimuli. Arrows representing conditional relations point from sample to comparison stimuli. The stimuli are arranged, for expository purposes, so that auditory "delta" or script L are matched to the letter on the left in each box, "sigma" or script O to the center letter, and "xi" or script G to the letter on the right; in all other instances, letters are matched to each other according to their relative positions in the boxes. The four solid arrows represent 12 conditional relations taught by explicit reinforcement procedures; the six broken arrows represent 18 emergent relations.

when "xi" is the sample. Then, in tests without reinforcement, the subjects match to each other those Set-B and Set-C letters that they had learned to match to the same dictated name: upper- and lower-case delta, upper- and lower-case sigma, upper- and lower-case xi.

Emergence of these new conditional discriminations signifies the formation of three three-member classes of equivalent stimuli, each class containing a dictated letter name from Set A, a Set-B letter, and a Set-C letter. Such auditory-visual classes have been demonstrated with human subjects and several kinds of stimuli (Mackay & Sidman, 1984; Sidman, 1971b, 1977; Sidman & Cresson, 1973; Sidman et al., 1974; Sidman & Tailby, 1982; Sidman et al., 1986). The existence of classes of equivalent stimuli makes it possible for the subjects, who are explicitly taught six conditional relations (three AB and three AC), to match the three B-samples to appropriate C-comparisons and vice versa (three BC and three CB relations); six new conditional relations emerge without having been explicitly taught.

The auditory stimuli in Set A cannot be presented simultaneously as comparisons, a methodological limitation that precludes BA and CA tests. In the lower triangle, however, all stimuli are visual. Subjects learn to select each Greek-letter comparison in Sets E and F conditionally upon a particular English script letter from Set D. Again, three three-member classes emerge, subjects matching those Set-E and Set-F letters to each other which they had learned to match to the same Set-D sample. Such visual classes have also been demonstrated with human subjects and several kinds of stimuli (Lazar, 1977; Lazar et al., 1984; Lazar & Kotlarchyk, 1980; Sidman et al., 1982, 1986; Spradlin et al., 1973; Stromer & Osborne, 1982; Wetherby et al., 1983). Because the Set-D stimuli are visual, one can evaluate the DE and DF relations for symmetry by testing whether subjects will match samples from Sets E and F to Set-D comparisons (ED and FD relations). Although symmetry has not yet been unequivocally demonstrated with nonhuman subjects (Sidman et al., 1982), humans do show symmetry in conditional relations (Lazar et al., 1984; Sidman and Tailby, 1982; Sidman et al., 1986; Stromer & Osborne, 1982; Wetherby et al., 1983).

In the lower triangle, then, the existence of classes of equivalent stimuli makes it possible for subjects who have been explicitly taught six relations (three DE and three DF) to match three Set-E samples to appropriate Set-F comparisons and vice versa (three EF and three FE relations) and to match each Set-E and Set-F sample to appropriate Set-D comparisons (three ED and three FD relations); 12 new conditional relations emerge without having been explicitly taught.

Each of the four solid arrows AB, AC, DE, and DF denotes three conditional relations that a subject has been explicitly taught. Each of the six broken arrows BC, CB, EF, FE, ED, and FD denotes three emergent relations. If the 12 explicitly taught relations are also equivalence relations, the subject will be capable of 18 new conditional discriminations. The ratio of emergent to explicitly taught conditional discriminations is 3:2. One may appreciate the potential

scope of the process of equivalence formation by considering the expansion of this ratio if a subject who has learned AB, AC, DE, and DF were then to be taught just three more conditional discriminations, denoted in Figure 7-2 by the solid arrow EC.

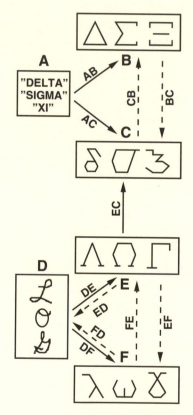

Figure. 7-2. The relations represented are as in Figure 7-1, with the addition of the three EC relations taught by explicit reinforcement procedures.

234

The subject now learns to select each comparison letter in Set C conditionally upon a particular sample from Set E; a member of each DEF class is matched to a member of each ABC class. If the new EC conditional relations were also equivalence relations, this linkage should combine the two groups of three three-member classes into one group of three six-member classes, each class containing one element from each of the six stimulus sets. The subject should then be able to match *any* two members of a class to each other.

Figure 7-3 depicts the potential for expansion of the emergent performances. Learning the three EC relations should add 42 new conditional discriminations to the subject's repertoire. In sum, the explicit teaching of 15 relations (three each in AB, AC, EC, DE, and DF) should generate 60 new relations (three denoted by each broken arrow). Combining the two groups of three-member classes into one group of six-member classes should therefore increase the ratio of emergent to explicitly taught conditional discriminations from 3:2 to 4:1. The present experiments explored several teaching and testing sequences to determine whether conditional-discrimination procedures would generate six-member classes of equivalent stimuli and to ascertain the composition of the emergent relations.

GENERAL METHOD

Subjects were pretested on conditional-discrimination and oral-naming procedures with familiar stimuli and for generalized identity matching with all letters that were to be used as experimental stimuli. Then, the baseline for the equivalence tests was established by teaching subjects the five groups of conditional discriminations denoted by solid arrows in Figure 7-2: AB, AC, DE, DF, and EC. Next, the existence of stimulus classes was evaluated by testing subjects for each of the 20 groups of conditional discriminations denoted by broken arrows in Figure 7-3; emergence of conditional relations FB and BF would demonstrate the existence of six-member classes and others would demonstrate five-, four-, and three-member classes and

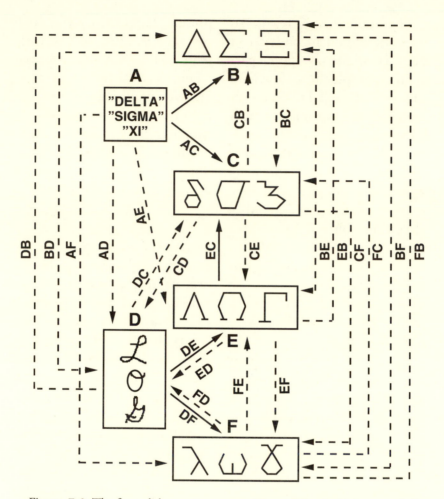

Figure. 7-3. The five solid arrows represent 15 conditional relations taught by explicit reinforcement procedures; the 20 broken arrows represent 60 emergent relations.

symmetry of the conditional relations. Finally, oral naming of the stimuli was tested. Variations in the procedures for establishing the baseline and in the method of alternating the teaching and testing phases will be noted.

Apparatus

Subjects sat before nine trans-lucent touch-sensitive keys onto which stimuli were projected from the rear. The keys, each 7.3 cm in diameter, were arranged in a circle of eight, with a ninth in the center. Sidman and Tailby (1982) have described additional features and dimensions of a similar projection and response system. The present experiments used only the center key and the lowest three keys in the circle. Automatic dispensers, mounted in an enclosure adjacent to the keys, delivered pennies or tokens into an open plastic receptacle below and at the right of the keys. The sound of chimes, mounted 1 m above the keys, helped to bridge the time pennies or tokens took to fall from the dispenser into the tray. A Nova minicomputer programmed the procedures. Data were also recorded online by printing counters, a 20-pen Esterline-Angus operations recorder, and an experimenter who was seated behind the subject.

Conditional-Discrimination Procedures

Each trial began with a sample stimulus, visual samples being on the center key and auditory samples being dictated and repeated by a tape loop (Fletcher et al., 1971). Visual and auditory samples never occurred together. When the subject pushed the sample key after a sample was presented, comparison stimuli appeared on the other three keys. With dictated samples, pressing the blank center key could not produce comparisons until at least one complete sample word had sounded. Each sample remained, along with the comparisons, until the subject pressed a comparison key.

Unless a reduced reinforcement probability or a probe trial precluded reinforcement, correct choices were followed by the sound of chimes, the disappearance of all stimuli, the delivery of a penny or token, and a 1.5-s intertrial interval. No chimes, penny, or token followed incorrect choices. Subjects traded their tokens for money, often buying snacks or toys after the session. They kept all money they did not spend.

Positions of correct and incorrect stimuli varied among the three comparison keys from trial to trial. All sample-comparison combinations and all correct keys were equally probable on successive trials, with the following restrictions: Starting with the first trial, within groups of three successive trials each key had to be scheduled as correct; trial sequences that included only two

237

different samples (during training) had no more than three consecutive trials with the same sample; with more than two samples, all possible combinations of sample and comparison stimuli had to occur before any could repeat.

Pressing any key during an intertrial interval postponed the next sample for 1.5 s. Once a sample had come on, the subject could not produce comparison stimuli by pressing sample and comparison keys simultaneously and had to break contact with all keys before a new sample press could be effective. Once comparisons had come on, pressing the sample no longer had programmed consequences. If the subject pressed an incorrect or blank key simultaneously with a correct comparison, the trial was scored as incorrect. A correct response was not defined until the subject had released the key for .2 s; pressure on another key during the preceding press or within .2 s of a release defined a simultaneous response. A computer programmed the procedures.

Oral Naming Procedures

Oral naming tests presented only samples, with no compari-

sons. Subjects pressed no keys but were asked, "Tell me what you see" or "What is it?" After each reply the experimenter, seated behind the subject, pressed a switch to initiate the intertrial interval and the slide change. Subjects received no chimes, pennies, or tokens, even for "correct" names. Their responses were recorded by the experimenter and on magnetic tape. As a reliability check, a second experimenter recorded the responses from the tape, in the absence of the visual stimuli to which the subject had been responding. There was never more than one disagreement between the two records in a 90-trial naming test.

Pretraining and Pretests

Subjects who were unfamiliar with the laboratory began with a program that taught them a circle versus ellipse discrimination, with stimuli appearing only on the outer keys (Sidman & Stoddard, 1966, 1967). Then, matching to sample was introduced with hues as stimuli. First, pressing the center key when a hue was projected on it brought the same hue onto one of the outer comparison keys; pressing the single comparison produced a reinforcer. Next, nonmatching comparison hues were also introduced and subjects quickly learned to select the one that was the same as the sample. Hue names were then dictated as samples, with the visual comparisons, after which oral naming of the hues was tested. In the final pretests, which used the visual stimuli illustrated in Figure 7-1, the sample and correct comparison were the same and the two incorrect comparisons were the other letters in the same set. All subjects performed accurately on all of these procedures, demonstrating their ability to do auditory-visual matching, oral naming, and generalized identity matching.

Baseline Teaching

Standard accuracy criterion. To advance from one teaching step to another, subjects had to achieve an overall score of at least 90% correct. In addition, they could make no more than one error on any trial type (combination of sample and comparisons).

The baseline. Subjects were taught the groups of baseline conditional discriminations represented by solid arrows in Figure 7-1. The sequence in which they learned the elements of this baseline varied among experiments. Figure 7-4 depicts the sample and comparison stimuli in the 15 trial types that all subjects were explicitly taught. These trial types would constitute a baseline into which probe trials would be inserted to evaluate the existence of equivalence relations.

TASK	SAMPLE	CORRECT	INCORRECT
AB1	"DELTA"	Δ	Σ, Ξ
AC1	"DELTA"	δ	σ, ʒ
EC1	Λ	δ	σ, ʒ
DE1	ℒ	Λ	Ω, Γ
DF1	ℒ	λ	ω, ɣ
AB2	"SIGMA"	Σ	Δ, Ξ
AC2	"SIGMA"	σ	δ, ʒ
EC2	Ω	σ	δ, ʒ
DE2	θ	Ω	Λ, Γ
DF2	θ	ω	λ, ɣ
AB3	"XI"	Ξ	Δ, Σ
AC3	"XI"	ʒ	δ, σ
EC3	Γ	ʒ	δ, σ
DE3	ƀ	Γ	Λ, Ω
DF3	ƀ	ɣ	λ, ω

Figure 7-4. The sample and three comparison stimuli (one correct and two incorrect) in the 15 baseline conditional discriminations that all subjects were explicitly taught (see Figure 2). The numbers 1, 2, and 3 specify the expected class membership of the sample and correct comparison in each trial type. These trial types were presented to the subjects in mixed sequences. Quotation marks around the name of a letter indicate that the stimulus was auditory.

At the beginning of each new teaching session, subjects had once again to meet the learning criterion on their most advanced performance. If they failed to do so, they were returned to an earlier teaching step before advancing through the teaching sequence again. The number of teaching trials and the duration of teaching sessions varied considerably but unsystematically from subject to subject and, within subjects, from phase to phase. Subjects sometimes required only the minimum number of trials to learn a baseline element and at other times needed review and reteaching before they could reach or maintain criterion performance. Most sessions lasted about 30 min but they ranged from 15 to 60 min in duration

Conditional-Discrimination Tests

Tests had 27 trials of a group of three untrained relations (each group denoted by a broken arrow in Figure 7-3) inserted as probes among 45 baseline trials (Figure 7-4). Subjects received no chimes, pennies, or tokens on probe trials. In preparation for unreinforced probes, the baseline reinforcement probability for two subjects (see Experiment 1) was gradually reduced to .20. The program for reducing the reinforcement probability while ensuring the maintenance of high baseline accuracy has been described by Sidman et al. (1986). All other subjects, however, had 27-trial tests with no reinforcement on any trials, baseline or probe. To ensure that they could maintain high accuracy, they had first to achieve the standard criterion on baseline trials without reinforcement. After extinction training and after tests, they were given enough hue-hue or picture-picture matching trials to make up for missed baseline reinforcements.

Sessions in which a test was scheduled began with a review of the baseline, with reinforcement. To proceed to the test, subjects had to meet the standard criterion. Any subject who failed several times to achieve criterion returned to an earlier teaching step and advanced through the teaching sequence again.

Oral naming tests. Each test had 90 unreinforced trials, six presentations each of the B-, C-, D-, E-, and F-stimuli.

240

EXPERIMENT 1

Conditional relations that are also equivalence relations will be reflexive, symmetric, and transitive. If the relations diagrammed in Figure 7-3 were equivalence relations, one could use transitivity to identify the sufficient prerequisites for the FB and BF relations: (1) For a subject to match Set-F samples to Set-B comparisons (FB) without being explicitly taught to do so, the FE, EC, and CB relations are prerequisites; (2) to match Set-B samples to Set-F comparisons (BF), the BC, CE, and EF relations are prerequisites; (3) BC and CB, themselves, require the explicitly taught AB and AC relations; EF and FE require DE and DF. Emergence of FB and BF therefore demands the involvement of all six sets of stimuli and would provide the first indication that the baseline teaching had established six-member classes.

In the event that six-member classes did form, the subject should then be able to do more than match the Set-B and Set-F stimuli to each other. Even without having been explicitly taught to do so, the subject should be able to match *any* two members of a class. All of the conditional discriminations denoted by the broken arrows in Figure 7-3 should emerge, providing final proof that the baseline teaching had established six-member stimulus classes.

Because six sets of stimuli are necessary for the FB and BF relations to emerge, these may be called *six-stage* equivalence relations (a terminology adapted from the paired-associate literature—e.g., Jenkins, 1963). The concept of stages, different from class size, is useful because *n*-member classes can exist even though no component relation requires more than three sets of stimuli (stages) for its derivation (e.g., see Lazar et al., 1984). Figure 7-5 classifies all of the potential relations in the present experiment according to stages and illustrates the actual conditional discriminations for which subjects were tested. At the upper left (six-stage) are the three BF and the three FB trial types; the five-stage section illustrates nine trial types in the three groups of relations (BD, DB, and AF) that require five sets of stimuli for their derivation (FA could not be tested because the Set-A stimuli

6-STAGE

TASK	SAMPLE	CORRECT	INCORRECT
BF1	Δ	λ	ω , δ
BF2	Σ	ω	λ , δ
BF3	Ξ	δ	λ , ω
FB1	λ	Δ	Σ , Ξ
FB2	ω	Σ	Δ , Ξ
FB3	δ	Ξ	Δ , Σ

5-STAGE

TASK	SAMPLE	CORRECT	INCORRECT
BD1	Δ	ℒ	θ , ♭
BD2	Σ	θ	ℒ , ♭
BD3	Ξ	♭	ℒ , θ
DB1	ℒ	Δ	Σ , Ξ
DB2	θ	Σ	Δ , Ξ
DB3	♭	Ξ	Δ , Σ
AF1	"DELTA"	λ	ω , δ
AF2	"SIGMA"	ω	λ , δ
AF3	"XI"	δ	λ , ω

4-STAGE

TASK	SAMPLE	CORRECT	INCORRECT
BE1	Δ	Λ	Ω , Γ
BE2	Σ	Ω	Λ , Γ
BE3	Ξ	Γ	Λ , Ω
EB1	Λ	Δ	Σ , Ξ
EB2	Ω	Σ	Δ , Ξ
EB3	Γ	Ξ	Δ , Σ
CF1	δ	λ	ω , δ
CF2	⊓	ω	λ , δ
CF3	3	δ	λ , ω
FC1	λ	δ	⊓ , 3
FC2	ω	⊓	δ , 3
FC3	δ	3	δ , ⊓
AD1	"DELTA"	ℒ	θ , ♭
AD2	"SIGMA"	θ	ℒ , ♭
AD3	"XI"	♭	ℒ , θ

3-STAGE

TASK	SAMPLE	CORRECT	INCORRECT
BC1	Δ	δ	⊓ , 3
BC2	Σ	⊓	δ , 3
BC3	Ξ	3	δ , ⊓
CB1	δ	Δ	Σ , Ξ
CB2	⊓	Σ	Δ , Ξ
CB3	3	Ξ	Δ , Σ
EF1	Λ	λ	ω , δ
EF2	Ω	ω	λ , δ
EF3	Γ	δ	λ , ω
FE1	λ	Λ	Ω , Γ
FE2	ω	Ω	Λ , Γ
FE3	δ	Γ	Λ , Ω
CD1	δ	ℒ	θ , ♭
CD2	⊓	θ	ℒ , ♭
CD3	3	♭	ℒ , θ
DC1	ℒ	δ	⊓ , 3
DC2	θ	⊓	δ , 3
DC3	♭	3	δ , ⊓
AE1	"DELTA"	Λ	Ω , Γ
AE2	"SIGMA"	Ω	Λ , Γ
AE3	"XI"	Γ	Λ , Ω

SYMMETRY

TASK	SAMPLE	CORRECT	INCORRECT
CE1	δ	Λ	Ω , Γ
CE2	⊓	Ω	Λ , Γ
CE3	3	Γ	Λ , Ω
ED1	Λ	ℒ	θ , ♭
ED2	Ω	θ	ℒ , ♭
ED3	Γ	♭	ℒ , θ
FD1	λ	ℒ	θ , ♭
FD2	ω	θ	ℒ , ♭
FD3	δ	♭	ℒ , θ

Figure 7-5. The sample, "correct," and "incorrect" stimuli in each probed conditional discrimination. Because there was no reinforcement on probe trials, comparisons indicative of the expected equivalence relations were designated as correct. The numbers 1, 2, and 3 specify the expected class membership of the sample and correct comparison in each trial type. The conditional discriminations are grouped according to their *n*-stage equivalence classification, the number of stimulus sets required for their derivation, except for those that require only symmetric baseline relations for their derivation. Quotation marks indicate auditory stimuli.

Table 7-1

Sequences in which subjects were taught each set of conditional discriminations. The identifiers, AB, AC, EC, DE, and DF refer to the relations diagrammed in Figure 7-2.

Conditional Relations	Subjects					
	E.H.	F.M.	N.O.	R.W.	J.S.	P.M.
AB	1	1	4	5	4	4
AC	2	2	1	4	5	5
AB,AC	3	3	—	6	6	6
DE	4	4	5	2	1	1
DF	5	5	2	1	2	2
DE,DF	6	6	—	3	3	3
AB,DE	—	—	6	—	—	—
AC,DF	—	—	3	—	—	—
AB,AC,DE,DF	7	7	7	7	7	7
EC	8	8	8	8	8	8
AB,AC,EC, DE,DF	9	9	9	9	9	9

were auditory); the four-stage section shows 15 trial types in the five groups of relations that require four sets of stimuli; the three-stage section has 21 trial types in seven groups of relations that require only three sets of stimuli for their derivation; the symmetry section illustrates the trial types in the three sets of relations that require only the symmetric property in the relation from which each is derived (CE from EC, ED from DE, and FD from DF).

The 60 conditional discriminations illustrated in Figure 7-5 comprise the entire test battery. Complete consistency of a subject's performance on these derived relations is required if the explicitly taught relations are to be said to have established six-member classes of equivalent stimuli.

METHOD

Subjects

Subjects were five normal children, whose sex (M or F) and age (years/months) at the start of the experiment were: N.O., F, 5/4; E.H., F, 5/6; R.W., M, 5/7; J.S., F, 6/2; F.M., F, 9/2; and one retarded adult with a medical diagnosis of Down's syndrome: P.M., M, 21/1 (mental age of 4-1 on the Peabody Picture Vocabulary Test).

Procedure

Table 7-1 gives the sequence in which subjects were taught the baseline conditional discriminations represented by solid arrows in Figure 7-2. Subject E.H., for example, first learned AB and then AC and then had trial sequences with both groups of trial types mixed; next, she learned DE, then DF, and then both of those together; next, AB, AC, DE, and DF trials were mixed; all subjects were taught the EC relations last and the final phase mixed all five groups of trial types. The three conditional discriminations within a group were taught in a carefully programmed sequence and groups were combined into a longer series of trials only after subjects met the standard accuracy criterion at each step (Sidman et al., 1986).

After learning the 15 baseline conditional relations, subjects were tested for the existence of six-member classes. The first test had the three FB trial types inserted as probes into the baseline and the second had the three BF trials as probes. The

subsequent testing sequence varied among subjects and will be described below. The baseline reinforcement probability during tests was .20 for Subjects P.M. and E.H. but was changed to zero for the latter after a few tests (see below); all other subjects were tested in extinction. Subjects E.H., F.M., and N.O. were tested for oral naming of the stimuli after they completed conditional-discrimination testing.

RESULTS

Conditional Discriminations

Subject E.H. Figure 7-6 summarizes Subject E.H.'s probe-trial performances in 27 consecutive tests. Matrices representing her first eight tests show how often she selected each comparison stimulus, given each sample. Beneath the column totals of each matrix, and underlined, are the test number, the relation that was tested, and the total number of "hits" per opportunity. For Tests 9 to 27 these data, not underlined, are tabulated without their corresponding matrices.

The matrix rows and columns have been arranged as follows: If the conditional relations the subject had been taught were also

COMPARISON STIMULI

	Δ	Σ	Ξ
λ	9	0	0
ω	7	2	0
ℵ	1	1	7
	17	3	7

1. FB: 18/27

	λ	ω	ℵ
Δ	9	0	0
Σ	1	5	3
Ξ	2	2	5
	12	7	8

2. BF: 19/27

	Δ	Σ	Ξ
ℒ	7	1	1
θ	3	4	1
♭	0	2	7
	10	7	9

3. DB: 18/26

	λ	ω	ℵ
"DELTA"	3	3	3
"SIGMA"	1	8	0
"XI"	2	1	6
	6	12	9

4. AF: 17/27

	ℒ	θ	♭
Δ	8	1	0
Σ	3	5	1
Ξ	1	0	8
	12	6	9

5. BD: 21/27

	Δ	Σ	Ξ
Λ	7	2	0
Ω	2	7	0
Γ	0	0	9
	9	9	9

6. EB: 23/27

	Δ	Σ	Ξ
ℒ	9	0	0
θ	0	9	0
♭	0	0	9
	9	9	9

7. DB: 27/27

	λ	ω	ℵ
λ	9	0	0
ω	2	7	0
ℵ	0	0	9
	11	7	9

8. FB: 25/27

SAMPLE STIMULI

9. BF: 27/27	10. BD: 26/27	11. AF: 27/27	12. EB: 26/27
13. BE: 26/27	14. FC: 27/27	15. CF: 26/27	16. AD: 27/27
17. CB: 27/27	18. BC: 27/27	19. FE: 27/27	20. EF: 26/27
21. DC: 27/27	22. CD: 25/27	23. AE: 26/27	24. CE: 27/27
25. FD: 26/27	26. ED: 27/27	27. BF: 26/27	E.H.

Figure 7-6. Subject E.H. Scores on the 27 probe trials in each of 27 consecutive tests. Matrices representing the first eight tests show how often the subject selected each illustrated comparison stimulus (columns), given each illustrated sample (rows). Quotation marks indicate auditory samples. Every test contained nine trials with each sample (in Test 3, the subject selected a blank key once, rather than one of the three comparison keys). Beneath the column totals of each matrix, and underlined, are the test number (1 for the first test, 2 for the second, etc.), the relation being tested (FB, BF, etc., corresponding to the broken arrows in Figure 3 and to the "tasks" in Figure 5), and the total number of hits per opportunity (18/27 in the first test, 19/27 in the second test, etc.). For Tests 9 to 27, these data (not underlined) are listed without the corresponding matrix.

equivalence relations, thereby creating three six-member stimulus classes, the uppermost sample and the leftmost comparison in any matrix would be members of Class 1; the center sample and comparison would be members of Class 2; the bottom sample and the rightmost comparison would be members of Class 3. Any comparison selection that was consistent with these class memberships was tabulated as a *hit*; all others were *false alarms*. Every test contained nine trials with each sample. Therefore, if the subject always selected a comparison according to these class specifications, the three diagonal cells of the matrix,

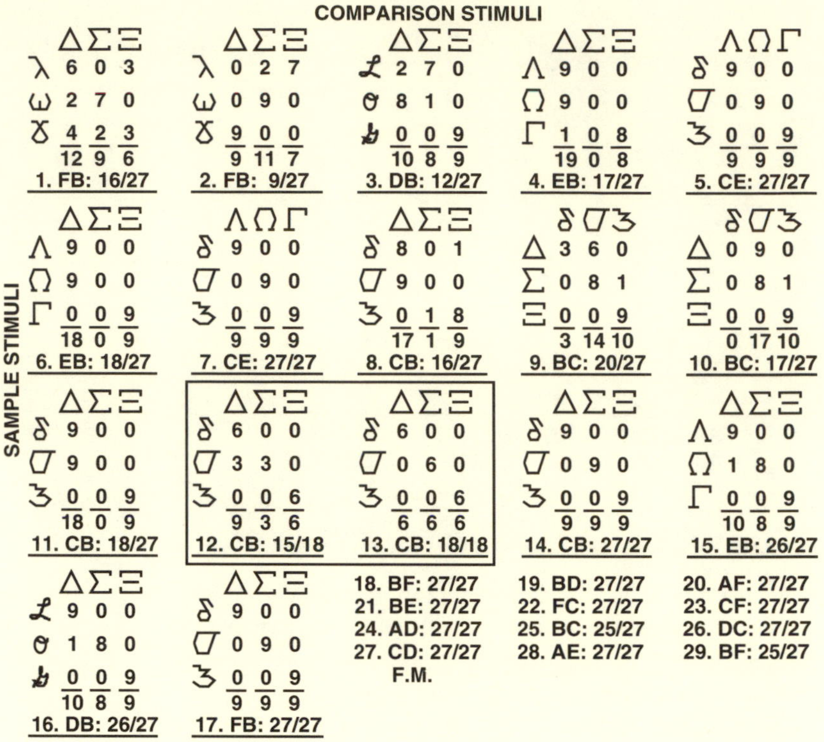

COMPARISON STIMULI

Matrix 1 — Δ Σ Ξ
λ 6 0 3
ω 2 7 0
ℵ 4 2 3
    12 9 6
1. FB: 16/27

Matrix 2 — Δ Σ Ξ
λ 0 2 7
ω 0 9 0
ℵ 9 0 0
    9 11 7
2. FB: 9/27

Matrix 3 — Δ Σ Ξ
ℒ 2 7 0
θ 8 1 0
♭ 0 0 9
    10 8 9
3. DB: 12/27

Matrix 4 — Δ Σ Ξ
Λ 9 0 0
Ω 9 0 0
Γ 1 0 8
    19 0 8
4. EB: 17/27

Matrix 5 — Λ Ω Γ
δ 9 0 0
℧ 0 9 0
Ʒ 0 0 9
    9 9 9
5. CE: 27/27

Matrix 6 — Δ Σ Ξ
Λ 9 0 0
Ω 9 0 0
Γ 0 0 9
    18 0 9
6. EB: 18/27

Matrix 7 — Λ Ω Γ
δ 9 0 0
℧ 0 9 0
Ʒ 0 0 9
    9 9 9
7. CE: 27/27

Matrix 8 — Δ Σ Ξ
δ 8 0 1
℧ 9 0 0
Ʒ 0 1 8
    17 1 9
8. CB: 16/27

Matrix 9 — δ ℧ Ʒ
Δ 3 6 0
Σ 0 8 1
Ξ 0 0 9
    3 14 10
9. BC: 20/27

Matrix 10 — δ ℧ Ʒ
Δ 0 9 0
Σ 0 8 1
Ξ 0 0 9
    0 17 10
10. BC: 17/27

Matrix 11 — Δ Σ Ξ
δ 9 0 0
℧ 9 0 0
Ʒ 0 0 9
    18 0 9
11. CB: 18/27

Matrix 12 — Δ Σ Ξ
δ 6 0 0
℧ 3 3 0
Ʒ 0 0 6
    9 3 6
12. CB: 15/18

Matrix 13 — Δ Σ Ξ
δ 6 0 0
℧ 0 6 0
Ʒ 0 0 6
    6 6 6
13. CB: 18/18

Matrix 14 — Δ Σ Ξ
δ 9 0 0
℧ 0 9 0
Ʒ 0 0 9
    9 9 9
14. CB: 27/27

Matrix 15 — Δ Σ Ξ
Λ 9 0 0
Ω 1 8 0
Γ 0 0 9
    10 8 9
15. EB: 26/27

Matrix 16 — Δ Σ Ξ
ℒ 9 0 0
θ 1 8 0
♭ 0 0 9
    10 8 9
16. DB: 26/27

Matrix 17 — Δ Σ Ξ
δ 9 0 0
℧ 0 9 0
Ʒ 0 0 9
    9 9 9
17. FB: 27/27

18. BF: 27/27	19. BD: 27/27	20. AF: 27/27
21. BE: 27/27	22. FC: 27/27	23. CF: 27/27
24. AD: 27/27	25. BC: 25/27	26. DC: 27/27
27. CD: 27/27	28. AE: 27/27	29. BF: 25/27

F.M.

(Left margin label: SAMPLE STIMULI)

Figure 7-7. Subject F.M. Probe-trial scores in each of 29 consecutive tests. Data from the first 17 tests are in matrix form. Below each matrix are the test number, the tested relation, and the hits per opportunity; for Tests 18 to 29, these data are listed without the corresponding matrix. The baseline in Tests 12 and 13 did not contain the EC relations and had only six trials with each sample.

extending from upper left to lower right, would each contain nine hits (as in Test 7).

Since random selection of the three comparisons would have produced only nine hits in the 27 opportunities, one might conclude that Subject E.H.'s 18 hits in her first FB test provided significant evidence for the existence of six-member stimulus classes. That evidence, however, is questionable. First, the matrix suggests a strong bias toward one comparison (nine hits and eight false alarms), especially in trials with two of the samples; nine hits therefore could reflect the comparison bias rather than the relation between sample and comparison. Then, in trials with the third sample, she almost always chose a particular one of the two remaining comparisons; given a 50% chance of choosing the one that was in the same class as the sample, this could have added another seven hits "by chance" to the total. The score of 18/27, therefore, may have reflected forms of stimulus control that were unrelated to the baseline conditional discriminations and cannot be accepted as evidence of stimulus-class formation.

The total number of hits remained relatively constant in the six-stage BF probes (Test 2) and the five-stage DB and AF probes (Tests 3 and 4) but the pattern of hits and false alarms varied. Early suggestions that one and perhaps two classes had formed were not sustained. The first four tests therefore provided no solid evidence for the existence of six- or five-member classes.

In Test 4, however, before starting to respond inconsistently, Subject E.H. scored hits on the first few probe trials. This observation raised the possibility that she had discriminated the zero reinforcement frequency on probe trials, in contrast to the occasionally reinforced baseline trials. Her comments also supported this possibility. Therefore, in order to prevent selective extinction on probe trials, she was given no reinforcements during subsequent tests, even on baseline trials.

The fifth test, five-stage BD probes, yielded more hits than before but the false-alarm rate was still high, so four-stage EB probes were given next. Matrix 6 provided encouraging evidence for the formation of four-member classes, so the five-stage DB test was repeated; Matrix 7 represented a perfect performance. Then, Test 8, a repetition of the FB probes, gave clear evidence for the existence of six-member classes.

Subject E.H. then completed the remaining tests, ending with a repetition of the BF probes (Test 27). Her consistent performances on the 60 emergent conditional discriminations (rarely as many as two false alarms) provided overwhelming evidence that three six-member stimulus classes had been established.

Subject F.M. Figure 7-7 summarizes Subject F.M.'s tests. Her first FB test gave little indication

247

of six-member classes and when the test was repeated, she scored only nine hits. Tests 3 and 4 (five-stage DB and four-stage EB) gave no convincing evidence of five- or four-member classes; in Test 4, she showed a comparison bias with two samples and with the third sample she nearly always chose the same one of the other two comparisons—a pattern, like Subject E.H.'s first test, of doubtful validity as an indicator of class formation.

The CE relations were tested next to determine whether an absence of symmetry in the explicitly taught EC relations might have prevented the ABC and DEF classes from combining. Test 5, however, demonstrated complete emergence of the CE relations. The next two tests were precautionary, Test 6 to determine whether the symmetry test, even though no reinforcement was given, might by itself have brought about the emergence of the EB relations, and Test 7 to ensure that the pattern of hits and false alarms on the EB retest had not adversely affected EC symmetry. Neither possibility was substantiated.

Then, in Test 8, the three-stage CB relations failed to emerge, the subject's hits and false alarms closely resembling her pattern in the EB probes. That pattern was not maintained, however, when the other three-stage relations, BC, were probed (Test 9). Because the number of hits increased, the BC probes were repeated (Test 10) but a new comparison bias only became more pronounced. A return to the CB probes (Test 11) reinstated the earlier pattern of choices.

Previous studies in this laboratory in which subjects had been taught the conditional discriminations AB, AC, DE, and DF but *not* EC (as shown in Figure 7-1) had rarely failed to document the emergence of BC and CB. The EC relations were therefore removed from the baseline and 18 CB probes were inserted into the abbreviated baseline. This test (Matrix 12) suggested a shift away from the earlier comparison bias toward control by individual samples, and a repetition of the CB probes in Test 13 found the subject scoring a hit on every trial. Then, upon a return to the original baseline, with the EC trials restored, she maintained her perfect CB performance.

COMPARISON STIMULI

SAMPLE STIMULI

	Δ	Σ	Ξ
λ	8	0	1
ω	8	1	0
Ⴚ	5	2	2
	21	3	3

1. FB: 11/27

	Δ	Σ	Ξ
ℒ	9	0	0
θ	9	0	0
♭	1	3	5
	19	3	5

2. DB: 14/27

	Δ	Σ	Ξ
Λ	9	0	0
Ω	9	0	0
Γ	1	0	8
	19	0	8

3. EB: 17/27

	Δ	Σ	Ξ
δ	9	0	0
ᒑ	3	6	0
Ꝫ	0	0	9
	12	6	9

4. CB: 24/27

	Δ	Σ	Ξ
δ	9	0	0
ᒑ	0	9	0
Ꝫ	0	0	9
	9	9	9

5. CB: 27/27

	δ	ᒑ	Ꝫ
Δ	9	0	0
Σ	0	9	0
Ξ	0	2	7
	9	11	7

6. BC: 25/27

	Δ	Σ	Ξ
δ	9	0	0
ᒑ	1	8	0
Ꝫ	0	0	9
	10	8	9

7. CB: 26/27

	Δ	Σ	Ξ
λ	8	0	1
ω	4	4	1
δ	2	3	4
	14	7	6

8. FB: 16/27

	Δ	Σ	Ξ
λ	7	2	0
ω	5	3	1
δ	4	2	3
	16	7	4

9. FB: 13/27

	Δ	Σ	Ξ
δ	8	1	0
ᒑ	0	8	1
Ꝫ	0	1	8
	8	10	9

10. CB: 24/27

	δ	ᒑ	Ꝫ
Δ	9	0	0
Σ	0	9	0
Ξ	1	2	6
	10	11	6

11. BC: 24/27

	Δ	Σ	Ξ
δ	9	0	0
ᒑ	0	9	0
Ꝫ	0	0	9
	9	9	9

12. CB: 27/27

	δ	ᒑ	Ꝫ
Δ	9	0	0
Σ	0	9	0
Ξ	0	0	9
	9	9	9

13. BC: 27/27

	Δ	Σ	Ξ
ℒ	9	0	0
θ	4	5	0
♭	1	1	7
	14	6	7

14. DB: 21/27

	Δ	Σ	Ξ
ℒ	9	0	0
θ	1	7	1
♭	0	1	8
	10	8	9

15. EB: 26/27

	Δ	Σ	Ξ
ℒ	9	0	0
θ	2	7	0
♭	0	0	9
	11	7	9

16. DB: 25/27

	Δ	Σ	Ξ
ℒ	9	0	0
θ	1	8	0
♭	0	1	8
	10	9	8

17. DB: 25/27

	Δ	Σ	Ξ
ℒ	9	0	0
θ	1	8	0
♭	0	0	9
	10	8	9

18. DB: 26/27

	Δ	Σ	Ξ
λ	9	0	0
ω	0	8	1
δ	0	0	9
	9	8	10

19. FB: 26/27

	λ	ω	δ
Δ	9	0	0
Σ	0	9	0
Ξ	0	0	9
	9	9	9

20. BF: 27/27

21. BD: 27/27   22. AF: 23/27   23. AF: 25/27   24. EB: 25/27   25. BE: 27/27
26. CF: 27/27   27. FC: 26/27   28. AD: 25/27   29. CD: 27/27   30. DC: 27/27
31. CE: 27/27   32. EF: 25/27   33. FE: 26/27   34. ED: 26/27   35. FD: 27/27
36. AE: 26/27   37. FB: 26/27

N.O.

Figure 7-8. Subject N.O. Probe-trial scores in each of 37 consecutive tests. Data from the first 20 tests are in matrix form. Below each matrix are the test number, the tested relation, and the hits per opportunity; for Tests 21 to 37, these data are listed without the corresponding matrix.

Once three-member classes had been established (although final proof did not come until the BC relations were probed in Test 25), the subject scored hits on nearly all trials in Tests 15-18, which went sequentially through four-stage EB, five-stage DB, and six-stage FB and BF probes. Then, moving back down through the five-, four-, and three-stage relations that had not been tested before, she documented the emergence of most of the relations needed to prove the existence of six-member classes. (She had to end her participation in the experiment before being tested for the EF, FE, ED, and FD relations.)

Subject N.O. Figure 7-8 summarizes Subject N.O.'s tests. Her first FB test showed a marked bias toward one comparison. In the next two tests, five- and four-stage (DB and EB), the hit and false-alarm pattern suggested forms of control that were unrelated to classes that the teaching procedures might have established. Test 4 then gave imperfect but encouraging evidence of three-stage CB relations, and Tests 5, 6, and 7 substantiated the existence of three-member ABC classes. Because testing the three-stage relations might have strengthened those prerequisites for the six-stage relations, the FB probes were given again in Tests 8 and 9 but still yielded no evidence of six-member classes.

After the unsuccessful six-stage FB probes, the next four tests (10-13) repeated the three-stage BC and CB probes until the subject achieved a 100% hit rate. Then, in five consecutive five-stage DB tests (14-18), her hit rate increased from 21/27 to 26/27. Finally, after the five-stage DB relations had emerged, FB and BF tests (19 and 20) provided solid evidence for the existence of six-member stimulus classes.

Untested relations were then probed, ending with a repeat of the FB probes (Test 37). Although the AF relations were weak at first, these improved on retesting (Tests 22 and 23) and the series of probes gave final proof of the formation of six-member classes.

Subject P.M. failed at first to demonstrate the emergence of equivalence relations in six-, five-, four-, or three-stage tests (Table 7-2, Tests 1-9); his only positive tests (4 and 6) were those for CE/EC symmetry. Then, even with EC removed from the baseline, three-stage relations in both the upper and lower triangles (CB and FE) proved deficient (Tests 10-11).

When only AB and AC were kept in the baseline, repeated testing (12-16) did bring about the emergence of BC and CB; then, with only EC removed from the baseline (17-18), the FE relations remained deficient even though CB was perfect. CB deteriorated again, however, when the EC relations were reinserted into the baseline (Tests 19-21). EC was removed once more, and repeated tests (22-29) succeeded in reinstating the CB

Table 7-2

Subject P.M. Hits per opportunity on successive tests. Under "Full Baseline," the indicated probes were inserted into the complete baseline, AB, AC, EC, DE, and DF (shown by the solid arrows in Figure 7-2);under "EC removed," the EC relations were removed from the full baseline; under "AB and AC," the baseline contained only AB and AC trial types.

Full Baseline	AB and AC	EC removed	Full Baseline
1. FB: 10/27	12. CB: 19/24	22. CB: 14/18	30. CB: 27/27
2. DB: 10/27	13. CB: 15/24	23. FE: 9/18	31. BC: 27/27
3. EB: 9/27	14. BC: 18/24	24. CB: 18/18	32. CB: 27/27
4. CE: 27/27	15. CB: 24/24	25. FE: 12/18	33. BC: 27/27
5. EB: 10/27	16. BC: 21/24	26. CB: 18/18	34. FB: 9/27
6. CE: 27/27	EC removed	27. FE: 12/18	35. CB: 26/27
7. CB: 18/27	17. CB: 18/18	28. CB: 18/18	36. BC: 27/27
8. BC: 13/27	18. FE: 12/18	29. FE: 12/18	37. DB: 9/27
9. CB: 14/27	Full Baseline		38. CB: 27/27
EC removed	19. CB: 23/27		39. BC: 26/27
10. CB: 12/18	20. CB: 23/27		40. EB: 13/27
11. FE: 12/18	21. CB: 20/27		41. EB: 10/27

but not the FE relations. Finally, with the full baseline and with repeated verification of the three-stage BC and CB relations, the six-stage FB, five-stage DB, and four-stage EB relations failed again to emerge (30-41). Subject P.M. was unable to return for more testing.

Subjects R.W. and J.S. also failed to demonstrate the emergent FB, DB, or EB relations that would have documented the formation of six-, five-, or four-member stimulus classes. They, too, had to leave the study before all questions raised by their data could be investigated but they had enough tests to verify two observations that were noted in other subjects' data: (1) The presence of EC in the baseline had a deleterious effect on the three-stage conditional relations; (2) BC and CB did emerge with continued testing in the context of a reduced baseline and remained intact in the context of the full baseline.

Oral Naming

Subject E.H.'s oral naming, tested after the series of equivalence probes, was also consistent. Given six trials with each of the 15 visual stimuli, she applied the names from Set A, calling the

Class-1 stimuli "delta," the Class-2 stimuli "sigma," and the Class-3 stimuli "xi."

Subject F.M. was old enough to have learned the names of upper-case script letters and in the naming test she called the Set-D letters "L," "O," and "G." She applied the Set-A names, "delta," "sigma," and "xi," however, to all Greek letters, even those in Sets E and F which she had learned to match to the script letters. She did not, therefore, give the same name to all members of any class. She was then given a second test in which she was asked, immediately after giving a Greek or English letter the same name as before, "Can you call it anything else?" She proved able to apply the names "L," "O," and "G" to the Greek letters in Classes 1, 2, and 3, respectively, and to apply the Greek names appropriately to the Set-D letters L, O, and G.

Subject N.O. called the letters in Classes 1, 2, and 3, "delta," "sigma," and "xi," respectively. Then, when asked for a second name, she always replied, "I don't know." Finally, when given 15 trials with each of the script letters in Set D and asked successively, "Is it an L?", "Is it an O?", and "Is it a G?", she answered "yes" and "no" indiscriminately.

EXPERIMENT 2

In Experiment 1, subjects learned each group of conditional discriminations separately, the three relations within a group being taught in a prescribed sequence and groups being combined only after subjects met the standard accuracy criterion at each step (Table 7-1). In Experiment 2, however, subjects were given the first 12 conditional discriminations all mixed together, with no restrictions on the order in which they were to be learned. The subjects were then tested for the three-member ABC and DEF classes (Figure 7-1) before those classes were linked together by teaching the EC relations (Figure 7-2).

METHOD

Subjects

Two normal human subjects served—one adult, P.H., M, 22/9, and one child, K.H., F, 10/2.

Procedure

The subjects continued through a lengthy sequence of

Table 7-3

Experiment 2. Hits per opportunity on successive tests. Baseline 1 did not include the EC relations.

Subject P.H. Baseline 1	Subject K.H. Baseline 1	Full Baseline	Full Baseline
1. BC: 18/18	1. CB: 18/18	9. AF: 25/27	18. BC: 27/27
2. EF: 17/18	2. FE: 17/18	10. EB: 27/27	19. EF: 27/27
3. CB: 18/18	3. BC: 18/18	11. BE: 26/27	20. FE: 25/27
4. FE: 17/18	4. EF: 18/18	12. CF: 27/27	21. AE: 27/27
Full Baseline	*Full Baseline*	13. FC: 27/27	22. ED: 27/27
5. FB: 8/27	5. FB: 27/27	14. AC: 27/27	23. FD: 26/27
6. FB: 11/27	6. BF: 26/27	15. CD: 27/27	24. CE: 26/27
7. FB: 21/27	7. DB: 25/27	16. DC: 27/27	25. BF: 26/27
8. FB: 15/27	8. BD: 26/27	17. CB: 27/27	
9. FB: 26/27			
10. FB: 27/27			
11. BF: 26/27			

the 12 AB, AC, DE, and DF trial types (Figure 7-1) mixed together until they attained the standard learning criterion. BC, CB, EF, and FE trials (Figure 7-5, three-stage) were then mixed into the baseline as tests for three-member ABC and DEF classes. Then, the three EC relations were mixed among the original twelve (Figure 7-2) until the subjects achieved criterion on the full baseline (Figure 7-4). Finally, they were tested for the existence of six-member classes, as in Experiment 1.

RESULTS

Conditional Discriminations
Subject P.H. The first column of Table 7-3 shows Subject P.H.'s

scores on 11 consecutive tests. His hit rates on the three-stage probes, before he was taught the EC relations, were uniformly high (Tests 1-4). After learning the full baseline, he scored only eight hits on his first six-stage probe (FB, Test 5). In successive FB tests, however, his scores increased. He eventually reached 100% in Test 10, and in Test 11 he was nearly perfect on BF also. He was unable to complete the conditional-discrimination test series, but his final performances were consistent with the formation of six-member stimulus classes.

Subject K.H. The scores for Subject K.H. on 25 consecutive probes are in the three righthand

253

columns of Table 3. She never gave more than two false alarms in any test. She scored nearly 100% on the three-stage probes (Tests 1-4) and then, with the full baseline, showed an immediate emergence of the six-stage FB and BF conditional discriminations (Testgs 5-6). Her nearly perfect scores in all of the remaining tests demonstrated all of the equivalence relations required to prove the formation of six-member classes.

Oral Naming

Oral naming was tested after Subject P.H.'s BF probes. He applied the Set-A names, "delta," "sigma," and "xi" appropriately to all of the Class-1, -2, and -3 letters in the upper triangle (Sets B and C). In the lower triangle he sometimes called the Class-1 stimuli in Sets D, E, and F "delta" and sometimes "L," and the Class-3 stimuli sometimes "xi" and sometimes "G," but he always called the Class-2 stimuli "sigma."

Subject K.H. gave the appropriate Greek names from Set A to all stimuli, including the Set-D English letters. When asked if she could call the letters anything else, she applied English

letter names only to set-D, saying that she could not call the other letters anything else (than the Set-A Greek names) or naming them by their shapes ("triangle" for upper-case delta, and so on).

EXPERIMENT 3

Subjects in Experiment 1 were first tested for six-stage equivalence after learning the full baseline, without having had lower-stage tests. Six-stage relations did not emerge, however, until prerequisites were tested and shown to be intact. Subjects in Experiment 2 were tested for three-stage relations in the context of a reduced baseline (Figure 7-1) before learning the full baseline. Six-stage relations emerged without additional testing of the prerequisites. In Experiment 3, the baseline was enlarged progressively; starting with AB and AC, subjects were taught conditional relations that were prerequisites for classes of gradually increasing size. After each consecutive teaching step, they were tested for the appropriate stimulus class before learning the next set of relations. Thus, they were successively

Table 7-4

Experiment 3. Teaching and testing sequences. Relations that were taught correspond to the solid arrows in Figure 7-3; tested relations correspond to the broken arrows.

Phase	Teach	Baseline	Test
1.	AB,AC	AB,AC	BC,CB (3-member classes)
2.	EC	AB,AC,EC	BE,EB (4-member classes)
3.	DE	AB,AC,EC,DE	BD,DB (5-member classes)
4.	DF	AB,AC,EC,DE,DF	BF,FB (6-member classes)
5.	—	AB,AC,EC,DE,DF	All remaining relations

taught the baseline relations AB, AC, EC, DE, and DF (Figure 7-2), with tests for three-, four-, five-, and six-member classes, respectively, after successive teaching phases.

METHOD

Subjects

Three normal children served: E.B., M, 5/3; C.J., F, 5/8; M.D., M, 5/10.

Procedure

After learning the baseline conditional discriminations AB and AC, the subjects were immediately tested for the three-stage relations BC and CB. The baseline was then progressively enlarged, one set of relations at a time, and conditional discriminations that would demonstrate four-, five-, and six-stage equivalence were probed successively.

Table 7-4 shows the sequence in which baseline conditional discriminations were taught and mixed with previously learned relations to form new baselines. The tests were given (with no reinforcement) immediately after subjects had learned each baseline. Probe trials were presented in a context of the smallest baseline that would be required to derive the probed relations. After the six-stage tests, the existence of six-member classes was verified by probing all remaining relations in the context of the full baseline. Finally, oral naming was tested.

RESULTS

Conditional Discriminations

Subject M.D. The first column of Table 7-5 shows high hit rates in tests for three-, four-, and five-member classes. (Although the

Table 7-5

Experiment 3. Subject M.D. Hits per opportunity on successive tests, with progressively increasing baselines. Probes are listed beneath the baseline relations in which they are embedded.

AB,AC	⊢ — — — — AB,AC,EC,DE,DF — — — — ⊣		
1. BC: 23/24	7. FB: 23/27	12. DB: 25/27	22. EF: 27/27
2. CB: 21/24	8. FB: 26/27	13. BD: 27/27	23. FE: 26/27
AB,AC,EC	9. BF: 22/27	14. AF: 26/27	24. DC: 27/27
3. EB: 25/27	10. BF: 22/27	15. EB: 27/27	25. CD: 27/27
4. BE: 24/27	11. BF: 26/27	16. BE: 27/27	26. AE: 27/27
AB,AC,EC,DE		17. FC: 27/27	27. ED: 27/27
5. DB: 26/27		18. CF: 26/27	28. FD: 26/27
6. BD: 26/27		19. AD: 27/27	29. BF: 26/27
		20. CB: 27/27	30. BF: 27/27
		21. BC: 27/27	

three-stage CB and the four-stage BE probes [Tests 2 and 4] did not quite meet the accuracy criterion, experimental error kept them from being repeated). The six-stage FB and BF probes in the context of the full baseline (second column of Table 7-5) required two and three tests, respectively (7-11), to reach criterion levels. Columns 3 and 4 of Table 7-5 show the subject proceeding with nearly 100% hit rates through all remaining tests (12-30), ending with a perfect score on the BF probes.

Subject E.B. The first column of Table 7-6 shows Subject E.B. proceeding through the three-, four-, and five-stage probes with few false alarms, requiring one repetition (Test 6) of the five-

stage DB probes. His FB probes (Column 2), although never far from the criterion level, were "shaky," so even though he attained a satisfactory hit rate in Tests 15 and 17 he was kept at this level until he met the criterion on two consecutive tests (19-20). Then (Test 21) he also gave a perfect score on the BF probes. He then proceeded with criterion performances through all remaining tests (22-41), ending with a satisfactory score on the BF probes.

Subject C.J. The three-stage BC and CB relations emerged immediately in Tests 1-2 and the four-stage EB and BE relations in Tests 3-5 (Table 7-7, Column 1). Subject C.J. then needed many repetitions of the

Table 7-6

Experiment 3. Subject E.B. Hits per opportunity on successive tests, with progressively increasing baselines. Probes are listed beneath the baseline relations in which they are embedded.

AB,AC	⊢ — — — — AB,AC,EC,DE,DF — — — — ⊣		
1. BC: 22/24	8. FB: 23/27	22. CB: 27/27	32. FD: 26/27
2. CB: 23/24	9. FB: 23/27	23. BC: 25/27	33. CE: 26/27
AB,AC,EC	10. FB: 24/27	24. BC: 26/27	34. EB: 25/27
3. EB: 26/27	11. FB: 24/27	25. EF: 26/27	35. BE: 26/27
4. BE: 26/27	12. FB: 23/27	26. FE: 27/27	36. CF: 26/27
AB,AC,EC,DE	13. FB: 22/27	27. DC: 26/27	37. FC: 25/27
5. DB: 24/27	14. FB: 22/27	28. CD: 27/27	38. AD: 26/27
6. DB: 25/27	15. FB: 25/27	29. AE: 25/27	39. DB: 25/27
7. BD: 27/27	16 FB: 24/27	30. ED: 26/27	40. BD: 27/27
	17. FB: 26/27	31. AE: 25/27	41. AF: 26/27
	18. FB: 22/27		42. BF: 25/27
	19. FB: 27/27		
	20. FB: 27/27		
	21. BF: 27/27		

five-stage DB and BD tests (Column 2, Tests 6-18). She met criterion on DB after three tests (6-8) but then BD remained just below criterion for five tests (9-13). At that point, her DB performance was also found to have regressed but regained criterion in three more tests (14-16). After that, two tests (17-18) carried BD also to a perfect score. Then (Column 3), three consecutive tests (19-21) saw her attain a perfect score on the six-stage FB relations, followed by immediate emergence of BF (Test 22).

Although Subject C.J. had to leave the experiment before completing all tests, several three-, four-, and five-stage relations did emerge with the full baseline (Column 4). Unlike other subjects, however, she did require retesting on the three-stage CB and EF relations (Tests 25-26, 27-29) before meeting criterion.

Naming

The three subjects applied names from Set A to all letters, calling the Class-1 stimuli "delta," the Class-2 stimuli "sigma," and the Class-3 stimuli "xi." In a second test, after giving each of those names, they were asked, "What else is it?" They answered consistently, "I don't know."

Table 7-7

Experiment 3. Subject C.J. Hits per opportunity on successive tests, with progressively increasing baselines. Probes are listed beneath the baseline relations in which they are embedded.

AB,AC	AB,AC,EC,DE	AB,AC,EC,DE,DF — — — — — ⊣	
1. BC: 24/24	6. DB: 24/27	19. FB: 19/27	23. DB: 26/27
2. CB: 24/24	7. DB: 18/27	20. FB: 23/27	24. BC: 26/27
AB,AC,EC	8. DB: 26/27	21. FB: 27/27	25. CB: 21/27
3. EB: 21/27	9. BD: 18/27	22. BF: 27/27	26. CB: 26/27
4. EB: 27/27	10. BD: 20/27		27. EF: 18/27
5. BE: 26/27	11. BD: 22/27		28. EF: 24/27
	12. BD: 23/27		29. EF: 27/27
	13. BD: 22/27		30. FE: 27/27
	14. DB: 19/27		31. AF: 26/27
	15. DB: 24/27		32. AD: 26/27
	16. DB: 26/27		
	17. BD: 24/27		
	18. BD: 27/27		

GENERAL DISCUSSION

Stimulus-class formation as an outcome of conditional-discrimination training has now been carried well beyond the original demonstration of three-member classes. Eight of the eleven subjects showed that the conditional relations they had learned were also equivalence relations. The first indication was the emergence of the FB and BF conditional discriminations, for which the prerequisites involved all six sets of stimuli (six-stage equivalence). Then, in test after test with no reinforcement being provided, the lower-stage relations emerged; with remarkable consistency, subjects matched stimuli according to class memberships that the original teaching had established. Teaching 15 conditional discriminations (five groups of three) had created three six-member stimulus classes, making the subjects capable of 60 new conditional discriminations that they had not been explicitly taught. The consistency of the 60 new relations, with respect to the baseline conditional discriminations, was more than sufficient to rule out irrelevant test-specific sources of control as explanations for the new behavior.

All but one of the successful subjects (Subject K.H., Table 7-3) needed repeated testing before proving capable of six-stage and sometimes even of lower-stage conditional discriminations. Although many subjects in previous studies have shown equivalence on their very first test, its emergence only after continued testing, even without reinforcement in the tests, has now been reported several times (Lazar et al., 1984; Sidman et al., 1986; Spradlin et al., 1973).

A related observation, confirming earlier findings with four-stage relations (Sidman & Tailby, 1982), was that whenever six-stage conditional discriminations failed to emerge, prerequisite relations, when tested, were also deficient. The missing or weak prerequisites often included even the three-stage relations needed to document three-member ABC or DEF classes. Once continued testing had caused missing prerequisites to emerge, however, it often proved possible to verify the formation of progressively larger classes. Sidman and his colleagues (1986) also reported that symmetry testing may have expedited the emergence of three-stage relations for which baseline symmetry was a prerequisite.

They noted, for example, with reference to the lower triangle in Figure 7-1, that giving subjects the ED and FD tests for symmetry of the baseline relations seemed to facilitate the emergence of the FE and EF relations.

It is possible that extended overlearning of the baseline conditional discriminations must take place before progressively larger stimulus classes can emerge. Also, no experiments have yet evaluated the relative efficacy of continued n-stage testing versus the testing of lower-stage prerequisites in the eventual formation of n-member classes. Nevertheless, it was clear in the present experiments that mere testing could facilitate the emergence of new conditional discriminations. Were it not for the absence of reinforcement during the tests, one might have supposed that final performances were being deliberately programmed by first teaching their prerequisites.

The actual observation, however, was that if any relations had somehow failed to develop, then their subsequent establishment, even through nonreinforced testing, also permitted higher-stage relations derived from them to emerge. The puzzling aspect of this observation was not the instructional programming—the production of new conditional discriminations by first establishing their prerequisites; the creation of classes of equivalent stimuli could account for the new relations (Sidman & Tailby, 1982). The puzzle was the emergence of any conditional discriminations, six-stage or lower-stage, as a consequence of testing them repeatedly without providing reinforcement.

A solution may lie in the answer to the question, "When do the classes of equivalent stimuli come into existence?" One possibility is that they form when the subjects learn the baseline conditional discriminations. Another, which seems more consistent with the present data, is that the classes do not exist until they are tested. Teaching the baseline relations may only create the potential for class formation, a potential that remains unrealized until the test itself. Although such a suggestion might seem unverifiable—how can one separate proof of class formation from the test?—observations in the present study do supply indirect evidence.

That the tests themselves provided the final conditions necessary for class formation was indicated first by the very fact that the emergence of equivalence relations sometimes required repeated testing. It seems incontrovertible that in such instances the classes formed subsequent to the initial test, not earlier when the subjects had only been taught the baseline relations.

A second relevant observation was that n-stage relations sometimes failed to emerge until lower-stage relations had been tested. Furthermore, once testing had established classes of n-1 members, previously nonexistent n-member classes often were manifested *immediately*. In this way, tests that demonstrated n-member classes were separated at least from lower-stage tests that were required to bring the n-member classes into existence, thereby providing almost a direct proof that the tests had generated the classes.

Strong rational support also exists for supposing that classes of equivalent stimuli form during the test rather than during the original teaching. Stimuli in the present experiment could have combined in various ways to form many classes besides those which arose from the equivalence relations. Other classes might have been based on stimulus characteristics like angles, lines, curves, or features determined by a subject's own stimulus-control history. Still other classes might have been determined, like those based on equivalence relations, by features of the experimental procedures.

One possibility arises because stimuli in Sets A and D were used only as samples during the original teaching, never as comparisons; Sets B, C, and F were always comparisons, never samples. Testing for "sample" or "comparison" classes with appropriate stimulus groupings might have demonstrated their existence also. For example, any AD trial (Figure 7-3) presented stimuli that had been used only as samples during training but which had come to differ with respect to class membership. With "delta" as the sample, then, subjects selected script-L on the basis of the Class-1 membership it shared with "delta," rejecting Class-2 and -3 letters O and G. Suppose, however, the subjects were given a different kind of test, again with "delta" as the sample but with the comparisons being script-O (from Set D), lower-case omega (from Set F), and upper-case omega (from Set E)—all Class-2 members. Now, they might well have selected script-O on the basis of the "sample class" membership it shared with "delta," rejecting "comparison class" members. Thus, the teaching procedures might have generated classes of equivalent stimuli, classes of samples, and classes of comparisons, but none of those classes need actually have existed in a subject's repertoire until an appropriate test actually called for it.

Class membership, therefore, need not be based solely on a relation between sample and "correct" comparison. Also relevant are contextual stimuli, of which the "incorrect" comparisons constitute an important category. If a stimulus can be a member of several classes, such contextual stimuli will determine the particular class to which it belongs at any moment. A subject may reject a comparison in one context and select it in another, even with the same sample. Uncontrolled physical or functional stimulus similarities, arising from the current experimental environment or from the subject's history, may transform a first-order conditional discrimination into a second- or higher-order relation.

The learning that apparently took place during the tests may well have represented a kind of sorting-out process, in which the stimuli chosen on some trials were determined by class memberships that proved to be invalid on other trials. This is speculation, clearly, but it is potentially verifiable, first by demonstrating that higher-order control is possible (Fucini, 1982), and second by experimentally manipulating various sources of control during the tests themselves. The latter has not yet been done.

All subjects in Experiment 1 failed to demonstrate six-member classes in their first tests and three never demonstrated those classes. Several observations indicated that teaching them the EC relations caused three-stage equivalences either to fail to emerge or to break down if they had previously emerged in the context of a reduced baseline. First, the failures of three-stage BC, CB, EF, and FE relations to

emerge were themselves most unusual in this laboratory. Then, when the EC relations were removed from the baseline, repeated testing brought about the eventual emergence of some three-stage relations; these deteriorated again when the EC relations were reinstated. Eventually, after two or more testing cycles (return to a reduced baseline, recover three-stage relations through retesting, and return to the complete baseline for continued testing), subjects were able to sustain their performance on two or more groups of three-stage relations, although BC and CB were more likely than EF and FE to be maintained; indeed, the FE relations never did emerge for Subject P.M.

Teaching EC in Experiment 3 and in an earlier study (Sidman & Tailby, 1982) succeeded in establishing four-member classes, with the integrity of the three-stage relations being maintained. Why did the EC relations interfere with three-stage equivalence in Experiment 1? A quantitative factor may have been at work. Teaching subjects the EC relations in Experiment 3 enlarged the already established three-member classes by only one member. In Experiment 1, however, teaching the EC relations was an attempt to double the size of the three-member classes by combining the ABC and DEF classes in one stroke. The number of members that can be added simultaneously to a class may be a parameter of class formation and may itself interact with a subject's age, experience, intellectual status, and other developmental or historical factors.

There was some indication, therefore, that the teaching and testing sequence can facilitate or hinder the formation of classes of equivalent stimuli. Enlarging the classes one member at a time and testing for class formation at each step, as in Experiment 3, may be the most effective method. Adding three new members all at once, however, may not only prevent six-member classes from forming but may prevent and even break down the original three-member classes. This speculation, too, remains to be confirmed; quantitative parameters of the training and testing procedures have yet to be worked out.

In previous experiments that involved three-member ABC classes, the names subjects applied to Set-B and Set-C stimuli were the dictated Set-A names to which they had become conditionally related. In the present experiment, six of the eight subjects who formed six-member classes applied names from Set A even to the letters in Sets D, E, and F. In addition to 60 new conditional discriminations, therefore, the procedures also generated 15 new simple discriminations, each stimulus in Sets B, C, D, E, and F controlling a naming response that was consistent with its class membership.

Classes of equivalent stimuli can form, however, even when subjects do not apply the same name to all members of a class (Lazar et al., 1984; Sidman et al., 1986). Such classes, therefore, need not be defined by reference to a response that all members control in common. The naming data of two subjects in the present experiments supported that conclusion. Subject P.H. (Experiment 2) applied the Set-A names appropriately to the Class-1, -2, and -3 stimuli in the upper triangle (Figure 7-2) and to the Class-2 stimuli in the lower triangle; sometimes, however, he gave the Set-A names and at other times he gave the English names of the Set-D letters to Class-1 and -3 stimuli in the lower triangle. For two of the classes, therefore, he did not give the same name to each member. In Experiment 1, Subject F.M. gave the English names to the Set-D letters but applied the Set-A names to all others in both the upper and lower triangles. Although in subsequent tests she proved capable of giving either the Set-A or the English letter names to all stimuli, her first naming test indicated that she had not originally given the same name to all members of any class.

Commentary

The *Six-Member Classes* paper dispelled any lingering doubts we might have had about the power of our analysis of equivalence relations. The analysis had to be taken seriously.

But not everyone did. Cognitivists in many areas—Psychology, Education, Child Development, Linguistics, and Artificial Intelligence, among others—characteristically postulate mental structures to account for complex human behavior. Here, in Figure 7-3, was an incredible structure—three six-member classes; 15 directly taught conditional relations giving rise to 60 new relations that the subjects had not been explicitly taught. The structure, however, consisted not of postulated mental elements but of directly observable relations among elements of the environment.

Figure 7-3, in combination with demonstrations of equivalence relations under contextual control (Chapter 12), prompted me to entitle an address at the 1985 convention of the American Psychological Association, "Equivalence Relations: *Mental* or Environ*mental* Structures?" I concluded the address by pointing out, "It is becoming clear that stimulus equivalence and the cognitive phenomena for which it serves as a basic paradigm can be shown to represent environmental structures. Those structures can be created, rearranged and combined, broken down, and prevented from forming by arranging relations among elements of the environment. The evidence is beginning to place mental structures right back where they started in the first place—in environmental structures."

Emergence of the structure depicted in Figure 7-3, inspiring though it was to the behaviorally oriented researchers who created it, presented a challenge. Every cognitivist to whom I have shown this structure and described its origins has dismissed it as theoretically uninteresting. It was a mere fact. In other fields of science, facts call for theories capable of encompassing them. In the study of cognition, facts appear to be the enemies of theory; can it be that they limit the creativity of the theorist?

Theory was involved, of course, in the *Six-Member Classes* paper. The theory, however, postulated neither hypothetical constructs nor intervening variables (MacCorquodale & Meehl, 1948). It assumed no unobserved or unobservable structures, entities, or processes. Nor did it propose a model. It simply suggested a rigorous behavioral definition of equivalence relations. The theoretical significance of the definition came from the predictions it generated.

In our earliest experiments, we thought we were making discoveries. The definition of equivalence relations that we eventually arrived at turned those seeming discoveries into inevitabilities. If our behavioral definition of equivalence relations possessed empirical validity, then all of the conditional discriminations represented by the dashed arrows in Figure 7-3 *had to* emerge from the explicitly taught baselines. If any one of those conditional relations failed to emerge, then one or more of the prerequisite relations would also have to be absent. Which of the more usual types of theoretical formulations in any area of Psychology has succeeded in predicting so much behavior so precisely? Which of those theories has shown us how to generate knowledge that is as complex as the representation in Figure 7-3? The thorough validation of the predictions that we achieved in the *Six-Member Classes* paper was an extraordinary theoretical triumph. (See Epilogue for a more comprehensive discussion of the descriptive system.)

From Coma to Equivalence

Theoretical triumph or not, the structure we had created in the *Six-Member Classes* paper was a "test tube" structure, not yet shown to be significant outside the laboratory. Could we demonstrate that it was really relevant to intellectual functioning? With respect to the measurement of behavioral development, I went out on a limb (Sidman, 1986b):

> [The development of stimulus equivalences] appears essential to the symbolic and semantic functions of language. It should be possible to evaluate the developmental significance of quantitative parameters: How many elements can a class of equivalent stimuli contain? How many new elements can be added simultaneously to a class? In how many classes can a stimulus share mem-

bership without destroying the integrity of the individual classes? One cannot fault current developmental scales for failing to consider these questions, because the processes of equivalence formation and maintenance are still active research topics. They do, however, point a way to the assessment of some rather complex cognitive functions through behavioral analysis. (pp. 50-51).

If stimulus equivalence is a fundamental building block in intellectual development, where better to document its significance than in people who are recovering from accident-induced intellectual deficit? Might parameters of stimulus equivalence serve as quantitative tools for evaluating the recovery of intellectual status in people who have suffered severe head injury? The challenge and the conviction that something could be done to meet it led to the initiation of a research project that produced some encouraging results. Dr. Michael Cataldo made the project possible, generously providing research and supporting resources at the John F. Kennedy Institute in Baltimore. There, Dr. John Eisely permitted us to work with patients who had been admitted to the pediatric rehabilitation inpatient service. Cleeve Emurian and I collaborated on this project for about a year. It was an interesting time, with me in Boston and Cleeve in Baltimore. I visited frequently and we also kept the telephone company in business that year.

The patients were youngsters who had suffered severe brain damage, usually in motor vehicle accidents. They would typically remain in coma for weeks. Then, slowly regaining consciousness but still passing through a period of complete sensory and motor helplessness, they would gradually become capable of small movements—eyes, fingers, arms, legs—and finally, sitting, standing, and moving about. Along with physical recovery came the gradual return of speech and intellectual functioning, often followed by a return to school.

Going on the supposition that class size is an important parameter in classes of equivalent stimuli, we attempted to determine whether this parameter would track patients' intellectual progress. The first problem was simply to find out whether a recovering patient would gradually become able to develop larger equivalence classes;

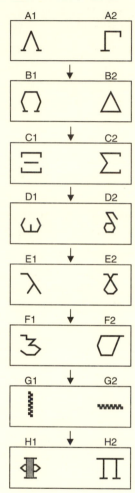

Figure 7-9. The baseline conditional discriminations in the *Recovery from Brain Injury* project. Arrows point from sample to comparison stimuli. Patients saw only the stimulus forms, not the alphanumeric stimulus designations.

would there be a limit to the number of class members in the early stages of recovery? If so, would that limit increase along with neurological improvement? If class size did increase gradually during a patient's recovery, we could then ask whether measurements of class size matched the practical criteria of everyday observation. If there seemed to be a correlation, it would then be feasible to ask whether laboratory tests of class size might prove substitutable for more complex indices of intellectual development. In the time we had, we were able to attack only the first of these possibilities.

Figure 7-9 summarizes the research plan. We would attempt to develop a baseline that had two classes, with as many as eight potential members in each class. Arrows pointing from sample to comparison stimuli indicate seven conditional discriminations, AB, BC, CD, DE, EF, FG, and GH. Our first task was to teach subjects a baseline, starting with AB and continuing as far toward GH as possible. Then, starting with CA, we would test for larger and larger classes.

For example, by matching C1 to A1 and C2 to A2, a subject would demonstrate two three-member classes, A1B1C1 and A2B2C2. We would then give the DA test for four-member ABCD classes. By successively testing EA, FA, GA, and HA, we could check for classes that could contain as many as eight members. Might recovering patients at first show a maximum class size and then gradually prove capable of larger and larger classes?

In fact, we found evidence that the recovery progression starts well before class size becomes testable. We were unable at first to teach several subjects even the simple form discriminations they had to be capable of before they could learn conditional discriminations. And then, having learned to discriminate the forms, they at first failed to learn the conditional discriminations that were to comprise the baseline for equivalence tests. Some patients, after learning the AB conditional discrimination, then failed at first to learn BC. This recovery-correlated progression—from simple to conditional discriminations and then to an increasing number of conditional discriminations—will be worth looking at more systematically.

When they came to the equivalence tests, several patients gave encouraging results but methodological problems kept getting in the way of clear interpretation. For example, after failing at first to progress from a class size of n to $n+1$ members (say, from CA to DA tests or from DA to EA), some patients seemed later to have become able to add the additional member. *Seemed* is appropriate here because after they passed the test for a larger class—say, DA—they then failed the previously successful test for the smaller class—in this case, CA. I eventually realized that I had made a bad mistake in trying to simplify the conditional-discrimination methodology by presenting only two comparison stimuli along with each sample. This left open a number of avenues both for false positives and false negatives in the test outcomes (Carrigan & Sidman, 1992; Johnson & Sidman, 1993; Sidman, 1987). Future research will have to avoid this trap.

Nevertheless, some of the data pointed in the right direction. After a number of frustratingly indecisive studies, Cleeve sent me the following letter, along with data, just before she went off on a vacation:

Friday, August 5, 1983
8:30 PM

Dear Murray,

It has been an incredible day. I am exhausted; it's late; and I'm still not done! But enclosed you will find the data we've been looking for. Yes, you read that right—the data we've been looking for!!

I would have loved to have reversed again *and* looked at repeated tests over time *and* run subtests, but time, time, time. Perhaps when I get back? We'll see.

The data are pretty—*five*-member is there, and strong, and *six*-member is not there and shows no signs of coming in. Both tests had the same baseline, had good baseline trial accuracy (100%/98%), and both were taken on the same day.

I'm enclosing copies [of Subject RVM's data]. I hope I made the right decisions on what to run, and that you are pleased. I am happy as a clam, but with no one to tell!

Why don't you come down to visit when I get back? We could talk about the high risk game of equivalence research, eat too many sundaes, and annoy the hell out of everyone by having so much fun doing our "work." (Keller would love that.)

My best to you both,
Cleeve

P.S. Trained 8-member baseline on Subject TJS today also and got 3-member equivalence at 90%. Under the same procedure, Subject RLE, earlier this week, came in at 0% on 3-member. (?!)

Figure 7-10 illustrates the rocky road we travelled with Subject RVM, a third-year high school student whose car had flipped over, leaving him unconscious and requiring respirator support. After about five weeks, a ventriculoperitoneal shunt helped him to begin recovery. Two months later, we began our teaching and testing procedures.

Each test, carried out without reinforcement, consisted of 20 probe trials inserted among baseline conditional-discrimination trials. Having learned the full baseline, Subject RVM almost immediately showed the emergence of three- and four-member classes (CA and DA tests, 8/1 and 8/2). Then, after doing badly on the first five-member test (EA on 8/2), he gave us the data that led to Cleeve's letter: On 8/3, he passed the five-member test, failed six-member tests (FA) on 8/4, showed five-member classes again on 8/5, and on the same day, failed the six-member test once again.

I was indeed pleased to see these data. Control subjects had shown themselves capable of developing classes that contained at least eight members. Now, for the first time, we had what looked like solid evidence for a limit to class size in one of our patients. When Cleeve

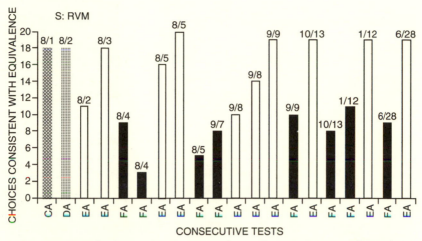

Figure 7-10. The bars represent 20-trial tests for emergent conditional discriminations. Tests are identified below each bar with reference to the baseline shown in Figure 7-9. Above each bar is the date (month/day) of the test, with the year advancing between the tests on 10/13 and 1/12. Cleeve's letter referred to tests up to and including those on 8/5.

returned from vacation, she resumed testing. After the one-month break, Subject RVM performed poorly on both six-and five-member tests (9/7 and 9/8) but then he consistently demonstrated five-member while failing to show six-member classes. One more piece of data that we would love to have seen would have been Subject RVM's eventual attainment of six-member but not seven-member classes. Unfortunately, continued testing became impossible because he returned home, which was quite a distance away.

And so, the challenge remains. Do equivalence relations play a significant role in intellectual development? The task is not to specify a role that is just theory-driven, nor even a role that is dictated by common-sense expectations, but to demonstrate a role empirically. Perhaps we can at least glean some knowledge from the tragic consequences of motor vehicle accidents and other forms of human violence. People recovering from brain injury give us opportunities to study behavioral growth—actually, regrowth—under controlled conditions that are not possible during the hectic and confusing course of development from infancy.

More on Nodes and Class Size

Besides stimulating a search for developmental significance, the *Six-Member Classes* paper raised some new theoretical considerations for us. It forced us also to look more closely at some findings that we had noted previously but had discussed and thought about only sketchily.

In the earlier *Class Expansion* paper (Chapter 6), we enlarged single-node three-member classes by adding one new stimulus to each class and by creating a second node in the baseline. Figure 6-2 illustrated the addition of D-stimuli to the ABC classes via the DC conditional discrimination and the transformation of C into a second baseline node. In the *Six-Member Classes* paper, however, Experiments 1 and 2 attempted to enlarge single-node three-member classes by adding three new stimuli to each class at once and by creating or adding three new nodes. Figure 7-1 illustrates the separate creation of ABC and DEF classes, with A and D functioning as Nodes 1 and 2; Figure 7-2 illustrates the (potential) combination of two three-member classes into one six-member class via EC, with C and E being transformed into Nodes 3 and 4.

Only when the experiments were well under way did we come to appreciate the possibility that adding three members at once to an existing class might be quite different than adding three members one at a time. It finally struck us that the enlargement of classes probably depends on the number of stimuli being added, the size of the classes to which stimuli are being added, and the number of nodes involved both in the original and final baselines. Thorough quantitative studies designed to disentangle these variables are still to be done.

Experiment 3 did suggest that enlarging existing classes one member at a time is more efficient than adding three new members at once. It remains unclear, however, whether the method of adding members to the baseline is the critical factor. The testing sequence may be more important. Later studies have suggested that testing for smaller classes first may facilitate the emergence of larger classes (Adams, Fields, & Verhave, 1993; Dube, Green, & Serna, 1993;

Fields, Adams, Newman, & Verhave, 1992; Fields, Adams, & Verhave, 1993; Fields, Adams, Verhave, & Newman, 1990, 1993; Kennedy, 1991). The conjecture at the end of Chapter 6 about a possible relation between baseline nodality and class size may therefore have to be qualified. The number of nodes in the baseline conditional discriminations may influence the likelihood of demonstrating an N-member class but only if one does not first test for—and demonstrate—subclasses that contain fewer than N members.

Delayed Emergence

Spradlin et al. (1973), in one of the early studies of equivalence relations in the conditional-discrimination context, had noted the gradual emergence of new conditional relations with repeated nonreinforced testing. For some time, this observation had remained unattended to—an anomaly in the literature. The gradual learning of a new conditional discrimination, without differential reinforcement, was one of those peculiar pieces of data that standard principles did not seem to account for. Before considering it seriously, experimenters and theorists wanted to see it replicated. After all, perhaps it just reflected an overlooked procedural defect.

But now, in the *Six-Member Classes* paper, we had strong replications; tests that were originally negative—that did not indicate equivalence—became positive with continued repetition Others were making the same observation (Devany et al., 1986; Fields et al., 1990; Lazar et al., 1984; Sidman et al., 1986; Sigurdardottir et al., 1990). It later turned out that tests in extinction sometimes turned positive abruptly rather than gradually (for example, Bush et al. 1989), so we changed our descriptive term from *gradual* emergence to *delayed* emergence of the derived conditional discriminations. The important point was that delayed emergence now had to be faced up to.

Along with the suggestion that the testing sequence may help determine whether new conditional discriminations emerge, the observation of delayed emergence of the new conditional discriminations brought up the question of what was happening during the tests. This question led us to ask, in the *Six-Member Classes* paper, "When do the classes of equivalent stimuli come into existence?" and to suggest that the classes do not exist until they are tested. McIlvane and Dube (1990) rightly took us to task for this unfortunate question. They pointed out that asking whether emergent behavior exists before we actually see it would lead us down the garden path of cognitivism—to the inference of structures located elsewhere than in the environment and in actual conduct. Their critique reminded me of a question that one of my teachers, W. N. Schoenfeld, used to ask when we attempted to locate behavior in some kind of a reservoir, like the reflex reserve (Skinner, 1938) or reverberating neural circuits (Lorente de Nó, 1938). "Where," he would ask us, "does the knee jerk go when the physician's hammer is not eliciting it?"

Instead, as McIlvane and Dube (1990, p. 14) pointed out, a behavioral analysis would conclude that "prior experience established the prerequisites for the emission of the new behavior at the appropriate time." Experimental analysis would ask about the nature of the prior experience and about what made the time appropriate.

As it turned out, I had come to a similar conclusion myself (Sidman, 1992a, pp. 23-25), but rephrasing the question does not make the problem go away. It is clear that repeated testing, even with the experimenter providing no reinforcement, can bring out new conditional discriminations that had failed to appear during earlier tests. In the *Six-Member Classes* paper, the need to deal with observations of delayed emergence led us to recognize that stimulus-class membership would inevitably come under contextual control. (Because the *Six-Member Classes* paper introduced the notion of contextual control in relation to delayed emergence, a brief discussion will be appropriate here. Contextual control will, however, be the main focus of Chapter 12.)

The basic notion is this: every stimulus is a member of many classes in addition to the classes our tests are designed to detect. Each stimulus will belong not only to the equivalence class for which explicit experimental procedures established the prerequisites, but will also be a member of other classes. Even though Sample A1, for example, joins one class along with Comparison B1, it may also hold membership in other classes along with Comparison B2 or B3. On a test trial too, each sample-comparison pair may belong to a different relation; the subject could choose a comparison on the basis of any of these. With tests being run in extinction, no differential consequence informs the subject whether a choice was correct or not.

Of the several classes to which a particular sample may belong in common with the comparisons, which will prevail during a particular test trial? Other aspects of the environment—the context— will select the prevailing class. Contexts may be historical, current, or both, and many test trials may be required before one of the possibilities proves to be relevant on *every* test trial. The relation that is possible on every trial will come eventually to provide the basis for choice. Hence, delayed emergence.

Let us take a somewhat fanciful example. After teaching a subject the baseline conditional relations A1B1, A2B2, A3B3, and A1C1, A2C2, and A3C3, we want to find out whether the conditional relations B1C1, B2C2, and B3C3 will emerge. On the first test trial, we present B1 as a sample and ask the subject to choose among comparisons C1, C2, and C3. Suppose the baseline had established B1 and C1 as members of the same class but, unknown to the experimenter, both B1 and C2 look like the subject's father. The subject therefore selects Comparison C2 instead of C1—an "incorrect" choice with respect to the equivalence relation being tested. On the next trial, Sample B2 and Comparison C3 are each constructed entirely of straight lines, while all of the other stimuli are made of curved lines. Again, the baseline had placed B2 into the same class as C2 but the subject selects C3 instead of C2 because of the rectilinear components—another "incorrect" choice. When the sample is B3, however, no paternal likeness, no component resemblances, and no other correspondences between it and any comparison are immediately evident. Without a competing class to get in the way of the experimentally established equivalence relation, the subject again selects C3—this time, a "correct" choice.

Later, when B2 again appears as a sample, although it is in the same rectilinear class as C3, that class has not proven relevant on other trials. The equivalence relation that had originated in the experimental baseline, however, is still a possible basis for choice, as it was on all other trials, and the subject now chooses Comparison C2—"correctly." And the next time the subject is faced with B1 as the sample, both the equivalence relation that originated in the baseline and a preexisting familial resemblance are again possible bases for choice. By this time, however, exposure to all of the trial types has established that the only consistent sample-comparison relation—the only one available on every trial—is the relation grounded in the baseline conditional discriminations, so the subject now chooses Comparison C1—a "correct" choice. From then on, the subject's comparison selection on every test trial becomes consistent with the expected equivalence classes because the test trials provide no other basis for choice that is consistently available.

Paul and Paul (1968) arrived at a similar conclusion about what had to be happening in paired-associate learning and in tests for transfer of such learning. In keeping with the then-dominant mediation theories of verbal and paired-associate learning, Paul and Paul (1968) talked not about *stimulus-stimulus (S-S) relations* and *stimulus classes* but about *stimulus-response (S-R) relations* and *response sets*, respectively; in the following, the translations are not difficult:

> It is tentatively suggested that the mediator(s) (verbalizable or not) activated by a particular S-R pair indexes or partially defines some specific relation between the S term and R term. If the S-R relation for each pair in the list is somewhat unique relative to other pairs in the list there should be minimal interpair effects (facilitation-interference) attributable to these relations. However, when various percentages of the pairs have some common relation there may be interpair effects attributable to this relation. An hypothetical example may clarify this point. If in one PA [paired associate] list each S-R pair is made up of common antonyms then the *relation* "opposite" activated by one pair and then by another will activate a *response set* "to give opposites." Presumably this set will facilitate performance since common antonyms are already in the subjects' response repertoire and because preexperimentally these

> responses can be discriminatively emitted to their appropriate stimuli. On the other hand, if, say, 30% of the pairs on a list were antonyms and the remaining pairs consisted of "opposite-producing stimuli" and nonantonym response terms, the antonym pairs might show poorer performance than these same pairs in the homogeneous list of antonyms. (p. 538).

One of the basic points made by Paul and Paul (1968), therefore, was that transfer tests may select or activate various different stimulus-control relations that subjects had learned during the experiment and/or before they entered the experimental situation. That a subject's choices may depend on experimentally unspecified relations has clearly been demonstrated by experiments on *unreinforced conditional selection*, in which subjects consistently related specific samples and comparisons even without having had any preexperimental history with those stimuli (Saunders, Saunders, Kirby, & Spradlin, 1988). Studies showing that reversal learning depends on the percentage of the baseline relations that participate in the reversed reinforcement contingency (Paul, 1966, 1968) led Paul and Paul (1968, p. 540) to a reasonable extrapolation: a subject's performance on any transfer-test trial is determined not just by that trial's stimuli (and their history) but also by the relations between other stimuli that have been presented on other test trials. It requires only a small additional step to arrive at experiments that would be even more immediately relevant to my suggestion that the delayed emergence of new conditional discriminations in equivalence test trials reflects a process in which the one consistent sample-comparison relation is sorted out from the many relations that are possible. In such experiments, the likelihood that the sought-for (by the experimenter) conditional discriminations will emerge, or the speed with which they emerge, should be (a) directly related to the percentage of test trials on which a choice was possible on the basis of the experimentally originated equivalence relation, and (b) inversely related to the total number of competing sample-comparison relations that are possible during the test.

One more question is also relevant to this interpretation of delayed emergence (Sidman, 1992a):

"Why," one must ask, "should a subject come consistently to select only those comparisons that are related in a consistent way to the samples?"

Here, a particular reinforcement history is required. In the experimental setting or in similar situations elsewhere, the subject must have learned, first, that each trial (or "problem") has a correct choice (or "answer"); and second, that each trial has only one correct choice. Without such a history, there is no reason why the subject's choices in a test without reinforcement should show any consistency at all, let alone the kind of consistency that the experimenter is looking for.

Such a selective process during the test can explain the delayed emergence of equivalence relations. It also permits another rather startling prediction: even without explicitly teaching any prerequisite conditional relations, one should be able to produce the emergence of any kind of stimulus class or any relation one wants between samples and comparisons during the nonreinforced tests. That is to say, given a subject with the appropriate general history noted above, it should be possible to teach anything one wants to teach about relations between stimuli without giving the subject any differential reinforcement. All that would be required are appropriately designed test trials.

Harrison and Green (1990) have provided an impressive confirmation of this prediction. They presented subjects with a series of two-choice conditional-discrimination trials, as illustrated in Table 7-8. Each trial had one of two possible samples, S1 or S2. Each trial also had one of two comparisons, C1 along with S1, and C2 along with S2. A second comparison, selected from a lengthy list, varied from trial to trial, but occasionally C1 and C2 were presented together. The subjects ended up always selecting C1 when S1 was the sample, and C2 when S2 was the sample. But the trials were run in extinction; no differential consequences were given for any of the

Table 7-8

Trial types (sample and comparison stimuli presented to the subjects without reinforcement (after Harrison & Green, 1990).

Samples	Comparisons
S1 ⟶	C1X1
S1 ⟶	C1X2
S1 ⟶	C1X3
*	*
*	*
*	*
S1 ⟶	C1Xn
S1 ⟶	C1C2
S2 ⟶	C2Y1
S2 ⟶	C2Y2
S2 ⟶	C2Y3
*	*
*	*
*	*
S2 ⟶	C2Yn
S2 ⟶	C2C1

subjects' choices. Consistency from trial to trial was the only possible basis for choice. (Harrison and Green then went on to show that the sample and the chosen comparison on each trial were related by equivalence.)

It remains now to determine how far this can be carried. In principle, there is no limit. It should be possible to generate any relation one wants between sample and comparison, for example, color, form, size, oddity, order, identity, or consistency of any arbitrary characteristic. All that should be required is to ensure that selections on the basis of any undesired relations are possible on only some of the trials, and that selection on the basis of the desired relations is possible on every trial.

This is what it means to assert that equivalence emerges during the test. [Experimentally established] equivalence is only one of the possible relations that may exist between sample and comparison stimuli. Whether equivalence or some other relation emerges during a test will depend on the structure of the test trials.... The only way to guarantee the emergence of equivalence relations is to test for them with test trials that permit no other consistent controlling relation between sample and comparison. (pp. 24-25).

Naming

The question of whether a common name for stimuli is a prerequisite for equivalence relations had still not been settled. But even if naming was not *necessary* for class formation, it seemed reasonable that naming could be *helpful*, particularly in multi-node baselines. It was our practice, therefore, to give naming tests only after subjects had completed the tests for emergent conditional discriminations. We hoped that if we did not deliberately elicit names for the stimuli, we might find that some subjects had formed classes without giving the same name to each class member.

Once again, the naming data proved suggestive but not definitive. Eight subjects formed six-member classes. Of these subjects, six applied the dictated names from Set A to all visual stimuli, including those in Sets D, E, and F. Unfortunately, the three subjects who failed to form six-member classes had to leave the experiment before receiving naming tests. Like Subject J.O. (Chapter 6,

Table 6-5), these subjects might have given the same name to potential members of a class even though the conditional-discrimination tests had failed to substantiate class formation.

Two of the subjects who formed six-member classes, however, did not always give the same name to each member of a class. Still, one of these subjects showed herself capable of giving consistent names to all members of a class, even though she did not do so when first asked for names. It was not clear, therefore, whether the results of naming tests reflected any process that was relevant to the conditional-discrimination tests or whether the naming and conditional-discrimination tests were independent of each other.

8

The Naming Puzzle and Other Matters

Background

The *Role of Naming* study (below) and the *Six-Member Classes* project (Chapter 7) went on together over a span of several years. Although the two investigations differed in their major emphases, they were closely related; data from each influenced what we did next in the other. The *Six-Member Classes* study was potentially of considerably greater importance so we wrote it up first. Then, before we could get the *Role of Naming* project out, Lazar et al. (1984) published a piece of similar work. Their data led them to conclusions like ours about the role of naming in establishing classes of equivalent stimuli and their publication priority must be acknowledged.

In questioning the role of naming in the formation of equivalence relations, we were concerned about the notion, analogous to the mediation hypothesis in the earlier paired-associate work, that subjects had to give all members of a class of equivalent stimuli the same name (for example, Jenkins, 1963; see also Chapters 4 and 6). Human subjects are, of course, likely to name stimuli that we present to them and naming may indeed foster original learning and eventual remembering (for example, Constantine & Sidman, 1975) and may facilitate equivalence relations (for example, Dugdale & Lowe, 1990). The reasons naming may serve these functions are not clear and deserve more research. The question, however, does not bear directly on the point that was at issue for us. Whether subjects do or do not name the stimuli is a more general problem than the one that concerned us in the *Role of Naming* study.

We wanted to know whether subjects who did not apply the same name to each potential class member would still form the classes. Is such naming more than just facilitative? Is it *necessary*? In our earlier studies, the dictated samples *gave* subjects what could have become the same name for each potentially related comparison. We now reasoned that if we used visual instead of auditory samples, thereby not giving subjects names to attach to the comparisons, they might apply different names even to comparisons that were related to the same sample. If they did, and still gave evidence of equivalence relations, we could conclude that equivalence did not require all related stimuli to receive the same label.

Because we wanted subjects who did not customarily resort to verbal reasoning when solving problems, we deliberately used subjects whose verbal sophistication was not fully developed; either they were only five years old or they were intellectually retarded. It was perhaps true of the five-year olds and was certainly true of our retarded subjects in this and earlier studies that chains of closely reasoned logic were not in their repertoires. We were well acquainted with our retarded subjects; we had worked with them for many years and our project staff had taught them most of their everyday living and academic skills (Mackay & Sidman, 1968; Sidman, 1970). Having learned AB and AC conditional discriminations, they were not likely to solve the BC and CB problems by going through a verbal chain like, "B1 and C1 must have the same name as A1 and must therefore go together." If all of the stimuli—A, B, and C—were visual, however, and our retarded subjects still showed the appropriate B- and C-stimuli going together, we would be hard put to ascribe the formation of ABC classes to a chain of verbal reasoning based on common names. In such instances, even if they did assign the same name to all members of a class, we would feel more confident that the common names were a result, not a cause, of the equivalence relations.

Our tactic, then, was to teach subjects two sets of conditional discriminations. In one set, the samples were auditory and the comparisons visual; the other set contained only visual stimuli. The first question was, "Would conditionally related pairs of stimuli in each set be included in an equivalence relation?" If the purely visual set of stimuli did give rise to equivalence relations, the second question would be, "Will subjects give the same name to each class member?" Finally, by teaching each subject one set of conditional discriminations with auditory samples and another set with visual samples, we could compare the emergence of conditional discriminations that were derived from auditory-visual and visual-visual baselines.

Matching-to-Sample Procedures and the Development of Equivalence Relations: The Role of Naming

Two normal children and four retarded youths were taught auditory-visual and visual-visual conditional discriminations and were then tested to determine whether the conditional relations were also equivalence relations. All subjects showed that conditionally related sample and comparison stimuli had become equivalent; the conditional discriminations generated two sets of three-member classes, one set containing both auditory and visual stimuli and the other containing only visual stimuli. In the auditory-visual classes, two of the retarded subjects failed to apply the name of the auditory stimulus to each visual stimulus in the same class; in the visual classes, all but one normal subject failed to apply a consistent label to all stimuli in a class. The formation of classes of equivalent stimuli does not, therefore, require that common names be applied to each member of a class. Although common naming responses were not necessary for equivalence, relations denoting symmetry and transitivity in the original conditional discriminations were shown to be prerequisites, as is demanded by the definition of equivalence.

Conditional-discrimination procedures, often called *matching to sample*, are commonly used to evaluate and even to teach comprehension. For example, if children can pick out appropriate colors, numbers, objects, and so on, on the basis of words or phrases that are spoken to them, one is likely to attribute auditory comprehension to them, to say that they understand the meaning of the spoken words. If they can also make those selections on the basis of printed or written words, one is likely to give them credit for reading comprehension, for understanding the meaning of text. The assumption one is making here is that the observed conditional relations (e.g., if [the word is] *red*, then [select] the red hue; if *green*, then green, etc.) are also equivalence relations; that the words are equivalent to their "referents." If the assumption of equivalence is correct, then one is justified in calling the conditional discriminations "matching to sample"; the child can indeed be said to be matching the selected objects or qualities to spoken or written words.

The process of analyzing conditional discriminations to determine whether they involve equivalence relations turns out to yield practical benefits. The analytic process itself teaches new stimulus-control relations without having to provide an explicit reinforcement history for those relations. In a recent study, for example, teaching children 15 arbitrary conditional discriminations by standard reinforcement techniques brought about the emergence of 60 new conditional discriminations that had never been directly reinforced (Sidman et al., 1985). A more complete understanding of the conditions responsible for this remarkable outcome will undoubtedly improve the efficiency of our techniques for teaching preacademic skills, simple vocabularies, and perhaps even advanced linguistic skills.

If a conditional-discrimination procedure is to generate not just conditional discriminations but true matching-to-sample performances, each conditional stimulus or sample must become equivalent to its correct comparison stimulus. The properties that define equivalence relations—reflexivity, symmetry, and transitivity—are behaviorally specifiable (Sidman et al., 1982; Sidman & Tailby, 1982). Generalized identity matching demonstrates reflexivity; a subject who has learned a conditional relation AB (if A, then B) must be able also to match A to itself (if A, then A) and B to itself (if B, then B). Symmetry requires functional sample-comparison interchangeability; having learned to match Sample-A to Comparison-B, a subject must then be able to match B as a sample to A as a comparison. Transitivity tests require a subject to learn two conditional relations, AB and BC, with comparison stimulus B in the first relation serving as the sample in the second; transitivity will then bring about the emergence of a new relation, AC, in which the subject matches the sample from the first relation to the comparison from the second. If stimuli are to be called equivalent, the relation between them must be shown to be reflexive, symmetric, and transitive; it must meet all three criteria.

The "triangles" in Figure 8-1 (ABC and DEF) outline a paradigm that has permitted symmetry and transitivity to be evaluated simultaneously, with many different stimuli (Lazar, 1977; Lazar et al., 1984; Lazar & Kotlarchyk, 1980; Mackay & Sidman, 1984; McDonagh et al., 1984; Sidman, 1971b, 1977; Sidman & Cresson, 1973; Sidman et al., 1974; Sidman & Tailby, 1982; Spradlin et al., 1973; Stromer & Osborne, 1982; Wetherby et al., 1983). In the upper triangle, the stimuli in Set A are auditory (dictated Greek letter names) and the B- and C-stimuli are visual (printed Greek letters). Subjects first learn to select each comparison in Sets B and C conditionally upon a sample from Set A. They are then tested to determine whether they have become able to match the letters in Sets B and C to each other. Sidman and Tailby (1982) have outlined the derivation of BC and CB matching from the symmetric and transitive properties of the AB and AC relations. By matching to each other those letters that they had learned to match to the same dictated name, subjects demonstrate the emergence of three three-member stimulus classes, each containing a dictated letter name from Set A, a letter from Set B, and a letter from Set C.

Testing for equivalence permits one to determine whether conditional discriminations have also generated semantic relations among the stimuli, as "symbolic matching" implies. The contingencies, however, specify only conditional relations. How can one account for the emergence of equivalence relations? Catania (1980) has noted, "Such equivalences must be important in verbal behavior, but it is not evident how their establishment is reducible to simpler discriminative processes" (p. 185). Yet, like fundamental discriminative and reinforcement processes, simple equivalence formation appears to be intact even in severe intellectual retardation. The present study attempted to identify behavioral prerequisites for the development of stimulus equivalence. In particular, is verbal mediation necessary?

In the paired-associate literature (e.g., Jenkins, 1963, 1965;

Jenkins & Palermo, 1964), response mediation has been postulated as the basic mechanism of stimulus equivalence, a theoretical orientation reflected in terms like *mediate association* (Peters, 1935), *mediated generalization* (Cofer & Foley, 1942), or *semantic conditioning* (Razran, 1939; Riess, 1940, 1946). Stimuli that do not resemble each other are presumed to become equivalent by virtue of being associated with the same response, in either a forward or backward (Ekstrand, 1966) direction.

Does naming mediate the emergence of equivalence from conditional relations? Although pretests show retarded and young normal subjects unable to name the B- and C-stimuli, and they usually do not name them aloud during conditional-discrimination training and testing, oral naming nearly always emerges when it is tested after subjects have learned the AB and AC relations (Mackay & Sidman, 1984; Sidman, 1971b; Sidman & Cresson, 1973; Sidman et al., 1974). They can apply the same name, taken from Set A, to each member of a class.

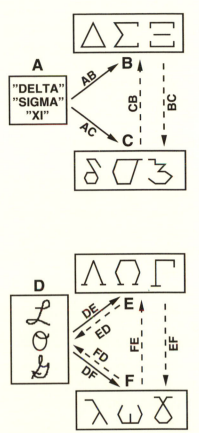

Figure 8-1. The equivalence paradigms in the present experiment. The stimuli are a set of dictated Greek letter names (Set A), four sets of printed Greek letters (Sets B, C, E, and F), and a set of English upper-case script letters (Set D). Each set has three stimuli. Arrows point from sample stimuli (only one presented at a time) to comparison stimuli. The solid arrows AB, AC, DE, and DF represent conditional relations that are explicitly taught to the subjects. The broken arrows CB, BC, FE, EF, ED, and FD represent conditional relations that are tested after the others have been explicitly taught.

Yet, naming of the B- and C-stimuli might be expected even in the absence of equivalence because subjects are explicitly taught relations between those stimuli and their auditory counterparts in Set A. The subjects' expressive vocabulary could be only a byproduct of the receptive vocabulary they had been taught via the crossmodal procedure. Although relations between the repertoires of the individual as listener and as speaker require considerable clarification (Guess, 1969; Guess & Baer, 1973; Lee, 1978, 1981a; Whitehurst, 1977), it is possible that names generated this way may play no role in the development of class membership.

Lazar (1977), Lazar and Kotlarchyk (1980), Spradlin et al. (1973), Stromer and Osborne (1982), and Wetherby et al. (1983) demonstrated that conditional discriminations can generate classes of equivalent stimuli even when all stimuli are visual, but these studies did not test naming. Although the procedure did not provide names, subjects might themselves have applied the same label to each member of a class, particularly if they had learned a label elsewhere for one of the class members (McDonagh et al., 1984). Lazar et al. (1984) have shown that normal children can develop purely visual stimulus equivalences without assigning a common name to each class member. Is this true also of the intellectually retarded? Would the use of visual rather than auditory stimuli in Set A prevent retarded subjects from applying common names to the different stimuli? Would those who have acquired only minimal verbal skills have to assign common labels before stimuli could become equivalent members of a class?

In the lower triangle (DEF) of Figure 8-1, all stimuli are visual. Subjects learned to select each Greek-letter comparison in Sets E and F conditionally upon English script samples from Set D. If the conditional relations DE and DF were also equivalence relations, subjects would prove capable of matching Set-E and Set-F letters to each other (EF and FE). Would they do this without giving the same name to each letter in a class? Since no names were dictated and all letters were unfamiliar to the subjects, they would not have been expected to apply the same label to different stimuli unless the procedures somehow generated such consistency. The present experiment exposed each subject to both of the paradigms in Figure 8-1, tested for the emergence of two sets of stimulus classes, ABC and DEF, and determined whether class formation required subjects to apply the same name to all stimuli in a class.

METHOD

The general plan (details are noted below) was:

1. Introduce subjects to the procedures and confirm their ability to do visual-visual and auditory-visual conditional discriminations, and oral naming, by pretesting them with familiar stimuli.

2. Evaluate reflexivity by testing generalized identity matching with all letters that are to be used as stimuli.

3. Establish baselines to be tested for symmetry and transitivity by teaching the four sets of relations denoted in Figure 8-1 by the solid arrows, AB, AC, DE, and DF.

4. Evaluate the subjects' performance on the four sets of relations denoted in Figure 8-1 by the broken arrows, BC, CB, EF, and FE; emergence of these new relations or their failure to emerge will prove whether the explicitly taught conditional relations are also equivalence relations.

5. Test the relations ED and FD, the symmetric counterparts of DE and DF.

6. Test the subjects' oral response to each stimulus in Sets B, C, D, E, and F.

Subjects

Two subjects, J.K. and W.R., were 5-year-old normal children. Four others were institutionalized retarded young men, 19 to 25 years old, whose medical diagnoses and mental ages on the Peabody Picture Vocabulary Test were: J.L., Down's Syndrome, 4 years; P.A., Down's Syndrome, 3 years 1 month; A.A., hydrocephalus, 4 years 5 months; M.D., microcephaly secondary to perinatal hypoxia, 8 years 9 months.

Apparatus

Subjects sat before a matrix of nine translucent touch-sensitive keys (windows) onto which stimuli were projected from the rear. The windows, each 7.3 cm in diameter, were arranged in a circle of eight, with a ninth in the center. Sidman and Tailby (1982) have described additional details and dimensions of this projection and response system. The present experiment used only the center window and the lowest three windows in the outer circle.

Matching-to-Sample Procedures

Each trial began with a sample stimulus. Visual samples appeared on the center window. Auditory samples were dictated from a tape at 2-s intervals (Fletcher et al., 1971); the center window remained dark until one sample had sounded and was then illuminated but blank. Visual and auditory samples never occurred in the same trial.

After a sample was presented, the subject had to press the center window to bring comparison stimuli onto the outer windows. With dictated samples, pressing the center window could not produce comparisons until at least one complete sample word had sounded. Each sample remained, with the comparisons, until the subject made a choice by pressing a comparison window.

Unless a reduced reinforcement probability or a probe trial (see below) precluded reinforcement, correct choices were followed by the sound of chimes, the disappearance of all stimuli, the delivery of a penny or token into an open receptacle below and at the right of the windows, and a 1.5-s intertrial interval. No chimes, penny, or token followed an incorrect choice. Subjects traded their tokens for money and often bought snacks or toys after the session. They kept all money they did not spend.

No trial presented more than three comparison stimuli. Positions of correct and incorrect stimuli varied among the three windows from trial to trial and each window had to be scheduled as correct before any could be correct again. In trial sequences that included only two different samples (during training), no more than three trials with the same sample could occur consecutively. With more than two samples, all possible combinations of sample and comparison stimuli had to occur before any could repeat. With those exceptions, all trial types—sample-comparison combinations—and all correct windows were equally probable on successive trials.

Pressing any window during an intertrial interval postponed the next sample for 1.5 s. Once a sample had come on, the subject could not produce comparison stimuli by pressing sample and comparison windows simultaneously and had to break contact with all windows before a new sample press could be effective. Once comparisons had come on, pressing the sample no longer had any programmed consequence but if the subject pressed an incorrect or blank window simultaneously with a correct comparison, the trial was treated as incorrect. The programming apparatus waited to define any response until the subject had released the window for .2 s; pressure on another window during the preceding press or within .2 s of a release defined a simultaneous response. A computer programmed the procedures.

Oral Naming Procedures

Oral naming tests presented only samples, with no comparisons. Subjects pressed no windows but responded to the instruction, "Tell me what you see," or "What is it?" After each response, the experimenter, seated behind the subject, pressed a switch to initiate the intertrial interval and the slide change. Subjects received no chimes, pennies, or tokens, even for correct names. Their responses were recorded by the experimenter and on magnetic tape. As a reliability check, a second experimenter recorded the responses from the tape, in the absence of the visual stimuli to which the subject had been responding.

Pretraining and Pretests

Subjects who were unfamiliar with the laboratory were introduced to the procedures by means of a program for teaching a circle versus ellipse discrimination, with stimuli appearing only on the outer windows (Sidman & Stoddard, 1966, 1967). Then, matching to sample was introduced with hues as stimuli. First, pressing the center window when a hue was projected on it brought the same hue onto one of the outer comparison windows; pressing the single comparison produced a reinforcer. Next, nonmatching hues were introduced on the other comparison windows and subjects quickly learned to select the one that was the same as the sample. Hue names were then dictated as samples, with the

Table 8-1

Sequences in which subjects were taught each set of conditional discriminations. The identifiers, AB, AC, DE, and DF refer to the relations diagrammed in Figure 8-1.

Conditional Relations	Subjects					
	J.K.	W.R.	A.A.	P.A.	J.L.	M.D.
AB	1	2	2	4	5	2
AC	2	1	1	5	2	5
DE	4	5	5	1	4	1
DF	5	4	4	2	1	4
AB+AC	3	3	3	6	—	—
DE+DF	6	6	6	3	—	—
AB+DE	—	—	—	—	6	3
AC+DF	—	—	—	—	3	6

visual comparisons. Finally, oral naming of the hues was tested. All subjects performed accurately on all of these procedures, demonstrating their ability to do identity matching, auditory-visual matching, and oral naming.

Stimuli in the final pretests are illustrated in Figure 8-1. On individual trials the sample and correct comparison were the same and the two incorrect comparisons were always other members of the same set. These tests evaluated generalized identity matching and reflexivity.

Baseline Teaching

Table 8-1 gives the sequence in which subjects learned the conditional discriminations represented by solid arrows in Figure 8-1. For example, Subject

J.K. first learned AB and then AC and then had trials with all of those auditory-visual relations; next, he learned DE, then DF, and then all of the visual-visual relations together. Each subject's final teaching phase, not shown in Table 8-1, mixed all of the relations, AB, AC, DE, and DF.

The teaching program was similar for each group of conditional relations. To advance from one step to another, subjects had to meet a standard accuracy criterion, an overall score of at least 90% correct with no more than one error on any trial type (combination of sample and comparisons).

In Step 1 of the first teaching phase, subjects who started, for example, with the AB relations had to match only two of the dictated samples—"delta" and "sigma" (these varied among subjects)—to appropriate Set-B comparisons; they rotated through six balanced sequences of 24 trials until they met the standard learning criterion. In Step 2, they went through sequences of 24 trials with another pair of samples—for example, "delta" and "xi"—until they met the same criterion. Step 3 presented the final pair of samples, "sigma" and "xi." Trials in these first three steps included only two comparison stimuli, one related conditionally to the current sample and the other to the second sample in the current pair.

The fourth teaching step contained 24-trial sequences that used all three samples but still presented only two comparisons per trial, one related conditionally to the current sample and the other to one of the two remaining samples in the current set. Once again, subjects had to meet the learning criterion before advancing to the next step.

Step 5 again used all three samples but each trial now included all three comparisons, one correct and two incorrect. When subjects once more met the accuracy criterion in a set of 24 trials, the first teaching phase was complete; they had learned the first three trial types.

Subjects next went through a similar series of steps with a second group of conditional relations, for example, AC. They first learned pairs of trial types with only two comparisons; then, they had sequences of trials with all three samples but still only two comparisons; finally, they had three comparisons per trial. This completed the second teaching phase.

The third phase mixed the six trial types that had already been taught into 48-trial sequences. By achieving the accuracy criterion at this step, Subject J.K., for example (Table 8-1), demonstrated that he could select either Set-B or Set-C letters conditionally upon dictated Set-A letter names.

The next three teaching phases proceeded like the first three, ending when subjects met the accuracy criterion in a 48-trial sequence of the remaining relations. They had then learned six more trial types. Subject J.K., for example, could then select either Set-E or Set-F letters conditionally upon script letters from Set D.

The same system was followed for each subject, regardless of the particular order in which the relations were taught. Finally, the 12 AB, AC, DE, and DF trial types were mixed into 72-trial sequences. When subjects met the standard criterion, their baseline training was complete. Figure 8-2 depicts the sample and comparison stimuli in the 12 trial types that all subjects were explicitly taught. Later, sequences of these 12 trial types would constitute a baseline into which probe trials would be inserted to evaluate the formation of equivalence relations.

TASK	SAMPLE	COMPARISONS CORRECT	INCORRECT
AB₁	"DELTA"	Δ	Σ , Ξ
AC₁	"DELTA"	δ	σ , ろ
AB₂	"SIGMA"	Σ	Δ , Ξ
AC₂	"SIGMA"	σ	δ , ろ
AB₃	"XI"	Ξ	Δ , Σ
AC₃	"XI"	ろ	δ , σ
DE₁	ℒ	Λ	Ω , Γ
DF₁	ℒ	λ	ω , δ
DE₂	θ	Ω	Λ , Γ
DF₂	θ	ω	λ , δ
DE₃	♭	Γ	Λ , Ω
DF₃	♭	δ	λ , ω

Figure 8-2. The sample and three comparison stimuli (one correct and two incorrect) in the 12 baseline trial types that all subjects were explicitly taught. Quotation marks indicate auditory (dictated) stimuli. Trial types were presented to subjects in mixed sequences

Reinforcement Probability

In preparation for unreinforced probes, the baseline reinforcement probability was gradually reduced to .2 in steps of .1. Subjects had to meet the standard accuracy criterion at each step. A computer program that generated the probabilities permitted no more than eight consecutive correct baseline trials to go unreinforced. It was occasionally necessary to halt a declining accuracy trend by increasing the reinforcement probability before reducing it again. Since no probe trials would be reinforced, the reinforcement probability on baseline trials during subsequent tests was increased enough to maintain the overall probability at .2. At the end of sessions with reduced reinforcement probabilities, subjects were given enough hue-hue or picture-picture matching trials, with all correct choices reinforced, to make up for correct baseline trials that had gone unreinforced.

After their tests with reduced reinforcement probabilities on baseline trials and no reinforcement on probe trials, some subjects had additional tests with no reinforcement on any trials, baseline or probe. To ensure that they would maintain accurate performances even under extinction, they had first to achieve the standard accuracy criterion in baseline trials without reinforcement. Extinction-training sessions also ended with enough reinforced hue-hue or picture-picture matching trials to make up for missed reinforcements.

Maintenance and Review

At the beginning of each new teaching session, subjects once again had to meet the learning criterion on their most advanced performance. Each session in which a test was scheduled began with a review of the baseline trial types. To proceed, subjects had to meet the standard criterion on these reviews. Any subject who failed several times to achieve criterion returned to an earlier teaching step and advanced through the teaching sequence again.

Tests

Equivalence. All subjects had two different conditional-discrimination tests, some receiving one first and some the other. One test inserted BC trials (samples from Set B, comparisons from Set C) and EF trials (samples from Set E, comparisons from Set F) as unreinforced probes into the sparsely reinforced baseline of AB, AC, DE, and DF trials; the other inserted CB and FE probes. The upper segment of Figure 8-3 shows the trial types in one test, with each of the three BC probes below its baseline AB and AC trial types, and each EF probe below its baseline DE and DF trial types. In the other test, the six CB and FE probes depicted at the bottom of Figure 8-3 replaced the BC and EF probe trials. Each test had 108 trials, six each of the 18 trial types (72 baseline and 36 probe trials). After the first two tests, the testing sequence varied among subjects and will be described in conjunction with the data.

Symmetry. Because the Set-A stimuli were auditory, it was not possible to present them simultaneously as comparisons; symmetry of the AB and AC relations, therefore, could not be evaluated by testing BA and CA. The Set-D stimuli, however, were visual; thus, symmetry tests ED and FD were possible. After equivalence was tested, the six

TASK	SAMPLE	COMPARISONS CORRECT	COMPARISONS INCORRECT
AB₁	"DELTA"	△	Σ , Ξ
AC₁	"DELTA"	δ	Ʊ , Ꙅ
BC₁(PROBE)	△	(δ)	(Ʊ , Ꙅ)
AB₂	"SIGMA"	Σ	△ , Ξ
AC₂	"SIGMA"	Ʊ	δ , Ꙅ
BC₂(PROBE)	Σ	(Ʊ)	(δ , Ꙅ)
AB₃	"XI"	Ξ	△ , Σ
AC₃	"XI"	Ꙅ	δ , Ʊ
BC₃(PROBE)	Ξ	(Ꙅ)	(δ , Ʊ)
DE₁	ℒ	Λ	Ω , Γ
DF₁	ℒ	λ	ω , ᵟ
EF₁(PROBE)	Λ	(λ)	(ω , ᵟ)
DE₂	θ	Ω	Λ , Γ
DF₂	θ	ω	λ , ᵟ
EF₂(PROBE)	Ω	(ω)	(λ , ᵟ)
DE₃	♭	Γ	Λ , Ω
DF₃	♭	ᵟ	λ , ω
EF₃(PROBE)	Γ	(ᵟ)	(λ , ω)
CB₁(PROBE)	δ	(△)	(Σ , Ξ)
CB₂(PROBE)	Ʊ	(Σ)	(△ , Ξ)
CB₃(PROBE)	Ꙅ	(Ξ)	(△ , Σ)
FE₁(PROBE)	λ	(Λ)	(Ω , Γ)
FE₂(PROBE)	ω	(Ω)	(Λ , Γ)
FE₃(PROBE)	ᵟ	(Γ)	(Λ , Ω)

Figure 8-3. The upper segment shows each of the three BC probes below its prerequisite AB and AC trial types and each EF probe below its prerequisite DE and DF trial types. In the other test, the BC and EF trials were replaced by the three CB and the three FE probes depicted in the lower segment. Baseline and probe trials were presented in mixed sequences. Correct and incorrect probe comparison stimuli (marked by parentheses) were designated as such on the basis of assumed stimulus equivalences.

ED and FD symmetry-probe trial types were inserted into the baseline in place of the equivalence probes.

Oral naming. Oral naming tests had 90 unreinforced trials, with six presentations each of the B-, C-, D-, E-, and F-stimuli.

RESULTS

Equivalence and Symmetry Tests

Each row in Table 8-2 summarizes the results of tests that are identified in the column headings. Baseline scores are combined for all tests shown in a given row. The first two tests evaluated the emergent BC, CB, EF, and FE performances; these revealed whether the original auditory-visual (AB and AC) and visual-visual (DE and DF) conditional relations were also equivalence relations. Subsequent ED and FD tests determined whether the original visual-visual relations DE and DF were symmetric.

In Tests 1 and 2, all except Subject P.A. demonstrated auditory-visual equivalences by making no more than two "errors" in either set of 18 BC or CB probe trials. The two 5-year-olds, Subjects J.K. and W.R., and

Table 8-2

Conditional-discrimination test scores (percentage correct) for each subject.

Subj.	Test No.	Equivalence				Symmetry		Baseline			
		Auditory-Visual		Visual-Visual		Visual-Visual		Auditory-Visual		Visual-Visual	
		BC	CB	EF	FE	ED	FD	AB	AC	DE	DF
J.K.	1-3	89	100	89	94	100	100	86	89	96	98
W.R.	1-3	100	89	94	94	94	100	97	94	98	98
J.L.	1-3	100	94	83	89	100	100	100	100	98	100
A.A.	1-2	89	94	67	56	—	—	100	100	89	100
	3	—	—	—	—	100	83	—	—	100	100
	4-5	100	100	89	83	—	—	97	100	100	100
	6-7[a]	100	100	89	100	—	—	100	100	100	100
M.D.	1-2	100	100	67	89	—	—	97	100	100	100
	3	100	—	67	—	—	—	100	100	100	100
	4	—	—	—	—	100	100	—	—	100	100
	5-6	100	100	94	100	—	—	100	100	100	100
	7-8[a]	100	100	94	100	—	—	100	100	100	100
P.A.	1-2	72	83	39	78	—	—	94	94	94	97
	3	94	—	61	—	—	—	100	100	89	100
	4-5	100	89	50	83	—	—	100	100	83	97
	6	100	—	50	—	—	—	89	94	83	100
	7	—	—	—	—	50	94	—	—	83	100
	8[b]	94	—	89	—	(100)	(100)	100	100	100	94

Note—Column headings refer to relations diagrammed in Figure 8-1. [a]Tests with no reinforcement. [b]Tests after reinforcement of the symmetry relations, ED and FD; parentheses indicate ED and FD scores after reinforcement.

Down's syndrome Subject J.L., also demonstrated visual-visual equivalences by their EF and FE performances. These subjects also proved capable of ED and FD matching, thereby showing symmetry in the baseline relations of the lower triangle.

Subjects, A.A., M.D., and P.A., the other retarded youths, proved at first to be considerably less capable of EF and FE matching. After continued testing, however, even without reinforcement on probes, they eventually did demonstrate both visual-visual and auditory-visual equivalence. Subject A.A. scored low in his first EF and FE tests (1 and 2) but after symmetry was tested (Test 3), his equivalence scores improved remarkably (Tests 4 and 5). Three months later, in tests with no reinforcement even on baseline trials, equivalence was stronger than ever (Tests 6 and 7).

Whether Subject A.A.'s improvement was the result of repeated equivalence testing or whether the symmetry tests also played a role is not clear, although the change was nearly complete immediately after one symmetry test. Subject M.D.'s data suggested more strongly that symmetry testing might have been responsible for the improvement in the equivalence tests. This subject's EF score was low (Tests 1 and 2) and remained so even when retested (3). After one perfect symmetry test (4), however, Subject M.D.'s equivalence scores were also nearly perfect (Tests 5 and 6) and remained so when retested one year later with no reinforce-

ment even on baseline trials (Tests 7 and 8).

Subject P.A. scored low at first both on auditory-visual and visual-visual equivalence tests (1 and 2). Because a repeated test (3) yielded a nearly perfect BC score and some improvement on EF, the full set of equivalence tests was given again (Tests 4 and 5). This repeated testing strengthened the auditory-visual equivalences, as demonstrated by the BC and CB performances, but visual-visual equivalence, which would have produced strong EF and FE performances, was still not evident. A sixth test did not improve the EF score. Subject P.A. then scored poorly on ED trials (Test 7), indicating a lack of symmetry in the original DE relations. He was therefore taught the ED and FD relations by means of the standard reinforcement techniques. Then (Test 8), he gave a strong EF performance, indicating the development of visual-visual equivalence.

Naming Tests

After completing the equivalence tests, each subject was asked to name the visual stimuli. Table 8-3 summarizes the naming responses. The scoring reliability—the percentage of agreement between the names that were directly recorded during the test and those recorded later from the tape transcription—fell between 92 and 100% for all except Subject P.A. (76%), who pronounced few words clearly. Even for Subject P.A., however, when each scorer's records were analyzed separately, the consistency (or inconsistency) of the recorded responses within each class was reliable.

The upper part of Table 8-3 lists responses to visual stimuli in the three auditory-visual classes, delta, sigma, and xi. Subjects J.K., W.R., J.L., and A.A. consistently responded with the name of the sample to which they had matched each visual stimulus, although Subject J.L. applied "sigma" somewhat indiscriminately. Subject M.D., however, applied no names in common to members of the delta or the sigma class, showing some consistency only with xi. Subject P.A. responded appropriately with "delta" only three times, with "sigma" nine times, and never with "xi".

The lower part of Table 8-3 gives the subjects' responses to stimuli in the three visual classes.

Subject J.K. was the only one to respond relatively consistently within each class and not between classes, although he was somewhat indiscriminate with delta. He responded, "delta", to stimuli in the script-L class 18 times (and four times to the script-O class); "xi" to members of the script-O class 12 times, and "sigma" to members of the script-G class 13 times. The consistent names he gave to stimuli in the all-visual classes were taken from the auditory samples in the other classes. To the extent that any of the other subjects did give common names to stimuli within a class, they, too, took the sample names from the auditory-visual relations. Subject J.L., for example, responded with "delta" 12 times (and with "sigma" once) to members of the script-L class and with "sigma" six times to the script-O class. Subject A.A., who also responded frequently with "sigma" and "delta," gave those names almost indiscriminately to members of all three visual classes.

DISCUSSION

All subjects eventually proved capable of the BC, CB, EF, and FE conditional discriminations,

Table 8-3

Naming responses to the visual stimuli (Figure 8-1). Stimuli are grouped by class membership, as determined by the equivalence tests. A number after a response indicates how often out of six opportunities the subject applied that name; absence of a number indicates only a single occurrence. A question mark indicates "I don't know" or a similar response; a single letter indicates that the subject gave that letter's name as a response; "usd" signifies the response "upside-down" in reference to the indicated letter; asterisks indicate undecipherable responses.

			Subject			
Stimulus	J.K.	W.R.	J.L.	A.A.	M.D.	P.A.
Auditory-Visual						
UC delta	Delta/6	Delta/4,Triangle,Sigma	Delta/5, Sigma	Delta/6	Triangle/6	C/2, Delta, U, O, *
LC delta	Delta/6	Delta/6	Delta/5, Sigma	Delta/6	?/6	Delta/2, A/2, C, *
UC sigma	Sigma/6	Sigma/6	Sigma/3, ?/3	Sigma/6	?/6	Sigma/6
LC sigma	Sigma/6	Sigma/6	Sigma/6	Sigma/6	?/5, xi	Sigma/3, Q, */2
UC xi	xi/6	xi/6	xi/6	xi/6	xi/6	A/3, S/2, T
LCxi	xi/6	xi/6	xi/6	xi/6	xi/4, Three/2	C/4, T, Z
Visual-Visual						
Script L	Delta/6	?/6	Delta/5, *	Sigma/3, Delta/3	?/6	Q/4, */2
UC lambda	Delta/6	usdV/6	Delta/5, Sigma	Delta/5, Sigma	?/6	A/6
LC lambda	Delta/6	usdY/5, ?	?/3, Delta/2, *	Delta/3, Sigma/3	?/6	Q/2, T, C, Key, *
Script O	xi/5,*	?/6	?/5, Sigma	Sigma/5, Delta	?/6	C/3, T/2, Key
UC omega	Delta/4, xi, ?	Horseshoe/5, usdV	?/3, Sigma/3	Ssigma/3, Delta/3	Chair/6	U/5, *
LC omega	xi/6	W/6	?/4, Sigma/2	Sigma/3, Delta/3	Three/6	U/6
Script G	Sigma/4, ?/2	?/6	?/6	Sigma/3, Delta/3	?/6	K/5, T
UC gamma	Sigma/6	usdL/4, usdV, ?	?/4, */2	Delta/3, Sigma/2, xi	?/6	F/6
LC gamma	Sigma/3, ?/3	?/6	?/6	Sigma/3, Delta/3	?/6	Fee/6

which had never been reinforced. The emergence of these new relations can be interpreted as a demonstration that both the auditory-visual and visual-visual conditional relations, which had been directly taught, were also equivalence relations. Conditionally related stimuli in Sets A and B had become equivalent members of a class and conditionally related stimuli in Sets A and C had become equivalent members of the same class. As a consequence of these equivalence relations, three three-member classes were created. The subjects were then able to match any pair of stimuli in the same class, even if they had not been reinforced for doing so. Similarly, conditionally related stimuli in Sets D and E and in Sets D and F had become equivalent members of a class, forming another group of three three-member classes and permitting the EF and FE relations to emerge without direct reinforcement.

One group of three-member classes contained both auditory and visual elements and the other contained only visual. The four retarded subjects and one of the two normal 5-year-olds did not give consistent names to

stimuli in the visual classes and two of the retarded subjects did not apply common names to members of the auditory-visual classes. The emergence of stimulus equivalence, therefore, did not require mediation by naming.

The name given by most subjects to each visual stimulus in the auditory-visual classes was determined by the dictated sample to which the visual stimulus had been conditionally related. Often, however, subjects applied those same labels to visual stimuli that had never been procedurally related to dictated names. The original training with auditory stimuli increased the likelihood that subjects would produce those stimuli as names. One may therefore question whether names, even when applied to members of an auditory-visual class, served as mediators. A parsimonious view would be that the emergence of stimulus classes and the emergence of common names for members of a class are independent consequences of the training procedures.

Several previous observations are consistent with this view: Sidman et al. (1974) noted new conditional relations emerging before subjects were able to name the stimuli. Sidman and Tailby (1982) observed that one subject, although able to name new stimuli that had been added to existing classes, had clearly never applied the names until the naming test; another subject, although able to name the stimuli, was unable to match them to their dictated names. An inference to be drawn from these observations and from the present results is that naming is neither necessary nor sufficient to establish equivalence relations. Naming responses may be products of the naming test itself, playing no role in the establishment of equivalence relations.

Given that a verbal label is not needed to define a class of equivalent stimuli, the formation of such classes even by retarded subjects who have severe language deficiencies might have been predictable. Equivalence has been shown to be possible in spite of severe language deficiency, however, only at the level of three-member classes. Still to be evaluated are class size, number of classes, number of members added simultaneously to a class, higher-order conditional control of class membership (Fucini, 1982), and interactions among such parameters. Quantitative studies of these and other variables may yet reveal limits that are correlated with developmental retardation.

Three retarded subjects required repeated testing before the classes of equivalent visual stimuli emerged and one also required repeated testing for the auditory-visual classes. This gradual emergence of equivalence relations even without reinforcement on the tests, first reported by Spradlin et al. (1973), is still only poorly understood. The present study, although it did not rule out control by irrelevant stimulus aspects, suggests that a delay in the emergence of equivalence is more likely for purely visual than for auditory-visual relations. It remains to be determined whether this observation is valid and, if so, whether it is a factor in retardation.

For Subjects A.A. and M.D., the demonstration that equivalence had emerged from the original conditional relations, DE and DF, seemed to be fostered by the symmetry tests, ED and FD. This apparent facilitation of equivalence by symmetry testing raises the possibility that a kind of instructional programming may be feasible even without reinforcement for the emergent relations. Symmetry is a prerequisite for equivalence; without symmetry the necessary transitive relations would not be possible (Sidman and Tailby, 1982). For example, the FE relations, which are required to validate DE and DF equivalence, can be derived from transitivity as follows: If FD and DE, then FE. The DE relations were directly taught but the FD relations could exist only if the explicitly taught DF relations were symmetric. Similarly, symmetry of the explicitly taught DE relations, shown by ED, would permit the derivation of EF: If ED and DF, then EF. If the necessary symmetries had somehow failed to develop until they were tested, then their establishment, even through nonreinforced testing, could have permitted transitivity and therefore equivalence to emerge.

The possibility that the derivation of conditional discriminations from equivalence relations might be facilitated by first establishing the prerequisite symmetric relations was strengthened by the ED test performance of Subject P.A., which

indicated that the original DE relations were not symmetric. Without DE symmetry, the transitive relation necessary to derive EF (if ED and DF, then EF) would not be possible. The EF relations did not, in fact, emerge for Subject P.A. until the prerequisite ED relations had been explicitly taught with reinforcement. The feasibility of such programming or shaping of equivalence relations requires the injection of a word of caution if the development of equivalence is to be used for classificatory purposes. As with other presumed tests of intellectual development, it will be necessary to apply the most effective instructional techniques before specifying limitations to potential growth.

Experiments that use more familiar stimuli than Greek letters make it more evident that the emergent BC, CB, EF, and FE relations exemplify reading comprehension. For example, if children are taught to select pictures conditionally upon dictated picture names (AB) and to select printed picture names conditionally upon the same dictated names (AC), then the emergence of equivalence from the directly taught conditional discriminations would

303

permit them to match the pictures to the printed words (BC and CB) even though they were never directly reinforced for doing so (e.g., Sidman, 1971b). Standard reading comprehension tests require children to match text to pictures.

Elementary reading comprehension, however, is usually taught by means of a "look-say," or oral-naming method; children are explicitly taught to give the same name to a picture and its corresponding printed name. Pictures and text thereby become functionally equivalent; both stimuli occasion the same oral response. Functional equivalence of picture and printed word is then supposed to permit the children to match the two—to read with comprehension—even with no direct reinforcement for doing so. The present results suggest that oral naming is not a necessary prerequisite for reading comprehension. One may question, then, whether the seeming success of the look-say method is related to functional equivalence at all. It is not at all clear why events that are related through a restricted commonality of function should then be

equivalent to each other in a broader context. Perhaps oral naming succeeds simply because a conditional relation is established between a picture and the product of the oral name—its sound—and between a printed word and the same sound. As in the present experiment, unrestricted equivalence, rather than a more narrow functional equivalence, would then be responsible for the derived performances. A similar interpretation has been suggested for teaching procedures that use name construction, writing, or signing instead of oral naming (Mackay & Sidman, 1984).

On more practical grounds, the teaching of reading comprehension via conditional discriminations, which involve only the presentation of stimuli and do not require the students to name the stimuli orally, eliminates the need for personal monitoring and reinforcement by a teacher. A computer can teach elementary comprehension, presenting the stimuli, recording the behavior, and providing consequences, thereby permitting the teacher to rotate among the students and apply procedures that do require personal attention.

* * * * * * * * * *

Commentary

Common Names

The experimental strategy in the *Role of Naming* study seemed to have worked. When the baseline conditional discriminations involved only visual stimuli, five of the six subjects did not give a common name to all members of a class. Even with auditory samples, two subjects did not label class members consistently. Conditional-discrimination tests documented classes of equivalent stimuli but subjects did not always give the same name to each member of a class.

These data, however, are not completely satisfactory. When we ask subjects to name stimuli after we have tested them for emergent conditional discriminations, they may not give the names they had applied (vocally or subvocally) during the tests (Dugdale & Lowe, 1990, p. 118; Stoddard & McIlvane, 1986, p. 157). For example, subjects who gave Greek letter names even to stimuli in the purely visual classes may have interpreted "What is it" as a request to classify those stimuli according to the dictated sample names we had given them. Perhaps they had originally classified them some other way.

This is a difficult matter to resolve. Many subjects do not overtly label stimuli during teaching and testing. Asking subjects to name stimuli while they are being taught or tested might produce naming that would otherwise not have occurred. And when unsolicited verbalizations do occur, we cannot tell whether they are among the causes or the effects of the equivalence relations.

Demonstrating that subjects fail to show equivalence relations until they are taught common labels for the stimuli is a step in the right direction (Eikeseth & Smith, 1992) but problems arise even there. For example, in the very process of teaching children to give the same name to a sample and its related comparison, one may inadvertently transform visual-visual into auditory-visual matching. Then too, if one teaches labels for stimuli by using terms like *goes with*, *is the name of*, *means*, *matches*, *is the same as*, and so forth, the instructions rather than the baseline conditional discriminations may be responsible for subsequently manifested equivalence relations. Additional complexity of interpretation is engendered by evidence that even auditory and visual elements of a complex stimulus may become members of the same stimulus class (Stromer & Mackay, 1990; Stromer & Stromer, 1990a, 1990b).

Showing that subjects who cannot name stimuli fail to develop equivalence relations might seem definitive. Such subjects, however, may well be limited in more ways than just their inability to name stimuli; they may also suffer other deficits that are incompatible with equivalence relations. Nonverbal retarded children (for example, Devany et al., 1986) may possess intellectual limitations that are correlated with or even spring from rather than cause their failure to demonstrate equivalence relations. Deaf children who have not learned sign language (Barnes, McCullagh, & Keenan, 1990) may also have suffered severe educational deprivation. People with stroke-induced dysphasias (Sidman, 1971a, pp. 420-422) may fail to demonstrate equivalence relations because their stroke caused other problems besides an inability to name stimuli orally or in writing. Even studies in which nonhuman subjects fail to form equivalence relations (for example, D'Amato et. al., 1985; Dugdale & Lowe, 1990; Lipkens et al., 1988; Sidman et al., 1982) may possess methodological limitations that have not yet been completely resolved—the nature of the stimuli, the subjects' training histories, and parameters of the conditional-discrimination procedures (Iversen et al., 1986; Sidman, 1980, 1987, 1992b; Sidman et al., 1982, p. 43).

In spite the interpretive difficulties that arise when naming tests are given after equivalence relations have been demonstrated, it would be imprudent to dismiss the naming data in Table 8-3 too quickly. It is not obvious that all of those data can be attributed to subjects' misinterpretations of what they were being asked to do, or to other methodological features that might have caused the subjects to give different names than those they had applied to the stimuli during the earlier conditional-discrimination tasks. Subject W.R., for example, did not give Greek letter names to the D-, E-, and F-stimuli. Instead, he named several of those stimuli quite accurately on the basis of their shape or their resemblance to letters of the English alphabet other than the sample letters. He seems not to have misunderstood the request, "What is it?" Subjects J.K. and A.A. arbitrarily assigned Greek letter names to stimuli in the visual classes but, when assigning the names, failed to maintain the class boundaries that their conditional-discrimination tests had demonstrated. Their naming was not consistent with those classes. And Subject M.D., who most often responded with "I don't know" even to members of auditory-visual classes, did give the sample name "xi" to lower- and upper-case xi, suggesting that although he was capable of such a classificatory scheme, it was not involved in his test performances. He also showed himself able to name stimuli on the basis of their shape but did not use this scheme, either, to differentiate the classes that his conditional-discrimination tests revealed. Taken together with earlier observations cited in the *Role of Naming* paper (pp. 301-302) and with later replications by Green (1990), these data cannot easily be declared irrelevant to the question of whether common names are necessary to mediate equivalence relations.

And then, too, another subject who was not in the *Role of Naming* study provided some highly suggestive additional data. He was a very bright 11-year-old who learned the seven visual-visual conditional discriminations that were illustrated in the preceding chapter (Figure 7-9). His HA test results indicated that he had established two eight-member classes. While going through the test, he said (without being asked), "This is very mysterious. I know I am picking the right ones but I can't figure out why I'm doing it." I would have hugged this subject even if he were not my grandson. For him, equivalence was not a matter of "figuring it all out" via a long verbal chain, with common names mediating symmetric and transitive relations from the H stimuli through six nodes all the way back to the A-stimuli. If verbal mediation was involved, this subject was unaware of it.

Auditory-Visual versus Visual-Visual Classes

Our evidence did not favor the notion that common names are necessary for equivalence relations. Still, with our retarded subjects, we did see indications that equivalence relations based on auditory-visual conditional discriminations showed themselves earlier in testing than did relations based on visual-visual conditional discriminations. Green (1990) reported similar differences between auditory-visual and visual-visual classes. The significance of these observations is not yet clear. It may be that common naming, although perhaps not necessary, can facilitate equivalence relations. Dictated A-samples in the auditory-visual conditional discriminations (Figure 8-1) might have provided subjects with names they could apply to each related B- and C-comparison, thereby expediting the ABC classes. Still, Subject M.D. in our *Role of Naming* study and several subjects in the Green (1990) study showed more rapid development of auditory-visual classes even though they did not label each class distinctively.

An interesting possibility is that differences in the readiness with which equivalence relations emerge from visual-visual and auditory-visual baselines might define a diagnostic category relevant to mental retardation. On the other hand, as Green (1990) pointed out, auditory-visual stimulus relations (for example, dictated names and objects) are taught even to infants, but intensive experience with arbitrary visual-visual relations (printed words and pictures or objects, upper- and lower-case letters, and so on) usually starts with academic instruction. Retarded learners, who typically do not progress academically as far as nonretarded learners, may therefore have less experience with visual-visual equivalences. Even so, differences in the results of tests for the formation of auditory-visual and purely visual classes may point the way toward effective educational interventions.

Auditory-visual versus visual-visual baselines: the learning sequence. A possible relation between crossmodal conditional-discrimination learning and the development of equivalence (and its likely relevance to mental retardation) remains a potentially fertile research area. One question that has yet to be assessed experimentally is the role played by subjects' experiences both with directly taught and with emergent intra- and intermodal conditional discriminations. In an attempt to determine whether subjects bring with them tendencies to treat the intra- and intermodal baseline conditional discriminations differently, we (Martha Willson-Morris, Barbara Kirk, and I) taught the AB, AC, DE, and DF baselines (Figure 8-1) by presenting trials of each in mixed order, without controlling the sequence in which subjects had to learn them. We were then able to graph a separate learning curve for each conditional discrimination, as if each were a different subject. We did not do this with enough subjects to reveal possible relations between the kind of history they brought to the laboratory and their sequence of learning the conditional discriminations, but we did find that the technique yields orderly data and is probably worth pursuing.

Two of the subjects took part in Experiment 2 of the *Six-Member Classes* paper (Chapter 7): K.H., a 10-year-old girl, and P.H., a

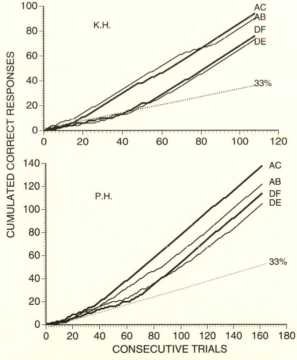

Figure 8-4. Subjects K.H. and P.H. Learning curves plotted separately for auditory-visual (AB, AC) and visual-visual (DE, DF) baseline conditional discriminations (Figure 8-1). Curves vary in thickness so that one may differentiate them more clearly. The horizontal-axis scales differ for the two subjects.

22-year old man, neither of them retarded. The other two subjects, also not retarded, were L.M., a 10-year-old girl, and B.V., a 9-year-old boy. Figure 8-4 shows the first two subjects' learning curves for each baseline conditional discrimination. Although Subject P.H. took considerably more trials than Subject K.H. to learn the baseline, both of them learned the auditory-visual conditional discriminations (AB and AC) before the visual-visual (DE and DF).

The other two subjects showed a different sequence (Figure 8-5). Neither of them learned the auditory-visual before the visual-visual baseline. Subject L.M., who took the fewest trials of all, learned the auditory-visual AB relations first and then the visual-visual DE relations. The slope of her auditory-visual AC curve then broke away from the chance level before the visual-visual DF curve did. Subject

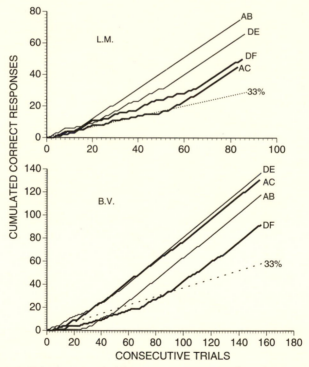

Figure 8-5. Subjects L.M. and B.V. Learning curves plotted separately for auditory-visual (AB, AC) and visual-visual (DE, DF) baseline conditional discriminations (Figure 8-1). Curves vary in thickness so that one may differentiate them more clearly. The axis scales differ for the two subjects.

B.V. showed little difference in his speed of learning the AC and DE conditional discriminations, one auditory-visual and the other visual-visual. Then, the auditory-visual AB relations clearly preceded the visual-visual DF relations. In subsequent tests, the intra- and intermodal classes (ABC and DEF, respectively) emerged immediately for Subjects K.H., P.H. (Table 7-3), and L.M. Subject B.V. required several repetitions of the tests before the classes emerged and the auditory visual classes developed first. There was, therefore, no discernible relation between the baseline learning sequences and the emergence of new conditional discriminations from auditory-visual versus visual-visual baselines.

Subject K.H. had shown herself able to label the ABC classes in accord with the auditory samples and the DEF classes in accord with the names of the English letter samples (Chapter 7, Experiment 2). In that same study, Subject P.H. named the ABC class members appropriately but gave inconsistent labels to members of the DEF classes. Both of these subjects had naming tests after they demonstrated six-member classes, so their data may not be strictly comparable to that of Subjects L.M. and B.V. In naming tests after the two three-member classes had emerged, Subject L.M. gave the appropriate Greek letter names to the B- and C-stimuli and the appropriate English letter names (Figure 8-1) to members of the DEF classes. Subject B.V. also named the B- and C-stimuli in accord with the dictated samples to which they had been related in the baseline conditional discriminations. Although he named all of the English letter samples (L, O, and G) correctly, he applied the appropriate sample name just to comparisons that had been related to the letter L; he labeled comparisons that had been related to O and G inconsistently. There seemed to be no relation, therefore, between the baseline learning sequences and the assignment of common labels to class members.

The only relation these data do suggest is between the assignment of common labels to class members and the overall speed of learning the baseline conditional discriminations. Subjects K.H. and L.M., the two who classified the stimuli by means of common labels, also learned the baseline conditional discriminations most rapidly. The possibility that common labels for samples and their related comparisons facilitate the learning of conditional discriminations remains a matter for further study.

Auditory-visual versus visual-visual baselines: conflict tests. Martha Willson-Morris, Barbara Kirk, and I also attempted to detect differences that might exist between auditory-visual and purely visual classes *after* subjects had learned the baseline conditional discriminations. This time, we were somewhat more successful. Figure 8-6 illustrates our plan. The baseline consisted of two sets of auditory-visual conditional discriminations, AB and AC, and two sets of visual-visual conditional discriminations, DC and DE. Although this three-node baseline (A, C, and D) had the potential for generating five-member classes, we were concerned here with the three-member components ABC and DCE. These potential classes would contain the C-stimuli in common. What would subjects do when faced with test trials in which they

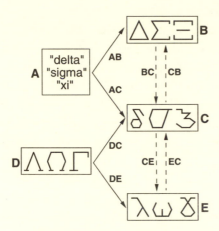

Figure 8-6. Auditory-visual (ABC) and visual-visual (DCE) classes, with the C-stimuli common to both. See text for details.

were presented with a C-stimulus as the sample along with the potentially related B- and E-stimuli as comparisons? On any given trial, would they select the B-comparison on the basis of its joint membership with the C-sample in the auditory-visual ABC class or would they select the E-comparison on the basis of its joint membership with the C-sample in the purely visual DCE class? Or would the joint membership of all stimuli in five-member classes prevent any such differences from showing up?

Our subjects were three nonretarded 5 to 6 year-old children. Baseline teaching was carried out as described in the *Role of Naming* study: Subjects V.E. and M.L. learned DC and DE (visual-visual) conditional discriminations first and Subject S.B. learned AB and AC (auditory-visual) first. After showing that they could do the whole baseline without reinforcement, the subjects were tested with BC, CB, CE, and EC probe trials to evaluate the three-member subclasses. Subject V.E. performed perfectly on his first CB and BC tests but required four repetitions of the CE and EC tests before these indicated equivalence relations. Subject M.L. required many repetitions of all the tests and he, too, showed the ABC classes emerging before the DCE classes. Subject S.B. needed a few repetitions of each test but gave no clear indication that one of the classes preceded the other.

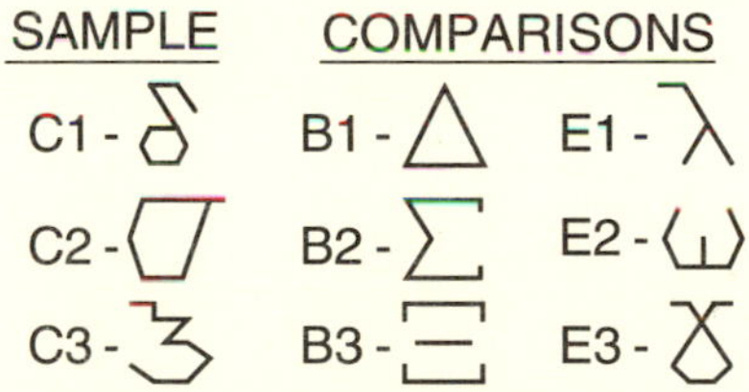

SAMPLE   COMPARISONS

C1 -   B1 -   E1 -

C2 -   B2 -   E2 -

C3 -   B3 -   E3 -

Figure 8-7. Conflict probe trials.

After the two three-member classes were confirmed, the children were given two-comparison "conflict probes" (Figure 8-7) in the context of baseline trials, all without reinforcement. In each conflict probe trial, the sample was a C-stimulus and the comparisons were the B- and E-stimuli that had been shown to be related to that C-stimulus. Subjects were tested several times to determine whether they would select the B-comparison from the auditory-visual class or the E-comparison from the purely visual class. Tests contained 27 trials, nine with each C-sample. Table 8-4 summarizes the results.

In all tests, the children chose B-stimuli (auditory-visual class members) more often than E-stimuli (visual class members). It was clear, however, that they recognized both comparisons to be correct, sometimes touching them simultaneously, sometimes touching a blank key, and occasionally even saying aloud, "They are both right." Because of these confusions (and, in the case of Subject S.B., because of many baseline errors during his first three conflict tests), we usually repeated the tests several times, often reviewing the class-formation tests between repetitions of the conflict probes.

Naming tests were given after the conflict probes were completed. Subject M.L. gave the Greek letter names "delta," "sigma," and "xi"

Table 8-4. Conflict probe test results.

Subject	Test Number	Number of Selections		
		B	E	Blank or Double
V.E.	1	18	5	4
	2	22	2	3
	3	21	6	0
	4	20	6	1
S.B.	1	14	8	5
	2	11	4	12
	3	16	10	1
	4	19	5	3
	5	14	6	7
	6	14	12	1
	7	21	6	0
	8	22	4	1
M.L.	1	19	7	1

appropriately to the B- and C-stimuli but always said, "I don't know," when asked about the D- and E-stimuli. In the conflict probes, therefore, he might have preferred the B-comparisons because they had the same names as the C-samples. On the other hand, Subjects V.E. and S.B. labeled all of the stimuli "delta," "sigma," or "xi" in conformity with the five-member classes that were to be expected from the baseline shown in Figure 8-6. These subjects, therefore, did not prefer the B-comparisons simply because they had the same names as the C-samples; the E-comparisons also had those names. Perhaps, however, subjects preferred the B-comparisons because they were more directly related to the names (via the baseline AB conditional discriminations); they could only have learned those names for the E-stimuli indirectly (via the emergent CE relations). If we had established larger classes and tested for conflict between E-stimuli and stimuli related to the dictated A-samples through additional nodes, subjects might have preferred the E-comparisons over stimuli whose names were even less directly related to the dictated A-samples.

We did not explicitly test for five-member ABCDE classes but several observations make it seem likely that those larger classes did form: Two children assigned the same name to each of the five visual stimuli that would be expected to constitute a single class; all of the children selected E-stimuli frequently, even though less often than B-stimuli; and children selected blank keys or both B- and E-stimuli simultaneously often enough to suggest strongly that the B-

and E-comparisons were both related to the C-samples. If five-member classes did form, as seems likely, then the conflict probes can be viewed as a method for attacking a number of interesting questions about the class memberships of stimuli.

For example, does it matter whether stimuli had been brought into the class via intermodal or intramodal baselines? That is to say, in addition to their membership in the verified equivalence classes, do the stimuli also retain membership in other classes that are grounded on the original baseline modalities? A similar question has been asked with respect to baseline nodality: do the stimuli in an equivalence class retain membership in other classes that are grounded on the number of baseline nodes that were needed to bring those stimuli into the class? Fields, Adams, and Verhave (1993) proposed a *within-class preference test* (another name for what I have called a *conflict-probe test*) to answer this question (see pp. 547-549). Also, does it matter how many different classes a stimulus belongs to? How does context determine class membership? And so on. The conflict-probe technique promises to provide a useful experimental tool for analyzing the histories that give rise to the multiplicity of classes every stimulus must belong to.

The Definition of Equivalence: A Cautionary Note

The strictest evidence for equivalence comes when a subject proves capable of all of the new conditional discriminations that document the properties of reflexivity, symmetry, and transitivity in the baseline relation. The BC and CB or the EF and FE conditional discriminations (Figure 8-1) are called a simultaneous or abbreviated test for equivalence because the emergence of these conditional discriminations requires the baseline to possess all of the properties of an equivalence relation. In Chapter 7, I discussed the possibility that such an abbreviated equivalence test might be more likely to be positive—to document equivalence—in a baseline containing N nodes if baselines containing fewer nodes are tested first. In the *Role of Naming* study, the possibility arose that even in a single-node baseline, equivalence might be fostered by testing individual properties first. For example, the prior demonstration of symmetry, even in tests without reinforcement, seemed to be necessary before Subjects A.A. and M.D. could perform accurately on the abbreviated equivalence tests (Table 8-2). So far so good. But then we went on to cite the data of Subject P.A. in support of the same point.

Subject P.A., too, failed on the EF tests for equivalence until he succeeded on the ED (and FD) symmetry tests (Table 8-2). The problem was that Subject P.A. was taught the ED relations *with explicit reinforcement*. As we realized later, if the conditional discriminations that document the properties of an equivalence relation are explicitly reinforced, rather than emergent, those conditional discriminations will not necessarily confirm an equivalence relation. For example, teaching ED need not give DE the property of symmetry; the ED and DE conditional discriminations might still represent completely independent performances. Only if ED emerges from DE without reinforcement can we infer with some certainty that the ED performance depends on DE—in this instance, through the property of symmetry. Because we cannot be certain, then, that Subject P.A.'s data documented symmetry, it is possible that our inclusion of Subject P.A. Among those in the *Role of Naming* study who demonstrated equivalence was incorrect

The need for caution in interpretation was brought home by a retarded teenager whom we (Willson-Morris, Kirk, and Sidman) taught to match six numerals as samples to upper- and lower-case letter comparisons (for example, 2 to A and a, 3 to D and d, 4 to E and e, and so on: Figure 8-8, AB and AC). With these arbitrary conditional discriminations as a baseline, we then tested

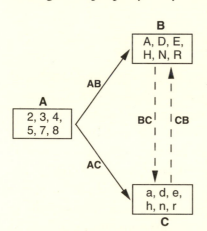

Figure 8-8. Arbitrary matching of numerals to upper- and lower-case letters (AB, AC), and equivalence tests of letter matching (BC, CB). See text.

to determine whether our subject would match the appropriate upper- and lower-case letters to each other (Figure 8-8, BC and CB).

Table 8-5 shows the data this boy gave us. In the first test, scores of 100% and 94% show his proficiency on the two baseline tasks he had been taught: matching the numerals to upper- and lower-case letters. The abbreviated equivalence tests required him to match upper-case samples to lower-case comparisons and vice-versa. He achieved only 33% and 29% correct on these, clearly *dis*confirming the formation of equivalence relations. This failure to validate equivalence made it imperative to test the baseline relations for symmetry: upper- or lower-case letters now served as samples, with numerals as comparisons. His scores of 25% and 29% indicated that he was unable to match the baseline stimuli when their sample-comparison roles were reversed; the baseline relations were not symmetric. The absence of symmetry was sufficient to explain our failure to observe equivalence in the abbreviated tests.

We then deliberately taught the boy—with reinforcement—to do the reverse matching tasks: letters as samples and numerals as comparisons. In the second set of tests, he did these and the original baseline almost perfectly. Nevertheless, even after having explicitly been taught the symmetric conditional discriminations, he still did not show equivalence (scores of only 67% and 33% on the abbreviated tests). We had to conclude that explicit training with interchanged samples and comparisons does not necessarily establish true

Table 8-5.
Baseline (numeral-letter), equivalence (letter-letter), and symmetry (letter-numeral) test results.

Samples	Comparisons	Percent Correct	
		Test 1	Test 2
2, 3, 4, 5, 7, 8	A, D, E, H, N, R	(100)	(100)
2, 3, 4, 5, 7, 8	a, d, e, h, n, r	(94)	(100)
A, D, E, H, N, R	a, d, e, h, n, r	33	67
a, d, e, h, n, r	A, D, E, H, N, R	29	33
A, D, E, H, N, R	2, 3, 4, 5, 7, 8	25	(100)
a, d, e, h, n, r	2, 3, 4, 5, 7, 8	29	(96)

symmetry. Such training may only generate additional but independent sets of specific conditional relations, not an equivalence relation. True symmetry requires the subject to be able to reverse samples and comparisons without having been explicitly taught to do so. The history is critical.

The history is critical for identifying not only symmetry but all of the other properties of an equivalence relation also. If the conditional discriminations indicative of reflexivity and/or transitivity and/or equivalence (the last indicated by the abbreviated test) are directly taught rather than emergent, then such teaching may only generate conditional discriminations that are completely independent of each other. The point is that we would not know whether pairs of conditionally related stimuli belonged to an equivalence relation or whether they were independent of each other. The application of mathematical set theory's generalized definition of the equivalence relation to the specifics of behavior analysis proves useful when it enables us to predict new performances that have not been generated by direct reinforcement contingencies. And so, although the mathematical formulation is silent about the history of the related pairs of events that make up an equivalence relation, that history determines whether or not the concept *equivalence relation* makes new behavior predictable or whether it is simply a useless label.

Two Clarifications

Retention. In the *Role of Naming* study, we reported the results of equivalence tests that were repeated after three months (Subject A.A.) and one year (Subject M.D.). The context did not make it clear, however, that these were not tests for retention of the equivalence relations; the baselines were always reviewed, with reinforcement, before the tests. Significant new discoveries are likely to emerge from investigations of the role of equivalence relations in remembering but our program has not yet moved in that direction. (See Saunders, Wachter, and Spradlin, 1988, and Spradlin, Saunders, and Saunders, 1992 for some relevant data and theory on equivalence and remembering.)

Reflexivity tests. As our research progressed, a number of changes took place in the ways we thought and talked about various aspects of equivalence relations. I noted some of the changes in previous chapters. A later development was the refinement of our conception of reflexivity, a development that is worth commenting on here because we were so explicit about the way we tested for reflexivity in the *Role of Naming* study. That way turns out to be irrelevant to our purpose.

A conditional relation is reflexive if each stimulus exhibits the *same conditional relation* with respect to itself. A reflexivity test trial might present a subject with both A1 and A2 as comparisons; which comparison will the subject choose when A1 or A2 is the sample? The test itself is simple enough but when is it to be carried out? In this and other studies, we evaluated reflexivity by means of pretests—identity-matching tests that we carried out before we taught subjects the baseline conditional discriminations. As we and others were to realize later (Saunders & Green, 1992; Carrigan and Sidman, 1992; Johnson & Sidman, 1993), the definition requires that reflexivity be tested not before but after we have taught the baseline conditional discriminations. This, of course, is true of tests for any property of an equivalence relation. Each test, whether for reflexivity, symmetry, or transitivity, is intended to determine whether the conditionally related pairs of baseline stimuli are included in an equivalence relation. The tests always evaluate the baseline. Pretests cannot identify properties of the baseline because the subjects will not at that point have learned or even encountered the baseline conditional discriminations. Pretests for reflexivity make no more sense than pretests for symmetry or transitivity. The results of any such tests will be determined by factors other than the baseline relations.

Significant consequences follow from maintaining a rigorous definition of reflexivity as a property of the baseline and from testing in accord with that definition. Reflexivity tests given before we have taught the baseline relations may yield what looks like a positive result—identity matching—for reasons that reflect historical rather than current experimental variables. On the other hand, reflexivity tests given after the baseline relations have been taught may yield results that look like matching or like nonmatching, depending on the nature of the baseline conditional relation. Either of these results may be consistent with reflexivity (Carrigan & Sidman, 1992; Johnson & Sidman, 1993). Thus, seemingly positive pretests (as in our *Role of Naming* study) or seemingly negative posttests (as in Dube, Green, & Serna, 1993, and Johnson & Sidman, 1993) could lead to erroneous conclusions about reflexivity.

9

Equivalence Relations and Contingency Analysis: The Analytic Units

Background

Early in 1984, I received a letter from Travis Thompson inviting me to participate in a conference in honor of Kenneth MacCorquodale. Travis wrote, "The topic of the conference concerns a matter of fundamental concern to behavioral science...namely, the nature of the fundamental units of analysis and their integration to form complex behavioral repertoires....If there is to be a major breakthrough in behavior analysis in the next decade, I believe it will be the formulation of laws of behavioral syntax which allow us to characterize the manner in which behavioral units combine to form integrated behavioral repertoires." He went on to suggest a topic for my presentation, *Functional Analysis of Emergent Verbal Classes*. My first thought was, "How did Travis know that this topic was at the top of my current repertoire?" Then I remembered that he had been one of the organizers of an earlier conference where I had given a presentation entitled *The Measurement of Behavioral Development* (Sidman, 1986b). There, I had tried to make the point that a rigorous analysis of development required the indentification of behavioral units whose status could be assessed at any developmental stage. But I had not then completed the analysis of behavioral units and I now welcomed the opportunity to take the next steps. Travis clearly had seen the direction in which my thoughts were moving. I was greatly encouraged by his desire to see the topic developed further.

In the first paragraph of the *Emergent Verbal Classes* paper (reproduced below), I wrote, "Self-analysis has not been a major recent preoccupation of Behavior Analysis." Since then, however, we have seen a veritable explosion of such self-analysis. In the past few years, three of the most prestigious behavior analytic journals have devoted all or nearly all of one or more issues to papers that have expressed considerable dissatisfaction with the current state of experimentation and theory in both applied and basic Behavior Analysis (for example, Baron, Perone, & Galizio, 1991; Behavior dynamics, 1992; Science, theory…, 1991). Much of the self-examination in these collections of papers was focused on negative critiques of current practices, although a few authors also proposed new procedural and theoretical approaches to be substituted for the old. Many of these papers will repay serious consideration. Because any developing field of science can be expected to undergo major changes, self-examination is always worthwhile. What has surprised me, however, about the general tenor of the self-criticism in these papers has been the almost complete absence of acknowledgment that current practices and principles possess any utility, that they, rather than or in addition to the proposed new approaches, might serve as a foundation for continued progress.

The death of B. F. Skinner undoubtedly triggered much of the self-examination within Behavior Analysis. Some of the negatively toned criticism can be attributed to a certain amount of position jockeying for a perceived leadership vacancy. This, of course, will pass. Although destructive criticism may bring notoriety, it contributes nothing lasting. And then, too, Skinner did not step into an empty leadership slot; he established a unique position that his own experimental and theoretical contributions defined. Much of the recent self-criticism that has been constructive reflects the recognition that we can no longer wait for Skinner's brilliant analyses to provide us with inspiration; we now have to do it ourselves. Given this imperative, my own predilection is not to abandon an empirical and theoretical framework that has proven itself productive but to take that system and try to add elements that seem to be missing. How does one decide what elements are missing and which of those we are ready to add?

Lee (1988) pointed out:

> Scientific knowledge is...knowledge of phenomena beyond ordinary observation.... [and] it is also reliable knowledge available to the anonymous observer and indifferent to whoever makes the observation.... [Nevertheless,] scientific inquiry begins with phenomena available to ordinary observers... [and] with a language available to ordinary speakers.... *We should expect [scientific] inquiry to start in what is known* and deliberately to surpass it [emphasis added]. (pp. 17-25)

Skinner's writings made it clear that he was aware of the relevance of his formulations to problems arising out of ordinary knowledge and that he felt it important to communicate that relevance to others (for example, Holland & Skinner, 1961; Skinner, 1953, 1957, 1968, 1971). My own interest in Skinner's work began when (and continued because) I saw how the science illuminated problems of everyday human conduct.

For example, my interest in what ordinary language classified as *anxiety,* and in conduct that was called *purposive,* led to my work on *avoidance* and other kinds of *coercively* controlled behavior (Sidman, 1953, 1960, 1964, 1966, 1989); clearly visible effects of *tranquilizing* drugs as *mood-changers* and as *anxiety reducers* led to my participation in the beginnings of the science of Behavioral Pharmacology (Sidman, 1955, 1956, 1959); observations of *language disorders* and other *psychological* changes in people who suffered central nervous system damage brought me into contact with hospitalized patients who had experienced strokes, patients with problems that challenged a science of behavior to provide rigorous definition and classification (Mohr et al., 1973; Mohr & Sidman, 1975; Sidman, 1971a; Sidman et al., 1971); long-standing concerns about our educational system led me into research on and application of effective teaching methods for both the handicapped and nonhandicapped (Mackay & Sidman, 1968; Sidman, 1970, 1985; Sidman & Sidman, 1965; Sidman & Stoddard, 1966, 1967); finally, the relevance of our work on equivalence relations to *reading comprehension,* and more broadly to *symbolic representation* and *meaning (semantic correspondence)* in *language* is in large part responsible for the continuation of that research program for more than 25 years.

I list these various involvements of mine not in a spirit of self-approbation but to illustrate how a simple yet classic approach can generate useful contributions without first throwing everything away. Other areas, their names taken from common language, and of general concern because they refer to happenings that touch the lives of many people, have been or could be approached in the same spirit: *memory, emotion, knowledge, intention, values, awareness, thinking, problem solving, development, intelligence, artificial intelligence, social interaction, culture,* and so forth. As more topics of common interest are brought in for analysis, additions to the basic structure of the science will inevitably be required and we can look forward to formulations that are more inclusive. Major changes in the science's basic structure, however, will be needed only if it is shown that matters available to general observation cannot *in principle* be handled. Behavior Analysis as it is currently formulated does not yet seem to have bumped up against any such built-in barriers to productivity. My hope was that the *Emergent Verbal Classes* paper would encourage both behavior analysts and others to take a constructive approach.

It is true that laboratory research on equivalence relations was examining phenomena that Behavior Analysis had not previously considered. Our formulation of those phenomena had introduced a new set of terms to the behavior analytic vocabulary. To some, our introduction of new terms and concepts seemed to suggest that we were discarding the old ones. In spite of the novelty of topic and terminology, however, I never felt that we were abandoning the system of behavioral analysis that was founded on the experimental, theoretical, and philosophical contributions of B. F. Skinner. Rather, I viewed the work on equivalence relations as a natural extension of that tradition. A major aim of the *Emergent Verbal Classes* paper was to show that the equivalence relation, while perhaps a new behavioral concept as we had defined it, was an outgrowth of the same kind of contingency analysis that had given rise to basic relational concepts like stimulus, response, reinforcement, discrimination, conditioned and generalized reinforcement, and conditional discrimination.

The study of equivalence relations has contributed some new data to Behavior Analysis and perhaps some new principles, but none of these requires the abandonment of data and principles that have already proven their worth. The enlargement of the analytic unit that is outlined in the *Emergent Verbal Classes* paper is just that—an *enlargement*. It encompasses equivalence relations and their contextual control but requires no fundamental change in the methods of analysis or in the underlying empirical and theoretical structure. In fact, I am convinced that the *Emergent Verbal Classes* paper provides a useful framework within which to organize the existing data and principles of Behavior Analysis. I believe it constitutes the outline for an elementary but inclusive text of Behavior Analysis and some day I may act on that conviction.

This is not to say that the *Emergent Verbal Classes* paper was the last word. Hardly. One of its major points—the notion that equivalence comes only from four-term contingencies—has in fact proven incorrect. But I will tell that part of the ongoing story later, in Chapters 10 and 11.

Functional Analysis of Emergent Verbal Classes

Since Skinner's classic treatment of the reflex concept (1931) and his explication of the generic nature of stimuli and responses (1935), the identification and analysis of basic behavioral units has received only intermittent attention. At first, thoughtful psychologists examined the problem out of their concern with the systematic status of the new Behaviorism (e.g., MacCorquodale & Meehl, 1948; Meehl, 1950) and with relations between Behaviorism and other approaches to the subject matter (e.g., Estes, Koch, MacCorquodale, Meehl, Mueller, Schoenfeld, & Verplanck, 1954; Goldiamond, 1962, 1966; Schoenfeld & Cumming, 1963). As experimental and applied Behavior Analysis grew in scope and power, however, the problem of behavioral units, seemingly of no practical importance, was swept under the rug. These developing sciences were busy devising powerful techniques for altering behavior both in and out of the laboratory, describing behavior of ever greater complexity, and advancing principles to coordinate and unify seemingly unrelated behavioral phenomena. They rarely paused to examine their own internal structure. With some exceptions (e.g., Catania, 1992; Goldiamond, 1975; Hineline, 1980; Lee, 1983; Schoenfeld, 1976), self-analysis has not been a major recent preoccupation of Behavior Analysis.

Therefore, where an opposing point of view, the Cognitive Sciences, might once have provoked searching evaluations and comparisons of both approaches, behavior analysts remained instead at the mercy of reinforcement contingencies that operated within their cultural, social, and political environments. Whether they fought or joined the opposition, few based their choice on rational grounds.

BEHAVIOR, COGNITION, AND THE PROBLEM OF ANALYTIC UNITS

After switching to cognitivism, many former behaviorists became content to leave the identification of stimuli and responses largely to the judgment of the individual experimenter or therapist. Soon, subjects and patients were even being asked to reinforce or punish themselves for their actions and thoughts (for critiques of these practices, see Catania, 1975, 1976; Goldiamond, 1976). Units of behavior no longer had to be capable of direct observation or measurement; experimenters and theorists found themselves able to "explain" the most complex behavior by appeal to representations, plans, and other mental structures, and to the innate capabilities and developmental sequences (programs) that are supposed to give mental attributes a life of their own. Behavior analysts who became *cognitive scientists, cognitive behavior modifiers*, or *cognitive therapists* also found that they no longer had to defend themselves against the epithet, *stimulus-response psychologist*.

Before taking the easy ways out—joining the opposition blindly, opposing it blindly, or ignoring it—behavior analysts might instead have gone to the trouble of examining the logic, assumptions, and research practices of both the cognitive approach and their own. If they had started with Cognitive Science, they would have found that it does not exist. There is no body of systematized principles, no unique set of data, no characteristic measurement techniques, and no typical investigative procedures to which a cognitivist can point and say, "That is my Science." The mind may possess a structure but the Science of Mind does not.

The basic units of cognition—representations, intentions, plans, rules, programs, and other mental structures—are linked to actual behavior only if that becomes necessary. When such necessity does arise—for example, in carrying out experiments—the logic of the linkage need not be compelling. For the cognitivist, behavior is important only as a product of mental processes, but criteria do not exist for determining whether different instances of behavior represent the same mental processes. Given an interest in some particular process, each observer is privileged to decide which behavior will provide the appropriate window into the mind.

A constructive view might be that: (a) Cognitive Science worries about important and interesting phenomena but has been too impatient, failing to accomplish the intellectually rigorous and prior task of laying a systematic foundation from which to synthesize complex processes; (b) Behavior Analysis, although it has moved swiftly even on the accelerated time scale of modern science and has developed a systematic foundation, still has not been impatient enough to attempt all of the syntheses of which it is capable. An easy criticism has been that Behavior Analysis deals well with uninteresting behavior but ignores everything that makes human beings superior to all other creatures. The concepts of stimulus and response have seemed impoverished, unable to capture the rich complexity of the human intellect. Behavior analysts, themselves, have not continued to examine the units of

their own science in sufficient depth to appreciate whether and how they might be able to account for just those phenomena that concern cognitive scientists.

At this particular time, therefore, it is appropriate to honor Kenneth MacCorquodale by returning to a consideration of matters to which he and his students have made major contributions. My own recent laboratory studies, also, have made it necessary for me to reexamine the basic units of Behavior Analysis and to evaluate how well those units might help systematize even phenomena that some hold to be nonbehavioral. I am going to attempt to describe what I believe are the basic units. For the most part, I shall merely summarize what is already known, my own contribution being, perhaps, to apply the notion that the units of analysis need not be fixed. By increasing the size and complexity of the analytic unit step by step, we can observe new relations emerging among the elements of the unit and between units. Ever more complex behavioral phenomena fall within the systematic framework.

THE RESPONSE

For behavior analysts, the primary object of observation and measurement, behavior itself, is usually conceptualized in any particular instance as a *response*. Although the response is a most complex unit of behavior, I have nothing useful to add to existing discussions of its definition (e.g., Catania, 1973; Estes et al., 1954; Goldiamond, 1962; Notterman & Mintz, 1965; Schoenfeld & Cumming, 1963; Skinner, 1935). By itself, however, the response has only limited utility as a unit of analysis. To measure behavior alone can be meaningful only in an environment that never changes. Indeed, its dictionary definition requires that a response be in reaction *to* something. Although one can *behave* in an unchanging environment, one can *respond* only to an environmental change. In the old stimulus-response Psychology, the unit of analysis was a *relation* between a response and a prior environmental event, an unconditioned or a conditioned eliciting stimulus. Functional analysis, however, has revealed and elaborated several relations between environment and behavior that go considerably beyond elicitation.

THE TWO-TERM CONTINGENCY

Skinner (1935, 1938) pointed out that an operant response is a class of organismic events that cannot be identified without reference to environmental consequences. He therefore retained the notion of a relation as the appropriate unit of analysis but his concept of the operant turned the original stimulus-response relation around. He proposed, instead, a response-stimulus relation, the now familiar two-term reinforcement contingency, as a basic unit for the analysis and description of operant behavior. Retention of the term, response, probably accounts in large part for the misconception that modern Behavior Analysis is constrained by a stimulus-response formula. The consequences of behavior—events that happen subsequent to a response—determine its future probability.

Figure 9-1 diagrams a two-term contingency. The upper line signifies that a particular

```
R1  (PRESS)  ──▶ C1 (COIN)

R2  (OTHER)  ─╫▶ C1 (COIN)
```

Figure 9-1. The two-term contingency (Reinforcement). R = Response; C= Consequence.

item of behavior, Response 1 (R1), is followed by a particular Consequence (C1). For example, a laboratory subject receives a coin after pressing a button. The second line shows why this relation between response and consequence is a *contingency*; the coin does not come (crossed arrow) if the subject does anything else (R2). The consequence follows the specified behavior, Response 1, and no other. Thus, we have: if press (and no other response), then coin. This behavior-consequence relation, modulated by many parameters (schedule, delay, amount, deprivation, alternative contingencies, and so on), will determine the future likelihood of the behavior.

Recognition of the two-term contingency as a unit of analysis, simple though it seems, must rank as a milestone in the development of behavioral analysis. Behavior that seemed controlled by future events, a puzzling scientific anomaly, could now be seen to have been generated by past contingencies. A major area of cognition, *purpose*, was for the first time placed in good scientific order. It was not even necessary to invoke hypothetical *expectations*, *anticipations*, or *intentions* to bring future determinants back into the present or the past; one could point instead to real contingencies that had already taken place.

Because the two-term unit of analysis specifies a causal relation between behavior and environment, we might learn much about particular people simply by cataloguing their repertoire of two-term contingencies, as aptitude and personality tests attempt to do. Identifying positive and negative reinforcers and the behavior to which these are characteristically related should indeed help to identify a person's interests and sources of satisfaction and how the person goes about achieving them. Applied behavior analysts, by conducting controlled observations to identify the relevant behavior-consequence relations in a client's repertoire, have achieved considerable success in defining and ameliorating problem behavior.

Useful as even a partial catalogue may be, however, it can

hardly satisfy our analytic needs. If parameters local to a two-term relation completely determined the probability that it would be active at any given moment, our behavior would be chaotic. Response would succeed upon response, the sequence being determined solely by momentary reinforcement probabilities, deprivation states, energy requirements, and so on. This, of course, is not what happens. Our environment not only provides consequences but selects from our repertoires the particular two-term units that are to be active at any moment.

THE THREE-TERM CONTINGENCY

The experiments that most thoroughly and successfully clarified the basic behavior-consequence relation (e.g., Ferster & Skinner, 1957; Skinner, 1938) did so by holding the subject's environment constant except for those changes that occurred subsequent to the behavior. It then became possible to introduce variations into the subjects' environment prior to or concurrently with the behavior. Behavior analysts usually conceptualize a variation in the subject's environment as a *stimulus*. Stimulus definition, like response definition, is a most complex matter and I shall not attempt here to amplify existing discussions (e.g., Estes et al., 1954; Lawrence, 1963; Prokasy & Hall, 1963; Ray, 1972; Ray & Sidman, 1970; Schoenfeld & Cumming, 1963; Sidman, 1969; Skinner, 1935; Stoddard & Sidman, 1971; Terrace, 1966). Rather, I shall focus on the familiar three-term relation, the analytic unit that emerges when one considers the two-term contingency in relation to the changing environment.

Figure 9-2 illustrates a three-term contingency. The upper half shows that the two-term contingency is now under the control of a third element, Stimulus S1. The subject can still press the button and produce the coin but only if the button has on it a particular geometric form, for example, a square (S1). The contrast with other stimuli, S2 (in the lower half of Figure 9-2), makes this three-term relation a contingency; the two-term relation holds true only in the presence of the square. When any other geometric form, a circle,

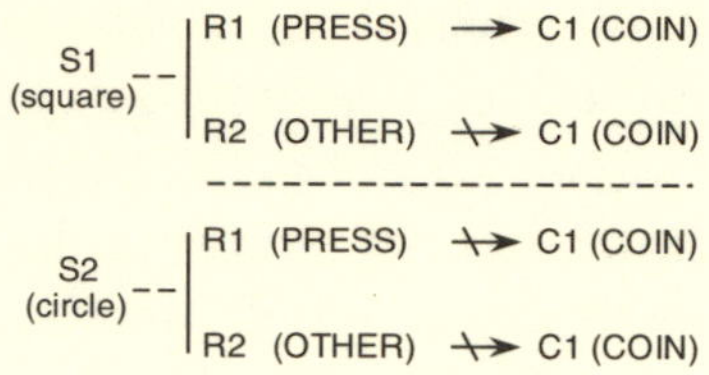

```
         | R1  (PRESS)  ----> C1 (COIN)
   S1   --|
 (square) | R2  (OTHER)  -/-> C1 (COIN)
         -------------------------
         | R1  (PRESS)  -/-> C1 (COIN)
   S2   --|
 (circle) | R2  (OTHER)  -/-> C1 (COIN)
```

Figure 9-2. The three-term contingency (Discrimination). R = Response; C = Consequence; S = Stimulus.

for example, is on the button, the two-term contingency does not exist; pressing the button will not produce a coin. Thus, we have the three-term contingency: if a square (and no other form) is on the button, then, if the subject presses (no other response will do), then a coin will follow.

As Skinner (1938) pointed out, the square does not elicit the response. Rather, since it increases the likelihood that a subject will produce a coin by pressing the button, the square activates that particular two-term contingency. The two-term relation is placed under *discriminative* control. This is how the environment establishes priorities, imposing order upon behavior by selectively altering the probability of two-term relations that exist in one's repertoire. In the process, the third term, S1, becomes part of an expanded unit of analysis. The three-term

contingency is the fundamental unit of *stimulus control*.

Why must we enlarge our analytic unit? Would it not suffice to treat S1 simply as a parameter of the two-term unit? Two considerations force us to acknowledge the larger unit. First, like the two-term relation, the three-term contingency itself can come under environmental control, increasing or decreasing in probability as an entity. This point will be elaborated below. Second, to define a response requires that we take the relation between it and its controlling environment as our unit. In the case of two-term contingencies, we need consider only the behavior-consequence relation, since the consequence is the only changing aspect of the subject's environment. In three-term contingencies, however, other aspects of the environment also vary. Discriminative control introduces an additional relation between environment and behavior and this new relation also enters into the response definition.

The problem of definition can be illustrated by reference to a familiar experimental arrangement for studying three-term contingencies, a procedure that requires only a slight reinterpretation of Figure 9-2. Suppose a subject has two buttons available, the square appearing unpredictably on one or the other; whichever button does not have the square on it has the circle. Both S1 and S2, therefore, are present simultaneously. The subject produces a coin by pressing the button on which the square appears.

It is easy enough to distinguish pressing the button (R1) from all other responses (R2), since only R1 produces the coin. Because this response definition requires a specification of the consequence, both terms, response and consequence, must be considered together as a single relation rather than as two independent units. But now we face the problem of distinguishing between two different responses of pressing a button, one "correct" and one "incorrect" (Sidman, 1978). The common-sense differentiation is "pressing the square" and "pressing the circle." Again, however, the response definition includes a stimulus specification. To define the response in a three-term contingency therefore requires that the response be related not only to C1 but to S1. All three components of the contingency must be considered together as a unit.

By adding a single term to its smallest analytic unit, Behavior Analysis significantly broadens its domain. For example, the three-term contingency encompasses those phenomena that have traditionally been included under *perception* (e.g., Goldiamond, 1962). Classical Psychophysics studies how quantitative and qualitative energy transformations of S1 affect the likelihood that certain three-term relations will hold true; given a history of reinforcement (C1) for saying, "Yes, I see it" (R1), in the presence of a flash of light (S1), what is the probability that flashes varying in intensity, duration, wavelength, and so on, will still occasion the same behavior-consequence relation? How do stimulus characteristics determine what we see, hear, smell, and so forth? Modern Psychophysics (Green & Swets, 1966) takes *biasing* factors into account—variables, for example, that modulate the behavior-consequence relation (Goldiamond, 1962)—in describing how stimulus energy affects the probability of a particular three-term unit; if the payoff for saying, "Yes," is greater than for saying, "No," we are likely to report seeing the flash even when it is actually too dim to affect our visual receptors.

When the third term, S1, is added to the analytic unit, a new process, conditioned reinforcement, enters the picture. A response that produces S1 as a consequence will activate the three-term unit of which S1 is the initiating component. Such activation of a three-term unit proves, itself, to be a reinforcer. S1 can now alter the future probability of behavior that precedes it (Skinner, 1938).

This new process, derived from the expanded analytic unit, enlarges the scope of Behavior Analysis still more. First, the environmental elements that can function as effective behavioral consequences become virtually limitless, extending from the "built in" reinforcing properties of basic biological necessities to subtly conditioned events like the sound of a cash register, the tone of a violin string, a syntactically correct verbal expression, or the blink of a listener's eye.

Second, generalized conditioned reinforcers (Skinner,

1953), each effective under many different deprivation states, support important categories of verbal behavior. Without generalized reinforcers, for example, our descriptions of the environment would be accurate only to the extent that they produced reinforcers that corresponded to our deprivation states at the moment. The three-term units in a person's repertoire would constitute demands for particular reinforcers rather than unbiased reports based solely upon S1. Generalized reinforcers make it possible for us to give accurate information no matter what our current states of deprivation may be. A special kind of three-term unit, the tact (Skinner, 1957), permits us to go beyond demands for particular reinforcers and instead to report the environment independently of our momentary deprivations.

Third, conditioned reinforcers can support second-order schedules. These treat the completion of a first-order schedule contingency, itself, as a response. That larger response, in turn, is made part of a second-order schedule contingency, each first-order element producing a brief conditioned reinforcer until the completion of the second-order schedule produces the terminal reinforcement. The imposition of such a structure on behavior may increase to a remarkable extent the quantity of behavior that the environment can maintain at low cost (Findley & Brady, 1965; Kelleher, 1966).

Fourth, by functioning simultaneously as the consequence in one three-term unit and as the initiating element in another, conditioned reinforcers permit three-term contingencies to be chained into complex sequences (Findley, 1962). Chaining can create three-term structures of almost limitless intricacy, the elements themselves involving combinations of contingencies (alternative, conjunctive, interlocking, concurrent, and many others) and the choice points in the sequence providing options from which the subject can select the element that is to come next. Such structures can include many different responses, stimuli, and reinforcers and can extend over large areas of space and long periods of time. The ability to synthesize them in the laboratory, therefore, permits direct behavioral observation and analysis of the topographical, spatial, and temporal structure of organism-environment interactions.

The three-term contingency is also the basic analytic *unit of cognition*. One infers *knowledge* from observations of stimulus control; we can be said to know a subject matter only if we behave differentially with respect to the materials defining that subject matter. It becomes reasonable, perhaps, to characterize individuals' knowledge repertoires by cataloguing their stimulus-control repertoires, the three-term contingencies through which their behavior has become related both to consequences and antecedents. We might assess how much a person knows by counting the number of three-term units in that individual's catalogue; we might judge the quality of the knowledge repertoire by classifying the units into categories to which we assign different values. To a large extent, that is what standard intelligence tests attempt to do.

Such a characterization would be far from complete, since the environment also sets constraints upon three-term contingencies. Alone, they do not carry a behavioral analysis far enough. An additional term is needed to describe and account for the environment's ability to select from our repertoires the particular three-term units of stimulus control that are to be active at any moment.

THE FOUR-TERM CONTINGENCY

If we allow an additional element of the experimental environment to vary, the simplest units of stimulus control, three-term contingencies, can themselves be placed under stimulus control. The upper half of Figure 9-3 shows that the three-term relation is now under the control of a fourth element, Stimulus S3. Suppose the subject still has the original two buttons available, a square on one and a circle on the other, but now we introduce a third button that is sometimes green (S3) and sometimes red (S4). The subject can still press the square and produce a coin but only if the new button is green.

Because other colors might also appear on the third button (as in the lower half of Figure 9-3), this four-term relation is a contingency; the three-term relation holds true only in the

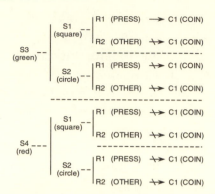

Figure 9-3. The four-term contingency (Conditional Discrimination). R = Response; C = Consequence; S = Stimulus.

presence of the green button. If that button is any other color, red, for example, the three-term contingency does not exist; the subject cannot produce a coin even by pressing a button that has a square on it. The three-term relation is placed under *conditional* control (Lashley, 1938). Thus we have the four-term contingency: if the third button is green (and no other color), then, if a square (and no other form) is on one of the two original buttons, then, if the subject presses it (no other response will do), only then will a coin follow.

The structure of the four-term unit reveals that conditional and discriminative control are different stimulus functions. A discriminative stimulus (S1) can be identified only by reference to a differential response (R1); the square can be said to exert discriminative control if its presence and absence are correlated with a change in behavior—the subject learns to press the button in the presence of the square but not in its absence. The conditional stimulus (S3) needs no additional differential behavior for its identification. The green hue can be said to exert conditional control if its presence and absence are correlated with a change in the control exerted by the square; even with a square on the button, the subject learns to press it only in the presence of the green hue. The diagram therefore shows no response intervening between S3 and S1. Even a *perceptual response* (e.g., Lawrence, 1963; Schoenfeld & Cumming, 1963), is superfluous in specifying the contingency. The stimulus-response relation gives way here to a stimulus-stimulus relation. Conditional stimuli do not control responses directly but determine the control that other stimuli exert over responses.

To appeal to an *association* between S3 and S1 in order to account for control by the hue (S3) would be, at worst, incorrect and misleading, and at best, incomplete. Rather, since it increases the likelihood that a subject will produce a coin by pressing the square, the green hue activates that particular three-term unit. Recognizing the different roles of discriminative and conditional stimuli, Cumming and Berryman (1965) pointed out that S1, as a discriminative stimulus, sets the occasion for the reinforcement of a specific response but that S3 functions as a "selector of discriminations, rather than of individual responses." They characterized the function of S3 as *instructional control.* That is how the environment establishes higher-order priorities, selectively altering the probability of three-term relations that exist in one's repertoire. In the process, the fourth term, S3, becomes part of still another expanded unit of analysis. The four-term contingency is the fundamental unit of what we might call *conditional, instructional,* or, as we shall see, of *contextual* stimulus control.

Again, it does not suffice to treat S3 simply as a parameter of the three-term unit. Like the two- and three-term relations, the four-term contingency itself can come under environmental constraint (see below). Nor are we dealing simply with stimulus compounds. One might suppose, for example, that the four-term contingency shown in Figure 9-3 could be reduced to a three-term contingency by specifying S1 as *green*-plus-*square* and S2 as either *green*-plus-*circle* or *red*-plus-*square*-or-*circle*. Stimulus compounding would combine S3 and S1, removing any need to expand the three-term unit of analysis. Collapsing Stimuli S3 and S1 into a single compound is not justifiable, however, when the two stimuli can be shown to function independently of each other (see below).

Cognitive scientists often criticize Behavior Analysis on the grounds that it cannot encompass important kinds of behavioral variability, those due to the effects of context. It is fashionable to interpret Behavior Analysis as a dogma that holds that behavior is simply a collection of reflexes, that given stimuli always elicit the same responses. The four-term analytic unit, however, contains within itself the elementary mechanism of contextual variation. Another name for conditional control might very well be contextual control. The significance of S1, for example, is no longer invariant but depends on other circumstances. The square only sets the occasion for the subject to obtain a coin if the environmental context includes the green hue. Four-term units consist of discriminations that are under contextual control.

Contextual control is particularly evident in language, where the significance of sounds, words, phrases, and so forth varies according to their context. Because the three-term unit of stimulus-control/cognition is fundamental to the analysis of all behavior, it brings general principles to bear upon the analysis of language. Contextual constraints upon a three-term contingency can therefore account for aspects of language that are themselves not linguistic in nature (Catania, 1980). The very establishment of contextual control, however, creates a potential for the emergence of a linguistic prerequisite, stimulus equivalence. Just as adding a third term to the analytic unit makes conditioned reinforcement possible, adding a fourth term also

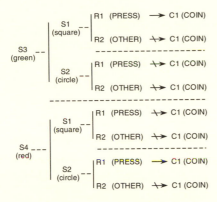

Figure 9-4. A balanced four-term contingency (Conditional Discrimination). R = Response; C = Consequence; S = Stimulus.

Figure 9-4 actually compresses into a single diagram two four-term contingencies of the type illustrated in Figure 9-3, one unit having S3 (green) as the fourth term and the other unit having S4 (red). Whether the subject can obtain a coin by pressing a square or a circle depends on the hue of the third button.

The expanded contingencies themselves specify only conditional relations: "if *green*, then press the *square* to produce the consequence" and "if *red*, then press the *circle*." The conditional relations, however, will also become equivalence relations. The green hue and the square will become equivalent members of one class, while the red hue and the circle will join as equivalent members of another class.

The emergence of equivalence from conditionality has some startling implications for a behavioral analysis, beginning with the very tests that are required to document equivalence. To determine whether equivalence relations have emerged from four-term units, one must test the conditional relations for the three properties, reflexivity, symmetry, and transitivity, which define equivalence (Sidman et al.,

generates a new process. The formation of *equivalence relations* (Sidman, 1971b) greatly extends the relevance of the four-term unit to language and other cognitive phenomena.

A small change in the four-term diagram will facilitate the exposition of equivalence relations. For an experimenter, the contingency outlined in Figure 9-3 is unbalanced; S3 provides a context in which the subject can press the square and produce a coin but S4 provides a context in which no behavior is effective. The arrangement in the bottom three lines of Figure 9-4 corrects the imbalance. The subject can now obtain a coin even in the context of S4 but the appropriate button has a circle on it.

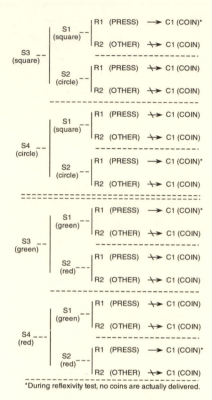

*During reflexivity test, no coins are actually delivered.

Figure 9-5. A test for reflexivity of the conditional relations in Figure 9-4.

1985; Sidman et al., 1982; Sidman & Tailby, 1982).

For a relation to be reflexive, it must hold true for each individual stimulus. If the conditional relations in Figure 9-4 between *green* and *square* and between *red* and *circle* are also equivalence relations, then reflexivity would require each stimulus to be conditionally related to itself. Reflexivity, therefore, translates behaviorally into

generalized identity matching. If equivalence has emerged from the explicitly constructed four-term units shown in Figure 9-4, then the units illustrated in Figure 9-5 will also be found in the subject's repertoire *even though the subject had never experienced those contingencies before.*

Since generalized identity matching is an empirical basis for the concept of sameness, we can see that sameness is a prerequisite for equivalence. Therefore, as will be noted below, it is also a prerequisite for the emergence of simple meanings, vocabularies, or semantic correspondences.

To help illustrate the other prerequisites for equivalence, we can set up a four-term contingency in which stimuli, although more familiar, are related to each other just as arbitrarily as those illustrated in Figure 9-4. In Figure 9-6, Stimuli S1 and S2 are printed words, *two* and *six*, while Stimuli S3 and S4 are printed digits, *2* and *6*. The subject can obtain a coin by pressing that button which has the word *two* on it if a third button has digit *2* on it; pressing *six* will produce the coin if the third button shows a *6.*

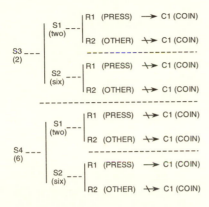

Figure 9-6. A four-term contingency (Conditional Discrimination). Like Figure 9-4 but with different stimuli.

As with the forms and colors, conditionality is explicit both in the contingency and in the relations between behavior and environment that the contingency generates. With numbers and number names, however, one may tend to forget that four-term contingencies do not always generate stimulus equivalence. Even here, it is necessary to test the relations for reflexivity, symmetry, and transitivity in order to document equivalence.

Generalized identity matching of the digits and of the names would demonstrate reflexivity. For symmetry, the second defining property of equivalence, to be demonstrated, the conditional relation must hold true even when the sample and

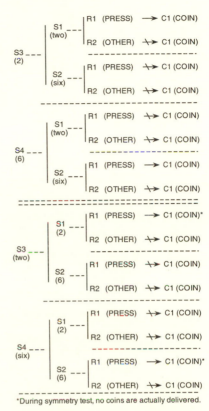

*During symmetry test, no coins are actually delivered.

Figure 9-7. A conditional discrimination and its symmetric counterpart.

comparison stimuli are interchanged. The upper section of Figure 9-7 reproduces the four-term units from Figure 9-6. Since those relations have the subject selecting the word *two* when given digit *2* as a sample and *six* when given *6*, symmetry would require the selection of the numbers when given the words as samples. The units illustrated in the bottom section of Figure 9-7

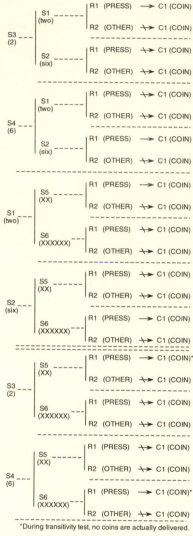

Figure 9-8. Four-term contingencies and a test for transitivity. R = Response; C = Consequence; S = Stimulus; X = Object.

units shown in the upper section *even though the subject had never experienced the new contingencies before.*

Symmetry translates behaviorally into reversibility of sample and comparison roles. If, therefore, equivalence has emerged from explicitly constructed four-term units of conditional control, subjects will prove capable of additional conditional discriminations that they had never been explicitly taught.

In order to determine whether the conditional relations are transitive, we must first establish two more four-term units. The upper section of Figure 9-8 shows the original contingencies, as in Figure 9-6. The center section shows two new discriminations, between the *quantities* two and six (X's represent quantities of objects). These discriminations depend on the printed words *two* and *six*. The subject can obtain a coin by pressing the button that has a picture of *two objects* if the third button shows *two* and by pressing the button that has *six objects* on it if the third button shows *six*.

Since the subject selects the comparison word *two* when given the number *2* as a sample

will be found in the subject's repertoire, having emerged from the explicitly established four-term and the comparison quantity *XX* when given the word *two* as a sample, transitivity would require the subject to select the quantity *XX* when given the number *2* as a sample. Similarly, given the relations, "if *6*, then *six*," and "if *six*, then *XXXXXX*," transitivity would produce "if *6*, then *XXXXXX*." Like reflexivity and symmetry, transitivity gives rise to new behavioral units (illustrated in the bottom section of Figure 9-8) *even though the subject has never explicitly been taught the additional conditional discriminations.*

When conditional relations possess the three defining properties of equivalence relations, the stimuli that have been related to each other become equivalent members of a class. Given equivalence, once the units in the top section of Figure 9-8 have been constructed, *2* and *two* become equivalent members of one class, while *6* and *six* join as equivalent members of another class. The formation of such classes permits us to say that a number and a name have the same meaning or that each is the meaning of the other. In this way, semantic correspondence emerges from nonlinguistic

if...then relations. Expanding the analytic unit from three to four terms establishes the potential for verbal classes to emerge.

Four-term contingencies, however, do not always generate stimulus equivalence. For example, semantic correspondences have not yet been observed to emerge from conditional discriminations taught to pigeons, Rhesus monkeys, or baboons (Sidman et al., 1982). Independent tests are necessary, therefore, to determine whether four-term units involve more than is immediately apparent—for example, to ascertain whether the numbers are indeed the meanings of the words.

The construction of four-term analytic units may accomplish still more than meets the eye. If, in addition to their conditional relations, the number and the word are equivalent members of a stimulus class and the word and quantity are equivalent within the same class, then all three stimuli will be equivalent. Given equivalence within all of the conditional relations diagrammed in Figure 9-8, the result will be two three-member stimulus classes, one containing the equivalent elements, *2, two,* and *XX,* and the

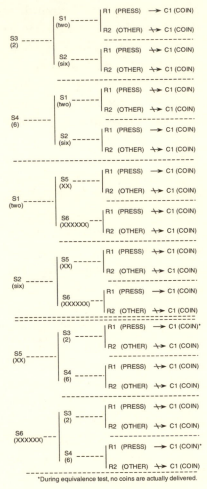

*During equivalence test, no coins are actually delivered.

Figure 9-9. Four-term contingencies and a test for stimulus equivalence.

other containing *6*, *six*, and *XXXXXX*.

A consequence of such class formation is that a subject, when tested, will match any member of a class to any other, even without ever having encountered the tested relation before. The sub-

ject will be capable of more new performances than those we have noted so far. Figure 9-9 illustrates what is actually a more global test for equivalence, eliminating the need to test separately for symmetry and transitivity. The upper and center sections of Figure 9-9 are the same as those in Figure 9-8. Again, we can ask whether more is happening here than the contingencies specify. In addition to the immediately observable conditional relations, is it also possible that the quantities are the meanings of the digits and the printed words?

Let us assume, on the basis of many experiments with human subjects, that equivalence relations hold among the conditionally related stimuli in the upper two sections of Figure 9-9. As a consequence, the subject will be capable of the new conditional discrimination shown in the bottom section even without having ever encountered the new contingencies before. Why? First, if the explicitly constructed relation in the center, "if *two* then *XX*" is symmetric, the subject's repertoire will automatically contain "if *XX* then *two*." Second, symmetry of the other explicitly constructed relation, "if *2* then *two*" (top section), will automatically place "if *two* then *2*" in the subject's repertoire. Given the two conditional discriminations generated by symmetry, "if *XX* then *two*" and "if *two* then *2*," transitivity will automatically place the new conditional discrimination, "if *XX* then *2*" (bottom section) in the subject's repertoire. A similar derivation is possible for "if *XXXXX* then *6*."

Furthermore, the subject will conform to the new contingencies even though the indicated consequences never actually occur. During the test, the subject receives no indication of what he or she is "supposed to do." Because *2*, *two*, and *XX* have become equivalent members of a class, a subject who has never experienced relations between digits and quantities and who is given no feedback during the test will nevertheless press *2* rather than *6* if the third button has a picture of two objects on it. Also, because *6*, *six*, and *XXXXXX* have become equivalent members of another class, the subject will press *6* if the third button depicts six objects.

Thus, we see meaning emerging from structures built out of four-term units. It is, indeed, an elementary form of meaning, yet it is a special property of language. Our subject can represent a quantity by a numerical symbol and can react to the symbol as if it were a quantity without having been taught explicitly to relate the two. Emergence of the new four-term units in the test justifies the assertion that the contingencies not only generated conditional discriminations but that they also taught the subject a meaningful two-word vocabulary. The procedures diagrammed in Figure 9-9 have successfully taught severely retarded students visual and auditory comprehension of 20 simple nouns, thereby starting them off with a 20-word vocabulary (Sidman, 1971b; Sidman & Cresson, 1973). With normal children and adults, the procedures have built stimulus classes containing as many as six equivalent elements (Sidman et al., 1985). A start has even been made in the direction of accounting for correct first-time occurrences of syntactic relations (Lazar, 1977; Lazar & Kotlarchyk, 1986).

Note also that once two stimuli have been explicitly related as sample and comparison in a four-term unit, they can then function individually, one without the other. In tests for reflexivity, symmetry, and transitivity and in the global test for equivalence, each stimulus serves its new function effectively in the derived units without ever before having been paired with the other stimulus component of the new unit. This observation documents the earlier assertion that it can be incorrect to treat sample and comparison stimuli as a unitary compound.

By reacting to a word as to an equivalent stimulus—the meaning of the word—a person can behave adaptively in an environment without having previously been exposed to it. The emergence of equivalence from conditionality permits Behavior Analysis to account for the establishment at least of simple semantic correspondences without having to postulate a direct reinforcement history for every instance. Instead of appealing to cognitions, representations, and stored correspondences to explain the initial occurrence of appropriate new behavior, one can find a complete explanation in the four-term units that are

the prerequisites for the emergent behavior.

Their lack of success in providing a useful account of contextual control has prevented cognitivists from programming computers to comprehend the English language. One could begin to solve that particular context problem by programming a computer to acquire a repertoire of four-term contingencies. The programmer would, of course, have to give the computer nonlinguistic capacities that would enable it to develop and maintain the two- and three-term units from which to synthesize four-term units. The computer would therefore have to be made sensitive to consequences, some "hard wired" into two-term contingencies and others derivable from three-term contingencies. Having first established these nonlinguistic prerequisites, a computer program for language comprehension would then have to give the machine a capacity for generating equivalence relations from four-term contingencies.

The emergence of equivalence from the four-term unit of conditional control sets the stage for the analysis of the contextual determination of meaning. By itself, the four-term contingency provides only a unit for describing the contextual control of three-term contingencies, a level of analysis that does not encompass the role of context in determining semantic correspondences. We might, for example, attempt to characterize people by constructing catalogues of the four-term units in their repertoires. Such catalogues would be of restricted utility because the environment also sets constraints upon four-term contingencies. We would find ourselves able to account for only a limited number of instances in which people display language comprehension in the absence of direct experience with a particular linguistic unit. By placing four-term contingencies themselves under environmental constraint, however, we can bring the emergence of meaning itself under contextual control.

Our computer program, too, if it were endowed only with the capacity to generate equivalence relations from four-term units, would be unable to cope with contextual constraints upon conditional control or upon the verbal classes that emerge from conditional control. The computer would be unable, for example, to handle the distinction between *soldier* and *sailor* as equivalent members of one class, *military forces*, and as nonequivalent members of other classes, e.g., *army* and *navy*. Only by making the computer sensitive to the contextual determination of equivalence relations can one expect it to comprehend language effectively.

Four-term units, therefore, still do not carry a behavioral analysis far enough. A fifth term is needed to describe the environment's ability to select conditional discriminations from our repertoire and to influence the meanings that are derived from conditional relations.

THE FIVE-TERM CONTINGENCY

If, then, an additional element of the experimental environment is allowed to vary, four-term contingencies, the simplest units of conditional control, can themselves be placed under conditional control. The upper half of Figure 9-10 shows that the four-term relation that Figure

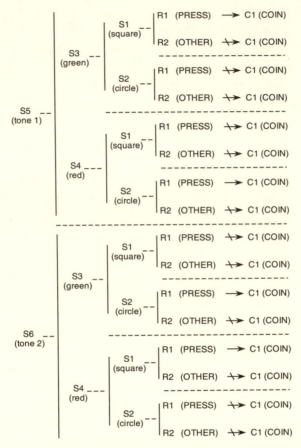

Figure 9-10. The five-term contingency (Second-Order Conditional Discrimination).

9-4 outlined is now controlled by a fifth element, Stimulus S5. The subject can still obtain a coin by pressing the *square* in the presence of a *green* hue or by pressing the *circle* in the presence of *red* but only if *Tone 1* is sounding. The bottom half of Figure 9-10 shows that if Tone 2 (S6) is on, the significance of the hues is reversed. The subject can now obtain a coin by pressing the *square* in the presence of *red* or by pressing the *circle* in the presence of *green*. Because the tones assume conditional control over the original conditional discrimination, the five-term contingency is the unit of *second-order conditional control.*

348

The five-term unit describes the influence that the environment exerts over conditional discriminations; conditional control by the hues over the form discriminations is itself conditional upon the tones. Four-term contingencies account for variations in the control that discriminative stimuli exert over response-consequence relations. Five-term contingencies, which leave discriminative control untouched, account for variations in the relations between conditional and discriminative stimuli. The four-term unit makes the stimulus control of behavior flexible; the five-term unit makes the conditional control of stimulus control flexible. Enlarging the unit of analysis step by step provides analytic tools that permit us to synthesize and account for any degree of breadth and complexity of behavioral variation that may be required.

The five-term analytic unit also describes a more powerful type of contextual control than does the four-term unit. If our original four-term unit generates equivalence relations, we can say, "*Green* means *square* and *red* means *circle*." Second-order conditional control—the five-term unit—now provides a mechanism that accounts for the contextual determination of these meanings.

With the five-term unit, we can still say, "*Green* means *square* and *red* means *circle*," but only in the context of *Tone 1*. When the context changes to *Tone 2*, the meanings also change; now, *green* means *circle* and *red* means *square*. Sometimes, then, *square* and *green* are equivalent members of one class and *circle* and *red* of another. At different times, however, one class includes *square* and *red* as equivalent members, while the other includes *circle* and *green*. The context, represented by Stimuli S5 and S6, shifts elements of the environment from class to class. Stimuli may therefore have multiple class memberships, changing in meaning from occasion to occasion.

Without contextual control by Tones 1 and 2, the common elements in each of the four small classes (*square* and *green*, *square* and *red*, *circle* and *red*, *circle* and *green*) would cause all of the hues and forms to combine into a single large class, for all practical purposes meaningless. For example, mercury can be classified both as a metal and a liquid. Contextual control, e.g., "Today's topic is oxidation (or flow patterns)," prevents other members of the class, metal, from entering into equivalence relations with members of the class, liquid. Mercury can therefore sometimes be equivalent to iron and sometimes to water without making those two elements equivalent to each other. Any program for making our language comprehensible to a computer will not only recognize verbal classes that conditional control generates but will take advantage of the contextual constraints that second-order conditional control imposes upon those verbal classes.

Only two behavior-analytic studies have so far explicitly explored or made use of contextual control over classes of equivalent stimuli (Fucini, 1982; Lazar & Kotlarchyk, 1986). Behavior Analysis has not yet proceeded beyond this point. Many questions remain. For example, what is the relation between the second-order conditional stimuli (the tones) and the other stimuli (the hues and geometric forms)?

The question can be clarified by following the two paths from S5 to C1 in the upper segment of Figure 9-10. These paths suggest that Tone 1 could become a common element of two three-member classes, one including *Tone 1*, *green*, and *square*, and the other, *Tone 1*, *red*, and *circle*. If these three-member classes did form, however, the common element would combine the two classes, hues and geometric forms all becoming equivalent to Tone 1 and to each other. Conditional control by *green* and *red* would be wiped out, as would discriminative control by *square* and *circle*, since all stimuli would have become equivalent, and the two-term contingency would be left uncontrolled; the five-term unit would "self destruct."

Similarly, Tone 2 would create and enter into a single class containing the hues and forms. With both tones now equivalent members of the large class, the whole contingency would be destroyed. Contextual control over classes of equivalent stimuli would be impossible.

Also, the paradigm illustrated in Figure 9-10 for increasing class size from two to three members would not be feasible.

There, however, may lie the solution to the problem. If the second-order conditional stimuli did *not* enter into equivalence relations with the other stimuli, maintaining only their conditional relations, then contextual control over meaning could be maintained without destroying the units from which meaning is derived. Different techniques than the one suggested by Figure 9-10 would then be required to increase the number of equivalent stimuli that a class encompasses (for example, Fields et al., 1984; Lazar et al., 1984; Sidman et al., 1985).

It is, of course, only conjectural that second-order conditional relations do not possess the properties of equivalence relations since it is by no means clear why equivalence should be precluded, but the experiments that are needed to provide the relevant data can be done. Even nonhuman subjects have demonstrated the existence of five-term units (Nevin & Liebold, 1966; Santi, 1978; Weigl, 1941); what remains is only to apply an equivalence-test paradigm that is slightly more complex than the one illustrated in Figure 9-9.

Other questions, too, are amenable to experimental analysis: Why does equivalence sometimes fail to emerge from four-term units? Third-order conditional control has yet even to be demonstrated; is it possible? Does the size of a stimulus class or the amount of overlap between classes affect the likelihood that contextual control will itself enlarge or merge the classes? Does the level of conditional control that one can attain or the number of equivalent stimuli that one can encompass within a single class constitute an intellectual marker? How does *stimulus equivalence*, as defined by the present analysis, interact with *functional equivalence*, defined as discriminative control exerted by two or more stimuli over a single response? And a more theoretical question, less obviously open to an experimental answer, concerns the new process that might be exposed by the five-term unit of analysis. Discriminative control makes conditioned reinforcement possible; conditional control generates stimulus equivalence; what new complexity does second-order conditional control bring within the purview of Behavior Analysis?

Along with the ever more complex interactions between environmental structures and behavior that become accessible as the analytic unit expands, the very exposure of questions, conundrums, and paradoxes may be regarded as an additional virtue of the analytic procedures. The delineation of obvious next steps and the clear exposure of lacunae in a systematic structure are characteristics of the most advanced sciences. As a consequence of its reluctance to analyze its own structure, Behavior Analysis has, perhaps, been overly reticent in establishing its position among the sciences.

✳ ✳ ✳ ✳ ✳ ✳ ✳ ✳ ✳ ✳

Commentary

Linear versus Nonlinear Diagrams

The contingencies described in the *Emergent Verbal Classes* paper were diagrammed as if they were linear, possessing a distinct beginning and proceeding to a well-defined completion. I did point out that the linearity can become quite complex, with many spatial and temporal options, branches, and combinations being included in the contingency (Brady, 1992; Findley, 1962, 1966). Nevertheless, some of the more careful thinkers about Behavior Analysis have been disturbed, and rightly so, about the use of linear notation to depict contingencies. Operant contingencies do not work that way. One type of nonlinearity, emphasized by Moxley (1982, 1983, 1984) and by Hineline (1986, 1990), arises because "The environment that occasions a behavior is changed by the effects produced by that behavior. These effects become part of the environment that occasions the next behavior" (Moxley, 1982, p. 48). Both Moxley and Hineline have recommended closed-loop rather than linear diagrams.

Not only is the operant contingency a closed loop, but the constituents of the loop change from occasion to occasion. Reinforcement both increases the likelihood that an act will be repeated and refines the effective discriminative stimulus. For example, with continued reinforcement, the part of the environment that occasions a child's "Daddy" will change from all men (or "non-mothers") to a particular man. Also, with repeated occurrences, the consequences of an act become part of the discriminative occasion for the next occurrence of the act. That is why giving an animal in the experimental chamber a "free" food pellet will cause the animal to press the lever again even after the act of lever pressing has been extinguished.

Another type of nonlinearity has been dealt with in the basic equation in matching theory (Herrnstein, 1970) by the inclusion of a term that represents the rate of "extraneous" reinforcement (for example, McDowell, 1988). This nonlinearity, emphasized by Goldiamond (1975, 1982), arises when the linearly depicted variables that influence a particular act do not suffice to explain that act. Goldiamond (1975) contrasts

> (1) the present *unilinear* framework which describes behavior by the contingencies into which it enters, and (2) a proposed framework of *alternative sets*, which requires description not only of behavior and its relation to environmental events, but also of alternative sets of behavior-environment relations. (p. 50)

With this kind of nonlinearity, the complete explanation of an act requires attention also to other acts and to variables that influence them. For example, a person's abnormal eating may sometimes be treated not just by altering food deprivation or by making food (or different kinds of food) contingent on desirable actions, but instead, by changing the person's interactions with his or her spouse and other family members. The strengthening of competing actions may weaken overeating. Also, the availability of new positive reinforcers and the elimination of preexisting negative reinforcers may cause the reinforcers contingent on overeating to become ineffective (Goldiamond, 1982, pp. 507-513).

If contingencies are actually nonlinear, and if the complete description of an action requires the consideration of alternative contingencies, one may ask, "Why continue to use linear diagrams?" The answer to this question has to do with the practicalities of analysis and of comprehension. No diagram, after all, can represent everything. Most diagrams are intended to illustrate features that have been abstracted from a larger context. As Goldiamond has pointed out (personal communication), the two-term contingency (Figure 9-1) does not really exist, not even in a well-controlled laboratory arrangement. It is, however, a useful abstraction.

Even though operant contingencies are nonlinear, the use of closed-loop diagrams to depict two-, three-, four-, and five-term contingencies would make the already complex linear diagrams in the *Emergent Verbal Classes* paper so intricate that they would become uninformative. The current complexity of these diagrams arises partly from an attempt to take into account the kind of nonlinearity that Goldiamond described. That is why each diagram includes an R2 (which represents alternative behavior), two kinds of consequences (C1 and not-C1), and two each of discriminative, conditional, and contextual stimuli (environmental alternatives). Much, however, has still been left out. A more complete picture would have included additional acts (Rn), consequences (Cn), and environmental elements (Sn), and would have indicated how the state of any of these options could affect the others. But by the time all possibilities had been worked into the diagrams, the more restricted points I was trying to make would have become hopelessly clouded. It is unfortunate that both behavior analysts and their critics often interpret such limited diagrams as though they were intended to represent a larger framework. It is just not feasible to imbed every instance of analysis within a diagram that also depicts everything else.

The Source of Equivalence

In the *Emergent Verbal Classes* paper, I depicted equivalence as emerging at the level of the four-term unit of analysis. No further explanation of equivalence was given. In a later paper (Sidman, 1990b),

Equivalence Relations and Contingency Analysis...

I asked, "Can we derive equivalence from more primitive behavioral functions, variables, or processes?" In that paper, I discussed the derivation of equivalence as follows (*from* Sidman, 1990b, pp. 104-107; 111-113).

Equivalence Relations: Where Do They Come From?

Logic as the Source of Equivalence

Perhaps a good place to start [a discussion of where equivalence relations come from] is one of those seemingly obvious notions that turn out to be incorrect. It is tempting to say that equivalence is simply a matter of logic, that each of the derived relations is a logical necessity. But no such logical necessity exists.

Table 9-1 shows that we can find relations characterized by any possible combination of the three requirements for equivalence. Only Relation 1 meets all the requirements. Here, we have a parallel relation between lines in a plane: Line A is parallel to Line B, and Line B to Line C. This relation is reflexive: each line is also parallel to itself. The relation is symmetric: Line B is also parallel to Line A, and Line C to Line B. And the relation is transitive: Line A is also parallel to Line C.

Relation 3, "greater than," is neither reflexive nor symmetric: a number cannot be greater than itself; and if A is greater than B,

Table 9-1. The Presence or Absence of the Defining Properties of Equivalence in Various Relations

Relations	Reflexivity	Symmetry	Transitivity
1. is parallel to (lines in a plane)	+	+	+
2. is brother of (all males)	–	+	+
3. is greater than (whole numbers)	–	–	+
4. is greater than or equal to (whole numbers)	+	–	+
5. lives next door to (people)	–	+	–
6. has at least one point in common with (lines in plane)	+	+	–
7. is highly correlated with (events)	+	–	–
8. is half of	–	–	–

B cannot be greater than A. But if A is greater than B, and B is greater than C, A will also be greater than C, showing the relation to be transitive.

Relation 5 is symmetric, but neither reflexive nor transitive. Reflexivity would require A to live next door to herself. But the relation is symmetric: if A lives next door to B, then B also lives next door to A. If A lives next door to B, and B lives next door to C, transitivity would require A to live next door to C, but the relation does not permit that juxtaposition.

Given a relation between A and B, then, logic does not demand reflexivity: A being related to B does not require A to bear that same relation to itself; in Relation 8, A may be one-half of B, but A cannot be one-half of itself. Nor does logic demand symmetry: A being related to B does not require that B bear the same relation to A; in Relation 7, A being perfectly correlated with B does not require B to be perfectly correlated with A. And logic does not require transitivity: given that A is related to B, and B to C, A does not have to bear that same relation to C; in Relation 6, Line A may share one point in common with Line B, and Line B may share one point in common with Line C, but Line A may still not intersect with Line C at all.

There is, therefore, no logical necessity for relations to be reflexive, symmetric, or transitive. Conditional relations are completely indeterminate in this respect. Given "if A then B" and "if B then C," the conditional relations "if A then A," "if B then A," and "if A then C" need not follow. Logic does not demand that conditional relations be equivalence relations. None of the derived relations have to emerge from conditional discriminations. To reason, "If A is related to B, and B to C, then C must be related to A" is simply incorrect.

Table 9-1 is not a logical but a behavioral construction. Our experience with these and other relations tells us whether they possess the properties of equivalence relations. This is not a case in which logical derivations account for behavior; rather, behavioral derivations justify the logic.

The relations emerging from the equivalence tests may even be regarded as a form of inductive inference; we might therefore entertain the possibility that equivalence is one of the behavioral processes that underlie inductive reasoning—but that is better saved for another occasion.

Verbal Behavior as the Source of Equivalence

Experiments on equivalence relations often find the subjects naming the stimuli. Also, subjects are often able to state rules that describe the emergent performances. It has been suggested, therefore, that naming, verbal rules, or both, may be necessary for the emergence of equivalence relations (Lowe, 1986).

Naming. Let us first look at the possibility that naming is critical for equivalence. It is not immediately clear what the function of the names might be. One possibility is that the same name assigned to several stimuli might mediate a common class membership for those stimuli. This was the hypothesized basis for the phenomenon of "mediated generalization," studied classically by paired-associate techniques (e.g., Jenkins, 1963, 1965). Indeed, when subjects—even monkeys—are explicitly taught to respond in the same way to conditionally related stimuli, the relations characteristic of equivalence do seem to emerge (McIntire et al., 1987). Definitive tests, however, remain to be carried out with nonhumans. Common names can surely facilitate the formation of stimulus classes for humans, but whether the names are necessary for equivalence is not yet certain (Lazar et al., 1984; Sidman et al., 1974; Sidman et al., 1986).

A common name for different stimuli does define a functional stimulus class, and I shall have more to say about the possible relation between functional classes and equivalence classes. But a significant problem arises when we do not explicitly teach the subject to give the same name to each stimulus that we are going to test for membership in an equivalence class. If the subject does give the same name to each class member, but without having been taught to do so, we then have to ask where the names came from. Under these circumstances, it is reasonable to suspect not that the common names gave rise to equivalence, but that equivalence gave rise to the common names.

Rules. A second possibility is that equivalence relations have to be rule governed (Skinner, 1969), i.e., that the derived relations must be products of verbal rules. Some subjects are able to describe the network of directly taught and derived relations even in complex, interlocking sets of conditional discriminations (Bush et al., 1989).

But once more, we must ask, "What comes first, the rules or the equivalence relations?" If the rule does come first, we must then ask where it came from. As we saw before, given a particular relation between A and B, and between B and C, there is no logical reason why that particular relation should also exist between C and A. Again, it is reasonable to suspect not that such rules give rise to equivalence, but that equivalence gives rise to the rules.

Skinner (1969) has stated that rules specify contingencies. The statement is surely true, but what is this process of "specification"? A behavioral interpretation has not been forthcoming. If equivalence gives rise to rules, then for a rule to specify a contingency may simply mean that the rule and the contingency are members

of an equivalence class. This is a behaviorally precise—and testable—proposition.

As with naming, existing evidence on the role of rules in generating equivalence is not definitive. Perhaps the question of whether verbal behavior (Skinner, 1957)—via naming, rules, or some other route—is necessary for equivalence will never be answered to everyone's satisfaction. It may not be possible to determine which is cause and which is effect. The question of verbal behavior's primacy would be settled—with a negative answer—if equivalence relations could be demonstrated unequivocally with nonhumans. It is important, therefore, to continue that search (D'Amato et al., 1985; Lipkens et al., 1988; McIntire et al., 1987; Sidman et al., 1982; Vaughan, 1988).

I, personally, have been convinced by some relatively "soft" data. I have seen four-member classes demonstrated by retarded subjects who did speak but only rarely, and then in utterances of only a few words, at most. Lengthy reasoning was not in their repertoires. They never performed long verbal chains like "A goes with B, and B goes with C;

therefore, C must go with A." But this is difficult to prove—perhaps impossible. My observations will become accepted only when many other experimenters acknowledge having seen the same thing happen with comparable subjects. The evaluation of clinical judgments can take a long time.

Functional Classes and Equivalence

[I am omitting this section of the *Where Does Equivalence Come From?* paper because in it, my discussion of the relation between functional classes and equivalence was particularly cloudy. I had not yet fully grasped the significance of the data from our initial experiment on this topic (Sidman, Wynne, Maguire, & Barnes, 1989). The relation between functional and equivalence classes, although not causal, is more intimate than I realized at the time. That relation, as I see it now, will be amplified in Chapters 10 and 11.]

Equivalence as a Fundamental Stimulus Function

If equivalence requires neither naming nor verbal reasoning, the possibility remains that equivalence is a fundamental stimulus function. We have some reason for suspecting this to be so, quite independently of our current inability to derive equivalence from something more basic.

The diagram in the upper right-hand segment of Figure 9-4 [used here in place of the original figure] shows a particular response (pressing a key) and no other producing a particular reinforcer (a coin). This is the reinforcement relation (Skinner, 1938), a two-term contingency between response and reinforcer.

Looking at the three right-hand columns in Figure 9-4, we see instances in which the response produces its reinforcer…only in the presence of a particular stimulus [S1 or S2]. This is the discrimination relation (Skinner, 1938; 1953), a three-term contingency that involves discriminative stimulus, response, and reinforcer. We know, too, that the discriminative stimuli also become conditioned reinforcers.

Moving to the left, we see another set of stimuli—[S3 and S4]. These determine which three-term contingency is in effect. This is the conditional-discrimination relation (Cumming

& Berryman, 1965), a four-term contingency that involves conditional stimulus, discriminative stimulus, response, and consequence. We know, too, that the conditional stimulus may also enter into an equivalence class along with its related discriminative stimulus [S3 with S1, S4 with S2].

The conditional relations are not just larger discriminative relations. The three- and four-term contingencies are fundamentally different. In the three-term contingency, the discriminative stimulus requires a differential response to relate it to the consequence. In the four-term contingency, however, the conditional stimulus requires no such differential response to relate it to the discriminative stimulus. The subject has to do nothing special in the presence of S3 in order to produce stimulus S1, or in the presence of S4 to produce S2.

The four-term relation, then, is different in kind from the three-term relation (Sidman, 1986a). The three-term contingency is a stimulus-response-reinforcer relation, and the four-term contingency adds a stimulus-stimulus relation (Sidman, 1978).

Just as the conditioned reinforcement function appears at the level of the three-term contintgency, equivalence relations appear at the level of the four-term contingency. And, just as the stimulus functions of reinforcement, discrimination, conditioned reinforcement, and conditional discrimination represent unanalyzable primitives in the description of behavior, equivalence may represent yet another primitive.

It may well be that we simply have to accept equivalence relations as a given. I do not believe we can ignore that possibility. It is, of course, true that related conditional and discriminative stimuli do not always form equivalence classes. They may, however, always start that way, with differential experience being required to break equivalence down; equivalence relations do come under contextual control (Bush et al., 1989). And so we have the possibility that the role of experience is not to create equivalence classes, but to break such classes down.

Given our failure so far to derive equivalence from something more basic, and given the qualitative change from stimulus-response to stimulus-stimulus relations in the transition from three- to four-term units of analysis, it does not seem unreasonable to suspect that equivalence relations emerge from conditional discriminations for the same reason our behavior is reinforceable, and for the same reason our behavior is controllable by discriminative and conditional stimuli—because contingencies of survival have made us that way.

＊ ＊ ＊ ＊ ＊ ＊ ＊ ＊ ＊ ＊

Commentary (continued)

Equivalence as a Basic Process

The *Where Does Equivalence Come From?* paper argued that equivalence relations cannot be accounted for by logic, and do not rely either on naming or verbal rules. The paper ended with the suggestion that equivalence relations, like the relations we call *reinforcement* and *discrimination*, are a product of survival contingencies. Later developments revealed that some of the arguments leading up to this conclusion were incomplete. Nevertheless, the discussion that is to come in Chapter 10, although it follows a different route, will lead to a similar conclusion: equivalence, while not derivable from more primitive behavioral functions, variables, or processes, is a direct outcome of reinforcement. I shall postpone further discussion of this point until Chapter 10, where I can develop it in a more orderly fashion.

Language as a Prerequisite for Equivalence

Dugdale (1988) and Dugdale and Lowe (1990) have advanced the strongest arguments for the necessity of vocal or subvocal naming in the establishment of equivalence relations. Their studies demonstrated clearly that equivalence relations can be facilitated by naming or by some aspect of the experimental procedures or instructions that lead a subject to name the stimuli. This distinction between the effect of naming per se and the variables that lead to naming has not yet been addressed experimentally. At present, therefore, it is not clear that linguistic naming by itself has been the critical factor in these studies. Indeed, if evidence (Schusterman & Kastak, 1993) that a California sea lion demonstrated equivalence relations holds up (see Chapter 5, pp. 165-175), and if it remains feasible to interpret Manabe and Kawashima's (1993) data with budgerigar subjects as demonstrations of equivalence relations (see pp. 466-471), the notion that language is necessary for equivalence will no longer be tenable. Perhaps, however, labeling—differential responding to the samples (and perhaps to the comparisons)—will facilitate equivalence even when the labels are nonlinguistic.

In discussing the relation between naming and equivalence, Dugdale and Lowe (1990) proposed a distinction between *naming* and *labeling*. They recommended that we use the term *naming* only when the relation between the name and the thing named is symmetric. For example, true naming is demonstrated when a child not only says "boy" upon seeing a boy but, having said (or heard) "boy," then points to a boy.

I find myself sympathetic to this suggestion. Although this example does not really represent a symmetric relation, the distinction is similar to one I had made earlier between the comprehension of written words and the oral naming of written words: one can name words without comprehending them, and one can comprehend words without being able to name them (Sidman, 1971b). I believe that Dugdale and Lowe's (1990) definition of true naming is a component of a larger picture. In Chapter 10, I will propose that differential responses in the analytic unit be included also in the equivalence relation. Such inclusion will require the relation between names and the stimuli that occasion them to be not only symmetric but reflexive and transitive as well. The equivalence relation will then include not only stimulus-stimulus pairs, but stimulus-response,

response-stimulus, and perhaps even response-response pairs. Including differential responses in the equivalence relation will remove the necessity for the distinction that Dugdale and Lowe had to make between stimulus-response symmetry and stimulus-stimulus symmetry. This revised conception of the equivalence relation will also establish theoretical grounds for the facilitation of equivalence by differential responses (pp. 413-414).

Generalized symmetry? Having postulated that true naming, a symmetrical stimulus-response relation, is necessary for stimulus equivalence, Dugdale and Lowe (1990) went on to ask where naming comes from. They pointed out that symmetrical stimulus-name relations arise naturally in the course of a child's language development, when the child is taught to be both a speaker and a listener— to say words and to comprehend those same words when others say them. Hayes, too (1991), has argued that such a history is necessary (although not sufficient) for equivalence relations. Dugdale and Lowe (1990) and Hayes (1991), therefore, attempt in this way to derive equivalence relations from an individual's linguistic experience. I believe, however, that they have overlooked a significant assumption that underlies their derivation. They assume that with enough name-event and event-name examples (which ordinarily occur extensively in a child's natural language community), a generalized relation of symmetry will emerge naturally.

As Hayes (1991) pointed out, the concern here is with arbitrary relations. Nonarbitrary relations are based on physical attributes like size, shape, color, quantity, and so on, while arbitrary relations like those between things or events and their names are dependent on one's learning history. The defining properties of arbitrary relations cannot be seen, heard, smelled, felt, and so on, or measured in physical dimensions. They are the product of arbitrary contingencies that are set up by the reinforcing community. I can understand how a sufficient number of examples may give rise to generalized nonarbitrary relations like *larger, brighter, heavier, more*, and so on. But I do not understand how any number of examples can give rise to generalized arbitrary relations like *reflexivity, symmetry, transitivity,* and so on. Because the exemplars would possess no measurable feature in common, it is not at all evident that one might be able to generalize an arbitrary relation solely from exemplars. What aspect of several examples of symmetric event-name relations would permit a new example to be recognized or produced?

Symmetry is a complex verbal construction, involving preestablished classes like *names, things, self, others,* and so on. The mere exposure of a verbally unsophisticated organism like a child or a nonhuman to a number of exemplars that have, themselves, not yet been appropriately classified does not seem to me sufficient to explain the emergence of a generalized concept of event-name symmetry on the basis of any known behavioral principle.

The key here is "known behavioral principle." It is true that not all of the data are in. Mere exposure to exemplars may yet prove sufficient to yield a generalized concept of symmetry. Schusterman and Kastak (1993), for example, may have generated symmetry by first giving their harbor seal reinforced experiences with tests for that relational property. In that event, it would not matter whether the emergent symmetry is shown in stimulus-response, response-stimulus, or stimulus-stimulus relations. That is to say, naming need not be involved. But, if classes defined by such relational properties can, like nonarbitrary classes, be generated merely by presenting exemplars to nonverbal or verbally unsophisticated individuals, this will itself define a new behavioral process, not derivable from anything more basic.

In attempting to derive equivalence relations from an individual's behavioral history, therefore, "exemplar theory" does not fulfill its intended purpose; it does not avoid the need to specify a behavioral process that is itself not derivable from anything more basic. Rather, it substitutes *generalized symmetry*, a behavioral phenomenon that has not yet been empirically confirmed, in place of the notion that equivalence, like other behavioral relations, is a direct outcome of reinforcement. (I shall have more to say in pp. 556-557 about the proposition that symmetry is a product of one's experience with examples.)

10

Equivalence Relations and the Unit of Analysis: Empirical and Conceptual Advances

As I noted in the introduction to Chapter 9, a major aim of the *Emergent Verbal Classes* paper was to show that the empirical phenomena predicted by our behavioral definition of the equivalence relation could be encompassed within a contingency analysis. In that paper, I described the equivalence relation as emerging at the level of the four-term contingency. I now believe that this restriction of equivalence to the four-term unit placed too strong a constraint on the relation between equivalence and the units of behavioral analysis. Also, in the *Where Does Equivalence Come From?* paper, I suggested that we have to consider seriously the possibility that equivalence is a basic stimulus function, not derivable from more fundamental processes. I now believe more strongly in this possibility. These developments in my conception of equivalence—the weakening of one belief and the strengthening of the other—are related, but definitive evidence is not yet in. Therefore, it may be helpful if, instead of directly stating the broader conception that is perhaps more valid than the original formulation, I reconstruct part of the course of my own thinking on the matter.

Two discoveries pointed toward the desirability of considering a more fundamental affinity than I had described in the *Emergent Verbal Classes* paper between the equivalence relation and the units of analysis. One of these discoveries started me off on the road to an expanded notion of the relation between equivalence and contingency-defined units, and the other discovery provided data that the expanded notion seemed to accommodate more efficiently.

The Equivalence Relation and the Reinforcer

The first key discovery was that the equivalence relation could include not only the four-term unit's conditional and discriminative stimuli but the reinforcing stimulus also (Dube, McIlvane, Mackay, & Stoddard, 1987; Dube, McIlvane, Maguire, Mackay, & Stoddard, 1989; Dube, Rocco, & McIlvane, 1989; McIlvane, Dube, Kledaras, de Rose, & Stoddard, 1992). To show this, it was necessary to modify the standard conditional-discrimination procedure by using what has come to be called *outcome-specific* reinforcement contingencies. The upper section of Figure 10-1 illustrates a standard conditional-discrimination procedure that does not involve outcome-specific reinforcement: a response that the experimenter has defined (R1) produces a reinforcer (SR1) that remains the same regardless of whether Comparison B1 (with Sample A1) or B2 (with Sample A2) is positive. The lower section of Figure 10-1 illustrates an outcome-specific reinforcement procedure: depending on which of the comparisons is positive, the defined response produces different reinforcers; in the presence of Sample A1, the subject touches Comparison B1 and produces Reinforcer SR1; in the presence of Sample A2, the subject touches Comparison B2 and produces Reinforcer SR2. (SR1 might be a candy and SR2 a cookie.)

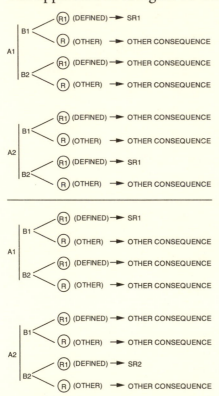

Figure 10-1. Standard (upper section) and outcome-specific (lower section) reinforcement procedures. (After McIlvane et al., 1992, Fig. 15.)

The outcome-specific reinforcement procedure makes it possible to test subjects for emergent conditional discriminations in which stimuli that had previously served as reinforcers now serve as samples or comparisons. In one kind of test trial, for example, the sample might be a candy (formerly, SR1) or a cookie (formerly, SR2). The comparisons in this test trial might be the former samples, A1 and A2, or the former comparisons, B1 and B2. When these tests are carried out, it is found that subjects will match SR1 to A1 and B1, and SR2 to A2 and B2. Such test results are to be predicted if equivalence-class membership extends also to the reinforcers (Dube, McIlvane, et al., 1987, 1989; McIlvane et al., 1992).

The finding that emergent conditional discriminations indicative of an equivalence relation can include the reinforcers is important in a number of contexts. For me, the demonstration suggested an exciting new possibility about the connection between equivalence and the analytic unit. The equivalence relation that the four-term contingency generates could now be seen to encompass three of the four elements of the unit: the conditional stimulus, the discriminative stimulus, and the reinforcing stimulus. What about the fourth element? Might the equivalence relation also include the defined (reinforced) response?

The Equivalence Relation and the Defined Response

A definitive experimental answer to the question of whether the equivalence relation includes all components of the four-term unit, including the defined response, will not be easy to obtain. Also, the question demands a more detailed examination of the terms *response* and *stimulus*: how can we make sense of the notion that a class might contain both responses and stimuli? Before reconsidering such fundamental concepts, I would prefer to have an empirical base— some compelling data—that called for a reappraisal. In the absence of such a base, let us do some armchair investigations. Figure 10-2 illustrates the final stages of an experiment that has not yet been done but that might provide some provocative data.

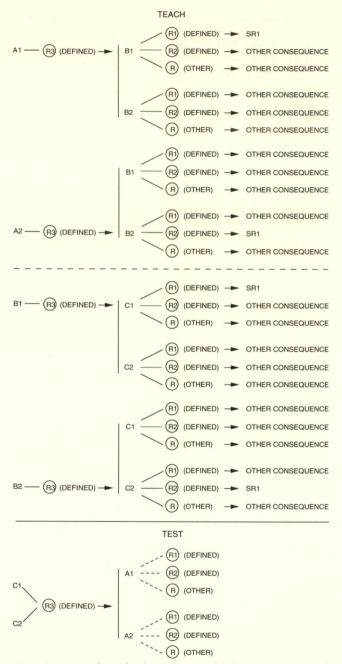

Figure 10-2. A proposed test for the inclusion of defined responses in the equivalence relation. See text for details.

The uppermost section of Figure 10-2 shows an AB conditional discrimination that includes just a single reinforcer (SR1) but *two defined responses* (R1 and R2) to the comparison stimuli. On any trial, the subject can produce comparison stimuli (B1 and B2) by touching the sample (A1 or A2). In the presence of Sample A1, the subject produces a reinforcer by touching Comparison B1, and in the presence of Sample A2 by touching Comparison B2. *Touching*, however, requires further specification; it is sometimes labeled R1, sometimes R2, and sometimes R3. Suppose we define R1 as *five consecutive touches, with the last four of the five having to be grouped within three seconds of the first*. And suppose we define R2 as *two consecutive touches, the second of which must come two to three seconds after the first*. Thus, R1 is defined as five touches within a period of three seconds; R2 is defined as two touches separated by two to three seconds. Sample keys need be touched only once, a defined response that is designated R3. After the subject has touched a comparison, the trial lasts for three more seconds, ending with reinforcement if the subject has touched only the correct comparison and if the touches have met the criteria for a correct response—R1 when the correct comparison is B1 or R2 when the correct comparison is B2. A trial ends without reinforcement if the subject has touched an incorrect comparison, if R2 occurs when R1 is correct, if R1 occurs when R2 is correct, or if the touches fail to meet the criteria for either R1 or R2. We can expect well-taught subjects to meet the criteria for R1 by touching the correct comparison five times in rapid succession, and for R2 by touching the correct comparison twice, spacing the touches two to three seconds apart. (In order to facilitate description, these examples use only two samples and two comparisons rather than the preferred three or more.)

The center section of Figure 10-2 (just below the dashed horizontal line) illustrates a BC conditional discrimination in which the former comparisons, B1 and B2, are now samples (and require only R3, a single touch); new stimuli, C1 and C2, are comparisons. The reinforcer is contingent on R1 when C1 is the correct comparison and on R2 when C2 is correct.

Having established a baseline of four-term AB and BC units, each with the same pair of defined comparison responses, we are in a position to ask whether emergent conditional discriminations will include the responses. A first approach might entail carrying out a CA equivalence test, as illustrated in the bottom section of Figure 10-2. In test trials (given without reinforcement), the sample is either C1 or C2, and the simultaneously presented comparisons are A1 and A2. As in the baseline conditional discriminations, the subject does not have to respond differentially to the test samples; touching C1 or C2 only once (R3) will produce comparisons A1 and A2. We can now observe not only whether subjects will touch A1 when C1 is the sample and A2 when C2 is the sample (the usual finding with only a single defined response), but also whether they will touch A1 five times in rapid succession (R1) and will touch A2 twice, with the two touches spaced two to three seconds apart (R2). (The subject has never been required to respond differentially to A1 and A2, a feature that the BA test for symmetry would also possess.) Will subjects act as though R1 belonged to the A1B1C1 class and R2 to the A2B2C2 class?

Although this exact experiment has not yet been done, pertinent data (Chapter 11) suggest that it is likely to support a conclusion that equivalence relations include the reinforced responses. More decisive, however, would be a test like the one outlined at the bottom of Figure 10-2 but with Responses R1 and R2 serving as samples in place of Stimuli C1 and C2. We could then observe directly whether Response R1 would lead a subject to select Comparison A1, and Response R2 to a selection of A2.

In order to carry out such a test, one would have to devise a way to make R1 and R2 occur reliably. One could then find out if the responses would serve as samples in equivalence test trials. The only way for an experimenter to ensure the reliable occurrence of particular responses at particular times is to place those responses under discriminative control by events in the external environment. Even though such a technique leads to problems of data interpretation, an example will repay close examination. The interpretive problems themselves led me to consider a more intimate connection than I had heretofore suspected between reinforcement and equivalence.

Let us first teach a subject the same four-term units as before, the AB conditional discrimination with two defined responses; in Figure 10-3, the uppermost section is the same as the corresponding section of Figure 10-2. Then, as shown in the next section, we teach the subject two three-term units, a simple D1D2 discrimination. This is a successive discrimination; on some trials we present D1 and on other trials we present D2—sometimes one and sometimes the other. When D1 is present, only R1 will produce the reinforcer; with D2 present, only R2 will produce the reinforcer. The purpose of this phase is to gain experimental control over the occurrence of R1 and R2. Then, having established the complete baseline—a four-term AB conditional discrimination and a three-term D1D2 simple discrimination—we are in a position to attempt an equivalence test in which R1 and R2 might function as samples.

The third section of Figure 10-3 (just below the solid horizontal divider) illustrates such a test. If the simple discrimination has been reliably established, R1 or R2 can be made to occur by presenting the subject with D1 or D2, respectively. When D1 is presented, the subject will touch it five times in rapid succession (R1); when D2 is presented, the subject will touch it twice, spacing the touches two seconds apart (R2). If R1 and R2 had become members of the A1B1 and A2B2 classes, respectively, then trials that occasioned R1 should lead a subject to select comparison A1, and R2 should lead to a selection of comparison A2.

It would be quite reasonable to expect these results, but whether or not to accept their interpretation is another matter. This seemingly direct test for the inclusion of defined responses in the equivalence relations turns out not to be as direct as one would like. The problem is this: one cannot be certain that a subject's choice of Comparison A1 or A2 is under the direct control of the defined responses, R1 and R2; the stimuli, D1 and D2, rather than or in addition to the responses they occasion, may be the effective samples. The background for this uncertainty—a reason for suspecting that D1 and D2 might control a subject's selections of A1 and A2 even

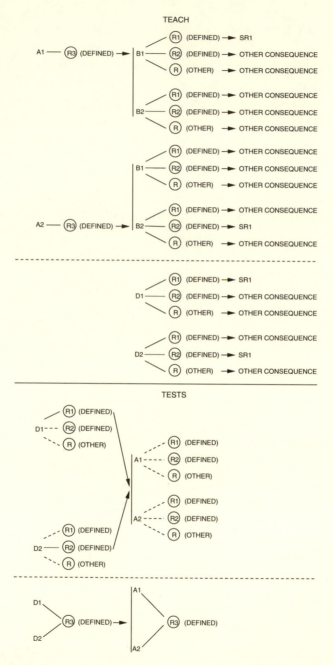

Figure 10-3. A proposed equivalence test in which defined responses might function as samples. See text for details.

though D- and A-stimuli had never even been presented at the same time to the subject before the test—comes from the second key discovery about the connection between equivalence and the unit of analysis.

The Equivalence Relation and the Three-Term Unit.

Another indication of a closer affinity between the equivalence relation and the analytic units came from experiments that either demonstrated or suggested strongly that three-term contingencies—simple rather than conditional discriminations—can establish the prerequisites for an equivalence relation (Barnes & Keenan, 1993; Cohen-Almeida, Galvão, & Sidman, in preparation; de Rose, McIlvane, Dube, Galpin, & Stoddard, 1988; de Rose, McIlvane, Dube, & Stoddard, 1988; Hayes, Devany, Kohlenberg, Brownstein, & Shelby, 1987; McIlvane et al., 1990; Sidman et al., 1989; Vaughan, 1988). Chapter 11 will discuss and evaluate these findings in more detail. At the moment, it will suffice to summarize an important conclusion to which they all point (some more directly than others): when two or more discriminative stimuli control the same two-term contingency (the same defined response and reinforcer), those stimuli can be shown to be related by equivalence. That is to say, *three-term contingencies can establish the prerequisites for an equivalence relation.*

Why should this finding cast doubt on the interpretation of the first test that is depicted in Figure 10-3? Uncertainty arises because one cannot be sure that the defined responses, R1 and R2, serve as samples in controlling the subject's choices between Comparisons A1 and A2 during the test. Because Stimuli D1 and D2 had never been explicitly related to any other stimuli, it was assumed that D1 and D2 themselves would not be related to A1 and A2. A closer look at the baseline (the two upper sections of Figure 10-3), however, will indicate why this assumption may not have been valid and will reveal grounds for doubting the interpretation of the test:

(1) The baseline contains two defined two-term contingencies. In one, R1 produces the reinforcer (SR1) and in the other, R2 produces the reinforcer.

(2) The baseline also contains four defined three-term contingencies, with B1, B2, D1, and D2 as the discriminative stimuli.

(3) Either of two discriminative stimuli, B1 or D1, controls one two-term contingency, and either of the other discriminative stimuli, B2 or D2, controls the other two-term contingency. That is to say, Stimulus B1 or D1 sets the reinforcing occasion for R1, and Stimulus B2 or D2 for R2.

(4) If discriminative stimuli that control the same contingency enter the same equivalence class (Chapter 11), the stimulus pair, B1D1, will be a member of one equivalence relation, and the B2D2 pair will be a member of another equivalence relation.

(5) Experiments on equivalence relations in four-term units have shown us that the B1A1 pair also will be a member of one equivalence relation, and the B2A2 pair will be a member of another equivalence relation.

(6) If the B1D1 and B1A1 pairs are members of the same equivalence relation, then we would expect the D1A1 pair to join that same relation; similarly, with the B2D2 and B2A2 pairs being members of an equivalence relation, we would expect the D2A2 pair to join that same relation.

(7) Given this reasoning, we might expect that the results of the original test would not change if we were to permit the subject to produce Comparisons A1 and A2 by touching D1 or D2 just once, *without the differential responses*. The bottom section of Figure 10-3 illustrates such a test; because the defined response, R3, is a single touch, it preempts R1 and R2 both to the samples and the comparisons. In this revised test, which does not involve Responses R1 and R2, Stimuli D1 and D2 alone might govern a subject's choices of Comparisons A1 and A2. If this happened, we would have to entertain the possibility that R1 and R2 had been irrelevant to the subject's comparison selections in the other

test. The seemingly different tests depicted in Figures 10-2 and 10-3, therefore, might in principle be the same.

This fundamental problem will dog any attempt to show that responses can serve as the conditional terms in a four-term contingency. Tested responses will always be under the control of stimuli. Therefore, one can never be certain that a response and not its controlling stimulus is the critical element.

Whenever I have run up against this kind of a blank wall—finding myself asking a question that seems unamenable to experimental test—I have found it useful to back off and reconsider the question itself. In this instance, I was searching for a way to find out whether equivalence relations include the defined response elements of the analytic unit, along with the conditional, discriminative, and reinforcing stimuli. In the process of trying to answer this question by placing differential responses under the control of conditional stimuli, I came up against the impossibility of completely separating the responses from the stimuli. Although it is possible to present conditional or discriminative stimuli while preventing the occurrence of particular responses to those stimuli, it is not possible to present the responses without their stimuli. Because the defined responses could not be made to occur in the absence of their controlling stimuli, I could not be certain whether responses or stimuli were the crucial elements in emergent four-term units. (See pp. 466-469, however, for a possible way around this difficulty.) Standard tests for the properties of equivalence relations, therefore, would not permit a definitive statement about the possible inclusion of responses in the equivalence relation.

Recognition of this problem turned my inquiry in another direction. Given the analytic uncertainties I had encountered, I wondered why it should matter whether we considered a defined response to constitute the effective sample in a four-term unit or whether we considered that response's controlling stimulus to constitute the effective sample. Since we cannot separate defined responses functionally from their controlling stimuli, why cling to a functional distinction? Why not include stimuli *and* responses in the equivalence relation? The language in which we then couched any particular analysis would depend simply on whether we chose to look at stimuli or responses.

This reasoning can be carried down from the four- to the three-term analytic unit. We can ask why we should not also consider both the occasion (discriminative stimulus) for a defined response *and* the response itself as potential components of element pairs in the equivalence relation. If a defined response that is controlled by a conditional stimulus can be included in the equivalence relation, why not also the defined response that is controlled by a discriminative stimulus?

It is important to note that I am not calling for the inclusion of unobservable or invented responses in the equivalence relation. This is not just a repetition of mediation theory's practice of postulating the occurrence of responses in order to satisfy theoretical needs. Defined responses are neither invented nor inferred. They are not only visible but are specified components of the reinforcement contingency. The contingency decrees that reinforcement be withheld unless the subject (or student) emits the defined responses. In the absence of those responses, the analytic unit of which they are components does not exist.

The three-term unit and the definition of equivalence. The inclusion of defined responses as elements of event pairs that make up the equivalence relation turns out to be more than just an arbitrary assignment of labels. Several theoretical and experimental advantages accrue immediately. One theoretically significant feature arises from the demonstration that discriminative stimuli can become related by equivalence even when they are involved only in three-term contingencies. This demonstration (to be discussed further in Chapter 11) calls into question our original behavioral definition of the equivalence relation. It is true that the required properties of reflexivity, symmetry, and transitivity can only be assessed directly by means of four-term contingencies; that is what led me in the *Emergent Verbal Classes* paper to describe equivalence as emerging at the level of the four-term unit. In the face of demonstrations that three-term contingencies can generate equivalence, however, I was compelled to drop the notion that equivalence emerges only at the level of the four-term unit.

Because the direct evaluation of reflexivity, symmetry, and transitivity requires four-term units, abandonment of the four-term unit as the necessary origin of equivalence might cause one also to abandon the set-theory definition of the equivalence relation. This would be unfortunate. After all, it is the evaluation of set theory's defining properties of the equivalence relation that gives rise to the extraordinary predictiveness we have been able to achieve. The old saw about "throwing out the baby with the bath water" applies here. (For further discussion of this matter, see pp. 536-538; 550-552.)

Furthermore, it turns out that the inclusion of responses in the equivalence relation not only permits but forces us to maintain our set-theory definition. This is because even though four-term units need not be involved in generating equivalence relations, it is still necessary to take the defining properties into account if we are to understand in principle how an inferred equivalence relation could have arisen from three-term units.

The advantages of retaining the set-theory definition of the equivalence relation even when direct assessment is not possible were exemplified above (pp.375-376). There, I pointed out that the results of the first test shown in Figure 10-3 would be equivocal because the effective samples might be the D-stimuli rather than or in addition to the defined responses. But how could the D-stimuli have come to control a subject's choices between the A-comparisons? For this control to have developed, Sample D1 would have had to become equivalent to Comparison A1, and Sample D2 to Comparison A2. We saw that this could not have happened without the involvement of the defined responses. The only way Stimuli D1 and D2 could have become equivalent to Stimuli A1 and A2, respectively, was via Responses R1 and R2. The D- and A-stimuli could become paired with each other indirectly via the DR, RB, and BA pairs. It is true that the emergence of conditional discriminations that define the properties of the equivalence relation could not be shown directly to require the defined responses, R1 and R2, but only by including those responses as elements of the event pairs that define the equivalence relation could we predict the emergent DA conditional discriminations.

That is why we would also predict emergent DA conditional discriminations in the test at the bottom of Figure 10-3 even though the test itself involves no differential responses; the only defined response, R3, is just a single touch. With D1 as the sample, we would still expect a subject to select comparison A1, and with sample D2, to select comparison A2. Only if we include the defined baseline responses in the equivalence classes do these DA pairings become predictable.

In addition to making emergent conditional discriminations predictable, the inclusion of differential responses in the equivalence relation yields another dividend. It permits us to escape the theoretical intricacies in which we involve ourselves when we hypothesize response mediation as the process responsible for emergent stimulus-stimulus relations. A major complexity of mediation theory is the requirement that the mediating responses must occur, although perhaps in a reduced form, whenever a subject demonstrates either baseline or emergent stimulus-stimulus relations. To maintain the necessary linear chain of stimulus–response–stimulus– and-so-on, mediation theorists had to assume the occurrence of unobserved responses between each related pair of stimuli. This assumption leads to greater and greater awkwardness in the necessary explanatory constructions as derived relations come to involve more and more baseline nodes. The very inelegance of mediation theories of stimulus equivalence ought to occasion some skepticism as to their explanatory utility.

Furthermore, mediation theorists had to assume the occurrence of backward conditioning (Ekstrand, 1966). Without accepting the reality of backward conditioning, mediation theory could not account for the AB and BC symmetry that was in turn required to account for the emergence of CA relations from an AB/BC baseline. Although backward conditioning is at best fragile, mediation theory requires it as an explanatory prop for the robust phenomena of symmetry and equivalence.

If, however, we simply include defined responses as elements of event pairs that constitute an equivalence relation, we need postulate no linear mediating process in baseline or emergent relations, no unobserved responses, and no backward conditioning to account for symmetry. (As we shall see, we need postulate no forward conditioning, either.) By definition, the equivalence relation will include all of the stimulus-stimulus, stimulus-response, response-stimulus, and response-response pairs that are directly taught and all of the pairs that emerge in the tests. We need nothing more than our behavioral definition of equivalence to predict the emergent relations. A potential equivalence relation can be thought of as a kind of bag that contains all the ordered pairs of events that constitute the relation (for example, Carrigan, 1986; Saunders and Green, 1992.). To document the relation, all we have to do is reach into the bag (using our conditional-discrimination tests as pincers) and pull out its member pairs. If even one of the defining pairs turns out to be missing, we have to conclude (assuming the absence of procedural artifacts) that the elements in the bag do not constitute an equivalence class.

The bag may be thought of as the name for the kind of relation that holds between the members of each pair: "is equal to," "is the blood relation of," "is associated with," "is linked to," "is conditional on," and so on. Each relation must first be defined independently of the equivalence tests. The *name* of the relation that holds between members of the component pairs of events is independent of the method for determining whether the set of pairs does or does not constitute an equivalence relation.

A variation of the experiment that we proposed in Figure 10-3 will help illustrate the advantage of this conception of the equivalence relation. The first part of the new baseline (the uppermost section of Figure 10-4) requires differential responses not to Comparisons B1 and B2 but instead, to Samples A1 and A2. Given Sample A1, the subject must touch it five times in rapid succession (R1) in order to bring up Comparisons B1 and B2; given Sample A2, the subject must touch it twice, spacing the touches two to three seconds apart (R2) to bring up the comparisons. The subject

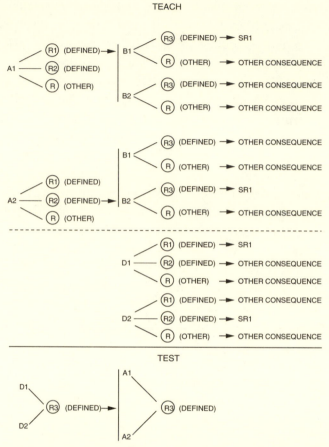

Figure 10-4. A proposed test for emergent DA relations, predictable if defined responses R1 and R2 are included in the equivalence classes. See text for details.

then has to touch the correct comparison only once (R3) to produce the reinforcer. The second part of the baseline (below the dashed divider) is the same as in Figure 10-3, a successive D1D2 discrimination: given Stimulus D1 or D2, the subject can produce the reinforcer by means of R1 or R2, respectively. The test in the bottom section of Figure 10-4 is also the same as before: again, R3 precludes the defined responses, R1 and R2; given Sample D1, will the subject select Comparison A1, and given D2, will the selection be A2?

Once again, the emergence of these DA conditional discriminations would become predictable if we assumed an equivalence relation that included the event pairs D1R1 and A1R1. For example, if D1R1 and A1R1 are members of the equivalence relation, then symmetry and transitivity would bring D1A1 into the relation. Similarly, D2A2 would become a member of another equivalence relation. Including the defined responses as elements of the equivalence class permits us to predict these test results (also, AD transitivity), and at the same time frees us from all the additional assumptions that an explanatory mediating process would require.

From this experiment comes another that will illustrate conclusively the need to examine more closely the relation between equivalence and the defined responses that the analytic unit includes. In predicting the test results in Figure 10-4, we did not have to mention the B-stimuli. Comparisons B1 and B2 served as discriminative stimuli for the reinforcement of R3 but played no special role in our prediction that the DA conditional discriminations would emerge in the test. Might we not achieve the same test results, then, if we eliminated the B-stimuli from the baseline? We could do this by allowing A1 and A2 to serve not as samples in four-term units but simply as discriminative stimuli in three-term units. Figure 10-5 illustrates such an experiment.

In the first baseline segment (above the dashed line), we teach a subject a simple A1A2 discrimination instead of a conditional discrimination. This is a successive discrimination, with A1 presented on some trials and A2 on others. With A1, only R1 will produce the reinforcer, and with A2, only R2. The second baseline

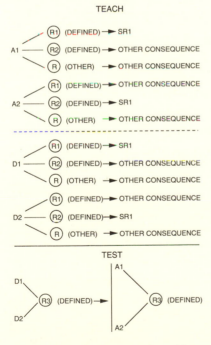

Figure 10-5. A proposed test, like that in Figure 10-4, but with no four-term units in the baseline. See text for details.

segment is the same as before, a successive D1D2 discrimination. Then, having established this baseline of two simple discriminations—three-term units—we carry out the same test as before (bottom segment of Figure 10-5). Will a subject still touch Comparison A1 when D1 is the sample, and A2 when D2 is the sample?

We can again predict the emergence of DA (and AD) conditional discriminations by assuming that the AR and DR relations in the baseline possess the three defining properties of an equivalence relation. For example, if A1R1 is symmetric, then by transitivity, D1R1 and R1A1 will yield D1A1. Only by including the defined responses in the equivalence relation can we explain how the explicit establishment of three-term units (simple discriminations) can lead to the emergence of untaught four-term units (conditional discriminations). Studies to be included in Chapter 11 will support the likelihood that the experiment summarized in Figure 10-5 will turn out as described.

Stimuli and Responses

What does the inclusion of responses in the equivalence relation have to say about the distinction between stimulus and response? It says that with respect to the equivalence relation, such a distinction is unnecessary. An equivalence relation is made up of pairs of events, with no restriction on the nature of the events that make up the pairs. The locus of those events, whether it be the living organism or the organism's living or nonliving environment, is irrelevant.

This does not mean there are no differences between stimuli and responses. Like all events, stimuli and responses can be members of many classes. Some classes may include one and not the other: the class of events that arise in the inanimate environment (we usually call these *stimuli*) does not include the acts of a living organism (we usually call these *responses*). A classification that distinguishes stimuli from responses on the basis of their locus is meaningful, particularly when behavior analysts are trying to define their subject matter. But then, the acts of one living organism (responses) can also function as environmental events (stimuli) that influence the acts of another living organism. Even here, however, taking events that are often classed together as responses and dividing them into classes that might be called *controlling* and *controlled* events is useful in applied, experimental, and theoretical analyses. Variations in context from occasion to occasion will determine whether an organism's act belongs to the *response* or to the *stimulus* class.

In the context of describing the membership of an equivalence class, the distinction between stimulus and response, or even between controlling and controlled events, loses its significance. Ordered pairs of the events that comprise an equivalence class constitute the membership of an equivalence relation. How the individual events that make up these ordered pairs are classified in other contexts has no bearing on whether the pairs belong to an equivalence relation. An equivalence relation may contain stimulus-stimulus, response-response, stimulus-response, and response-stimulus pairs.

Including stimuli and responses in the same equivalence class is not the same as equating stimulus and response in the context of a conditioning paradigm (for example, Jenkins, 1963). Theories of conditioning, whether Pavlovian or operant, account for the characteristics of acts by appeal to temporal or contingent relations between acts and environmental events or between different kinds of environmental events (between responses and reinforcing stimuli, between discriminative stimuli and responses, between conditioned and unconditioned stimuli, and so on). Fixed temporal sequences of events characterize many of the relations that are involved in conditioning. In reinforcement and discrimination, for example, one element of the relation must occur before or simultaneously with the other. Even when related elements do not occur in fixed temporal sequences, as when a state variable like deprivation alters reinforcer effectiveness and changes the probability of many responses (Meehl, 1992; Skinner, 1938, pp. 22-25), or when constant stimuli remain present throughout the establishment of conditioned behavior (Goldiamond, 1962, pp. 295-297), the relations are characterized by a unidirectional causal influence. One element of the relation is the controlling event and the other the controlled. Inclusion of event pairs in an equivalence relation, however, implies neither temporal nor causal directionality.

In analyzing equivalence relations, then, we do not sometimes call an event a stimulus and at other times a response. Rather, we discard both of those terms. Equivalence relations have their own defining characteristics, none requiring the stimulus/response dichotomy.

The independence of equivalence relations from the arrows of time and causality removes any need to distinguish between stimuli and responses when specifying the membership of an equivalence class. Therefore, in determining whether events are members of an equivalence class, we do not have to consider whether those events are related via conditioning. What we achieve here is more than just a way around the theoretical and empirical complexities that concepts like response mediation and backward conditioning introduce. The concepts of *equivalence class* and *equivalence relation* require us to consider *neither* backward *nor* forward conditioning. We need not conceptualize equivalence relations in terms that are relevant to conditioning.

Equivalence and the Reinforcement Contingency

Demonstrations that equivalence-class membership can include reinforcing stimuli (Dube, McIlvane, Mackay, & Stoddard, 1987; Dube et al., 1989; Dube et al., 1989; McIlvane et al., 1992) led me to ask whether the equivalence relation might include not just the conditional, discriminative, and reinforcing stimuli that constitute a four-term analytic unit, but also the defined responses in the unit. In attempting to answer this question, one proposed experiment led to another, but none have yet been carried out precisely as I described them. Nevertheless, outlining those experiments did lead me to recognize a shortcoming in our original conception of the equivalence relation: The statement in the *Emergent Verbal Classes paper* (Chapter 9) that equivalence emerges at the level of the four-term unit was not correct. To show that this statement was incorrect required me to cite in advance of Chapter 11 some closely related experiments that *have* been carried out and that involved three-term units. Then, the likelihood that equivalence relations could form at the level of the three-term unit led to questions about our original definition of equivalence relations that was based on the three properties of mathematically defined equivalence. Behavioral definition of those properties entailed conditional discriminations—four-term units. The utility of the definition was then shown to *require* the inclusion of responses as members of some of the event pairs that make up the equivalence relation. With defined responses included in the equivalence class, the original definition turned out to be indispensable in explaining how equivalence could develop out of three-term units. And so we came full circle.

Still remaining is the question of where equivalence relations come from. An important part of the answer to this question almost leaps out at us now that we have included in the equivalence relation all the elements of the analytic unit. Question: where does that unit come from? Answer: the reinforcement contingency creates the unit and with it, the equivalence relation. The establishment of equivalence relations is, then, one of the outcomes of reinforcement contingencies.

A terminological note. It must be recognized that to speak of the "establishment" of equivalence relations is a circumlocution, taken in the interest of linguistic brevity; it saves words and eliminates awkward sentence constructions. *Equivalence relation* refers neither to a theoretical entity nor (Chiesa, 1994, p. 150) to processes or entities that are beyond observation, but rather, summarizes a set of observed regularities. Strictly speaking, reinforcement contingencies do not *create* equivalence relations; rather, they create prerequisites, or the potential, for demonstrating the properties that define an equivalence relation. Additional factors, like the test conditions, contextual control, and a subject's behavioral history will help determine whether and how that potential is realized (for example, Hayes, 1991, p. 27; Saunders and Green, 1992; Sidman, 1986a, pp. 239-241; 1992a, pp. 23-25).

An equivalence relation, therefore, has no existence as a *thing*; it is not actually *established, formed,* or *created*. It does not *exist*, either in theory or in reality. It is defined by the emergence of new—and

predictable—analytic units of behavior from previously demonstrated units. But the set of ordered pairs that defines whether or
not any particular relation is also an equivalence relation does not
constitute a theoretical entity. Those pairs of events are directly
observable in conditional-discrimination tests for the properties that
define an equivalence relation. To give a set of observations a name,
and then to transform the name into an explanation for those very
observations, adds exactly zero to our store of knowledge or our
understanding.

The equivalence relation is not itself a unit of behavior from which
more complex units are built. Nor is the equivalence relation a structure that is composed of more basic units. Although the diagrams
that are typically used to depict experimental procedures may give a
misleading impression of sequential or mediated learning processes,
the definition of an equivalence relation does not require the
component pairs to possess any temporal or structural property that
might define a *mediating* event, a temporal or spatial *sequence*, an
association, a *link*, an *associative link*, a *distance*, a *chain,* a *network*, a
conditioned stimulus, a *conditioned response*, or any other kind of
presumed basic structure or unit of behavior.

For all of these reasons, then, when I speak of the role of contingencies in "establishing" equivalence relations I am not making a
statement about the problem of *when* an equivalence relation "comes
into existence," or is "formed." As McIlvane and Dube (1990) have
pointed out, this is not an issue of real substance (see also Sidman,
1992a, pp. 22-25). To say that an equivalence relation has been
established, or formed, or created is to say no more than that the
potential has been created for the emergence of new analytic units
that are predictable on the basis of the properties that define an
equivalence relation.

Equivalence as an outcome of reinforcement contingencies. The *Where
Does Equivalence Come From?* paper (Chapter 9) asked, "Can we
derive equivalence from more primitive behavioral functions, variables, or processes?" I ended by suggesting that the equivalence
relation, like the relations we call reinforcement and discrimination,

is a product of survival contingencies. The suggestion was that we form equivalence relations because we are built that way. I felt that this suggestion had to be considered seriously because I could see no satisfactory derivation of equivalence from more primitive behavioral functions, variables, or processes. Indeed, in a later paper (Sidman, 1992a) I suggested that individual learning experiences may be required not for forming equivalence relations but rather, for breaking them down. Now, the discussion in Chapter 10, following a different route, has led to the conclusion that equivalence is a direct outcome of reinforcement. But although reinforcement contingencies generate equivalence relations, reinforcement itself can be accounted for only as a product of survival contingencies (Skinner, 1965). The recognition that reinforcement contingencies establish equivalence relations is consistent with a conception of equivalence as a primitive function. The notion, along with some of its systematic consequences, can be elaborated as follows.

Reinforcement can have many outcomes. Reinforcers are events which, when contingent on an act, increase the likelihood that the act will reoccur whenever the context reoccurs. Many writers have fleshed out this sparsely worded definition, making its implications for systematic behavioral analysis more evident (for example, Catania, 1992; Holland & Skinner, 1961; Keller & Schoenfeld, 1950; Skinner, 1938). The concepts of emotion and motivation extend the basic definition from a change in the probability of the single act (or class of acts) upon which a reinforcer is contingent to simultaneous changes in the probability of many different acts (Meehl, 1992; Skinner, 1938). Also, by including in the basic definition the context in which reinforcement occurs, we arrive at the three-term contingency as the basic unit of behavioral analysis. And so, along with an increase in response probability, the three-term unit—simple discrimination—is an inherent characteristic of reinforcement. Discrimination is actually part of the definition of reinforcement.

Why does a reinforcer increase the probability of the act that produces it? How is it that many different acts change in probability as a function of reinforcer-related variables? Behavior Analysis does not try to derive these phenomena from more basic behavioral processes. They are all products of survival contingencies, and the answers to such questions are going to come from other sciences—from other levels of analysis and other methods of investigation. The observations that make these questions important for other sciences, however, are behavioral. Behavior Analysis is therefore concerned to define more precisely the phenomena to which the terms reinforcement, motivation, and emotion are to be applied.

Reinforcement also helps to determine what we see, hear, smell, and so on, and perception is therefore an area to which Behavior Analysis can contribute directly. Nevertheless, the fact that we do sense certain aspects of our environment and not others is an outcome of evolutionary processes. Behavior Analysis accepts as a given the fact that we respond to different kinds of energy in our environment, but leaves it to other sciences to study the various kinds of sensory equipment that we are born with and that make such discriminations possible.

Similar considerations may apply to equivalence relations. Reinforcement contingencies select the particular elements that constitute a unit of analysis. As we have seen, the equivalence relation consists of ordered pairs of the unit's elements. The analytic units and the equivalence relations that reinforcement has established comprise an individual's repertoire of acts and discriminations. To the extent that we have had similar experiences each of us will demonstrate the same units and the same equivalence relations. To the extent that our experiences have differed, each of us will possess different repertoires of units and equivalence relations. The facts that analytic units and equivalence relations are established at all, however, are species characteristics. Because the study of equivalence relations is relatively new, the extent of the generality of this characteristic across species is as yet unknown. The capacity for demonstrating equivalence relations can be regarded as a most useful gift from our inheritance, and the anatomic and chemical substrates of that capacity can be expected to become an ongoing concern of sciences other than Behavior Analysis. Sciences that deal with structural and functional neuroanatomy, biochemistry, and genetics have not yet begun to ask questions about equivalence relations. When they do, behavioral studies of equivalence relations will provide the data that these other levels of analysis must consider.

The conception that equivalence relations come about as a consequence of reinforcement contingencies raises a number of questions, some that require theoretical elaboration and some that suggest new experiments. I shall complete Chapter 10 with a discussion of several of these matters.

Equivalence Relations and Conditioned Reinforcement

The inclusion of reinforcers and defined responses as elements in the ordered pairs of events that make up an equivalence relation increases the explanatory and predictive power of our definition of equivalence. In the *Emergent Verbal Classes* paper I had listed conditioned reinforcement, along with primary reinforcement and discrimination, as a stimulus function that is not derivable from anything more basic. Behavior Analysis accepts as a given the fact that the reinforcing function of a stimulus can be passed on to other events. One of the consequences of including equivalence relations among the basic outcomes of reinforcement, however, is that conditioned reinforcement then becomes derivable.

Because the distinction between conditioned reinforcers (often called secondary or learned reinforcers) and primary reinforcers is not always clear, some definitions are in order. I propose these not as matters of principle but only to simplify the following discussion. The term *conditioned reinforcement* arises from the observation that events can become reinforcers even though they do not originally function as such. I shall apply the term *conditioned reinforcers* to events that are known to have acquired their reinforcing function. I shall reserve the term *primary reinforcer* for the terminal events in operant and Pavlovian contingencies. These may actually be conditioned reinforcers, so calling them primary implies nothing about the origin of their reinforcing function. I call them primary when we are not concerned with the source of their reinforcing function and if they are involved somehow when another event acquires a reinforcing function. They are primary, therefore, only in relation to that other event.

How do we derive the relation that we call conditioned reinforcement from the equivalence relation? If a reinforcement contingency has created an equivalence relation, our definition of equivalence leads us to expect a positive result when we test each pair of the analytic unit's elements for emergent conditional relations that are consistent with the defining properties. We should expect, for example, to demonstrate not only the conditional relation that the contingency establishes between discriminative stimulus and reinforced response, but also its symmetric counterpart, the relation between response and discriminative stimulus. This particular response-stimulus pair is of special importance because its elements are involved in the relation that we call conditioned reinforcement. We should also expect the event pair, discriminative stimulus and reinforcer, to be a member of the equivalence relation.

Several studies have shown that functions possessed or acquired by one element of the analytic unit are transferred to other elements of the unit. To account for these observations by postulating a process called *transfer of function*, however, adds unnecessary complexity to the analysis. Instances that we attribute to a transfer process can be accounted for more parsimoniously as the merger of overlapping classes. Here, we return once more to set theory, and adapt for our own behavioral purposes not only the concept of the equivalence relation but also of set union (Gellert et al., 1977, pp. 320-322). If a member of Class I also belongs to Class II, then (unless other factors come into play; see below) class union will bring the other members of Class I also into Class II. Thus, if a conditional relation is also an equivalence relation and the sample stimulus in the equivalence class joins a syntactic class, becoming, for example, a "first" or a "second," the comparison that is related to that sample will also join the syntactic class (for relevant data, see Green et al., 1991; Lazar, 1977; Lazar & Kotlarchyk, 1986; Sigurdardottir, Green, & Saunders, 1990; Wulfert & Hayes, 1988). Similarly, if the sample in a conditional relation also serves as a positive discriminative stimulus in a three-term unit, the conditionally related comparison will join the same discriminative-stimulus class as the sample (de Rose, McIlvane, Dube, Galpin, & Stoddard, 1988; de Rose, McIlvane, Dube, & Stoddard, 1988).

A like analysis can be applied to instances that have been described as a transfer of the reinforcing function by means of an equivalence relation (Hayes et al., 1987; Hayes, Kohlenberg, & Hayes, 1991). Instead of invoking a transfer process, we need only recognize that two classes overlap: First, the equivalence class that includes both the discriminative and reinforcing stimulus components of the analytic unit, and second, the reinforcer class. Because the reinforcing stimulus is a member of both classes, the two merge, bringing the discriminative stimulus into the reinforcer class. Indeed, all of the classes to which individual members of the unit belong will merge (unless, as noted below and in Chapter 12, contextual control prevents such mergers). Discriminative stimuli, for example, will function as reinforcers and reinforcers will function as discriminative stimuli. Although the behavioral observation will be the display of new functions by elements of the analytic unit, no transfer process as such need be invoked.

Conditioned reinforcement, then, is to be expected as a direct consequence of: (a) our definition of the equivalence relation; (b) the inclusion of equivalence relations among the direct effects of reinforcement contingencies; and (c) the merger of classes that takes place when members of the analytic unit whose event pairs define the equivalence relation also belong to other classes. Unlike the basic reinforcing, discriminative, emotional, and motivational functions of events, the conditioned-reinforcement function can be derived from other behavioral processes—in this instance, equivalence class formation and the merger (union) of classes (for more on class union, see pp. 457-463; 515-524; 529).

The Two-Term Response-Reinforcer Unit

The suggestion that equivalence relations, along with the analytic unit, are a direct outcome of reinforcement contingencies came about in part because of observations that equivalence could arise not only from four-term but also from three-term contingencies. Consistent with these observations is the inclusion of defined responses in the equivalence class. It is noteworthy, however, that the original suggestion sets no limit on the number of elements that a unit has to contain if the contingency is to give rise to an equivalence relation. What about the two-term contingency between act and reinforcer? Might this contingency also give rise to equivalence relations? (Even to ask this question requires that the analytic unit's defined response be involved in the equivalence relation.) At present, we have to answer the question in the affirmative.

The increase in response probability that helps to define reinforcement always takes place in a discriminative context. That context, along with the increase in probability, must also be specified in the definition of the contingency. Still, even though the two-term contingency does not exist in isolation, it can serve as a useful analytic device. In any specific instance, we may be more interested in the relation between response and reinforcer than in the relation between discriminative stimulus and response or between discriminative stimulus and reinforcer. That is why I have almost always used the qualifier *analytic* when speaking about the units that reinforcement contingencies create. Even though three- or four-term units, too, may be components of still larger units, it can still be advantageous to analyze the smaller units separately. We may therefore learn something useful by asking whether two-term contingencies can give rise to equivalence relations.

For example, suppose we have taught a subject to perform several different acts, each producing the same reinforcer. We would then be in a position to examine a set of two-term units, each containing a different act but the identical reinforcer. Skinner's specification of a response class that is formed by a set of acts each producing the same reinforcer (Skinner, 1938, p. 38), along with the suggestion that the response-reinforcer pair within each two-term analytic unit belongs to an equivalence relation, permit the derivation of new empirical phenomena. If the response-reinforcer pair within each analytic unit belongs to an equivalence relation, and if each of these pairs possesses an element in common, all of the two-element equivalence classes will merge. We will then be able to demonstrate new relations that would document the merger of equivalence classes. We might, for example, do the following experiment.

Let us start with a subject who has a joystick that can always be moved in any of four directions: horizontally to the left (Response L) or right (Response R), or vertically up (Response U) or down (Response D). Let us also start with two reinforcers, SR1 and SR2, that the subject has shown are equally preferable. In Phase I of the experiment, we teach the subject that Responses L and U will produce SR1 and Responses R and D will produce SR2. In the course of this teaching, we sometimes lock the joystick so that, for example, it will not move to the left but only up, down, or to the right, or neither left nor right but only up or down, and so on, with all possible combinations of locked and unlocked movements of the joystick occurring equally often.

Then, in Phase II, we lock the joystick so that it will move *only* to the left. Also, Response L now produces not SR1 but SR3, a reinforcer that the subject prefers over both SR1 and SR2.

The test comes in Phase III. The subject has never produced SR3 except by means of Response L, but we now lock the joystick so that it will move in each direction *except* to the left. In which direction will the subject now move the stick? If Responses L and U had become members of the same equivalence class in Phase I, when they both led to the same reinforcer, then Response U should become the replacement for Response L in Phase III even though Response U had never produced SR3.

This test does not directly evaluate any of the defining properties of an equivalence relation. The subject's selection of Response U when Response R is blocked becomes predictable, however, if one assumes that the two-term contingency generates equivalence relations and that the common reinforcer element causes the two-member equivalence classes to merge.

We could evaluate equivalence relations somewhat more directly by testing for the emergence of new three-term units. For example, in Phase III, we might sometimes present SR1, SR2, or SR3 not as reinforcers but as discriminative stimuli. Which of the available responses would each of these discriminative stimuli occasion? If the two-term contingencies had generated equivalence relations, then each explicitly taught (or emergent) response-reinforcer pair and its symmetric reinforcer-response pair would be members of the same relation. Discriminative stimuli SR1 and SR3 would occasion both Responses L and U, and SR2 would occasion Responses R and D.

We could test for the properties of an equivalence relation more directly by making use of four-term units, but these examples will suffice to illustrate how one might go about determining whether two-term response-reinforcer contingencies, like three- and four-term contingencies, create equivalence relations. This does not mean that the complexity of the contingency is unimportant. Further elaboration of the conditions under which a reinforcement contingency does and does not establish prerequisites for the demonstration of equivalence relations may show the size of the analytic unit to be a significant variable. Unit size may in turn interact with variables such as animal species, human diagnostic category, and learned contextual restrictions.

The Two-Term Stimulus-Reinforcer Unit

All of the analytic units discussed so far have included at least one defined response, the act that produces the reinforcer. The defined response is, of course, essential when specifying a particular stimulus as a conditioned or primary reinforcer. In the above derivation of the conditioned reinforcement function (p. 391), however, it was not necessary to mention the defined response. It was sufficient to include the unit's discriminative stimulus and terminal event among the components of the equivalence class and to include the terminal event in the reinforcer class also. Merger of the reinforcer class and the equivalence class to which all of the unit members belong brings the discriminative stimulus into the reinforcer class.

Highlighting this particular component of the equivalence relation—discriminative stimulus and primary reinforcer—as critical for the derivation of conditioned reinforcement brings up questions about the nature of the unit that is required for the creation of conditioned reinforcers. The above derivation of conditioned reinforcement adds some new dimensions to an old controversy: Can a stimulus become a conditioned reinforcer without also serving or having served as a discriminative stimulus? Must a conditioned reinforcer also control or have controlled a defined response or need it only have been paired with an existing reinforcer? (For literature reviews and extensive discussion of this and related questions, see Dinsmoor, 1983; Kelleher and Gollub, 1962.)

The discriminative stimulus and the primary reinforcer are the very events that Pavlovian conditioning requires (Pavlov, 1927). What is the relation between conditioned reinforcement and the Pavlovian, or respondent (Skinner, 1938) contingency? Does the establishment of a conditioned reinforcer require a three-term operant contingency or does a two-term respondent contingency suffice? And if a respondent contingency is enough to create a conditioned reinforcer, where does equivalence come into the picture?

A respondent contingency specifies only two events, the conditioned stimulus and the reinforcer (unconditioned stimulus). Unlike operant contingencies, respondent contingencies involve only environmental events and are independent of any act performed by the subject. *If Stimulus 1 then Stimulus 2* and *if not Stimulus 1 then not Stimulus 2* describes the respondent contingency. Responses are measured but play no role in the contingency. Although Pavlovian conditioning creates a new stimulus-response relation, the contingency that brings about this new relation specifies only two terms, both of them stimuli. This two-term respondent unit— conditioned stimulus and reinforcer—is apparently sufficient for the creation of conditioned reinforcers for operant behavior. Catania (1991) has defined *conditioned reinforcer* as "a stimulus that functions as a reinforcer *because of* [emphasis added] its contingent relation to another reinforcer." Is it possible, then, that the event pair, discriminative stimulus and primary reinforcer, is critical for the creation of a conditioned reinforcer not because of the pair's membership in an equivalence relation but because the pair is a respondent unit that happens to be enclosed within an operant unit?

In determining whether the discriminative stimulus and the operant reinforcer act as Pavlovian conditioned and unconditioned stimuli, respectively, we must take into account some procedural differences between operant and respondent conditioning. Although the pairing of discriminative stimulus and primary reinforcer within an operant three-term contingency may look like an instance of respondent conditioning, appearances here can easily prove deceptive. Parameter values within the operant paradigm are rarely optimal for respondent conditioning (for reviews of the parameters that are relevant in various respondent conditioning procedures, see Domjan and Burkhard, 1982, pp. 42-99; Henton and Iversen, 1978, pp. 29-96; Kling, 1971, pp. 554-565). For example, the duration of the discriminative stimulus is seldom fixed at a value that would encourage respondent conditioning. Because the discriminative stimulus usually remains present until the subject emits the defined response, stimulus duration can vary and can differ considerably from an optimal value. Even if the discriminative stimulus duration is held constant, variations in the time interval between it and the defined response and in the duration of the response will cause a varying delay of reinforcement. It is not clear, then, that discriminative control—a three-term analytic unit—necessarily brings about Pavlovian conditioning. Although a discriminative stimulus for an operant may serve at the same time as a Pavlovian conditioned stimulus (Shapiro, 1960, 1961; Williams, 1965), the inevitability of such a dual function remains questionable. And if the discriminative stimulus in an operant three-term unit does not serve simultaneously as the conditioned stimulus in a respondent two-term unit, then the conditioned reinforcement function of that discriminative stimulus cannot be attributed to Pavlovian conditioning.

Pavlovian conditioning may therefore not be necessary for the creation of conditioned reinforcers, but it does appear to be sufficient. Pavlovian conditioned stimuli can function as conditioned reinforcers for operant behavior. It is possible, of course, that conditioned reinforcers arise from more than one source, perhaps from respondent contingencies *and* from equivalence relations that operant contingencies create. In any event, given that respondent contingencies can create conditioned reinforcers, it becomes relevant to ask how this comes about. Briefly stated, respondent conditioning occurs when the conditional pairing of conditioned and unconditioned stimuli causes the conditioned stimulus to elicit a response that it would not have elicited without the pairing. This definition of respondent conditioning says nothing about transfer of a reinforcement function to the conditioned stimulus even in a respondent unit, let alone about such transfer to the discriminative stimulus in an operant unit. Whether the Pavlovian unconditioned stimulus extends its reinforcing function either to conditioned or discriminative stimuli has generally been regarded as a matter to be determined empirically. Might it be possible, however, that the establishment of equivalence relations can provide a theoretical foundation for predicting such transfer?

To answer this question, it will be useful to look more closely at the Pavlovian conditioning process itself. Suppose we were to include the creation of an equivalence relation among the outcomes of the two-term Pavlovian contingency. That is to say, suppose the conditional relation *if conditioned stimulus (CS) then unconditioned stimulus (UCS)* also possesses the properties of an equivalence relation. If this conception is correct, we can derive both operant and Pavlovian conditioned reinforcement in exactly the same way—as the result of the formation of equivalence relations and the merger of equivalence and reinforcer classes.

How can we know whether respondent conditioning brings about equivalence relations? An experiment by Shipley (1935) strongly suggests that it can. Shipley presented subjects sometimes with a light (CS1) and sometimes with a tone (CS2), with each CS followed by a tap to the cheek (UCS1) that caused the subject to blink. Then only the light was presented, followed by a shock to the finger (UCS2) that elicited finger withdrawal. In subsequent test trials, the tone, too, which had never been paired with the shock, was found to elicit finger withdrawal. The original conditioning had apparently established the tone and light as equivalent, so that any function subsequently acquired by one was automatically acquired by the other.

More direct evidence of equivalence relations in the context of respondent conditioning would be desirable. Suppose we begin like Shipley (1935), first establishing two respondent units in which different conditioned stimuli, CS1 and CS2, are separately paired with the same unconditioned stimulus, UCS1 (CS1-UCS1 and CS2-UCS1). Then, to complete Phase I of our experiment, we establish two more respondent units, again with different conditioned stimuli but the same unconditioned stimulus: CS3-UCS2 and CS4-UCS2. Panel I in Figure 10-6 illustrates these CS-UCS pairings. (Not illustrated here are the response measurements that would be required to confirm that respondent conditioning actually occurred.)

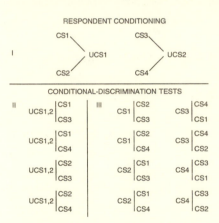

Figure 10-6. A proposed experiment to determine whether equivalence relations can be an outcome of Pavlovian conditioning.

Our question now is whether the relations that these two-term respondent contingencies establish are also equivalence relations. If they are, we would expect one relation to include all of the ordered pairs that can be made up from CS1, CS2, and UCS1, and the other to include all of the ordered pairs that can be made up from CS3, CS4, and UCS2. We could find out whether the respondent contingencies had created equivalence relations, then, by testing for conditional relations between event pairs that were not directly involved in the contingencies. Emergence of the conditionally related pairs UCS1-CS1, UCS1-CS2, UCS2-CS3, and UCS2-CS4 would show the directly established pairs (Figure 10-6, Section I) to be symmetric. Emergence of the pairs, CS1-CS2, CS2-CS1, CS3-CS4, and CS4-CS3, would show the directly established relations to be both symmetric and transitive.

In the test phases of the experiment, then, we shift to four-term operant contingencies. (Intermediate phases would have taught the subject the conditional-discrimination procedure and perhaps also would have established the former respondent stimuli as samples and comparisons, independently of each other.) Section II of Figure 10-6 shows unreinforced test trials that start with either UCS1 or UCS2 being presented not as a reinforcer but as a sample stimulus. By touching the sample, a subject produces any one of four pairs of comparisons, each comparison having been used in Phase I as a conditioned stimulus in a respondent contingency. If the respondent conditioning had established prerequisites for equivalence relations, then with UCS1 as the sample, symmetry of the baseline relations would bring about selections of CS1 or CS2, depending on which was available. Similarly, UCS2 as the sample would control selections of CS3 or CS4.

Section III shows tests for emergent relations between former conditioned stimuli. If the conditional CS-UCS relations that the respondent contingencies had established were also equivalence relations, test trials will show the subject selecting comparisons that had been directly related to the same reinforcer as the sample: CS2 when CS1 is the sample, CS1 when CS2 is the sample, CS4 when CS3 is the sample, and CS3 when CS4 is the sample. And finally, identity matching tests (not included in Figure 10-6) will indicate whether the baseline relations show reflexivity, the third property of equivalence relations.

More complex experimental arrangements would permit additional tests for the properties that define equivalence relations. For example, after Phase I, one might establish CS1 and CS3 as conditional stimuli in new four-term contingencies, with the other elements of the new four-term units not having been involved in the Phase I respondent contingencies. Then, after the usual kinds of tests had shown the emergence of the new conditional discriminations that would be required to document equivalence relations, one could substitute CS2 and CS4 for CS1 and CS3, respectively, and again test for the defining conditional discriminations. If CS1 and CS2 had become members of the same equivalence class because of their respondent conditioning histories, then ordered pairs in which CS2 was a member would also be included in the equivalence relation that the four-term contingency established. For that reason, CS2 would be substitutable for CS1 in the emergent conditional discriminations and CS4 would be substitutable for CS3.

Experiments like these would tell us whether respondent conditioning establishes the prerequisites for equivalence relations. If it does, then the acquisition of a Pavlovian reinforcing function by conditioned stimuli becomes predictable. Merger of the equivalence class and the reinforcer class would turn all members of the equivalence class into reinforcers. Second-order respondent conditioning too, in which a conditioned stimulus functions also as a reinforcer, then becomes not just an empirical finding but a predictable one.

We have seen how the establishment of equivalence relations can give rise to conditioned reinforcers within operant or within respondent units. But how does one get from respondent to operant conditioned reinforcement? How does a conditioned stimulus that has acquired a reinforcing function in a respondent unit also come to function as a conditioned reinforcer in an operant unit?

The solution to this problem comes when we acknowledge an assumption that previous discussions about the respondent/operant distinction have rarely stated explicitly (but see Crawford, Holloway, & Domjan, 1993, pp. 56-57; Donahoe, Burgos, & Palmer, 1993, pp. 21-23). This is the assumption that respondent and operant reinforcers are interchangeable. Even though we define respondent and operant reinforcement differently, we have assumed that reinforcers in a respondent two-term contingency will be able to function also as reinforcers in operant three-term contingencies.

This assumption is difficult and perhaps impossible to test directly, which may explain why it has been infrequently acknowledged. An experimenter cannot duplicate all stimulus and response parameters when comparing operant and respondent conditioning. One reason for this is that operant contingencies require the defined response to occur before reinforcement can be delivered, but in respondent contingencies reinforcement delivery is independent of any response. The absence versus presence of a response-reinforcer relation, depending on whether the unit is created by a respondent or an operant contingency, would itself be expected to influence the relative reinforcing effectiveness of the unit's terminal event. Because of such problems, the assumption that a particular respondent reinforcer will also function as an operant reinforcer must by qualified by a statement like, "All other relevant factors being equal...."

With such a qualification, the interchangeability of an event's respondent and operant reinforcing function permits one to account for the observation that a conditioned reinforcer in a respondent unit may also function as a conditioned reinforcer in an operant unit. Formation of the equivalence class and merger of the equivalence and reinforcer classes brings the CS into the reinforcer class along with the UCS. Then, all other relevant parameters being equal, the CS, like the UCS, will be able to serve as a reinforcer in an operant unit also. A similar derivation would also account for findings that Pavlovian conditioned stimuli may also serve as operant discriminative stimuli (Bower & Grusec, 1964; Mellgren & Ost, 1969). Unless the operant and respondent reinforcer classes included the same events, not even the creation of equivalence relations by each type of contingency would permit the derivation of operant conditioned reinforcement (and discrimination) from Pavlovian conditioning procedures.

Pavlovian Conditioning Derived?

An even more tentative possibility must be added to these speculations about relations between equivalence and respondent conditioning. I pointed out above that second-order respondent (Pavlovian) conditioning can be derived from the assumption that the two-term respondent contingency establishes an equivalence relation. Can we extend the same reasoning to first-order respondent conditioning? Might it be possible to view the defining feature of respondent conditioning itself as a derived phenomenon?

The defining feature of respondent conditioning has been the observation that the conditional pairing of CS and UCS causes the conditioned stimulus to elicit a new response. But if the CS-UCS pairing creates an equivalence relation, then the establishment of the equivalence relation, rather than the creation of a new stimulus-response relation, can perhaps be taken as the defining feature of Pavlovian conditioning.

Such a change in the definition of Pavlovian conditioning is desirable because it helps resolve a discrepancy that has always existed between our descriptions of the respondent conditioning procedure and the result of that procedure. We describe the establishing operation as a CS-UCS contingency and we define the outcome, conditioning, as the elicitation of a new response by the CS. The definition of respondent conditioning requires a response but the establishing contingency does not include a response. (This discrepancy does not exist between our description of the operant conditioning procedure—the response-reinforcer contingency, in context—and our definition of operant conditioning—increased response probability, in context. Here, the establishing contingency and the definition of conditioning specify the same events.) By removing the response from our definition of respondent conditioning and substituting the creation of an equivalence relation that includes the CS-UCS pair, we bring the descriptions of procedure and result into harmony. The events specified by the contingency and by the definition are the same.

This conception works best when the conditioned and unconditioned responses are similar. Just as the CS can be shown to acquire a reinforcing function from the formation of the equivalence relation and the merger of equivalence and reinforcer classes, the CS could also be shown to acquire the eliciting function of the UCS from a merger of the equivalence and elicitor classes. Our behavioral application of the mathematical definitions of equivalence relations and of class (set) union permits us to predict not only the acquisition of a reinforcing function by the conditioned stimulus but the acquisition of an eliciting function also. In predicting the acquisition of an eliciting function by the conditioned stimulus, however, we are predicting the occurrence of Pavlovian conditioning itself.

When conditioned and unconditioned responses are dissimilar, however, (for example, Schoenfeld, Matos, & Snapper, 1967; Siegel, Hinson, & Krank, 1978; Wasserman, 1973) the conception is not quite so straightforward. Observations that conditioned and unconditioned responses may differ markedly make it clear that the form of the conditioned response is not determined solely by the unconditioned stimulus. Other variables must also enter the picture. There are many likely candidates for interaction with respondent conditioning: (a) built-in mechanisms of defense or preparation, as in classical eyeblink and salivary conditioning, respectively; (b) processes that bring about compensatory adjustments, as when certain drugs act as UCS (Guha, Dutta, & Pradhan, 1974); (c) factors that define CS/UCS relevance, as when food aversions are learned more readily for certain CS/UCS combinations than for others (Garcia & Koelling, 1966); (d) functions of general biological utility, as when the conditioned response is the release of a hormone that enhances reproductive efficiency (Graham & Desjardins, 1980); (e) interactions between respondent and operant conditioning (Henton, 1978); and others.

Differences between conditioned and unconditioned responses are to be expected as soon as one recognizes that unconditioned and conditioned stimuli belong also to other classes. When the features that define these other classes have been selected by survival contingencies, a respondent contingency in the laboratory may produce results that seem independent of current experimental conditions. Nevertheless, even when multiple class membership has produced a difference between conditioned and unconditioned responses, respondent conditioning may still have brought CS and UCS into the same equivalence class. A critical experiment here would take the form shown in Figure 10-6 but with the added stipulation that the conditioned responses to CS1 and CS2 differ from the recorded response to UCS1 and that the conditioned responses to CS3 and CS4 differ from the recorded response to UCS2. If respondent conditioning establishes an equivalence relation, the tests will show the emergence of the conditional discriminations that the defining properties of the equivalence relation require, in spite of the discrepancy between the responses to conditioned and unconditioned stimuli. If, however, different responses to CS and UCS prevent the defining conditional discriminations from emerging, the notion that respondent conditioning can be *defined* as the creation of an equivalence class by the CS-UCS pairing will have to be abandoned.

And so, I arrived at a point in my own thinking that I find rather astonishing. Although some have suggested that equivalence relations can be accounted for by associative, respondent, or respondent-like conditioning processes (Barnes, 1994; Cofer & Foley, 1942; Hall, 1990; Hayes, L.J., 1992; but see Hayes & Hayes, 1989, for a negative reaction to this suggestion), the above reasoning has led to an opposite possibility—that respondent conditioning can be accounted for by the formation of equivalence relations. Experiments (some suggested above) that are needed to evaluate this speculation have yet to be done. But the speculation is not completely uninformed. Some relevant data, although not yet definitive, do exist (see Cofer and Foley, 1942, and Jenkins, 1963, for reviews and evaluations of early experiments on stimulus equivalence and Pavlovian conditioning; see also Dougher, Augustson, Markhan, Wulfert, & Greenway, in press). If, however, it can be shown that respondent contingencies can create units whose pairs are not members of an equivalence relation, then my suggestion that the establishment of equivalence relations might define respondent conditioning will have to be abandoned. Although the creation of equivalence relations by respondent contingencies may still be demonstrable, and may still serve as a basis for the derivation of conditioned reinforcement, any failures of such demonstrations would negate the utility of a definition of respondent conditioning that *required* the formation of equivalence relations.

Failures to Demonstrate Equivalence in Operant Units

If the operant reinforcement contingency is the origin of equivalence relations, how can it be that reinforcement sometimes fails to establish an equivalence relation? The most serious kinds of failures would appear to be those in which human subjects who had learned, say, a baseline of four-term units yielded negative results when tested for the emergence of conditional discriminations that would show unit members to be related by equivalence. Such instances abound.

With some subjects, initial tests have yielded negative results, with repeated tests being necessary to document equivalence. This phenomenon of *delayed emergence* has a plausible explanation (discussed in pp. 274-279; 511-512). Sometimes, however, we see subjects—even highly intelligent subjects—failing completely to show evidence of equivalence relations after having mastered a baseline of four-term units. For these subjects, reinforcement contingencies that gave rise to conditional relations did not give rise to equivalence relations.

Although I speculated above that the establishment of an equivalence relation might be taken as the defining feature of respondent conditioning, I did not suggest the same kind of definition for operant conditioning. One reason for my reluctance to offer that new definition of operant conditioning was the very observation now under discussion, that reinforcement sometimes creates an analytic unit without at the same time causing the elements of the unit to be related by equivalence. Any failure of a reinforcement contingency to generate an equivalence relation tells us that although such contingencies may be necessary for equivalence, they are not sufficient. Other factors must also help to determine whether the components of the analytic unit can be shown to be members of an equivalence class.

It is, in fact, not difficult to see why the standard experimental arrangements may lead to negative results in tests for equivalence. Suppose we teach a subject the baseline conditional relations A1B1, A2B2, B1C1, and B2C2. In a typical experiment, every unit the contingency establishes contains the same defined response, the *touch*, and the same reinforcer, *SR1*. In the presence of conditional stimulus A1, the subject *touches* discriminative stimulus B1 (and not B2) and produces the reinforcer *SR1*; in the presence of conditional stimulus A2, the subject *touches* discriminative stimulus B2 (and not B1) and produces the reinforcer *SR1*; in the presence of conditional stimulus B1, the subject *touches* discriminative stimulus C1 (and not C2) and produces the reinforcer; *SR1*; in the presence of conditional stimulus B2, the subject *touches* discriminative stimulus C2 (and not C1) and produces the reinforcer *SR1*. With the same defined response (*touch*) and reinforcer (*SR1*) being included in each equivalence class, we can expect the classes that the contingencies establish to merge. The equivalence relation will then include not only the sought-for emergent conditional relations A1B1, B1C1, A1C1, and so on, along with their symmetric counterparts, but will also include all of the other possible conditional relations: A1B2, B1C2, A1C2, and so on. Because of their relation to the same reinforcer and the same defined response, all of the stimuli in all of the units that the reinforcement contingencies create will be related to each other.

As Saunders and Green (1992) pointed out,

> If this pattern emerges [merger of two intended classes into one large equivalence class], the usual tests for equivalence are inappropriate because on each test trial, both comparisons are correct with respect to showing an equivalence class. Responding on all…tests for symmetry and transitivity most likely will vary from trial to trial, indicating the equivalence of all members of the large set. Normally, such a pattern of apparently unsystematic responding is accepted as evidence that equivalence has not developed (p. 237).

And so, if the contingencies establish one large equivalence class, the usual tests for the emergent relations that would demonstrate equivalence will yield negative results.

Saunders and Green (1992) suggested some reasons why one large equivalence class *might* emerge instead of the separate classes that the experimenter intends. My suggestion is more drastic. One large equivalence class *must* emerge when the establishing contingencies share the same reinforcer and defined response. Failures to obtain positive results in the usual tests for equivalence relations are therefore to be expected. This very reason for expecting failures imposes on us an obligation to explain not the occasional negative results but rather, to explain why the standard experiment usually succeeds in demonstrating equivalence.

The problem is like the one that arises in conjunction with five-term contingencies that establish second-order conditional discriminations (Chapter 9, pp. 350-351 and Figure 9-10; also Chapter 12). In a five-term unit the separate class membership of the first-order conditional stimuli would become compromised because each second-order conditional stimulus would be related to all of the first-order conditional stimuli. This would bring all of the first- and second-order conditional stimuli together into a single class. With all first-order conditional stimuli becoming members of the same class, the discriminative stimuli would also join that class. It would then not only be impossible to demonstrate the intended equivalence relations, but impossible to create the units themselves. With all stimuli and responses that are involved in the contingencies becoming equivalent, differential control by conditional and discriminative stimuli would be wiped out. Second-order conditional control would be impossible to demonstrate.

Without second-order conditional control, however, we would be seriously handicapped in adapting to the complex environments in which we live. If five-term units were not demonstrable in the laboratory we would have to wonder about our own competence as experimenters (Chapter 12). What is happening here is an incompatibility between the differential stimulus control that the reinforcement contingencies call for and the formation of a single large equivalence class. Given that reinforcement contingencies do create five-term units, we have to conclude that the incompatibility is usually resolved in favor of differential control (see pp. 350-351; 507-508; 530).

The use of a single reinforcer and/or defined response to establish two or more analytic units creates a similar but even larger problem. Because all elements of all of the intended units would be related to the same reinforcer and/or defined response, they all would gain membership in the same equivalence class. Not only would five-term units be impossible to establish, but no units of any size would be possible. Bringing all components of a unit into a single large equivalence class would prevent any differential stimulus-stimulus or stimulus-response relations. Duby et al. (1987), having demonstrated that emergent conditional discriminations indicative of an equivalence relation could include the reinforcers, recognized this problem as follows:

> Consider the units established by typical conditional-discrimination procedures: A1—B1—R—F1 and A2—B2—R—F1. Both units terminate with F1. If A1, B1, and F1 form a class and if A2, B2, and F1 also form a class, then…all of the stimuli (A1, A2, B1, B2, and F1) should become members of the same class. Such an outcome might be expected to interfere with subsequent discrimination among these stimuli; if A1 and B2 were members of the same stimulus class, for example, one might expect a subject sometimes to select B2 conditionally upon A1. Of course, this does not happen ordinarily. As many studies of conditional discrimination document, programmed four-term contingencies effectively establish units that maintain their integrity despite sharing a common reinforcing stimulus with other units. (p. 173).

We have here what seems to be an immense gulf between theory and data. After all, in spite of common reinforcers and common defined responses, reinforcement contingencies do establish the specified units. Also, we do find members of those units to be differentially related by equivalence.

Once more, the data tell us that even when different analytic units contain elements in common, the differential control specified by the reinforcement contingencies counteracts any tendency of those elements to combine into one large equivalence class. The very definition of a reinforcer requires that the specified unit be created; if it is not, then the event that is presumed to be a reinforcer is not performing that function. When class formation is incompatible with the creation of the unit, the primary function of reinforcement—the creation of the unit—will prevail. Continuing directly from the above quotation, Dube et al. (1987) point out:

> Subjects cannot effectively meet the contingencies if they relate stimuli that are followed by the same reinforcer (i.e., in the example given above, relation of A1 and B2 would result in errors and hence extinction). In addition, contingencies may establish specific four-term units that are simply conditional "If…then…" performances, without stimulus class formation…. (p. 173).

In establishing AB and BC baseline relations, then, in preparation for reflexivity, symmetry, and transitivity tests, we create the following four-term units:

$$A1 — B1 — R1 — SR1 \qquad B1 — C1 — R1 — SR1$$
$$A2 — B2 — R1 — SR1 \qquad B2 — C2 — R1 — SR1$$

The very success of the reinforcement contingencies in bringing about these conditional discriminations tells us that a single large equivalence class encompassing all elements of the four units has not been created. Also, the equivalence tests usually document two separate classes, A1B1C1 and A2B2C2. Distinctive units and distinctive equivalence classes could have come about only if R1 and SR1 had dropped out of those classes, thereby resolving the conflict between unit and class formation. The incompatibility between the reinforcement contingencies and the formation of a single large class causes the inclusion of the same reinforcer and response elements in all of the units to result not in class union but rather, in the separation of the common elements from the class. Instead of remaining with the A-, B-, and C-stimuli and bringing the elements of all units into a single class, the reinforcer and the defined response separate out. This selective dropping out of common elements from the equivalence classes is highly adaptive because it permits the AB and BC relations to maintain compatibility with the differential reinforcement contingencies.

Under what circumstances, then, might we generate conditional relations that are not also equivalence relations? The very formation of four-term units like those shown above tells us that the defined response and the reinforcer had dropped out of the contingency-generated equivalence classes. But then, failures to document conditional and discriminative stimulus pairs as members of an equivalence relation would tell us that those stimuli, too, had dropped out of the classes. Therefore, when conformity with differential reinforcement contingencies requires some unit members to drop out of the equivalence class, it looks as though other members of the class may also drop out, even those whose membership in the class is compatible with the contingencies. When this happens, the end result is a generalized rather than a selective breakdown of the equivalence relation.

Such a generalized breakdown is perhaps most likely in experiments with nonhuman subjects and with very young or handicapped human subjects who have not often experienced the necessity for—and the utility of—a differential breakdown of contingency-generated equivalence classes. This supposition is consistent with the suggestion that it is not the formation but the breakdown of equivalence relations that requires experience (Sidman, 1992a, p. 22).

Is all this just theoretical nit-picking? Not quite. It gives us some verifiable notions about how equivalence relations come to be, and about how reinforcement contingencies operate. We can start, for example, with the assumption that is outlined above: a conditional-discrimination procedure that involves just one reinforcer and one defined response does at first generate one large equivalence class, but the demands of the reinforcement contingency cause the response and reinforcer elements eventually to drop out of that class; then, without common elements to cause their union, the remaining components can form the smaller classes A1B1 and A2B2 within each unit. If this picture is accurate, then at some point before a subject has succeeded in learning a conditional discrimination, appropriate tests will show all elements of the not-yet established units to be members of a single equivalence class. What might constitute an appropriate test?

Many options are available. In one, we might precede a subject's exposure to the four-term contingencies by teaching a three-term unit:

$$B1\text{---}R2\text{---}SR2$$

in which the response R2 produces the reinforcer SR2 in the presence but not in the absence of discriminative stimulus B1. Then, we teach the subject an AB conditional discrimination that involves neither R2 nor SR2:

$$A1 — B1 — R1 — SR1$$
$$A2 — B2 — R1 — SR1$$

At various stages while the subject is being taught this conditional discrimination, we insert three-term-unit probe trials but substitute other stimuli from the intended four-term units in place of B1. At some point, the elements A1, A2, B2, and SR1 should become substitutable for B1 because all should have become members of one large equivalence class. As the new four-term units begin to form, however, only A1 will remain substitutable for B1. A2 and B2 will eventually separate out into their own class and SR1 will come to belong neither to the A1B1 nor the A2B2 classes.

Repetitions of this experiment with the same subject but with different conditional and discriminative stimuli can be expected to cause a progressively earlier breakdown of the large equivalence class. This accelerated breakdown of the large class into smaller classes will also cause subjects to learn new conditional discriminations more rapidly. Continued experience can be expected eventually to prevent the large class from forming at all

It should also be possible to diminish or even eliminate the necessity for an all-encompassing class to form in the first place. This should be the outcome if the contingencies specify different reinforcers and defined responses for each four-term unit. Subjects will then learn the conditional discriminations more easily. This prediction has been confirmed in a number of studies that used outcome-specific reinforcers (Trapold, 1970; for reviews of subsequent work, see McIlvane et al., 1992; Peterson, 1984). Yet to be tested are procedures in which each discriminative stimulus not only leads to a different reinforcer but also controls a different response. Facilitated learning of conditional discriminations when each conditional stimulus controls a different response has received some confirmation, (Cohen et al., 1981; Cohen et al., 1976; Urcuioli, 1985; Urcuioli & Honig, 1980; see Carter & Werner, 1978). An alternative explanation for these data, however, all obtained with nonhuman subjects, is that the subjects' responses simply took over the conditional-stimulus function without facilitating class formation. It has been suggested that with human subjects, conditional-discrimination learning is facilitated when different responses are defined not only for the conditional stimuli but for the discriminative stimuli also (Lowenkron, 1984, 1989). We can expect the greatest facilitation when all of these procedures are combined— when the contingencies specify a different reinforcer in each four-term unit, a different defined response to each conditional stimulus, and a different defined response to each discriminative stimulus. Such contingencies should prevent an all-inclusive class from forming and should thereby remove any need for an initial all-inclusive class to be broken down.

The use of unique reinforcers and defined responses for all stimuli should not only hasten the learning of conditional discriminations but may even facilitate the demonstration of equivalence relations with nonhuman subjects (Manabe & Kawashima, 1993). Having human subjects name the stimuli is also a way to arrange differential defined responses, and may help to explain the facilitation both of conditional discriminations and of equivalence relations by children (Dugdale & Lowe, 1990). Indeed, verbal naming may have a special status because it is a type of defined response that does not require physical support from the environment. Along with their effectiveness in breaking down the all-inclusive classes that would otherwise prevent or hinder both equivalence relations and the differential units that reinforcement contingencies specify, the ready availability of spoken words for emission perhaps contributes to the high frequency of naming even when the contingencies do not explicitly require it.

11

Equivalence and the Three-Term Unit

Background

In Chapter 10, I pointed out that equivalence relations have been shown to include all possible ordered pairs of the stimuli in a four-term analytic unit (conditional discrimination)—the conditional, discriminative, and reinforcing stimuli. Then, theoretical considerations along with some obtained and some anticipated empirical findings were advanced to support the inclusion of the unit's defined responses, too, among the components of the ordered pairs that make up an equivalence relation. These findings, actual and speculative, gave rise to the proposal that the contingency responsible for establishing the analytic unit is also responsible for the equivalence relation. (See p. 387, for a cautionary terminological note.)

Both of these proposals, (a) that defined responses be included as components of the equivalence relation's event pairs and (b) that the reinforcement contingency creates the equivalence relation, were said to be supported by findings that three-term contingencies (simple discriminations) and perhaps even more restricted contingencies (response-reinforcer and stimulus-reinforcer) could also establish equivalence relations. If the four-term units that are needed for direct documentation of the reflexive, symmetric, and transitive properties that define an equivalence relation can emerge from three-term (and perhaps two-term) contingencies that specify different reinforcers or defined responses, then, it was argued, reinforcers *and* defined responses would have to be included among the components of the relation. Only then could the emergence of equivalence from three- and perhaps two-term units be accounted for. In support of this argument, Chapter 11 will present reasons for concluding that (a) two or more discriminative stimuli that control the same two-term contingency will be related by equivalence; (b) discriminative stimuli that control different responses, even though correlated with the same reinforcer, will partition themselves into different equivalence classes; (c) discriminative stimuli that are correlated with different reinforcers, even though controlling the same response, will partition themselves into different equivalence classes; and (d) equivalence relations can emerge from three-term units.

Before presenting our data, however, it will be necessary to retract a conclusion we had drawn from some of the earlier published findings. I make this retraction here rather than in the later Commentary so that readers can take it into consideration when first encountering the questionable data and their original interpretation in the *Functional Classes* paper (below).

Equivalence Relations and Functional Classes: A Retraction

It should come as no surprise when I point out that the *Functional Classes* paper (Sidman et al., 1989) to be presented below had a different rationale than to help explain the emergence of equivalence relations from simple discriminations. Indeed, the need for such explanation did not become apparent to me until additional research had been carried out (Cohen-Almeida, 1993; Cohen-Almeida & Sidman 1991; Galvão, Sidman, & Cohen-Almeida 1992). The original impetus for the experiments in the *Functional Classes* paper came from a study by Vaughan (1988), who had been kind enough to send me a prepublication copy of his report. That it took only one year for my collaborators and me to complete and publish a derivative study gives some indication of the significance I attached to Vaughan's contribution. Yet, I must admit that it was only after we had completed the *Functional Classes* paper and then followed it up with an even more definitive set of studies (pp. 454-463) that I came to understand more fully the implications of Vaughan's work.

416

Does partition imply equivalence? As indicated earlier, I had become acquainted with the mathematical formulation of the equivalence relation after our experimental program was well underway. My understanding of the mathematics, therefore, went only as far as was needed for a systematic formulation of the data on hand at the time. That is to say, the conceptualization had been data-driven, and the data at that time had all been obtained by means of conditional-discrimination procedures.

Vaughan (1988), using simple- rather than conditional-discrimination procedures, pointed out that (a) his subjects (pigeons) had learned to partition a large set of stimuli into two subsets, and (b) mathematically, a partition implies an equivalence relation. That sent me back my math textbooks, where I found "...a simple theorem...of fundamental importance....the basis of the *principle of identification by abstraction*....If R is an equivalence relation on a set S, then there exists a partition P of S such that [elements of the set] lie in the same class of P if and only if aRb holds. Conversely, if P is a partition of S, then the relation...is an equivalence relation." (Gellert et al., 1977, p. 324). In other words, a partition implies an equivalence relation and an equivalence relation implies a partition.

Once one faces up to it, this reciprocal implication makes sense intuitively, even to a nonmathematician: if a group of things, events, or qualities is separated off (partitioned) from other groups, there must be some basis for the separation; *with respect to that basis* (identification by abstraction), the elements of the group are equivalent to each other. Partition is another word for classification, or categorization, and if classification is possible, pairs of components within each class are included in an equivalence relation. For example, if we classify a set of differently shaped and differently sized objects according to their colors, then, with respect to color, the red objects are equivalent to each other, the green objects to each other, the blue objects, and so on. Classification is, of course, possible on grounds other than physical identity; stimuli that are physically different in all respects may be classified on the basis of, say, a common function. Vaughan's pigeons presumably partitioned a set of stimuli on the basis of their function—in this instance, the two-term contingency (reinforcement or nonreinforcement for pecking) that each stimulus controlled. To distinguish such functional classes from others that might be possible, I shall use the term *contingency classes*.

And so, both mathematically and behaviorally, partition and equivalence look like two faces of the same coin. (Others, too, have pointed this out: Hall & Chase, 1991; Saunders & Green, 1992.) In the *Functional Classes* paper (below), however, we had not yet come to appreciate the correspondence between the equivalence relation and the partition in both mathematics and behavior. We asked in that paper whether a behaviorally defined partition of a set into functional classes (in this instance, contingency classes) necessarily implies equivalence relations. After all, behavioral extensions of mathematical set theory are analogues, and analogues do not share all properties. Therefore, it was worth asking by experiment whether a partition implies an equivalence relation behaviorally as well as mathematically. (Eventually, as is pointed out on pp. 550-553, I realized that we were not really appealing to analogy but rather, were assuming the behavioral observations—like observations in other areas of knowledge—to be specific examples encompassed by the generalized mathematical formulation.)

But we did not realize that the question had a deeper significance. If it turned out that the behavioral definitions of the equivalence relation and the partition did *not* match the mathematical defini-tions, then the utility of the mathematically derived behavioral definition of equivalence, while not negated, would be severely restricted. Where mathematical set theory nicely integrates the notions of equivalence relation and partition, behavior analysis would have the awkward task of dealing with equivalence and categorization separately. Partly because of the formulation in the *Functional Classes* paper, perhaps, this confusion has already begun to show itself, particularly in the exploitation of an inferred process, *transfer of function*, that is said to bridge the gap between equivalence class and functional class. An enormous integration of data and elegance of theory would be achieved if it could be shown that the partition implies equivalence—that functional classes imply equivalence relations—not only in mathematics but in behavior also.

The retraction. Unfortunately, one subject's data in the *Functional Classes* paper (below) seemed to dash any hope of such integration and elegance. Because we had not yet come to recognize fully the advantages of a concordance between mathematical and behavioral formulations of equivalence, we accepted that subject's data without the careful scrutiny that deviant findings usually require. Later, however, we found that procedural artifact was likely to have been responsible for that subject's performance (Galvão, Calcagno, & Sidman, 1992). The conclusion in the *Functional Classes* paper that the partition and the equivalence relation do not represent the same behavioral process had to be abandoned.

In the experiment, three subjects had learned to partition a set of discriminative stimuli into two classes. In subsequent conditional-discrimination tests, two of the subjects also showed the members within each class of the partition to be related by equivalence. The third subject failed to show the emergent conditional discriminations that would have demonstrated equivalence relations. It will be helpful at this point to reproduce and comment on some of the probably invalid conclusions we drew from that subject's data. In the *Functional Classes* paper (Sidman et al., 1989) the second paragraph from the end reads as follows:

> The 3rd subject in the present experiment formed functional classes without being able to demonstrate equivalence relations between class members. Why this subject differed from the others is not known, but the lesson he taught is clear: A set of stimuli partitioned into subsets of functionally equivalent members does not represent the same behavioral process as conditional-discrimination tests for equivalence relations, even with human subjects (p. 273).

On later reflection, it became clear that our procedure of testing without reinforcement was probably responsible for this subject's failure to show the emergent conditional discriminations. For me particularly, this is an embarassing admission because I had previously discussed at some length (see Chapter 6, the *Remarks* paper, pp. 186-189) the problems inherent in interpreting negative results that are obtained in tests without reinforcement (or positive results in tests with reinforcement). But I was deceived here because the subject, while failing to show emergent conditional discriminations, continued to partition the stimuli accurately on baseline trials and, without reinforcement, to perform accurately on baseline conditional discriminations. What I had not realized was that this subject's reinforcement was probably coming from doing what was expected of him; this reinforcer disappeared when the tests presented new tasks. Without reinforcement, the tests provided no indication of what was expected or whether he was meeting any expectations (Galvão, Calcagno, et al., 1992). He therefore showed the usual effects of extinction. What is important here is not just that someone who should have known better made a methodological error but that the conclusion drawn from that error is no longer valid. This subject's data do not permit us to say that the partition and the equivalence relation are behaviorally distinct. If that conclusion should turn out to be valid (see, for example, Dube, McDonald, and McIlvane, 1991), it will not be on the basis of data from the *Functional Classes* paper.

The final paragraph of the paper suggested two reasons why equivalence relations and functional classes need not represent the same behavioral process. We pointed out:

> If the two kinds of equivalence need not coexist, it follows that even when they do, a conclusion that they represent the same behavioral process is not justified. Given that the behavioral definitions and the behavioral tests for functional equivalence and for equivalence relations differ drastically, this should not come as a great surprise. It is perhaps more useful to examine the relations between two distinct processes than to attempt to gloss over such obvious differences (p. 273).

We might have gone on to add: "To the extent, however, that drastic differences between the procedures for defining and testing functional equivalence and equivalence relations justify a theoretical inference that the two represent different behavioral processes, an opposite empirical finding would take on even greater significance. A seemingly unlikely empirical confirmation of a relation marks a greater scientific advance than does a highly predictable confirmation. As I have indicated elsewhere, 'Every demonstration that a behavioral phenomenon is independent of variables that one has reason to suspect would be important factors serves to extend the generality and reliability of that phenomenon', and 'The less plausible some consequence of a finding, A, appears, the greater will be our confidence in A if that consequence is verified', and 'When several seemingly isolated experimental findings are shown to be related, each of the individual components of the system gains in stature' (Sidman, 1960/1988, pp. 83, 128, 130). By showing empirically that functional classes *do* imply equivalence relations in behavior, *in spite of* their different definitions and testing procedures, we would achieve a remarkable degree of theoretical elegance, empirical predictability, and potential data integration. A finding of congruence between the mathematical and behavioral definitions of equivalence—and therefore, between the equivalence relation and the partition—would constitute the most powerful demonstration yet achieved of the utility of the mathematically derived formulation." I now believe that this conclusion, rather than its opposite, is to be drawn from the *Functional Classes* paper (below) and from the other data cited in the Commentary.

✳ ✳ ✳ ✳ ✳ ✳ ✳ ✳ ✳ ✳

Functional Classes and Equivalence Relations

Three adult subjects were taught a set of two-choice simultaneous discriminations, with three positive and three negative stimuli; all possible combinations of positive and negative stimuli yielded nine different pairs. The discriminations were repeatedly reversed and rereversed, the former positive stimuli becoming negative, and the former negative stimuli becoming positive. With all subjects, a reversal of the contingencies for one pair of stimuli became sufficient to change their responses to all of the other pairs. The reversals had produced functional stimulus classes. Then, all subjects showed conditional discriminations emerging between members of a functional class; given a sample from one class and comparisons from both classes, they selected the comparison that was in the same class as the sample. Next, two of the subjects showed that the within-class conditional relations possessed the symmetric and transitive properties of equivalence relations; after having been taught to relate new stimuli to existing class members, the subjects then matched other class members to the new stimuli. Subsequent tests of two-choice discriminations showed that the conditional discriminations had transferred functional-class membership to the new stimuli. The third subject, who did not show equivalence relations among functional-class members, was also found to have lost the within-class conditional relations after the equivalence tests.

After learning arbitrary conditional discriminations, human subjects demonstrate new conditional relations that they were never explicitly taught (e.g., Sidman, 1971b; Spradlin et al., 1973). These emergent conditional discriminations provide behavioral definitions of the three formal properties of equivalence relations: reflexivity, symmetry, and transitivity (e.g., Sidman, 1990b; Sidman et al., 1985; Sidman & Tailby, 1982).

So far, studies of equivalence relations have used conditional discriminations to test for reflexivity, symmetry, and transitivity. Vaughan (1988) has suggested another way to view and to test for equivalence classes. He first taught pigeons to peck at any of a set of positive stimuli, and to refrain from pecking at any of a set of negative stimuli. Then, after repeatedly reversing the discriminations, he observed the pigeons changing their responses to all of the stimuli after experiencing the reversed contingency with just a few.

This result indicated that the pigeons had partitioned the stimuli into two subsets. Mathematically (with some qualifications), such a partition implies equivalence. The behavioral analogue of the partition is the functional class. With respect to the behavior that stimuli in the class control in common, they are substitutable for each other (Goldiamond, 1966). In Vaughan's experiment, when a few stimuli in one set became discriminative for pecking, and a few in the other set for not pecking, responses to the rest of the stimuli in each set also changed appropriately. The discrimination reversals had generated two functional classes.

What is not yet clear, however, is whether functional classes (identified by their members' common behavioral functions)

and equivalence classes (identified when relations among their members meet the three defining features of equivalence relations) are behaviorally the same. As Vaughan (1988) pointed out, "Mathematically, an equivalence relation and a partition are two ways of looking at the same mathematical structure. It remains to be seen to what extent behavioral analogues share that literal structure" (p. 42).

A reasonable first approach to this question would be to inquire whether members of equivalence classes also form functional classes. This question, which can be asked only when subjects form equivalence classes, has been answered in the affirmative with humans (Lazar, 1977; Lazar & Kotlarchyk, 1986; Mackay, 1985; Mackay & Sidman, 1984; Silverman, Anderson, Marshall, & Baer, 1986; Wulfert & Hayes, 1988). The present study asks the opposite question: Do relations among members of a functional class meet the reflexivity, symmetry, and transitivity criteria that define equivalence relations? Although Vaughan's reversal technique permits this to be asked with nonhumans, the present experiments used human subjects.

METHOD

The basic methodology was the same for all subjects. Differences will be noted in conjunction with the presentation of results. The experimental plan was the following.

1. Teach the subjects several two-choice simultaneous discriminations. Continue reversing these discriminations until the subjects make an error just at the beginning of each reversal. This will establish the two functional classes.

2. Determine whether the subjects will match members of a functional class to each other.

3. If conditional relations between functional-class members do emerge, teach the subjects conditional relations between some of the functional-class members and new stimuli. Test the relations between other functional-class members and the new stimuli for equivalence.

4. Return to the two-choice discrimination procedure, with stimulus pairs that include the new stimuli, and test the functional-class membership of the new stimuli. Did the new stimuli join the same functional classes

as the stimuli to which they were shown to be equivalent?

Subjects

Subject DJK was female, 22 years old, and a student in speech pathology. Subjects PJV and JDB, males in their upper teens, were students at the New England Center for Autism. Although Subjects PJV and JDB were quite skilled socially and verbally, the concepts *odd* and *even* were unfamiliar to them— a necessary condition, because odd numbers were to constitute one class and even numbers the other class. Before the experiment, these subjects were asked several times whether numbers to be used were odd or even, and to select the odd and even members of number pairs; their replies and selections were inconsistent. After the experiment, Subject PJV was taught the concepts, but only with great difficulty; attempts to teach Subject JDB have so far been unsuccessful.

Apparatus

The equipment has been described in detail elsewhere (Bush et al., 1989). In brief, a computer monitor displayed five

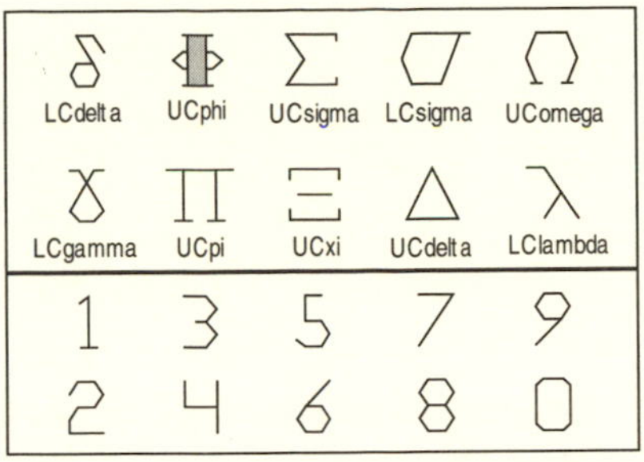

Figure 11-1. The upper section shows the stimuli used with Subject DJK and the Greek letter names used to identify them in the text. UC and LC indicate upper- and lower-case. Class-A stimuli are in the first row and Class-B stimuli in the second. The lower section shows the numerals used as stimuli with Subjects PJV and JDB; one class contained odd numbers and the other, even.

keys; the key in the center had a key above, below, to the left, and to the right of it. Sample stimuli always appeared in the center, and comparisons in three of the surrounding keys. The position of the blank key varied from trial to trial. Figure 11-1 illustrates the stimuli, which were computer-generated forms that resembled Greek letters (used with Subject DJK) or numerals (used with Subjects PJV and JDB). When subjects touched a transparent screen mounted over the face of the monitor, the computer recorded the location of the touch.

Procedures

Reinforcement. The monitor continuously displayed the number of points a subject had earned. A "beep" sounded along with each addition to the point counter. At the end of every session, points were exchanged for money at the rate of two pennies per point for Subject DJK and one penny per 15 points for Subject PJV. The beeps (and perhaps the points) sufficed to keep Subject JDB working at high levels of accuracy. At the end of every session, the two boys were also given 50 cents to spend immediately in a candy/snack dispenser.

Instructions to subjects. When subjects first sat at the terminal all five keys were displayed, but the center key was blank and only one outer key contained a stimulus. Subjects were told only, "Touch it." Eventually, all subjects touched the key that contained a stimulus, producing the beep, the first point on the counter, and another stimulus on another key. The counter was then brought to their attention; they were told that sometimes a point would be added, the monetary value (if any) of the points, and that the money (if any) would be paid at the end of the session. Then, they were once again told, "Touch it." They were occasionally asked, "How many points do you have?" Because tests were carried out in extinction (see below), subjects were told before each test, "This time you will not get any beeps or points, but you can make up the points on some easy ones later."

Preteaching. The customary backchaining procedures (e.g., Bush et al., 1989), using stimuli that differed from those to be used later, taught the subjects the conditional-discrimination procedures. If the subject touched a correct comparison and reinforcement was scheduled (see *Tests in Extinction*, below), the sample and comparison stimuli disappeared, the computer beeped and added a point to the reinforcement counter, and a .68-s intertrial interval began. Neither beeps nor points followed errors, and the intertrial interval was the same as on correct trials. The procedure was noncorrection.

Standard learning criteria. Each combination of sample and comparison stimuli was defined as a trial type. For example, one trial type might have the numeral 1 as a sample and the numerals 2 and 3 as comparisons; another trial type might have the same sample with the comparisons 2 and 5; another might have 3 as the sample with 2 and 5 as comparisons. Trial types in simple discriminations (see below) had no sample; stimuli appeared only on two comparison keys. The definition of a trial type did not include a specification of key location.

A block of trials included one occurrence of every trial type that was required in a particular experimental phase (see Results), and consecutive blocks contained different sequences of trial types and correct keys. No trial type was repeated on consecutive trials; no key was correct on consecutive trials. (At the beginning of the experiment, when there were only two trial types, no trial type could occur on more than three consecutive trials.) Subjects completed a preteaching or teaching phase by meeting the following criteria: an overall accuracy of at least 95% and no trial type with more than one error during six consecutive trial blocks. Occasionally, if the experimenters were unsure of the stability of a subject's performance, the number of criterion trial blocks was increased.

Delayed-cue procedure. Each new discrimination was taught by a variant of the delayed-cue procedure (Touchette, 1971). During the first block of trials, all incorrect comparisons disappeared after .1 s, leaving the correct key obvious. After every errorless trial block, a longer interval elapsed before the incorrect comparisons disappeared. Eventually, subjects began to select the correct comparison while the incorrect stimuli were still present. Once subjects had become familiar with the delayed-cue procedure during preteaching, they learned subsequent discriminations nearly errorlessly.

Tests in extinction. Test trials that assessed emergent conditional discriminations were inserted as probes among baseline trials of conditional discriminations that the subject had been explicitly taught. In tests, however, neither beeps nor points followed any trials, baseline or probe; no differential consequences followed correct or incorrect choices; baseline and probe trials were always mixed

in unpredictable sequences. After each test, subjects were given enough trials of simple auditory-visual and visual-visual number and number-name matching to make up for the points they had missed.

Before the first test with probe trials, baseline conditional discriminations that had been explicitly taught were tested without beeps or points, using the same number of unreinforced trials that subsequent tests would require. Subjects had to meet the standard accuracy criteria.

Simple discriminations. After preteaching, subjects were taught the first of three two-choice simultaneous discriminations. The trials used no samples. Stimuli appeared simultaneously on two comparison keys that varied in position from trial to trial; blank keys were nonfunctional. One stimulus was from the group designated as Class A (for Subject DJK) or Odd (for the other subjects), and the other stimulus was from the Class-B or Even group (Figure 11-1). Later, when the second and third simple discriminations were added, all stimuli designated as one class were positive, and all stimuli in the other class were negative. Touching the correct stimulus—one from the group designated as the positive class—produced a beep and a point. Reinforcement, the delayed-cue procedure, trial sequence restrictions, error specifications, and the standard learning criteria were the same as in conditional-discrimination trials. Subjects had no problem when presented with simple discriminations.

Discrimination reversals. When subjects met the standard learning criteria, the first discrimination was reversed and rereversed until they met the reversal accuracy criteria (see below). Then, a second two-choice discrimination was taught, after which the subjects were given all four possible combinations of positive and negative stimuli from the first two discriminations. A second series of discrimination reversals was then carried out with these four trial types and their reversed counterparts. Then, a third two-choice discrimination was taught, after which the subjects were given all nine possible combinations of positive and negative stimuli from the three discriminations. A third series of discrimination reversals was then carried out

with these nine trial types and their reversed counterparts.

Reversal accuracy criteria. The subject's selections of stimuli from the group designated as the positive class continued to be reinforced until the subject met the standard learning criteria, described above. The contingencies were then reversed, with the other group being designated as the positive class. Contingencies continued to be reversed until the subject met the following additional criteria on at least three consecutive reversals: First, no more than one error could be made in the first block of trials; this gave the subject one opportunity to find out or to confirm that the contingencies had been reversed. Second, no more than one subsequent error could occur; this permitted one "error of inattention" after the first block.

After meeting the standard learning criteria, the subject moved to another seat while the experimenter selected parameters for the next set of trials. During reversal phases, stimuli accompanying this change of seating position permitted subjects to anticipate reversals of the contingencies.

Equivalence and the Three-Term Unit

RESULTS

Functional Stimulus-Class Training

The first question was: Will all stimuli correlated with the same consequence (reinforcement or nonreinforcement) become members of a functional class? A replication of Vaughan's (1988) findings would pave the way for

an investigation of relations between functional and equivalence classes.

The experimenters classified the stimuli (Figure 11-1) into subsets; stimuli within a subset always functioned together as positive or negative. For Subject DJK, the Greek letters were divided into Class A and Class B; for Subjects PJV and JDB, the

Table 11-1

The discriminations taught to Subject DJK (Greek letters) and to Subjects PJV and JDB (numerals). In original discriminations, Class A letters or odd numbers were positive; in reversals, Class B letters or even numbers were positive. Greek letters are designated by their names (some abbreviated—see Figure 1); LC and UC indicate lower- and upper-case. Plus and minus signs indicate the positive and negative stimulus in each pair. Underlining indicates new discriminations. Stimuli within a class functioned together as positive or negative. When discriminations were combined (Phases II and III), stimulus pairs were presented in mixed orders.

Phase	Subject DJK		Subjects PJV, JDB	
	Class A/Class B	*Class B/Class A*	*Odd/Even*	*Even/Odd*
I	<u>LCdel + /LCgam −</u>	LCgam + /LCdel −	<u>1 + /2 −</u>	1 + /2 −
II	<u>UCphi + /UCpi −</u>	UCpi + /UCphi −	<u>7 + /4 −</u>	4 + /7 −
	UCphi + /LCgam −	UCpi + /LCdel <u> </u>	7 + /2 −	4 + /1 −
	LCdel + /UCpi −	LCgam + /UCphi −	1 + /4 −	2 + /7 −
	LCdel + /LCgam −	LCgam + /LCdel −	1 + /2 −	2 + /1 −
III	<u>UCsig + /UCxi −</u>	UCxi + /UCsig −	<u>3 + /8 −</u>	8 + /3 −
	UCsig + /UCpi −	UCxi + /UCphi −	3 + /4 −	8 + /7 −
	UCsig + /LCgam −	UCxi + /LCdel −	3 + /2 −	8 + /1 −
	UCphi + /UCxi −	UCpi + /UCsig −	7 + /8 −	4 + /3 −
	UCphi + /UCpi −	UCpi + /UCphi −	7 + /4 −	4 + /7 −
	UCphi + /LCgam −	UCpi + /LCdel −	7 + /2 −	4 + /1 −
	LCdel + /UCxi −	LCgam + /UCsig −	1 + /8 −	2 + /3 −
	LCdel + /UCpi −	LCgam + /UCphi −	1 + /4 −	2 + /7 −
	LCdel + /LCgam −	LCgam + /LCdel −	1 + /2 −	2 + /1 −

429

numerals were classed as odd or even. Class-A or odd stimuli were positive whenever new discriminations were introduced. Table 11-1 shows the discriminations and reversals that the subjects learned in each phase of functional stimulus-class training.

With the delayed cue procedure, the subjects learned each new discrimination quickly and usually errorlessly. After learning the first discrimination in Phase I, they all met the reversal accuracy criteria with few errors, and those all occurred on the first trial after a reversal. Subject DJK made no errors in the final two reversals.

After subjects learned the second discrimination, positive and negative stimuli from the two discriminations were combined; Phase II in Table 11-1 shows all four stimulus pairs in which Class-A letters or odd numbers were positive and the four pairs in which the Class-B letters or even numbers were positive. Subjects DJK and PJV again met the reversal criteria almost errorlessly, often without an error even after a reversal. Subject JDB, however, after only two errors on the first reversal (one on the first trial), began to make

many errors, sometimes as many as 15, before meeting the learning criteria in the next series of Phase II reversals. After 17 reversals, however, his performance became more accurate, and three of the final four reversals in Phase II were errorless.

After the subjects learned the third discrimination, the three discriminations were combined; each block of trials contained all nine stimulus pairs in which Class-A or odd stimuli were positive (Table 11-1, Phase III). Subject DJK made five errors in the first block of combined trials, and one subsequent error, before meeting the learning criteria. Then, she made errors only on Trials 1 and 8 in the first reversal; the next three were errorless. At the start of the next session, the same set of contingencies prevailed (no reversal), and she made errors on Trials 1 and 2. Given one final reversal, she made no errors.

Subject PJV made no errors when the three discriminations were combined. He then made an error on Trial 1 of the first reversal and few errors on the final three reversals, none in the first block of nine trials. Subject JDB made three errors when the three discriminations were combined into nine trial types, but he then went on to meet the reversal criteria in Phase III nearly errorlessly.

With each reversal, the subjects shifted their selections to stimuli from the other class, sometimes after an error on the first trial, and often with no errors. They continued to select members of the class that Trial 1 had shown to be positive (or to reject members of the class that Trial 1 had shown to be negative). Because a reversal of the contingencies for one pair of stimuli became sufficient to change their response to all the other pairs, the subjects could be said to have partitioned the stimuli, Greek letters or numerals, into functional classes.

After Phase I, the subjects could not have met the reversal accuracy criteria unless the functional classes had formed. They therefore demonstrated functional classes as early as Phase II, which involved only two positive and two negative stimuli—four trial types.

By making no errors even on Trial 1 in the final reversals of Phases II and III, the subjects also showed that they had learned to anticipate the contingency

changes; the reversals themselves had come under the conditional control of "between-run" stimuli (changing of seats, etc.). This conditional control over the contingency reversals does not differ in principle from conditional control exerted by the first unreinforced trial; both give the subjects the same "instruction." If functional classes based on the reinforcement contingency had not formed, no conditional control by between-run stimuli could have developed.

Conditional Relations Within Functional Classes.

The next tests determined whether the subjects would match functional-class members to each other. In the previous simple discriminations and reversals, the subjects had been selecting members of the same class on virtually every trial. Now, if they were suddenly tested for conditional discriminations without reinforcement to guide their choices, they could be expected to continue selecting comparison stimuli from just one class—ignoring the samples. To prevent the subjects from treating the probes as simple rather than conditional discriminations,

Table 11-2

Subject DJK. Section I shows the functional classes that were established during discrimination reversals, and, in parentheses, the stimuli that were to be added to each class later. In Sections II and III, stimuli are identified by class name and stimulus number, as designated in Section I (for example, LCdel is A1, UCxi is B3, etc.). Section II shows the trial types in the tests for conditional relations within functional classes. Sections III and IV show the trial types in equivalence tests after new stimuli were related conditionally to functional class members (Test 1) and to each other (Test 2). Plus and minus signs indicate positive and negative comparison stimuli.

	I. Functional Classes		II. Conditional discriminations within functional classes				
					Comparisons		
				Baseline		Probe	
Stimulus	Class A	Class B	Sample	+	−	+	−
1	LCdel	LCgam	A1	A1	B1	A2	B2
2	UCphi	UCpi	B1	B1	A1	B2	A2
3	UCsig	UCxi	A2	A2	B2	A1	B1
(4)	(LCsig)	(UCdel)	B2	B2	A2	B1	A1
(5)	(UCome)	(LClam)					

III. Equivalence Test 1						IV. Equivalence Test 2					
New baseline			Probe			New baseline			Probe		
	Comp.			Comp.			Comp.			Comp.	
Sample	+	−	Sample	+	−	Sample	+	−	Sample	+	−
A4	A1	B1	A3	A4	B4	A5	A4	B4	A2	A5	B5
B4	B1	A1	B3	B4	A4	B5	B4	A4	B2	B5	A5
						A4	A1	B1			
						B4	B1	A1			

a baseline of reinforced identity matching was established first, with the stimuli being the same functional-class members that were to be used in the tests. All subjects showed themselves immediately capable of identity matching, thereby demonstrating reflexivity.

Section I of Table 11-2 shows the three stimuli in each functional class that the discrimination reversals had established for Subject DJK (and two stimuli that were to be added to each class later). In Sections II, III, and IV of Table 11-2, stimuli are denoted by their class and their number, as specified in Section I of the table (e.g., LCdel is A1, LCgam is B1, UCsig is A3, etc.).

Section II of Table 11-2 shows the trial types in the test for conditional discriminations within the functional classes. Only two stimuli from each class were used, leaving the others available for later equivalence tests. The left column lists the four sample stimuli, and the next two columns show the comparisons in identity-matching baseline trials. The two right columns show the probe comparisons. Probe trials tested symmetric relations between Stimulus 1 and Stimulus 2 within each class; the samples in one pair of probe trial types functioned as comparisons in the other pair.

Subject DJK made no "errors" in the 72-trial test (nine presentations of each baseline and probe trial type), always selecting a comparison that was in the same functional class as the sample. Such selections were arbitrarily called "correct." When tested, therefore, conditional relations emerged between functional-class members.

Section I of Table 11-3 shows the three numerals in each functional class that the discrimination reversals had established (and two numerals that were to be added to each class later) for Subjects PJV and JDB. Section II shows the identity baseline trial types and the probe trial types that tested for emergent conditional discriminations within the functional classes. Again, only two stimuli from each class were used.

Subject PJV made no baseline errors and only two errors in the 36 probe trials. Subject JDB made no baseline errors in his first test, but only 24 of the 36 probe trials were correct. In subsequent tests, however, probe selections became highly accurate and stable. In six consecutive tests, each with 36 probes, Subject JDB scored 24, 30, 30, 34, 35, and 33 correct. By choosing an odd comparison when the sample was odd and an even comparison when the sample was even, Subjects PJV and JDB showed conditional relations emerging between functional-class members.

Table 11-3

Subjects PJV and JDB. Section I shows the functional classes that were established during discrimination reversals, and, in parentheses, the numerals that were to be added to each class later. Section II shows the trial types in the tests for conditional relations within functional classes. Sections III and IV show the trial types in equivalence tests after new stimuli were related conditionally to functional class members (Test 1) and to each other (Test 2). Subject JDB did not go beyond Test 1. Plus and minus signs indicate positive and negative comparison stimuli.

I. Functional Classes		II. Conditional discriminations within functional classes				
			Comparisons			
			Baseline		Probe	
Odd	Even	Sample	+	−	+	−
1	2	1	1	2	7	4
3	4	2	2	1	4	7
7	8	7	7	4	1	2
(5)	(0)	4	4	7	2	1
(9)	(6)					

III. Equivalence Test 1

New baseline			Probe		
	Comp.			Comp.	
Sample	+	−	Sample	+	−
5	1	2	3	5	0
0	2	1	8	0	5

IV. Equivalence Test 2

New baseline			Probe		
	Comp.			Comp.	
Sample	+	−	Sample	+	−
9	5	0	7	9	6
6	0	5	4	6	9
5	1	2			
0	2	1			

The First Equivalence Test

The emergence of conditional discriminations within functional classes, although a necessary first step, did not suffice to demonstrate equivalence relations among the class members. Given that subjects will match any stimulus in a functional class to any other member of that class, the emergence of symmetric relations was inevitable; equivalence was not needed to account for any of the symmetries. The same may be said of transitivity.

Symmetry and transitivity could be tested, however, by first teaching the subjects conditional relations between class members and new stimuli. These new relations could then be directly tested for equivalence. Therefore, each subject was taught a conditional discrimination in which the samples were new stimuli and the comparisons were original members of the functional classes. Subjects were then tested for the emergence of a conditional discrimination in which the samples were other class members and the comparisons were the new stimuli.

Subject DJK. The new samples were Stimuli A4 and B4 (LCsig and UCdel, listed in Section I of Table 11-2). The subject was taught to relate one new sample, A4 (LCsig), to an original Class-A member, A1 (LCdel), and the other new sample, B4 (UCdel), to an original Class-B member, B1 (LCgam). The left side of Section III in Table 11-2 shows that the baseline for Equivalence Test 1 consisted of the trial types in the new conditional discrimination.

In probe trials (Table 11-2, right side of Section III), the samples were Stimuli A3 (UCsig) and B3 (UCxi), original class members that had not yet taken part in any conditional discriminations. Comparisons were the

new stimuli, A4 and B4, that served as samples in the baseline. During the 36-trial test, Subject DJK made no errors. On the 18 probes, she always selected Stimulus A4 (LCsig) when A3 (UCsig) was the sample, and B4 (UCdel) when B3 (UCxi) was the sample.

The diagram in Figure 11-2 helps to clarify how these results must have come about. As indicated by the upper (solid) arrow in the center, the subject had been explicitly taught to relate the new samples, LCsig (A4) and UCdel (B4), to functional-class members LCdel (A1) and LCgam (B1), respectively. The lower (dashed) arrow in the center denotes conditional relations between functional-class members, LCdel and UCsig in Class A and LCgam and UCxi in Class B. Although these particular relations between functional-class members had neither been taught directly nor tested, they can reasonably be assumed on the basis of the positive within-class tests that had used other class members (Table 11-2, Section II).

If the conditional relations represented by the center arrows were symmetric, as demanded by

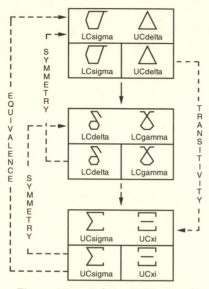

Figure 11-2. Subject DJK. Conditional relations involved in the first equivalence tests. Sample stimuli are enclosed in individual boxes to indicate that they were presented separately; pairs of comparisons are enclosed in the same box to indicate that they were presented together. (The names were not shown to the subjects.) Each arrow points from samples to comparisons. The solid arrow indicates the directly taught conditional discriminations; dashed arrows indicate emergent relations (see text).

equivalence, samples could serve as comparisons and comparisons as samples; this would yield the derived relations denoted by the innermost dashed arrows at the left. Transitivity of these derived relations would then bring about the emergent conditional discrimination in the first equivalence test, as indicated by the

leftmost arrow. This is termed a test for equivalence, however, rather than transitivity, because it requires the derived symmetry relations, whereas simple transitivity (not tested here, but indicated by the arrow at the right) might be found even if the relations depicted in the center were not symmetric. The conditional relations demonstrating equivalence could have come about only if the relations between class members were symmetric and transitive.

Subjects PJV and JDB. The new samples were the numerals 5 and 0. Subjects PJV and JDB learned to relate one new sample, 5, to an original odd class member, 1, and the other new sample, 0, to even class member 2. The new conditional discrimination formed the baseline for Equivalence Test 1 (Table 11-3, left side of Section III). In the probe trials (Table 11-3, right side of Section III), class members 3 and 8, not yet used in any conditional discriminations, were samples, and the comparisons were the new stimuli, 5 and 0, that served as samples in the baseline.

During the first 36-trial test, Subject PJV made two errors, both on probes. In a second test, he again made two probe errors. On 89% of the 72 probes, he selected 5 when 3 was the sample and 0 when 8 was the sample.

Figure 11-3 indicates how equivalence could have brought about the emergence of the untaught conditional discrimination. The uppermost (solid) arrow in the center shows the conditional discrimination that had been explicitly taught, and the lower (dashed) arrow shows the conditional discrimination that was to be expected on the basis of the within-class tests (Table 11-3, Section II). If these conditional relations were also equivalence relations, the derived symmetric relations (denoted by the two innermost arrows on the left) would, via transitivity, yield the conditional relations that emerged in the equivalence test (outermost arrow).

After showing the emergent conditional discrimination within the functional classes, Subject JDB differed from the other subjects in his remaining tests. In the first test for equivalence (Table 11-3, Section III), Subject JDB made 10 errors on the 18 baseline trials and 12 on the 18 probes. A second test pro-

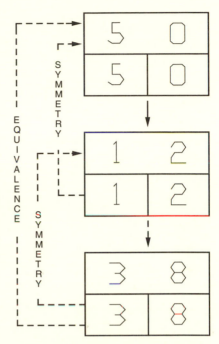

Figure 11-3. Subject PJV. Conditional relations involved in the first equivalence test. Sample stimuli are enclosed in individual boxes to indicate that they were presented separately; pairs of comparisons are enclosed in the same box to indicate that they were presented together. Each arrow points from samples to comparisons. The solid arrow indicates the directly taught conditional discriminations; dashed arrows indicate emergent relations (see text).

duced only a slight improvement in the baseline. The baseline was therefore retaught and was maintained in the next two tests. In the probes, however, the subject showed a complete comparison stimulus preference, selecting 5 whether the sample was 3 or 8.

Subject JDB's remaining data need only be summarized: On subsequent tests, the baseline again deteriorated. The subject started to respond as though the instructions, "No beeps and no points," meant, "Do everything wrong"; his scores approached zero. With beeps and points, however, he rarely made errors. Even when given his familiar number matching without reinforcement, he consistently selected the wrong choice. Correct performances were finally produced by asking him before each choice, "What is the right answer," and then, when he named the correct comparison, telling him, "Touch it." These instructions were gradually faded out, the baseline for the equivalence test was reintroduced, the number of extinction trials per test was gradually increased, and Subject JDB was once again given equivalence tests.

During these tests, he maintained the baseline, and in the first test, made only one error on the probes. In three more tests, however, his probe score deteriorated to 50%, and remained at that level for four more tests. Unlike the other subjects, Subject JDB's test for equiva-lence relations was clearly negative.

At the start of almost every test session, Subject JDB had been given the simple discriminations and a reversal. With the exception of occasional errors on Trial 1, his performance was perfect in 25 repetitions of these reversal tests. A breakdown of the functional classes, therefore, was not responsible for his failure to show equivalence.

If, however, conditional relations no longer existed within the functional classes, then conditional discriminations that would have shown equivalence could not have been expected to emerge; the relations denoted by the lower dashed arrow in the center of Figure 11-3 would not have existed. The subject was therefore retested for conditional relations within the classes, with baseline and probe trials as indicated in Table 11-3, Section II.

All subsequent baseline identity-matching performances were perfect. On 24 probe trials in each of two tests, however, Subject JDB was correct at first on only 15 and then on 12 trials. The two probe trial types that had 7 or 4 as samples were then eliminated but in 11 more tests with this reduced set of probes, the subject settled down to scores of 50%.

To check on the possibility that some peculiarity of the stimuli was responsible for the negative results, functional-class members 3 and 8 were substituted for 7 and 4 in the probe trials. In the first test for the new conditional discriminations, the subject scored only 11 correct out of 19 trials (an experimenter error produced a smaller number of trials than was planned), and in the second test, scored only 10 correct out of 24 trials.

Subject JDB, therefore, formed and maintained the functional classes throughout testing, and at first showed conditional relations between class members. After he learned to match new stimuli to class members, however, the new stimuli failed to enter the classes; equivalence relations between class members could not be demonstrated. These negative equivalence tests were consistent with negative retests for conditional relations between class members.

The Second Equivalence Test

For two subjects, the first equivalence test showed that the conditional relation between each new stimulus and one functional-class member was also an equivalence relation. Having become equivalent to one class member, the new stimulus also entered into conditional relations with other class members. To demonstrate this interaction between functional classes and equivalence classes required the establishment of two three-member equivalence classes. A more stringent test was attempted next.

Subject DJK. This subject was taught conditional discriminations in which two more new stimuli, A5 (UCome) and B5 (LClam), were related to the former new stimuli, A4 (LCsig) and B4 (UCdel). These trial types, along with the baseline trial types from the first equivalence test, comprised the baseline for the second equivalence test (Table 11-2, left side of Section IV).

In probe trials (Table 11-2, right side of Section IV), the samples were existing class members A2 (UCphi) and B2 (UCpi), which had been used in testing for conditional discriminations within the functional classes (Table 11-2, Section II).

The most recently introduced stimuli, A5 and B5, served as comparisons in probe trials.

In 36 baseline trials, Subject DJK made no errors. With only one exception during the 18

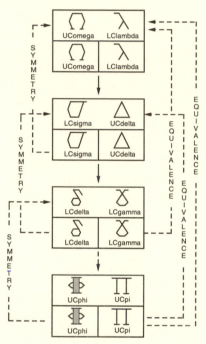

Figure 11-4. Subject DJK. Conditional relations involved in the second equivalence test. Sample stimuli are enclosed in individual boxes to indicate that they were presented separately; pairs of comparisons are enclosed in the same box to indicate that they were presented together. (The names were not shown to the subjects.) Each arrow points from samples to comparisons. The solid arrows indicates directly taught conditional discriminations; dashed arrows indicate emergent relations (see text).

probe trials, Subject DJK always selected A5 (UCome) when A2 (UCphi) was the sample and B5 (LClam) when B2 (UCpi) was the sample.

Figure 11-4 illustrates the directly taught and derived relations that made this outcome possible. The upper solid arrow in the center shows the conditional relations that Subject DJK had been most recently taught (Table 11-2, Section IV), with the newest stimuli (A5 and B5) as samples and the former new stimuli (A4 and B4) as comparisons. The solid arrow below shows the relations she had learned in preparation for the first equivalence test (Table 11-2, Section III), with the first pair of new stimuli (A4 and B4) as samples and existing class members (A1 and B1) as comparisons. The lowest (dashed) arrow in the center denotes conditional relations between existing class members that were never explicitly taught but were demonstrated in the earlier within-class tests (Table 11-2, Section II). The dashed arrows at the left of Figure 11-4 denote the three symmetric counterparts of the relations depicted in the center. On the right side, the two innermost dashed arrows denote the derived equivalence relations that each pair of symmetric relations would make possible. If the conditional discriminations had indeed generated these equivalence relations, their combination would yield the results observed in the second equivalence test, indicated by the dashed arrow at the far right. This more stringent test required three-member classes of equivalent stimuli to combine into four-member classes, each with two nodes (Fields & Verhave, 1987; Fields, Verhave, & Fath, 1984).

In the second equivalence test, the newest stimuli, A5 (UCome) and B5 (UClam), entered the functional classes because their explicitly taught conditional relations with the previous new stimuli, A4 (LCsig) and B4 (UCdel), were also equivalence relations. In turn, Stimuli A4 and B4 had to have joined the classes via equivalence relations with original class members during the first test.

Subject PJV. In preparation for Subject PJV's second equivalence test, he was taught conditional discriminations relating two more new stimuli, 9 and 6, to the first new stimuli, 5 and 0.

The newest trial types, along with those that had been introduced as the baseline for the first equivalence test, comprised the baseline for the second equivalence test (Table 11-3, left side of Section IV). Samples in the probe trials (Table 11-3, right side of Section IV) were original class members 7 and 4, which had been used in testing for conditional discriminations within the functional classes (Table 11-3, Section II). Comparisons in the probes were the most recently introduced stimuli, 9 and 6.

In 54 trials, Subject PJV made one error (on a baseline trial). On all 18 probes, he selected 9 when 7 was the sample and 6 when 4 was the sample. Figure 11-5 illustrates the directly taught and derived relations that made this outcome possible. The center arrows show the conditional relations the subject had either been explicitly taught (solid arrows) or (dashed arrow at the bottom center) that he had demonstrated in the within-class tests (Table 11-3, Section 2). Given that the conditional relations were also equivalence relations, their symmetric counterparts (indicated by the dashed arrows

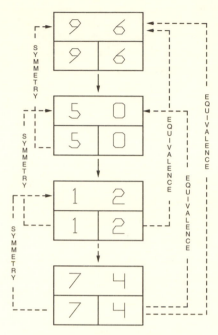

Figure 11-5. Subject PJV. Conditional relations involved in the second equivalence test. Sample stimuli are enclosed in individual boxes to indicate that they were presented separately; pairs of comparisons are enclosed in the same box to indicate that they were presented together. Each arrow points from samples to comparisons. The solid arrows indicates directly taught conditional discriminations; dashed arrows indicate emergent relations (see text).

at the left) would, via transitivity, give rise to the equivalence relations indicated by the innermost arrows at the right. These derived relations, each indicating a three-member equivalence class, would, in turn, yield the four-member classes documented in the second equivalence test, as

indicated by the dashed arrow at the far right. Again, the new stimuli had apparently entered the functional classes through their conditional relations with existing class members, even when the existing members had gained that status only through conditional discriminations.

Final Functional-Class Test

Not yet directly confirmed was the actual inclusion of the new stimuli in the existing functional classes that had been established on the basis of the differential reinforcement contingencies. Simple discrimination tests would show whether the new stimuli that had been related to functional-class members via conditional discriminations had actually joined the functional classes. New trial types presented each new stimulus along with each original class member, and with each other, adding 16 stimulus pairs to the nine that had comprised the final phase of functional stimulus-class training (Table 11-1, Phase III).

The two left columns of Table 11-4 list all of the Greek-letter stimulus pairs, with Class A or Class B positive, for Subject

Table 11-4

Functional class test. The 25 stimulus pairs presented as simple discriminations and reversals (+ and – indicate positive and negative stimuli) to determine whether the new stimuli had entered the classes. Underlining identifies the new stimuli.

Subject DJK		Subject PJV	
Class A positive	Class B positive	Odd positive	Even positive
LCdel + /LCgam –	LCgam + /LCdel –	1 + /2 –	2 + /1 –
LCdel + /UCpi –	UCpi + /LCdel –	1 + /4 –	4 + /1 –
LCdel + /UCxi –	UCxi + /LCdel –	1 + /6 –	6 + /1 –
LCdel + /UCdel –	UCdel + /LCdel –	1 + /8 –	8 + /1 –
LCdel + /LClam –	LClam + /LCdel –	1 + /0 –	0 + /1 –
UCphi + /LCgam –	LCgam + /UCphi –	3 + /2 –	2 + /3 –
UCphi + /UCpi –	UCpi + /UCphi –	3 + /4 –	4 + /3 –
UCphi + /UCxi –	UCxi + /UCphi –	3 + /6 –	6 + /3 –
UCphi + /UCdel –	UCdel + /UCphi –	3 + /8 –	8 + /3 –
UCphi + /LClam –	LClam + /UCphi –	3 + /0 –	0 + /3 –
UCsig + /LCgam –	LCgam + /UCsig –	5 + /2 –	2 + /5 –
UCsig + /UCpi –	UCpi + /UCsig –	5 + /4 –	4 + /5 –
UCsig + /UCxi –	UCxi + /UCsig –	5 + /6 –	6 + /5 –
UCsig + /UCdel –	UCdel + /UCsig –	5 + /8 –	8 + /5 –
UCsig + /LClam –	LClam + /UCsig –	5 + /0 –	0 + /5 –
LCsig + /LCgam –	LCgam + /LCsig –	7 + /2 –	2 + /7 –
LCsig + /UCpi –	UCpi + /LCsig –	7 + /4 –	4 + /7 –
LCsig + /UCxi –	UCxi + /LCsig –	7 + /6 –	6 + /7 –
LCsig + /UCdel –	UCdel + /LCsig –	7 + /8 –	8 + /7 –
LCsig + /LClam –	LClam + /LCsig –	7 + /0 –	0 + /7 –
UCome + /LCgam –	LCgam + /UCome –	9 + /2 –	2 + /9 –
UCome + /UCpi –	UCpi + /UCome –	9 + /4 –	4 + /9 –
UCome + /UCxi –	UCxi + /UCome –	9 + /6 –	6 + /9 –
UCome + /UCdel –	UCdel + /UCome –	9 + /8 –	8 + /9 –
UCome + /LClam –	LClam + /UCome –	9 + /0 –	0 + /9 –

DJK; the two right columns list the stimulus pairs, with odd or even numbers positive, for Subject PJV. Tests contained 75 trials; three 25-trial blocks presented the stimulus pairs in mixed orders—three presentations of each pair. All responses consistent with the experimentally defined contingencies (Class-A or Class-B positive; odd or even positive) were reinforced.

443

On her first 75-trial test, with Class-B stimuli positive, Subject DJK made two errors, one on Trial 1, before she had any indication of which class was positive, and one on Trial 3. Neither of these errors involved new stimuli. When the contingencies were reversed, she made one error, but not until Trial 24.

On Subject PJV's first test, with odd numbers positive, he made just one error, on Trial 40. On the reversal, he made two errors. One, on Trial 4, did not involve a new stimulus; the other, on Trial 20, did.

The first pair of new stimuli had been conditionally related to two existing class members, and the second pair of new stimuli had then been conditionally related to the first pair. The simple discrimination tests demonstrated directly that the new stimuli had indeed joined the functional classes. Both subjects, therefore, showed that the conditional discriminations had transferred functional-class membership appropriately to the new stimuli.

GENERAL DISCUSSION

When changes in the contingencies controlled by one pair of stimuli are sufficient to change the subject's behavior with respect to other pairs, classes of functionally equivalent stimuli are demonstrated. When explicitly taught conditional relations give rise to untaught conditional discriminations that show the original relations to be reflexive, symmetric, and transitive, classes of stimuli related by equivalence are demonstrated. Do these behavioral analogues of two mathematical ways of looking at equivalence represent the same behavioral process?

With three human subjects, successive reversals of a set of two-choice simultaneous discriminations established two functional classes. This systematically replicated Vaughan's (1988) study, which was done with pigeons as subjects. The subjects were then given conditional-discrimination tests for equivalence classes.

For two subjects, members of the functional classes did prove to be related by equivalence. The tests given to these subjects, and the results, illustrate the kinds of investigation that are needed to ascertain whether relations between members of a functional class meet the defining criteria for equivalence relations. Related studies are those of de Rose, McIlvane, Dube, Galpin, and Stoddard (1988) and de Rose, McIlvane, Dube, and Stoddard (1988), who showed that conditional relations between a positive discriminative stimulus and a neutral stimulus transferred the discriminative function to the formerly neutral stimulus. In those studies, however, the existence of functional classes had to be inferred from the transfer test.

Studies similar to the present one, but with nonhuman subjects, will be required to help answer the theoretical question of where equivalence relations come from (Sidman, 1990b). It has been suggested that linguistic competence may be required for subjects to demonstrate the formal properties of equivalence (Devany et al., 1986; Lowe, 1986). On the other hand, it has also been suggested that equivalence relations may underlie some aspects of language (Sidman, 1986a, 1990b). This problem may never receive a satisfactory resolution. For example, would the absence of language explain a subject's failure to show equivalence, or

would that failure help explain the absence of language? A demonstration that nonhumans can form equivalence relations would, however, settle the issue; it would be clear, then, that equivalence relations do not require language.

Nonhuman subjects have not yet shown the emergent conditional discriminations that would demonstrate equivalence relations (e.g., D'Amato, Salmon et al., 1985; Lipkens et al., 1988; Sidman et al., 1982). (In the one seeming exception, reported by McIntire et al., 1987, the "emergent" performances had actually been directly taught to the subjects; this provocative study, however, deserves to be followed up.) A continued search with nonhuman subjects may yet provide the key to the problem of which is primary, equivalence or language. Studies like those of de Rose et al. (1988) and the ones reported here remain to be done with nonhumans. Only then will it be known whether functional classes formed by nonhumans share properties in common with equivalence relations. Positive outcomes of such tests would prove language to be unnecessary for the formation of equivalence relations.

The third subject in the present experiment formed functional classes without being able to demonstrate equivalence relations between class members. Why this subject differed from the others is not known, but the lesson he taught is clear: A set of stimuli partitioned into subsets of functionally equivalent members does not represent the same behavioral process as conditional-discrimination tests for equivalence relations, even with human subjects.

If the two kinds of equivalence need not coexist, it follows that even when they do, a conclusion that they represent the same behavioral process is not justified. Given that the behavioral definitions and the behavioral tests for functional equivalence and for equivalence relations differ drastically, this should not come as a great surprise. It is perhaps more useful to examine the relations between two distinct processes than to attempt to gloss over such obvious differences. It may turn out, for example, that the most important function of equivalence relations is to transfer new stimuli—for example, words—into already existing functional classes.

Commentary

I suggested (pp. 419-421) that Subject JDB's failure to demonstrate equivalence relations between functional-class members was probably the outcome of a procedural artifact (generated by testing in extinction, as in Galvão, Calcagno, and Sidman, 1992). If that is correct, the other two subjects' data can be taken as strong support for the notion that a behaviorally defined partition does imply an equivalence relation—that the partition and the equivalence relation are two sides of the same coin behaviorally as well as mathematically. *Functional class* is a behavioral name for *partition class*, and set elements that are included in a partition class must be related by equivalence. The empirical reconciliation of equivalence relations with functional equivalence is especially powerful just *because* the two are defined and measured (tested) differently. The less plausible a prediction, the more significant its confirmation (Sidman, 1960/1988, pp. 129-131).

A functional class has been said to be defined when different discriminative stimuli in a set of three-term contingencies (simple discriminations) occasion the same response (for example, Goldiamond, 1966, pp. 214-215). Two additional qualifications, however, are necessary before the control of a single response by several stimuli can be said to demonstrate a functional class.

First, it must also be shown that other discriminative stimuli do not occasion the same response as do the members of the presumed functional class: "Classes of objects or events, differently responded to, develop different concepts....Generalization *within* classes and discrimination *between* classes—this is the essence of concepts" (Keller & Schoenfeld, 1950, p. 155); "Stimulus classes may be established through similar (for members of the same class) and differential (for different classes) contingencies..." (Goldiamond, 1962, p. 293). Like the definition of a single stimulus, the definition of a stimulus class requires that stimuli presumed to lie within and outside the class exert differential control.

Second, to define a functional class simply as a set of stimuli each of which controls the same response limits the utility of the *class* concept. Even when several stimulus-response relations share the same response, the relations may remain independent of each other (Kennedy & Serna, unpublished manuscript). If the designation *functional class* is to serve as more than just a label, it must be shown that "contingencies applied to one member of a class will tend to affect other members of that class" (Goldiamond, 1962, p. 303). Only then does it become useful to say that an experimenter-defined stimulus class is also a stimulus class for the subject (Goldiamond, 1962, p. 293; see also Dougher & Markham, 1994, pp. 72-73; Dube, McDonald, & McIlvane, 1991, p. 7).

Barnes and Keenan (1993) pointed out, "After a discriminative response is explicitly trained to one member of an equivalence class, that same response may then transfer to the other members of the class without additional training" (p. 61). This is part of the definition of a *functional* class; if stimuli are members of a functional class, this kind of transfer *must* take place. As I indicated earlier (pp. 392-393) and will reiterate below (Chapters 12; Epilogue), the more general observation that a variable applied to one member of a class will also affect other members—what has been termed *transfer of function* (for example, Dougher & Markham, 1994, pp. 73-76)—can be predicted on the assumption that the contingency has established equivalence relations. Instead of attributing such instances to a separate process of function transfer, we can view them as the transfer of stimuli from one class into another via equivalence relations and class union. Our ability thereby to predict functional equivalence from equivalence relations, and vice-versa, adds tremendous empirical utility and theoretical elegance to the behavioral definitions of the equivalence relation and the partition that are derived from mathematical set theory.

The Repeated Reversal Procedure

In the Vaughan (1988) paper and in our *Functional Classes* paper, the members of each class controlled not just a common response but a common response consequence also. I have therefore been calling these classes *contingency classes*. Figure 11-6 brings out the

Equivalence and the Three-Term Unit

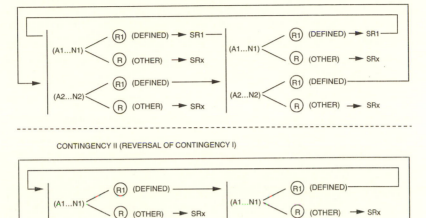

Figure 11-6. A diagrammatic representation of the repeated reversal procedure. See text for details.

essential procedural elements in the repeated reversal technique for establishing contingency classes. The procedure involves two subsets of discriminative stimuli, A1...N1 and A2...N2; a single defined response, R1 (for example, pecking or touching); undefined responses, R; a single defined reinforcer, SR1; and undefined reinforcers, SRx.

In Contingency I (upper section of Figure 11-6), stimuli from potential Class 1 are positive; in their presence, R1 produces SR1, which is followed by the next trial. Stimuli from potential Class 2 are negative—in their presence, R1 produces only the next trial. Undefined responses (R) produce no defined consequences. Contingency II (lower section of Figure 11-6) is a reversal of Contingency I; stimuli from potential Class 2 are positive and those from potential Class 1 are negative. Any set of trials will have either Contingency I or II in effect.

Suppose we start with Contingency I. In each trial of a successive "go/no-go" discrimination procedure (as in Vaughan, 1988), the subject will be presented with a Class-1 *or* a Class-2 stimulus; in each trial of a simultaneous discrimination procedure (as in our

449

Functional Classes paper), the subject will be presented with a Class-1 *and* a Class-2 stimulus. To simplify the discussion, let us assume that reinforced responses are under the control of the positive rather than the negative stimulus (S-plus rather than S-minus control; Carrigan & Sidman, 1992). In both the go/no-go and the simultaneous discrimination procedures, when the subject emits the defined response R1 (for example, a touch, peck, name, stimulus displacement, or the like) under the control of a Class-1 stimulus, SR1 will be forthcoming and the procedure will advance to the next trial. A defined response that is controlled by a Class-2 stimulus will not produce SR1 but will only advance the procedure to the next trial. No other (undefined) response will produce an experimentally defined consequence; only a defined response will bring on the next trial (preceded or not by a reinforcer).

Sets of Contingency-I trials, with Class-1 stimuli positive and Class-2 stimuli negative, continue until the subject meets some predetermined performance criterion. Then, Contingency II goes into effect, with Class-2 stimuli now positive and Class-1 stimuli negative. Each time the predetermined criterion is reached, the contingency reverses again. The first trial in a series "tells" the subject which contingency is in effect. Eventually, within a few trials after each reversal (Vaughan, 1988) or even starting as early as the second post-reversal trial (our *Functional Classes* paper; also, Paul, 1970; Paul, Hoffman, & Dick, 1970), the subject begins to respond appropriately to members of the experimenter-defined classes that had not yet been correlated with the recently reversed contingency. When this happens, it can be said that the experimenter-defined functional stimulus classes are also functional classes for the subject. (For a somewhat less direct way to probe for functional classes by means of discrimination reversals, see the discussion by Dube, Callahan, and McIlvane, 1993, p. 438, of an experiment by Nakagawa, 1992.)

Simple or conditional discriminations? The main object of the *Functional Classes* paper was to find out whether members of a functional class that was established by means of repeated discrimination reversals would be related by equivalence. As a first approach to this problem, we asked, "Will subjects match Class-1 stimuli to each other and Class-2 stimuli to each other?" It turned out that subjects did match stimuli that belonged to the same functional class. It looked as though three-term contingencies might have been sufficient to establish equivalence relations; untaught conditional relations between functional class members seemed to have *emerged*. We realized later, however, that these seemingly emergent performances may actually have been directly taught before we tested them (Galvão, Sidman, & Cohen-Almeida, 1992).

Figure 11-6 illustrates this possibility in a general way. Reinforcement for selecting a member of the positive class always follows a trial in which selection of a stimulus from the same class was reinforced or in which selection of a stimulus from the other class went unreinforced. One can therefore view the repeated reversal procedure itself not as a simple- but rather as a conditional-discrimination procedure. A stimulus that is correlated with reinforcement (or nonreinforcement) on one trial might come to serve as a sample, with discriminative stimuli on the following trial serving as comparisons. (Because of the intertrial interval, this would be a *delayed* matching-to-sample procedure.) If the experimenter carefully varies the trial-to-trial stimulus sequences, all possible sample-comparison pairs of Class-1 stimuli will eventually be correlated with the defined reinforcer when Contingency I is in effect, as will all possible Class-2 sample-comparison pairs when Contingency II is in effect.

Figure 11-7 provides a more detailed illustration over a hypothetical series of trials. Trial 1, not having been preceded by another trial, must be viewed as a simple discrimination trial (unless other cues—see below—have signalled a contingency shift). The positive stimulus in Trial 1 can then serve as a sample, with comparisons being presented in Trial 2 (after the intertrial delay). For example, in Contingency I (the left column), a subject may select comparison B1 in Trial 2 because selecting B1 had always been reinforced when A1 was positive in the preceding trial; in Trial 3, the subject may again select B1, this time because selecting comparison B1 had always been reinforced when it was presented after sample B1; on

CONTINGENCIES

Trial	I S+	I S-	II S+	II S-
1	A1	A2	A2	A1
2	B1	B2	B2	B1
3	B1	B2	B2	B1
4	A1	A2	A2	A1
5	A1	A2	A2	A1
6	C1	C2	C2	C1
⋮				
n	α1	α2	α2	α1
n+1	ω1	ω2	ω2	ω1

Figure 11-7. A hypothetical series of trials in which the positive stimulus on one trial might serve as a sample, and the choices on the next trial might serve as comparisons. See text.

occasions like Trial 4, with A1 as one of the comparisons and B1 as the sample (from Trial 3), reinforcement had followed selections of A1; then, in Trials 5 and 6, selecting A1 and C1, respectively, had been reinforced whenever A1 (from Trial 4 or 5, respectively) was the preceding sample. A similar analysis can be made for Contingency II (the right column of Figure 11-7). Under both contingencies, a subject will experience many more sample-comparison sequences than Figure 11-7 illustrates, the number depending on how many stimuli are to be included in each class. Generally, as expressed in the bottom two rows, a subject's reinforced selection of each member of an experimenter-defined class will have followed a reinforced selection of every other member of the class; every α1–ω1 pair (Contingency I) and every α2–ω2 pair (Contingency II) will be directly correlated with reinforcement.

Reinforcement contingencies in effect during the repeated reversal procedure may therefore teach subjects directly what appear later to be emergent conditional discriminations. If the tested conditional relations had been directly taught, a conclusion that their "emergence" was consistent with equivalence relations between functional class members would have no force. More immediately, one would have to wonder whether the repeated reversal procedure had really generated functional classes or whether the subject had simply learned a large number of unrelated conditional discriminations, with no subject-defined classes having been established at all. This was especially possible in our *Functional Classes* study because each experimenter-defined class contained only three stimuli; the subjects had many opportunities to learn all nine possible sample-comparison pairs within each class (18 pairs in all) via direct reinforcement. Whether this can be said also of the subjects in the Vaughan (1988) study is not so clear. Because each experimenter-defined class had 20 stimuli, Vaughan's pigeons would have had to learn 400 sample-comparison pairs within each class (800 in all). Some subgroupings of stimuli, however, were likely on the basis of physical similarities and this would have lessened considerably the number of specific pairs that subjects needed to learn. Also, the pigeons had hundreds of opportunities (80 trials per session for approximately 800 sessions) to learn each distinctive sample-comparison pair.

The possibility that the repeated reversal procedure might have involved conditional rather than simple discriminations raises two questions: First, did the procedure merely create independent pairs of conditionally related stimuli rather than classes of functionally related stimuli? Second, if the procedure did generate functional classes, were four-term contingencies (conditional discriminations) necessary or did three-term contingencies (simple discriminations) suffice? Proof that three-term contingencies were sufficient would require a rethinking of the notion that equivalence relations arise only at the level of the four-term analytic unit.

Tests for Functional Classes.

The Functional Classes study. As noted above, a definitive solution to the first problem—to determine whether a true partition emerges during the repeated reversal procedure or whether the procedure simply generates a set of independent sample-comparison relations—requires a test of whether all members of a presumed class are similarly affected by any contingency that is applied to just one member. This, of course, is what the baseline repeated reversal procedure was itself supposed to demonstrate. It looked as though some discrimination reversals were cued by the contingency reversal in other discriminations—evidence for a partition. But now we see that all discrimination reversals might have been the outcome of explicitly reinforced conditional discriminations—indicating not a partition but rather, conditional sample-comparison relations that were directly taught during each baseline discrimination shift.

In our *Functional Classes* study, we followed one of several possible courses to determine whether true partitions had emerged from the repeated reversal procedure. Having established what seemed to be functional classes, we then related one presumed class member conditionally to a new stimulus and tested whether the new stimulus had entered the class. Our results for two subjects indicated that the repeated reversal procedure had indeed established stimulus classes and not merely a set of unrelated sample-comparison pairs. Whether we can draw that same conclusion when the repeated reversal procedure is used with nonhuman subjects, as in the Vaughan (1988) study, still remains to be determined.

At the time of the *Functional Classes* study, however, we had not yet actually become aware of the possibility that the baseline repeated reversal procedure might involve four-term and not just three-term contingencies, and so we still viewed the functional classes as having been created by means of three-term contingencies. Nevertheless, it was clear that we had used four-term contingencies both to bring new stimuli into the classes and to test for the inclusion of the new stimuli in the classes. We wondered, therefore, whether it might be possible not only to establish functional classes but both to transfer new stimuli into those classes and to test for the enlargement of the classes while using only three-term contingencies. (Remember, we had not yet recognized that the repeated reversal procedure might involve four-term contingencies.)

One approach to this question might be to replicate systematically our *Functional Classes* study and the Vaughan (1988) study while making sure that the subject never encountered some of the experimenter-defined class members on consecutive baseline trials. If the seeming partition actually depended on direct reinforcement contingencies, keeping certain pairs of positive stimuli from occurring on consecutive baseline trials would prevent such direct reinforcement. For example, change the trial sequences illustrated in Figure 11-7 by never presenting A1 and B1 as positive stimuli on successive trials. Then, because those stimuli had never before been presented on consecutive baseline trials, subjects could not class them together in later tests on the basis of directly reinforced A1-B1 or B1-A1 (sample-comparison) relations.

If, however, such test trials did show A1 and B1 to belong to the same subset, this evidence of a true partition could have come about only if each stimulus was also related by equivalence to other members of the subset. For example, if both A1-C1 and B1-C1 pairs were members of an equivalence relation, then the A1-B1 and B1-A1 pairs would also have become members of the relation.

Although this exact experiment has not yet been done, we did carry out three follow-up studies in which we used similar methods for preventing stimuli from being directly related to each other as samples and comparisons during the repeated reversal training procedure (Cohen-Almeida & Sidman, 1991; Galvão, Sidman, & Cohen-Almeida, 1992). In describing these additional studies (below), I shall take some liberties in their sequence of presentation: the third experiment to be described was actually done first, and the first to be described was the third to be done. Why this turnabout? It had dawned on us only gradually that the partition we seemed to have generated by means of the repeated reversal procedure might instead represent a set of directly reinforced and independent sample-comparison relations, and so we did not at first design an experiment explicitly to check this possibility. Later, we saw that our rationale for the two experiments that we did first—a desire to see how far we could go with what we then considered to be three-term units—might not have been valid. We also saw, however, that those experiments were still relevant to the question of whether the repeated reversal procedure generated true partitions. And so, I will first summarize the experiment that we designed explicitly to help determine whether the apparent partition was actually a set of unrelated conditional discriminations that the subjects had learned through direct reinforcement. The other studies will then be seen to support the same conclusions as the first.

Procedural changes. In our new studies, we made two major procedural modifications. The first was to present subjects with three

AB Discrimination Training

Trial	Shift 1 S+	S-	S-	Shift 2 S+	S-	S-	Shift 3 S+	S-	S-
1	A1	A2	A3	A2	A1	A3	A3	A1	A2
2	B1	B2	B3	B2	B1	B3	B3	B1	B2
3	B1	B2	B3	B2	B1	B3	B3	B1	B2
4	A1	A2	A3	A2	A1	A3	A3	A1	A2
5	A1	A2	A3	A2	A1	A3	A3	A1	A2

BC Discrimination Training

Trial	Shift 1 S+	S-	S-	Shift 2 S+	S-	S-	Shift 3 S+	S-	S-
1	B1	B2	B3	B2	B1	B3	B3	B1	B2
2	C1	C2	C3	C2	C1	C3	C3	C1	C2
3	C1	C2	C3	C2	C1	C3	C3	C1	C2
4	B1	B2	B3	B2	B1	B3	B3	B1	B2
5	B1	B2	B3	B2	B1	B3	B3	B1	B2

AC (and CA) Tests

Trial	Shift 1 S+	S-	S-	Shift 2 S+	S-	S-	Shift 3 S+	S-	S-
1	A1	A2	A3	C2	C1	C3	A3	A1	A2
	↓??			↓??			↓??		
2	C1	C2	C3	A2	A1	A3	C3	C1	C2

Figure 11-8. Discrimination shifts during AB and BC discrimination training and AC (and CA) tests. See text.

rather than two stimuli per trial; one stimulus was positive and two were negative. Now, with the reinforcement contingency specifying one of three stimuli to be positive on any trial, we abandoned the term *reversal* to indicate a contingency change and instead used the more general term, contingency (or discrimination) *shift*. After a discrimination shift, all formerly positive stimuli become negative and a set of formerly negative stimuli becomes positive. Figure 11-8 illustrates three such contingency shifts for each of several discriminations. For example, in Shift 1, the stimuli in experimenter-designated Class 1 are positive and those in Classes 2 and 3 are negative; in Shift 2, the stimuli in Class 1 become negative along with those in Class 3, while the stimuli in Class 2 become positive; in Shift 3, the Class-2 stimuli become negative along with those in Class 1, while the Class-3 stimuli become positive. (In the experiments, shifts are programmed in varying sequences.)

The second procedural change was to signal to the subjects the positive stimulus in one of the discriminations. This was done by flashing the positive stimulus on and off a few times in the first trial of every set of trials. For example, suppose a subject was being taught discriminations A and B, with the contingency designated as Shift 1 in effect (upper left segment of Figure 11-8). Stimulus A1 or B1 would always be positive, with A2 and A3 or B2 and B3 negative. On the first trial of every set, Stimulus A1 (or B1) would flash. Then, when Shift 2 went into effect, Stimulus A2 (or B2) would

456

flash on the first trial of every set. Similarly, on Shift 3, Stimulus A3 (or B3) would flash on the initial trial.

With the current contingency signalled by the flashing stimulus on Trial 1, a subject would never have to experience extinction before making contact with a shifted contingency. Once functional classes had emerged, therefore, subjects would be able to go through a complete set of baseline trials errorlessly, no matter which stimuli were positive. Also, a flashing stimulus on Trial 1 could indicate to the subject the class that contained the positive stimuli even in tests that provided no differential reinforcement.

Procedurally independent AB and BC classes. In one study that included these procedural changes (Galvão, Sidman, & Cohen-Almeida, 1992), we attempted to establish baseline AB and BC classes while preventing the A-stimuli from serving as samples for C-comparisons and the C-stimuli from serving as samples for A-comparisons. We then tested to determine whether appropriate A-, B-, and C-stimuli had all become members of the same functional classes—A1B1C1, A2B2C2, and A3B3C3. Because AC relations could not have been directly reinforced, such classes could come about only if both the A- and C-member of each class had become related to the same B-stimulus.

Baseline performances were established by first giving subjects repeated discrimination shift training with the A- and B-stimuli, as in the uppermost segments of Figure 11-8 (AB discrimination training). When they reached a criterion of errorless performance during six consecutive contingency shifts, they were then given the same kind of training with the B- and C-stimuli, as in the center segments of Figure 11-8 (BC discrimination training). No baseline set of trials ever included both A- and C-stimuli, so these could not have become directly related as samples and comparisons from one trial to the next. The question at issue was: would this separation of the A- and C-stimuli during repeated shift training prevent A1 and C1 from being classed together, or A2 and C2, or A3 and C3?

To answer this question, we gave the subjects AC and CA tests (with no differential reinforcement) like those illustrated in the

457

bottom segments of Figure 11-8. For example, having been cued on the first test trial of Shift 1 to select A1, would a subject then select C1 on subsequent trials that presented C stimuli? Then, in Shift 2, after being cued to select C2, would the subject shift to A2? And after having been cued in Shift 3 to select A3 on the first trial of a test set, would the subject then select C3? Such discriminative control would not be expected if it depended on the AC and CA relations having been directly reinforced during the baseline training.

Data from at least some of our subjects told us that functional classes—true partitions—had emerged from the discrimination shift training; A1 "went with" C1, A2 with C2, and A3 with C3. Because the A- and C-stimuli had never been presented on consecutive trials during shift training, the only way the AC classes could have come about was via the common relation of the A- and C-stimuli to the B-stimuli. The discrimination shift procedure had indeed generated true partitions.

It is important to note, however, that this demonstration of true partitions does not settle the question of whether the repeated discrimination shift procedure generates conditional discriminations. Although our experiment did show the AC and CA classes to be derived—not directly taught during baseline AB and BC training—those classes might still have been derived from four-term units. We cannot be certain, then, whether the baseline AB and BC classes were the outcome of deliberately programmed three-term contingencies or of unplanned four-term contingencies. Experiments that will answer this question in the context of the discrimination shift procedure have not yet been done.

Procedurally independent ABC and AX classes. In a second study, we used a slightly different method to find out whether the discrimination shift procedure would bring about true partitions even when members of the presumed subsets could not have become directly related as sample and comparison on consecutive training trials. Subjects were first taught the three sets of A, B, and C discriminations that are illustrated in the uppermost segments of Figure 11-9 (ABC discrimination training). After repeated

ABC Discrimination Training

Shift 1			Shift 2			Shift 3		
S+	S-	S-	S+	S-	S-	S+	S-	S-
A1	A2	A3	A2	A1	A3	A3	A1	A2
B1	B2	B3	B2	B1	B3	B3	B1	B2
C1	C2	C3	C2	C1	C3	C3	C1	C2

AX Discrimination Training

Shift 1			Shift 2			Shift 3		
S+	S-	S-	S+	S-	S-	S+	S-	S-
A1	A2	A3	A2	A1	A3	A3	A1	A2
X1	X2	X3	X2	X1	X3	X3	X1	X2

XB Tests

Shift 1			Shift 2			Shift 3		
S+	S-	S-	S+	S-	S-	S+	S-	S-
X1	X2	X3	X2	X1	X3	X3	X1	X2
B1	B2	B3	B2	B1	B3	B3	B1	B2

XC Tests

Shift 1			Shift 2			Shift 3		
S+	S-	S-	S+	S-	S-	S+	S-	S-
X1	X2	X3	X2	X1	X3	X3	X1	X2
C1	C2	C3	C2	C1	C3	C3	C1	C2

Figure 11-9. Discrimination shifts during ABC and AX discrimination training, and XB and XC tests. See text.

discrimination shifts, the subjects eventually demonstrated what appeared to be three functional classes, A1B1C1, A2B2C2, and A3B3C3; depending on which of the A- (or B- or C-) stimuli flashed in the first trial of a set, they then selected a stimulus from that class on every subsequent trial.

Then, the subjects were taught three sets of A and X discriminations (Figure 11-9: AX discrimination training). The A-stimuli were the same as those presented during ABC discrimination training, but the X-stimuli were new to the subjects.

After this training, they demonstrated what appeared to be three more functional classes, A1X1, A2X2, and A3X3; depending on which of the A- (or X-) stimuli flashed on the first trial, subjects selected the other stimulus from that class on all subsequent trials.

Our goal here was to determine whether the AX training would bring the X-stimuli into the previously established ABC classes, even though the X-stimuli could never have become related to the B- and C-stimuli as samples or comparisons during consecutive training trials. The two lower segments of Figure 11-9 illustrate the tests that were designed to answer this question (XB tests and XC tests). If the ABC and AX training had established true partitions, and if class union via the ABC and AX training had brought the X-stimuli into the ABC classes, then subjects' choices of B- and C-stimuli during the tests could be expected to depend on the X-stimulus that had flashed in the first test trial. That is indeed what we observed: if X1 flashed, subjects then chose B1 or C1, depending on which was available; if X2 flashed, they chose B2 or C2; and if X3 flashed, they chose B3 or C3. True partitioning had taken place; each X-stimulus had joined the appropriate subset of the partition even though the X-stimuli could not have become directly

459

related to B- and C-elements of the subset during successive baseline trials.

Procedurally independent ABC and XYZ classes. Another experiment (Cohen-Almeida, 1993; Cohen-Almeida & Sidman, 1991), although somewhat more complex in design, asked the same question: "Can the repeated discrimination shift procedure by itself bring about the merger of independent functional classes?" In Figure 11-10, the three rows above the horizontal line outline the baseline training phases of the experiment. We used the repeated discrimination shift procedure first to establish two independent sets of three three-member classes, the ABC and XYZ classes. Subjects were first taught the three groups of A, B, and C discriminations that are illustrated in the uppermost row of Figure 11-10 (ABC discrimination training). As in the previously described experiment, the subjects eventually demonstrated what appeared to be three three-member functional classes, A1B1C1, A2B2C2, and A3B3C3. Next, with the same procedure, the subjects were taught the three groups of X, Y, and Z discriminations that are illustrated in the second row (XYZ discrimination training). At the completion of this training, they demonstrated what appeared to be three more three-member functional classes, X1Y1Z1, X2Y2Z2, and X3Y3Z3. During baseline training, A, B, and C discrimination trials were never mixed with X, Y, and Z trials.

In the final baseline training phase, which we thought of as "merger training," we used the discrimination shift procedure to generate a set of three two-member classes, each class now to include one stimulus from both of the previously established three-member classes. Subjects were taught the three sets of AX discriminations that are illustrated in the third row of Figure 11-10 (AX discrimination training [merger]). At the end of this training, they demonstrated what appeared to be three more functional classes, A1X1, A2X2, and A3X3; depending on which of the A- (or X-) stimuli flashed on Trial 1, subjects selected one of the two stimuli from that class on every subsequent trial in that set.

Equivalence and the Three-Term Unit

ABC Discrimination Training

	Shift 1			Shift 2			Shift 3	
S+	S-	S-	S+	S-	S-	S+	S-	S-
A1	A2	A3	A2	A1	A3	A3	A1	A2
B1	B2	B3	B2	B1	B3	B3	B1	B2
C1	C2	C3	C2	C1	C3	C3	C1	C2

XYZ Discrimination Training

	Shift 1			Shift 2			Shift 3	
S+	S-	S-	S+	S-	S-	S+	S-	S-
X1	X2	X3	X2	X1	X3	X3	X1	X2
Y1	Y2	Y3	Y2	Y1	Y3	Y3	Y1	Y2
Z1	Z2	Z3	Z2	Z1	Z3	Z3	Z1	Z2

AX Discrimination Training (Merger)

	Shift 1			Shift 2			Shift 3	
S+	S-	S-	S+	S-	S-	S+	S-	S-
A1	A2	A3	A2	A1	A3	A3	A1	A2
X1	X2	X3	X2	X1	X3	X3	X1	X2

AY Test

	Shift 1			Shift 2			Shift 3		
	S+	S-	S-	S+	S-	S-	S+	S-	S-
Merger	A1	A2	A3	A2	A1	A3	A3	A1	A2
Probe	Y1	Y2	Y3	Y2	Y1	Y3	Y3	Y1	Y2

XB Test

	Shift 1			Shift 2			Shift 3		
	S+	S-	S-	S+	S-	S-	S+	S-	S-
Merger	X1	X2	X3	X2	X1	X3	X3	X1	X2
Probe	B1	B2	B3	B2	B1	B3	B3	B1	B2

ZC Test

	Shift 1			Shift 2			Shift 3		
	S+	S-	S-	S+	S-	S-	S+	S-	S-
Probe	Z1	Z2	Z3	Z2	Z1	Z3	Z3	Z1	Z2
Probe	C1	C2	C3	C2	C1	C3	C3	C1	C2

BY Test

	Shift 1			Shift 2			Shift 3		
	S+	S-	S-	S+	S-	S-	S+	S-	S-
Probe	B1	B2	B3	B2	B1	B3	B3	B1	B2
Probe	Y1	Y2	Y3	Y2	Y1	Y3	Y3	Y1	Y2

Figure 11-10. Discrimination shifts during ABC, XYZ, and AX discrimination training, and AY, XB, ZC, and BY tests. See text.

The goal of this training was to find out whether the explicit merger of just one element from each independent class into a new class (merger training) had caused all elements of the two independent sets of three three-member classes to come together into one set of three six-member classes. Would subsequent tests with the discrimination shift procedure show that the originally independent three-member functional classes had merged to form larger classes? Such mergers would again demonstrate that the discrimination shift procedure had established functional classes even though most of the class members had never been presented on consecutive baseline training trials.

The four rows below the horizontal divider in Figure 11-10 outline the merger tests. In AY and XB tests (the first two rows below the divider), one of the stimuli that had been used in merger training was flashed in Trial 1 (depending on the shift that was being programmed, this was A1, A2, or A3 in AY tests and X1, X2, or X3 in XB tests). If the ABC and XYZ classes had merged, subjects could be expected to select a Y- or a B-probe stimulus that would have joined the same class as the flashed A- or X-merger stimulus. This was indeed what subjects did; these test results were consistent with class merger.

The ZC and BY tests (bottom two segments of Figure 11-10) were more rigorous in that all of the stimuli were probes; none had been directly involved in the original AX merger training. In ZC tests, none of the stimuli had even been involved in previous merger tests. Nevertheless, if the ABC and XYZ classes had merged, subjects could be expected to select a C- or a Y-stimulus that the merger would have placed in the same class as the flashed Z- or B-stimulus. Here again, subjects did select C- or Y-stimuli that were consistent with class merger.

In all of the discrimination shift experiments, subjects' baseline discrimination reversals seemed to be cued by the contingency reversal in one or more other discriminations. Nevertheless, it was still necessary to verify this finding in contexts other than the original discrimination shift baseline. That is to say, would all members of a presumed class be similarly affected by *any* contingency that is applied to just one member (Goldiamond, 1962, p. 303)? In the later experiments, therefore, we went beyond the original baseline and brought new stimuli into classes that the baseline procedure had established. (Although such tests are commonly called *transfer tests*, I pointed out on pp. 392-393 that their results fit a description that is in accord with the mathematical set theory notions of *equivalence relation* and *class union*, and that the additional concept of *transfer* is unnecessary.) All of the later experiments were consistent in demonstrating that the discrimination shift procedure can generate true partitions. The functional classes were genuinely emergent— not a result of the direct reinforcement of sample-comparison relations in consecutive baseline trials.

Because not all of our subjects yielded this result, however, caution is warranted. Until we gain more understanding of the conditions that facilitate or prevent true partitions, experimenters will have to give explicit tests before unequivocally attributing seemingly generalized discrimination shifts to a subject's categorization of stimuli into equivalence classes or any other kind of emergent classes. Such tests are particularly needed with nonhuman subjects (but see below).

Functional Classes and Equivalence Via Three-term Contingencies

Although I had previously cited the above experiments as indicators that three-term contingencies can establish prerequisites for equivalence relations, we see now that the discrimination shift procedure may not support that statement. We did find that the procedure can generate true partitions—and, therefore, equivalence relations, but we still cannot be certain whether those equivalence relations are the outcome of our deliberately programmed three-term contingencies or of unplanned four-term contingencies. Whether the discrimination shift procedure is more accurately to be described as a simple- or as a conditional-discrimination procedure has yet to receive a rigorous test. Until repeated discrimination reversals are shown to involve only three-term units, we are not justified in using that procedure to support our proposal that three-term units suffice for discriminative stimuli to become related by equivalence.

It is necessary, therefore, to turn to other experiments to answer the question of whether equivalence relations can be demonstrated in a context solely of three-term analytic units. Several investigators have reported relevant studies, although no single one has provided a definitive answer to the question. Each of these experiments used somewhat different procedures and various teaching/testing sequences but all were predicated on the same basic strategy. An example is diagrammed in Figure 11-11, in which the teaching/testing sequence goes as follows: (a) establish simple discriminations (three-term units) with a single defined reinforcer, SR1 (SRx indicates consequences other than SR1), and with discriminative Stimuli A1 and A2 controlling different defined responses, R1 and R2, respectively; (b) establish conditional discriminations (four-term units) with a single defined response, R3; sample Stimulus B1 is conditionally related to Comparisons C1 and D1, and Sample B2 to C2 and D2; (c) establish conditional discriminations, again with the single defined response, R3; Stimulus A1, now a sample, is conditionally related to Comparison C1, and A2 is related to C2; (d) finally, test to determine whether other stimuli that had been conditionally related (directly or indirectly) to C1 (for example, B1 and D1) can now be substituted for A1 as a discriminative stimulus in the three-term unit, and whether B2 and D2 could be substituted for A2.

Each reported variation of this strategy has shown that if a discriminative stimulus in a three-term unit serves also as an element in a four-term unit, the other members of the four-term unit will join a discriminative stimulus class along with the common element (Barnes & Keenan, 1993; de Rose, McIlvane, Dube, Galpin, & Stoddard, 1988; de Rose, McIlvane, Dube, & Stoddard, 1988; Dougher, Augustson, Markham, Wulfert, & Greenway, in press; Hayes et al., 1987). Although these experiments have usually been reported as examples of function transfer, it is possible, as I have discussed before, to dispense with the transfer-of-function concept and consider the results as demonstrations that simple-discrimination

Equivalence and the Three-Term Unit

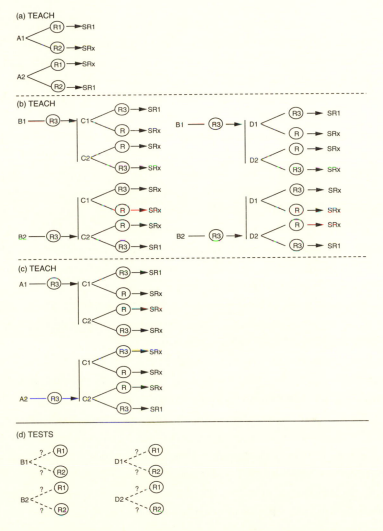

Figure 11-11. A teaching/testing sequence for determining whether equivalence relations can be demonstrated in a context solely of three-term analytic units. See text.

procedures can establish equivalence classes and that conditional-discrimination procedures can enlarge those classes via set union. Although I was late in grasping the significance of these data, it is clear now that they require us to recognize that three-term units may engender equivalence relations.

Still, however, the experimental contexts in these studies did not consist *solely* of three-term units. Although simple discriminations sufficed to demonstrate equivalence classes and class enlargement, conditional discriminations were used to enlarge the classes. Our conclusion that three-term units are sufficient for equivalence relations would be bolstered considerably if we could be confident that four-term units were not involved at all. One of the experiments that was proposed in Chapter 10 (Figure 10-5) might take us closer to our goal. That experiment would still make use of four-term units but only in tests without reinforcement; conditional discriminations would never be taught directly but would themselves emerge from simple discriminations. If successful, the experiment would take on a dual significance: (a) it would add weight to the proposition that defined responses, along with the stimulus members of an analytic unit, participate in the equivalence relation (Chapter 10), and (b) it would bring us a step closer to our goal of evaluating the possibility that three-term units suffice for the establishment of equivalence relations.

With respect to showing equivalence in the context of three-term units, perhaps the most definitive experiments so far have been reported by Kawashima (1993) and by Manabe and Kawashima (1993). These experiments are exciting on other grounds also: (a) the subjects were birds (budgerigars—a type of parakeet); if the data hold up, they will add to other recent evidence for the formation of equivalence relations by nonhumans (Schusterman & Kastak, 1993); (b) the procedures appear to demonstrate that defined responses are included in equivalence classes; (c) those defined responses need be neither linguistic nor even vocal; (d) the inclusion of responses in the equivalence class is a consequence rather than a cause of the equivalence relations; (e) finally, some aspects of the data suggest that accurate conditional discriminations do not require differential defined responses to the samples.

Figure 11-12 outlines one of these experiments. A subject was first taught a simple discrimination, with two defined responses (as illustrated above the horizontal divider): in the presence of a red

Equivalence and the Three-Term Unit

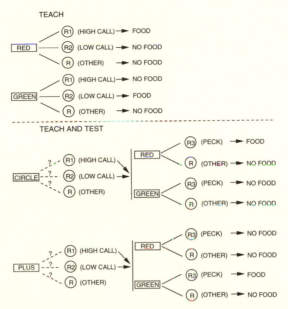

Figure 11-12. An outline of one of the Manabe and Kawashima (1993) experiments. See text.

discriminative stimulus the bird could produce food by vocalizing a high-pitched call (R1); in the presence of a green stimulus, by vocalizing a low-pitched call (R2). Then, as shown below the horizontal divider, the bird was taught a conditional discrimination in which a form—a circle or a plus sign—served as the sample, with the red and green stimuli now serving as comparisons. In the presence of the circle, the bird could produce food by pecking once at the red comparison and in the presence of the plus by pecking once at the green comparison. These conditional-discrimination teaching trials, however, also included the following test.

After a sample form was presented, the bird had to vocalize either the high or the low call before the red and green comparisons could appear. The critical feature of this procedure was that the effectiveness of the vocalization did not depend on the sample that was presented; regardless of whether the sample was the circle or the plus, either the high call or the low call (but no other response) would produce the red and green comparisons—and the opportunity to peck for food. The question being asked was: even though differential responses were not required, would each sample come to control a different call—would the bird give a high-pitched call in the presence of the circle and a low-pitched call in the presence of the plus sign? That is to say, would each of the sample forms come to control the same call that its related comparison color had controlled during the previous simple-discrimination training?

Some birds appeared to give a positive answer to this question. In the presence of the circle, they usually gave the high call and in the presence of the plus, the low call—even though either call in the presence of either sample would have sufficed to produce the comparisons. And so, although conditional discriminations were involved in this experiment, the four-term contingencies did not require subjects to respond differentially to the samples. The high and low vocalizations that the circle and plus controlled had to have come from the three-term contingencies that taught the bird to vocalize differentially in response to red and green. This "transfer of naming" from the colors to the forms could have come about only if the simple-discrimination procedure had generated equivalence relations and if the defined responses were included in the equivalence classes. The reasoning goes as follows:

(1) the three-term contingencies (Figure 11-12, upper section) established Equivalence Relations 1 and 2 (note that the subjects here were nonhumans);

(2) in the three-term units, the discriminative stimuli and the vocal responses were elements of event pairs that belonged to Equivalence Relations 1 and 2. Thus, the three-term contingencies established the red stimulus and the high vocalization as an event pair in Equivalence Relation 1 and the green stimulus and the low vocalization in Equivalence Relation 2;

(3) the four-term contingencies (Figure 11-12, lower section) established Equivalence Relations 3 and 4 (one way to check this assumption would be to do a symmetry test with the colors as samples and the forms as comparisons);

(4) the conditional and discriminative stimuli in the four-term contingencies were elements of event pairs that belonged to Equivalence Relations 3 and 4. Thus, the four-term contingencies established the circle and the red stimulus as an event pair in Equivalence Relation 3 and the plus and the green stimulus in Equivalence Relation 4;

(5) Equivalence Classes 1 and 3 contained the red stimulus and Classes 2 and 4 contained the green stimulus. The common stimuli brought about class union, a merger of Class 1 with Class 3 and of Class 2 with Class 4.

(6) With the merger of the classes, the circle, the red stimulus, and the high vocalization became elements of event pairs that defined one equivalence relation, and the plus, the green stimulus, and the low vocalization another. And so, even though the four-term contingencies did not require the birds to respond differentially to the circle and plus, they did so because each call, its directly related stimulus, and its indirectly related stimulus were now included together in one of the enlarged equivalence classes.

The ingenious procedure that Figure 11-12 illustrates gets around the difficulty I had encountered earlier in trying to determine whether defined responses are to be included as elements of the equivalence relations (p. 377). The problem I had run up against was the impossibility of determining whether the critical element was the response or its controlling stimuli. Manabe and Kawashima (1993) circumvented this problem by leaving some flexibility in the defined response to each stimulus and then observing whether the orderliness that emerged was consistent with the formation of equivalence relations and with the inclusion of defined responses in the equivalence classes. If my interpretation of these experiments is correct, they provide the most definitive demonstration so far that three-term contingencies are sufficient for equivalence relations. Also—and perhaps this is more important—we have, for the first time, unequivocal evidence that defined responses are to be included in the equivalence classes.

Furthermore, several aspects of the experiments done by Manabe and Kawashima (1993) are relevant to the notion that equivalence relations require verbal mediation (Dugdale & Lowe, 1990) or that a history of exposure to symmetric relations is necessary (Dugdale & Lowe, 1990, p. 135; Hayes, 1991, p. 26; Hayes & Hayes, 1989, p. 167). First of all, of course, these experiments seem to have shown equivalence relations with nonhuman subjects (for an even more direct demonstration, see Schusterman and Kastak, 1993). If that observation is correct, then verbal responses were not likely to have been involved, even though the defined responses were vocal. Other experiments suggest that it would be unwarranted to conclude from the data I have described so far that equivalence relations require mediation by vocal—if not actually linguistic—responses. Those experiments (Kawashima, 1993), using nonverbal response patterns—fast and slow pecking generated by fixed-ratio and DRL (spaced-responding) reinforcement schedules—yielded results like the studies that involved vocal responses. As for the notion that equivalence depends on an extensive reinforcement history with respect to symmetrical relations between stimuli or between stimuli and responses, it seems unlikely, too, that the birds in these studies had much, if any, such experience (see pp. 364-365; 556-558 for discussions of that point on other grounds).

Second, the design of the Manabe and Kawashima (1993) studies shows that the inclusion of responses in the equivalence class is a consequence rather than a cause of the formation of equivalence relations. Because the four-term contingency did not require the birds to respond differentially to the two samples, the source of the response differentiation that developed must have been the subjects' experience in other contexts than the four-term contingency itself. Those other experiences could only have come from the prior simple-discrimination training that established the first equivalence classes. Because of the union of those classes with the classes that conditional-discrimination training established—a union brought about by the colors that were common to both classes—the defined responses fitted themselves into the enlarged classes without playing any role in generating them.

Consistent with the conclusion that differential sample responses are not prerequisites for equivalence was the observation that subjects in the Manabe and Kawashima (1993) studies sometimes performed accurately on the conditional discrimination (selected the correct comparisons) before they started to vocalize accurately in response to the samples. The circle-red and plus-green relations, therefore, could not have required mediation by the vocal responses. Thus, accurate conditional discriminations and, presumably, equivalence relations that the four-term contingencies generate, need not depend on differential responses to the sample stimuli.

The Manabe and Kawashima (1993) studies may eventually be found to possess less significance than I have attached to them here. Indeed, it is rare that a single set of experiments answers all possible questions. Until the budgerigar studies are published in full, giving others the opportunity to examine all aspects of the procedures and to view the details of the data from which the conclusions are drawn, one is justified in reserving judgment. For example, one may question the performance criteria that were used to justify a conclusion that the subjects responded differentially to the sample stimuli; I have shown elsewhere that even a score as high as 75 to 80 percent correct may signify a performance that is actually quite different from the one being evaluated (Sidman, 1969, 1980). Also, with reference to Figure 11-12, it would be of interest to know if the birds vocalized in response to the comparison stimuli—before or after they pecked. They had, after all, been taught to vocalize in response to those stimuli during the previous simple-discrimination training. If they continued to vocalize to the color comparisons, the vocalizations might have moved forward to the form samples through a conditioning process and not because of their membership in equivalence classes (although this would have been less likely when differential response patterns that were generated by reinforcement schedules were used instead of vocalizations, as in Kawashima, 1993).

Still to come is the experiment that will demonstrate equivalence by means solely of three-term contingencies without resorting at all to conditional discriminations. Such an experiment is simple enough in principle, although it may be technically difficult to control for

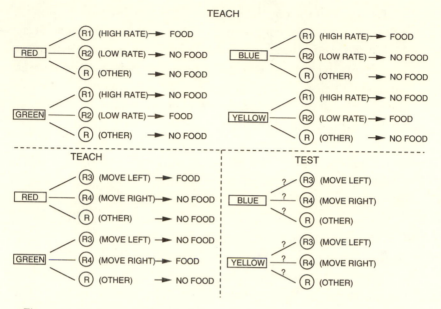

Figure 11-13. A proposed equivalence experiment that involves no conditional discrimination. See text.

inherent similarities among responses or stimuli. Figure 11-13 outlines the procedures (subjects could be either human or nonhuman).

During the first teaching phase (shown above the horizontal divider in Figure 11-13), the subject is taught to touch an illuminated (white) key at a high rate (R1) when a red or a blue lamp is lit, and to touch at a low rate (R2) when the lamp is green or yellow (touching when the key itself is dark has no defined consequence, even if the lamp is lit). This phase of the experiment fulfills the first part of the definition of a functional-class, or partition: more than one stimulus controlling the same response. If these three-term contingencies bring about true partitions, the red and blue discriminative stimuli will be members of one equivalence class and the green and yellow stimuli will be members of another class.

To set up a test for the second part of the definition of a partition, the subject is taught a different response in the presence of one member of each potential class. During this second teaching phase (Figure 11-13, left side, below the horizontal divider), the key is dark and the subject is taught to move a joystick to the left (R3) in the presence of the red discriminative stimulus, and to move the stick to the right (R4) when the discriminative stimulus is green. Or, instead of moving a joystick, other discriminated responses may be defined, a requirement being that the subject be unable to perform the original high- and low-rate responses, R1 and R2, while the new responses, R3 and R4, are being taught or tested, and vice versa. One way of fulfilling this requirement would be to darken the key or remove the joystick at appropriate times. Then, the original responses will not extinguish while R3 and R4 are being taught nor will the two sets of responses compete during subsequent tests.

In the test phase (Figure 11-13, right side, below the divider), the other members of each presumed class, the red and blue stimuli, are presented. If the three-term contingencies had established a true partition, the subject will now be found to move the joystick to the left (R3) in the presence of the blue stimulus and to the right (R4) in the presence of yellow. That is to say, without having been explicitly established as discriminative occasions for the new responses, the blue and yellow lights will control the same new responses that explicit three-term reinforcement contingencies had brought under the control of other members of their respective classes.

If the results of this experiment confirm a subject's partitioning of the stimuli into two classes, and if, as discussed on pp. 417-419, a behavioral partition implies an equivalence relation, then we will have an unequivocal demonstration of equivalence in the context entirely of three-term contingencies. In turn, such a demonstration makes sense if the ordered pairs of events that define the equivalence relation include the defined responses. Then, after the first teaching phase, Equivalence Relation 1 would include all possible ordered pairs made up of the red stimulus, the blue stimulus, and R1; Equivalence Relation 2 would include all possible ordered pairs made up of the green, yellow, and R2 elements. The second teaching phase would explicitly add the red-R3 and the green-R4 pairs to the equivalence relations, thereby enlarging Relations 1 and 2 by adding all possible ordered pairs that included R3 or R4, respectively.

The general experimental plan outlined in Figure 11-13 has been used before (for excellent reviews, see Jenkins, 1965, pp. 82-85; Jenkins & Palermo, 1964, pp. 148-149). It is difficult to generalize from the earlier studies: some involved mixtures of operant and respondent procedures and others involved overt or covert naming, with the reinforcement history of the names playing a critical role. In general, however, the earlier studies encourage the expectation of positive results in the experiment that Figure 11-13 outlines. I hope to have that experiment under way soon after this book appears in print. In any subsequent journal report, however, editorial custom will not permit me to reveal that the inspiration for the experiment came from the development of my thoughts during the writing of this book. And so, for those interested in how experiments come to be conceived, I have traced my thought processes in this and the two preceding chapters. If someone else gets the experiment done first, I will be pleased because it will confirm that my lengthy description of the process was useful.

12

Equivalence Relations in Context

Background

The *Contextual Control* experiments to be described in this chapter were actually done before the *Functional Classes* study (Chapter 11) and before the thoughts I outlined in Chapter 10 had begun to crystallize. I am presenting the study out of order because, although I have conjectured about the contextual control of equivalence relations in earlier chapters, the considerations underlying the *Contextual Control* experiments and the procedures they introduce mark off a new direction for experimental, applied, and theoretical investigations of equivalence. And yet, although these experiments set us off on a new track, we have to recognize that contextual control has been with us all along. Furthermore, it will have to be taken into account in all studies and formulations of equivalence relations that are yet to come. And so, it provides a fitting conclusion to our research story, serving as a connecting link between what has gone before and what is still to be done.

Since our original work was reported at the 1986 convention of the Association for Behavior Analysis, a number of others have published studies dealing with the same topic (Gatch & Osborne, 1989; Green, 1987; Hayes et al., 1991; Kennedy & Laitinen, 1988; Kohlenberg, Hayes, & Hayes, 1991; Lynch & Green, 1991; Serna, 1987; Sigurdardottir, 1992; Steele & Hayes, 1991; Wulfert, Greenway, & Dougher, 1994; Wulfert & Hayes, 1988). Some of these studies have corrected shortcomings in our *Contextual Control* paper and others have raised new considerations. I shall have more to say about a few of these.

Contextual control is not just a laboratory phenomenon. We can see examples all around us, some relevant particularly to equivalence relations and some more general. Things and events in our environment affect us in different ways under different circumstances—in different contexts: a child may either embrace or flee from a parent, depending on cues from the day's events or from a posture or a tone of voice; being relatively far away when a traffic signal at an intersection turns yellow, one may slow one's car in preparation for a stop, but if one is close to the intersection, one may step on the accelerator in order to get across before the signal turns red; the words *disk problem* may bring us either to the computer repair shop or to the hospital. With respect to equivalence relations in particular, we all recognize that varying conditions can change the meaning of words and other symbols: if we are building a house, *scale* may refer to a measuring stick but if we are preparing a meal, to something that has to be cleaned from a fish; at home, *family tree* may send one to a list of one's human relatives and ancestors but in an anthropology class, to a list of nonhuman ancestors; for a mathematician, the Greek letter *pi* may usually represent a geometric constant but on some occasions, just an initial in the name of her college sorority. The options we have available will also help determine which class a particular thing or event belongs to: faced with a decision about which airline to use, we scan the schedules, selecting airline X if airline Y is the only other option but rejecting X if airline Z has a flight at the time we want; in the presence of mother and sister, a child may unerringly identify daddy but in a group of brothers and uncles, the child may be confused. Common experience informs us about contextual control. Everyday observation tells us that things, events, and symbols can be classified in more than one way, depending on what the situation calls for. Both lay and professional communities will justifiably be dissatisfied with, and probably distrustful of the validity of any behavioral formulation that fails to take contextual control into account.

The following experiment, then, did not simply ask whether contextual control is real. It had, after all, been demonstrated already in the laboratory, with conditional-discrimination procedures and even with nonhuman subjects (Nevin & Liebold, 1966; Santi, 1978). But now there were new questions to ask: would conditional relations that were placed under contextual control turn out also to be equivalence relations? If they did, would the emergent conditional discriminations that defined equivalence relations fall under the same contextual control as the baseline conditional discriminations that had been explicitly taught?

Contextual Control of Emergent Equivalence Relations

Three college students in Experiment 1, and one student in Experiment 2 learned visual conditional discriminations under contextual control by tones; the visual comparison stimulus that was correct with a given sample stimulus depended on whether a high tone or a low tone was present. Two of the subjects in Experiment 1 then demonstrated the emergence of two sets of contextually controlled three-member classes of equivalent stimuli, and the subject in Experiment 2 showed the emergence of contextually controlled four-member classes; the class membership of each stimulus varied as a function of the tones. Class membership was demonstrated by the subjects' performance of new conditional discriminations that they had never been directly taught. In Experiment 2, the procedures attempted to ensure that the tones and visual stimuli exerted second-order conditional control, and did not simply form compounds with each of the visual stimuli, but the subject's verbal description of the tasks suggested that this attempt might not have been successful. It could not be ascertained, therefore, whether the tones exerted contextual control as independent second-order conditional stimuli or simply as common elements of auditory-visual stimulus compounds.

With human subjects, equivalence classes containing words, pictures, objects, designs, and other stimuli readily emerge from conditional discriminations that share samples or comparisons (e.g., Devany et al., 1986; Lazar, 1977; Lazar et al., 1984; McDonagh et al., 1984; Sidman et al., 1985; Sidman & Tailby, 1982; Stromer & Osborne, 1982; Wetherby et al., 1983). For example, the upper part of Figure 12-1 summarizes a procedure for establishing three classes of equivalent stimuli, each class containing the names of three historical figures. The classes to be established are:

Class 1: A1, B1, C1 (Renoir, Constable, Pollock)

Class 2: A2, B2, C2 (Twain, Voltaire, Byron)

Class 3: A3, B3, C3 (Churchill, Kennedy, De Gaulle).

These classes can be expected to emerge after a student is taught the AB and BC conditional discriminations indicated by the solid arrows that point from sample to comparison. First, a sample is presented with the comparison stimuli Constable (B1), Voltaire (B2), and Kennedy (B3), and the subject learns: If the sample is Renoir (A1), then pick Constable (B1); if the sample is Twain (A2), then choose Voltaire (B2); and if Churchill (A3), then Kennedy (B3).

(Throughout these experiments, subjects were exposed to the reinforcement contingencies in standard conditional-discrimination procedures. Although the contingencies may well generate verbal rules—e.g., "match people by occupation"—the subjects were not explicitly given any rules.) Next, with a former comparison, B1, B2, or B3, as the sample, and with C1, C2, and C3 as comparisons, the subject learns: If Constable (B1), then Pollock (C1); if Voltaire (B2), then Byron (C2); and if Kennedy (B3), then De Gaulle (C3).

The CA conditional discriminations indicated by dashed arrows in Figure 12-1 (a C-stimulus as sample and the A-stimuli as comparisons) can then provide a test for equivalence relations. If the conditional relation between Sample A1 and Comparison B1 is also an equivalence relation, and if Sample B1 and Comparison C1 enter into the same equivalence relation as B1 and A1, then, without additional explicit teaching, the subject will select Comparison A1 when C1 is the sample. For example, having learned to choose Constable (B1) when Renoir (A1) was the sample, and Pollock (C1)

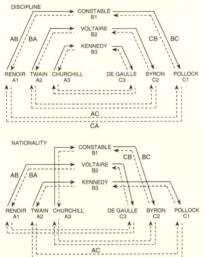

Fig. 12-1. Contextually controlled classes of equivalent stimuli. The context of "discipline" or "nationality" determines class membership for particular stimuli.

when Constable (B1) was the sample, the subject will then select Renoir (A1) when Pollock (C1) is the sample. Similarly, with Byron (C2) as the sample, the subject will select Twain (A2); and with De Gaulle (C3), Churchill (A3).

From a CA test performance consistent with the dashed arrows in Figure 12-1, one can infer that the AB and BC conditional relations met the requirements of symmetry and transitivity that equivalence demands (Sidman et al., 1982; Sidman & Tailby, 1982). A thorough evaluation of equivalence, however, would also test the symmetric and transitive relations as depicted by the remaining dashed arrows in Figure 12-1. Testing for BA (a B-stimulus as sample and the A-stimuli as comparisons) and CB (a C-stimulus as sample, and the B-stimuli as comparisons) would indicate whether the AB and BC relations were symmetric. An AC test (an A-stimulus as sample and the C-stimuli as comparisons) would indicate whether the relations were transitive.

Stimuli need not confine their membership to a single equivalence class. The bottom half of Figure 12-1, for example, shows the same A-, B-, and C-stimuli, with the solid arrows again indicating the conditional discriminations that are to be taught explicitly. But the AB and BC relations are different. Now, the sample, Renoir (A1), goes with the comparison Voltaire (B2), and Voltaire (B2) with De Gaulle (C3). Similarly, the other conditional discriminations relate each sample to a new comparison. If the new conditional discriminations also generate equivalence relations, new equivalence classes should emerge:

Class 1: A1, B2, C3 (Renoir, Voltaire, De Gaulle)

Class 2: A2, B3, C1 (Twain, Kennedy, Pollock)

Class 3: A3, B1, C2 (Churchill, Constable, Byron).

The CA test now shows the subject selecting Twain (A2) with Pollock (C1) as the sample, Churchill (A3) with Byron (C2), and Renoir (A1) with De Gaulle (C3). The symmetry tests (BA and CB) and the transitivity test (AC) should also reflect the new AB and BC conditional discriminations.

For the A, B, and C stimuli to belong simultaneously to both sets of equivalence classes diagrammed in Figure 12-1 would require some kind of contextual control. For example, without such control, the top diagram would have Renoir (A1) equivalent to Constable (B1), but the bottom diagram would have Renoir equivalent to Voltaire (B2). Sharing the same sample, Renoir (A1), would place Constable (B1) and Voltaire (B2) in the same class. With Voltaire (B2) and Twain (A2) also sharing class membership in the upper diagram, and with Twain (A2) and Kennedy (B3) in the same class in the lower diagram, Twain (A2), Kennedy (B3), Voltaire (B2), Constable (B1), and Renoir (A1) would merge into one class. Ultimately, all the stimuli would become equivalent to each other. The six stimulus classes (three in the upper diagram and three in the lower) would collapse into one, and the subject's behavior when confronted with any of the conditional discriminations would become unpredictable.

But, of course, that need not happen. Anyone familiar with these names knows that the diagrams can coexist. The labels Discipline (upper diagram) and Nationality (lower diagram) indicate topical contexts. If we are discussing disciplines, Renoir, Constable, and Pollock go together as artists; Twain, Voltaire, and Byron as writers; and Churchill, Kennedy, and De Gaulle as heads of state. If we are discussing nationality, Renoir, Voltaire, and De Gaulle go together as French; Twain, Kennedy, and Pollock as American; and Churchill, Constable, and Byron as British.

The contextual labels place the original first-order conditional discriminations under second-order conditional control. With discipline as the topic, for example, the relations, "if Renoir, then Constable," "if Constable, then Pollock," and so on, hold true. With nationality as the topic, however, the relations, "if Renoir, then Voltaire," "if Constable, then Byron," and so forth, hold true.

A few studies of second-order conditional discriminations have been reported (Fucini, 1982; Lazar & Kotlarchyk, 1986; Nevin & Liebold, 1966; Santi, 1978; Weigl, 1941). It remains to be shown, however, that emergent equivalence classes also can be under second-order control.

Will contextually dependent classes of equivalent stimuli emerge from contextually controlled conditional discriminations? With AB and BC conditional discriminations brought explicitly under contextual control, will the new conditional discriminations (CA, BA, CB, and AC) that emerge without explicit teaching also prove to be under contextual control?

In each of the two experiments reported here, we attempted to teach subjects first-order conditional discriminations that were themselves under second-order control. With any particular sample, one comparison was the correct choice in the presence of a high tone, and a different comparison was correct in the presence of a low tone. Tests then determined whether the emergent conditional discriminations that defined equivalence relations had also come under control by the tones.

EXPERIMENT 1

In Experiment 1, we sought to determine whether teaching subjects conditional discriminations under second-order control would produce classes of

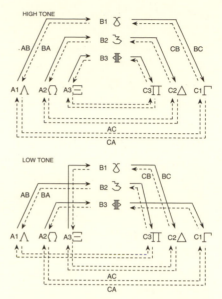

Fig. 12-2. Procedure for Experiment 1. The solid arrows indicate the conditional discriminations taught directly (AB and BC). The dashed arrows indicate emergent conditional discriminations which would demonstrate that the trained conditional discriminations had also generated equivalence relations (CA), and symmetry (BA and CB) and transitivity (AC) of the AB and BC relations. Conditional relations between visual stimuli differ in the presence of the high and low tone.

equivalent stimuli that were also under second-order control. The procedures depicted in Figure 12-2 are like those in Figure 12-1 except that experimental stimuli have been substituted for the names. Tones provided the context, a high tone for the relations in the top diagram, and a low tone for the relations in the bottom diagram. All other stimuli were visual forms that resembled Greek letters.

The subjects learned 12 conditional discriminations: three AB and three BC relations in the high tone and three AB and three BC relations in the low tone. For example, with a high tone and A1 as the sample, the correct comparison was B1, but with a low tone, the correct comparison was B2. If the stimuli in the conditional discriminations had become members of equivalence classes, the explicitly taught relations would be reflexive, symmetric, and transitive (Sidman et al., 1982; Sidman & Tailby, 1982). Reflexivity, testable by generalized identity matching (in which the subject matches each stimulus to itself) can be assumed for the normal adult subjects in this study. Symmetry can be tested by reversing the roles of samples and comparisons (dashed arrows, BA and CB, in Figure 12-2). For example, having learned the AB relations (an A-stimulus as sample and the B-stimuli as comparisons), will subjects show the expected BA relations (a B-stimulus now serving as sample, and the A-stimuli as comparisons)? Also, will they show the CB relations that would demonstrate BC symmetry? Finally, after the subjects have learned AB and BC, will the AC relations (also indicated by dashed lines in Figure 12-2) show the expected transitivity?

CA is called a test for equivalence because it tests simultaneously, although indirectly, for symmetry and transitivity of the AB and BC relations. If the explicitly taught relations did not possess these properties of equivalence relations, we would have no basis for predicting the subject's performance on the CA test. To verify this theoretical assumption, however, we must also test the relations directly for symmetry and transitivity.

Performances consistent with the CA relations shown in the upper and lower diagrams of Figure 12-2 suggest the emergence of conditionally controlled stimulus classes—classes dependent on a context. For example, with a high tone and C2 as the sample, the correct comparison would be A2, but if the tone were low, the correct comparison would be A3. (We use the term *correct* merely to refer to the comparison whose selection by the subject in the presence of a given

483

sample would indicate the formation of equivalence classes.)

Labels corresponding to "French, British, and American," or "Painter, Writer, and Statesman," are, of course, not available for the stimuli in Figure 12-2. Whether such labels, which define functional stimulus classes (Goldiamond, 1966), are required to mediate the emergence of equivalence relations is an important question that has not yet been answered satisfactorily (Devany et al., 1986; Dugdale & Lowe, 1990; Lazar et al., 1984; McIntire et al., 1987; Sidman et al., 1974; Sidman et al., 1986). The present study, like other investigations of emergent equivalence relations, may highlight this question but was not designed to provide an answer.

METHOD

Subjects

The subjects, all between 18 and 25 years old, were three Northeastern University undergraduates, recruited by a notice on a bulletin board. Subject AXP, a male premedical student, participated in eight teaching and 19 testing sessions. Subject JLR,

a female nursing student, had eight teaching and nine testing sessions. Subject JXT, a female student in the criminal justice program, had seven teaching and seven testing sessions. The duration of each session ranged from .5 to 1.5 hours.

Apparatus

A Digital Equipment Corporation LSI 11/03 computer presented stimuli, managed contingencies, and recorded and analyzed data. Visual stimuli, displayed on the 11-in (28-cm) monitor of a Heathkit H19 computer terminal, were constructed from elements of that terminal's graphics character set. White lines 1 mm wide defined five rectangular "keys" arranged in a matrix shaped like a cross; the key in the center of the monitor had a key above, below, to the left, and to the right of it. The key outlines, 3.3 cm wide and 3.8 cm high and spaced .6 cm apart horizontally and 1 cm apart vertically, remained displayed throughout an experimental session. Visual samples always appeared in the center key, and comparisons appeared in three of the four surrounding keys. One of the comparison keys was always blank (no stimulus within the outline), with the position of the blank key varying from trial to trial.

A transparent touchscreen (TSD Display Products, Inc., Model TF-12H) was mounted inside the casing and over the face of the monitor. When subjects touched the visually displayed stimuli, the computer program recorded the location of each touch on the screen as being within a particular key or in the area outside the keys.

Auditory stimuli were two readily discriminable tones, one high and one low, presented by a voice synthesizer (AstroTronics Model 001-0007). The tonal qualities were generated by adjusting several of the parameters available on the synthesizer. Tones were discontinuous, lasting 1 s and repeated at .5-s intervals throughout a trial.

Throughout the experimental session, the number of points a subject had earned was displayed as a three-digit number on a white background 2.3 cm wide and 6 mm high in the lower left corner of the monitor. At the end of each session, points were exchanged for money at the rate of 2 cents per point. Subjects earned amounts ranging from $5 to $15 per session.

Procedure

Instructions to subjects. When first seated before the screen, which showed all keys but with a stimulus on only one of the outer (comparison) keys, the subject received no verbal instruction except, "Touch it." Nothing happened unless the subject pressed the key that contained the stimulus. Sometimes the instruction had to be repeated—as when the subject pressed a blank key and then stopped—but eventually the subject touched the key that contained a stimulus, producing the beep, the first point on the counter, and another stimulus on another key. The counter was then brought to the subject's attention, and he or she was told that sometimes a point would be added to the counter, that each point was worth 2 cents, and that the amount of money indicated by the counter would be paid at the end of each session. The subject was then told again, "Touch it."

When the subject was reliably pressing only the key with a stimulus, the nature of the trials changed. Each trial now began

485

with a stimulus on the center (sample) key; touching the sample key brought a single stimulus onto one of the comparison keys. As before, touching the comparison key that displayed a stimulus produced the beep, a point, and the next trial. When the subject was reliably touching the sample and comparison in sequence, he or she was ready for conditional-discrimination trials that presented stimuli on the sample key and on more than one comparison key at a time. This preliminary phase was accomplished without any additional verbal instructions. The stimuli differed from those to be used later in the experiment.

All questions, at the start or later, about what to do next were answered with generalities like, "Keep going," "Give it a try," "See for yourself," or "Do your best," and questions about the purpose of the experiment were answered with a promise to explain everything at the end. During the first few sessions, the subject was occasionally asked, "How many points do you have?"

Preteaching and teaching contingencies. Trials began with a visual sample displayed in the center key. In second-order conditional discriminations either the high or the low tone accompanied the visual sample. By touching the sample, the subject produced three comparisons in the surrounding keys. The remaining key stayed blank. Visual samples remained present, and auditory stimuli continued to be repeated throughout the trial. When the subject touched a comparison key, the trial ended: All stimuli disappeared, a .68-s intertrial interval occurred, and the next trial began. If the subject touched a correct comparison on a trial in which reinforcement was scheduled, the computer beeped and added a point to the reinforcement counter before the intertrial interval began. When reinforcement was not scheduled, neither beeps nor points were given.

Errors were recorded if the subject touched an incorrect comparison or touched both the correct and an incorrect comparison within .1 s. Touching the blank comparison key or the area outside the keys had no programmed effect (except during the delayed-cue procedure described below). Responses during the intertrial interval reset the interval, delaying the onset of the next trial.

Trial sequences. The computer program that managed the procedures presented trial sequences that were subject to the following restrictions: With each combination of sample and comparison stimuli defined as a trial type (the number of trial types in a session depended on the current phase of the experiment), each trial block included one occurrence of every trial type; no trial type occurred on consecutive trials; no key was correct on consecutive trials; and every block of trials contained a different sequence of trial types and of correct keys.

Delayed-cue procedure. Conditional discriminations were taught by a variation of the delayed-cue technique (Touchette, 1971). Each trial began with the presentation of a sample, and when the subject touched the sample key, the comparisons appeared. On the first several trials, however, the incorrect comparisons disappeared immediately (.1 s), leaving only blank keys with the sample and the correct comparison. Pressing a blank key that had contained an

incorrect comparison was treated as an error, but this rarely happened; the disappearance of the incorrect comparisons made the correct choice obvious. Each time the subject completed a block of trials without error, the interval between presentation of the comparisons and removal of the incorrect comparisons increased, the amount of the increase growing larger as the subject progressed. The interval could have become as long as 20 s, but before waiting that long, subjects always began selecting the correct comparison while the incorrect comparisons were still on the screen. When a subject responded correctly prior to the removal of the incorrect comparisons for 16 consecutive trials, the delayed cue was dropped from that particular teaching phase. Once subjects had become familiar with the delayed-cue procedure, they often learned subsequent conditional discriminations almost errorlessly.

Standard learning criteria. Subjects completed any teaching phase by meeting the following criteria: an overall accuracy of at least 95% during six consecutive trial blocks and no more than one error in any trial type during those six blocks.

Preteaching. Preteaching familiarized subjects with the equipment, trial and reinforcement procedures, first- and second-order conditional discriminations, and the delayed-cue procedure. With visual stimuli that differed from those to be used later in the experiment, they learned first-order conditional discriminations, first with visual samples and then with auditory samples (the same tones that were to be used later). Then they learned second-order conditional discriminations that combined the visual and auditory samples. At the end of preteaching, subjects were matching visual samples and comparisons, with the correct comparison on a given trial depending on whether the high or the low tone was present. They had also learned to use the delayed-cue procedure efficiently when faced with new trial types.

Teaching. With the delayed-cue procedure, subjects first learned the conditional discriminations labeled AB in Figure 12-2. When the tone was high and the visual sample was an uppercase lambda (A1), subjects

learned to choose lowercase gamma (B1). But with a low tone sounding with uppercase lambda (A1), subjects learned to choose lowercase xi (B2). Similarly, with A2 and A3 as samples, the correct comparison depended on whether the high or the low tone sounded during the trial. In this way, the visual-visual AB conditional discriminations came under tonal control.

Once subjects met the learning criterion on the AB conditional discriminations, they continued to review them at the start of each session while learning the BC tasks, the latter also under control by the tones. After attaining criterion on BC, they received a series of mixed AB and BC trials until they again met the learning criterion. These AB and BC trials served as a baseline into which probes were inserted to assess whether the relations that had not been explicitly taught had emerged. Variations in the teaching sequence will be described in conjunction with the results.

Extinction pretest. Because all tests were given in extinction, it was necessary to make sure that subjects would maintain their high accuracy on the baseline conditional discriminations even in the absence of a beep and a point for correct responses. Before testing began, subjects were told, "This time you will not get any beeps or points, but you can make up the points on some easy ones later." Then, on completing the same number of unreinforced trials that were to be used in subsequent tests, the subjects were allowed to make up their missed points by matching numbers and number names. Once subjects had demonstrated the standard accuracy criterion without reinforcement, testing of emergent conditional discriminations began. After each test, subjects were given enough number-matching trials to make up for their missed reinforcements during the unreinforced baseline trials of the test.

Probe tests. Before any test, subjects reviewed the baseline conditional discriminations that they had been taught explicitly. During these reviews, subjects received the usual beeps and points after correct choices. Only when they met a review criterion of at least 95% accuracy with no more than one error per trial type in three consecutive blocks of trials was a test given.

The trials that assessed emergent relations were usually presented as probes mixed with trials of the baseline conditional discriminations (exceptions are noted below). On each trial, the sample appeared, the subject touched the sample, the comparisons appeared, the subject touched a comparison, and the trial ended. After the intertrial interval, the next trial began. Without points or differential feedback on any trial, subjects received no direct instruction about correct choices on probe trials.

In earlier experiments in this laboratory, probe trials had been interspersed among intermittently reinforced baseline trials. Occasionally, however, subjects discriminated the differential reinforcement contingencies, maintaining high accuracy on their baselines but showing selective extinction on the probes (e.g., Subject EH in Sidman et al., 1985). This observation gave rise to the current extinction procedure for both baseline and probe trials.

Subjects received tests for CA (combined test of symmetry and transitivity), AC (test of transitivity), and BA and CB (tests of symmetry). The sequence of tests varied with subjects and will be described with the results.

Verbal reports. After all tests for emergent relations were completed, some subjects reported verbally on their performance. Probe trials were presented in extinction and subjects were asked to describe what they were going to do and why. The conversations were recorded on tape and later transcribed.

RESULTS

Except where noted below, tests had 18, 36, or 54 probes interspersed among AB and BC baseline trials, and the subjects' accuracy on baseline trials remained above 90%. Figures 12-3 and 12-4 are cumulative records of the probe trials for Subjects JLR and JXT. The curves cumulate "hits" and "false alarms" (see below) within single tests only. Subject AXP's data are described in the text.

The records of probe trials in all CA tests of equivalence have their origin near the lowest line; probes assessing transitivity begin on the line labeled AC; and probes assessing symmetry begin either on the line labeled BA or

CB, depending on the relation tested. The origin of each cumulative record is displaced an arbitrary distance along the appropriate test axis.

On each trial, the subject's choice of a comparison stimulus that was consistent with the relation being tested was considered a "hit," and caused the line to move up one notch; a perfect performance produced a vertical line as in Test 7 (Figure 12-3). Every choice inconsistent with the relation being tested was considered a "false alarm" (not an incorrect rejection, because no choice was incorrect), and caused the line to move one notch to the right; the lower the slope of the line, the greater the number of selected comparisons inconsistent with the relation being tested.

Because each record includes both high-tone and low-tone probes, an intermediate slope (e.g., Test 1 in Figure 12-3) could have represented a subject's consistent selection of comparisons indicative of relations under the control of only one tone. For example, the subject might have responded as though the tone were always high. In fact, this pattern never occurred, so inter-

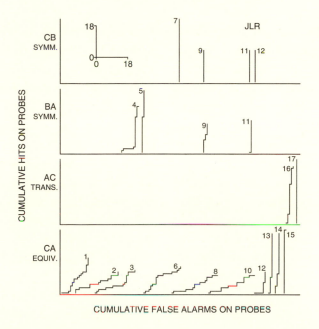

Fig. 12-3. Cumulative records of Subject JLR's responses on probe trials. Each "hit" (response consistent with the relation being tested) causes the line to move one vertical step. Each "false alarm" (response consistent with one of the relations not being tested) causes the line to move one step to the right. Hits and false alarms cumulate within each test; the scale is shown at the upper left. The numbers beside each record indicate the sequence of tests. Two records with the same number indicate a test that included probes for both relations.

mediate slopes always indicate a mixture of hits and false alarms on probes with both high and low tones.

Subject JLR

Subject JLR received 17 tests (Figure 12-3). The first was the CA test of equivalence. Would the CA conditional discriminations, not explicitly taught to the subject, emerge under the control of the tones, as diagrammed in the upper and lower sections of Figure 12-2? The steplike record, with only 21 hits in the 36 probe trials, indicates a failure of equivalence to emerge. Repeated in Tests 2 and 3, the CA probes continued to show no convincing evidence of equivalence.

Test 4 checked the explicitly taught AB relations for symmetry by probing with BA trials in the presence of one or the other tone. The low slope of the line

491

during the early trials of Test 4 showed that symmetry was not immediately present, but the abrupt change to a nearly vertical line showed symmetry emerging suddenly. Test 5, a repetition of the BA test, produced 35 hits in the 36 trials.

Might the emergence of the BA conditional discriminations, indicating AB symmetry, have brought in equivalence? A repetition of the CA probes in Test 6 indicated that it had not; only 15 of the subject's 36 choices were hits.

Test 7 yielded a perfect score on 36 CB probes, indicating symmetry of the BC relations, but in Test 8, a score of only 10 hits in 36 CA probes indicated that the positive symmetry tests had not been sufficient to generate equivalence. To ensure that both sets of explicitly taught relations, AB and BC, had retained their symmetric properties, BA and CB symmetry probes were mixed in Test 9. Symmetry was intact in both, but Test 10 still showed no equivalence. Test 11 confirmed that the emergent BA and CB relations endured.

Symmetry of the AB and BC relations had never been shown at the same time that the CA relations were being probed. Test 12, therefore, included CB symmetry probes with the CA equivalence probes. Subject JLR's choices were hits on all 18 of the CB probes. Her first five choices on the CA trials were false alarms, but 12 of her remaining 13 choices were hits; equivalence emerged during this test. Also, after a few hits on the CA probes, even without beeps or points, Subject JLR said, "It took me long enough, but I've got it now."

Tests 13, 14, and 15 confirmed the emergence and maintenance of the CA conditional discriminations indicative of equivalence. Then, AC probes in Tests 16 and 17 demonstrated that the AB and BC relations were transitive, a property that was required (along with symmetry) if the emergence of the CA relations was to be confirmed as a valid indicator of equivalence.

In her verbal reports, Subject JLR gave names to all the stimuli and was able to describe all of the sample-comparison relations and their derivations, in accordance with Figure 12-2.

Subject AXP

Subject AXP had 43 tests (not shown), during which he showed symmetry for the trained AB and BC relations but never showed transitivity (AC) or equivalence (CA) under contextual control of the tones. Nor was his responding consistent with stimulus classes generated by one tone alone. A full graphical presentation of Subject AXP's extensive test data would be more distracting than illuminating.

In Tests 1 through 5 (CA probes for equivalence), he never scored more than 11 hits in 36 probes. The AB and BC conditional discriminations had not generated equivalence relations. The AB and BC relations were then tested for transitivity by presenting the subject with AC probes in Tests 6 and 7; the AC relations did not emerge.

Subsequent tests yielded evidence neither of transitivity (AC) nor of AB symmetry (BA). The BA conditional discriminations indicative of AB symmetry under tonal control did emerge, however, when tested with only AB trials in the baseline. Then, a return to the full baseline of AB and BC trials confirmed that the AB relations had become symmetric, as had the BC relations.

A long series of tests then presented various combinations of probes, but equivalence (CA), although tested 18 more times, still did not emerge. Nor did transitivity emerge, although reassessed four more times with the AC probes. Testing came to a halt when personal circumstances kept Subject AXP from continuing the experiment.

Subject AXP's verbal reports did not indicate any consistent names for the stimuli, nor did he describe any of the emergent sample-comparison relations. He stated that he was unable to describe what he was doing, but could draw it and, subsequently, drew a diagram of the samples and specific comparisons he had been choosing. Neither his statements nor his drawings outlined any general rules.

Subject JXT

The data for Subjects JLR and AXP had suggested that the testing sequence and the combinations of baseline trials and probes can influence the emergence of new relations, even though the tests are carried out in extinction. A previous study (Sidman et al., 1985) had given rise to a similar suggestion. Accordingly, in an attempt to facilitate the emergence of contextually controlled

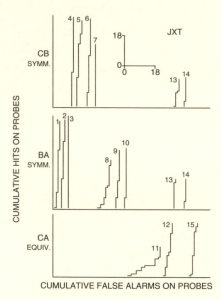

Fig. 12-4. Cumulative records of Subject JXT's responses on probe trials. Each "hit" (response consistent with the relation being tested) causes the line to move one vertical step. Each "false alarm" (response consistent with one of the relations not being tested) causes the line to move one step to the right. Hits and false alarms cumulate within each test; the scale is shown in the upper section. The numbers beside each record indicate the sequence of tests. Two records with the same number indicate a test that included probes for both relations.

equivalence, Subject JXT was given a different teaching and testing sequence. It is not possible, at present, to determine whether these procedural modifications had any effect on the subject's performance.

After Subject JXT met the learning criterion on the AB conditional discriminations and demonstrated continued accuracy in extinction, she received BA symmetry probes mixed with a baseline of AB trials. Her nearly 100% hit rate in Tests 1 through 3 (Figure 12-4) showed symmetry of the AB relations. Subject JXT then learned the BC conditional discriminations and demonstrated continued accuracy in extinction. The subsequent CB probes in Tests 4 through 6, mixed with a baseline of BC trials, showed symmetry of the BC relations.

AB and BC trials were then reviewed separately until Subject JXT met criterion on each. Then she was given the mixed baseline of AB and BC trials until she met the learning criterion and maintained her accuracy in extinction. Testing for emergent relations then resumed with the full AB and BC baseline.

In Test 7, Subject JXT scored 100% hits on CB probes for symmetry of the BC relations, with the full baseline. In Tests 8 through 10, the BA probes for AB symmetry (also with the full baseline) showed progressive improvement and stabilization of the hit rate.

Having shown symmetry for each of the directly taught relations, Subject JXT was given the CA probes for equivalence with the full baseline (Test 11). Although the first part of the test gave no evidence of equivalence, the hit rate did increase at the end. Test 12 then confirmed the emergence of equivalence, with the subject scoring 31 hits in 36 choices on the CA probes.

An injury prevented Subject JXT from participating in the experiment for the next several weeks. When she returned, she once more showed AB and BC symmetry in Tests 13 and 14, which inserted BA and CB probes into the full baseline. Test 15 reaffirmed the emergence of equivalence. Subject JXT did not return for further testing; transitivity was never tested directly, and no verbal reports were obtained.

DISCUSSION

Of three subjects who were explicitly taught AB and BC conditional discriminations with contextual control by tones, two showed that the teaching and testing had generated contextually controlled equivalence relations. New CA, BA, CB, and AC conditional discriminations emerged under tonal control. One subject demonstrated tonal control in BA and CB symmetry tests, but gave no evidence of transitivity or equivalence in the AC and CA tests.

Teaching two subjects the AB and BC conditional discriminations created six three-member classes of equivalent stimuli, with the high tone common to one set of three classes, and the low tone common to the other. Control by the tones made multiple class membership possible for the visual stimuli, each one becoming a member of two classes. For example, in the presence of the low tone, Stimulus A1 participated in one equivalence class along with B1 and C1, and in the presence of the high tone, participated in another class along with B2 and C3 (Figure 12-2).

If some kind of contextual control did not determine the class membership of Stimulus A1 at any particular moment, Stimuli B1, C1, B2, and C3

495

would all have become equivalent to each other because of their shared equivalence relation with A1; the subjects would have had no basis for performing the new conditional discriminations as they did. The tones kept the classes from interacting. These findings provide an affirmative answer to the major question that initiated the study: if conditional discriminations are brought explicitly under contextual control, will new conditional discriminations that define equivalence relations also emerge under contextual control?

The data also raise several questions that remain unanswered. For example, why did Subject AXP not show the same results as the others? His academic competence indicated that he was perfectly capable of forming equivalence relations. Perhaps the answer is to be found in his verbal report, in which he neither gave names to the stimuli nor described any rules for relating the stimuli. Still, it has not yet been demonstrated that verbal mediation is necessary for equivalence relations to emerge from conditional discriminations. The opposite— that equivalence relations are necessary for verbal rules to emerge—is, at present, equally likely.

Another unanswered question concerns the nature of the contextual control. One possibility is that the high and low tones functioned as second-order conditional stimuli, with the explicitly arranged contingencies placing each in control of the original first-order conditional discriminations (depicted by the solid arrows in Figure 12-2), and each then coming to control the emergent relations also (depicted by the dashed arrows in Figure 12-2).

An alternative interpretation does not attribute second-order control to the tones. It is possible that the tones never developed an independent function of their own, but simply entered into stimulus compounds with the visual stimuli. They may just have changed the stimuli in the first-order conditional discriminations from purely visual to auditory-visual compounds. For example, instead of matching the visual Sample A1 to visual Comparison B1 under the control of the high tone and the same visual sample to visual Comparison B2 under the control of the low tone, the subjects may have been matching one compound sample (A1 + high tone) to a compound comparison (B1 + high tone) and another compound sample (A1 + low tone) to a compound comparison (B2 + low tone). If these compounds had formed, the subjects could be said to have learned only first-order and not second-order conditional discriminations.

It is clear that the A- and B-stimuli did not simply form stimulus compounds with each other; the AC and CA tests showed the A-stimuli to be effective in the absence of the explicitly related B-stimuli, and the CB tests showed the B-stimuli to be capable of functioning independently of the A-stimuli. Similarly, the AC, CA, and BA tests showed that the B- and C-stimuli did not have to function together as compounds. A tone, however, was present in every test; the tones, therefore, were never shown to function independently of visual samples and comparisons with which they had been explicitly combined. Contextual control by the tones may have come about solely because one tone or the other was an element of every stimulus.

The tones, then, may never really have served as second-order conditional stimuli. They may simply have made the specification of the first-order conditional stimuli more complex, and for that reason never have exerted independent control over emergent equivalence relations. Would it be possible to establish second-order conditional control by stimuli that were capable of functioning independently? This question helped shape the next experiment.

EXPERIMENT 2

The first purpose of Experiment 2 was to determine whether emergent contextual control could be confirmed with another subject. The second purpose, an attempt to produce unequivocal second-order control over the emergent conditional discriminations, dictated a more complex procedure. Experiment 2 was an attempt at systematic, rather than direct replication of Experiment 1, in that it required the emergence not of three-member but of four-member classes under contextual control.

True second-order control required that the tones exert

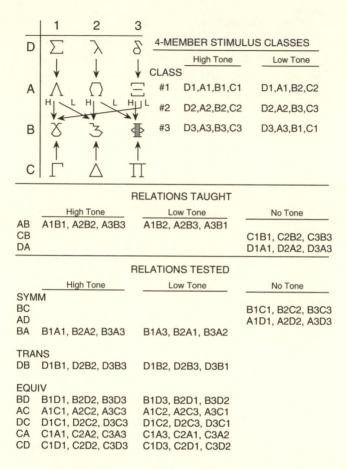

Fig. 12-5. Procedure for Experiment 2. The upper left portion diagrams DA, AB, and CB, the relations taught directly; the letter H denotes relations in the high tone, and L denotes the low tone. The upper right portion shows the expected stimulus classes contextually controlled by tones. The middle portion shows the relations taught with and without tones. The bottom shows the tests for symmetry, transitivity, and equivalence with and without tones.

contextual control independently of the particular visual stimuli with which they had been combined during the original teaching. One way to validate such independence would be to generate emergent conditional discriminations that involved new combinations of tones and visual stimuli. These would be analogous to the emergent relations between visual stimuli that had never been explicitly related to each other during teaching. The procedure illustrated at the top of Figure 12-5 was designed to permit such definitive tests for true second-order control over emergent conditional discriminations. As before, the AB conditional discriminations were taught in the presence of either the high or the low tone. Stimuli C and D were related to Stimuli B and A, respectively, in the absence of the tones. Would the tones then control the class membership of the C- and D-stimuli with which they had never before been combined?

As in Experiment 1 with the tones present, arrows in Figure 12-5 point from sample (A-stimuli) to comparisons (B-stimuli), with the high (H) or low (L) tone indicated beside each arrow. For example, when A1 was the sample, the subject learned to select Comparison B1 in the presence of a high tone and Comparison B2 in the presence of a low tone. The tones also determined the comparison he was to select when the sample was A2 or A3.

The subject learned the CB and DA conditional discrimina-tions *without any tones*. With the B-stimuli as comparisons, he was taught to select B1 whenever C1 was the sample, B2 with C2 as the sample, and B3 with C3. Similarly, with the A-stimuli as comparisons, he learned to select A1 whenever D1 was the sample, A2 with D2, and A3 with D3. All relations that were explicitly taught are listed in the center section of Figure 12-5.

If the explicit teaching had generated equivalence relations, the DA and CB conditional discriminations would be symmetric; emergent AD and BC conditional discriminations would be independent of the tones (bottom section of Figure 12-5). AB symmetry, however, would generate two sets of BA conditional discriminations, one set accompanied by the low tone, and the other set by the high tone (as in Experiment 1). All other emergent conditional discriminations would have to include C- or D-stimuli as samples or comparisons and would also have to involve the AB or BA relations.

In the DB transitivity test, the tone would, for example, determine whether D1 as the sample would lead the subject to select

Comparison B1 or B2. It is of particular interest here that while the original conditional discriminations were being taught, no tones accompanied the D-stimuli. Similarly, in the CA equivalence test (because this test requires symmetry of the AB relations, it is more than just a transitivity test), the tones would control the emergent CA conditional discriminations, even though the C-stimuli and the tones had not been presented together during the original teaching. The CD and DC tests for four-member equivalence classes are the most demanding, because the original teaching had involved neither the samples nor the comparisons in conditional discriminations that included tones.

The four-member stimulus classes under tonal control are shown in the upper right section of Figure 12-5. Given equivalence, six four-member classes will form, each tone controlling three classes. The subject would be able to match any member of a class to any other, even without having been directly taught to do so.

All of the new relations that could be expected to emerge af-ter the explicit teaching are listed in the bottom section of Figure 12-5. Control by the tones over emergent conditional discriminations in which C- or D-stimuli served as samples or comparisons would suggest that the tones could function independently of the A- and B-stimuli with which they had been combined during the original teaching. This, in turn, would suggest that the tones had not simply entered into compounds with the visual stimuli but instead were exerting second-order contextual control over the emergent equivalence relations.

METHOD

Subject

Subject EXY was a 25-year-old male foreign student enrolled as an undergraduate in a local school of music.

Apparatus

All equipment was identical to that of Experiment 1, except that there was no touchscreen to identify responses. Instead of touching the screen to indicate the stimulus he was selecting, the subject pressed one of five keys on the numerical data pad on the keyboard below the monitor on which the stimuli appeared. The keys, arranged in a cross, corresponded in position to the stimuli. The subject was told to "choose one of these [stimuli on the monitor] by pressing the corresponding one of these [keys on the keyboard]—the one that is in the same relative position as those up there."

Procedure

The preteaching and teaching contingencies, the delayed-cue procedure, the procedural parameters, and the standard learning criterion were the same as in Experiment 1. Subject EXY tended to work for longer sessions than the subjects in Experiment 1 and rarely earned less than $15 per session. He participated in four teaching and three testing sessions.

After preteaching, Subject EXY first learned the AB conditional discriminations with the tones, as illustrated in Figure 12-5. With any sample (an A-stimulus), the tone (high or low) determined the comparison (one of the B-stimuli) that the subject was to select. After reaching the learning criterion, the

subject continued to review the AB conditional discriminations at the start of subsequent sessions.

The subject then learned the CB conditional discriminations without any tones present. AB trials (with tones) and CB trials (without tones) were then mixed. Next, the DA conditional discriminations were taught without tones. The final baseline, reviewed at the start of each session, contained trials of all of the explicitly taught conditional discriminations—AB with high tone, AB with low tone, and CB and DA without any tone.

The subject then received the extinction pretest, meeting the learning criterion on the baseline without any beeps or points. Finally, he went through a series of tests for emergent conditional discriminations. As in Experiment 1, trials that assessed emergent relations were presented as probes mixed with baseline trials. Again, all testing was done in extinction.

The sequence of tests will be described with the results. After the tests were completed, verbal reports were requested, taped, and transcribed.

Results

Figure 12-6 presents Subject EXY's probe data, obtained in 20 tests that had 18 or 36 probes interspersed among AB, CB, and DA baseline trials. Baseline accuracy remained above 95%. Again, hits and false alarms are cumulated within single tests only.

Subject EXY started with two CD tests, each containing 36 probe trials. Tones had never before accompanied the C samples or the D comparisons. If the original teaching had established the prerequisites for the emergence of tonal control over four-member classes of equivalent stimuli (Figure 12-5), Sample C1 would lead the subject to select Comparison D1 in the presence of the high tone and Comparison D3 in the low tone; with Sample C2, the subject would select Comparison D2 in the high tone and D1 in the low tone; and with Sample C3, he would select D3 in the high tone and D2 in the low tone.

The first two tests did not fulfill these expectations; the low, steplike slopes of curves 1 and 2 (Figure 12-6) indicate a failure of equivalence to emerge. Tests 3

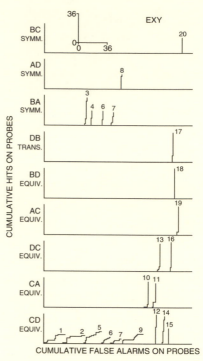

Fig. 12-6. Cumulative records of Subject EXY's responses on probe trials. Each "hit" (response consistent with the relation being tested) causes the line to move one vertical step. Each "false alarm" (response consistent with one of the relations not being tested) causes the line to move one step to the right. Hits and false alarms cumulate within each test; the scale is shown in the upper section. The numbers directly above each record indicate the sequence of tests. Two records with the same number indicate a test that included probes for both relations. Note change in scale from previous graphs.

(36 trials) and 4 (18 trials) probed the AB conditional discriminations for symmetry by presenting BA trials with the tones. The AB

relations proved symmetrical, but CD conditional discriminations indicative of equivalence still did not appear in Test 5. Tests 6 and 7 combined BA and CD probes (18 trials of each), but the results did not change; the AB relations maintained their symmetry, but the CD relations still did not emerge. Test 8, which presented 18 AD probe trials without any tones, showed that the DA relations were symmetric, but another CD probe in Test 9 still yielded no evidence of equivalence.

If CD relations indicative of four-member equivalence classes are to emerge, AB symmetry (under tonal control) and DA symmetry (independently of the tones) are required (Figure 12-5). BA and AD tests had already documented these necessary symmetries. Also required are the BD and CA relations that would signify two sets of three-member equivalence classes (ABD and ABC); the four-member classes could not be expected to emerge in the absence of either set of smaller classes. Given the AB and DA symmetry that the emergent BA and AD relations had already demonstrated, transitivity of BA and AD would bring about the necessary BD relations. Given the explicitly taught CB relations and the AB symmetry that the emergent BA relations had demonstrated, transitivity of CB and BA would bring about the necessary CA relations.

Because probes of the BD and CA conditional discriminations test simultaneously for symmetry and transitivity, they are equivalence tests. The BD probes for the ABD class require both the BA and AD relations to be symmetric if equivalence is to emerge, but the CA probes for the ABC class require only BA symmetry. The presumably simpler CA relations were therefore tested next.

After the first three false alarms at the beginning of Test 10, Subject EXY said, "Oh, I think I have something," and the remaining probes documented the existence of the three-member ABC class. In Test 11, the subject again scored mainly hits on the CA probes.

In Test 12 the subject was once more given the CD probes; this time, the 36 trials contained only one false alarm. Six previous tests had failed to yield CD relations indicative of four-member ABCD classes, but after the three-member ABC classes had emerged, the CD relations showed themselves immediately.

Tests 13-20 included two replications of the CD probes (Tests 14 and 15) and probed all of the previously untested conditional discriminations that were necessary to document four-member equivalence classes. Tests 13 and 16 confirmed the four-member classes by demonstrating the necessary DC relations; the DB relations in Test 17 showed that the DA and AB relations were transitive, and the BD relations in Test 18 confirmed the three-member equivalence class ABD. Test 19 probed the AC relations, confirming the three-member ABC class that Tests 11 and 12 had shown by means of CA probes; and in Test 20, BC probes demonstrated the symmetry of the CB relations.

In his verbalizations elicited after the tests, Subject EXY used names for each of the stimuli and described the relations among stimuli exactly as they are illustrated in Figure 12-5.

DISCUSSION

Once more, the question that initiated the study received a positive answer: Classes of equivalent stimuli that emerge from contextually controlled conditional discriminations will themselves be under contextual control. The contextual control permitted stimuli to become members of more than one class without causing the classes to combine. Experiment 2 confirmed this finding with a third subject, extending it to the more complex case of emergent four-member classes.

There remains the secondary question of whether the contextual control could be attributed to second-order conditional discriminations. Although tones had never been present while Subject EXY was explicitly being taught conditional discriminations that involved C- or D-stimuli, the emergent CD, DC, CA, AC, DB, and BD conditional discriminations did depend on the tones. For example, with C1 as the sample and the D-stimuli as comparisons, the subject selected D1 in the presence of the high tone and D3 in the low tone. Similarly, in each emergent conditional discrimination, the tone controlled the class membership of the C- and D-stimuli.

On the face of it, the tones seemed to be controlling equivalence relations even between visual stimuli that had never been presented with tones while conditional discriminations were being explicitly taught. If this were correct, true second-order conditional control would have been demonstrated. The reason for the tentative nature of this conclusion lies in the subject's descriptions of the rules he was following during probes for emergent conditional discriminations. (Because it was recognized that the subject's verbal description might itself influence what he subsequently did, reports were not elicited until all of the conditional-discrimination procedures had been completed.)

In a CD trial, for example, with only the low tone and Sample C1 present (D3 was the correct choice after the subject produced the comparisons), Subject EXY was asked, "What are you going to do?" He said the following (paraphrased, and with the alphanumeric stimulus designations shown in Figure 12-5 substituted for the names he used): "When I see C1 [the sample], I immediately think about B1. And *a low tone, with B1, connects to A3*. If I push C1, A3 will be on one of the squares. If A3 is not there, D3 is connected to A3, so I will push D3. D3 is connected to A3, and *A3 with a low tone makes B1*, which is connected to C1." (Subject then pressed the sample to produce the comparisons, and selected D3.)

Even though the tone was present from beginning to end, the subject mentioned it only while describing the AB and BA relations, never while referring to the CB or DA relations. He spoke of D3 being related to A3 and C1 to B1 without including the tone in his description. The tone was noted only in describing AB relations. Could he have learned to disregard the tone in conjunction with the C- and D-stimuli and to take it into account only in conjunction with the AB relations? If so, that might invalidate the assumption that the tones exerted direct second-order control over the emergent CD relations. The subject's performance can then be described as a chain in which his verbal rule, interacting with the experimental stimuli, acted as a complex set of discriminative stimuli (Skinner, 1969, pp. 122, 142-148) to determine his final choices. The tones might have controlled the emergence only of the segment of the rule that dealt with the AB conditional discriminations.

Whether the verbal rules stated by the subject played a pivotal role in the emergence of equivalence relations is, of course, only conjectural, depending on several assumptions whose validity has not yet been demonstrated. These can only be outlined briefly here. First, does equivalence, in general, require that the individual be able to verbalize the relationships? Second, even if such verbalization proves not generally necessary, might it be required for the emergence of larger classes, and particularly for multinodal classes (Fields & Verhave, 1987)?

Third, were the emergent (or the directly-taught) conditional discriminations in this experiment actually rule governed? The reports were retrospective, created perhaps by the experimenter's very act of requesting them and therefore not even existing during the previous experimental procedures. Fourth, although the contingencies outlined in Figure

12-5 did generate the stated rules, it cannot be known whether those rules, if they did exist before the requested verbal reports, then operated independently of the contingencies that generated them. And finally, one can ask the chicken-and-egg type of question: Which comes first, the rules or the equivalence relations? If one is indeed necessary for the other, which is primary?

To discuss potential solutions for these problems is not appropriate here. Yet, even with these unanswered questions about possible interactions between equivalence relations and rule-governed behavior, it is unwise at this juncture to ignore the likelihood that the formulation of a helpful set of rules became possible only when the subject learned to disregard the tones except when considering the AB relations. This may have occurred during the CA probes in Test 10 (Figure 12-6), when he said "I think I have something," and was perhaps more likely to happen during a test for three-member than for four-member classes. In that event, the tones could not be said any more definitely than in Experiment 1 to have functioned as second-order conditional stimuli in exerting their contextual control.

GENERAL DISCUSSION

In the present experiments, we sought to determine whether contextually controlled conditional discriminations can produce emergent equivalence relations that are also under contextual control. Three of four subjects gave a positive answer to this question, even though it could not be determined unequivocally whether the tones exerted contextual control as independent second-order conditional stimuli or simply as common elements of compound first-order conditional and discriminative stimuli.

A major impetus for the present study came from an analysis of the potential role of second-order conditional stimuli in accounting for the contextual control of emergent equivalence classes (Sidman, 1986a). This analysis raised the question of why the context itself does not become a member of all the emergent classes and, by virtue of its common membership, condense all of the classes into

one. In the present study, for example, if the tones exerted independent second-order control over the directly taught and the emergent conditional discriminations, why did the tones not enter into equivalence relations with the A- and B-stimuli? If they did, all stimuli would be related to the tones and therefore to each other and would become members of a single equivalence class. Why did this not happen?

The most likely reason is that the contingencies themselves prevented it. Differential stimulus control—discrimination—requires that the controlling stimuli be different. If all stimuli became equivalent to each other, the subjects would have no basis for responding differentially; neither the simple nor the conditional discriminations that the reinforcement contingencies specified would have been possible for the subjects. A conflict therefore exists between the reinforcement contingencies that call for differential stimulus control and the formation of equivalence classes that impart the same function to all members of a class. As the most likely winners of such a conflict, the reinforcement contingencies perhaps counteract the tendency of the stimuli to combine into one large equivalence class.

A similar consideration arises in conjunction with the observation that different reinforcers correlated with each sample-comparison pair bring the reinforcers into the sample-comparison equivalence class (Dube et al., 1987). In the more common experimental procedure in which all conditional discriminations share a common reinforcer, one might expect all of the stimuli to become related to each other because of their relation to the same reinforcer. Again, as in the case of a common second-order conditional stimulus, one can appeal to the incompatibility between class formation and the reinforcement contingencies to explain why the use of a common reinforcer does not preclude the establishment of conditional discriminations or the emergence of independent equivalence classes.

The considerations just noted assume second-order conditional control by the contextual stimulus. The incompatibility between class formation and the contingencies does not arise when a subject is learning simple discriminations or first-order conditional discriminations. It becomes a problem only when second-order control is being established. Another reason, therefore, that a common element (tone or reinforcer) might not bring all the stimuli into a single equivalence class comes from the possibility, discussed in conjunction with Experiments 1 and 2, that the common elements simply enter into stimulus compounds with each visual sample and comparison. In the present experiments, the tones would then not have become second-order conditional stimuli. In that case, the conflict between second-order conditional control and the formation of equivalence classes would not have arisen, or, if it did, would have resolved itself. This potential conflict may even increase the likelihood that the formation of stimulus compounds will preempt the establishment of second-order conditional discriminations.

✳ ✳ ✳ ✳ ✳ ✳ ✳ ✳ ✳

Commentary

The Verbalization of Contingencies

The Journal reviewers of the *Contextual Control* paper were uneasy about our use of Subject EXY's verbalizations as indicators of what might have been happening during the tests (p. 505). I was sympathetic to their unease. It looked as though we might be falling into the mechanistic trap of inventing links in a cause-effect chain to explain the test results (see, for example, Chiesa, 1994, pp. 95-123; Lee, 1988, pp. 160-161). Indeed, what we were doing here was to pay our respects to the notion that equivalence relations might require the verbalization of rules by the subject. During a test, such rules might then serve as mediating elements in a chain of events that started with the presentation of a sample stimulus and ended with the subject's choice of a comparison. If we did not discuss that possibility ourselves, others would surely do so.

We also went on, however, to delineate the complexities that would have to be overcome before one could accept the necessity of verbal mediation of equivalence relations. Furthermore, if the data (Schusterman & Kastak, 1993) that show nonhumans to be capable of the emergent performances that define equivalence remain convincing, the question of the necessity of verbal mediation will lose its significance. Still, even if equivalence does not *require* verbal mediation, we must not lose sight of the fact that the statement of a verbal rule *can* establish equivalence relations. This caution is relevant not just when formulating theory but also when performing experiments. As I have pointed out elsewhere (Sidman, 1992a):

> One can instruct an experimental subject as follows: First, "Stimulus A1 goes with Stimulus B1, and B1 with C1"; second, "Any two or more stimuli that go with the same stimulus also go with each other." Such instructions can, of course, suffice to yield a positive equivalence test, not because of experimental contingencies but because of the subject's experiences before coming into the laboratory. Indeed, if the subject has a particular verbal history,

the relation "goes with" may already be an equivalence relation, and the second instruction will not even be necessary; just telling the subject that particular stimuli "go with" each other may be sufficient to establish equivalence relations.

It is not clear, however, that verbal rules are necessary for the establishment of equivalence relations. That rules can give rise to equivalence relations does not mean that equivalence relations require rules. Also, to say that the derived relations indicative of equivalence must be products of verbal rules begs the question of where the verbal rules come from, and of how oral, written, or signed statements can generate behavior that is consistent with contingencies a listener or reader has never experienced....

...Until we have answered the question of whether rules give rise to equivalence, or equivalence makes rules possible, we are going to have to be careful about our experimental procedures in investigations of equivalence. If we tell our subject that stimuli "go with" each other (or that they "match each other," "belong together," "are the same," "go first" or "go second," etc.), the data may then tell more about the subject's verbal history than about the effects of current experimental operations. (pp. 21, 22).

Unfortunately, a number of published experiments, although directed at important conceptual issues, suffer from the problem of over-instruction of the subjects. It is sometimes not clear whether demonstrations of equivalence (or failures to demonstrate equivalence) have anything to do with the presumably relevant experimental arrangements. Instructions to the subject may establish a context that brings into play historical contingencies that interact with or completely override current experimental contingencies.

On a more theoretical note, it is worth repeating that the inclusion of responses in the equivalence class (Chapter 10) permits one to dispense with the notion that labels or more complex verbalizations "mediate" equivalence relations. If responses are granted status as components of the event pairs that make up an equivalence relation, then to attribute a mediating function to responses would accomplish no more than would the attribution of a mediating function to stimulus components. With defined responses taking their place along with conditional, discriminative, and reinforcing stimuli as members of the class, any necessity for the causal chain that is implied by the concept of mediation disappears; the concept itself becomes excess baggage.

To say that verbal mediation is unnecessary for equivalence is not to say that verbal labels and rules are always irrelevant. To deny what Luria (1957) has termed "the abstracting and generalizing, analyzing and synthesizing power of language" (cited in Vocate, 1987, p. 135), would be contrary to everyday observation. But how does language help us to abstract, to generalize, to analyze, and to synthesize, and how does it come to do so? The mere acknowledgment of those powers does not explicate the role of verbalization in such complex behavioral phenomena as simple and conditional observing, remembering, conceptualizing, categorizing and relating, ordering, inducing, deducing, and others. It is possible, for example, that attaching labels to stimuli in a single-node equivalence class and expressing rules for relating those labels may help one subsequently to expand the class in accord with multinodal contingencies. Why verbalization should have such a facilitating effect is an interesting and important problem but its interest and importance are not restricted to equivalence phenomena. Surely, that facilitation involves something more than just the establishment of links in a causal stimulus-response chain (Skinner, 1957, pp. 107-129).

More on Delayed Emergence

All subjects in the *Contextual Control* experiments showed delayed emergence of equivalence. That is to say, they had to experience the tests several times before conditional discriminations indicative of equivalence relations emerged. I had previously proposed that delayed emergence might reflect the fact that stimuli can belong to other classes in addition to the experimentally established equivalence classes that are being tested (pp. 274-279). Some of these classes may be products of the subject's extraexperimental history (Sidman, 1992a, pp. 23-24); others, although irrelevant to the aims of the study, may nevertheless have been created within it. Equivalence tests usually provide no context that would select a particular one from among the many classes that might be possible. Any of these classes may therefore serve as bases for relating sample and comparison stimuli during test trials. A well-designed test will arrange test trials so that the experimentally established equivalence class provides the only basis for classification that remains possible—that "works"—on *every* trial. Thus, the grounds for relating the sample and a comparison may vary from one test trial to the next until finally, the subject hits on a consistent basis—the experimentally established equivalence relation that remains possible from trial to trial.

Although "hitting on" a basis for classification need not be verbal, it may still be verbalizable. Subject JLR's statement after a few consecutive correct (but not reinforced) choices, "It took me long enough, but I've got it now" (Figure 12-3, Test 12), suggests that a selection process may well have been going on—that the absence of a consistent basis for choice had left her doubtful, her doubt being resolved when she recognized that she had finally achieved consistency from trial to trial. Without any feedback from the test procedure itself, what other grounds could have led her to say, "...I've got it now"?

Where Does Contextual Control Come From?

Although the sources of equivalence have been a matter of theoretical dispute (for example, Dugdale & Lowe, 1990; Hayes & Hayes, 1989; Sidman, 1990b), the contextual control of equivalence relations has been generally agreed to have an experiential basis. I have gone so far as to suggest that experience may be required not to make equivalence possible but rather, to break down or prevent specific equivalence relations (Sidman, 1986a, p. 113). Instead of asking, "Where does equivalence come from?" I have found it useful to ask instead, "What breaks down or precludes an equivalence relation?" To answer this question in any particular instance, look for contingency-engendered contextual control.

Without experientially based contextual control, simple and conditional discriminations and equivalence classes—partitions—would be impossible; multiple class membership, giving rise to class union, would take events that we had to discriminate and bring them instead into one large equivalence class where they would all be treated alike. Everyday observation tells us, however, that events can belong to more than one class even while those classes remain independent of each other. In such instances, what breaks down or prevents class union?

In addition to the problem that is raised by multiple class membership, other observations also lead us to contextual control. For example, (Sidman, 1992a):

> [How can it be that] humans do not always test positively for equivalence? Also, why do phenomena that equivalence is supposed to underlie not always happen? For example, the words, "Route 128" on the map, and the road on which we are driving are equivalent when we are trying to find our way to an unfamiliar place, but we do not try to drive our car onto the words, or to illuminate the road with a reading light. We do not try to eat the word, "bread," or to swat the word, "fly."
>
> To account for such seeming anomalies, we remind ourselves, and demonstrate experimentally, that equivalence relations come under contextual control (Bush et al., 1989; Kennedy & Laitinen, 1988; Sidman, 1986a; Wulfert & Hayes, 1988). Other circumstances determine whether, and when, stimuli are equivalent. (p. 22).

Hayes, in making contextual control the foundation of a "relational control theory of stimulus equivalence" (Hayes, 1991; Hayes & Hayes, 1989), has expressed a similar view (1991):

> Arbitrarily applicable relational responding must to some degree be under conditional control. If relational responding can be applied arbitrarily, and if it is not under conditional control, nothing would prevent all types of relational responding from occurring with regard to all events. For example, if stimulus equivalence occurred automatically whenever conditional discriminations were encountered, eventually the great variety of conditional discriminations in normal life would yield stimulus equivalence among virtually all stimuli. Everything would be in one gigantic class. This obviously does not happen, and it is contextual control that prevents it from happening. (p. 27).

Even without accepting relational-frame theory (see pp. 554-561 for a brief discussion of that theory) or its contention that "Stimulus equivalence can be interpreted as a special case of a network of relational frames" (Hayes, 1991, p. 32), one can remain fully in accord with the thesis that contextual control prevents equivalence from running wild, and with the observation that contextual control arises from experience.

But it *is* possible for equivalence to run wild in the laboratory, with the stimuli and defined responses falling into one all-encompassing equivalence class:

> Following some sequences of match-to-sample baseline training trials, equivalence relations could arise in such a way that one large equivalence class emerges instead of the two or more that were intended by the experimenter. When this occurs, test performances may appear to indicate that no equivalence classes emerged, even if a general relation of equivalence arose from the training (Saunders & Green, 1992, p. 236; see also Chapter 10, pp. 407-411).

And so, some instances in which humans seem not to test positively for equivalence in the laboratory may also reflect the absence of contextual control. The failure of laboratory contingencies to generate contextual control can account for some seeming failures of equivalence classes to develop. Outside the artificial conditions of the laboratory, experientially based contextual control accounts for the observation that all-encompassing equivalence classes rarely if ever form. What kinds of experience are we to look for, then, as sources of contextual control?

Compound samples and second-order conditional stimuli. In our *Contextual Control* experiments, context might have been defined by second-order conditional stimuli or by distinctive elements of compound samples. Later studies give more conclusive examples of contextual control by second-order conditional stimuli (for example, Kohlenberg et al., 1991; Lynch & Green, 1991; Steele & Hayes, 1991). Demonstrations that elements of compound samples can enter individually into equivalence relations (Stromer & Mackay,

1992; Stromer, McIlvane, & Serna, 1993; Stromer & Stromer, 1990a,b) give rise to the reasonable suggestion that such elements can also provide contextual control. With our new recognition that equivalence does not require four-term analytic units, but can arise also from three-term contingencies (Chapter 10), the location of contextually controlling stimuli in the third or the fourth term of the unit no longer poses a general theoretical problem. It becomes an issue only when one attempts to identify the source of control in a particular experimental or applied analysis.

Comparison stimuli. Another source of contextual control is possible in most experiments and in many nonexperimental situations. This is because the definition of any discrimination—simple or conditional—requires the specification both of positive and negative stimuli (*positive*: correlated with a particular reinforcer; *negative*: not correlated with that reinforcer), and because the definition of any class—any partition—requires both positive and negative exemplars (*positive*: members of a particular class; *negative*: not members of that class). The negative events that help define a discrimination or a class can also supply a context that limits discriminative control by the positive events or that circumscribes class membership. More specifically, when we establish a conditional discrimination with A1 as the sample, B1 as the positive comparison, and B2 as the negative comparison, the conditional A1B1 relation may hold *only* in the context of B2. Furthermore, the conditionally determined A1B1 pair may turn out to be a member of an equivalence relation *only when* B2 is also in the picture.

Even in our earliest mathematically-derived formulation of behavioral equivalence relations we had recognized the possibility that a full description of a particular conditional relation might require specification of the negative comparison[s], and we had pointed out that failures to demonstrate equivalence might result from superordinate control by negative comparisons. For example, "If a complete definition of the conditional relation had to include incorrect stimuli, then a valid symmetry test would require sample and correct comparison to be interchangeable only when the original incorrect comparison was also present" (Chapter 5, p. 142). Somewhat later (p. 261): "Also relevant are contextual stimuli, of which the 'incorrect' comparisons constitute an important category." To flesh out the actualities of contextual control and to provide a laboratory model that would permit its investigation, one of my graduate students set off on what turned out to be her doctoral dissertation research (Fucini, 1982). In this study, which, unfortunately, has never been written for publication, Fucini started by demonstrating class union. She then set up baseline contingencies that established contextual control by negative stimuli in conditional discriminations, and went on to show that (a) such control could prevent class union, and (b) contextual control by negative stimuli could separate classes that had previously merged. Here is an outline of the main features of those experiments—omitting various control procedures that checked for unwanted conditional relations that can obscure description when only two comparisons are used (Carrigan & Sidman, 1992; Johnson & Sidman, 1993; Sidman, 1987).

The conditional discriminations that were taught to the subjects (mostly children, aged 5 to 6 years) in the first part of the study were like many of those described earlier. In the upper part of Figure 12-7, however, the four boxes group each sample and its conditionally-related comparisons separately in order to delineate more clearly the equivalence classes that might be expected to emerge from the teaching phase of the experiment. During teaching phases, the sample on every trial—A1, A2, D3, or D4—was an auditory stimulus and the comparisons were visual. Arrows connect samples and positive comparison stimuli, with simultaneously presented comparisons shown side by side in adjoining boxes. On trials that presented Comparisons B1 and B2 together (the uppermost boxes), subjects could procure a reinforcer by selecting B1 in the presence of Sample A1 and by selecting B2 in the presence of A2; on trials with Comparisons X and C2, X was correct with Sample A1, and C2 with Sample A2. On trials that presented Comparisons X and E4 together (the two lower boxes), subjects could procure a reinforcer by selecting X in the presence of Sample D3 and by selecting E4 in the

TEACH

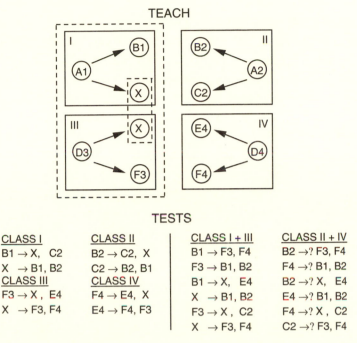

TESTS

CLASS I	CLASS II	CLASS I + III	CLASS II + IV
B1 → X, C2	B2 → C2, X	B1 → F3, F4	B2 →? F3, F4
X → B1, B2	C2 → B2, B1	F3 → B1, B2	F4 →? B1, B2
CLASS III	CLASS IV	B1 → X, E4	B2 →? X, E4
F3 → X , E4	F4 → E4, X	X → B1, B2	E4 →? B1, B2
X → F3, F4	E4 → F4, F3	F3 → X , C2	F4 →? X , C2
		X → F3, F4	C2 →? F3, F4

Figure 12-7. Teaching trials are shown within the four solid-line boxes. In these boxes, arrows connect samples and comparisons that become related via directly programmed reinforcement contingencies. Dashed-line boxes enclose the two representations of Stimulus X, and the two classes that might be expected to merge because they both contain X. Test trials are diagrammed below the boxes. In the test trials for Classes I, II, III, IV, and for the combined Classes I + III, arrows denote sample-comparison relations that would indicate positive test outcomes (the second comparison in each pair would be "incorrect" for that sample). Because Classes II + IV are not expected to merge, tested sample-comparison relations in the right-hand column are not expected to be consistent—denoted by question marks beside the arrows.

presence of D4; on trials with Comparisons F3 and F4, F3 was correct with Sample D3, and F4 with Sample D4. These contingencies could be expected to generate four three-member equivalence classes, each shown within its box and identified by a Roman numeral.

Fucini first confirmed the four classes by demonstrating the emergent conditional discriminations that are summarized in the two left-hand columns of test trials in the lower section of Figure 12-7. A positive test trial would find subjects relating the sample (shown at the left of the arrow) to the comparison the arrow points to. A subject would relate the other comparison stimulus to a different sample in another type of trial, indicating membership of that comparison in a different class. For example, Classes I and II would be—and were—confirmed when subjects, presented with Comparisons X and C2, chose X when B1 was the sample but chose C2 when B2 was the sample; and when given Comparisons B1 and B2, they chose B1 when X was the sample but B2 when C2 was the sample. Similar findings confirmed Classes III and IV. (Note that these are what we have called *combined* or *global* tests for equivalence because a positive outcome requires both symmetry and transitivity; for the same reason, we have sometimes called such tests simply *equivalence* tests.)

The distinctive aspect of this arrangement was the membership of Stimulus X in both Classes I and III. Because of this common element, Classes I and III might be expected to merge (as in the *Class Expansion* paper, Chapter 6). Classes II and IV, however, would have been expected to maintain their independence from each other and from the other classes because they contained no element in common. The next phase of the experiment, then, consisted of tests for class merger, as shown in the two columns of test trials in the lower right section of Figure 12-7. A merger of Classes I and III would find subjects relating members of Class I to members of Class III (and vice-versa) but not to members of Class II or IV. Therefore, the arrows in the Class I + III column connect each sample from Class I or Class III to its related Class III or Class I comparison, respectively. Tests for the merger of Class II or IV with other classes, however, would prove negative; subjects would not in any consistent or predictable way relate samples from Classes II or IV to comparisons from other classes. Hence the question marks beside the arrows in the Class II + IV column. To illustrate, when presented with F3 and F4 as comparisons, subjects would consistently select F3 when B1 was the sample but would select neither F3 nor F4 consistently when B2 was the sample. The test data fulfilled both of these sets of expectations: consistent and predictable conditional relations emerging between elements of Classes I and III, and either no consistent relations or an unpredictable pattern of relations between elements of Classes II or IV and any other class.

A merger of classes I and III might not have taken place, however, if subjects had learned during the teaching phases not just to select X in the presence of the appropriate sample but to take the negative stimulus into account also. For example, subjects might have learned to relate Sample A1 to Comparison X, but only when C2 was the other comparison. If C2 had acquired such contextual control, the relation between B1 and X would have emerged only when C2 was the other comparison and might not have emerged if E4 had been presented as a comparison along with X. Similarly, subjects might have learned to relate Sample D3 to Comparison X only when E4 was the other comparison. The new relation between F3 and X would then have emerged only when E4, but not C2, was the other comparison. Tests for Class I, as given, could not have revealed such contextual control by negative comparison stimuli because those tests never presented subjects with the latter kind of options—Comparisons X and E4 along with Sample B1, and Comparisons X and C2 along with Sample F3.

In tests for the merger of Classes I and III, however, some trials did pair X and E4 as comparisons when B1 was the sample. With C2 failing to appear as a comparison along with X on such trials, contextual control by C2 would have prevented the demonstration of an emergent relation between Sample B1 and Comparison X. Similarly, the relation between Sample F3 and Comparison X might have failed to emerge during Class I + III merger tests when the other comparison was C2 rather than E4. And so, if the comparison that was presented along with X had acquired contextual control, the merger of Classes I and III could not have taken place; the tests for B1F3 and F3B1 relations would have turned out negative. None of these possible negative results, however, were observed. The actual union of Classes I and III demonstrated that the possibility of contextual control by negative stimuli in the baseline conditional discriminations had not been realized. Therefore, the next experiment established such contextual control explicitly, with a view to finding out whether it would prevent the union of Classes I and III.

TEACH

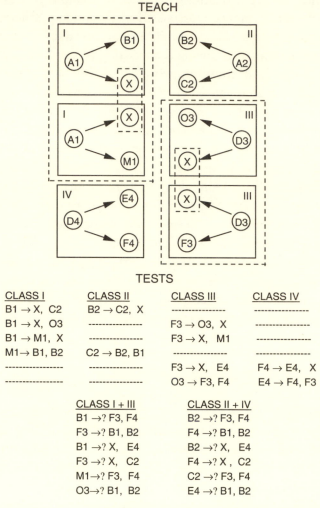

TESTS

CLASS I	CLASS II	CLASS III	CLASS IV
B1 → X, C2	B2 → C2, X	----------------	----------------
B1 → X, O3	----------------	F3 → O3, X	----------------
B1 → M1, X	----------------	F3 → X, M1	----------------
M1→ B1, B2	C2 → B2, B1	----------------	----------------
----------------	----------------	F3 → X, E4	F4 → E4, X
----------------	----------------	O3 → F3, F4	E4 → F4, F3

CLASS I + III	CLASS II + IV
B1 →? F3, F4	B2 →? F3, F4
F3 →? B1, B2	F4 →? B1, B2
B1 →? X, E4	B2 →? X, E4
F3 →? X, C2	F4 →? X , C2
M1→? F3, F4	C2 →? F3, F4
O3→? B1, B2	E4 →? B1, B2

Figure 12-8 about here. Teaching trials are shown within the solid-line boxes, where arrows connect samples and comparisons that become related via directly programmed reinforcement contingencies. Broken lines enclose the two classes that might be expected to merge because they both contain the element, X; the two representations of stimulus X within each expected class are also enclosed within broken lines. In the test trials for Classes I, II, III, IV, arrows connecting each sample to one of the comparisons denote sample-comparison relations that would indicate positive test outcomes. Because none of the classes are expected to merge, the tested sample-comparison relations in the merger trials (combined Classes I + III, and II + IV) are not expected to be consistent—denoted by question marks beside the arrows.

520

The new feature in the second experiment was the inclusion of negative stimuli in the programmed reinforcement contingencies; subjects had to attend to the incorrect comparisons during the teaching phases. Figure 12-8 shows how this was done. The contingencies that established Classes I and II in the first experiment are diagrammed in the uppermost pair of boxes and those that established Classes III and IV are in the bottom pair (with Class III, however, now in the right column and Class IV in the left column). Negative stimuli were brought into the contingencies by means of the trial types in the center boxes. Subjects learned that when A1 was the sample, Comparison X was positive if C2 or O3 was the other comparison but not if M1 appeared with X. When the sample was D3, Comparison X was positive if the other comparison was M1 or E4 but not if O3 was shown along with X.

If the new contingencies gave rise to equivalence relations, one consequence would be the enlargement of Classes I and III, as shown by the pairs of boxes enclosed within broken lines. Class I would grow to include Sample A1 and the comparisons directly related to A1—B1, M1, and X—the last, however, only if the other comparison was C2 or O3 and not M1. Class III would grow to include Sample D3 and the stimuli directly related to D3—F3, O3, and X—the last, however, only if the other comparison was M1 or E4 and not O3. Classes II and IV would remain unchanged.

A second consequence would be the prevention of a merger of Classes I and III, even though X was a member of both. This is because X would belong to each class under different circumstances—in different contexts.

Fucini confirmed the composition of the four classes by demonstrating the emergent conditional discriminations that are summarized by the first six rows of test trials in the lower section of Figure 12-8. As before, a positive test trial would find subjects relating the sample (shown at the left of the arrow) to the comparison the arrow points to. Subjects would relate the other comparison stimulus to a different sample (in another type of trial), indicating membership of that comparison in a different class. For example, Classes I and III would be—and were—confirmed and differentiated from each other when subjects, presented with Comparisons X and M1, chose X if F3 was the sample but chose M1 if B1 was the sample; and when given X and O3 as comparisons, they chose X if B1 was the sample but O3 if F3 was the sample. Other test trials, like those in the first experiment, confirmed Classes II and IV and differentiated them from Classes I and III.

This time, the membership of Stimulus X in both Classes I and III would not be expected to bring about a merger of those classes. Contextual control by negative comparison stimuli in the baseline conditional discriminations would keep X in Class 1 as long as the other comparison was C2 or O3 and in Class 3 as long as the other comparison was M1 or E4. And again, Classes II and IV would be expected to maintain their independence from each other and from the other classes because they contained no element in common. All of the tests for class merger, therefore, would be expected to prove negative.

Class merger test trials are shown at the bottom of Figure 12-8. In the absence of class union, no predictable consistency would be expected in a subject's choice of comparisons on any of these test trials. This unpredictability is indicated by the question mark beside each arrow. A merger of Classes I and III would have found subjects relating samples from Class I to comparisons from Class III, and vice-versa, but such relations were not observed in the tests. Because class union would have placed Stimulus X in both classes, without restriction, subjects would have been expected to select X if the sample was B1, even though the other comparison was E4; and again, to select X if the sample was F3, even though the other comparison was C2. The failure to observe such consistency in the tests confirmed the separation of Classes I and III. And, as was expected, tests for the merger of Class II or IV with other classes also proved negative. In the second experiment, therefore, deliberately programmed contextual control by the comparison stimuli succeeded in preventing the class merger that had taken place in the first experiment when such contextual control was absent.

The final question to be answered was whether contextual control by the comparison stimuli could not only prevent class union but could also break down a union that had already taken place. To answer this question, Fucini used the subjects from the first experiment—who had not shown contextual control—and exposed them to the procedures of the second experiment. In the first experiment, the baseline contingencies had left open the possibility of contextual control by the comparisons but had not required it. Although the possibility existed, it did not materialize; the merger of Classes I and III had shown the absence of contextual control. In the third experiment, contextual control was built into the reinforcement contingencies. Would the explicit establishment of contextual control bring about a separation of the two classes that had previously merged?

After establishment of the baselines shown in Figure 12-8, the first tests confirmed the maintenance of the four classes (with the expected enlargement of Classes I and III). On the other hand, tests for class union were now negative; subjects no longer matched stimuli from Class I to stimuli from Class III, or vice versa, and the selection or rejection of comparison Stimulus X depended on the other comparison. The explicit establishment of contextual control by the comparison stimuli had succeeded in breaking down the original class union; Classes I and III were now separated from each other.

Whenever we find ourselves able to bring a phenomenon under experimental control, turning it on and off at will, the hope always is that we are dealing with something real. Indeed, the experience of scientists in general has taught them that the laboratory *is* part of the real world, that laboratory findings involve processes that operate everywhere. Although the laboratory rarely mirrors the outside world exactly, it does provide a distilled version of real phenomena, relatively unencumbered by variables that ordinarily make analysis difficult or even impossible. And so, even though some will argue that the experiments I have just described do not take all relevant factors into account, I find myself viewing them as a controlled demonstration of what happens in nature. They show me clearly that contextual control does not create equivalence relations but rather, that context prevents lower-level contingencies from generating potentially maladaptive equivalence relations, and breaks down equivalence relations that other contingencies have already generated.

Contextual Control and Negative Equivalence Tests

I noted before that seemingly negative equivalence tests may reflect a failure of laboratory contingencies to generate contextual control. The opposite may also happen: negative equivalence tests may reflect an experimenter's failure to recognize the actuality of contextual control. Consider the contingencies that are outlined in the left section of Figure 12-9. Studies of equivalence frequently use this type of baseline. When the sample is A1, the correct comparison is either B1 or C1, depending on which is presented to the subject; when the sample is A2, the correct comparison is either B2 or C2, again depending on which is available for the subject to choose. To determine whether the baseline relations A1B1, A1C1, A2B2, and A2C2 are symmetric, we give test trials in which the sample is one of the former comparisons—B1, C1, B2, or C2—and the comparisons are the two former samples—A1 and A2. Such trials test for emergence of the relations B1A1, C1A1, B2A2, and C2A2; if the original relations are symmetric, we expect the subject now to select A1 if the test sample is B1 or C1 and to select A2 if the sample is B2 or C2. These expectations are based on the assumption that we have described the baseline conditional discriminations accurately. If we overlook that assumption, negative test results may lead us to conclude erroneously that the baseline relations were not symmetric. Inaccurate specification of the relations generated by the baseline contingencies may arise from several sources.

Failures to recognize contextual control. In most studies, our description of the baseline relations specifies only pairs of stimuli, each composed of a sample and its correct comparison—for example, A1B1. For a conditional relation that involved nothing more than stimulus pairs, a valid symmetry test would indeed have to probe only for the B1A1 relation. But for a baseline relation that was controlled by context, an accurate description of the relation would have to include at least one more stimulus—the context. If the conditional relation between Sample A1 and Comparison B1 depended on the presence of Comparison B2, the standard test for the symmetry of the A1B1 relation—the B1A1 probe—is likely to prove negative because of the absence of B2. Although the negative result would accurately document the absence of symmetry in the tested equivalence relation, the tested relation would not be the actual relation. And so, the negative result would not justify a conclusion that the baseline contingencies had failed to generate a symmetric relation.

Such a misconception of the relation that is being tested can also negate the validity of the standard transitivity/equivalence tests, which probe for the emergence of BC and CB relations. For example, the baseline contingencies bring A1 into relation with both B1 and C1 but under different circumstances—the presence, respectively, of B2 or C2. If a complete description of the baseline relations required negative stimuli to be specified as context, the contextual differences—a negative B stimulus in the AB pairs and a negative C stimulus in the AC pairs—might keep the AB and AC pairs from belonging to the same equivalence relation. In that case, seeming transitivity and equivalence tests would be meaningless, their results predictable, if at all, only on grounds other than equivalence. (See Carrigan and Sidman, 1992, pp. 195-198, for other instances in which inclusion of the AB and BC pairs in different equivalence relations makes transitivity/equivalence tests meaningless.)

Sample-comparison relations: one-to-many and many-to-one. A frequently used paradigm for studying equivalence relations has each sample being related to more than one comparison, a "one-to-many" arrangement. The diagram on the left side of Figure 12-9 shows examples—in this instance, one sample to two comparisons. The diagram on the right side illustrates another paradigm. Here, more than one sample is related to each comparison, a "many-to-one" arrangement—in this instance, two samples to one comparison. In the terminology of Fields et al. (1984), the one-to-many design uses samples as nodes and the many-to-one design uses comparisons as

"ONE-TO-MANY"   "MANY-TO-ONE"

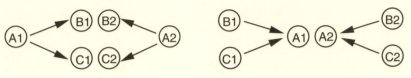

Figure 12-9. AB and AC baselines in two arrangements for studying equivalence relations. Arrows point from samples to correct comparisons. On the left side ("one-to-many"), each sample is related to two comparisons; on the right side ("many-to-one"), two samples are related to each comparison.

nodes. The many-to-one paradigm has begun to appear more frequently in published reports because of findings that it is sometimes more effective in generating the kinds of emergent performances that document equivalence relations (Barnes, 1994; Saunders, Saunders, Williams, & Spradlin, 1993; Saunders, Wachter, & Spradlin, 1988; Spradlin & Saunders, 1986; Spradlin et al., 1992; Urcuioli & Zentall, 1993).

This difference between the one-to-many and the many-to-one paradigms has been called an effect of "directionality," a term that is a product of an implicit (sometimes explicit) linear chaining, linking, stimulus-response, or associative conception of the derived "network" of emergent conditional discriminations that define an equivalence relation (for further discussion of such conceptions, see pp. 83-86, 110-111, 114, 352-354, 380-381; 539). For example, instead of illustrating the many-to-one arrangement as in the right side of Figure 12-9, one might simply reproduce the left-hand diagram with the arrows reversed in direction. But changing the direction of the arrows alters in no way the procedures for establishing baseline conditional discriminations. The direction in which arrows point in our laboratory notebooks makes no contact with our experimental subjects. The emphasis on a seeming directionality is an instance of theory not only becoming divorced from reality but actually keeping us from looking at factors in the historical or current environment that might underlie different outcomes of the two paradigms.

A difference between the two paradigms that does make contact with the subjects' behavior in equivalence tests appears when we probe for emergent BC and CB conditional discriminations. After establishing a one-to-many baseline, we test for sample-comparison relations between B- and C-stimuli that had previously functioned only as comparisons; after establishing a many-to-one baseline, we test for relations between stimuli that had previously functioned only as samples. As has been pointed out elsewhere (Lazar & Scarisbrick, 1993; Saunders & Spradlin, 1989; Saunders et al., 1993; Sidman et al., 1982, Exp. 4), the conditional-discrimination procedure we have been using involves successive discriminations between sample stimuli and simultaneous discriminations between comparison stimuli. With a many-to-one baseline, therefore, the tests for emergent relations ask for simultaneous discriminations between stimuli (comparisons) that had previously been presented to the subject separately (as samples); with a one-to-many baseline, the tests do the opposite, asking for successive discriminations between stimuli (samples) that the subject previously had always seen together (as comparisons).

This change in the nature of the discriminations from baseline to tests—from simultaneous to successive discriminations or vice-versa—seems of greater potential relevance than "directionality." Contrary to a suggestion offered by Barnes (1994, pp. 117-118), differences between simultaneous and successive discriminations are procedural, not theoretical, and are relevant not just to equivalence relations but to the more general domain of stimulus control. Any description of equivalence phenomena must not only be internally consistent but must also fit into that more general framework of data and principles. A literature on successive- versus simultaneous-discrimination procedures does exist (for example, Bitterman, Tyler, & Elam, 1955; Spence, 1952; Weise & Bitterman, 1951) but definitive experiments remain to be done.

Yet another factor that might cause one-to-many and many-to-one baselines to yield different equivalence test results can be pin-pointed by taking into account the possibility of contextual control by negative stimuli in the baseline conditional discriminations. All sample-comparison relations would then come under the control of different negative stimuli in the one-to-many paradigm: the A1B1 relation under the contextual control of Comparison B2; the A1C1 relation under the control of Comparison C2; the A2B2 relation under the control of Comparison B1; and the A2C2 relation under the control of Comparison C1. As I pointed out above, this kind of contextual control in the one-to-many baseline would bring the AB and AC pairs into different equivalence relations, making the results of BC and CB tests unpredictable on the grounds of equivalence.

In the many-to-one paradigm, however, contextual control by comparisons would place all sample-comparison pairs that constituted a potential equivalence relation under the control of the same negative stimulus: B1A1 and C1A1 pairs would both depend on the presence of Comparison A2; B2A2 and C2A2 pairs would both depend on the presence of Comparison A1. The B1A1 and C1A1 pairs would still be members of one equivalence relation; B2A2 and C2A2 would be members of another. Even with contextual control by the negative stimuli, the results of BC and CB tests in the many-to-one paradigm would permit valid inferences about equivalence relations.

Contextual control by negative stimuli in the one-to-many situation is therefore more likely to bring about varied and uninterpretable equivalence test results than in the many-to-one situation. Seeming failures of the one-to-many paradigm to generate equivalence relations may, then, reflect not a theoretical insufficiency in one or another method of describing equivalence relations but rather, a failure to recognize the possible role of contextual control by negative stimuli in the baseline conditional discriminations.

Contextual Control and the Mathematical Logic of Equivalence

In the process of doing the series of experiments described in this book—and while doing the book itself—changes took place in my own thinking about equivalence. One development was my increasing appreciation of mathematical set theory's utility for describing and predicting behavioral phenomena (see pp. 550-553 for further discussion of the correspondence between general mathematical formulations and behavioral particulars). One of the extensions from the mathematical definition of the equivalence relation was the introduction of the set-theory concept of class *union* to describe what had previously been talked of as *transfer of function* (pp. 392-393). This permitted the substitution of a descriptive for a theoretical term, eliminating a presumed behavioral process—transfer of function—that had previously been used to explain emergent performances but that required explanation itself.

Class union refers to the merger of classes that possess one or more elements in common. But the possession of one or more elements in common does not always result in class union. When it does not, set theory talks about class *intersection*. In analyzing behavior, we have to go beyond the descriptive terms and ask why the possession of common elements sometimes results in class union and sometimes in class intersection. Contextual control provides the answer to this question. It prevents the merger of smaller into larger classes and it breaks down larger into smaller classes. Contextual control determines whether the possession of an element in common will bring about a union or an intersection of classes— whether classes will combine, bringing the common element into the larger class, or whether classes will remain separate, with the common element sometimes belonging to one and sometimes to the other.

Contextual control, however, is a product of behavioral, not mathematical processes. The mathematics of set theory permits a substantial degree of descriptive consistency and predictive accuracy in the behavioral analysis of equivalence relations even when those relations come under contextual control, but the mathematics does not predict when or how control by context arises. It may arise in conjunction with simple or compound discriminative stimuli, first- or second-order conditional stimuli, primary or conditioned reinforcers, setting stimuli, or any other members of an analytic unit. It is subject to all of the factors—reinforcement variables, temporal and schedule variables, stimulus and response variables, motivational variables, and so on—that enter into the establishment of the analytic unit itself. Contextual control arises *because* the reinforcement contingencies permit or demand it. Unlike the equivalence relation itself, which, although it is the product of a reinforcement contingency is not actually incorporated in its conditions, control over the relation by context is a condition that the contingency does specify.

That is the background of the suggestion that was advanced in the *Contextual Control* paper for a resolution of the problem of "why the context itself does not become a member of all the emergent classes and, by virtue of its common membership, condense all of the classes into one" (p. 507). Because equivalence relations are not directly specified in a reinforcement contingency, it is possible for a conflict to exist between the two outcomes of a contingency: (a) the creation of an analytic unit and (b) the formation of an equivalence relation. In a five-term unit, for example, if the contextual stimulus (the second-order conditional stimulus), by virtue of being an element common to all of the equivalence classes that the contingency makes possible, were to cause a union of those classes, then the subject would be unable to meet the terms of the contingency. On the one hand, the contingency calls for differential control by discriminative stimuli in each three-term unit and by conditional stimuli in each four-term unit; on the other hand, the contingency creates equivalence classes containing a common contextual element that could wipe out differential control by bringing all discriminative and conditional stimuli together into a single class. Our suggestion was that creation of the unit takes priority. The explicit inclusion of differential stimulus control in the contingency counteracts the formation of equivalence classes; the latter are not only not explicitly included in the contingency but would actually prevent the conditions that are included from being met. And so, behavioral processes determine which aspect of the mathematically derived description is applicable; in this instance, whether control by context brings about class union or class intersection.

Epilogue

My story, of course, is not over, but I am not sure I shall ever be able to contribute anything more fundamental than the studies I have described here. Many people have been investigating equivalence relations in behavior and are continuing to do so, and I hope more will enter the field. They will clarify unsolved problems and will extend the methodology, data, and theory to new areas of research and application. They will also consider philosophical ramifications and will construct new theoretical frameworks. Their stories, too—past and future—should be told either directly, as I have done, or indirectly as components of more complete reviews of the field.

But several matters did not come to the fore during the telling of the story and some readers will be looking for these. Throughout the narrative, I tried to indicate directions in which I thought it important for basic research to move but except while discussing the earliest experiments, I said little more about new applications that might be feasible. Also, I talked little about the nature and role of theory in advancing our knowledge of equivalence phenomena. Perhaps I can still contribute constructively to these matters. Let me end by expanding previous discussions of possible applications and of theoretical formulations.

Equivalence Relations Outside the Laboratory

In experiments on such matters as concept formation, classification and categorization, remembering, equivalence, and many other aspects of learning, laboratory subjects have shown themselves capable of truly astonishing performances. Subjects have included not only college students and bright older children but also children younger than six years and both adults and children with severe learning disabilities. Nonhuman subjects, too, have revealed unsuspected capabilities. What distinguishes the studies of equivalence relations from most other areas of experimentation is the emergence in the laboratory of startlingly complex performances that have not been explicitly taught to the subjects. (Another type of emergent learning can be seen in the work on exclusion, as in Dixon, 1977; McIlvane and Stoddard, 1981, 1985.) I noted in several places that this feature of our work on equivalence relations played a major role in the decision to continue in that area. What I did not emphasize was the gulf between many subjects' accomplishments inside and outside the laboratory. Techniques that succeed in teaching so much even to supposedly unteachable people have become standard in the laboratory but have not been adopted by those whose major responsibility is to carry out instruction outside the laboratory. The separation between research and application in education can be characterized not merely as a gulf but as an abyss.

From research to pedagogy. In all areas of medicine and engineering, practitioners keep up with research publications in order to make use of new discoveries. They adapt, modify, combine, and, where necessary, develop them further. I know of no service area except education in which practitioners habitually disregard fundamental research. It is true that the engineering and administrative details necessary for any large-scale application of laboratory-derived principles and teaching methods have yet to be worked out, but administrators of pedagogy have characteristically shown themselves unwilling to take on that responsibility. Even when educators do acknowledge the possible relevance of research, they insist that the basic researchers also carry out the task of arranging for and accomplishing the potential applications.

It has been painful for me and my colleagues to experience this widespread disregard for our work on equivalence by school administrators and by the faculties of institutions that are supposed to train the teachers of children. Particularly disappointing has been the failure to apply our techniques to the teaching of children who show learning deficiencies associated with mental retardation, autism, and some kinds of congenital and accidental brain damage. Many of our experiments have used such people as subjects, not only because their relatively unsophisticated language repertoires and simpler behavioral histories make their data more easily interpretable but because they are of interest and concern in their own right—they need all the help that is available.

The stakes, therefore, are too high for us to retire into our laboratories and give up the struggle to influence educational practice. Efforts to reach the teaching establishment must still be made. One path might be to join those who are reacting to the deficiencies of our public educational system by proposing that it be handed over to private enterprise. Unfortunately, there is no indication so far that the advocates of privatization are any more open than is the current educational establishment to the practical use of laboratory-derived teaching methods. A second option, short of abandoning basic research and instead, gaining teacher certification in order to work within the system, is to try to improve our channels of communication. Attempts to present research findings in nontechnical language have been made (for example: Hamblin, Buckholdt, Ferritor, Kozloff, & Blackwell, 1971; Holland et al., 1976; Skinner, 1968; Stromer, Mackay, & Stoddard, 1992; Sulzer-Azaroff & Mayer, 1986, 1991), but applications based on equivalence research have not yet been featured in texts for teachers.

A third option is also available for the possible improvement of communication between researchers and educators. It is only fair to point out that the incredibly effective teaching methods that have become commonplace in experimental work on equivalence relations have been demonstrated only in piecemeal fashion. Because most of the laboratory teaching has been intended only to establish representative behavioral baselines for research purposes, the kinds of performances that have been taught have varied from study to study. One experiment, for example, might have taught subjects to read and to understand spoken and written color names; another might have taught the relations among a restricted sample of spoken and written numbers, number names, and quantities; still others might have taught the same kinds of relations among a sample of objects or pictures and their spoken and written names, between the names of a few people and their pictures, or between some of the spoken and written words in two or more languages. As yet, however, nobody has taken all these individual relations, enlarged the samples beyond the few specimens that had sufficed for research purposes, and put them together into a single "curriculum." If these and other important kinds of equivalence relations and procedures for teaching them were put together into an instructional sequence, designed both for computer and table-top application, and the whole package were handed to educators, then, perhaps, a fruitful collaboration between classroom and laboratory might begin. It is worth a try.

Laboratory and classroom. Efficient as the teaching techniques used in equivalence research have proven, the relaxation of requirements for experimental rigor outside the laboratory brings about an even greater efficiency. Conditions and procedures in the classroom need not be as austere as in the laboratory. For example, it is not necessary to wait until pupils reach some rigorous learning criterion and then prepare them to work without reinforcement so that we can test whether the performances we are most interested in have emerged. Because research has already shown that the procedures work, teaching and testing can be mixed from the beginning, with consistent reinforcement both for baseline and emergent performances. As teachers, we do not have to prove that the emergent performances would have come about even if we had not reinforced them.

Similarly, use of the techniques in the classroom does not require laboratory-like constancy of method or environment. Reinforcements can vary; instructions can be given (with care; once having received instructions, pupils sometimes come to depend on them); with language proficient pupils, verbal rules can often short-circuit lengthy trial-and-error sequences; the presence of other students, alterations of the physical surroundings, and other situational variations that would be considered unacceptable in the laboratory may even facilitate the newly learned performances in more extensive environments. In general, any supposition that a teacher has to act like a basic scientist when applying scientific discoveries is unwarranted.

Still, even though laboratory methods are often devised not for practical teaching but for the study of fundamental behavioral processes, the techniques are then available for application outside the laboratory. Most schools of Education, departments of Psychology, and even some degree or training programs in Behavior Analysis, however, give no instruction on how to apply laboratory findings in the classroom or in other educational environments. They teach neither research-validated procedures nor their underlying principles. Behavior analysts, psychologists, and teachers must therefore educate themselves and continue independently to refresh their knowledge about effective instructional technologies that come out of research laboratories.

Research done with computers, and even with nonhumans, is not out of bounds. A behavior analyst worthy of certification will know how to adapt simple- and conditional-discrimination procedures from automated to table-top use. Clinicians whose first concern is the clients' welfare will be able to adapt useful methods even from studies done with nonhumans. For years, experimenters have been teaching nonhuman subjects behavior of a complexity that many had considered beyond the capacity of children or people classified as retarded. Children, both those with and those without special needs, have suffered from the educational establishment's failure to meet this challenge.

Theoretical Matters

As I indicated in Chapter 1, my colleagues and I were greatly surprised when our first severely retarded subject showed himself suddenly able to read and understand twenty printed words. We continued to be surprised as the story unfolded and revealed new and evermore complex features of emergent relations among words, things, events, and other aspects of our subjects' environments, particularly between elements that bore no physical resemblance to each other. I can perhaps be excused for viewing what we saw in the first and in subsequent experiments as something new: no other experimental behavior analysts had given the emergence of arbitrary environmental relations any attention at all; neither the phenomenon nor the methods for generating it had ever been listed among the tools available for applied behavior analysis; and no theoretical behavior analysts had ever cited the phenomenon as something predictable on the basis of known data or theoretical formulations. I can perhaps also be excused for some exasperation at a few theorists who, having been shown the phenomenon, then treated it as something that was to have been predicted or expected. I had to wonder why none of them had ever done or even thought of the experiments. There have been times when I have seriously entertained the uncharitable notion that whenever new phenomena are found or demonstrated, theoretical vultures move in to explain them away or to trivialize them.

The descriptive system. It will not surprise anyone, then, to find that for me, the equivalence relation is neither a theoretical entity nor an entity or process that is beyond observation. My own theorizing has been directed not so much at an explanation of equivalence relations but rather, at the formulation of a descriptive system—a consistent, coherent, and parsimonious way of defining and talking about the observed phenomena. Mathematical set theory contains tools that allow me to meet all of these goals—consistency, coherence, and parsimony. My colleagues and I therefore adapted set theory's definition of the equivalence relation, a definition that has a large number of regularities already built in. That is to say, the regularities themselves define the equivalence relation. Any relation that is to be called an equivalence relation *must* show those regularities. This necessity gives the descriptive system one of the flavors of an explanatory theory; it permits us to make predictions. The predictions, however, are already incorporated in the definition. The behavior-analytic task is to find out whether the regularities the descriptive system requires are in fact observed. That those regularities have been so reliably confirmed continues to astonish me. I know of no formal theory that makes so many behavioral observations so consistently predictable.

In the course of writing the present story, I also found other components of mathematical set theory to be useful for the description of equivalence phenomena. In particular, the fundamental concepts of set union and set intersection permit us to include within the same descriptive system behavioral phenomena that had previously seemed to require the postulation of a separate process—*transfer* of function. Many kinds of functions have perfectly adequate behavioral definitions: events that are involved in a reinforcement contingency may exert a primary or conditioned reinforcing function, a simple or conditional discriminative function, a setting function, an eliciting function, and so on. Events that perform a particular function become partitioned off into a class whose members are related by equivalence. Different classes that possess members in common may merge into a single class—set union—or may remain independent—set intersection. Contextual components of the contingency determine whether set union or intersection takes place. None of this requires more than a description of the events that make up an observable reinforcement contingency.

Still, there is more to equivalence relations than mathematical set theory can describe. If equivalence relations are a product of reinforcement contingencies, all behavioral variables that are relevant to reinforcement contingencies must be relevant also to equivalence relations. Beyond this truism, some investigators have suggested that the mathematically derived description of equivalence relations is incomplete because new—previously unknown—behavioral variables or theoretical principles are involved. Any discovery of new variables is, of course, an exciting event. Nevertheless, such discoveries may introduce interpretive complexities and require difficult conceptual changes. It is wise, therefore, to follow a conservative course and search carefully for alternative explanations before trying to work a new variable into an existing formulation. Several instances in the literature on equivalence are worth noting.

Structural determinants: directionality. A variable that some have called *directionality* was suggested by studies in which the emergence of new conditional discriminations seemed to depend on whether the baseline consisted of individual samples being conditionally related to many comparisons, or of individual comparisons being related to many samples (for a review, see Fields, Adams, &

Verhave, 1993). In specifying the ordered stimulus pairs that make up an equivalence relation, the mathematics takes no account of which member of a pair is listed first; the AB pair has no properties that differentiate it from the BA pair in the same relation. Behavioral evidence for such differentiation would suggest that the mathematical properties do not completely describe equivalence relations in behavior. But, as I indicated in Chapter 12, the effects of directionality might have explanations that are based on known behavioral variables and principles of stimulus control. For one thing, some tests for emergent relations require subjects to shift from simultaneous to successive discriminations or vice versa, the type of shift depending on whether the original training established relations between one sample and many comparisons or between many samples and one comparison (pp. 526-527). Also, contextual control by negative stimuli may make equivalence tests of a one-to-many baseline less likely to produce interpretable results than tests of a many-to-one baseline (pp. 527-528). If such discriminative shifts and/or contextual control were shown to account for the effects of directionality, no new variable would have to be cited and the mathematical description would retain an undiminished utility. Because definitive tests of these possibilities are yet to be made, we have to reserve judgment about the status of directionality as a primary variable.

Structural determinants: nodal distance. A second proposed new variable has been called *nodal distance* (again, see Fields, Adams, & Verhave, 1993, for a review). A *node* is a stimulus that is paired by explicit reinforcement contingencies with at least two other stimuli: if we establish AB and BC pairs, B is a node; if we also establish CD pairs, both B and C are nodes. Nodal *distance* simply specifies the smallest number of baseline nodes that are required for particular new stimulus pairs to become members of a relation: AC pairs can be derived from a baseline that involves only node B, so there is one unit of nodal distance between A and C; emergent AD pairs require the baseline nodes B and C, so there are two units of nodal distance between A and D. (How to fit emergent pairs that define symmetry and reflexivity into this system is a problem that need not concern us here.)

Like *directionality*, the term *nodal distance* arises from a linear-associative conception of stimulus control. I find the term uncongenial because I have not been convinced either that the concept of association is useful for describing equivalence phenomena (pp. 110-111) or that stimulus control in general is best characterized as a linear process or structure. The implication that hypothetical structural entities are at work can be avoided by specifying not a *distance between* stimuli but rather, the least *number* of nodes that must be involved in the conditional discriminations that are needed for a particular stimulus pair to be included in an equivalence relation. That is to say, for *nodal distance*, substitute *nodal number*. Nodal distance is a property of a hypothetical structure but nodal number is directly observable in the experimental procedures. Before the term *node* was introduced (Fields et al., 1984; Fields & Verhave, 1987) the analogous term *stage* had become common in the mediated-generalization literature (for example, Jenkins, 1963). Sidman and Tailby (1982) and Sidman et al. (1985) borrowed that term and talked about *n-stage* relations. Here, however, in order to maintain contact with the literature on nodal effects, I shall use the concept of nodal number.

Nodal number might affect equivalence relations in two general ways. The first: whether or not we can include a particular stimulus pair in an equivalence relation may be determined by the number of nodes that are required to derive the pair. This possibility seems to me not unreasonable; the likelihood that a relation between two stimuli will emerge may well be inversely related to the minimum number of nodes that are required to generate the relation. Indeed, nodal number was first suggested as a variable by studies in which the emergence of new conditional discriminations that helped define an equivalence relation seemed to depend on the number of necessary nodes in the baseline relations (Dube, Green, & Serna, 1993; Fields et al., 1990; Kennedy, 1991; Saunders, Wachter, & Spradlin, 1988; Sidman et al., 1985, 1986; Sidman & Tailby, 1982). Such a finding would raise no problem for a description of equivalence relations that is based on set theory. The mathematics does not pretend to provide a basis for predicting whether or not a particular set of baseline contingencies will generate equivalence relations. It only tells us how to describe an equivalence relation and, therefore, how to find out whether particular event pairs belong to that relation (see, for example, Carrigan, 1986; Saunders & Green, 1992).

Nevertheless, I am not yet satisfied with the currently available data. Do they definitely show nodal number to be primarily responsible for the reported effects? I see several experimental and interpretative problems. First, the use of only two comparisons per trial in some of the experiments creates a potential for uncertainty in interpreting equivalence test results because subjects can meet the requirements of the baseline reinforcement contingencies in two ways: by selecting correct stimuli or by rejecting incorrect stimuli (Carrigan & Sidman, 1992; Johnson & Sidman, 1993). As conditional discriminations are added to a baseline, the probability increases that a subject's bases for choice will vary—it becomes more likely that some comparisons will be chosen by selection and others by rejection. Such inconsistency can be expected to increase the variability among test outcomes as the number of nodes increases. One way to reduce the likelihood that a subject will choose by rejection is to present more than two comparisons per trial. In one study (Kennedy, 1991), a change from two to three comparisons greatly decreased the influence of nodal number on the outcome of equivalence tests. I would therefore like to see more of the relevant experiments repeated with three or more comparison stimuli per trial.

Second, in some experiments, the particular comparison pairs that were presented to subjects during test trials may have favored the emergence of some conditional relations over others. Also, varying the negative stimuli that are presented along with a particular positive comparison during tests may bring about test results that are independent of the baseline contingencies (Harrison & Green, 1990). Positive and negative comparison stimuli in any test trial should be given equal reinforcement histories. Again, when this precaution was taken (Kennedy, 1991, Experiment 2), the influence of nodal number was greatly reduced. It is not clear, however, whether the reduction came about because of the restrictions on the negative stimuli, the shift to three comparisons per trial, or both factors.

Third, many of the nodal-number effects that some of these studies claimed to show are small, particularly when the special zero-node case (symmetry testing) is left out of consideration. (Symmetry tests are special in that they ask subjects to relate stimuli that they had already learned to relate during baseline training.) A continuous relation between nodal number and the emergence of new conditional discriminations was not at all evident, the major effect seeming to occur between one and two nodes. The question that must be asked here is, "What happens when the number of required baseline nodes increases from one to two but does not happen at higher nodal levels?" Is it possible that an exposure to one- and two-node tests teaches subjects something that then helps them with tests for emergent relations that require more than two nodes? If this is so, it might be possible to demonstrate nodal-number effects more conclusively by testing first for the emergence of relations that require many nodes, without having given previous tests.

My fourth problem, related to the third, is that with repeated testing, equivalence has been eventually demonstrated regardless of nodal number. That is to say, nodal number appeared primarily not to influence whether new performances emerged but rather, how long it took for them to emerge (delayed emergence; see pp.273, 511-512). An evaluation of this finding requires a more complete understanding of the phenomenon of delayed emergence. The appropriate question posed by these data, then, is not, "Does the number of nodes determine whether two stimuli become related by equivalence?" but rather, "How does the number of nodes interact with variables that produce delayed emergence?" Attempts to answer this question will also help to determine whether the critical factor is nodal number itself or other variables that are correlated with nodal number.

A final problem with some of the existing data on the possible influence of nodal number in the establishment of equivalence relations comes from the confounding of nodal number with another feature of the baseline: stimulus pairs that are required for the emergence of other pairs may themselves be either derived or directly taught. Sidman and Tailby (1982) cited an example in conjunction with the two-node baselines shown in Figure 6-2 (p. 196). There, subjects were taught AB, AC, and DC conditional discriminations. Two derived two-node pairs of conditionally related stimuli, BD and DB, were possible. The derivation of BD required two sets of conditional relations, BC and CD—both of them also derived. The other derived two-node pair, DB, differed: of its two sets of requisite conditional relations, only one, CB, was itself derived; the other, DC, had been directly taught. Even when nodal number remains constant, this kind of difference may cloud any conclusion that dissimilarities between the stimulus-pair members of an equivalence relation can be attributed to variations in the number of required nodes.

It remains to be proven that the inclusion of a higher-level event pair in an equivalence relation is influenced by whether the requisite lower-level pairs have themselves to be derived or are directly taught. In an extreme case, having taught subjects AB, BC, CD, and DE conditional discriminations, we would be more likely to observe emergence of the three-node AE pairs (transitivity test, requiring no other derived relations) than the three-node EA pairs (equivalence test, requiring at least four other derived relations). This question must be cleared up before we can say with confidence that nodal number by itself is a factor in the delayed emergence of derived stimulus-stimulus relations.

There is yet a second way in which it has been suggested that nodal number might influence equivalence relations: even after stimulus pairs have been shown to be included in an equivalence relation, those pairs may still differ from each other as a function of the number of nodes that each had required. That is to say, differences in the number of required baseline nodes may induce permanent dissimilarities among the pairs of stimuli that make up a given equivalence relation. Fields et al. (1993, pp. 702-703) suggested that the stimulus pairs within a given equivalence relation may differ in their "relatedness," their "associative strength," or the "partial substitutability" of their components.

Epilogue

Again, a terminological confusion needs clarification: the notion that the members of a class can be differentially related to each other. Any class is defined by one or more characteristics that are common to all of its elements. Members of a class must, by definition, be substitutable for each other. They are, however, substitutable only with respect to the properties that define the class—the bases for the partition. Members of a class that is defined, say, by the color red need not be equal in any other respect; objects that are red are likely to differ from each other in shape, size, and many other properties. Without the common characteristic, however, the class does not exist—cannot be defined. To say that the members of a class differ in their relatedness, then, is either a contradiction in terms or must refer to differences in features other than those which define the class.

It should come as no surprise, then, when differences are found between the pairs of elements that constitute an equivalence relation. Such differences are to be expected on the grounds that any given pair will belong to more than one relation—any given element will belong to more than one class. We might, for example, teach a subject to select an appropriate comparison color, regardless of its shape, when given the sample word *red, green,* or *blue.* Standard tests for emergent relations are then likely to show the subject matching former comparisons to each other on the basis of their color, regardless of the shapes of the stimuli. Given a test trial in which a red square is the sample and a red circle, a green triangle, and a blue square are the comparisons, the subject can be expected to select the red circle; both it and the sample are in the class *red* and the subject has learned that the shapes are irrelevant.

Suppose we then teach the same subject to select an appropriate comparison shape, no matter what its color, when given the sample word *square, circle,* or *triangle.* The subject will now select a shape, regardless of color, when given a shape name, and will select a color, regardless of shape, when given a color name. What will happen when we repeat the same test trial as before? The sample is again a red square and the comparisons are a red circle, a green triangle, and a blue square. Given the subject's history, the red square sample will now be in the same class as two of the comparisons, the red circle and the blue square. Which will the subject choose? Which class will predominate? That is to say, which aspect of the stimuli will control the subject's selection, the red color or the square shape? A similar situation prevails in the Stroop test (Stroop, 1935), in which subjects have color-naming problems when they are shown color names that are printed in other colors—for example, the word *blue* printed in red ink. Whether color, shape, or some other aspect of the stimuli will predominate in determining a subject's choice cannot be predicted without additional information. Differences in context are required to resolve the conflict that arises when the sample in a conditional discrimination belongs to more than one comparison class or when several comparisons belong to the same class.

Mathematical set theory cannot predict which features of a set of stimuli will be abstracted as the basis for a partition. That is a matter for contingencies of reinforcement and other factors to determine. Although the mathematics can describe the conflicting relations, thereby permitting us to predict which pairs of elements will belong to each relation, the relations themselves arise from the contingencies. Similarly, the contextual control that resolves the conflicts arises not from the mathematics but from the reinforcement contingencies. The existence and resolution of such conflicts, therefore, poses no problem for a description of equivalence relations that is based on mathematical set theory. Lasting differences among the stimulus-pair constituents of an equivalence relation are to be attributed not to inadequacies in the descriptive system but to reinforcement contingencies that bring any given stimulus pair into various equivalence relations.

Given this admonition, how does it affect the way we look at data that seem to point to differences between members of a stimulus class? In particular, we may ask whether an understanding of the findings requires the postulation of a hypothetical structure.

As a prerequisite for meaningful discourse, we have to assume that the experiments germane to this question did not suffer from possible procedural deficiencies like: (a) confounding of number of nodes with reinforcement history or recency of training or testing;

(b) the possibility that negative-stimulus variations during testing, rather than conditional relations established during training, were responsible for some test results; (c) an interaction between nodal number and instructions to the subjects like "Choose stimuli that *go together*"; (d) stimulus-control uncertainties that go along with the use of two comparisons per trial; and (e) confounding of number of nodes with the nature of the prerequisite relations (derived versus directly taught). It is not clear that any of the studies reported so far have been free of all such potential problems; to carry out conclusive experiments turns out to be a delicate matter (for reviews, see Fields, Adams, & Verhave, 1993; Fields, Adams, Verhave, & Newman, 1993).

Still, two sets of findings occasion considerable interest. Fields, Adams, and Verhave (1993) described the first of these as *post-class formation transfer tests*. Although the findings that have been published (Fields, Adams, Verhave, & Newman, 1993) are at best tentative, variations of the procedure will undoubtedly be used again. An example of the tactic is: (a) teach a subject AB, BC, CD, and DE conditional discriminations; (b) demonstrate the emergence of conditionally related stimulus pairs that define an equivalence relation, one set containing all the ordered pairs made up of Stimuli A1, B1, C1, D1, and E1, and the other of Stimuli A2, B2, C2, D2, and E2 (although an example that is limited to only two classes of stimuli may complicate interpretation of an actual experiment, such a limitation facilitates exposition); (c) teach the subject a simple discrimination in which one member of each class—for example, A1 and A2—serves as a discriminative stimulus for a new defined response: R1 or R2, respectively; (d) administer simple-discrimination tests to determine whether other stimuli in the two classes will also occasion the new responses. If they do, does the likelihood of Class 1 members occasioning R1 and of Class 2 members occasioning R2 depend on the number of nodes that were needed to bring each stimulus into its class?

In the following discussion of this example, I refer only to Class 1 but corresponding statements must also be applicable to Class 2. Indeed, to say that only Class 1 members occasion the new response can lead to serious errors of interpretation. This is because the observation that Stimuli B1...E1 (all or some) occasion R1 does not by itself justify a conclusion that R1 has transferred from A1 to other stimuli on the basis of class membership. One must show that Stimuli B2...E2 do not also occasion R1. If members of both B1...E1 and B2...E2 classes controlled the same response, a partition of those stimuli with respect to R1 could not be said to have taken place. A related problem must also be noted: to observe that a Class 1 member—say, Stimulus E1— occasions not R1 but R2, and that Stimulus E2 occasions not R2 but R1, signifies that those stimuli are partitioned on the basis of the response that each controls. Such a finding, even though unexpected, cannot be dismissed as a mere failure of transfer. Rather, it indicates that more is involved in the new partition than just nodal number.

What has happened in the example described above is that we have made A1 a potential member of two classes: the original A1B1...E1 class and the subsequently established A1R1 class. We then asked two questions: first, will the inclusion of A1 in both the A1B1...E1 and the A1R1 classes bring about union or intersection of the two classes? second, will nodal number help to determine whether class union or intersection takes place?

In reply to the first question, several transfer-of-function studies suggest that class union is more likely than intersection. If, however, well-controlled studies show that the likelihood of class union depends on the number of nodes that were required to bring a stimulus into the A1B1...E1 class, then the second question will have received a positive answer—indicating that more must be known before one can answer the first question with any confidence. We will have discovered that nodal number is a parameter in tests for class union. (A demonstration that nodal number determines only how many test trials are required to demonstrate class union would change the problem to one of specifying the interactions between nodal number and variables that are involved in delayed emergence.) Although the demonstration of nodal number as a new variable would mark an important discovery, the structural parameter *distance* would not be required. Nodal number, as an observable feature of the set of contingencies, would suffice.

Epilogue

In a second type of study, *within-class preference tests*, the available data are somewhat more solid. Here is an example of the basic tactic (Fields, Adams, & Verhave, 1993, pp. 705-707; see also pp. 312-315 for what I have called *conflict tests*): first, as in the transfer studies, (a) teach a subject AB, BC, CD, and DE conditional discriminations, and (b) demonstrate the emergence of conditionally related stimulus pairs that define an equivalence relation, one set containing all the ordered pairs made up of Stimuli A1, B1, C1, D1, and E1, and the other of Stimuli A2, B2, C2, D2, and E2; then, (c) conduct within-class preference tests in which, for example, a subject is given a trial with E1 as the sample and C1 and B1 as comparisons. With all the stimuli in the same class, which comparison will the subject choose? The consistent finding has been that subjects select the comparison that is most like the sample with respect to the number of nodes that were required to bring it into the class.

Without in any way attempting to diminish the potential importance of this finding, we must still ask where it fits into a formulation of equivalence phenomena. I suggest that the class preference test neither increases nor lessens our ability to specify the pairs of elements that are necessary to define a particular equivalence relation. Rather, it tells us something about other classes to which an element may belong.

Suppose we do an analogous experiment by setting up the classes *red* and *green*, with the shape of the stimuli irrelevant. Then, in a test, we present a red square as the sample and, as comparisons, a red circle and a red triangle. With all stimuli belonging to the class *red*, which comparison will subjects choose? Choices will depend on factors that have not been identified: perhaps a subject will select the circle because it resembles the square in area more closely than the triangle does—with respect to area, the square and circle are partitioned into a class from which the triangle is excluded; or perhaps a subject will select the triangle because, like the square, it is rectilinear—with respect to linearity, the square and triangle are partitioned into a class from which curvilinear forms are excluded.

In the within-class preference tests that have actually been done, nodal number may serve the same function as shape does in our hypothetical experiment. The important discovery here is not that the members of the original class differ in that they also belong to other classes, but that nodal number may serve as the basis for a classifying the stimuli. In principle, this finding is no different from other discoveries that factors inherent in the procedures we use to establish and test for equivalence relations can also serve as a basis for partition: the sequence in which stimuli are added to a class, or experimental versus control stimuli (Stikeleather & Sidman, 1990); sample versus comparison stimuli (p. 261); control by the positive versus control by the negative comparison (Carrigan & Sidman, 1992; Johnson & Sidman, 1993); physical resemblances between stimuli (cited in Sidman, 1987, p. 15; also, Barnes, 1990); contextual control by negative comparisons or other aspects of the experimental environment (pp. 515-524); and the class membership of the elements of a compound sample (Pérez-González, 1994).

The within-class preference test does not even preserve the integrity of the originally demonstrated class. Any partition must create at least two classes, and a demonstration of one must always involve a demonstration of the other; for every positive discriminative stimulus, there must also be a negative. The within-class test does not fulfill this requirement because it presents the subject with stimuli from only one partition class. In forcing a subject to choose between stimuli from the same class, we are forcing a discrimination on grounds other than the feature that defines the class. Suppose we have given within-class preference tests, as described above, and found that a subject always selects the comparison that is most like the sample with respect to the number of nodes that were required to bring it into the class. This finding would tell us that when we preempt the original partition by presenting stimuli from only one class, nodal number can take over as a basis for classification. When it does, nodal number will be independent of the original partition classes. For example, with respect to nodal number, Stimuli E1 and E2 would be in the same class. If, then, we were to present E2 rather than E1 as a sample, we would still expect the subject to select C1 and not B1, and with E1 rather than E2 as the sample, to select C2 and not B2. With respect to nodal number, E2 is closer to C1 than to A1, and E1 is closer to C2 than to A2.

And so, in one arbitrary partition that the original baseline contingencies established, Stimulus E1 was shown to belong to a different class than stimulus E2; in another partition, based on nodal number, those stimuli were members of the same class. During test trials, other stimuli would provide a context that would determine which partition was in effect. What is new here is not the self-contradictory notion that differences exist among stimuli that have been classified as equivalent but rather, the finding that nodal number can serve as an alternate basis for classifying the stimuli.

Class size as a variable. Spradlin et al. (1992) suggested that class size—the number of pairs of elements that are included within an equivalence relation—may help determine whether a stimulus pair that a subject has forgotten will ultimately be remembered. For example, suppose we have taught a subject AB and AC conditional discriminations and the standard tests have shown all of the emergent relations necessary to define an equivalence relation. Then, after some time has elapsed, we find that the subject no longer remembers the AB baseline pairs. If, however, the AC (baseline) and CB (derived) conditional discriminations are still intact, and if those relations are transitive, the original AB pairs may eventually re-emerge. As Spradlin et al. (1992) elaborated:

> To take the example one step further, one can expand the set of conditional discriminations to include four stimuli [AB, AC, and DC]. If all of the derived relations are demonstrated, and if A-B relations are disturbed, the A-B relations are derivable as long as either the A-C [baseline] and B-C [derived] relations are intact or the A-D [derived] and B-D [derived] relations are intact.
>
> As the number of stimuli within each equivalence class increases, the number of possible ways of recovering the A-B relations is increased dramatically. As long as some key relations within the class have been tested and demonstrated and as long as the "to be recovered" relations are presented in sessions including these intact relations, it is easy to see how recovery might occur across repeated tests under extinction conditions (pp. 33-34).

Still in need of experimental verification is the attractive notion that the larger an equivalence relation (the more ordered pairs that make up the relation) the more likely we are to recall the conditional discriminations from which the pairs are derived. Also still to be verified is a somewhat more restricted version of this notion: we are more likely to remember a set of conditional discriminations that are involved in an equivalence relation than we are to remember the same number of independent conditional discriminations. Confirmation of these suggestions would bring another new variable, class size, into our picture of equivalence relations.

Although the mathematics assigns no role either to nodal number—the number of nodes that are required to bring an element into a class—or to class size—the number of ordered pairs that make up an equivalence relation, a final confirmation of the relevance of those variables would raise no problems for the mathematically derived description of equivalence relations. Indeed, the potential relevance of nodal number and class size as behavioral determinants is revealed only in the context of set-theory descriptions and predictions of equivalence relations and classes. That is to say, although the mathematical description is neutral with respect to any effects of nodal number and class size, it is the mathematical description that exposes the potential importance of those variables..

The mathematics and the behavior. When applied to the analysis of behavior, the mathematical theory of sets seems to agree closely with behavioral reality. That this correspondence exists is in itself remarkable. How is it that purely mathematical conceptions fit observed behavioral phenomena so well?

The same question, of course, has been asked in Physics and other natural sciences. As many philosophers have pointed out (for example, Whitehead, 1925):

> When we think of mathematics, we have in our mind a science devoted to the exploration of number, quantity, geometry, and in modern times also including investigation into yet more abstract concepts of order, and into analogous types of purely logical

relations. The point of mathematics is that in it we have always got rid of the particular instance, and even of any particular sorts of entities. So that for example, no mathematical truths apply merely to fish, or merely to stones, or merely to colours. So long as you are dealing with pure mathematics, you are in the realm of complete and absolute abstraction....

Mathematics is thought moving in the sphere of complete abstraction from any particular instance of what it is talking about....

The certainty of mathematics depends upon its complete abstract generality....[For example] it is a general abstract truth of pure mathematics that any group of forty entities can be subdivided into two groups of twenty entities. We are therefore justified in concluding that a particular group of apples which we believe to contain forty members can be subdivided into two groups of apples of which each contains twenty members. (pp. 31-33).

How does such abstraction come about? Abstraction requires the discrimination of elements, qualities, or properties that different instances possess in common. Discrimination is a behavioral process, based largely on experience. Whitehead (1925) clearly recognized this relation between direct experience and mathematical abstraction:

...We can now see what is the function in thought which is performed by pure mathematics. It is a resolute attempt to go the whole way in the direction of complete analysis, so as to separate the elements of mere matter of fact from the purely abstract conditions which they exemplify.

The habit of such analysis enlightens every act of the functioning of the human mind. It first (by isolating it) emphasizes the direct aesthetic appreciation of the content of experience. This direct appreciation means an apprehension of what this experience is in itself in its own particular essence, including its immediate concrete values. This is a question of direct experience, dependent upon sensitive subtlety. There is then the abstraction of the particular entities involved, viewed in themselves, and as apart from that particular occasion of experience in which we are then apprehending them. Lastly there is the further apprehension of the absolutely general conditions satisfied by the particular relations of those entities as in that experience. These conditions gain their generality from the fact that they are expressible without reference to those particular relations or to those particular relata which occur in that particular occasion of experience. They are conditions which might hold for an indefinite variety of other occasions, involving other entities and other relations between them. Thus these conditions are perfectly general because they refer to no particular occasion, and to no particular entities (such as green, or blue, or trees) which enter into a variety of occasions, and to no particular relationships between such entities. (pp. 36-37).

We arrive, then, at the notion that the seemingly mysterious correspondence between mathematical and behavioral formulations of equivalence relations is actually built into set theory itself. Numbers and other kinds of elements are not related except via behavior, and in its treatment of relations, mathematical theory takes that behavior as a given: "In colloquial usage the term 'set' is taken, as a rule, to mean a collection of things that in some sense or another belong together or are akin. This latter aspect is difficult to make precise and is therefore omitted from the mathematical concept" (Gellert et al., 1977). That is to say, even in mathematical theory, no relations exist until some behavior has occurred. Particular discriminations then give rise to the abstraction of commonalities, often expressed in linguistic forms—words. From these words, we derive higher-order abstractions, a thought process that itself becomes available to us via equivalence relations. It is equivalence relations that make purely verbal constructions possible—words or phrases that have no immediate referents except other words or phrases.

It should not surprise us, then, if we find behavioral and mathematical formulations of equivalence to be consistent with each other. Those mathematical abstractions that prove useful in describing behavior are the ones that have made valid assumptions about behavior in the first place. The generalized concepts of classes, of equivalence and other kinds of relations, and of the various elementary components of mathematical set theory arose originally out of specific everyday observations. (For a set-theory formulation of order relations in behavior, see Green, Stromer, and Mackay, 1993.) Whether or not they are conscious of what they are doing, many pure mathematicians are also keen observers of behavior.

Epilogue

Whitehead's conception that pure mathematics is concerned with general abstractions from matters of fact (see above) is also relevant to the sometimes expressed opinion that the mathematically-derived behavioral definition of equivalence relations which I and my colleagues have offered is just "Sidman equivalence." The implication is that the definition, if not capricious, is, at the least, arbitrary, with no stronger a priori justification than any other definition. Far from being arbitrary, however, the mathematical definition of the equivalence relation possesses tremendous generality: "Equivalence relations are found not only in every corner of mathematics, but in almost all the sciences" (Gellert et al., 1977). To adopt the mathematical definition is to take the position that behavior is included among the many real-world specifics that the abstractions of mathematical set theory encompass. This position, although conceivably incorrect, is hardly arbitrary. Given the general empirical support for the mathematical formulation, the a priori denial of its relevance to behavior is considerably more arbitrary than its acceptance.

The origin of equivalence relations. Elementary mathematical set theory describes the abstract properties of equivalence relations, and I have argued that behavioral phenomena like those described in this book exemplify the mathematical abstraction. But although set theory informs us how to find out whether any particular event pair belongs to an equivalence relation, it is silent about the origin of equivalence relations themselves. Questions about testing for equivalence relations are to be distinguished from questions about prerequisites for the development of equivalence. I have dealt with the latter problem by treating equivalence relations parsimoniously as a natural product of reinforcement contingencies. One consequence of this treatment is that all of the variables that modulate the effects of reinforcement contingencies can be expected to be found relevant also to equivalence relations, even though those variables may have no place in the mathematical description.

A second consequence is that no additional experience on the part of the individual need be invoked in order to account for the observation that the components of a reinforcement contingency are related by equivalence. My suggestion (Chapter 10) was that equivalence relations are a built-in effect of reinforcement contingencies but that the breakdown of particular equivalence relations is a product of contextual control which, in turn, comes about through experience (Chapter 12). The problem then becomes not how to explain the origin of equivalence relations in general but how to explain those particular instances in which some or all of the events involved in a reinforcement contingency fail to become members of the same equivalence class. Experience is responsible for the removal or preclusion of events from an equivalence class.

Others, however, have argued that special kinds of experiences are necessary precursors of equivalence relations. The position has been expounded by Hayes (1986, 1991), and Hayes and Hayes (1989) in the form of *relational frame* theory. This theory treats the relation of equivalence as but one member of the larger class of relations in which elements of the environment may take part. (Opposition, difference, order, and so on are examples of relations other than equivalence.) Relational frame theory holds that the establishment of any arbitrary relation, including equivalence, is itself a learned operant. One's experience with examples of a particular kind of relation is said to establish a relational frame: "Relational frames are specific kinds of *learned arbitrarily applicable relational responses*" (Hayes, 1994, p. 12). It becomes possible, therefore, to talk about "framing relationally" (Hayes, 1994, p. 11). And when summarizing the outcome of the kind of learning history that is held to make equivalence relations possible, it becomes appropriate, in relational frame theory, to talk about "equivalencing." A similar experiential derivation, consistent with mediation theory, was noted by James and Hakes (1965), who talk about "the *strategy of mediation* as a method for learning equivalences" (p. 93, emphasis added). Finally, like all learned behavior, relational frames come under contextual control: "For equivalence to work, *equivalencing itself must be under conditional control*" (Hayes et al., 1987, p. 371).

Relational frames are not supposed to represent actual variables, or things, but are to be conceptualized as summary terms for the experiential history and for the set of properties that characterize a particular type of relational responding. Within a given context, a relational frame is said to possess the properties of mutual entailment, combinatorial entailment, and transfer of functions. I list the essential features of these properties here.

(1) The observation that defines mutual entailment: given that A is related to B (the AB relation, usually directly learned), B will also be related to A (the derived BA relation). Unlike the property of symmetry that enters into the mathematical definition of an equivalence relation, mutual entailment does not require the derived BA relation to be the same as the AB relation (for example, if the AB relation is "larger than," the BA relation will be "smaller than").

(2) The observation that defines combinatorial entailment: given the directly learned relations AB and BC, we will also find the derived relations AC and CA.. Again, unlike the relations that help to define equivalence, neither the directly learned relations nor the derived relations need be the same (for example, if the relation AB is "uncle of" and the relation BC is "father of," then the derived BA relation will be "nephew of," the CB relation will be "son of," the AC relation will be "great-uncle of" and the CA relation will be "great-nephew of").

(3) The observation that defines transfer of function: given a psychological function, F, and that A—>F, and given any derived relation that involves A, like AC, then we may find that C—>F. Although the entailment processes that characterize a relational frame are held to be learned on the basis of experience with examples, and therefore *to involve no new behavioral principles* [emphasis added], transfer of function is recognized as a new source of behavioral control: "The transfer of functions through such relations [for example, equivalence or higher-order concepts like relational frames] instantiates a new behavioral principle, because these [transferred] functions are based on a learned process" (Hayes, 1992, pp. 111-112).

Relational frame theory can be seen as an attempt to account for observations that our actions come under the control of environmental events that are related not only by equivalence but in other ways also. It is the first such general formulation that springs from a behavior-analytic orientation. And yet, I have waited until nearly the end of my story before bringing it in. Why the delay? Although I find much that is congenial in this attempt to formulate a general theory of the kinds of stimulus control that involve relations between controlling stimuli, I have been unable to resolve some of the problems that I see in relational frame theory's treatment of equivalence relations.

First of all, I have difficulty with the notion that the process by which equivalence relations come about—"equivalencing"—must itself be a learned response. To say that a particular equivalence relation is arbitrary (for example, the relation between a word and its referent) is to say that the related elements have nothing in common except the relation itself. The accomplishments of mathematicians show us that linguistically proficient organisms can indeed abstract the properties of arbitrary relations and come up with a list of features that other similarly proficient organisms (behavior analysts?) can look for in any specific instance. But surely, this is not the behavior of equivalencing that relational frame theory postulates; relational framing is not supposed to require a background of highly sophisticated linguistic proficiency. As I have asked before (pp. 364-365), however, what makes it possible for linguistically unsophisticated organisms (like young children, people with severe mental retardation, or nonhumans) to abstract the shared features from a set of specific instances of reflexivity, symmetry, and transitivity when those very words—sophisticated abstractions that define the relation—remain outside of their repertoires? This is not to say that young children or nonhumans are incapable of equivalence relations; far from it, since every partition implies an equivalence relation (pp. 417-419). But I find it difficult to see how a common response (equivalencing?) to exemplars that have nothing in common except the relation could arise in the absence of a highly complex verbal repertoire.

Epilogue

A linguistically naive organism's abstraction of commonalities from a set of exemplars that share no physical feature requires more of an explanation than just a history of experience with the exemplars. It is certainly possible to teach specific equivalence relations nonlinguistically, like *sameness*, for example, and to teach other kinds of arbitrary relations, too, like *opposition* and *difference*; all of these involve control by physical characteristics of stimuli. If, however, we were to find that linguistically impoverished organisms could derive the concept *equivalence relation* just from a reinforcement history with paired elements that shared no feature beyond the relation itself, that very finding would require an explanation that is not currently available among the principles of behavior analysis. If, for example, experience with exemplars was responsible for the observation of equivalence relations with a sea lion as subject (Schusterman & Kastak, 1993), then such an experiential outcome will require its own explanation. Before generalization from physically unlike exemplars by a nonverbal organism is itself understood, it would be unwise to use that phenomenon as the explanatory basis for other phenomena.

Perhaps in recognition of this problem, relational frame theory holds that only symmetry is necessary for equivalence. The assumption is made that "...with enough examples of specifically trained symmetrical responding, and transfer of functions in terms of that, a more general form of [symmetrical] responding may emerge" (Hayes, 1991, p. 26). It is still necessary to ask how a nonverbal abstraction can arise merely from experience with exemplars of symmetric relations between stimuli that have nothing in common except the relation of symmetry itself. Mediation theories of equivalence recognized the problem and dealt with it directly by postulating explicit or implicit response mediation to account for generalization from unlike exemplars (Jenkins, 1965, pp. 72-85). A close analogy to relational frames is also to be found in the notion of *response sets*, which Paul and Paul (1968, p. 537) described as "A vast repertoire of preexperimentally acquired habits and sets of self-instructions which can be activated by specific aspects of the learning task, including experimental instructions and procedural variables." The notion of *transfer-activated response sets* (Paul & Paul, 1968) is an even more direct precursor of *relational frames*. I am left with the uncomfortable feeling that to interpret equivalence as a learned response is, despite protestations to the contrary, merely to summarize a complex set of variables by postulating a hypothetical entity—in this instance, an inferred but undemonstrable response—as a mediator of equivalence relations.

I also have difficulty with the view that only symmetry is critical for equivalence, and with the related conception that equivalence is but a special case of the more general relational frame formulation: "The kind of symmetry described in the equivalence literature is a specific instance of mutual entailment....stimulus equivalence can be interpreted as a special case of a network of relational frames." (Hayes, 1991, pp. 31, 32). These notions seem to provide an option for understanding equivalence without having to make use of the mathematical formulation, but in throwing away the mathematically derived description, one also throws away its predictive power. It is important, therefore, to ask, "To what end?" Even if relational frame theory permitted the same predictions as the mathematical description (see, for example, Barnes, 1994), the concept of an equivalence frame requires a complex set of interrelated background assumptions: a hypothetical act of equivalencing; the presumption that the act can be learned from a set of discriminations (abstractions) that are based on direct experience with mutual and combinatorial entailment in arbitrary relations, and on direct experience with the transfer of functions—itself a hypothetical process; and the postulation of reflexivity, a property unique to equivalence relations. Even without considering the adequacy of these assumptions, one must ask what is to be gained by substituting them for the single assumption that equivalence relations in behavior are instances of the class that elementary mathematical set theory describes.

Furthermore, in the general relational frame conception, specific relations within a frame need not be the same as each other, whether they are directly learned or derived (p. 555). In coordination (see below), however, the relation between all stimuli must be the same;

the relation between A and B must be the same as the relation between B and C, and so on. Also, the relation must be reflexive; the relation that holds between any pair of elements must also hold between each element and itself. From what source except the mathematical definition of the equivalence relation are these special requirements derived? In spite of all of the additional assumptions in relational frame theory, one still has to return to the set-theory definition of the equivalence relation for these special properties of equivalence relations. For me, the mathematical description of the equivalence relation has an elegance and simplicity that relational frame theory is unable to match.

Another problem arises from statements to the effect that the equivalence relation is best conceived of as the outcome of a special type of relational frame—the frame of *coordination*: "[Coordination is a relation] of identity, sameness, or similarity; this is that.... The frame of coordination yields an equivalence class..." (Hayes, 1991, pp. 29, 31). It is true that the relation of equality (sameness) may be learned at a young age, but equality is only one example of an equivalence relation. Equivalence itself is more general, including, for example, the relations, "is parallel to," "is congruent to" (for triangles in a plane), "has the same teacher as" (an equivalence relation only if each has but one teacher), "is conditional upon" or "is paired with" (depending on context). Indeed, it is always possible to ask whether any relation is *also* an equivalence relation. Equivalence, therefore, has a characteristic that makes it something more than just another member of the class of all possible relations: any relation may turn out also to be an equivalence relation. Set theory provides means for detecting such instances. For example, set theory shows equality to be an equivalence relation. Based on that observation, I would suggest not that coordination yields equivalence, but that coordination is itself but one example of equivalence.

And finally, the special process of transfer of functions is not only critical to relational frame theory but is advanced as the area which provides evidence that the effects of relational frames "deserve...to be treated as a new phenomenon involving a new principle" (Hayes, 1991, p. 39). I have suggested, however, that the set-theory abstractions, class union and intersection, make it possible to describe the transfer of functions without having to invoke a special behavioral process of function transfer. The notion that equivalence relations are built into reinforcement contingencies, but are precluded or broken down by context, implies also that class union is a primary outcome of reinforcement contingencies that share components, but that context can transform class union into intersection. That is to say, class merger is primary, and is precluded or broken down by context. And so, as with equivalence relations, observations that have given rise to the hypothetical process, transfer of functions, can be treated simply as specific cases of mathematical abstractions; the descriptive concepts of class union and intersection replace the hypothetical process of transfer of function.

What about experimental findings that purport to show stimulus equivalence as but one among many kinds of relations that relational frame theory can account for? Experiments by Steele and Hayes (1991) were intended to show that subjects will select different stimuli from a group of comparisons, depending on whether a contextual stimulus calls for a sample-comparison relation of sameness, opposition, or difference. The general experimental approach in these studies constitutes a valuable contribution: first, establish contextual control over different relations (for example, same/opposite or same/different) with nonarbitrary stimulus sets (for example, lines of different length or height, squares of different sizes, different numbers of dots, and so on); then, use the contextual stimuli to control arbitrary conditional discriminations; and finally, examine the effects of the contextual cues on derived arbitrary relations. Even after a number of interpretive problems (most of them noted in the report) are taken care of, it would be surprising if the original findings were not replicable. Suppose, for example, we teach a subject to relate Samples A1 and A2 to Comparisons B1 and B2, and Samples B1 and B2 to Comparisons C1 and C2, all on the basis of sameness in the presence of Context S, and on the basis of difference in the presence of Context D. Then, when we test the possible derived relations, we would expect to find that the comparison choice that any given sample controls would depend on whether the context was S or D.

Interesting and valuable though these findings are, it is difficult to see how they are supposed to "demonstrate the existence of relational frames" (Steele & Hayes, 1991, p. 549). Relational frame theory is not unique in stressing contextual control. Earlier experiments had shown that particular stimulus pairs could be members of various equivalence relations, with context determining which relation prevailed at any given time. The Steele and Hayes studies went a step further by showing that the contextually controlled arbitrary relations to which particular stimulus pairs belonged did not have to be equivalence relations. But the fact that a stimulus pair can be brought via contextual control into such differing relations as same, opposite, different, and so forth, can be handled by any formulation of equivalence that recognizes the role of context.

Nor do demonstrations of contextual control serve to place all types of relations under the same theoretical umbrella. Each relation has its own properties; placing those properties within the borders of an empty frame and then giving the frame a label does not account for them.

These differences of opinion about the origin of equivalence relations should not obscure the large area of concordance that exists among the various formulations when it comes to the empirical evaluation of the relations between stimuli. The mathematically-derived but procedurally-based analysis that my colleagues and I have proposed for the description of equivalence relations, the application of a similarly derived procedural analysis by Green et al. (1993) to describe order relations, and the expansion of the procedural analysis by Steele and Hayes (1991) to describe other kinds of relations are all in harmony with each other. The empirical findings are robust and procedurally interrelated. I believe that this analytic consistency will prove more productive and lasting than the theoretical controversies.

Equivalence, meaning, symbolism, and reference. My frequent references to meaning, symbolism, and reference, particularly in the

Introduction, should not be taken as suggestions that these terms represent independent entities. They neither explain behavior nor do they represent behavioral properties, principles, or processes that require explanation. The major behavioral question they raise is, "Why do we use (say or write) such terms?" Theory becomes involved when I suggest that whenever people do use these terms, we will find (by appropriate tests) that the words and their referents will be related by equivalence. This is a relatively straightforward proposition, easily checked by means of the methods described in these pages. Nevertheless, terms like meaning, symbolism, and reference make many behavior analysts uneasy because they are usually treated as explanatory concepts, not as behavior that requires explanation itself. My own thinking about these terms was greatly clarified by the need to respond to friendly but sharp doubts that Willard Day expressed about my usage of them. I reproduce here some excerpts from our correspondence on these matters—a correspondence that his sudden passing left uncompleted. The discussion illustrates both the sources of a sophisticated thinker's (Day's) unease and the gradual sharpening of my own conception that his unease generated.

It all started when Willard, in a nice note to me about the *Functional Analysis* paper (Chapter 9), also expressed some distress about my frequent reference to "meaning." Here is my reply:

October 10, 1986

Dear Willard,

I must confess that I thought my references to "meaning" might get a reaction from you. But you can be sure that when you do react to something I say, I sit up and take notice; your judgment is always meaningful to me. Look at it this way: sometimes kids act up just because they need help.

So here is my problem. I am perfectly at home with Skinner's definition of meaning as the determining conditions of verbal behavior, and with his objections to "reference" as an explanation. And yet, it seems to me also true that "meaning," in at least one of its traditional senses—semantic meaning—is based on a real datum. Your words, "...you toss me quite distinctly overboard..." produce the same effect on me that you could have produced by sending me to stand in the corner for misbehaving. The term, "rule-governed behavior," summarizes the observation that with words, you can get people to do things even without their having experienced the relevant contingencies. In this sense, words have meanings; they refer to things, actions, and events. How *do* I handle this observation?

In the simplest case, a word does become equivalent to "the thing it stands for." That is why people call words "symbols." When I was last in Brazil, I reacted to 10,000 cruzeiros—which I had seen before only as a term in print—as I would ordinarily react to a dollar bill. My grandson, whom I have just taught to match a picture of a cow to the written word, cow, now says "moo" when he sees the word, even though he had never done that before. Now, I do not regard "symbol" as an explanation for anything, but I do regard it as a name for something real, an observed phenomenon that *requires explanation*.

Is it really wrong to talk about "meaning" in these senses? Should we invent some other term to take its place? I think the equivalence paradigm demonstrates one way that symbols do become established as such, one way that words can come to "mean" what they "stand for." The phenomena are real; we see them all about us and we can reproduce them in the laboratory. I think the phenomena are important in their own right, and I think they are also "a special property of language" in the sense that they help to make language as powerful as it is.

I am, in fact, quite worried about the rapidly escalating power of language to replace conduct that is tied more to unmediated cause-effect relations with the environment. Words seem actually to be usurping reality in our culture. Symbols seem to be achieving independence from their former referents, as people more and more accept the images in place of the substance. We see it in the untruths and irrelevancies that characterize advertising and we see it in a president who is able to get away with statements that describe exactly the opposite of what is really happening. Meaning, in its traditional sense, is becoming warped, and I think that behavior analysts had better get involved.

Am I really way off the mark in using "meaning" this way? If I am, then I will have to find some other way to talk about the same things, because I think they are important matters.

Murray

Both Willard and I spent a good part of the next few months traveling, but his reply finally came:

June 16, 1987

Dear Murray,

...This is to thank you for your good letter of October 10, in which you pour your heart out about notions having to do with meaning, the equivalence paradigm, and "the rapidly escalating power of language." ...It's a super piece of your thought, I think. Also, it kept working away at me all winter, and together with the effect of Steve Hayes' related written work, led me ultimately to prepare the enclosed paper on "the problem of meaning," the last ten pages or so of which I read at the ABA convention in Nashville a couple of weeks ago.

...I don't think I would have written my ABA paper the way I did, if it had not been for your letter, which gave me the confidence to go ahead and try to speak relatively openly about my thoughts along this line....there was a lot of passion in the paper—a lot of emotion.... But all in all, I find in retrospect I feel good about what I had to say.

At any rate, the ABA paper I enclose makes clear what I think the next step should be in trying to develop the implications of the equivalence-class research. What is your response to this suggestion? What are your views now? How would you suggest I try to adjust mine?

Willard

I will not reproduce all of Willard's ABA paper (which apparently was never published). After citing a number of statements in my *Functional Analysis* paper, he goes on to say:

> In these examples Sidman really does stay fairly close to talking about arrangements of experimental operations. But he is too decent and too honest a person not to be up-front about the fact that what he sees his research really pointing to is the experimental investigation of the emergence and development of meaning. Even more explicit incursions into linguistics territory are made by Steve Hayes and his associates.
>
> ...What I see in all this is that behavior analysts are beginning to take off into realms of professional inquiry which my personal history makes me want to associate primarily with linguistics, to say nothing of such metaphysical disciplines as logic, or the philosophy of language.
>
> ...I guess I've said most of what I have to say about what I think the serious problem of meaning is as far as the analysis of behavior

is concerned. In sum that is that, if we are going to try to advance new theories of the nature of language, then we should try to place these views within the relevant context of existing linguistic work.

Specifically, my suggestion would be that we first find out, and then be up-front about, the way in which issues under respectable professional discussion in the areas of linguistics and the philosophy of language impinge upon our research activities....

More of the details of Willard's discussion in his ABA paper come out in my reply to his letter:

January 14, 1988

Dear Willard,

You must be wondering what happened to me. I should have written to you a long time ago, but your letter of June 16 was so full of good things—information, thoughts, and questions—that I just had to put off answering until I could sit down and think a bit.

...I enjoyed reading your ABA paper and I hope you are continuing to think about those matters. The burgeoning areas of rule-governed behavior and stimulus equivalence need your kind of thoughtful consideration now, before too many of us have gone off the deep end and have done irreversible damage. As far as I, personally, am concerned, I believe that some of the comments in your paper give me too much credit. I really know very little about linguistics, and I hope I do not have to master that field because linguists do not appear to be interested in verbal behavior. How do the following thoughts strike you?

I know that linguists are always talking about meaning, and about many kinds of meanings. But it is not true that anyone else who talks about meaning must therefore become embroiled in linguistics. One of my concerns starts with just some everyday observations: First, people somehow make sense to each other (I am sure we would both give the same behavioral definition of "make sense") when they ask and are then told what the meaning (the referent) of a word is. Second, I notice that people can act effectively in relation to unfamiliar aspects of the world around them simply as a result of words that others have spoken or written (I think this is the same observation that makes Skinner talk about rule-governed behavior). These are common, unscientific observations of the sort that Vicki Lee talks about as the starting point for a scientific curiosity. Because behavior analysts and linguists both begin with the same observations about things that happen in the world, that does not mean their respective treatments of the observations need have anything in common, or even that one treatment must be correct and the other wrong. Certainly, my own reaction to these observations is not an attempt to advance a new theory of the nature of language; I do not believe I deserve either credit for such an attempt or blame for going about it improperly.

If linguists claim that my reactions to these everyday observations have carried me into their turf, that is perfectly fine; I have no objections, and hope I have been of use to them. But if linguists object that I am simply reinventing the wheel, then I claim it is their responsibility to show how they had already incorporated my notions into their field. I do not believe that can be true, because linguists are just not interested in my reasons for being curious about the everyday observations I noted above. Even in the unlikely event that the opposite were true—that linguists were able to use my data or interpretations to resolve any of their problems—my pleasure at such an outcome would still not place me under any obligation to become involved in linguistics.

The fact that professionals in several fields argue about "the concept of meaning" is really irrelevant to me. My word "referent" need have no relevance to the linguistic concept of reference—a concept that I am sure is much more sophisticated than the simple observations that concern me....I am not attempting to reformulate the concept, nor do I even appreciate a necessity for doing so. When I talk about "referent" and "symbol," I am referring to behavioral units that anyone can easily observe. They are in no sense "key concepts" that have to be "fleshed out."

Having made those simple observations about our behavior with respect to words, I come up with a simple-minded theory that might help us understand at least one aspect of what is going on when people offer a referent as the meaning of a word. I have not presented the theory so explicitly before (but I shall, soon, unless you convince me that I should not), but I do not believe I have ever said or written anything that goes beyond what I am now about to say.

First, I venture to claim that whenever we talk about word-meaning-referent, an equivalence relation will be found to exist between the word and its referent. This is the selfsame equivalence relation that elementary mathematics defines quite elegantly and precisely in terms of reflexivity, symmetry, and transitivity. (Note: bidirectionality—symmetry—is not enough.)

Epilogue

Second, I offer a behavioral counterpart for each element of the three-part mathematical definition of an equivalence relation. This makes behavioral tests available that permit us to determine in any specific instance whether the relation we call "meaning" exists between two aspects of the environment—but particularly between a word and some other event, object, or environmental feature. Having the tests available makes it possible now for us to investigate how such relations become established. This, of course, is exactly the concern that differentiates linguist and behavior analyst.

The third part of the theory suggests that the formation of equivalence relations helps to make rule-governed behavior possible. Skinner has stated that "rules specify contingencies," but he has never explained how such "specification" comes about. I am suggesting that equivalence relations make "specification" possible.

These theoretical notions may or may not stand up; they may or may not prove useful. But I do not think they require me to become a linguist or that they turn me into a cognitivist.

Now, how about Steve's position? I certainly do not go along with all of his statements, but I think I understand where they come from. An important question that I have not yet resolved is the explanatory status of equivalence relations. It is a "which comes first, chicken or egg?" kind of problem. Do equivalence relations help us to explain some aspects of verbal behavior—for instance, the "specification" of contingencies by rules—or does verbal behavior—for example, rules—make equivalence relations possible? Most people believe the latter (you, too, I would guess from the first part of your ABA paper), but I am not certain; surely, verbal chains can mediate equivalence relations, but are they necessary? Some of my observations make me feel that equivalence relations can emerge from certain experiences even without the involvement of verbal behavior. If this is so, I am left with the suspicion that the formation of equivalence relations, like reinforcement, discrimination, and other stimulus functions, may be a product of evolution, and not derivable from more basic behavioral processes.

Steve's notion of "relational frames" is, I think, simply an attempt to explain the emergence of equivalence relations by appeal to behavioral history. I, like you, see relational frames as a cognitive structure, and I think that as Steve runs up against the continual modifications he will have to make in that concept, he, too, will agree that it is a smokescreen rather than a clarification. It is not at all clear how a frame is established, and, once established, how a frame can then make it possible for words to govern our interactions with environmental contingencies we have never before experienced. But at this point, I believe that relational frames represent his attempt to explain how equivalence relations are to be derived from already known behavioral processes, and to explain why the same procedures will produce equivalence relations for some subjects and not for others.

So, does all this clarify anything? One thing should be obvious: I take your comments very seriously. I may end up agreeing or disagreeing, but whatever you say is worth thinking about. I look forward to the next development.

Murray

Willard's reply, this time, came quickly:

1/26/88

Dear Murray,

Thanks so much for your careful review of your research interests concerning stimulus equivalence and rule governed behavior. I'm sure it will be ultimately very helpful in enabling me to locate the sources of my frustrations along these lines. I have a hunch my difficulties will not be so much at all with the theoretical reasoning outlined on p. 3 of your letter, but with the basic notions and vocabulary in terms of which the problem gets oriented to begin with in the second complete paragraph on p. 2. My student Edie McCoy was in my office when I opened your letter, so I just started reading your letter out loud to her from its beginning. When I got to the end of the sentence on p. 2 beginning: "One of my concerns starts…", I stopped reading. Edie describes what happened after I stopped reading in her letter to you (enclosed).

Could I ask you to let me (us) know what response you might have to Edie's letter? We feel we are no longer able to look at verbal behavior in terms of words, meanings, and referents because of the import old B.F.'s book has had upon us. I enclose a photocopy of some early pages in *Verbal Behavior* [pp. 7-10]. I need to know what you do with *that* material before I can look at how you are interested in the equivalence findings and conceptualization. Can you resonate to how having deeply incorporated *Verbal Behavior* into our thinking, we take the following sentence from your letter to refer only secondarily to rule governed behavior: "Second,…people…act effectively as a result of words others have spoken…" E.g., there's an auroch over that hill. No rules nowhere. No rules nowhere.

Willard

Epilogue

Here is the letter that Willard enclosed from Edie McCoy:

Dear Professor Sidman:

Willard Day asked me to describe for you an incident occasioned by your recent letter to him.

I am a graduate student here at UNR, and I have been studying with Dr. Day for the past couple of years. I was in his office when he received your letter, and he read parts of it aloud to me. He read your statement: "One of my concerns starts with just some everyday observations: First, people somehow make sense to each other (I am sure we would both give the same behavioral definition of 'make sense') when they ask and are then told what the meaning (the referent) of a word is."

Then he stopped reading, sat quietly for a moment, and then turned to me and said something like, "All right, I have a word for you, and I want you to tell me its meaning." He searched around his desk for notepaper, wrote the word once, scrutinized it carefully, wrote it again, and then reached for his dictionary. I, meanwhile, sat and watched this performance with the feeling of scrambling around within myself to get set for my move in this game we were suddenly playing, extremely curious to know what word would prompt the look of mischief on his face and wondering when he reached for the dictionary if the word would be Japanese.

He handed me the paper, upon which he had written *syzygy*. I said I had encountered the word before, but, beyond the sense of "I've seen this somewhere and he has reason to think I might recognize it" I had no recollection of how the word was defined or in what circumstances it had previously appeared.

He read the dictionary definition to me. (He was almost chuckling now.) It sounded like the word is some kind of astronomy term, used to describe the conjunction or opposition of the moon with the sun or other stars. He said, "I think it's a wonderful word." I wanted to know if he knew how I might have met it before. He said it came from the work of a mutual friend of ours on the campus, a counseling psychologist, and that he had recently read it in a paper she had sent to him.

What I want to do in this description is capture for you in verbal stop-action photography the moment within the interaction of two people when the word, and the interaction centered on the word, existed, but just at the split second before the dictionary was opened and the definition read (the referent identified?). It seems to me that the incident raised the possibility that the word had meaning for me before it "had" a referent.

To complete the story of *syzygy*, it happened that I went to lunch with the author of the paper right after that time with Dr. Day. As we were leaving the restaurant engaged in a conversation about the process of graduate training, she used the word, and the way she spoke it made me feel that the word functioned for her explanatory system the way *discriminative stimulus* or such like central term might function in a behaviorist's conversation. I asked her about *syzygy*, and she spoke in terms of the word's identification of counter forces pulling against each other, a component I don't remember at all in the definition Dr. Day had read. And she also told me that the word had first become important to her years ago when she was writing her dissertation, and that one of the members of her committee, a literary person, objected to the term because it was too harsh.

I think my answer, today, to the question Willard asked me two days ago: "What does *syzygy* mean," is contained in my account of what has happened.

Sincerely,
Edie McCoy

The exchange was heating up. Edie McCoy's letter certainly did identify the major source of Willard's discomfort when he encountered my and other behaviorists' talk about meaning. My reply was not long delayed:

February 15, 1988

Dear Willard,

My printer has been repaired, and I am enclosing a more readable copy of my previous letter. Perhaps the poor print quality was responsible for some of your reactions; at any rate, matters do seem to have gotten out of hand. When you feel you have to address me as someone who has either not experienced the impact of Skinner's book or does not appreciate that work, then something is wrong somewhere. The key is perhaps in your statement that you have to know how I feel about the passages (from Skinner) you sent me before you can look at how I am interested in the equivalence findings and conceptualization. I come from the opposite direction. My work on equivalence came first, and its relevance to Skinner's formulation of verbal behavior followed the empirical findings. That is the way I have always worked. One consequence of my approach from data to theory rather than from theory to data is that I do not first try to define meaning and then use that definition to explain equivalence; rather, I define equivalence empirically and then use that definition to help explain meaning. Perhaps I am wrong about the relevance of equivalence relations to verbal behavior, but there should be no mistake about the explanatory direction.

I assign no independent existence to meanings; I give meaning no *explanatory* status whatsoever. I look at the statement, "The meaning of syzygy is…" in the same way that I look at the statement, "The sun sets over the horizon." Both are inaccurate and explain nothing. We know that is so about the sunset because scientists considered the statement interesting enough to concentrate their efforts in identifying the physical variables responsible for its emission. I believe it important also to identify the behavioral variables responsible for people's statements that syzygy and other sounds or visual patterns "have meanings." Skinner has done much to clarify that situation, and his definition of "meaning" as the variables responsible for an utterance is something that I, no less than you, have come to take for granted. What Skinner has not done, and what probably will never be done completely, is to identify *all* of the relevant variables. (If that ever is done, the science of behavior will become a closed book; nothing will be left to be discovered.) To say that Skinner has not given the whole story is not to deny or reduce the importance of his accomplishments. I feel that my work offers him the ultimate form of respect by building upon the foundation he laid down.

What you seem to be saying, however, is that we should pay no attention whatsoever to what is going on behaviorally when people say that some word, phrase, sentence, symbol, experience, etc. means something. You do not seem to want me to apply the empirical phenomenon of equivalence relations to help explain the fact that people make such statements. That is not a responsible position, and I find it hard to believe you are really taking it. Certainly, you must realize that a science of behavior has to make contact with everyday life if it is to be treated respectfully, and if it also is to have an effect on the world. People are always going to ask about and give meanings. A science of behavior that tries to make them stop doing so is not only asking for derision but is probably suicidal. What would happen if astronomers tried to decree it unlawful to talk about sunsets?

For me, the field of equivalence relations opens up a whole new set of variables that help explain the emission of utterances like "A means B." Not all instances to which people apply the term "meaning" are explainable as equivalence relations, but many important cases are. I believe it is extremely interesting that when people match words to objects, equivalence relations between those words and objects can be demonstrated, but that this is not true when nonhumans do the same matching. Does this not suggest that perhaps "meaning," like "sunset," can have a legitimate meaning? Furthermore, equivalence relations help explain the *first-time* occurrence of much verbal behavior that has never been involved in actual reinforcement contingencies—for example, the enlargement of vocabularies, new syntactical arrangements, the development of rules. In my chapter that occasioned the start of this exchange between us, I was simply indicating that the phenomenon I was explicating was relevant to such utterances. And I am certain that other phenomena, not yet explored by behavior analysts, will also prove relevant; I cannot believe that we know everything. (Actually, I consider the problem of first instances the most serious omission in Skinner's formulation of behavior in general; I believe that equivalence relations help to fill the gap.)

And so, answering your query by way of a summary of the above, I do not feel that I ever asked anyone to look at verbal behavior in terms of words, meanings, and referents. I am actually somewhat bewildered that you ever thought so. What I *have* done is to use the formation of equivalence relations to help explain what is going on when people talk about words, meanings, symbols, and referents. Just as Edie's account helps to explain what syzygy means to her, the whole complicated network of data and theory about equivalence relations helps to explain what meanings, symbols, and referents mean to me. I think the same should be true for you and Edie, and for everybody else. Perhaps I am wrong about that, but if so, my mistakes are not the ones you attributed to me.

Murray

That was the last direct interaction between me and Willard Day. I worried that my vehemence might have upset him. But a short time later, I incorporated the gist of my final statements in an address to the Northern California Association for Behavior Analysis. After the talk, Edie McCoy came up from the audience and introduced herself. She indicated that she was pleased with what she had heard me say and that she was sure Willard would be, also.

As I indicated in the *Introduction*, there is more to science than the customary publications reveal. My original writings never mentioned the spirited interchange between me and Willard Day but, as will be obvious to any reasonably diligent reader of this book, that interaction greatly sharpened my conceptualization of equivalence relations. The story about my research on equivalence relations in behavior would have been incomplete had I left Willard Day out of the picture.

References

Adams, B. J., Fields, L., & Verhave, T. (1993). Effects of test order on intersubject variability during equivalence class formation. *The Psychological Record*, **43**, 133-152. (272)

Axelrod, S. (1992). Disseminating an effective educational technology. *Journal of Applied Behavior Analysis*, **25**, 31-35. (66)

Barnes, D. (1994). Stimulus equivalence and relational frame theory. *The Psychological Record*, **44**, 91-124. (406, 526, 527, 558)

Barnes, D., & Keenan, M. (1993). A transfer of functions through derived arbitrary and nonarbitrary stimulus relations. *Journal of the Experimental Analysis of Behavior*, **59**, 61-81. (375, 448, 464)

Barnes, D., McCullagh, P. D., & Keenan, M. Equivalence class formation in non-hearing impaired children and hearing impaired children. *The Analysis of Verbal Behavior*, **8**, 19-30. (306)

Barnes, T. (1990). *Equivalence without symmetry? A stimulus artifact.* Unpublished M. A. thesis, Northeastern University, Boston. (548)

Baron, A., Perone, M., & Galizio, M. (1991). Analyzing the reinforcement process at the human level: Can application and behavioristic interpretation replace laboratory research? [Main article, followed by responses, pp. 95-155]. *The Behavior Analyst*, **14**, 95-105. (322)

Behavior dynamics [Special Issue]. (1992). *Journal of the Experimental Analysis of Behavior*, **57**(3). (322)

Birch, H. G. (1962). Dyslexia and and the maturation of visual function. In J. Money (Ed.), *Reading disabilityy: Progress and research needs in dyslexia* (pp. 161-169). Baltimore, MD: Johns Hopkins. (24, 46, 105)

Birch, H. G., & Belmont, L. (1964). Auditory-visual integration in normal and retarded readers. *American Journal of Orthopsychiatry*, **34**, 852-861. (25, 46, 105)

Birch, H. G., & Belmont, L. (1965). Auditory-visual integration, intelligence, and reading ability in school children. *Perceptual and Motor Skills*, **20**, 295-305. (25, 46, 105)

Bitterman, M. E., Tyler, D. W., & Elam, C B. (1955). Simultaneous and successive discrimination under identical stimulating conditions. *American Journal of Psychology*, **68**, 237-248. (527)

Bloom, L. (1974). Talking, understanding, and thinking. In R. L. Schiefelbusch & L. L. Lloyd (Eds), *Language perspectives—acquisition, retardation, and intervention* (pp. 285-311). Baltimore, MD: University Park Press. (115)

Bower, G., & Grusec, T. (1964). Effect of prior Pavlovian discrimination training upon learning an operant discrimination. *Journal of the Experimental Analysis of Behavior*, 7, 401-404. (403)

Brady, J. V. (1992). Continuously programmed environments and the experimental analysis of human behavior. *Cambridge Center for Behavioral Studies monograph series: Progress in behavioral studies*, Monograph #1, pp. 6-35. (352)

Brown, P. L., & Jenkins, H. M. (1968). Auto-shaping of the pigeon's keypeck. *Journal of the Experimental Analysis of Behavior*, 11, 1-8. (134)

Bush, K. M. (1993). Stimulus equivalence and cross-modal transfer. *The Psychological Record*, 43, 567-584. (35)

Bush, K. M., Sidman, M., & de Rose, T. (1989). Contextual control of emergent equivalence relations. *Journal of the Experimental Analysis of Behavior*, 51, 29-45. (xi, 117, 273, 359, 361, 424, 426, 513)

Carrigan, P. F. (1986). *Conditional discrimination and transitive relations: A theoretical and experimental analysis*. Unpublished doctoral dissertation, Northeastern University, Boston. (381, 540)

Carrigan, P. F., Jr., & Sidman, M. (1992). Conditional discrimination and equivalence relations: A theoretical analysis of control by negative stimuli. *Journal of the Experimental Analysis of Behavior*, 58, 459-504. (vii, 167, 269, 319, 320, 450, 516, 525, 540, 548)

Carter, D. E., & Eckerman, D. A. (1975). Symbolic matching by pigeons:Rate of learning complex discriminations predicted from simple discriminations. *Science*, 187, 662-664. (128)

Carter, D. E., & Werner, T. J. (1978). Complex learning and information processing by pigeons: A critical analysis. *Journal of the Experimental Analysis of Behavior*, 29, 565-601. (413)

Catania, A. C. (1973). The concept of the operant in the analysis of behavior. *Behaviorism*, 1, 103-116. (329)

Catania, A. C. (1975). The myth of self-reinforcement. *Behaviorism*, 3, 192-199. (327)

Catania, A. C. (1976). Self-reinforcement revisited. *Behaviorism*, 4, 157-162. (327)

Catania, A. C. (1980). Autoclitic processes and the structure of behavior. *Behaviorism*, 8, 175-186. (286, 338)

Catania, A. C. (1991). Glossary. In I. H. Iversen & K. A. Lattal (Eds.), *Techniques in the behavioral sciences: Experimental analysis of behavior, Part 2*. (pp. G1-G44). Amsterdam: Elsevier. (397)

Catania, A. C. (1992). *Learning* (3rd ed.). Englewood Cliffs, NJ: Prentice Hall. (326, 389)

Cerutti, D. T., & Rumbaugh, D. M. (1993). Stimulus relations in comparative primate perspective. *The Psychological Record*, 43, 811-821. (173)

Chiesa, M. (1994). *Radical behaviorism: The philosophy and the science*. Boston: Authors Cooperative. (7, 387, 509)

Chomsky, N. (1965). *Aspects of the theory of syntax*. Cambridge, MA: MIT Press. (220)

References

Cofer, C. N., & Foley, J. P. (1942). Mediated generalization and the interpretation of verbal behavior: I. Prologomena. *Psychological Review, 49,* 513-540. (81, 82, 85, 287, 406)

Cohen, L. R. (1969). Generalization during acquisition, extinction, and transfer of matching with an adjustable comparison. *Journal of the Experimental Analysis of Behavior, 12,* 463-474. (167)

Cohen, L. R., Brady, J., & Lowry, M. (1981). The role of differential responding to samples in matching-to-sample and delayed matching performance. In M. L. Commons & J. A. Nevin (Eds.), *Quantitative studies of operant behavior: Discriminative properties of reinforcement schedules* (pp.345-364). Cambridge, MA: Ballinger. (139, 413)

Cohen, L. R., Looney, T. A., Brady, J. H., & Aucella, A. F. (1976). Differential sample-response schedules in the acquisition of conditional discriminations by pigeons. *Journal of the Experimental Analysis of Behavior, 26,* 301-314. (136, 413)

Cohen-Almeida, D. (1993). *Simple discrimination tests for the merger of functional classes.* Unpublished M.A. thesis, Northeastern University, Boston. (416, 460)

Cohen-Almeida, D., & Sidman, M. (1991). Simple discrimination tests for transfer of functional class membership. (Poster at ABA, Atlanta, GA). (375, 416, 455, 460)

Constantine, B. (1981). *An experimental analysis of stimulus control in simple conditional discriminations.* Unpublished doctoral dissertation, Northeastern University, Boston. (154, 155, 167)

Constantine, B., & Sidman, M. (1975). The role of naming in delayed matching to sample. *American Journal of Mental Deficiency, 79,* 680-689. (281)

Crawford, L. L., Holloway, K. S., & Domjan, M. (1993). The nature of sexual reinforcement. *Journal of the Experimental Analysis of Behavior, 60,* 55-66. (402)

Cumming, W. W., & Berryman, R. (1965). The complex discriminated operant: Studies of matching-to-sample and related problems. In D. I. Mostofsky (Ed.), *Stimulus generalization* (pp. 284-330). Stanford, CA: Stanford University Press. (77, 161, 167, 337, 360)

D'Amato, M. R., Salmon, D. P., Loukas, E., & Tomie, A. (1985). Symmetry and transitivity of conditional relations in monkeys (*Cebus apella*) and pigeons (*Columba livia*). *Journal of the Experimental Analysis of Behavior, 44,* 35-47. (166, 168, 306, 359, 445)

Davenport, R. K., & Rogers, C. M. (1970). Intermodal equivalence of stimuli in apes. *Science, 168,* 279-280. (164, 167)

Day, W. (1992). *Radical behaviorism: Willard Day on psychology and philosophy.* Reno, NV: Context Press. (85)

de Rose, J. C., McIlvane, W. J., Dube, W. V., Galpin, V. C., & Stoddard, L. T. (1988). Emergent simple discrimination established by indirect relation to differential consequences. *Journal of the Experimental Analysis of Behavior, 50,* 1-20. (375, 393, 445, 464) de Rose, J. C., McIlvane, W. J., Dube, W. V., & Stoddard, L. T. (1988). Stimulus class formation and functional equivalence in moderately retarded individuals' conditional discrimination. *Behavioural Processes,* 17, 167-175. (375, 393, 445, 464

Devany, J. M., Hayes, S. C., & Nelson, R. O. (1986). Equivalence class formation in language-able and language-disabled children. *Journal of the Experimental Analysis of Behavior,* 46, 243-257. (86, 273, 306, 445, 478, 484)

Dinsmoor, J. A. (1983). Observing and conditioned reinforcement. *The Behavioral and Brain Sciences,* 6, 693-728. (397)

Dixon, L. S. (1977). The nature of control by spoken words over visual stimulus selection. *Journal of the Experimental Analysis of Behavior,* 27, 433-442. (60, 532)

Domjan, M., & Burkhard, B. *The principles of learning and behavior.* Monterey, CA: Brooks/Cole. (398)

Donahoe, J. W., Burgos, J. E., & Palmer, D. C. (1993). A selectionist approach to reinforcement. *Journal of the Experimental Analysis of Behavior,* 60, 17-40. (402)

Dougher, M. J., Augustson, E. M., Markham, M. R., Wulfert, E., & Greenway, D. E. (in press). The transfer of respondent eliciting and extinction functions through stimulus equivalence classes. *Journal of the Experimental Analysis of Behavior.* (464)

Dougher, M. J., & Markham, M. R. (1994). Stimulus equivalence, functional equivalence, and the transfer of function. In Hayes, S. C., Hayes, L. J., Sato, M., & Ono, K. (Eds.), *Behavior analysis of language and cognition* (pp. 71-90). Reno, NV: Context Press. (448)

Dube, W. V., Callahan, T. D., & McIlvane, W. J. (1993). Serial reversals of concurrent auditory discriminations in rats. *The Psychological Record,* 43, 429-440. (450)

Dube, W. V., Green, G., & Serna, R.W. (1993). Auditory successive conditional discrimination and auditory stimulus equivalence classes. *Journal of the Experimental Analysis of Behavior,* 59, 103-114. (35, 229, 272, 320, 539)

Dube, W. V., McDonald, S. J., & McIlvane, W. J. (1991). A note on the relationship between equivalence classes and functional stimulus classes. *Experimental Analysis of Human Behavior Bulletin,* 9, 7-11. (420, 448)

Dube, W. V., McDonald, S. J., McIlvane, W. J., & Mackay, H. A. (1991). Constructed-response matching to sample and spelling instruction. Journal of Applied Behavior Analysis, 24, 305-317. (77)

Dube, W. V., & McIlvane, W. J. (1989). Adapting a microcomputer for behavioral evaluation of mentally retarded individuals. In J. A. Mulick & R. F. Antonack (Eds.), *Transitions in mental retardation* (Vol. 4, pp. 104-127). Norwood, NJ: Ablex. (65)

Dube, W. V., McIlvane, W. J., Callahan, T. D., & Stoddard, L. T. (1993). The search for stimulus equivalence in nonverbal organisms. *The Psychological Record,* 43, 761-778. (166)

References

Dube, W. V., McIlvane, W. J., Mackay, H. A., & Stoddard, L. T. (1987). Stimulus class membership established via stimulus-reinforcer relations. *Journal of the Experimental Analysis of Behavior, 47*, 159-175. (368, 369, 386, 409, 410, 508)

Dube, W. V., McIlvane, W. J., Maguire, R. W., Mackay, H. A., & Stoddard,L. T. (1989). Stimulus class formation and stimulus-reinforcer relations. *Journal of the Experimental Analysis of Behavior, 51*, 65-76. (368, 369, 386)

Dube, W. V., Rocco, F. J., & McIlvane, W. J. (1989). Delayed matching to sample with outcome-specific contingencies in mentally retarded humans. *The Psychological Record, 39*, 483-492. (368, 386)

Dugdale, N. A. (1988). *The role of naming in stimulus equivalence: Differences between humans and animals.* Unpublished Ph.D. thesis, University of Wales. (362)

Dugdale, N. A., & Lowe, C. F. (1990). Naming and stimulus equivalence. In D. E. Blackman & H. Lejeune (Eds.), *Behaviour analysis in theory and practice: Contributions and controversies* (pp. 115-138). Hove, England: Erlbaum. (63, 113, 126, 166, 281, 305, 306, 362, 363, 364, 414, 470, 484, 512)

Eckerman, D. A. (1970). Generalization and response mediation of a conditional discrimination. *Journal of the Experimental Analysis of Behavior, 13*, 301-316. (167)

Eikeseth, S., & Smith, T. (1992). The development of functional and equivalence classes in high-functioning autistic children: The role of naming. *Journal of the Experimental Analysis of Behavior, 58*, 123-133. (305)

Ekstrand, B. R. (1966). Backward associations. *Psychological Bulletin, 65*, 50-64. (111, 222, 287, 380)

Epstein, R., Lanza, R. P., & Skinner, B. F. (1980). Symbolic communication between two pigeons *(Columba livia domestica). Science, 207*, 543-545. (125)

Estes, W. K. (1969). New perspectives on some old issues in association theory. In N. J. Mackintosh and W. K. Honig (Eds.), Fundamental issues in associative learning (pp. 162-189). Halifax: Dalhousie Univ. Press. (108)

Estes, W. K., Koch, S., MacCorquodale, K., Meehl, P. E., Mueller, C. G., Schoenfeld, W. N., & Verplanck, W. S. (1954). *Modern learning theory: A critical analysis of five examples.* New York: Appleton-Century-Crofts. (326, 329, 331)

Fantuzzo, J., & Atkins, M. (1992). Applied behavior analysis for educators: Teacher centered and classroom based. J*ournal of Applied Behavior Analysis, 25*, 37-42. (66)

Farthing, G. W., & Opuda, M. J. (1974). Transfer of matching-to-sample in pigeons. *Journal of the Experimental Analysis of Behavior, 21*, 199-213. (142, 167)

Fawcett, S. B. (1991). Some values guiding community research and action. *Journal of Applied Behavior Analysis, 24*, 621-636. (66)

Ferster, C. B., & Skinner, B. F. (1957). *Schedules of reinforcement.* New York: Appleton-Century-Crofts. (331)

Fields, L., Adams, B. J., Newman, S., & Verhave, T. (1992). Interactions among emergent relations during equivalence class formation. *Quarterly Journal of Experimental Psychology*, **45B**, 125-138. (273)

Fields, L., Adams, B. J., & Verhave, T. (1993). The effects of equivalence class structure on test performances. *The Psychological Record*, **43**, 697-712. (273, 315, 537, 538, 545, 547)

Fields, L., Adams, B. J., Verhave, T., & Newman, S. (1990). The effects of nodality on the formation of equivalence classes. *Journal of the Experimental Analysis of Behavior*, **53**, 345-358. (273, 539)

Fields, L., Adams, B. J., Verhave, T., & Newman, S. (1993). Are stimuli in equivalence classes equally related to each other? *The Psychological Record*, **43**, 85-105. (273, 542, 545)

Fields, L., & Verhave, T. (1987). The structure of equivalence classes. *Journal of the Experimental Analysis of Behavior*, **48**, 317-332. (226, 441, 506, 539)

Fields, L., Verhave, T., & Fath, S. (1984). Stimulus equivalence and transitive associations: A methodological analysis. *Journal of the Experimental Analysis of Behavior*, **42**, 143-157. (226. 351. 441. 525. 539)

Findley, J. D. (1962). An experimental outline for building and exploring multi-operant behavior repertoires. *Journal of the Experimental Analysis of Behavior*, **5**, 113-166. (335, 352)

Findley, J. D. (1966). Programmed environments for the experimental analysis of human behavior. In W. K. Honig (Ed.), *Operant behavior: Areas of research and application* (pp.827-848). New York: Appleton-Century-Crofts. (352)

Findley, J. D., & Brady, J. V. (1965). Facilitation of large ratio performance by use of conditioned reinforcement. *Journal of the Experimental Analysis of Behavior*, **8**, 125-129. (335)

Fletcher, F. G, Stoddard, L. T., & Sidman, M. (1971). A system for unlimited repetitive presentation of auditory stimuli. Journal *of* Experimental Child Psychology, 11, 165-169. (48, 92, 199, 237, 290)

Fodor, J. A., Bever, T. G., & Garrett, M. F. (1974). *The psychology of language*. New York: McGraw-Hill. (220)

French, G. M. (1965). Associative problems. In A. M. Schrier, H. F.Harlow, & F. Stollnitz (Eds.), *Behavior of nonhuman primates* (pp.167-210). New York: Academic Press. (164)

Fucini, A. (1982). *Stimulus control of class membership*. Unpublished doctoral dissertation, Northeastern University, Boston. (262, 302, 350, 481, 516)

Galvão, O., Calcagno, S., & Sidman, M. (1992). Testing for Emergent Performances in Extinction. *Experimental Analysis of Human Behavior Bulletin*, **10**, 18-20. (419, 420, 447)

Galvão, O., Sidman, M., & Cohen-Almeida, D. (1992). Does the repeated-reversals procedure establish functional classes? (Poster at ABA, SanFrancisco, CA). (416, 451, 455, 457)

References

Garcia, J., & Koelling, R. A. (1966). Relation of cue to consequence in avoidance learning. *Psychonomic Science*, 4, 123-124. (405)

Gatch, M. B., & Osborne, J. G. (1989). Transfer of contextual stimulus function via equivalence class development. *Journal of the Experimental Analysis of Behavior*, 51, 369-378. (475)

Gellert, W., Küstner, H., Hellwich, M., & Kästner, H. (1977). *The VNR concise encyclopedia of mathematics*. New York: Van Nostrand Reinhold. (123, 392, 417, 552, 553)

Gershenson, C. W., & Joseph, B. (1990, May). *The formation of conditional discriminations and equivalence classes by individuals with Alzheimer's disease.* Poster presented at the meeting of the Association for Behavior Analysis, Nashville, TN. (117)

Geschwind, N. (1965a). Disconnexion syndromes in animals and man: Part I. Brain, 88, 237-293. (25, 46, 105)

Geschwind, N. (1965b). Disconnexion syndromes in animals and man, Part II. Brain, 88, 585-644. (21, 25, 31, 46)

Geschwind, N. (1972). Language and the brain. Scientific American, 226, 76-83. (21, 24, 46)

Geschwind, N. (1979). Specializations of the human brain. Scientific American, 241, 180-199. (21, 46)

Gibson, E. J. (1965). Learning to read. *Science*, 148, 1066-1072. (79)

Gibson, E. J., Gibson, J. J., Pick, A. D., & Osser, H. (1962). A developmental study of the discrimination of letter-like forms. *Journal of Comparative and Physiological Psychology*, 55, 897-906. (77)

Ginsburg, N. (1957). Matching in pigeons. *Journal of Comparative and Physiological Psychology*, 50, 261-263. (167)

Goldiamond, I. (1962). Perception. In A. J. Bachrach (Ed.), *Experimental foundations of clinical Psychology* (pp. 280-340). New York: Basic Books. (77, 170, 221, 326, 329, 333, 385, 447, 448, 463)

Goldiamond, I. (1966). Perception, language, and conceptualization rules. In B. Kleinmuntz (Ed.), *Problem solving* (pp. 183-224). New York: Wiley. (326, 423, 447, 484)

Goldiamond, I. (1975). Alternative sets as a framework for behavioral formulations and research. *Behaviorism*, 3, 49-86. 326, 353)

Goldiamond, I. (1976). Self-reinforcement. *Journal of Applied Behavior Analysis*, 9, 509-514. (327)

Goldiamond, I. (1982). Training parent trainers and ethicists in nonlinear analysis of behavior. In R. F. Dangel & R. A. Polster (Eds.), *Parent training: Foundations of research and practice* (pp. 504-546). New York: Guilford Press. (353)

Graham, J. M., & Desjardins, C. (1980). Classical conditioning: Induction of luteinizing hormone and testosterone secretion in anticipation of sexual activity. *Science*, 210, 1039-1041. (405)

Gray, L. (1966). Backward association in pigeons. *Psychonomic Science,* **4**, 333-334. (150)

Green, D. M., & Swets, J. A. (1966). *Signal detection theory and psychophysics.* New York: Wiley. (333)

Green, G. (1987). Contextual control of stimulus equivalence with preschool children. *Dissertation Abstracts International,* 47, 2652B-2653B. (Order No. DA8719421). (475)

Green, G. (1990). Differences in development of visual and auditory-visual equivalence relations. *American Journal on Mental Retardation,* **95**, 260-270. (307, 308)

Green, G. (1991). Everyday stimulus equivalences for the brain injured. In W. Ishaq (Ed.), *Human behavior in today's world* (pp. 123-132). New York: Praeger. (117)

Green, G., & Sigurdardottir, Z. G. (1990, May). *Long-term remembering of equivalence classes and sequence classes by two brain-injured adults.* Paper presented at the meeting of the Association for Behavior Analysis, Nashville, TN. (117)

Green, G., Sigurdardottir, Z. G., & Saunders, R. R. (1991). The role of instructions in the transfer of ordinal functions through equivalence classes. *Journal of the Experimental Analysis of Behavior,* **55**, 287-304. (116, 392)

Green, G., Stromer, R., & Mackay, H. A. (1993). Relational learning in stimulus sequences. *The Psychological Record,* **43**, 599-616. (552, 561)

Grossman, D. (1989). *See under: Love.* (Translated from the Hebrew by Betsy Rosenberg). New York: Farrar Straus Giroux. (4)

Grover, D. E., Horton, D. L., & Cunningham, M., Jr. (1967). Mediated facilitation and interference in a four-stage paradigm. *Journal of Verbal Learning and Verbal Behavior,* **6**, 42-46. (183)

Guess, D. (1969). A functional analysis of receptive language and productive speech: Acquisition of the plural morpheme. *Journal of Applied Behavior Analysis,* **2**, 55-64. (32, 58, 90, 288)

Guess, D., & Baer, D. M. (1973). An analysis of individual differences in generalization between receptive and productive language in retarded children. Journal of *Applied Behavior Analysis,* 6, 311-329. (90, 288)

Guha, D., Dutta, S. N., & Pradhan, S. N. (1974). Conditioning of gastric secretion by epinephrine in rats. *Proceedings of the Society for Experimental Biology and Medicine,* **147**, 817-819. (405)

Hall, G. (1990). Reasoning and associative learning. In D. E. Blackman & H. Lejeune (Eds.), *Behaviour analysis in theory and practice: Contributions and controversies* (pp. 159-180). Hove, England: Erlbaum. (406)

Hall, G. A., & Chase, P. N. (1991). The relationship between stimulus equivalence and verbal behavior. *The Analysis of Verbal Behavior,* **9**, 107-119. (418)

Hamblin, R. L., Buckholdt, D., Ferritor, D., Kozloff, M., & Blackwell, L. (1971). *The humanization processes: A social, behavioral analysis of children's problems.* New York: Wiley. (533)

References

Harlow, H. F. (1959). Learning set and error factor theory. In S. Koch (Ed.), *Psychology: A study of a science* (Vol 2, pp. 492-537). New York: McGraw-Hill. (169)

Harrison, R.J., & Green, G. (1990). Development of conditional and equivalence relations without differential consequences. *Journal of the Experimental Analysis of Behavior, 54*, 225-237. (278, 540)

Hayes, L.J. (1992). Equivalence as process. In S. C. Hayes & L. J. Hayes (Eds.), *Understanding verbal relations* (pp. 97-108). Reno, NV: Context Press. (406)

Hayes, L. J., Tilley, K. J., & Hayes, S. C. (1988). Extending equivalence class membership to gustatory stimuli. *The Psychological Record, 38*, 473-482. (35)

Hayes, S. C. (1986). The case of the silent dog—verbal reports and the analysis of rules: A review of Ericsson and Simon's *Protocol Analysis: Verbal Reports as Data. Journal of the Experimental Analysis of Behavior, 45*, 351-363. (63, 174, 554)

Hayes, S. C. (1989). Nonhumans have not yet shown stimulus equivalence. *Journal of the Experimental Analysis of Behavior, 51*, 385-392. (170)

Hayes, S. C. (1991). A relational control theory of stimulus equivalence. In L. J. Hayes & P. N. Chase (Eds.), *Dialogues on verbal behavior* (pp. 19-40). Reno, NV: Context Press. (63, 167, 174, 364, 387, 470, 513, 514, 554, 557, 558, 559)

Hayes, S. C. (1992). Verbal relations, time, and suicide. In S. C. Hayes & L. J. Hayes (Eds.), *Understanding verbal relations* (pp. 109-118). Reno, NV: Context Press. (555)

Hayes, S. C. (1994). Relational frame theory: A functional approach to verbal events. In S. C. Hayes, L. J. Hayes, M. Sato, & K. Ono (Eds.), *Behavior analysis of language and cognition* (pp.9-30). Reno, NV: Context Press. (554)

Hayes, S. C., Devany, J. M., Kohlenberg, B. S., Brownstein, A. J., & Shelby, J. (1987). Stimulus equivalence and the symbolic control of behavior. *Mexican Journal of Behavior Analysis, 13*, 361-374. (375, 393, 464, 554)

Hayes, S. C., & Hayes, L. J. (1989). The verbal action of the listener as a basis for rule-governance. In S. C. Hayes (Ed.), *Rule-governed behavior: Cognition, contingencies, and instructional control* (pp. 153-190). New York: Plenum. (406, 470, 512, 513, 554)

Hayes, S. C., Kohlenberg, B. S., & Hayes, L. J. (1991). The transfer of specific and general consequential functions through simple and conditional equivalence relations. *Journal of the Experimental Analysis of Behavior, 56*, 119-137. (397, 475)

Henton, W. W. (1978). Review of classical-operant conditioning, parameter by parameter. In W. W. Henton & I. H. Iversen, *Classical conditioning and operant conditioning: A response pattern analysis* (pp. 19-96). New York: Springer-Verlag. (405)

Henton, W. W., & Iversen, I. H. *Classical conditioning and operant conditioning: A response pattern analysis.* New York: Springer-Verlag. (398)

Herrnstein, R. J. (1970). On the law of effect. *Journal of the Experimental Analysis of Behavior*, **13**, 243-266. (353)

Hineline, P. N. (1980). The language of behavior analysis: Its community, its functions, and its limitations. *Behaviorism*, **8**, 67-86. (7, 326)

Hineline, P. N. (1986). Re-tuning the operant-respondent distinction. In T. Thompson & M. D. Zeiler (Eds.), *Analysis and integration of behavioral units* (pp. 55-79). Hillsdale, NJ: Lawrence Erlbaum Associates. (352)

Hineline, P. N. (1990). The origins of environment-based psychological theory. *Journal of the Experimental Analysis of Behavior*, **53**, 305-320. (352)

Hogan, D. E., & Zentall, T. R. (1977). Backward associations in the pigeon. *American Journal of Psychology*, **90**, 3-15. (131, 137, 141, 150, 161, 166)

Holland, J. G., & Skinner, B. F. (1961). *The analysis of behavior.* New York: McGraw-Hill. (323, 389)

Holland, J. G., Solomon, C., Doran, J., & Frezza, D. A. (1976). *The analysis of behavior in planning instruction.* Reading, MA: Addison-Wesley. (77, 533)

Hollis, J. H., Carrier, J. K., Jr., & Spradlin, J. E. (1976). An approach to remediation of communication and learning deficiencies. In L. L. Lloyd (Ed.), *Communication assessment and intervention strategies* (pp. 265-294). Baltimore, MD: University Park Press. (65)

Holmes, P. W. (1979). Transfer of matching performance in pigeons. *Journal of the Experimental Analysis of Behavior*, **31**, 103-114. (131, 137, 161, 166)

Iversen, I. H. Matching-to-sample performance in rats: A case of mistaken identity. *Submitted for Publication.* (167)

Iversen, I. H., Sidman, M., & Carrigan, P. (1986). Stimulus definition in conditional discriminations. *Journal of the Experimental Analysis of Behavior*, **45**, 297-304. (167, 306)

James, C. T., & Hakes, D. T. (1965). Mediated transfer in a four-stage, stimulus-equivalence paradigm. *Journal of Verbal Learning and Verbal Behavior*, **4**, 89-93. (182, 183, 554)

Jenkins, J. J. (1963). Mediated associations: paradigms and situations. In C. N. Cofer, and B. S Musgrave (Eds.), Verbal behavior and learning: Problems and processes (pp. 210-245). New York: McGraw-Hill. (58, 62, 85, 88, 89, 90, 108, 111, 112, 179, 181, 183, 206, 222, 241, 281, 286, 358, 385, 406, 539)

Jenkins, J. J. (1965). Mediation theory and grammatical behavior. In S. Rosenberg (Ed.), *Directions in psycholinguistics* (pp. 66-96). New York: Macmillan. (180, 222, 286, 358, 474, 557)

Jenkins, J. J., & Palermo, D. S. (1964). Mediation processes and the acquisition of linguistic structure. In U. Bellugi & R. Brown (Eds.), *The acquisition of language. Monographs of the Society for Research in Child Development,* **29**, (1, Serial No. 92), 141-169. (85, 86, 179, 222, 287, 474)

Jensen, A. R. (1971). The role of verbal mediation in mental development. Journal *of* Genetic Psychology, **118**, 39-70. (58)

References

Johnson, C., & Sidman, M. (1993). Conditional discrimination and equivalence relations: Control by negative stimuli. *Journal of the Experimental Analysis of Behavior*, **59**, 333-347. (vii, 167, 224, 269, 319, 320, 516, 540, 548)

Johnston, J. M., & Pennypacker, H. S. (1980). *Strategies and tactics of human behavioral research*. Hillsdale, NJ: Lawrence Erlbaum Associates. (183)

Joseph, B., & Thompson, T. (1990, May). *The formation of equivalence relations by persons with Prader-Willi and Down Syndrome*. Poster presented at the meeting of the Association for Behavior Analysis, Nashville, TN. (117)

Joyce, B., & Joyce, J. (1990, May). *Stimulus equivalence: An approach for training children with TBI*. Poster presented at the meeting of the Association for Behavior Analysis, Nashville, TN. (117)

Kahn, D., & Birch, H. G. (1968). Development of auditory-visual integration and reading achievement. *Perceptual and Motor Skills,* **27**, 459-468. (25, 46, 105)

Kastak, D., & Schusterman, R. J. (1992). Comparative cognition in marine mammals: A clarification on match-to-sample tests. *Marine Mammal Science*, **8**, 414-417. (175)

Kastak, D., & Schusterman, R. J. (1993). Immediate transfer of visual identity matching-to-sample in two California sea lions (*Zalophus californianus*). Manuscript submitted for publication. (175)

Kawashima, T. (1993). Personal communication. (466, 470, 471)

Kelleher, R. T. (1966). Conditioned reinforcement in second-order schedules. *Journal of the Experimental Analysis of Behavior*, **9**, 475-485. (335)

Kelleher, R.T., & Gollub, L. R. (1962). A Review of Positive Conditioned Reinforcement. *Journal of the Experimental Analysis of Behavior*, **5** (Suppl.), 543-597. (397)

Keller, F. S., & Schoenfeld, W. N. (1950). *Principles of Psychology.* New York: Appleton-Century-Crofts. (81, 389, 447)

Kennedy, C. H. (1991). Equivalence class formation influenced by the number of nodes separating stimuli. *Behavioural Processes,* **24**, 219-245. (273, 539, 540)

Kennedy, C. H., & Laitinen, R. (1988). Second-order conditional control of symmetric and transitive stimulus relations: The influence of order effects. *The Psychological Record,* **38**, 437-446. (475, 513)

Kennedy, C. H., & Serna, L. A. (unpublished manuscript). Establishment, reversal, and indirect transfer of new discriminative functions for stimuli controlling incompatible responses. (448)

Kirshner, H., & Sidman, M. (1972). Scanning patterns in aphasic patients during matching-to-sample tests. *Neuropsychologia,* **10**, 179-184. (61)

Kjeldergaard, P. M. (1968). Transfer and mediation in verbal learning. In T. R. Dixon & D. L. Horton (Eds.), *Verbal behavior and general behavior theory* (pp. 67-96). Englewood Cliffs, NJ: Prentice-Hall. (85)

Kling, J. W. (1971). Learning: Introductory survey. In J. W. Kling & L. A. Riggs (Eds.), *Woodworth & Schlosberg's experimental psychology* (pp. 551-613). New York: Holt, Rinehart and Winston. (398)

Kohlenberg, B. S., Hayes, S. C., & Hayes, L. J. (1991). The transfer of contextual control over equivalence classes through equivalence classes: A possible model of social stereotyping. *Journal of the Experimental Analysis of Behavior, 56*, 505-518. (475, 514)

Lashley, K. S. (1938). Conditional reactions in the rat. *Journal of Psychology, 6*, 311-324. (336)

Lawrence, D. H. (1963). The nature of a stimulus: Some relationships between learning and perception. In S. Koch (Ed.), *Psychology: A study of a science* (Vol. 5, pp. 179-212). New York: McGraw-Hill. (139, 331, 337)

Lazar, R. (1977). Extending sequence-class membership with matching to sample. *Journal of the Experimental Analysis of Behavior, 27*, 381-392. (110, 116, 117, 146, 193, 229, 233, 286, 288, 345, 392, 423, 478)

Lazar, R. M., Davis-Lang, D., & Sanchez, L. (1984). The formation of visual stimulus equivalences in children. *Journal of the Experimental Analysis of Behavior, 41*, 251-266. (35, 116, 229, 233, 234, 241, 259, 263, 273, 281, 286, 288, 351, 358, 478, 484)

Lazar, R. M., & Kotlarchyk, B. J. (1986). Second-order control of sequence-class equivalences in children. *Behavioural Processes, 13*, 205-215. (116, 131, 146, 233, 286, 288, 345, 350, 392, 423, 481)

Lazar, R. M., & Scarisbrick, D. (1993). Alexia without agraphia: A functional assessment of behavior in focal neurologic disease. *The Psychological Record, 43*, 639-650. (527)

Lee, V. L. (1978). Teaching generalized receptive and productive behind-front discriminations to two retarded children. *Journal of Applied Behavior Analysis, 11*, 529. (115, 288)

Lee, V. L. (1981a). Prepositional phrases spoken and heard. *Journal of the Experimental Analysis of Behavior, 35*, 227-242. (62, 115, 288)

Lee, V. L. (1981b). Terminological and conceptual revision in the experimental analysis of language development: Why? *Behaviorism, 9*, 25-53. (62)

Lee, V. L. (1983). Behavior as a constituent of conduct. *Behaviorism, 11*, 199-224. (326)

Lee, V. L. (1988). *Beyond behaviorism.* Hillsdale, NJ: Lawrence Erlbaum Associates. (20, 323, 509)

Leicester, J., Sidman, M., Stoddard, L. T., & Mohr, J. P. (1971). The nature of aphasic responses. *Neuropsychologia, 9*, 141-155. (7, 8, 13, 183)

Lindsley, O. R. (1992). Why aren't effective teaching tools widely adopted? *Journal of the Applied Analysis of Behavior, 25*, 21-26. (66)

Lipkens, R., Kop, P. F. M., & Matthijs, W. (1988). A test of symmetry and transitivity in the conditional discrimination performances of pigeons. *Journal of the Experimental Analysis of Behavior, 49*, 395-409. (166, 306, 359, 445)

References

Lissauer, H. (1890). Ein fall von seelenblindheit nebst einem beitrage zur theorie derselben. *Archives of Psychiatry, 21*, 222-270. (10)

Lorente de Nó, R. (1938). Analysis of the activity of the chains of internuncial neurons. *Journal of Neurophysiology, 1*, 187-194. (274)

Lowe, C. F. (1986, May). *The role of verbal behavior in the emergence of equivalence relations.* Paper presented at the meeting of the Association for Behavior Analysis, Milwaukee, WI. (63, 113, 358, 445)

Lowenkron, B. (1984). Coding responses and the generalization of matching to sample in children. *Journal of the Experimental Analysis of Behavior, 42*, 1-18. (414)

Lowenkron, B. (1989). Instructional control of generalized relational matching to sample in children. *Journal of the Experimental Analysis of Behavior, 52*, 293-309. (414)

Luria, A. R. (1957). The role of language in the formation of temporary connections. In B. Simon (Ed.), *Psychology in the Soviet Union.* Stanford, CA: Stanford University Press. (511)

Lynch, D. C., & Green, G. (1991). Development and crossmodal transfer of contextual control of emergent stimulus relations. *Journal of the Experimental Analysis of Behavior, 56*, 139-154. (475, 514)

MacCorquodale, K., & Meehl, P. E. (1948). On a distinction between hypothetical constructs and intervening variables. *Psychological Review, 55*, 95-107. (266, 326)

Mackay, H. A. (1985). Stimulus equivalence in rudimentary reading and spelling. *Analysis and Intervention in Developmental Disabilities, 5*, 373-387. (423)

Mackay, H. A., & Brown, S. M. (1971). Teaching serial position sequences to monkeys with a delayed matching-to-sample procedure. *Journal of the Experimental Analysis of Behavior, 15*, 335-345. (167)

Mackay, H. A., & Sidman, M. (1968). Instructing the mentally retarded in an institutional environment. In G. A. Jervis (Ed.), Expanding concepts in mental retardation (pp. 164-169). Springfield: Charles C Thomas. (34, 47, 91, 282, 323)

Mackay, H. A., & Sidman, M. (1984). Teaching new behavior via equivalence relations. In P. H. Brooks, R. Sperber, & C. McCauley (Eds.), *Learning and cognition in the mentally retarded* (pp. 493-513). Hillsdale, NJ: Lawrence Erlbaum Associates. (117, 233, 286, 287, 304, 423)

Mackay, W. E. (1979). *Stimulus class formation with an oddity procedure.* Unpublished master's thesis, Northeastern University. (163)

Manabe, K. & Kawashima, T. (1993). *The role of vocal operant and auditory stimuli on stimulus equivalence in budgerigars.* Poster presented at the meeting of the Association for Behavior Analysis, Chicago, IL. (363, 414, 466, 467, 469, 470, 471)

McDonagh, E. C., McIlvane, W. J., & Stoddard, L. T. (1984). Teaching coin equivalences via matching to sample. *Applied Research in Mental Retardation, 5*, 177-197. (117, 286, 288, 478)

McDowell, J. J. (1988).Matching theory in natural human environments. *The Behavior Analyst*, **11**, 95-109. (353)

McIlvane, W. J., & Dube, W. V. (1990). Do stimulus classes exist before they are tested? *The Analysis of Verbal Behavior*, **8**, 13-17. (274, 388)

McIlvane, W. J., Dube, W. V., Kledaras, J. B., de Rose, J. C., & Stoddard, L. T. (1992). Stimulus-reinforcer relations and conditional discrimination. In S. C. Hayes & L. J. Hayes (Eds.), *Understanding verbal relations* (pp. 43-67). Reno, NV: Context Press. (368, 369, 386, 413)

McIlvane, W. J., Dube, W. V., Kledaras, J. B., Iennaco, F. M., & Stoddard, L. T. (1990). Teaching relational discrimination to individuals with mental retardation: Some problems and possible solutions. *American Journal on Mental Retardation*, **95**, 283-296. (77, 375)

McIlvane, W. J., & Stoddard, L. T. (1981). Acquisition of matching-to-sample performances in severe retardation: Learning by exclusion. *Journal of Mental Deficiency Research*, **25**, 33-48. (60, 532)

McIlvane, W. J., & Stoddard, L. T. (1985). Complex stimulus relations and exclusion in mental retardation. *Analysis and Intervention in Developmental Disabilities*, **5**, 307-321. (532)

McIntire, K. D., Cleary, J., & Thompson, T. (1987). Conditional relations by monkeys: Reflexivity, symmetry, and transitivity. *Journal of the Experimental Analysis of Behavior*, **47**, 279-285. (170, 171, 358, 359, 445, 484)

McIntire, K. D., Cleary, J., & Thompson, T. (1989). Reply to Saunders and to Hayes. *Journal of the Experimental Analysis of Behavior*, **51**, 393-396. (170)

Meehl, P. E. (1950). On the circularity of the Law of Effect. *Psychological Bulletin*, **47**, 52-75. (326)

Meehl, P. E. (1992). Needs (Murray, 1938) and state-variables (Skinner, 1938). *Psychological Reports*, **70**, 407-450. (385, 389)

Mehegan, D. (1994). War of words erupts over 'rape' review. *Boston Globe*, January 6, pp. 45, 50. (5)

Mellgren, R. L., & Ost, J. W. P. (1969). Transfer of Pavlovian differential conditioning to an operant discrimination. *Journal of Comparative and Physiological Psychology*, **67**, 390-394. (403)

Mohr, J. P., & Sidman, M. (1975). Aphasia. In S. Arietti (Ed.), *American handbook of Psychiatry* (Vol. 4, pp. 279-298). New York: Basic Books. (323)

Mohr, J. P., Sidman, M., Stoddard, L. T., Leicester, J., & Rosenberger, P. B. (1973). Evolution of the deficit in total aphasia. *Neurology*, **23**, 1302-1312. (62, 183, 323)

Moore, R., & Goldiamond, I. (1964). Errorless establishment of visual discriminations using fading procedures. *Journal of the Experimental Analysis of Behavior*, **7**, 269-272. (74)

Moxley, R. (1982). Graphics for three-term contingencies. *The Behavior Analyst*, **5**, 45-51. (352)

Moxley, R. (1983). Educational diagrams. *Instructional Science*, **12**, 147-160. (352)

References

Moxley, R. (1984). Graphic discriminations for radical functional behaviorism. *Behaviorism*, **12**, 81-95. (352)

Nakagawa, E. (1992). Effects of overtraining on reversal learning by rats in concurrent and single discriminations. *The Quarterly Journal of Experimental Psychology*, **44B**, 37-56. (450)

Nevin, J. A., & Liebold, K. (1966). Stimulus control of matching and oddity in a pigeon. *Psychonomic Science*, **5**, 351-352. (351, 477, 481)

Nissen, H. W., Blum, J. S., & Blum, R. A. (1948). Analysis of matching behavior in chimpanzee. *Journal of Comparative and Physiological Psychology*, **41**, 62-74. (164)

Notterman, J. M., & Mintz, D. E. (1965). *Dynamics of response*. New York: Wiley. (329)

O'Leary, C. A. (1994). *Stimulus equivalence in the tactile modality*. Unpublished honors thesis, Washington and Jefferson College, Washington, PA. (35)

Paul, C. (1966). Verbal discrimination reversal as a function of overlearning and percentage of items reversed. *Journal of Experimental Psychology*, **72**, 271-275. (277)

Paul, C. (1968). Verbal discrimination reversal as a function of overlearning and percentage of items reversed: An extension. *Journal of Verbal Learning and Verbal Behavior*, **7**, 270-272. (277)

Paul, C. (1970). Acquired equivalence of correct alternatives after verbal discrimination learning. *Journal of Experimental Psychology*, **86**, 123-125. (450)

Paul, C., Hoffman, C. D., & Dick, S. (1970). Acquired (conditional) equivalence: A basis for response-set effects in verbal-discrimination reversal performance. *Journal of Experimental Psychology*, **85**, 361-367. (450)

Paul, C., & Paul, H. (1968). Transfer-activated response sets in verbal learning and transfer. *Psychological Review*, **75**, 537-549. (276, 277, 557, 558)

Pavlov, I. P. (1927). Conditioned reflexes: An investigation of the physiological activity of the cerebral cortex. London: Oxford University Press. (397)

Pérez-González, L. A. (1994). Transfer of relational stimulus control in conditional discriminations. *Journal of the Experimental Analysis of Behavior*, **61**, 487-503. (548)

Peters, H. N. (1935). Mediate association. Journal of Experimental Psychology, 18, 20-48. (58, 62, 87, 287)

Peterson, G. B., (1984). How expectancies guide behavior. In H. L. Roitblat, T. G. Bever, & H. S. Terrace (Eds.), *Animal cognition* (pp. 135-148). Hillsdale, NJ: Erlbaum. (413)

Polis, A. R., & Beard, E. M. L. (1973). *Fundamental mathematics for elementary teachers: A behavioral objectives approach*. New York: Harper & Row. (123)

Postman, L. (1971). Transfer, interference and forgetting. In J. W. Kling & L. A. Riggs (Eds.), *Woodworth & Schlosberg's Experimental Psychology* (3rd ed., pp. 1019-1132). New York: Holt, Rinehart & Winston. (85)

Prokasy, W. F., & Hall, J. F. (1963). Primary stimulus generalization. *Psychological Review*, **70**, 310-322. (331)

Ray, B. A. (1972). Strategy in studies of attention: A commentary on D. I. Mostofsky's Attention: contemporary theory and analysis. *Journal of the Experimental Analysis of Behavior,* 17, 293-297. (331)

Ray, B. A., & Sidman, M. (1970). Reinforcement schedules and stimulus control. In W. N. Schoenfeld (Ed.), *The theory of reinforcement schedules* (pp. 187-214). New York: Appleton-Century-Crofts. (77, 331)

Razran, G. H. S. (1939). A quantitative study of meaning by a conditioned salivary technique (semantic conditioning). *Science,* 90, 89-90. (287)

Rescorla, R. A. (1980). *Pavlovian second-order conditioning: Studies in associative learning.* Hillsdale, NJ: Lawrence Erlbaum Associates. (110)

Riesen, A. H., & Nissen, H. W. (1942). Nonspatial delayed response by the matching technique. *Journal of Comparative Psychology,* 34, 307-313. (164)

Riess, B. F. (1940). Semantic conditioning involving the galvanic skin reflex. *Journal of Experimental Psychology,* 26, 238-240. (287)

Riess, B. F. (1946). Genetic changes in semantic conditioning. *Journal of Experimental Psychology,* 36, 143-152. (287)

Rodewald, H. K. (1974). Symbolic matching-to-sample by pigeons. *Psychological Reports,* 34, 987-990. (131, 137, 161, 166)

Rosenberger P. B., Mohr, J. P., Stoddard, L. T., & Sidman, M. (1968). Inter- and intramodality matching deficits in a dysphasic youth. *Archives of Neurology,* 18, 549-562. (26)

Santi, A. (1978). The role of physical identity of the sample and the correct comparison stimulus in matching-to-sample paradigms. *Journal of the Experimental Analysis of Behavior,* 29, 511-516. (351, 477, 481)

Saunders, K. J. (1989). Naming in conditional discrimination and stimulus equivalence. *Journal of the Experimental Analysis of Behavior,* 51, 379-384. (170)

Saunders, K. J., Saunders, R. R., Williams, D. C., & Spradlin, J. E. (1993). An interaction of instructions and training design on stimulus class formation: Extending the analysis of equivalence. *The Psychological Record,* 43, 725-744. (526, 527)

Saunders, K. J., & Spradlin, J. E. (1989). Conditional discrimination in mentally retarded adults: The effect of training the component simple discriminations. *Journal of the Experimental Analysis of Behavior,* 52, 1-12. (77, 527)

Saunders, K. J., & Spradlin, J. E. (1990). Conditional discrimination in mentally retarded adults: The development of generalized skills. *Journal of the Experimental Analysis of Behavior,* 54, 239-250. (77)

Saunders, R. R., & Green, G. (1992). The nonequivalence of behavioral and mathematical equivalence. *Journal of the Experimental Analysis of Behavior,* 57, 227-241. (167, 319, 381, 387, 408, 418, 514, 540)

Saunders, R. R., Saunders, K. J., Kirby, K. C., & Spradlin, J. E. (1988). The merger and development of equivalence classes by unreinforced conditional selection of comparison stimuli. *Journal of the Experimental Analysis of Behavior,* 50, 145-162. (277)

References

Saunders, R. R., Wachter, J., & Spradlin, J. E. (1988). Establishing auditory stimulus control over an eight-member equivalence class via conditional discrimination procedures. *Journal of the Experimental Analysis of Behavior, 49*, 95-115. (318, 526, 539)

Savage-Rumbaugh, E. S., Rumbaugh, D. M., & Boysen, S. (1978). Symbolic communication between two chimpanzees *(Pan troglodytges). Science,* **201**, 641-644. (125)

Savage-Rumbaugh, E. S., Rumbaugh, D. M., Smith, S. T., & Lawson, J. (1980). Reference: The linguistic essential. *Science,* **210**, 922-925. (173)

Scandura, J. M. (1971). *Mathematics: Concrete behavioral foundations.* New York: Harper & Row. (123)

Schoenfeld, W. N. (1976). The "response" in behavior theory. *Pavlovian Journal of Biological Science,* 11, 129-149. (326)

Schoenfeld, W. N. (1994). *Religion and human behavior.* Boston: Authors Cooperative. (7)

Schoenfeld, W. N., & Cumming, W. W. (1963). Behavior and perception. In S. Koch (Ed.), Psychology: the study of *a science* (Vol. 5, pp. 213-252). New York: McGraw-Hill. (89, 108, 109, 139, 326, 329, 331, 337)

Schoenfeld, W. N., Matos, M. A., & Snapper, A. G. (1967). Cardiac conditioning in the white rat with food presentation as unconditional stimulus. *Conditional Reflex,* **2**, 56-67. (404)

Schusterman, R. J. (1988). Language and counting in animals: Stimulus classes and equivalence relations. *Behavioral and Brain Sciences,* 11, 596-597. (126)

Schusterman, R. J. (1990). Stimulus equivalence and cross-modal perception: A testable model for demonstrating symbolic representations in bottlenose dolphins. In J. Thomas & R. Kastelein (Eds.), *Sensory abilities of Cetaceans* (pp. 677-684). New York: Plenum. (126)

Schusterman, R. J., & Gisiner, R. C. (1989). Please parse the sentence: Animal cognition in the Procrustean bed of linguistics. *The Psychological Record,* **39**, 3-18. (126)

Schusterman, R. J., Gisiner, R., Grimm, B. K., & Hanggi, E. B. (1993). Behavior control by exclusion and attempts at establishing semanticity in marine mammals using match-to-sample paradigms. In H. L. Roitblat, L. M. Herman, & P. E. Nachtigall (Eds.), *Language and communication: Comparative perspectives* (pp. 249 - 274). Hillsdale, NJ: Lawrence Erlbaum Associates. (126)

Schusterman, R. J., & Kastak, D. (1993). A California sea lion (*Zalophus californianus*) is capable of forming equivalence relations. *Psychological Record,* **43**, 823-839. (126, 173, 174, 175, 363, 364, 466, 470, 509, 557)

Science, theory, and technology: Varied perspectives [Special section]. (1991). *Journal of Applied Behavior Analysis,* 36(3). (322)

Serna, R. W. (1987). An investigation of the five-term contingency and the conditional control of equivalence relations. *Dissertation Abstracts International,* 48, 2126B. (Order No. DA8719451). (474)

Shapiro, M. M. (1960). Respondent salivary conditioning during operant lever pressing in dogs. *Science,* **132,** 619-620. (398)

Shapiro, M. M. (1961). Salivary conditioning in dogs during fixed-interval reinforcement contingent upon lever pressing. *Journal of the Experimental Analysis of Behavior,* 4, 361-364. (398)

Shipley, W. C. (1935). Indirect conditioning. *Journal of General Psychology,* **12,** 337-357. (399, 400)

Sidman, M. (1953). Avoidance conditioning with brief shock and no exteroceptive warning signal. *Science,* 118, 57-58. (37, 323)

Sidman, M. (1955). Technique for assessing the effects of drugs on timing behavior. *Science,* **122,** 925. (323)

Sidman, M. (1956). Drug-behavior interaction. *Annals of the New York Academy of Sciences,* **65,** 282-302. (323)

Sidman, M. (1959). Behavioral pharmacology. *Psychopharmacologia,* 1, 1-19. (323)

Sidman, M. (1960). Normal sources of pathological behavior. *Science,* **132,** 61-68. (323)

Sidman, M. (1960/1988). *Tactics of Scientific Research: Evaluating Experimental Data in Psychology.* New York: Basic Books. Boston: Authors Cooperative (reprinted). (16, 42, 183, 421, 447)

Sidman, M. (1964). Anxiety. Proceedings of the American Philosophical Society, **108,** 478-481. (323)

Sidman, M. (1966). Avoidance behavior. In W. Honig (Ed.), *Operant behavior: Areas of research and application* (pp. 448-498). New York: Appleton-Century-Crofts. (323)

Sidman, M. (1969). Generalization gradients and stimulus control in delayed matching to sample. *Journal of the Experimental Analysis of Behavior,* **12,** 745-757. (77, 331, 471)

Sidman, M. (1970). Behavior shaping with the mentally retarded. In N. R. Bernstein (Ed.), Diminished people: The problems and care of the mentally retarded (pp. 263-276). Boston: Little, Brown. (34, 47, 91, 282, 323)

Sidman, M. (1971a). The behavioral analysis of aphasia. *Journal of Psychiatric Research,* **8,** 413-422. (62, 306, 323)

Sidman, M. (1971b). Reading and auditory-visual equivalences. Journal of Speech and Hearing Research, 14, 5-13. (ix, 47, 48, 53, 57, 70, 84, 88, 105, 108, 131, 146, 162, 193, 220, 233, 286, 287, 304, 339, 345, 363, 422)

Sidman, M. (1977). Teaching some basic prerequisites for reading. In P. Mittler (Ed.), *Research to practice in mental retardation: Vol. 2. Education and training* (pp. 353-360). Baltimore, MD: University Park Press. (ix, 233, 286)

Sidman, M. (1978). Remarks. *Behaviorism,* **6,** 265-268. (223, 333, 361)

Sidman, M. (1980). A note on the measurement of conditional discrimination. *Journal of the Experimental Analysis of Behavior,* **33,** 285-289. (77, 140, 306, 471)

References

Sidman, M. (1981). Remarks. *Behaviorism, 9,* 127-129. (x, 185)

Sidman, M. (1985). Aprendizagem-sem-erros e sua importância para o ensino do deficiente mental [Errorless learning and its significance for teaching the mentally handicapped]. *Psicologia, 11(3),* 1-15. (323)

Sidman, M. (1986a). Functional analysis of emergent verbal classes. In T. Thompson & M. D. Zeiler (Eds.), *Analysis and integration of behavioral units* (pp. 213-245). Hillsdale, NJ: Lawrence Erlbaum Associates. (xi, 361, 387, 445, 507, 512, 513)

Sidman, M. (1986b). The measurement of behavioral development. In N. A. Krasnegor, D. B. Gray & T. Thompson (Eds.), *Advances in behavioral pharmacology, Vol. 5: Developmental behavioral pharmacology* (pp. 43-52). Hillsdale, NJ: Lawrence Erlbaum Associates. (321)

Sidman, M. (1987). Two choices are not enough. *Behavior Analysis, 22,* 11-18. (269, 306, 516, 548)

Sidman, M. (1989). *Coercion and Its Fallout.* Boston, MA: Authors Cooperative. (120, 323)

Sidman, M. (1990a). *Tactics:* In reply.... *The Behavior Analyst, 13,* 187-197. (183)

Sidman, M. (1990b). Equivalence relations: Where do they come from? In D. E. Blackman & H. Lejeune (Eds.), *Behaviour analysis in theory and practice: Contributions and controversies* (pp. 93-114). Hillsdale, NJ: Lawrence Erlbaum Associates. (xi, 354, 422, 445, 512)

Sidman, M. (1992a). Equivalence relations: Some basic considerations. In S. C. Hayes & L. J. Hayes (Eds.), *Understanding verbal relations* (pp. 15-27). Reno, NV: Context Press. (274, 277, 387, 388, 389, 412, 509, 511, 513)

Sidman, M. (1992b). Adventitious control by the location of comparison stimuli in conditional discriminations. *Journal of the Experimental Analysis of Behavior, 58,* 438-458. (167, 169, 306)

Sidman, M. (1993). Stimulus equivalence in and out of the laboratory. In A. Brekstad & G. Svedsäter (Eds). *Proceedings from the 21st Annual Congress of the European Association for Behaviour Therapy, Oslo, Norway, September, 1991* (pp. 42-59). Slependen, Norway: Norwegian Association for Behaviour Analysis. (78)

Sidman, M., & Cresson, O. (1973). Reading and crossmodal transfer of stimulus equivalences in severe retardation. American Journal of Mental Deficiency, 77, 515-523. (ix, 70, 88, 90, 105, 108, 131, 146, 162, 193, 220, 233, 286, 287, 345)

Sidman, M., Cresson, O., Jr., & Willson-Morris, M. (1974). Acquisition of matching to sample via mediated transfer. *Journal of the Experimental Analysis of Behavior, 22,* 261-273. (ix, 62, 70, 146, 220, 221, 233, 286, 287, 301, 358, 484)

Sidman, M., & Fletcher, F. G. (1968). A demonstration of auto-shaping with monkeys. *Journal of the Experimental Analysis of Behavior, 11,* 307-309. (134)

Sidman, M., Kirk, B., & Willson-Morris, M. (1985). Six-member stimulus classes generated by conditional-discrimination procedures. *Journal of the Experimental Analysis of Behavior, 43*, 21-42. (x, 35, 116, 285, 339, 345, 351, 422, 478, 489, 493, 539)

Sidman, M., Rauzin, R., Lazar, R., Cunningham, S., Tailby, W., & Carrigan, P. (1982). A search for symmetry in the conditional discriminations of rhesus monkeys, baboons, and children. *Journal of the Experimental Analysis of Behavior, 37*, 23-44. (ix, 77, 110, 192, 231, 233, 285, 306, 340, 343, 359, 445, 480, 483, 527)

Sidman, M., & Stoddard, L. T. (1966). Programming perception and learning for retarded children. In N. R. Ellis (Ed.), *International review of research in mental retardation* (Vol. 2, pp. 151-208). New York: Academic Press. (73, 238, 291, 323)

Sidman, M., & Stoddard, L. T. (1967). The effectiveness of fading in programming a simultaneous form discrimination for retarded children. *Journal of the Experimental Analysis of Behavior, 10*, 3-15. (73, 169, 238, 291, 323)

Sidman, M., Stoddard, L. T., Mohr, J. P., & Leicester, J. (1971). Behavioral studies of aphasia: Methods of investigation and analysis. *Neuropsychologia, 9*, 119-140. (8, 19, 48, 62, 183, 323)

Sidman, M., & Tailby, W. (1982). Conditional discrimination *vs.* matching to sample: An expansion of the testing paradigm. *Journal of the Experimental Analysis of Behavior, 37*, 5-22. (x, 110, 116, 131, 146, 233, 234, 237, 259, 260, 262, 285, 286, 289, 302, 303, 340, 422, 478, 480, 483, 539, 542)

Sidman, M., Willson-Morris, M., & Kirk, B. (1986). Matching-to-sample procedures and the development of equivalence relations: The role of naming. *Analysis and Intervention in Developmental Disabilities, 6*, 1-19. (xi, 233, 234, 240, 244, 259, 263, 266, 273, 358, 484, 539)

Sidman, M., Wynne, C. K., Maguire, R. W., & Barnes, T. (1989). Functional classes and equivalence relations. *Journal of the Experimental Analysis of Behavior, 52*, 261-274. (xi, 360, 375, 416, 419)s

Sidman, R. L., & Sidman, M. (1965). *Neuroanatomy: A Programmed Text* (Vol. 1). Boston, MA: Little, Brown. (323)

Siegel, S., Hinson, R. E., & Krank, M. D. (1978). The role of predrug signals in morphine analgesic tolerance: Support for a Pavlovian conditioning model of tolerance. *Journal of Experimental Psychology: Animal Behavior Processes, 4*, 188-196. (404)

Sigurdardottir, Z. G. (1992). *Establishing classes of Icelandic nouns using a stimulus equivalence paradigm.* Unpublished doctoral dissertation, Northeastern University, Boston. (117, 475)

Sigurdardottir, Z. G., Green, G., & Saunders, R. R. (1990). Equivalence classes generated by sequence training. *Journal of the Experimental Analysis of Behavior, 53*, 47-63. (116, 273, 392)

References

Silverman, K., Anderson, S. R., Marshall, A. M., & Baer, D. M. (1986). Establishing and generalizing audience control of new language repertoires. *Analysis and Intervention in Developmental Disabilities, 6,* 21-40. (423)

Skinner, B. F. (1931). The concept of the reflex in the description of behavior. *Journal of General Psychology, 5,* 427-458. (326)

Skinner, B. F. (1935). The generic nature of the concepts of stimulus and response. *Journal of General Psychology, 12,* 40-65. (326, 329, 331)

Skinner, B. F. (1938). *The behavior of organisms: An experimental analysis.* New York: Appleton-Century-Crofts. (82, 274, 329, 331, 332, 334, 360, 385, 389, 394, 397)

Skinner, B. F. (1953). *Science and human behavior.* New York: Macmillan. (77, 323, 334, 360)

Skinner, B. F. (1957). *Verbal behavior.* New York: Appleton-Century-Crofts. (2, 5, 62, 82, 115, 125, 165, 323, 334, 359, 511)

Skinner, B. F. (1965). The phylogeny and ontogeny of behavior. *Science, 153,* 1205-1213. (389)

Skinner, B. F. (1968). *The technology of teaching.* New York: Appleton-Century-Crofts. (77, 323, 533)

Skinner, B. F. (1969). *Contingencies of reinforcement: A theoretical analysis.* New York: Appleton-Century-Crofts. (359, 506)

Skinner, B. F. (1971). *Beyond freedom and dignity.* New York: Knopf. (323)

Skinner, B. F. (1974). *About behaviorism.* New York: Knopf. (82, 125)

Skinner, B. F.(1989). *Recent issues in the analysis of behavior.* Columbus, OH: Merrill. (82)

Spence, K. W. (1952). The nature of the response in discrimination learning. *Psychological Review, 59,* 89-93. (527)

Spradlin, J. E., Cotter, V. W., & Baxley, N. (1973). Establishing a conditional discrimination without direct training: A study of transfer with retarded adolescents. *American Journal of Mental Deficiency, 77,* 556-566. (35, 116, 146, 152, 196, 229, 233, 259, 273, 286, 288, 302, 422)

Spradlin, J. E., Karlan, G. R., & Wetherby, B. (1976). Behavior analysis, behavior modification, and developmental disabilities. In L. L. Lloyd (Ed.), *Communication assessment and intervention strategies* (pp. 225-263). Baltimore, MD: University Park Press. (65)

Spradlin, J. E., Saunders, K. J., & Saunders, R R. (1992). The stability of equivalence classes. In S. C. Hayes & L. J. Hayes (Eds.), *Understanding verbal relations* (pp. 29-42). Reno, NV: Context Press. (318, 526, 549)

Spradlin, J. E., & Saunders, R R. (1986). The development of stimulus classes using match-to-sample procedures: Sample classification versus comparison classification. *Analysis and Intervention in Developmental Disabilities, 6,* 41-58. (526)

Steele, D., & Hayes, S. C. (1991). Stimulus equivalence and arbitrarily applicable relational responding. *Journal of the Experimental Analysis of Behavior,* **56**, 519-555. (475, 514, 560, 561)

Stikeleather, G., & Sidman, M. (1990). An instance of spurious equivalence relations. *The Analysis of Verbal Behavior,* **8**, 1-11. (548)

Stoddard, L. T. (1982). An investigation of automated methods for teaching severely retarded individuals. In N. R. Ellis (Ed.), *International review of research in mental retardation* (Vol. 11, pp. 163-208). New York: Academic Press. (77)

Stoddard, L. T., & McIlvane, W. J. (1986). Stimulus control research and developmentally disabled individuals. *Analysis and Intervention in Developmental Disabilities,* **6**, 155-178. (113, 305)

Stoddard, L. T., & Sidman, M. (1967). The effects of errors in children's performance on a circle-ellipse discrimination. *Journal of the Experimental Analysis of Behavior,* **10**, 261-270. (77, 167)

Stoddard, L. T., & Sidman, M. (1971). Stimulus control after intradimensional discrimination training. *Psychological Reports,* **28**, 147-157. (331)

Stromer, R., & Mackay, H. A. (1990). Arbitrary stimulus relations and delayed identity matching to complex samples. *Experimental Analysis of Human Behavior Bulletin,* **8**, 22-25. (306)

Stromer, R., & Mackay, H. A. (1992). Spelling and emergent picture-printed word relations established with delayed identity matching to complex samples. *Journal of Applied Behavior Analysis,* **25**, 893-904. (514)

Stromer, R., Mackay, H. A., & Stoddard, L. T. (1992). Classroom applications of stimulus equivalence technology. *Journal of Behavioral Education,* **2**, 225-256. (65, 533)

Stromer, R., McIlvane, W. J., & Serna, R. W. (1993). Complex stimulus control and equivalence. *The Psychological Record,* **43**, 585-598. (515)

Stromer, R., & Osborne, J. G. (1982). Control of adolescents' arbitrary matching-to-sample by positive and negative stimulus relations. *Journal of the Experimental Analysis of Behavior,* **37**, 329-348. (229, 233, 234, 286, 288, 478)

Stromer, R., & Stromer, J. B. (1990a). The formation of arbitrary stimulus classes in matching to complex samples. *The Psychological Record,* **40**, 51-66. (306, 515)

Stromer, R., & Stromer, J. B. (1990b). Matching to complex samples: Further study of arbitrary stimulus classes. *The Psychological Record,* **40**, 505-516. (306, 515)

Stroop, J. R. (1935). Studies in interference in serial verbal reactions. *Journal of Experimental Psychology,* **18**, 643-661. (544)

Sulzer-Azaroff, B. & Mayer, G. R. (1977). *Applying behavior analysis procedures with children and youth.* New York: Holt, Rinehart and Winston. (76)

Sulzer-Azaroff, B. & Mayer, G. R. (1986). *Achieving educational excellence using behavioral strategies.* New York: Holt, Rinehart and Winston. (533)

References

Sulzer-Azaroff, B. & Mayer, G. R. (1991). *Behavior analysis for lasting change.* Fort Worth, TX: Holt, Rinehart and Winston. (533)

Terrace, H. S. (1966). Stimulus control. In W. K. Honig (Ed.), *Operant behavior: Areas of research and application* (pp. 271-344). New York: Appleton-Century-Crofts. (77, 331)

Touchette, P. E. (1971). Transfer of stimulus control: Measuring the moment of transfer. *Journal of the Experimental Analysis of Behavior,* 15, 347-354. (74, 427, 487)

Trapold, M. A. (1970). Are expectancies based upon different positive reinforcing events discriminably different? *Learning and Motivation,* 1, 129-140. (413)

Underwood, B. J. (1949). *Experimental psychology.* New York: Appleton-Century-Crofts. (83)

Urcuioli, P. J. (1985). On the role of differential sample behaviors in matching-to-sample. *Journal of Experimental Psychology: Animal Behavior Processes,* 11, 502-519. (413)

Urcuioli, P. J., & Honig, W. K. (1980). Control of choice in conditional discriminations by sample-specific behaviors. *Journal of Experimental Psychology: Animal Behavior Processes,* 6, 251-277. (139, 413)

Urcuioli, P. J., & Nevin, J. A. (1975). Transfer of hue matching in pigeons. *Journal of the Experimental Analysis of Behavior,* 24, 149-155. (167)

Urcuioli, P. J., & Zentall, T. R.. (1993). A test of comparison-stimulus substitutability following one-to-many matching by pigeons. *The Psychological Record,* 43, 745-759. (526)

Vaughan, W., Jr. (1988). Formation of equivalence sets in pigeons. *Journal of Experimental Psychology: Animal Behavior Processes,* 14, 36-42. (359, 375, 416, 417, 422, 423, 429, 444, 448, 449, 450, 453, 454)

Vocate, D. R. (1987). *The theory of A. R. Luria.* Hillsdale, NJ: Lawrence Erlbaum Associates. (511)

Wasserman, E. A. (1973). Pavlovian conditioning with heat reinforcement produces stimulus-directed pecking in chicks. *Science,* 181, 875-877. (404)

Weigl, E. (1941). On the psychology of so-called processes of abstraction. *Journal of Abnormal and Social Psychology,* 36, 3-9. (351, 481)

Weinstein, B. (1941). Matching-from-sample by rhesus monkeys and by children. *Journal of Comparative Psychology,* 31, 195-213. (164, 167)

Weinstein, B. (1945). The evolution of intelligent behavior in rhesus monkeys. *Genetic Psychology Monographs,* 31, 3-48. (164, 167)

Weise, P., & Bitterman, M. E. (1951). Response selection in discrimination learning. *Psychological Review,* 58, 185-190. (527)

Wepman, J. M. (1962). Dyslexia: Its relationship to language acquisition and concept formation. In J. Money (Ed.), *Reading disability: Progress and research needs in dyslexia* (pp. 179-186). Baltimore, MD: Johns Hopkins. (24, 46, 105)

Wetherby, B., Karlan, G. R., & Spradlin, J. E. (1983). The development of derived stimulus relations through training in arbitrary-matching sequences. *Journal of the Experimental Analysis of Behavior,* **40**, 69-78. (116, 229, 233, 234, 286, 288, 478)

Whitehead, A. N. (1925). *Science and the Modern World.* New York: Macmillan. (550, 551)

Whitehurst, G. J. (1977). Comprehension, selective imitation, and the CIP hypothesis. *Journal of Experimental Child Psychology,* **23**, 23-38. (288)

Williams, D. R. (1965). Classical conditioning and incentive motivation. In W. F. Prokasy (Ed.), *Classical conditioning.* New York: Appleton-Century-Crofts. (398)

Wulfert, E., Greenway, D. E., & Dougher, M. J. (1994). Third-order equivalence classes. *The Psychological Record,* **44**, 411-439. (475)

Wulfert, E., & Hayes, S. C. (1988). Transfer of a conditional ordering response through conditional equivalence classes. *Journal of the Experimental Analysis of Behavior,* **50**, 125-144. (116, 117, 392, 423, 475, 513)

Yerkes, R. M. (1928). The mind of a gorilla: Part III. Memory. *Comparative Psychology Monographs* ,**5** (2, Serial No. 24). (19)

Zentall, T. R., & Urcuioli, P. J. (1993). Emergent relations in the formation of stimulus classes by pigeons. *The Psychological Record,* **43**, 795-810. (172)

Zygmont, D. M., Lazar, R. M., Dube, W. V., & McIlvane, W. J. (1992). Teaching arbitrary matching via sample stimulus-control shaping to young children and mentally retarded individuals: A methodological note. *Journal of the Experimental Analysis of Behavior,* **57**, 109-117. (78)

Index

Note: page numbers for cited authors are given in Reference section.

Index

Skinner, B. F. 322, 324, 565
sound barrier 24
speaker 116
species characteristics 390
stages 206–208, 210, 219, 241–243, 260, 539
stimulus class 343
stimulus compounds 338, 346, 496–497
stimulus control 332
stimulus equivalence 112, 222
stimulus location 163, 166–170, 174
  and labeling 171–172
stimulus mediation 89
stimulus naming 281
stimulus specification
  as part of response definition 333
stimulus-class formation 195
stimulus-response distinction 384–386, 386
stimulus-response theories 108
stimulus-stimulus association theories 108
stimulus-stimulus learning 109
stimulus-stimulus relations 86, 119, 337
stored correspondences 346
strategy of mediation 554
Stroop test 544
substitutability 80, 542
subvocal naming 113
successive discrimination 76, 152, 527
sunset 571
survival contingencies 362, 389, 390
symbol 563, 566, 572
symbolic matching 128, 286
symbolic reference 2–13
symmetry 111, 125, 126, 130, 192, 231, 341–342, 566
  emergence from exemplars 162–163, 174–175, 364–365, 470, 556–558
symmetry and transitivity
  combined test 131, 193, 194, 224–225, 315, 343–345, 518
  independent tests 197
symmetry tests
  and reinforcement contingencies 187–189
syntactic class 392
syntactic relations 345
syzygy 569, 570, 571

T

teaching efficiency 219
teaching machine 59, 73
theory 165, 265–266, 410, 513, 531, 535–573, 570
Thompson, Travis 321
three-term contingency 331–336
  distinguished from four-term contingency 360–361
three-term unit 331–336
training node 226
transfer of function 392, 393, 399, 418, 448, 463, 464, 529, 537, 555, 559
transfer of training 186
transfer triangle 96, 98
transfer-activated response sets 558
transitivity 111, 130, 156, 192, 232, 342–343
trial-initiation key 134
true matching 123, 126, 285
two-term contingency 329–331
two-term unit 329–331

U

units of cognition 327
unreinforced conditional selection 277
unreinforced probes 139, 158, 204, 419–420, 447, 489

V

ventriculoperitoneal shunt 270

605

verbal classes 343
   contextual control of 350–351
verbal constructions 6–7
verbal learning 88
verbal mediation 470, 496
visual classes 233, 283, 287
visual comprehension 44–47, 345
visual-visual equivalence 301
vocabulary 340, 345

W

Walter Reed Army Institute of Research 177
whole-word method 78
within-class preference test 315, 547–550
word naming 90
words and symbols 2–13

Y

yes-no procedure 154–155